BARRON'S
HOW TO PREPARE FOR THE
CDL
COMMERCIAL DRIVER'S LICENSE
BUS DRIVER'S TEST
by
Mike Byrnes
and Associates
BARRON'S

All inquiries should be addressed to:
Barron's Educational Series, Inc.
250 Wireless Boulevard
Hauppauge, New York 11788

Library of Congress Catalog Card No. 91-17117

International Standard Book No. 0-8120-4521-1

Library of Congress Cataloging-in-Publication Data

How to prepare for the commercial driver's license (CDL) : bus driver's test / by Mike Byrnes and Associates.
p. cm.
Includes Index.
ISBN 0-8120-4521-1
1. Bus driving – Examinations, questions, etc.
2. Bus drivers – Licenses – United States.
I. Mike Byrnes & Associates.
TL232.3.H68 1991
629.28′333′076 – dc20 91-17117
CIP

PRINTED IN THE UNITED STATES OF AMERICA

1234 100 98765432

Table of Contents

Acknowledgments

We would like to thank the following people, who dropped what they were doing to answer questions we had about the fine points of commercial driver licensing, transportation regulations, and bus driving: Clint Langston, Westward Insurance; Dennis Wylie and Ted Schultz, The Essex Corporation; Jeannine Bleicher, Arizona Motor Transport Association; Phil Forgan, Department of Transportation; George Dobbins, Arizona Department of Transportation; Keene Freidley, Arizona Department of Transportation; Michael Weede, Arizona Department of Transportation; Tom Piowarsy, Phoenix Union High School District; Dom Spataro, Federal Highway Administration; Richard Camp, Central Area VoTech, Drumwright, Oklahoma; Glen Grootegoed and William Brewer, Western Truck School and Nonie Ray. Thank you all.

Special recognition is due Carlos Gonzalez, graphic artist, who labored many late hours to portray vehicles and equipment in faithful detail, down to the lug nuts. For those who are interested in that sort of thing, he used CorelDraw! © on an IBM-compatible computer.

Preface

This book has been written to help you, the bus driver, pass the Commercial Driver's License tests. You must pass these tests to get your Commercial Driver's License (CDL). (Truck drivers should read the companion book, *How To Prepare For The Commercial Driver's License Truck Driver's Test.)*

In this book, you will learn what the CDL is. You'll learn who must have one. You'll find out how to apply for a CDL.

We'll give you the information our government says you must have to get a commercial driver's license.

And, we'll offer you tips on taking the CDL tests.

Last, we hope to do this in a way that's painless, maybe even enjoyable.

This book is in three main parts:

Part One – general information about the CDL, and the tests you must take to get one; plus **PASS**, a plan to help you prepare for those tests

Part Two – facts about commercial driving that you must have at your command to pass the CDL tests

Part Three – sample CDL tests for practice, plus tips on making "Test Day" worry-free. Answer Keys for the practice tests follow Chapter 16.

We, the authors, are honored that you have chosen this book to prepare for the CDL. We know how important this license is to you. We also know how valuable your time is. We pledge to give you every bit of help we can. We won't waste your time with information you don't need. We want you to pass the CDL. Your success is our success.

We have many years of experience in preparing people for successful careers as commercial vehicle drivers. Now there's an added step toward that career: getting a CDL. This book will help you with that one important extra step.

We'd also like to congratulate you on your decision to prepare yourself for the CDL. Many drivers skip this step. They take the test unprepared. They may think that their driving experience or training is enough. But their test results show that this isn't true. Even experienced drivers with good driving records fail the CDL tests. The failure is not because they don't know how to drive. Many times, they simply don't do well on tests.

Figure: P-1 Preparing for the CDL Tests means brushing up on the facts, and practicing your driving skills.

Many people don't do well on tests, even when they know their stuff. They don't recognize the correct answer, even when they know what it is, because of the way the question or answer is worded. Perhaps that's been your experience. If so, preparing for the CDL tests with **PASS** is a smart move. You will not only get the facts you need for the tests, you will also learn how to be a good test-taker. You will learn skills you can use on any type of test, now and in the future.

So let's get to it.

Figure P-2 Drivers of vehicles like these need Commercial Driver's Licenses.

A BRIEF INTRODUCTION TO THE CDL

What is the Commercial Driver's License anyway? Very simply, the Commercial Driver's License grants a **license** to **certain drivers** to drive **certain vehicles.** Let's take that piece by piece to see what it means to you.

License

When you receive a driver's license, any kind of driver's license, some body of government has granted you permission to drive. In this case, it's a state government. That makes driving a regulated activity.

Why should the government regulate driving? Shouldn't we all be allowed to drive if we wish? Let's take a closer look at that question.

What if you could not hear or see well? What if you did not know the rules of the road or refused to obey them? You would be an unsafe driver, a danger to others on the road. To ensure everyone's safety, the state government judges your fitness to drive before granting you a license. You are given permission to drive. It's not a right granted to everyone.

What is a **commercial** driver's license? A commercial driver's license is different from a car or motorcycle driver's license. It gives certain drivers the license to drive certain vehicles. These are commercial vehicles.

Certain Vehicles

What vehicles are **commercial** vehicles? Briefly, these are:

- vehicles with gross vehicle weights of 26,001 pounds or more
- trailers with gross vehicle weights of 10,001 pounds or more
- vehicles that transport hazardous materials that require placards
- buses designed to carry 16 or more people (including the driver)

Later in this book, we will examine the definition of "commercial vehicle" in greater detail.

Certain Drivers

And who are those "certain drivers"? Only those drivers who pass the Commercial Driver's License tests may hold a CDL. There are different CDLs for different driving jobs, and tests that go with them. You might take all the tests, or only a few. **All** commercial vehicle drivers must pass at least the basic knowledge test.

Sounds reasonable enough. But what if you have been driving for 20 years and have a perfect record? Or perhaps you have just gotten a perfect score on the final exam in a tough training program? Shouldn't that be enough? Why do you need a special license?

There are many reasons for a Commercial Driver's License law. Here are three:

- public safety
- driver quality
- national standards

Public Safety

In 1986, the United States Congress passed the Commercial Motor Vehicle Safety Act. This act was in response to public concern over safety on roadways. Heavy vehicles seemed to be in more accidents every year. The facts proved it.

Look at Figure P-3. It shows the increase of accidents involving heavy trucks over the years from 1982 to 1986.

Heavy trucks also seemed to be in more fatal accidents than other vehicles. Figure P-4 bears this out. Trucks were involved in more fatal accidents than cars. This is true even though there are more cars on the road than trucks.

The facts also showed that accidents were more often due to driver error than equipment failure.

The number of buses on the highway is much smaller than the number of trucks. So bus accidents are only a small part of national accident figures (see Figure P-5). However, since bus accidents involve passengers, bus safety is still of great importance to the public.

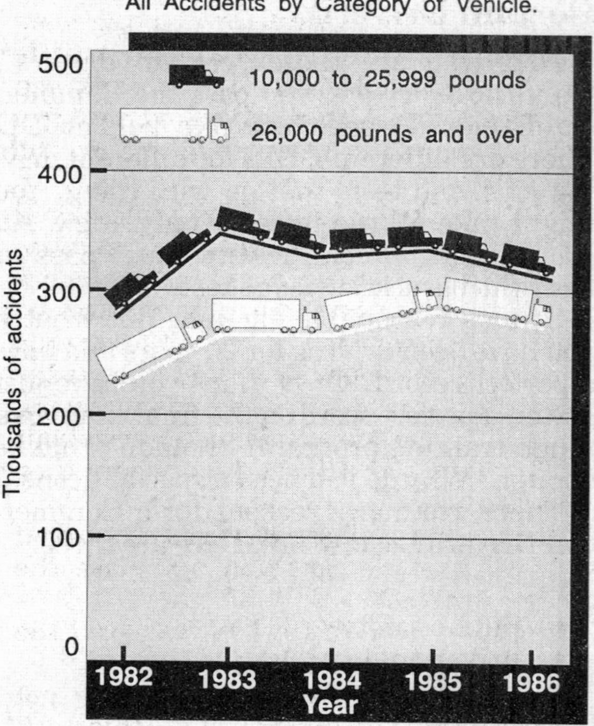

Figure P-3 Truck accidents by category of truck.

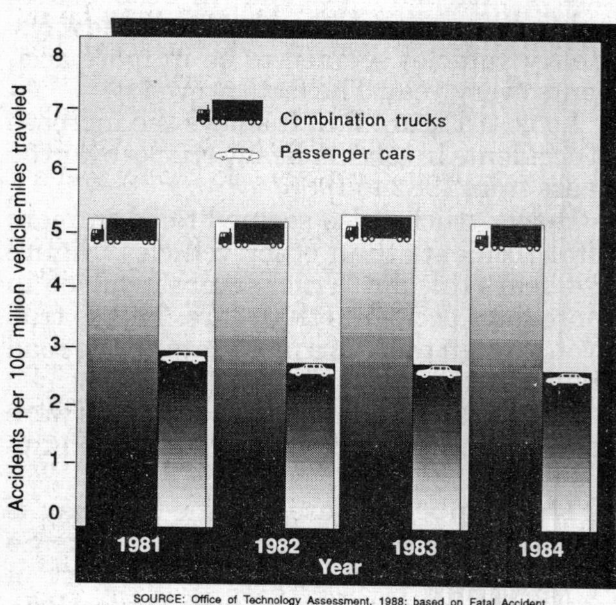

Figure P-4 Vehicles involved in fatal accidents.

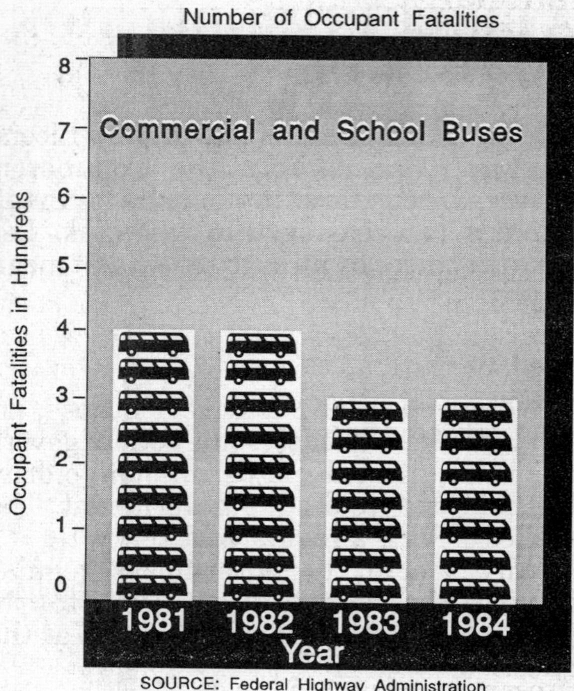

Figure P-5 Types of motor vehicles involved in accidents.

The goal of the Commercial Motor Vehicle Safety Act was to improve driver quality and to remove unsafe and unqualified commercial drivers from the road. In accordance with the suggestion of people in the bus industry, this act covers bus drivers as well as truck drivers.

Driver Quality

Trucks and buses are much more dangerous pieces of equipment today than ever before. They're heavier, bigger, and can travel at higher speeds. Would you want to be on the road with a driver who didn't know how to stop such a vehicle safely? Neither does anyone else. So the Commercial Motor Vehicle Safety Act seeks to remove unqualified drivers from the road. All drivers of commercial vehicles must show they have a minimum of knowledge and skill. This is shown through testing.

But we said earlier that it is the state that gives out licenses, not the federal government. This is still true. What the Commercial Vehicle Safety Act of 1986 did was set standards that all states must follow in granting licenses.

National Standards

States did not always use the same standards when giving out driver's licenses. As of July 1988, only 32 states issued some form of a classified driver's license. (A classified license is one that states what type of vehicle the license holder may drive.) Of these 32 states, only 12 required a behind-the-wheel test to obtain the license. Some of the remaining states accepted proof of training, either on the job or through a school, instead of a license test. Some states required neither testing nor training.

So you see, there were no standards. It was easier to get a license in some states than in others.

With the CDL, states may still give almost any type of test they choose. They may accept training or a good driving record as a substitute for part of the test. You will find, though, that most, if not all, states will give some form of test.

The federal government has offered states a model test to follow. Most states do follow this model. We have used this same model in this book. Later, we will tell you how to find out whether your state follows this model, and what to do if it doesn't.

THE PRIDE'S BACK INSIDE!

Figure P-6 From Now On, Only The Best Will Drive...

You will still get your license from your state. When you do, you'll have to have the same basic knowledge and skills that drivers in all the other states must have. The Commercial Driver's License Test will test those skills.

Think of it this way. Driving a heavy vehicle used to be a simple job. Now, there are a great many laws covering driving. The equipment is complicated. Traffic conditions leave no room for error. Driving is no longer simple. The driver of a heavy vehicle must be better informed and more skilled than ever before. Other drivers want to feel safe and confident when they are on the road.

It's much like other forms of professional licensing. Doctors, lawyers, and accountants all must pass licensing exams before they can go into practice. The license assures consumers that these professionals have at least the basic skills and knowledge required to do their job. Now the motoring public will have the same confidence about the heavy vehicle drivers with whom they share the road.

You may always have thought of yourself as a professional. Now you will have the license to prove it.

Need more convincing? We've saved the best argument for last: It's the law.

Let's be honest. You are probably not delighted about having to take this test. You may resent it. You may be fearful about it. But you have to take it. So put those bad feelings aside. Resentments and fears won't help you. You need all your energy to prepare. The whole process will go much better if you approach it positively.

Here's one last thing to consider. Preparing for and taking the CDL test may be a new activity for you. It will at least be different from what you do every day. Unless you just got out of school yesterday, reading and taking practice tests will be out of your normal routine. So it may feel a little strange.

Think of it as a new exercise program. At first, it may seem hard. You may feel sore after the first few sessions. But the longer you stay with it, the stronger you will get. As you grow stronger, it will get easier. You will begin to feel good about it and about yourself. This feeling will carry over to everything else you do. It will carry you through actually taking the CDL test.

Yes, it's a pain. We know there are a thousand things you'd rather be doing. But it has to be done, and you can do it. You know you can. So, to steal a line from a popular athletic shoe commercial: "Just do it!"

PART ONE

CHAPTER 1

Introduction

When you have finished this chapter, you will be able to provide the correct answers to questions about:

- the contents of this book
- what is **PASS**
- how **PASS** can help you pass the CDL Tests

When you were in school, your teacher may have said, "Now class, you won't be tested on what I'm about to present. You don't have to take notes. Just sit back and listen."

You may have wondered why Teach was wasting your time with the stuff if it wasn't going to be on the test. Or you may have been happy to relax and enjoy the presentation. Either way, it was nice to know you didn't have to memorize the material.

Well, it's only fair to tell you that you won't be tested on the information in this part. But that doesn't mean you can skip it. Even if you are short on time, we urge you to read it. Part One introduces you to **PASS,** one of many valuable tools that will help you absorb the material in Part Two. But Part One doesn't have a test.

Now you can relax and enjoy Part One.

WHAT'S IN THIS BOOK

Were you surprised by the size of this book? Are you wondering if there really is so much to learn before taking the CDL Tests? Are you thinking, "I hope I don't have to read all of it"?

You may not have to. We'll show you how to determine just how much of this book you do need. This is one feature of the **PASS** system you'll use to prepare for your CDL tests.

Here's a quick explanation of just what does make this book so large.

This book is in three parts.

If this book were a meal, Part One would be the appetizer. Part One has some general information about the CDL law. In Part One, we also outline the **PASS** system. This is a technique you'll apply to getting through the rest of the book. Perhaps you don't have much spare time in which to prepare for the CDL tests. You will appreciate the way **PASS** helps you make the most of that time. **PASS** will help you stay on track and stay motivated.

PASS includes tips on how to read. Perhaps you don't think there's any particular trick to this. You may be in for a surprise. We'll also show you how to take a test, any test. Here again, there may be more to this than you think.

Part Two is the meat of our meal. It contains all the facts you must digest before taking the CDL tests. You may already know much of this material. When it comes to taking the CDL tests, how these facts are stated is important. We've seen that many people who take the CDL tests are already well informed about driving. All the same, they do poorly on the tests. This is because they do not recognize the right answer when they see it. Part Two will help you overcome this problem. Even if you find that the material sounds familiar, you should read it carefully.

Part Three is dessert. We'll serve a few last-minute tips to make your Test Day go smoothly. We'll also offer lists of other CDL test preparation resources and aids. Just as dessert after a meal is optional, so are many of the resources in Part Three.

HOW TO USE THIS BOOK

When you first opened this book, did you look at the table of contents? If you didn't, please do that now. Then return to this page.

The table of contents does two things:

- It tells you how the book is organized.
- It lets you know what to expect.

Organization

The table of contents lists chapters and chapter subheadings. Then it shows on which page each chapter and chapter subheading begins. This becomes useful if you want to read the chapters out of order, instead of from page 1 right to the end. Use the table of contents to go straight to the chapter you need to read.

We suggest that you read the chapters in order. You will find that each chapter builds on the one before it. Still, if there's a chapter you're itching to get to, go ahead and scratch that itch. You can always reread it in sequence later.

What to Expect

The table of contents also gives you an overview of the entire book. It's helpful to have an overview of material you are trying to learn. An overview gives you an idea about what you can expect. Reading the table of contents may increase your curiosity. You may find yourself thinking, "I wonder what that's going to be about." All this helps you to focus. If you have questions, you will seek answers. Then you will retain more of what you have read.

Did any questions occur to you when you read the table of contents? Grab a piece of paper and write them down. We'll use them later.

TIP *Don't have any paper handy? Then write the questions in the margins or inside covers of this book. If this is your book, you should feel free to write in it.*

As you can see, Part Two is the largest. This part contains the material that the CDL tests cover. Looks like a lot, doesn't it? We'll show you how to break it down into manageable bites.

To save time, you may be tempted to skip the rest of Part One. We don't advise this. The ideas in Part One will help you cut Part Two down to size. You may discover there are chapters in Part Two you don't need to spend much time on. In Part One, we show you how to identify those chapters. We think you will find the rest of Part One worthwhile.

HOW TO USE THIS BOOK – USING PASS

This is your book, and you can use it in any way you wish. You may choose to read the chapters out of order. You may read only those chapters that look interesting and skip the ones that don't. But we suggest you read this book using the **PASS** method. Doing so will give you the best preparation for the CDL tests.

PASS

The letters **PASS** stand for two things. One is the word "pass." This is your final goal. It's your reason for reading this book in the first place. You want to pass the CDL.

PASS also stands for Personal Action System for Success. It's the system we suggest you use to get from page 1 to the end.

Figure 1-1 This is your book. Use it however it best helps you to prepare for the CDL tests.

PASS is personal. We will show you techniques everyone can use. How you use them will be unique, just as you are unique. You are starting out with a certain level of knowledge and experience. This level is different from that of anyone else preparing to get a CDL license. We'll show you how to prepare in a way that's tailored to your needs. You may need all of this book, or only some of it. **PASS** will help you decide. It will be a personal decision.

PASS requires action. You must take an active role in preparing for your CDL. Just having this book isn't enough. (If simply owning a book were enough, everyone who bought a diet book would instantly lose weight.) You must use it. Throughout the book we will give you exercises and tasks. We'll tell you to do something. Don't skip over these exercises. Do them. There are always good reasons behind them.

For example, when we say "write it down," we **mean** write it down. We don't mean read it over, or think about it. The reason is that making a mental note of it is just not the same. Writing is a great reinforcer. Often, jotting down a note is all you need to do to remember something. You may never even go back to the note itself. Just writing it down is enough to implant it in your memory.

Also, the act of writing keeps you in motion and alert. It helps you stay focused on what you are doing. When you remain in one position for a stretch of time, you can fall half-asleep and not know it. Writing will snap you back to attention.

Earlier, we asked you to read the table of contents. We said you should write down any questions that occurred to you. Did you do it? Did you read the table of contents? Did you write down your questions?

If you did, great! You're an active learner and will get a lot out of the time you spend preparing for your CDL Tests.

If you didn't, get with it! Your family and friends, your employer, your state, even the authors of this book want to see you get your CDL. We're ready to help. But you have to make some effort, too.

PASS is a system. It's a step-by-step plan for moving towards a goal. Having a plan ensures you won't skip over something important. It keeps you from duplicating your efforts. Your time is important. Don't waste it doing something twice when once would have been enough.

PASS is success. That's the goal. The main goal of this entire effort is to pass the CDL. Getting your CDL will be the ultimate success. If that's some time off, you may find it hard to keep this goal in focus. So along the way, there will be mini-goals to aim for, and mini-successes to keep you motivated.

In Chapter Two, we'll get into **PASS** in greater detail. We'll show you how to create a **PASS** that's all your own.

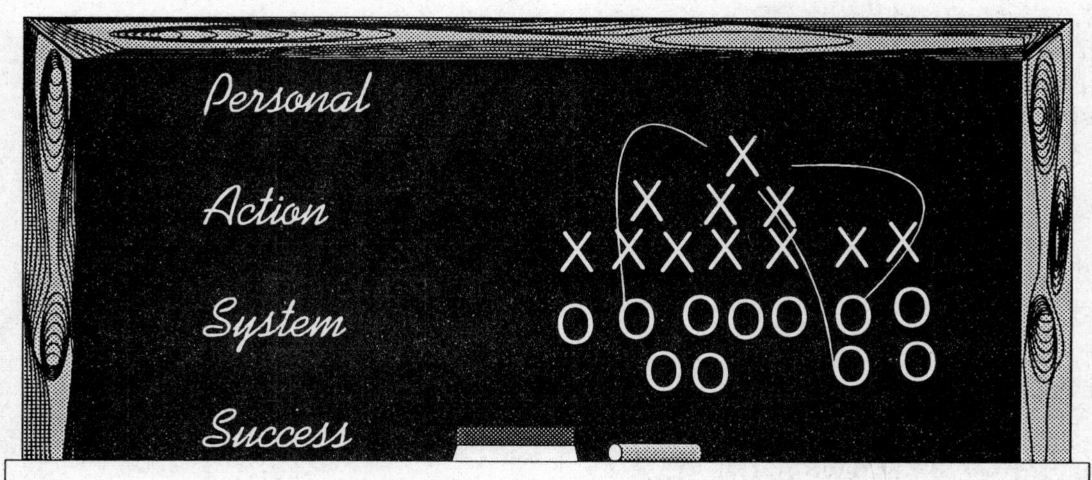

Figure 1-2 Use **PASS** to prepare for the CDL tests.

CHAPTER 2

Using **PASS**

When you have finished this chapter, you will be able to provide the correct answers to questions about:

- how to get the most information from reading
- success strategies for taking tests
- what other resources will help you prepare for the CDL tests
- how much you already know about subjects tested by the CDL
- how to measure the progress of your preparation
- what agencies exist to help you get your CDL
- how to apply for a CDL

To complete this chapter you will need:

- scrap paper
- pencil and eraser
- calendar with room to write on
- colored pens, markers, pencils, or crayons

In Chapter One we introduced **PASS,** the Personal Action System for Success. In this chapter, we will show you how to design one for yourself.

THE PERSONAL PART OF PASS

We said that **PASS** was personal. This means you can tailor it to your needs and preferences. Each person preparing for the CDL tests is different. Your skills, knowledge, and experience are different from your co-worker's, your friend's, or your spouse's. You have different blanks that need filling in.

Your preferences are different, too. Some people like to read. Some people don't. Some people like to work alone. Others do better in a group. Some people can chug along quite nicely under their own power. Other people need a little pat on the back now and then to keep going.

Which type are you? Maybe you're not so sure. Let's find out. In this section, you'll take stock of your needs and make note of your preferences.

Needs

First, how much do you already know about driving? Have you been driving for some time? Have you just finished a training program? Your knowledge may be fresh and quite complete. You may feel confident about your knowledge.

Or maybe you've been out of the driver's seat for a while. Perhaps it's been some time since you had any formal training. It's likely you're just not sure of what you do know or you're wondering whether it's going to be enough. The quickest way to get a reading on where you stand would be – you guessed it – take a test.

Throughout this book you will find many tests. We'll offer you tests both before you read a chapter and after. If you simply don't like tests, you may think of them as inspections. In fact, we'll call them **PASS** Pre-trip and **PASS** Post-trip Inspections. Here's how tests and inspections are alike.

A vehicle inspection is a routine part of the driver's job. It's required by law, and it's important for safety's sake. You will likely inspect your vehicle both before you begin your shift and after. In this book, you'll inspect your knowledge both before and after you read a chapter.

When you pre-trip your vehicle, you take stock of your equipment before going to work. You are mainly looking for defective or missing equipment. When you pre-trip yourself before starting a chapter, you will be looking for defective or missing areas in your knowledge about the chapter's subject.

Then, when you post-trip your vehicle, you're checking to see what, if anything, has changed since you last looked. It's the same with the **PASS** Post-trip test. You'll be looking for changes. You'll be checking for any change in your knowledge about the subject covered by the chapter you just read. Before we go any further, then, let's pre-trip your knowledge about bus driving.

Sample CDL Knowledge Test

The following is a sample CDL knowledge test. It contains questions similar to the ones on an actual CDL Knowledge Test. The questions are similar in terms of type of question and the information covered. You may take all the time you need to complete the test. However, do complete the test in one sitting, much as you would under true test conditions. Time yourself to see how long it takes.

You may not use any notes or reference materials while you are taking this sample test. You may not ask help from another person. You can't do any of these things when taking the CDL Knowledge Test.

This sample test is made up of one type of test question, the multiple choice question. First read the numbered question or statement. Then read the three choices – A, B, or C. If the numbered item is a question, pick the lettered item that answers the question correctly. If the numbered item is a statement, pick the lettered item that completes the statement and makes it true.

Write your answers on a separate sheet of paper, not on the test itself. That will make it easier to score. You can find an answer sheet for this purpose on page 21 at the end of this chapter. Carefully tear or cut it out of your book along the dotted line. When you have finished marking your answers on this answer sheet, turn to page 10. That's where you will find the answers. Score your own test. You can find out what different scores mean to you by turning to page 21.

Mark your answer sheet with the date you took the Sample CDL Knowledge Test for the first time. Fill in the time you spent taking the test, and write down your score. Store it away because we will come back to it later.

Figure 2-1 Test your knowledge "pre-trip," like inspecting your vehicle pre-trip.

SAMPLE CDL KNOWLEDGE TEST

1. If you do not have a Hazardous Materials Endorsement on your Commercial Driver License, you may _____.

A. never haul hazardous materials
B. haul hazardous materials when the load does not require placards
C. haul hazardous materials when the load will not cross state lines

2. You are driving a 40-foot vehicle at 45 mph on dry pavement in clear daylight weather. To be safe, the least amount of space you should keep in front of your vehicle is the distance you travel in _____.

A. three seconds
B. four seconds
C. five seconds

3. The best way to handle a tailgater is to______.

A. speed up to put more space between you and the tailgater
B. increase the space in front of your vehicle
C. signal the tailgater when it is safe to pass you

4. When steering in order to avoid a crash,______.

A. apply the brakes while turning
B. don't turn any more than needed to clear whatever is in your way
C. avoid countersteering

5. Driving down a steep hill calls for extra caution. You should______.

A. shift down and use your brakes
B. use your brakes only
C. shift to a lower gear

6. If the road you are driving on becomes slick with ice, you should______.

A. downshift to stop
B. stop driving as soon as it is safe to do so
C. drive at a varying speed

7. You wish to turn right from one two-lane, two-way street to another. Your vehicle is so long that you must swing wide to make the turn. The proper way to make this turn is shown by Picture______.

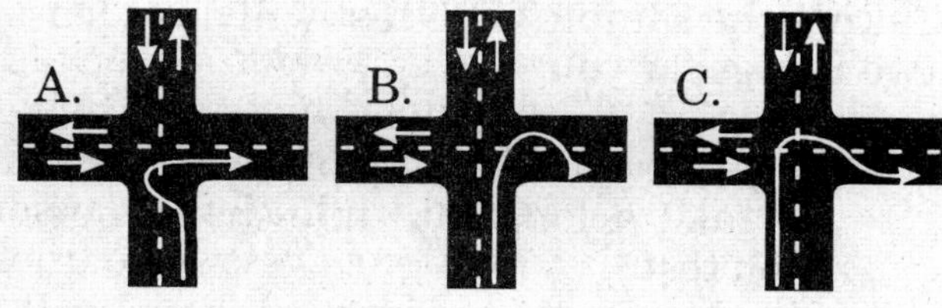

8. When the roads are slippery, you should______.

A. drive alongside other vehicles
B. decrease the distance that you look ahead of your vehicle
C. make turns as carefully as possible

9. A load's center of gravity______.

A. is a problem only if the vehicle is overloaded
B. should be kept as high as possible
C. can make a vehicle more likely to roll over on a curve

10. Heading down a long, steep hill, your brakes begin to fade, then fail completely. You should______.

A. downshift
B. pump the brake pedal
C. look for an escape ramp or escape route

11. Medical certificates must be renewed every______.

A. year
B. two years
C. four years

12. To correct a rear-wheel acceleration skid,______.

A. apply the brake
B. increase acceleration to the wheels
C. stop accelerating and push in the clutch

13. To avoid a crash, you drove onto the right shoulder. You are driving on the shoulder at 40 mph. The safest way to return to the pavement is______.

A. make sure the pavement is clear. Come to a complete stop. Then steer back onto the pavement.
B. brake hard to slow the vehicle. Then steer sharply onto the pavement.
C. still moving at 40 mph, steer very gently back onto the pavement.

14. Which of these statements about overhead clearance is true?

A. If the road surface causes the vehicle to tilt, you should drive close to the shoulder.
B. You should assume posted clearance signs are correct.
C. A vehicle's clearance can change with the load carried.

15. Which of these statements about tires is true?

A. Tires of mismatched sizes should not be used on the same axle.
B. Radial and bias-ply tires can be used together on the same axle.
C. A tread depth of 2/32 inch is safe for the front tires.

16. You can put out a_____fire with water.

A. tire
B. gasoline
C. electrical

17. While driving at 50 mph on a straight, level highway, a tire blows out. The first thing you should do is_____.

A. begin light braking
B. stay off the brake until the vehicle slows down on its own
C. quickly steer onto the shoulder

18. You must not permit standing riders_____.

A. in front of the standee line
B. within two feet of an emergency exit
C. within two feet of any window

19. Hydroplaning_____.

A. only occurs when there is a lot of water
B. only occurs at speeds above 55 mph
C. is more likely if tire pressure is low

20. What is the proper way to test for leaks in a hydraulic brake system?

A. Step on the brake pedal and the accelerator at the same time and see if the vehicle moves.
B. Move the vehicle slowly and see if it stops when the brake is applied.
C. With the vehicle stopped, pump the pedal three times, apply pressure, then hold for five seconds and see if the pedal moves.

Scoring the Sample CDL Knowledge Test

Count the number of questions you answered incorrectly. Include in the count of wrong answers any questions you did not answer (left blank).

ANSWERS

1. B	**5.** C	**9.** C	**13.** A	**17.** B
2. C	**6.** B	**10.** C	**14.** C	**18.** A
3. B	**7.** B	**11.** B	**15.** A	**19.** C
4. B	**8.** C	**12.** C	**16.** A	**20.** C

Sample CDL Test Scoring

Five or more wrong answers: less than 80 percent
Four wrong answers: 80 percent
Three wrong answers: 85 percent
Two wrong answers: 90 percent
One wrong answer: 95 percent
No wrong answers: 100 percent

Using Your Sample CDL Knowledge Test Score

How did you do on the Sample CDL Knowledge Test? Did you really take it? You should.

The sample test is very much like the CDL Knowledge Test offered by many states. All states must ask at least 30 questions. Many will ask more. Most will have multiple-choice questions like the ones on our Sample CDL Knowledge Test. Taking the sample CDL test will do at least two things for you:

- it gives you a feeling for what it's like to take a long multiple-choice question test
- it gives you an idea of how well-prepared you already are for an actual CDL Knowledge Test

Here's how to interpret your score:

Less than 80 percent – If you scored less than 80 percent, you did not pass the sample test. Don't go crazy! You took this test with very little preparation. Remember, we said many experienced and skilled drivers have failed the CDL Knowledge Test because they took it without preparation.

California was the first state to start commercial driver licensing. In the first few months of testing, failure rates were around 57 percent. Word quickly got out that you needed to prepare for this test. As more people did, failure rates dropped. A recent report stated that failure rates were down to 15 percent in some areas.

Your score may not surprise you. You may already have known you would need some preparation for the CDL Knowledge Test. As you put your **PASS** plan together, give yourself plenty of time to go through this book thoroughly. Pledge to work intensively through this book and the other resource materials we suggest. Plan to do every exercise and take every practice test until you get perfect scores. Allow yourself time to give extra effort to the subject areas that you missed on the sample test. Then you can tackle the actual CDL tests with confidence.

Between 80 and 100 percent – You passed the sample test. You can feel good, but don't get too cocky. What about the questions you missed? Do you want to risk missing them on the real CDL Knowledge Test? Pinpoint those subject areas and plan to give them special attention.

If you scored 100 percent, congratulations! You are already well prepared to take the CDL Knowledge Test. Just the same, you should work through the rest of this book. After all, this was just a 20-question sample test. There will be at least 30 questions on the actual CDL Knowledge Test. You want to be prepared for them all.

Your **PASS** plan might use a "scan" or "review" technique, which we'll describe later. This technique will allow you to target those areas where your knowledge is the weakest. Or you may wish to do a more thorough preparation, just to be sure.

Turn now to the **PASS** Planner on page 22. Find the section marked Sample Test Score. If your score on the sample test was less than 80 percent, write "3" in the blank space. If you scored between 80 and 100 percent, mark "2." If you received a perfect score on the sample test, mark "1."

Time Needed

One factor that will influence your **PASS** plan is time. How much time will you need?

Stop and think for a moment. How do you learn new things? Think back to the last time you had to learn something new. Let's say it was a work-out program. How did you go about learning the exercises? Did you sign up for a class or get a trainer? Or did you sit down with a how-to book you got from a bookstore and work it out for yourself?

These methods are good. Neither is better than the other. If you tend to learn new things by reading about them, working with this book will feel quite natural. You will like being able to use it anytime, anywhere. You won't need any special equipment or have to wait for an instructor to be available.

If you would rather be "shown how" than "read about how," you may wish there were some kind of "gym" you could go to in order to "train" for the CDL tests. Maybe you don't have access to that kind of help, though, and have chosen this book as the next best thing. It's true that you won't have the advantage of using your preferred learning method. You'll have to make allowances for that.

Keep in mind, though, that you will have the advantage of being able to work whenever and wherever you want. When you finish this book, you may find you like the reading learning method more than you used to.

Turn again to the **PASS** Planner on Page 22. If reading is your preferred learning method, mark a "1" in the space next to "Learning Method." Mark a "2" if you don't have a strong opinion either way. Mark a "3" if your preferred method is to work with a trainer or instructor.

Now add the two factors together. Your final answer will fall in a range from 2 to 6.

This book will take anywhere between 28 and 90 hours to complete. How long it will take you depends on your needs and your level of commitment.

If you just finished a formal training program, much of the information in this book will sound familiar. Your preparation for the CDL tests may be more like a review. If it has been some time since you had any formal training, you may find many of the terms and ideas in this book sound new. This will be true even if you are a good, experienced driver. You may need to go over the material more than once.

Your commitment to give your full attention to this work will help shorten the time you need to spend on it. If you allow yourself to be distracted, you will have to go over the material more than once to absorb it.

To get a rough idea of how much time you are likely to need, look at your final score on the **PASS** Planner. The higher your **PASS** Planner score, the more time you should plan to spend preparing for the CDL tests. If you scored 5 or 6, you should plan to take the full 90 hours. If you scored 2 or 3, you might complete the book in as few as 30 hours. If you scored 4, plan to take about 50 hours to finish the program.

These are merely estimates. Your experience may be different. There is no "right" answer. The real amount of time you will need to prepare for the CDL tests is however much time it takes for you to feel confident. Take all the time you need, and all the time you can afford to spend.

Preferences

Think back to the last time you were in school or in a formal training program. Perhaps you had early morning classes, and you're just not a morning person. Maybe the only time you could study was at night, and you're not a night person. Did you think you could have done a whole lot better if only you could have set the schedule?

Now you can. These are some of the issues we're getting at when we talk about preferences. If you think the best time for a **PASS** session would be two o'clock in the morning, then by all means, that's when you should have it. Your spouse may think you're nuts at first. You'll just have to explain that this is what works best for you.

Find it hard to work alone? Many people do. Try teaming up with someone else who must prepare for the CDL tests. Having a study buddy can help you stay focused and on track. It can make the whole process just a little more pleasant. Your buddy's skills and experience will likely be different from yours. This different viewpoint can be valuable. And when you just feel like complaining, it's most satisfying to complain to someone who understands what you're talking about.

You can choose where you want to work. It can be at home, in the public library, in the park – wherever suits you. In the section on System, we'll have some suggestions for a work space that will aid the preparation process. You can pick the tip that most appeals to you.

THE ACTION PART OF PASS

Action is a very important part of **PASS.** You can't just put this book under your pillow and expect the knowledge to seep into your head while you sleep. You must go after it. Tell yourself you are going to pass the CDL tests, come hell or high water.

Set a date on which you plan to take the tests. Then state your goal: "I will pass the CDL tests on (date)." Write it down. Post it someplace where you will see it every day. Try the bathroom mirror or the refrigerator door. Writing down your goal statement will fix it in your mind. Looking at it every day will keep your motivation high.

Get the support of the people around you. Tell your co-workers what you are doing. Explain it to your spouse or your kids. This will do three things for you.

First, it will put them on notice that you are going to be busy with this program, at least for a while. They will understand when you can't spend as much time with them as you usually do.

Second, they may be able to help you. For example, you may need to take some time away from your household chores. If the other members of your family understand your goal, they won't mind taking up the slack until you pass the CDL tests.

Last, explaining CDL testing and licensing to someone else will help you understand it. After all, you have to have the facts yourself before you can share them with someone else.

Collect the resource materials and tools you will need. You may need other books besides this one. When you do, they are listed at the beginning of each chapter. Have them all in place before you get down to work.

You'll be taking notes as you read, so you'll need blank paper, blank index cards, or a notebook. (Of course, you will also need a pen or pencil to write with.) You will also find a color highlighter, colored pens, pencils, markers, or crayons helpful.

Come Hell or High Water

One evening out on a country road, a driver delivering a bus ran into some bad weather. It started to rain, and the roads became very slick. Soon rain was coming down so heavily, he could barely see. The roads were so wet that hydroplaning was a real danger. He finally decided that to go on was suicide. He saw a farmhouse in the distance and headed toward it, thinking maybe someone there could tell him where he could stop for the night.

The farmer's family agreed it would be foolish for the driver to go on. Since there were no motels anywhere nearby, they offered to put him up for the night. The driver gratefully accepted.

The rain continued all night. Our bus driver had never seen anything like it. At last he fell asleep and dreamed of arks and pairs of animals.

The morning sun coming through his window woke him up. He also heard a strange noise, like a small motor. He looked out the window. The rainwater in the front yard was nearly six feet deep. Even stranger than that was a straw hat that floated on the surface. It would start at the south end of the yard and move slowly north. Then it would turn around and work its way back south. Back and forth along the surface of the water covering the yard went this straw hat.

The driver dressed quickly and ran downstairs. He found the farmer and his wife in the kitchen fixing breakfast.

Figure 2-3 Gramps promised to mow the lawn come hell or high water.

"You'll never believe what I saw," he said to the farmer. Then he told him about the water and the straw hat. The farmer was neither surprised nor amazed.

"Oh that," he said. "That's just Gramps. He promised to mow the lawn today, come hell or high water."

THE SYSTEM PART OF PASS

Now that you have a goal, you need a plan to reach that goal. You need a way to measure your progress toward that goal, and a way to tell when you have reached the goal.

Find Time to Work

In the section on the personal part of **PASS,** you figured out how much time you will need to complete the program. How much time do you have?

When you were in school, learning and studying were your job. You were supposed to devote the entire day to them. Now that you are an adult, you have other jobs. Other responsibilities take up your day. You may already be driving for a living. Perhaps you are working at some other job until you can get your driving career off the ground. You may have a family to care for. You may have all these demands on your time, and more besides. It's the rare adult who has four or eight hours every day to devote completely to learning.

Wondering where you are going to find the time to prepare for the CDL tests? If so, it would be helpful now to identify when it is you do have free time. Use the Free Time Locator on page 20. Using a red pencil, pen, marker, or crayon, "X" out all the time periods that are taken up by work, chores, eating, and sleeping. In the block, describe briefly what you will be doing at that time. Block out any time periods that are not "free time."

With a green marker, highlight the time periods that remain. You might identify some free early morning hours after the family has gone off to work or school. Maybe there's some time available in the evening, just before dinner or late at night when the house is quiet. No matter when these hours occur, you will commit them to preparing for the CDL tests.

If you are a driver with an irregular work schedule, you may find this exercise tough to complete. If you don't know when your duty shifts will be, you may not be able to identify when you will have free time. In that case, approach this exercise from another angle. Think back over the past few weeks. When were you off duty, not driving? You may need to map a few weeks to see any pattern of free time.

Even after doing the exercise this way, you may not find any pattern of free time. You know it's there, though. You know you have times when you are neither driving, sleeping, or maintaining your equipment and when you are off duty. Make a commitment to use these off-duty hours to prepare for the CDL tests.

If, after all this work, you don't seem to have any free time, then you will have to make some. Take a second look at the blocks you marked with a red "X." Are any of these leisure activities? You may have to give them up, at least until you've gotten your CDL.

Do you have some responsibilities that can be shared or given to someone else? Can you get a friend or family member to take over some of your chores? One of your **PASS** actions was to tell those close to you about your plan to prepare for and pass the CDL tests. If you did that, you paved the way for asking for help. Can you hire a neighbor's kid to mow the lawn for a few weeks? Can you get your spouse to make a few grocery shopping runs or cook a few meals? Anything that will free up a few hours will help.

In a pinch, maybe you have vacation time you can use to prepare for the CDL tests. No, it won't be the same as taking the family camping or going to Hawaii. But getting your CDL is important, and Hawaii will still be there next year.

When do you plan to take the CDL tests? Is your test date some weeks or months away? If so, then you can squeeze in your **PASS** sessions whenever you get the chance. If you plan to take the tests in a few days, you're working with a tighter schedule. Use the methods we've just described to carve some time out of your day to work toward your goal.

Set Mini-Goals

Your final goal for all this work is to pass the CDL tests and get your license. But achieving this goal is out in the future, some weeks away. You need something more immediate to aim for. Setting up some mini-goals will help you move along. It will break up a large task into smaller, more manageable units.

What should these mini-goals be? You could aim to finish a certain number of pages in each session. You could aim to continually improve your score on the **PASS** Post-trips. Whatever these mini-goals are, they should be within your ability to achieve. In other words, don't make them too hard. If you do, you will only fail each time. That will not make you eager to begin the next session. The point of these mini-goals is that you should end each session with a feeling of achievement. Then you will look forward to the next one.

In the section you just finished, you named a date to take the CDL tests. You have also used the **PASS** Planner to estimate how much time you need to prepare. You can combine these two pieces of information to set mini-goals. Here's a simple example of how this is done.

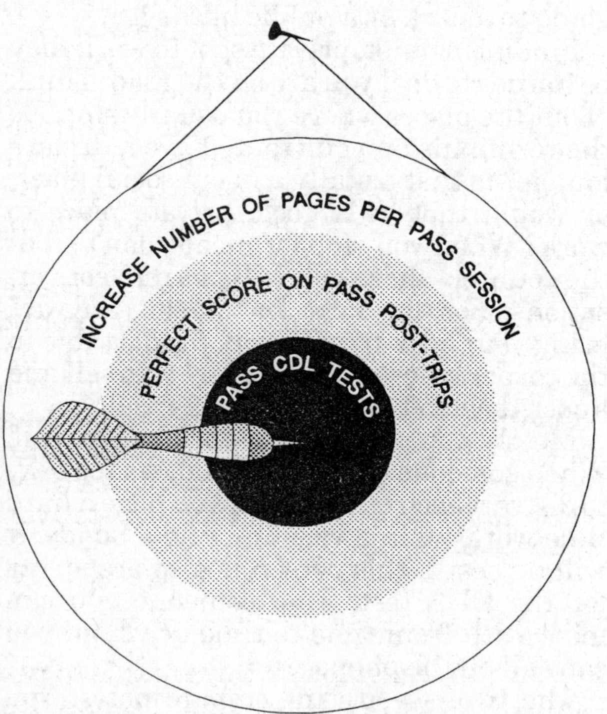

Figure 2-4 Aim to achieve your goals.

Let's say you plan to take the CDL tests in 15 days. That's about two weeks away. Let's also say you figured you would need 90 hours to prepare. If you divide 90 by 15, you find you should spend six hours each day from now until Test Day preparing for the CDL tests. Your mini-goals, then, would be to spend six hours a day preparing for the CDL.

What if you don't have six hours a day free? We'll answer that in the next section. For now, work out for yourself what your mini-goal is for each day.

Set a Schedule

Earlier, you used the Free Time Locator to find out when you have time available to prepare for the CDL tests. Now you will combine that information with your mini-goals and make up a schedule. Making a schedule will help you use the time you do have to work toward your goals. It will help you stay on track.

For this exercise, you will need a calendar. It should be large enough so there is writing space for each day. If you don't have a large calendar, sketch one out on scrap paper, or use the calendar form in this chapter.

Pencil in your mini-goals. Let's use the example we gave earlier as an illustration. In that example, Test Day, the final goal, is 15 days away. Therefore, write "Pass CDL Test" on the calendar day 15 days away from today. The mini-goal from that example was six hours of CDL preparation each day. You should therefore write "CDL prep = 6 hours" on each calendar day until Test Day.

Fill in the calendar with your Personal Test Day and mini-goals.

Now compare the calendar with your Free Time Locator. It's likely you will find you do not have an equal amount of spare time each day. You will have to adjust your goals to suit reality. If you have no free time one day, you will have to make up the time somewhere else. You may have to add an extra hour here and there to make up for the missed session. You may even have to double up on some days. You will probably find that you must devote most or all your days off to preparing for the CDL tests.

Use your calendar, your needs and mini-goals, and the Free Time Locator to schedule appointments with yourself. Be as exact as you can about the starting and ending times each day.

Do this exercise even if you were not able to predict your free time with much accuracy. Make your schedule as complete as you can in spite of this.

Chart Your Progress

Now that you've made up your schedule, be sure to use it. Put it someplace where you will see it often. It will help keep you on track. You should avoid falling behind. Falling behind will only make you feel anxious. Being nervous will not enhance your learning ability.

Yes, emergencies do happen. In spite of your best intentions, you may have to miss a session. Take immediate steps to catch up. Don't allow yourself to fall too far off the schedule.

When you do complete a session, cross it off your calendar with a big, colorful "X." It may sound silly, but you will be surprised at how good this simple act feels. It's part of ending each session on a positive note. It's part of recognizing your achievements.

From time to time, review the progress you have made. You will likely notice that your skills are improving. You may be getting higher and higher scores on the **PASS** Post-trips. You may find that you can cover more pages in one session than you could at the beginning. This is good. It's these improved skills that will help you pass the CDL tests. But you won't know your skills are improving if you don't keep track of your progress. Time your sessions, and record the number of pages you completed and your scores on the **PASS** Post-trips.

Your Work Space

The space in which you work can help you or hurt you. You'll base your decision about where you will do your preparation in part on your needs and preferences.

Most people have the best success with this type of work when they have a minimum of distractions. That means don't try to read this book and watch TV at the same time. You'll probably remember more about what you watched than what you read.

On the other hand, you might not want to be in a room that's completely silent. When you first begin this program, you may find yourself easily distracted by little noises around you, such as traffic outside or people talking in the next room.

A radio or stereo can be helpful. Find something to listen to that is neutral; you don't want music you like so well that you end up humming along with the radio instead of reading. What you are looking for is something that will block out the other, more disturbing noises. This masking sound is called "white noise." "Easy-listening" music is often a good choice. Have it on at a low volume.

As you improve your powers of concentration, you will be able to do without the "white noise." You will be able to tune out the little distracting noises that used to disturb you, all by yourself.

Find a space where you can work without interruption. If you are working at home, try the bedroom or kitchen. Ask your housemates, spouse, or children not to disturb you. You may have to leave home to study if you cannot find the privacy you need. Try going to a park or a public library.

Finding a quiet, private spot to work may be harder to do if you are on the road. Think about the places where you usually stop. Do the terminals on your route have a driver's lounge? Is that usually a noisy, social place, or would that be a good, private place to work? When you stop for meals, don't sit at the counter where you will get into conversations. For the next few weeks, anyway, bring your book in with you. Find a table in the corner where you can be by yourself and knock down a few pages over a meal.

Mostly, you will want to work by yourself. When someone else is with you, it's too easy to distract each other. But if you have a hard time working in a vacuum, find a buddy. It will be best if this person is also preparing for the CDL test. Find someone you can meet with from time to time or whom you can call on the phone.

The two of you can compare notes. You may have understood something that was a problem for your partner (or the other way around). Talking it out could clear up the matter.

If you are the competitive type, set up a little challenge. It could be just the extra spark you need to get cracking when you are tempted to goof off. Just knowing your buddy will ask you about your progress will keep you from skipping a session.

Or, just call up your partner to complain about what a chore this all is and get that off your chest. Then, get back to work.

Figure 2-5 Keep your CDL preparation supplies handy.

Get in the Mood

Here are some tips that help you focus on the task at hand and make it more pleasant. Like making big, red "X"s on your calendar, these tips may seem silly at first. But they do help you focus on your work.

Pick out something special that you will use only when you work on this program. It could be a colorful calendar that you will devote to this project. Maybe it's a special coffee cup. Put on your "lucky shirt." Whatever it is, it will remind you that you are working on your CDL test preparation, and only that.

If possible, try to work at the same time every day. This helps form a habit. When you start having the feeling that it's time, crack the books. That way you start work already warmed up mentally.

Have all the supplies you need with you before you begin. If you have a work space all to yourself that won't be disturbed, that's great. Make sure all your books, paper, markers, and munchies are in place. Then you won't have to get up in the middle of a sentence to get a cup of coffee, a pencil, or whatever. These interruptions will only break your train of thought. When you sit back down again, you will have to backtrack. That wastes time.

If you don't have a work space all your own, at least collect all your supplies in a box or tote bag that you can carry with you. That will keep everything ready and at hand when you do see a chance to work.

Aim for sessions that last about 45 minutes. After 45 minutes of undisturbed work, stand up and stretch. Walk around the room. Sitting for long periods of time forces your muscles into a fixed position. This in turn causes fatigue, which makes it hard to concentrate. So read for 45 minutes, then get up, stretch, and take a few deep breaths. Then if you have time, go for another 45-minute session.

TIP *Speaking of breaks, when was the last time you took one? Have you been reading along for more than 45 minutes without stopping? If so, now would be a good time to get up and stretch. Then come back to this page.*

When working for 45 minutes at a time gets easier, increase the number of 45-minute sessions you string together. The goal is to get better at focusing your attention for long stretches of time. It will probably take longer than 45 minutes to complete the CDL tests. You must be able to stay sharp and focused for the length of the test sessions.

As you get closer to your test date, make your **PASS** work sessions more like actual test-taking. If you have been using "white noise" to help you concentrate, practice working without it. Go through several sessions without coffee, soda, or snacks. If you're a smoker, practice going without a cigarette. Rules at the test site may forbid you to smoke or drink during the CDL tests. In this case it would be good practice for you to be able to go without. You will not be able to concentrate on the test if all your energy is focused on wanting a cigarette.

End your work session on a positive note. We've mentioned this before. Part of the trick is knowing when to quit. Once you have met your goal for the session, stop there. If you have gone through the number of pages you set out to do and have passed the **PASS** Post-trip, call it a day.

You may be tempted to try getting ahead. If you try to do too much, though, you may trip yourself up. If you get overtired and don't do as well as you wanted to, you'll just end up feeling defeated. Again, if you have achieved what you have set out to do, that's enough. Pat yourself on the back, "X" out that mini-goal on your calendar, and put the work away until the next session.

Be in Good Physical Condition

You will have an easier time preparing for and taking the CDL tests if you are in good physical condition. Does that surprise you? Did you say, "What am I training for, the Olympics?" It's true, though. If your health is generally good, you will be able to concentrate for longer periods. You will remember more of what you read. You will be more alert, sharper, better able to make decisions. So think of it as training for the Olympics, if you like. Do what you can to get – and stay – in good health and good physical condition.

THE SUCCESS PART OF PASS

The main goal of this program is, of course, to pass the CDL tests. The ultimate reward will be getting your Commercial Driver's License. On the way to achieving your final goal, you have set mini-goals. Just as you have mini-goals, you will have mini-successes.

Celebrate those successes. Crossing off a completed work session is one way of doing that. Here are some others.

Design a reward system for yourself. It doesn't have to be anything fancy or expensive. It can be a favorite food or a video you have been wanting. It can be an article of clothing or some small accessory. Make a list of small items that please you. Whenever you achieve a mini-goal, reward yourself with an item from that list.

Share your successes with those around you, especially those who have helped you. Thank your family members or friends for their support with a card, a celebration meal, or a movie. Don't forget your **PASS** partner, if you have one.

Remember that success is achieving a goal, whatever the goal is. Your goal is to pass the CDL tests. It's not to get a perfect score on the tests. You don't have to get 100 percent; you simply have to pass. So if you pass with 80 percent, feel good about it. That was all you had to do.

You don't even have to pass the tests on the first try. Of course you would prefer to pass the first time. It's time-consuming and costly to have to take the tests more than once. Yet people fail the tests on the first try and pass them on the second. Why? Often it's because taking tests like these was such a new experience for them. On the second try, they had enough familiarity with the testing process to pass easily.

Plan to pass the CDL tests the first time. But if you don't pass, don't give up and look for some other career. You'll probably pass the second time. It's nothing to feel bad about. The important thing is to pass them.

To sum up, **PASS** is a system to help you tackle learning something new. The letters **PASS** stand for **P**ersonal **A**ction **S**ystem for **S**uccess.

It's personal, because you make a judgment about how much you need to learn in order to pass the CDL tests. You decide how hard you have to work to learn it. You take into account your own preferences and style.

It's action because you don't just sit back and wait for the knowledge to come to you. You go after it aggressively. It's a system because you don't take aimless stabs at preparing for the CDL Tests. You make a plan, and you follow that plan.

It's success because you are going to pass the CDL tests. You are going to get your license.

So much for **PASS,** and Chapter Two. In Chapter Three, you'll learn about **SEX.** Before you go on to Chapter Three, take a short break.

MONTH YEAR

Sunday	Monday	Tuesday	Wednesday	Thursday	Friday	Saturday

Free Time Locator

Instructions: Using a red pencil, pen, marker or crayon, "X" out all the time periods that are taken up by work, chores, eating and sleeping. In the block, describe briefly what you will be doing at that time. Block out any time periods that are not "free time".

Time	MON	TUES	WED	THURS	FRI	SAT	SUN
6:00 AM							
7:00 AM							
8:00 AM							
9:00 AM							
10:00 AM							
11:00 AM							
NOON							
1:00 PM							
2:00 PM							
3:00 PM							
4:00 PM							
5:00 PM							
6:00 PM							
7:00 PM							
8:00 PM							
9:00 PM							
10:00 PM							
11:00 PM							
MIDNIGHT							
1:00 AM							
2:00 AM							
3:00 AM							
4:00 AM							
5:00 AM							

Sample CDL Knowledge Test Answer And Self - Scoring Form

Test taken on:

SCORE

Start Time:
End Time:

Time spent on test:

Instructions: Mark the date you took the Sample CDL Knowledge Test at the top of this form. Note the time you started and finished the Test. Calculate the time spent taking the Test. Mark the answer you choose. Then, use the Answer Key to score your Test. Mark your final score at the top.

Test Item	Answer Choices A	B	C	Self - Scoring Correct	Incorrect
1.				☐	☐
2.				☐	☐
3.				☐	☐
4.				☐	☐
5.				☐	☐
6.				☐	☐
7.				☐	☐
8.				☐	☐
9.				☐	☐
10.				☐	☐
11.				☐	☐
12.				☐	☐
13.				☐	☐
14.				☐	☐
15.				☐	☐
16.				☐	☐
17.				☐	☐
18.				☐	☐
19.				☐	☐
20.				☐	☐

Cut Here

PASS Planner

Sample Test Score	______
Learning Method	+ ______
TOTAL	______

CHAPTER 3

Using **SEX** To Prepare For The CDL Tests

When you have finished this chapter, you will be able to provide the correct answers to questions about:

- reading techniques that result in maximum recall
- the difference between a dictionary and a glossary
- how to use a dictionary and a glossary
- what is a "PASS Billboard"

To complete this chapter you will need:

- a dictionary
- pencil or pen
- blank paper or notebook
- colored pencils, pens, markers, or highlighters

Are you here at Chapter 3 already? We thought we told you to take a little break after Chapter 2. Bet you couldn't wait to read about SEX. Well, now that we have your attention, we must confess that SEX isn't what you thought it would be.

The letters in SEX stand for **S**can, **E**xamine and e**X**tract. It's the technique we suggest you use to get the most out of this book or any book you use to learn something new. Just as with the more romantic sex, you may think there's not much to know about the subject. Or, you may feel that you already know everything you need to know. We think you'll be surprised.

If, on the other hand, you have had a good grounding in how to read, these techniques may sound familiar. If so, feel free to move rapidly through the material.

BE RELAXED AND ALERT

You will get the most from your **PASS** sessions if you are relaxed and alert when you begin. Avoid working when you are tired or tense from the day's stresses.

Warm-Ups

If you are tired, try some light exercise. If you've ever been involved in a work-out program, you may already know a warm-up routine that would work. Any one of the following will also help you to feel more awake: Take a cool shower; go for a brisk 20-minute walk, jog or bicycle ride; jump rope or do "jumping jacks." Get just enough exercise to get your circulation going again but not so much that you tire yourself out!

Stretches

To relieve stress, try some simple stretching exercises. Stand and raise your arms straight up over your head. Really reach for the ceiling. Then let go. Bending from the hips, reach straight out in front of you. Straighten up. Reach to the left, then to the right. Bend over from the hips and reach toward your toes. Don't bounce or strain to touch your toes. Just hang there for a few minutes. Then come up slowly and take a deep breath.

Neck Rolls

Neck rolls are a stress-reliever you can do when seated. Here's how to do them. Slowly allow your head to droop forward, as if you

Figure: 3-1 Neck rolls will help relieve stress.

were going to rest your chin on your chest. Then, just as slowly, raise your head back up. Slowly, tilt your head to the right, as if you could touch your right ear to your right shoulder. Raise your head back up. Slowly, drop your head back and look up at the ceiling. Bring your head back to the face-forward position. Last, tilt your head to the left. Repeat the whole series five times.

Next, keeping your neck straight, swivel just your head to the right and look along the line of your right shoulder. Swivel slowly back and to the left. Return to the face-forward position. Then repeat the movement, beginning at the left this time. Do this five times also.

As you do the neck rolls, breathe deeply. Breathe in slowly and deeply through your nose. Breathe out through your mouth.

Clear Your Mind

Imagine your mind is a blackboard and you are erasing it so you can start your **PASS** session with a clean slate. Or, picture yourself gathering up your worries and preoccupations and putting them in a box. See yourself putting the box on a shelf. You know you can get the box down and work on those problems later. For now, though, you are going to be 100 percent involved in preparing for the CDL tests.

Get Ready

Make a small ritual of getting down to work. Think of it as suiting up for a ball game. This little ritual puts you in a frame of mind to focus on one thing only.

Gather all your supplies. Make sure you have everything we discussed in Chapter 2. To review, that would be:

- this book
- pencils, pens, and markers
- paper or index cards for taking notes
- your **PASS** calendar and schedule

You should also have a dictionary. A small, paperback dictionary is all you need.

Your supplies should also include any manuals you may have gotten from your state Department of Motor Vehicles or from your employer or both.

If you own a calculator, have that on hand, too. You can manage without one, but if you happen to own one, you will find it handy.

Settle down in the work area you have set aside for your **PASS** sessions. If you are in a public place, clear the area immediately around you. Make some room to spread out your books and papers. Remove as many distractions from view as possible.

BE SYSTEMATIC

Now you have everything in place and are ready to get to work. So you start with word one and read until your eyes fall out, right? Wrong. We suggest you be more systematic than that.

First, take the **PASS** Pre-trip. Take stock of what you already know about the subject and what you don't. As you read the chapter, be on the lookout for answers to the Pre-trip questions you missed.

Next, instead of simply reading the chapter, we suggest you use SEX: scan, examine, and extract.

PASS Billboard

Everything You Ever Wanted to Know About Dictionaries

All the reading strategies in the world won't help you if you don't understand the meaning of the words you read. Fortunately, there's help. It's called a dictionary.

Many people reject the use of a dictionary because they don't understand what it's for or how to use it. A dictionary has words, and their meanings, called definitions. It contains other information, such as how to pronounce words and use them in sentences. In many dictionaries, you can also find out something about the history of the word, where it came from.

For the most part, you will be interested in definitions and pronunciations.

Dictionaries are set up in alphabetical order. That means words that begin with the letter "A" are at the beginning, and words that begin with "Z" are at the end. The word's second letter further organizes the order of the words. So, a word like "aardvark," whose second letter is "a," would come before a word like "abalone," whose second letter is "b." But "azure" (which begins with "a") still comes before "bath" (which begins with "b").

You can estimate where in the dictionary you will find a word on the basis of its spelling. Then you use the words at the top of the pages to guide you further. The guide words tell you the first and last words you will find on that particular page. When the word you are looking for falls between the two guide words (in alphabetical order), you know you are on the right page.

For example, you may be reading this sentence: "Check the wheel seal for leaks." You want to know the meaning of the word "seal." First, find the section of the dictionary that has words beginning with "s." Next, use the guide words to find the pages with words beginning "se...." Say you find a page with the guide words "sea/sealant." This tells you the first word on this page is "sea," and the last word is "sealant." "Seal" comes after "sea" and before "sealant" alphabetically, so you know you have found the correct page.

The first piece of information you usually find is how the word is broken up into segments called syllables. This information is most useful in writing. For the most part, you will only be interested in syllables as far as pronunciation is concerned. To pronounce a word correctly, you must know which segment, or syllable, gets the emphasis.

Take the word "present" as a very simple example. There are two syllables to this word: "pre" and "sent." If you give the first syllable the emphasis (PREsent), you have the word "present," as in, "The governor is present at today's State Safe Driver Awards Dinner." If you stress the second syllable (preSENT), you have the word "present," as in, "I now present to you the winner of the State Safe Driver Award."

The next type of information the dictionary usually gives you is more details on how to pronounce the word. You'll see some symbol to tell you which syllable gets the emphasis. Other symbols stand for different sounds. An explanation of what the symbols mean is usually at the bottom of the page. You'll often find example words that give you an idea of the sound a symbol stands for.

Using our example of "seal," you may find the symbol for the sound of the "ea" is an "e" with a horizontal line over it. The example at the bottom of the page shows this is the sound of "ea" as in the word "be." "Seal" is a fairly easy word, and you probably already know how to say it. But you will find the pronunciation guide helpful with a word like "synchromesh."

Next, you'll often find information about what "part of speech" the word is, like "n." for noun or "adj." for adjective. In other words, how is it used in a sentence? For our purposes here, you probably already know how the word is used in a sentence. You

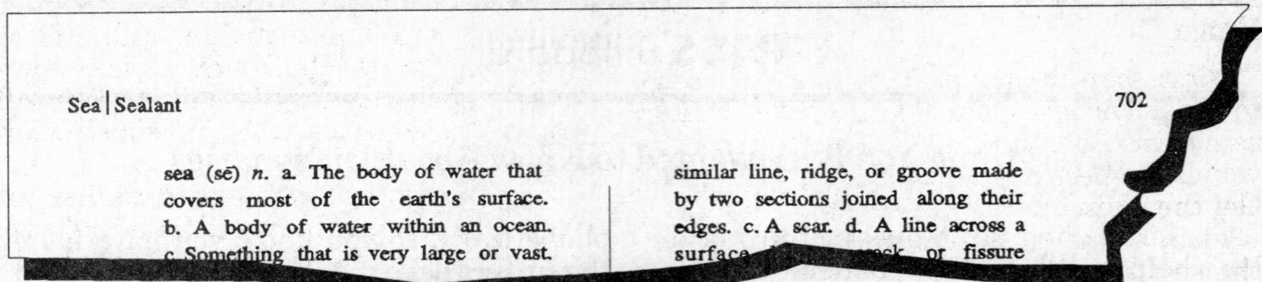

Sea | Sealant 702

sea (sē) *n.* a. The body of water that covers most of the earth's surface. b. A body of water within an ocean. c. Something that is very large or vast.

similar line, ridge, or groove made by two sections joined along their edges. c. A scar. d. A line across a surface ... or fissure

Figure 3-2 Words at the top of the page guide you through the dictionary.

want to know what it means. Fortunately, that's usually the next piece of information.

Following the definition, you may find some more symbols. These have to do with the history of the word. Most of our English words have roots in a foreign language.

But back to the definition. Many words have more than one meaning or have different shades of meaning. The most common definition is given first. The least common one is given last. How can you tell which definition is the one you want? Try each definition in your sentence to see which one makes sense.

Let's say your dictionary gives you three definitions for "seal." The first is, "a small disk of wax or lead with an imprint." The next definition is, "a sea mammal with flippers." The last definition is, "a device used to prevent air or moisture leaks."

Use each of these definitions in your sentence. Remember our example sentence? It was: "Check the wheel seal for leaks."

Try the first definition in the sentence. Clearly, we are not talking about imprinted wax here, so this definition is not the one you want. Try the second one. Since we're not talking about ocean life, this definition is no help, either. Definition Number Three is therefore the one we're after. Now you know that the "seal" in a wheel is a device that prevents leaks.

What if your dictionary doesn't have any definitions that make sense? A small dictionary may not. That's because some of the words in this book are technical terms. They're not used in common speech. How then would you find out what such words mean?

This is when a glossary comes in handy. A glossary is a mini-dictionary of special or technical words, words with meanings that are unique to a particular use. Many words used in the transportation industry fit this description. Take, for instance, words like "pancake" or "pigtail." These words have special meanings when used in connection with buses. You may not always find these meanings in an ordinary dictionary.

We include a glossary with this book. The glossary is organized much like a dictionary. It defines technical terms and common words that have special meanings when used in the business of transporting passengers. You need both a dictionary and a glossary to get the full meaning of what you read here. Make sure you include both in your list of CDL test preparation supplies.

Scan

First, scan the material you have chosen to read. Perhaps your goal for one **PASS** session is to read the chapter on doing vehicle inspections. Read the chapter title. Get the main topic firmly in your mind.

Look at the table of contents. What are the sections that make up the chapter on vehicle inspections? One is "State and Local Requirements." Right away, this tells you something about the subject this chapter covers. Even before you begin to read the chapter, you know there are two different requirements for inspections, state and local.

Read the objectives at the start of the chapter. They tell you what you can expect to know when you are done. They are mini-goals for the chapter. Keep these objectives, these mini-goals, in mind as you read. Mentally cross them off as you achieve them.

You will also find a list of supplies you'll need to complete the chapter. Gather the supplies before you sit down. That way you won't have to interrupt your train of thought to go hunting for a pencil.

Now scan the chapter pages. Note the main topic headings and the subtopic headings. Take a brief look at any charts, tables, or illustrations. Start getting warmed up to the subject.

As you scan, do any questions occur to you? Write them down. You'll look for the answers later when you read the chapter. That will help you to read more closely and keep you from just skimming over the material.

Examine

Now that you have some familiarity with the topic, get down to serious business. This is the time for close reading. Use the list of questions you formed when you scanned. Keep the objectives in mind. Look for the answers to these questions.

Use your highlighter or marker as you read. If this is your book, you should feel free to mark it up in any way that helps you. Find an answer to one of your questions? Highlight it. Read something that you find surprising or new? Highlight it. If you find a section you don't quite understand, circle it. Come back to it later. It may make more sense then. If it's very difficult or technical, you may have to read it several times before you understand it.

Use your dictionary or glossary when you come to an unfamiliar word. Highlight the word, and write the definition in the book's margin. Or write the new words and their definitions on your notepaper or in your notebook.

eXtract

When you have finished the number of pages you set out to cover, take the time to review in your mind what you have read. Write a little summary in your notebook. Get a hold of your study buddy, your spouse, even one of your kids. Make a short oral report to them on what you have read. If you can explain it to someone else, it's a good sign you understand it yourself.

Now take the **PASS** Post-trip. Pretend this is an actual test and you can't look up the answers. Then score yourself. Did you miss any questions? If so, turn to the table of contents or the index. Find the part of the chapter that deals with the subject of the questions you missed.

Reread that information. Try to figure out why you missed it. Did you simply not read it with enough attention? Maybe you didn't understand it completely the first time. Highlight that section of the chapter with a different color. You may need to come back to those sections more than once before you feel you have grasped the information.

Before you conclude a **PASS** session, do one last review. Scan the pages all over again. Include in your scan all the material you highlighted. Review the definition of the words you looked up.

You've finished reading when you have:

- met all the objectives stated at the top of the chapter
- answered all the questions that occurred to you during the scan
- answered the **PASS** Pre-trip questions correctly
- answered all the **PASS** Post-trip questions correctly

TOOLS FOR SUCCESS

This book has been written to do more than just provide information. The information is presented in a way that's easy to read. We hope you will find the book organized in a way that makes sense.

This book includes many helpful tools. You've already been introduced to some of these tools. They are the table of contents, the glossary, the objectives, and the list of supplies. Here are some others.

Index

We've mentioned the index, which you can find at the back of this book. The index is like a table of contents. It lists the subjects covered by this book and the pages where you can find them discussed. The index is more detailed than the table of contents. Also, the subjects are listed in alphabetical order. The table of contents, on the other hand, follows the order in which the subjects appear in the book, from first page to last.

Illustrations

You'll find many charts, tables, diagrams, and other illustrations in this book. You know the old saying, "A picture is worth a thousand words." You'll find illustrations that help explain ideas or procedures or describe equipment. Examine these closely.

The pictures have a dual numbering system. Each picture, or figure, has a number, followed by a dash, followed by another number. The first number is the chapter number. The second number is the order in which the picture appears in that chapter. So Figure 3-1 is in Chapter 3, and it's the first picture you will find there. Figure 3-3 is the third picture in Chapter 3. Figure 8-3 is the third picture in Chapter 8, and so on. From time to time, you will be told to "see..." or "refer to..." a figure. The numbering system will help you find it quickly.

Some pictures are included simply to give you a mental break from all this reading.

Index

A

Figure 3-3 A section of this book's Index.

PASS Billboards

You may have been wondering what are those **PASS** Billboards you've been seeing. **PASS** Billboards are much like the billboards you see along the roadside. Sometimes they have very important, useful information. Driving through a strange town late at night, you may have welcomed billboards that told you about nearby motels or cafes. Sometimes billboards are just silly stuff you barely notice before turning your eyes back to the road.

Our **PASS** Billboards contain information that's a little off the beaten track of the main subject. Sometimes they are helpful hints or alternative techniques. Other times they contain extra information that will broaden your understanding of the subject.

If it doesn't disrupt your train of thought too much, read them as you come to them. Otherwise, come back and read them when you finish the chapter.

Once in a while, the **PASS** Billboard offers a story or joke that, like some of the cartoons you see, give you a break from the more serious reading. Read them when you feel yourself becoming mentally tired. They will refresh you and help you to feel more alert.

PASS Billboards are set off from the main text with a special border.

PASS Tips

From time to time, you will see some special messages. These are **PASS** tips. Like **PASS** Billboards, they are extra material or helpful hints. Unlike **PASS** Billboards, they are shorter, and more directly related to what you are reading at the time.

Tests

You may not have thought of a test as a helpful tool. Tests do help you learn, however, by measuring your progress.

There are several ways to measure what you have retained from your reading. You could try writing a copy of the chapter from memory. Then you could compare it to the original to see how you did. You could recite the chapter from memory to someone who is reading along in the book. That person could tell you how close your recall comes to the real thing. These methods would take a lot of time and could even be thought of as overkill. After all, you're not concerned with whether you remember every word. All you want to know is whether you recall the important ideas and facts.

A simpler way to do this is to answer a few questions. These questions address the major points and items of information. Yes, that is a test. But there is no pass or fail to most of the tests given in this book. They are truly measuring tools, yardsticks of what you remember. If you answer all or most of the questions correctly, you know you have retained much of what you read. If you can only come up with a few correct answers, you know you did not retain much.

Why didn't you? Only you can answer that. Perhaps you were not reading with your full attention. Maybe you were distracted. Perhaps you read too quickly or skipped over sections that didn't look important. Whatever the reason, you have learned something useful. The next time you read something, if you want to remember more of it, you will have to go about reading a different way.

All these tests do many things for you:

- they give you practice taking tests.
- they give you examples of different kinds of tests.
- they help you measure your progress in your own **PASS**.

The more you practice taking tests, the more relaxed and confident you will be about taking the CDL tests, or any test for that matter. Remember, one of the goals is simply to reduce your anxiety about taking tests. Practice – rehearsals, if you prefer – will help achieve that goal.

The **PASS** Pre-Trips and Post-trips are offered in different forms. There are true/false, multiple-choice, and matching questions. These are not the only kinds of test questions, but they are the most common. The CDL tests you will take could use any of these types. They may combine several types. They could even use them all.

PASS Billboard

How to Learn from A Picture

Along with words, you'll find pictures in this book. Some of them are charts or tables that offer you a different way to look at facts or figures. Many are technical illustrations. That is, they are drawings of equipment parts, sometimes even entire systems. Once you have examined the picture, you should be able to locate or recognize the same parts or systems on an actual bus.

You could stare at the picture for an hour or two until the image is burned into your brain. But there's a better, faster way to learn from a picture. Refer to Figure 3-4 as you read about this method.

Pick a system for scanning the picture. You could use vertical (up-and-down) or horizontal (side-to-side) rows, whichever you like. Here's how the horizontal pattern works.

Start at the top left. Work your way across the top, toward the right edge of the picture. Follow the arrows and labels that name each part. Say the name of the part out loud (or, if you are not alone, at least say it to yourself). Move your eyes down a little and scan back towards the left edge of the picture. Continue moving your eyes back and forth across the picture until you arrive at the bottom right, having looked at all the parts.

Using Figure 3-4 as an example, start with the oil pressure gauge at the top left.

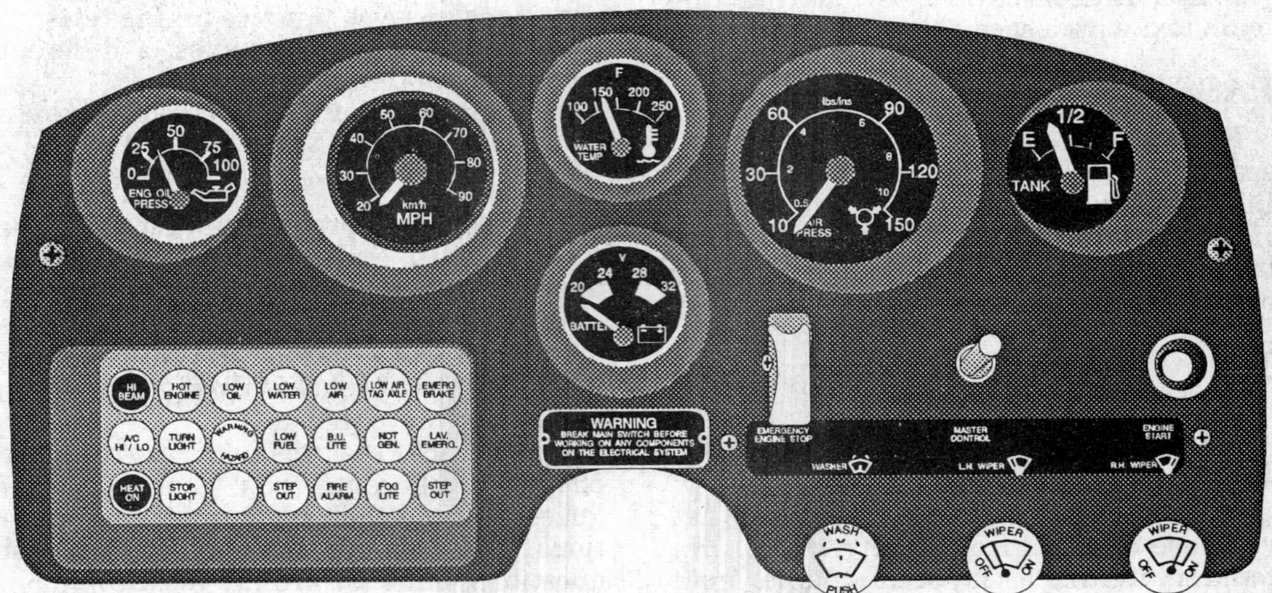

Figure 3-4 Example bus dashboard.

Move your eyes to the right along the instrument cluster at the top, to the fuel gauge at the right. Now move your eyes to the controls down the right side of the picture. Start with the starter button and scan across to the tell-tale panel at the left. Moving back toward the right, study the controls leading to the windshield wiper controls.

Use the same scanning pattern to memorize the different lights on the tell-tale panel.

As you look at the illustration, say the name of each part. Describe it aloud or to yourself. You might say something like this: "Fuel gauge. Circular, with needle. Needle points to left for empty, to the right for full."

Scan the picture several times, until you think you have it down. Then cover up the picture. Get a sheet of paper and a pencil. Sketch the picture as you remember it. You don't have to be an artist. Just get all the parts with their labels in roughly their sizes and shapes and in their approximate positions.

Now compare the picture with your sketch. How much did you recall? If it was a complex system, you may have missed something. Make a note to return to the picture and repeat the exercise from time to time until you can recall every part perfectly.

It doesn't matter which pattern you choose. All the pattern does is give you a system so you see every part of the picture. It keeps you from missing anything. Pick a pattern, and use the same pattern each time. Use the same pattern to sketch or recall the picture that you used to study it in the first place.

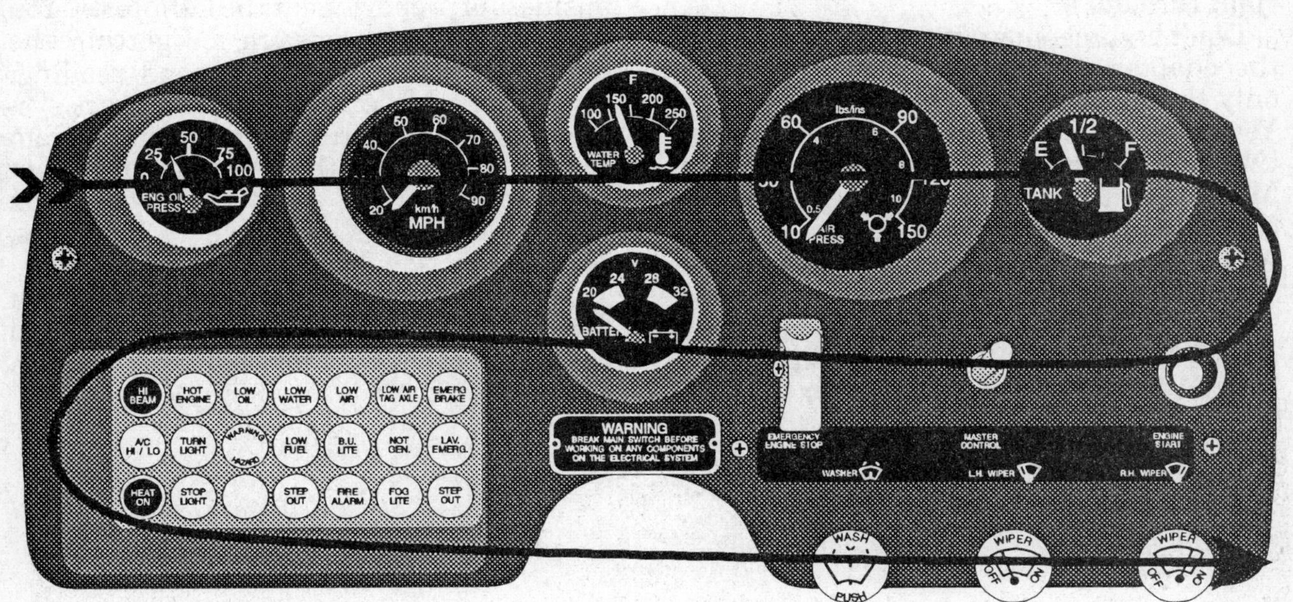

Figure 3-5 Use a scanning pattern to "learn" from a picture.

You will use different methods for answering each type of test question. One of the things we will do in Chapter 4 is show those methods.

Last, these tests help you measure your progress. The **PASS** Pre-trip is a special type of test. While the **PASS** Post-trip tells you how far you have come, the Pre-trip tells you where you were when you started. The **PASS** Pre-trip will help you take stock of how much you already know about the subject you are about to tackle.

We promised you we would not waste your time. Why spend time and energy on what you already know? If you are pressed for time, the **PASS** Pre-trip will help you decide what parts of this book you can go over lightly. Then you can spend the rest of your valuable time where it is needed the most.

The **PASS** Pre-trip will ask three questions about the chapter's subject. You may be able to answer all three questions easily. If so, you can expect the chapter to seem familiar to you. You should be able to sail right through it.

Don't assume, however, that you can skip the chapter entirely. After all, these are only three out of many possible questions. You may feel confident about only one or two of your answers to the **PASS** Pre-trip. Make special note of the questions you could not answer. Pay particular attention to the parts of the chapter that cover those subjects.

Most likely, you will not be able to answer any of the questions. That's to be expected. If you were already well-prepared for the CDL tests, you wouldn't need this book in the first place. If you can't answer any of the **PASS** Pre-trip questions, resolve to pay close attention to the chapter that follows. You may find that, through experience or training, you already know the material. You may simply need to learn different terms or slightly different procedures.

The **PASS** Post-trip will measure whether you have achieved your goal. That goal is usually to learn something or some things about the subject in the chapter. The **PASS** Post-trip will include the three questions that made up the **PASS** Pre-trip. Once you have finished the chapter, you should be able to answer those questions correctly. If you miss these questions a second time, that calls for a close review of the chapter.

There is no "good" or "poor" in your results on either test. Your scores are for your eyes and for your use only. They are simply to guide you in your CDL test preparation efforts.

You're just about ready to tackle the real business of preparing for the CDL tests. You have at least one system for getting the most out of the time you spend reading. That's the scan, examine, and extract system. You have a strategy for learning from illustrations. That's the scan pattern system we described in this chapter. You know you have several tools available to help you, such as a dictionary.

You need only one more piece before you dive in. That's the secret of taking, and passing, tests. We will reveal that secret in Chapter 4.

CHAPTER 4

About Tests

When you have finished this chapter, you will be able to provide the correct answers to questions about:

- the purpose of tests
- the different types of tests
- the different types of test questions and answers
- the way tests are scored
- common test-taking mistakes and how to avoid them
- smart guessing
- what makes the CDL tests special
- how to use the sample tests in this book

To complete this chapter you will need:

- a dictionary
- pencil or pen and eraser
- blank paper or notebook
- colored pencils, pens, markers, or highlighters

In Chapter 3, we introduced the subject of tests. After reading Chapter 3, you may have a different view of tests. Now you see how they can be tools to help you learn.

Thinking about tests you have taken in the past, you may feel some were a real challenge, some hard, some even impossible. You may not have felt very positive about them at all. Some tests are harder than others. Why is that so? There are several reasons. One is that the questions test very fine details of the subject you have studied. You may not have studied with an eye for such fine detail. Another reason is the test questions may be complex. One single question might test several points of information. You have to be able to cover each point to answer the question correctly.

Some tests are hard because they are simply bad tests. They were badly written. Creating a test is harder than you might think. It's not uncommon to find poor tests where answer choices don't really fit the question. Or the test may ask questions about material that wasn't covered. Another thing that test writers do is write trick questions. They have the mistaken idea that this makes a more challenging test. All it does is make an unfair test.

You shouldn't have any of these problems with the sample tests in this book. They were not written to trick you. Every effort was made to make them fair and appropriate questions. You can feel confident about using them to measure your progress.

Nor should you have these problems with your CDL tests. You may find the CDL test questions hard, especially if you are not fully prepared. They may test your knowledge of certain details, and they may be complex questions. You would be unlikely to find the test questions tricky or unfair, though.

Even when asked good, fair test questions, people still manage to give the wrong answers. It may surprise them to find they failed the test. They may claim they worked very hard to prepare for it. When you ask them more about it, you find that they did prepare well. So why did they fail?

It's because there is more to passing a test than simple preparation. There is a wrong way and a right way to take a test. In this chapter, we will show you some of the common mistakes test-takers make. That will help you avoid making those mistakes.

We'll dissect different types of test questions. Knowing how the question was put together will make finding the right answer that much easier.

There are many forms of tests and types of test questions. We'll focus on those you are likely to find on CDL tests.

TYPES OF TESTS

To get your CDL license, you will take two types of tests. These are knowledge tests and performance (skills) tests. Knowledge tests test what you know. Skills tests test what you can do.

Knowing and doing are not the same. What if you are a new, inexperienced driver? You may know how to double-clutch, that is, you can list all the steps involved in double-clutching. Knowing how may not be enough to keep you from grinding the gears when you try to put your knowledge into practice, however.

If you are an experienced driver, you may be able to double-clutch quite smoothly. But try to explain what you are doing to someone else without showing them. It might be harder to explain double-clutching than it is to do it. You may find you don't know all the steps.

The CDL law requires drivers to have certain knowledge and certain skills. It's not enough to "know" how to back your vehicle. You'll have to show you can do this maneuver and do it safely. On the other hand, knowing the details of the Safety Act is enough. There's no performance test for this.

Some aspects of being a licensed commercial driver will be tested by both knowledge and skills tests. One example is vehicle inspection. You will be asked knowledge questions about vehicle inspections. You will also be asked to do a vehicle inspection.

The Knowledge Test is the first CDL test you will take. You must pass the Knowledge Test before you can take any skills tests. So let's look at knowledge tests first.

Knowledge Tests

There are many ways to test what people know. You could ask them to give a report, for example. The method the CDL Knowledge Test uses is to ask you questions and check to see if your answers are correct.

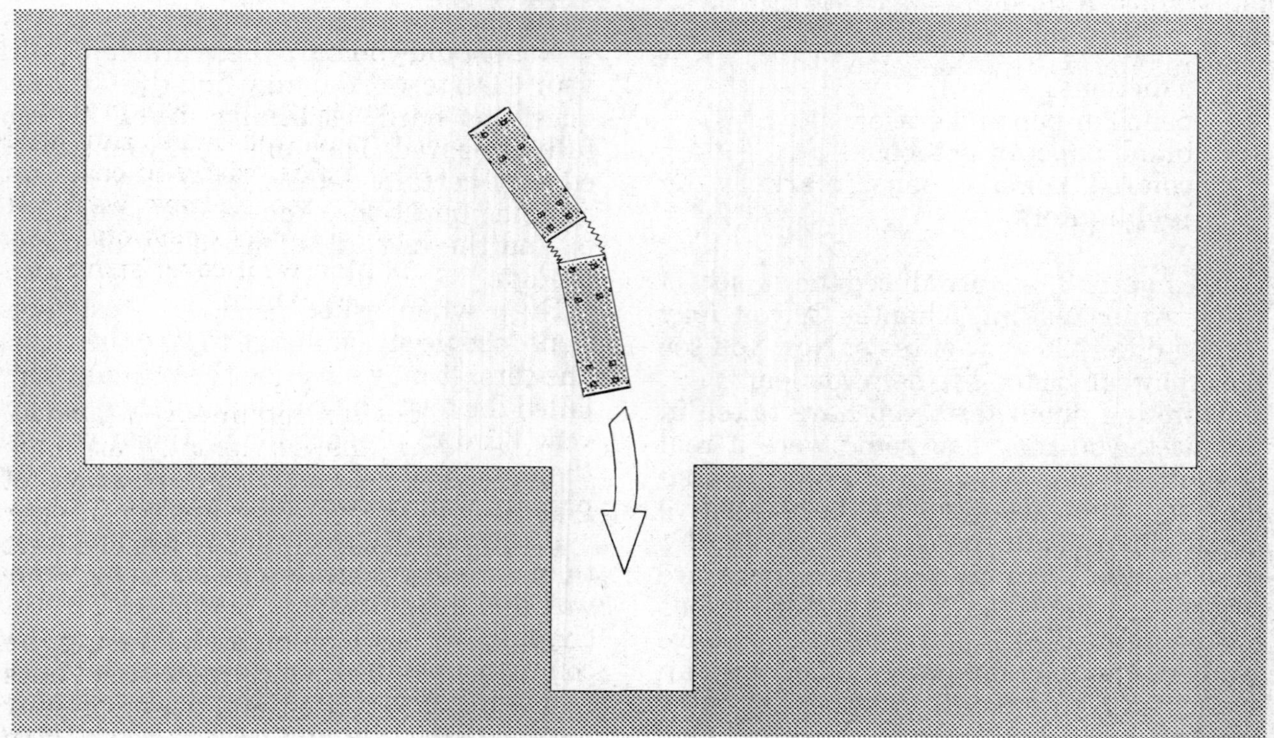

Figure 4-1 It's not enough to "know" how to back your vehicle. You'll have to show you can do it.

The most common way to present such questions is in a written test. On the CDL Knowledge Test you will be given a form with the questions. You may put your answers right on the same form, or you may be given a separate form on which to put your answers.

You will record your answers in one or more ways, based on the type of questions asked. You may have to write out a sentence or two. You may be asked to look at a selection of possible answers and pick the one or ones that you think answer the question correctly. You may be told to check off or circle the right answer.

The examiner may give you an answer form that will be scored by machine. This will be a form with many numbered or lettered boxes. Using a pencil, you fill in the box that has the same number or letter as your answer choice. A machine compares the pencil marks you make with a form that has been filled out correctly. The places where your form does not match are scored as incorrect answers.

You may take your CDL Knowledge Test on a computer. Don't let this concern you. It doesn't make the CDL test harder or special. It's just a different way of presenting the questions to you and recording your answers. You will not be expected to have any experience with computers to do this. You will be given any information you need about taking a test on a computer at the time you take the test. You'll probably find you enjoy taking a test this way.

Figure 4-2 Taking the CDL Knowledge Test.

Some states make an oral test available. Instead of your reading the questions from a form, an examiner will read the questions to you. You will tell the examiner what your answer is instead of writing it down.

You may have to make special arrangements to take an oral exam in your state. Check with your Department of Motor Vehicles in advance if this option interests you.

TYPES OF TEST QUESTIONS

There are many different types of test questions. In your schooling, you likely have run into all of them at one time or another. Here are some of the most common types:

- essay
- matching
- fill-in-the-blank
- true/false
- multiple-choice

Your CDL Knowledge Test will probably have multiple choice questions. But we'll discuss the other types briefly in case you run into those types, too. For now, we'll just introduce you to these test question types. Later in the chapter, we'll cover strategies you can use to answer them.

Essay

An essay question requires you to write or recite your answer, usually at some length. This gives you the advantage of being able to express your answer in your own words. A disadvantage is you don't get any suggested answer choices to jog your memory.

Questions you may be asked during the Skills Tests are like essay questions. That's because you will recite your answers in your own words. No one will prompt you or give you hints about what the right answer is.

Matching

Matching tests offer you two lists. One list contains the questions. These can be words, phrases, or sentences. The other list contains the answers. These can also be words, phrases, or sentences. You are supposed to match one item from the first list with one item from the second. Usually, it's a one-to-one match. That is, both lists have the same number of items. You should not have any unmatched items left over when you are finished.

Matching questions are a good way to test your understanding of terms. You match the term with its definition. You may also be asked to match a regulation to a description of what that regulation requires or when it passed into law. You may even be asked to pick an item from one list that completes a sentence in the other list, making it a true sentence. This is like a fill-in-the-blank question, which we'll discuss next.

In matching questions, you must find your answer among the list of suggested answer choices. You cannot supply an answer that isn't on the list, even if you think it's a better answer. On the plus side, having a list of answer choices in front of you may aid your recall.

Fill-in-the-blank

In this type of test question, you are given a statement that is missing a word or several words. You write out the word or words that are missing. Often, you are given a list of words or phrases to choose from. One of the words or groups of words on the list correctly completes the sentence. You must choose the item that completes the statement and makes it true.

True/False

This type of test question usually presents you with a statement. You must decide whether the statement is true or false. It sounds easy, but don't be fooled. The statement can be quite complex. It may have several parts and conditions. All the parts of the statement must be true for the entire statement to be true. If any part of the statement is false, the entire statement is false.

Multiple-Choice

This is a very common type of question on a knowledge test. It's one you're likely to find on many CDL Knowledge Tests.

The multiple-choice question begins with a part called a stem. This can be a question or a statement. It can be complete or incomplete. It is followed by two or more answer choices. You choose the answer that completes the statement and makes it true. If the stem is a question, you pick the correct answer from the list of choices.

TYPES OF TEST ANSWER CHOICES

So much for types of test questions. Let's look at answer choices. There's a little more to this than just "the right answer" and "the wrong answer."

As we said, on an essay question, you can phrase the answer in your own words. How you phrase your answer usually doesn't matter, so long as you give the examiner enough evidence that you have the knowledge being tested.

On the other types of test questions, you have to choose an answer from a list of choices. These answers are written in someone else's words. They may not be your words. You may not find the answer phrased quite the way you would have phrased it. Nevertheless, you have to choose one of the items on the list.

More than other types of test questions, multiple-choice questions can have different types of test answer choices. You may run into them all on your CDL Knowledge tests. They are:

- only one answer is correct
- one answer is the best answer
- all of the answers are correct
- none of the answers is correct

Only One Answer Is Correct

On most multiple-choice tests, only one answer choice is correct. All the others are wrong. There will usually be a note or instruction if this isn't the case.

One Answer Is the Best Answer

You may be instructed to choose the best answer or something similar. Don't make the mistake of thinking this is the same as the right answer. More than one answer may be correct. But one answer will clearly be the best response.

This is best described by example. Try this multiple choice question:

1. When you approach an intersection marked by a red octagonal stop sign, you should ______ before you proceed through the intersection.

A. come to a full stop
B. come to a full stop and check for other traffic
C. come to a full stop, check for other traffic, and wait for the intersection to clear

As you can see, choice A isn't wrong, but it's not the correct choice for this question. If you were to choose it, you would be marked wrong.

Answer B is a better answer. At a stop sign, you should stop and check for other traffic. This still isn't the correct choice for this test question, though.

The correct answer is choice C. Of the three answers, it has the most complete description of what you should do at a stop sign. You should not only stop and check for other traffic, you should proceed only if the intersection is clear.

These types of questions are often used to test your knowledge of a procedure or system. Sometimes it's simply not enough for you to know only one step of the procedure or one piece of the system. You must know the entire procedure or system for your knowledge to be any good. A test question that asks you to recall all the steps or parts truly tests the completeness of your knowledge.

All the Answers Are Correct

Sometimes, when all the answer choices seem to be correct, they are. Some test questions offer an answer choice that reads "all of the answers are correct" or "all of the above." When you see "all of the above," it's the last of a series of answer choices. If the answers that came before it in the series are all correct, you would choose "all of the above."

Here's an example of "all of the above": Which of the following terms describes a type of tire?

A. bias
B. belted bias
C. radial
D. all of the above

The correct answer is "D." All three terms, bias, belted bias, and radial, describe types of tires. This is a type of "best answer" question. The best answer is "all of the above." It is the only answer that would be correct. Yes, it's true that "belted bias" is a type of tire. You may think it's correct to choose "B" as an answer choice. While "B" is not wrong, it is also not "the best answer." You would be marked wrong for choosing "B" as your answer. Again, the best answer, the only right answer in this case, is "all of the above."

None of the Answers Is Correct

Here is another variation on the best answer test question. It's the opposite of "all of the above." This is the test question where none of the answer choices is correct. Be very careful with this type of test question. You must be absolutely sure that no answer choice is correct before you choose "none of the above."

SCORING KNOWLEDGE TESTS

Most knowledge tests are scored by counting the number of questions that were answered correctly. These are compared with the total number of questions on the test. This comparison is expressed as a percentage. If you took a 100-question test and answered 85 of the questions correctly, you would get a score of 85 percent. A score of 70 percent on a 50 question test means you answered 35 of the 50 questions correctly.

You may have received a letter score, like A, B, or C, on tests you took in school. Here, the letter represents a group of percentages. For instance, the letter A might represent the group of scores from 90 percent to 100 percent. Someone scoring 91 percent would receive an "A," and so would someone scoring 99 percent. However, your score on the CDL Knowledge Test will probably be expressed as a percentage.

On most tests, you must answer a certain number of questions correctly to pass the test. Federal law states that you must score 80 percent or better to pass the CDL Knowledge Test. Your state may require CDL applicants to achieve even higher scores in order to pass the test.

PASS Billboard

Changing Test Scores to Percentages

You'll be keeping track of your progress by scoring your **PASS** Post-trips. It would be handy to change your scores to percentages. If you don't remember how to calculate a percentage, use this chart.

Number of right answers	**Number of questions**									
	100	90	80	70	60	50	40	30	20	10
100	100%	–	–	–	–	–	–	–	–	–
90	90	100	–	–	–	–	–	–	–	–
80	80	89	100	–	–	–	–	–	–	–
70	70	78	88	100	–	–	–	–	–	–
60	60	67	75	86	100	–	–	–	–	–
50	50	56	63	71	83	100	–	–	–	–
40	40	44	50	57	67	80	100	–	–	–
30	30	33	38	43	50	60	75	100	–	–
20	20	22	25	29	33	40	50	67	100	–
10	10	11	12	14	15	20	25	33	50	100

SKILLS TESTS

In addition to Knowledge Tests, you will take Skills Tests to get your CDL. You will be tested on your ability to do certain maneuvers, such as backing and turning. You will also be tested on your skill in driving in traffic.

Sometimes a knowledge test will be combined with a skills test. As you do an inspection, for example, the examiner may ask you questions about the systems you are inspecting. In a sense, you will be taking two tests at the same time. You will not only show you can do a proper inspection, you will also show you have good knowledge of your equipment.

SCORING SKILLS TESTS

Skills tests are a little harder to score than knowledge tests. There are many ways to do a maneuver. Which is the correct way? Take the skill of making right turns. Is it enough simply to get your vehicle around the corner? Is part of the skill how long it takes to turn the corner? Does it count if you scrape the curb or go out into the middle of the intersection? What about the examiner who is measuring your skill? Will two people score the same skill the same way?

Yes, it's hard to score skill tests – but not impossible. The answer to all the questions we just asked about scoring performance tests is "standards." In order for skills tests to be scored fairly, standards have been set for what is considered a "good" performance.

Let's look at right turns again. Most people would agree that it's not good to scrape the curb. So this condition is made part of the standard for scoring the test. The test then would not simply be "Make a right turn," it would be "Make a right turn without scraping the curb." To pass the test,

Figure 4-3 You'll be tested on your skill in driving in traffic.

you must meet both conditions. You must make the turn and you must avoid scraping the curb.

You can feel confident that your CDL Skills Tests have been carefully designed. They will have specific and detailed descriptions of what skills are expected. In making a right-hand turn, for example, your vehicle's rear wheels should come as close to the curb as possible without scraping it. You should also not turn too wide. If you scrape the curb, or turn wider than five feet, your level of skill is not considered "passing."

Conditions like these ensure a fair test and fair scoring. They mean everyone who takes the test is judged by the same standards. They make it possible to measure your level of skill, rather than your looks, your jokes, the attractiveness of your vehicle, or some other factor.

These conditions keep the examiner's personal feelings out of the picture. It doesn't matter how the examiner would have made that turn. It doesn't matter whether the examiner likes you or likes the make of the bus you drive. All the examiner has to decide is whether your performance met all the conditions set in the test.

You will often be told what the conditions are. For the right-hand turn test, the examiner might say, "You must make a right-hand turn without scraping the curb and without turning wider than five feet away from the curb."

You will also be told whether you must meet all the conditions or only most of them. Sometimes it takes only one error to fail a test. This is the case on some of the CDL Skills Tests. Breaking a traffic law or causing an accident during the Skills Test results in automatic failure.

TEST-TAKING TIPS

The best test-taking tip we can give is "prepare well." There's nothing like having a good grasp of the material that will be tested. Along with that, these tips will help you not to make careless errors.

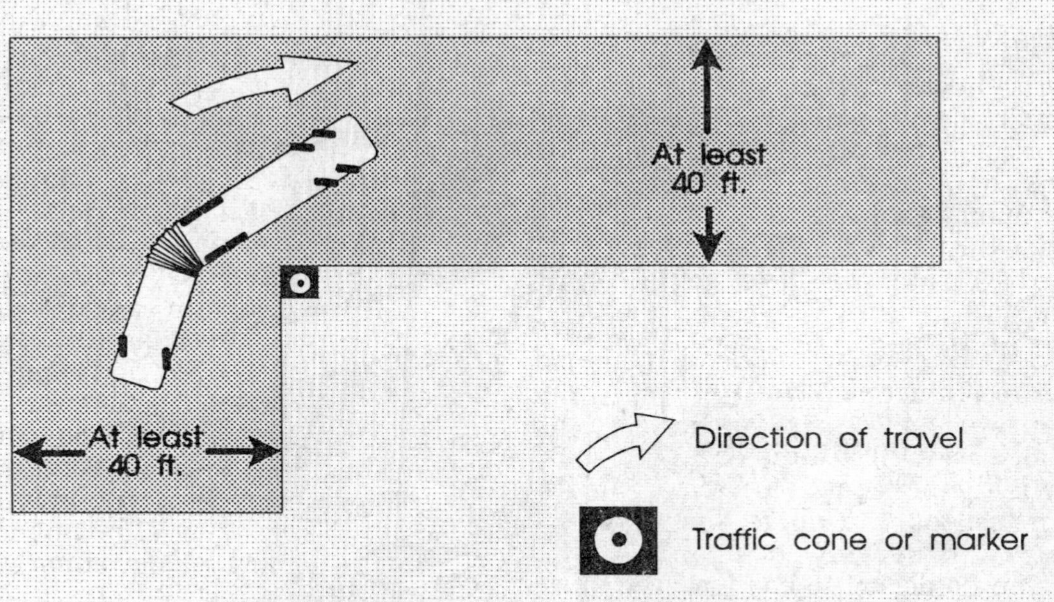

Figure 4-4 The CDL Skills Tests are scored to specific standards.

Understand the Instructions

Before you begin any test, make sure you understand the instructions. On a written test, read any information that comes before the questions. That's where you will find instructions to choose "the right answer" or "the best answer."

If no instructions have been given, ask the examiner. Ask whether you should use a pencil or pen to take the test. Find out whether you may use scrap paper. Will there be a time limit? Don't make a pest of yourself. Do ask enough questions so you think you understand the test conditions.

Don't Rush

If there is no time limit, relax and take all the time you need. Rushing will cause you to make careless errors. Take each question or skill test item one at a time. Clear your mind of the other parts of the test.

Read Carefully

Read Knowledge Test questions carefully. Before you answer, be certain you understand what's being asked. Read any suggested answers just as carefully. When two or more answers seem alike, describe to yourself the difference between them.

Answer the Easy Ones First

Unless you are told to do otherwise, scan through written tests quickly. Answer all the questions you can answer off the top of your head. Then work on the trickier ones. Finally, before you hand in the test, review the easy ones just to make sure you didn't misread them or write down "A" when you meant to write "B."

Avoid Careless Errors

When filling out answer sheets that are separate from the question forms, avoid careless errors. Make sure the number of the question on the question form and the number on the answer blank match. It's not uncommon for test-takers to put the right answer in the wrong answer space. That throws off the entire answer form and makes all the answers that follow wrong. Use your scrap paper, a spare pencil, or your finger to line up the question with the right answer blank.

Write Neatly

Write neatly. Mark your answer choices with firm, bold marks. This is especially important when the answer form will be "read" by a machine. The machine can't read marks that are too light or that fall outside the fill-in area. These marks will be scored as wrong answers.

Don't Change Your Answer

It's recommended that you don't change an answer choice once you have made it. Usually, your first decision about the answer is the best one. More often than not, when test-takers change an answer, they change it to the wrong one.

If you do decide to change your answer, erase the old answer completely. Make sure it's clear that your new answer is the one you mean.

Again, with machine-scored tests, this is vital. If you do not erase completely, the machine may see two answer choices marked. This will be scored as a wrong answer, even if one of the answers happens to be the right choice.

Figure 4-5 Rushing through the CDL tests will only cause you to make careless errors.

Don't Leave Blanks

Don't leave any blanks on written tests. If you don't know the answer, plan to come back to the question later. Often, other questions on the test will refresh your memory of the subject. Even if that doesn't happen, you can make a smart guess. We'll cover that next. Before you leave the question, though, make a circle, "X," arrow, or some other mark beside the question or answer blank. That makes it easier to find when you want to tackle it again. It also helps you to see that you have left something blank so you don't hand in the test with questions left unanswered.

It's really not to your advantage to leave any blanks. If there are four answer choices, even if you make a wild guess, you have a one-in-four chance of hitting the right one. You can improve your chances with smart guessing.

Smart Guessing

To make a smart guess, eliminate any answer choices you know are wrong. Does one of the remaining answer choices have words like "all," "every," "always," or "never"? Consider that answer carefully. It's rare that something is always so or never the case. You may be able to eliminate this answer choice after all.

That narrows your choices. You may be left with only two choices instead of four. A wild guess will then give you a 50-50 chance of getting the right answer. By now, one of the remaining two answers may look pretty good to you. You may feel quite certain it's the right one after all.

Penalties for Guessing

The only time you want to leave questions unanswered is if there is a penalty for guessing. Some tests are scored as the percentage of right answers compared with the number of total questions answered. This is different from tests where the right answers are compared with the total number of questions **asked.** On such a test, it's better to leave a question blank if you don't know the answer.

There will usually be some information on the test that tells you when there is a penalty for guessing. Your CDL Knowledge Tests will not likely have such penalties. Unless you are told otherwise, make smart guesses on the questions that have you stumped.

TIPS FOR DIFFERENT TEST QUESTION TYPES

Matching

On a matching test, look for any instructions first. You may be told that the first list is a list of terms and you are to match terms to their definitions. Or each list may have a heading that describes the items in the list. Look for clues about what relationship the two lists have to each other.

If there are an equal number of items in each list, you probably have to make a one-to-one match. If there are more items offered on the answer list than there are on the question list, this isn't the case. You will clearly have some left over. Or you may have fewer answers than there are questions. In that case, some answers are used more than once. You guessed it – these variations make the test more challenging.

Scan the lists quickly. Make any matches that jump out at you. If you have scrap paper, you may want to use pieces of it to cover up any answer choices you have eliminated in this first pass. Or draw a line through them (unless you're told not to write on the form). Since you have already used them, you don't need to consider them as answers for any of the other questions. If you remove them from view, you reduce the chance of mistakenly choosing them a second time.

Next, work on any remaining unmatched question items. Taking each one in turn, try to answer it without looking at the answer choices. If the question item is a term, define it. If it's a regulation, what does it regulate? If it's an item of equipment, what does it do, and so on.

Look over the list of matching choices. Do you see your definition there? If so, match the two. Draw a line through or cover up the answer you have chosen.

Continue to make all the matches you can. Skip over any you can't answer at all. Come back to those when you have done all the easy ones. By then you will have eliminated more answer choices. You'll have a short list of answers to choose from, instead of the entire range.

Consider each of the answer choices with the remaining questions. Examine the questions and answers closely. You may notice some things right away that help you to make the correct matches. Take these three sample matching question and answer choices.

Term	Definition
1. duals	A. riding on the surface of water
2. hydroplaning	B. two tires on one axle
3. check valve	C. a part of the braking system

The first item, "duals," seems to be asking about a group of things. Only one of your remaining answers refers to a group. That is "two tires on one axle." That's the correct match for "duals."

Notice also that "hydroplaning" seems to be asking about an action, rather than a thing. "Riding on the surface of the water" is the only answer choice left that is also an action rather than a thing. That's the correct match for "hydroplaning."

Now you're left with one question, "check valve," and one answer, "a part of the braking system." Match those two up and you are done.

Use this logic if you are simply flat out stuck on some test questions. Stop racking your brain for definitions you don't know. Take a mental step back and simply look at the words. Try to find any way in which they relate to each other or seem alike. That may lead you to the match the test is asking you to make.

True/False

Usually true/false questions are worded as statements. You decide whether they are true statements or not. Sometimes true/

false questions are worded as questions. An example would be, "Are on-duty drivers who take narcotics prescribed to them by a doctor breaking the law?" If you would answer the question "yes," your answer should be "true." If you would answer the question "no," your answer should be "false." (In this case, the answer is "yes." The "question" is "true.")

Remember that all parts of the statement or question must be true, for you to say it's a true statement. If any part is false, then "false" is your answer. Take this true/false question, for example:

1. It is safe for an on-duty driver to take over-the-counter cold remedies without a prescription.
   A. True
   B. False

The answer to this question is "B. False." Yes, it's true that over-the-counter cold remedies can be taken without prescription. But it's not true that on-duty drivers can take them safely. Many of these medications cause drowsiness. It would not be safe for a driver to take them while driving. If the driver in the question were "off duty," the answer to the question would be "A. True."

Be on the lookout for words like "always," "every," "never," "all," and "complete." These words should make you read the statement very carefully. Be certain that your answer, true or false, covers every possible case, since a question like this does not allow for any exceptions.

True/false questions look easy. That's why it's especially important to read them closely.

Multiple-Choice

Multiple-choice questions are a little easier to answer if you follow a system. We'll assume we're dealing with the "only one answer is correct" type of question.

First, read the question to yourself. Then read the question with the first answer choice. Does the combination make a true statement? If so, this answer choice is correct. If not, go on to the next choice.

Read the question with each answer choice in turn. Note which combinations make a true statement. Most times, only one answer will make a true statement of the question stem. If more than one answer seems to be correct, use the elimination and smart-guessing techniques already described to narrow the choices.

Read "best answer" test questions and their answer choices very carefully. Describe to yourself the difference between the answer choices. Does one include more details than the others? If all the details are true, this may be the best answer. An answer that is a lot shorter, or a lot longer, than all the rest is often the correct answer.

All the Answers Are Correct

Be careful when one of the answer choices is "all of the above." Just because "all of the above" is an answer choice doesn't mean it's the correct one. Select it only if you have convinced yourself that all the answer choices are correct. It may be that one or more of the answer choices is indeed wrong.

Try each answer choice with the question. Make certain that each one completes the question and makes it a true statement or answers the question correctly. If all the answer choices meet this test, then the answer choice to select is "all of the above."

PASS PRACTICE TESTS

Throughout the rest of this book, you will find many sample tests on which to practice. You'll have a chance to work with true/false, matching, and multiple-choice questions. Try all the techniques described in this chapter.

After you have scored your own tests, examine the questions you missed. Did you make careless errors, or were you simply not prepared enough? Keep track of your results. See whether practice helps you make fewer careless errors.

You'll also find some practice skills tests. They will include specific conditions your performance must meet to be considered "passing." Keep these conditions in mind when you self-score your performance.

This concludes Part One. You've covered test preparation and test-taking in general. In Part Two, you'll get into preparation specifically for taking the CDL tests. Before we leave Chapter 4, though, there's one last item to cover.

In the following chapters, you may read about facts or procedures that differ from what you already know or do. The terms used for equipment or maneuvers may not be the ones you are familiar with or use. That doesn't mean you are wrong.

Your way may be just fine. You may even be better informed. But to get a CDL, you'll have to do things by the book. You must speak the language used by the CDL Tests and the examiners.

When you find a way of doing something or describing something that's different from what you are used to, make a special note of it. Review it and get it firmly in your mind. You don't want to be surprised by it on the test. If you're looking only for answers phrased your way, you won't recognize the right answers when you see them.

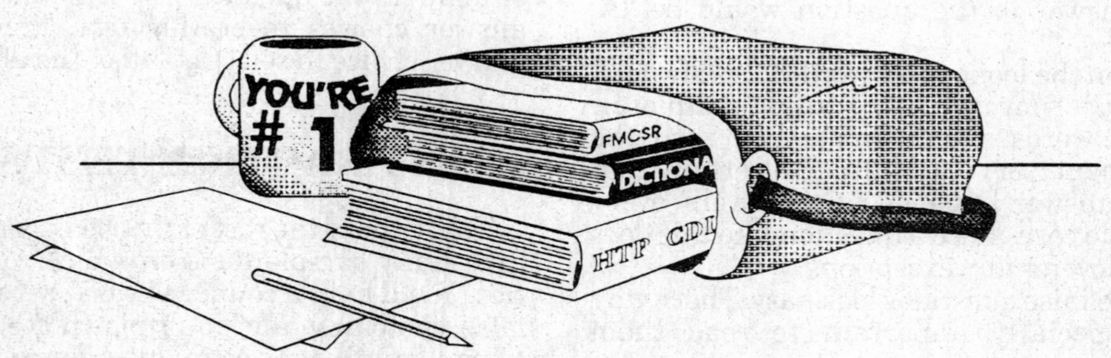

PART TWO

CHAPTER 5

Commercial Driver Licensing

When you have finished this chapter, you will be able to provide the correct answers to questions about:

- what is the Commercial Driver's License
- who must have a Commercial Driver's License
- how to get a Commercial Driver's License
- penalties for not having a Commercial Driver's License
- areas of knowledge and skill covered by the Commercial Driver's License
- Commercial Driver's License Tests
- other Safety Act rules regarding commercial driver licensing

To complete this chapter you will need:

- a dictionary
- pencil or pen
- blank paper or notebook
- colored pencils, pens, markers, or highlighters
- a CDL preparation manual from your state Department of Motor Vehicles, if one is offered
- driver license manual from your state Department of Motor Vehicles
- Federal Motor Carrier Safety Regulations pocketbook (or access to U.S. Department of Transportation regulations, Parts 383, 387, and 390–399 of Subchapter B, Chapter 3, Title 49, Code of Federal Regulations)

PASS PRE-TRIP

Instructions: Read the three statements. Decide whether each statement is true or false. If it is true, circle the letter A. If it is false, circle the letter B.

1. If you do not have a Hazardous Materials Endorsement on your Commercial Driver's License, you can never haul hazardous materials.

A. True
B. False

2. It is legal to have a Commercial Driver's License from more than one state if you lived in that state when you got that license.

A. True
B. False

3. There is a national Commercial Driver's License required by federal law, but your home state may decide not to adopt the CDL.

A. True
B. False

How did you do with these first **PASS** Pre-trip questions? Did you feel confident about your answers? More likely, you may have felt you didn't know the first thing about commercial driver licensing. Don't worry. When you finish this chapter, you will know the answers to the **PASS** Pre-trip questions and more besides.

The Commercial Driver Licensing program took a lot of effort and compromise to develop. It can seem rather complicated just reading about it. In practice, though, commercial driver licensing is quite simple. As a commercial driver, you'll have little trouble deciding how it applies to you. You'll find the Commercial Driver's License program easy to live with.

CDL BACKGROUND

The Commercial Driver's License is a special type of driving license. Before we explore this special license, it would be helpful for you to have a clear understanding of just what is a driver's license – any type of driver's license.

Driver Licensing

A driver's license is permission to drive granted by a body of government. That makes driving a regulated activity.

To get your license to drive any heavy vehicle, you go to the Motor Vehicles Department of your home state. This is because it is your state that grants you the license to drive. It's not the city, county, or Federal government.

Commercial Driver Licensing

A Commercial Driver's License (CDL) grants permission to people who have passed one or more tests. By passing, they have shown that they have the knowledge and skill to drive certain types of vehicles in certain conditions. The CDL law is quite specific about types of vehicles, conditions, and drivers concerned. We'll cover these later in this chapter.

The Pride's Back Inside! From Now On, Only the Best Will Drive...

You may have already noticed the "Pride ... " slogan and the thumbs-up symbol on CDL materials. This slogan and symbol are part of the CDL program's theme. It was developed by The American Association of Motor Vehicle Administrators (AAMVA) jointly with the regulated motor carrier community.

The slogan and symbol recognize the special skill and preparation it takes to

---

PASS Billboard

Abbreviations and Acronyms

You will see many abbreviations and acronyms in this book. An abbreviation is a shortened form of a word. For example, "Dept." is an abbreviation. It is a shortened form of the word "Department." You can tell it's an abbreviation because it ends with a period. This is true whether it appears at the beginning, in the middle, or at the end of a sentence.

An acronym is a word formed from the first letters of several words in a group. Taking the first letters of the words in the group "Department of Transportation" forms the acronym "DOT." You can tell it's an acronym, and not a word by itself, because it appears in all capital letters.

In this book, you will always be properly introduced to the abbreviation or acronym. First you will see the whole word, name, or group of words spelled out. That will be followed by the abbreviation or acronym enclosed in curved brackets called parentheses. After the abbreviation or acronym has been introduced in this way, it will be used throughout the book with no further explanation.

THE PRIDE'S BACK INSIDE!

Figure 5-1 The symbol of PRIDE.

drive a heavy vehicle. Commercial drivers handle complex and costly equipment. Whether they transport expensive cargo, passengers, or hazardous materials, they must do so safely. They must drive with regard for the public and the environment, as well as their own safety.

It takes special skill and knowledge to do many important jobs in today's society. Airline pilots, police officers, and other professionals prepare for and take tests to earn special licenses. They take pride in that special testing and licensing. Now the licensed commercial driver can also take pride in being a member of a recognized skilled profession.

FMCSR PART 383, COMMERCIAL DRIVER'S LICENSE STANDARDS

The CDL is part of the Federal Motor Carrier Safety Standards. These standards are, in turn, part of a larger body of regulations. These are the regulations set by the U.S. Department of Transportation in Subchapter B, Chapter 3, Title 49 of the Code of Federal Regulations (CFR).

If you have a Federal Motor Carrier Safety Regulations (FMCSR) pocketbook, you are familiar with other standards. Driver log books (hours of service) are covered in Part 395 of the FMCSR. Vehicle inspections are Part 396. The Commercial Driver Licensing laws are Part 383 of the FMCSR.

This may be starting to seem like just so much alphabet soup. You are expected to know it, though.

TIP *You should, at least once, read these regulations in their official language. If you would like your own copy of the FMCSR, you can order one from any number of companies that supply materials to the transportation industry. You could also contact either the U.S. Government Printing Office or your local motor transport association. The address of the U.S. Government Printing Office is:*

U.S. Government Printing Office
Superintendent of Documents
Washington, D.C. 20402
Telephone: (202) 783-3238

You'll find the address and telephone number of each state motor transport association listed in Appendix C at the end of this book.

TIP *An appendix in a book is extra material. Like our **PASS Billboards,** it's material you may find helpful or may not need at all. That's why you will usually find appendices (that's the plural of appendix) at the back of a book, after the main material. This book has several appendices.*

The FMCSR is a compact book and usually is not very expensive. Title 49 CFR, on the other hand, is larger and more costly. You can find what you want to know for your CDL test in the FMCSR.

If you can't afford or get your own copy of the FMCSR, check with the reference librarian at your local public library. The library will either have an FMCSR or a copy of Title 49 CFR or both. You can't take either out of the library, however. You can only look at them there. You will really be a lot better off with your own copy. You will refer to the FMCSR often to prepare for your CDL.

CMVSA 1986

In 1986, the Congress of the United States of America passed the Commercial Motor Vehicle Safety Act (CMVSA). The goal of this act was to improve driver quality and remove unsafe and unqualified commercial motor vehicle (CMV) drivers from the highway.

The Federal Highway Administration (FHWA) of the U.S. Department of Transportation (DOT) responded to this Act by changing some regulations and adding Part 383 to the FMCSR. These changes fall into two main areas of interest to commercial drivers:

- the single license law
- commercial driver testing and licensing

These changes occurred at the federal level of government. It's still state governments that issue licenses to CMV drivers. Each state's licensing standards must comply with the federal regulations, however. Within certain limits, states may develop their own tests and licenses for commercial drivers. These tests and licenses must, however, at least meet the federal requirements. State standards can be higher or more demanding than the federal standards, but they can't be lower or less demanding.

The bottom line is, although it is state governments that issue driving licenses, there is a national Commercial Driver's License required by federal law. Effective April 1, 1992, your home state must have a CDL program that meets the federal requirements.

These requirements are set out in Part 383 of the FMCSR. If you have a copy of the FMCSR, follow along as we discuss each section of that part.

PASS Billboard

"May," "should," and "must" are common words that you are used to in everyday language. They are often used as if they mean more or less the same thing. Most of the time that doesn't matter.

When laws are written, however, the meaning of words must be very clear. "May," "should," and "must" have unique and specific meanings when used in a legal sense. They refer to three different levels of permission.

"May" refers to a relaxed level of permission. When a law says you may do something, it means you are allowed. If there is more than one action possible, the choice is yours to make. This is usually used when some conditions have been set. If the situation meets the condition, then you may choose to act or not to act.

Take, for instance, a law that says you may make a right turn at a red light. This means there is nothing that would stop you, legally, from making that turn. Of course, there may be reasons, besides whether it is legal or not, that you wouldn't want to make that right turn. Perhaps you're concerned that oncoming traffic turning left will turn into your lane, so you stop at the red light and wait for a green light before you turn. As far as the law is concerned, though, a right turn at a red light is permitted.

Sometimes, you might see the word "can" used instead of "may." "Can" refers to ability rather than permission. That is, you might have permission to do something but not the ability. You might have permission to make a right hand turn, but if your steering system breaks down, you might not have the ability to make it. This is splitting hairs, though. It's all right to

Figure 5-2 Some laws state you "may" make a right turn at a red light.

assume that if a law says you "can" do something, it means the same as you "may" do something.

"Should" gives you a little less permission than "may." It carries recommendations with it. It's usually used with some conditions. The "right on red" law could more accurately be stated, "You should stop at a red light. If it is safe to do so, after you have stopped, you may make a right turn at a red light." The recommendation is that you stop at the red light. The condition is that it must be safe to proceed. Once the situation has met that condition, you have permission to choose whether to turn or not.

The recommendation in "should" laws is more than an idle suggestion. It's usually best to do what is recommended. Although you have permission to make your own choice, you will rarely get into trouble if you just do what the law would prefer you to do.

The last level of permission is "must." A law that states you must do something (or must not do something) gives you no choice at all. Don't even bother to think about it, to second-guess it, or make excuses. Just do it (or don't do it if the law says you must not). If the law says, "You must stop at a red light," then stop. Don't think, "Well, I'm the only one on the road, so I may as well go ahead." It doesn't matter if you are the only one who has been on that road in 20 years. The law says, "You must stop." So stop.

Keep the differences between these words in mind when you read about regulations or try to decide their meaning.

There's one last word you'll see often in the FMCSR but rarely hear in everyday speech. That word is "shall." As used in the FMCSR, it gives the same level of permission as "must."

Purpose and Scope

The purpose and scope of the CDL program is described in FMCSR Part 383, Subpart A (General), Section 383.1. As you know by now, the purpose has two targets. They are:

- help reduce or prevent truck and bus accidents, deaths, and injuries by requiring drivers to have a single commercial motor vehicle driver's license
- disqualifying drivers who operate commercial motor vehicles in an unsafe manner

How does the CDL program achieve this? We'll answer that question briefly, then address each point in greater detail later in the chapter.

First, a CMV driver may have only one CMV driver's license. This is known as the single license requirement.

Next, drivers must notify their current employers and their home states of certain convictions.

Drivers must provide previous employment information when they apply for jobs as CMV drivers.

Employers must not hire anyone with a suspended license to operate a commercial motor vehicle.

Persons convicted of certain criminal acts or traffic violations are subject to fines, suspensions, loss of license, and other penalties.

Commercial motor vehicle drivers must pass tests and receive a special license.

States must give knowledge and skills tests to all qualified applicants for commercial driver's licenses.

There are different types of licenses, called endorsements, for different types of vehicles and cargoes.

Drivers must meet specific knowledge and skill requirements to be licensed to drive certain vehicles and haul certain cargo.

Commercial driver licensing tests must meet specific standards. Commercial driver's license applicants must achieve a stated minimum score on these tests.

States must keep records on licensed commercial drivers.

Section 383.3 states that the rules in FMCSR Part 383 apply to all who operate commercial motor vehicles in interstate, foreign, or intrastate commerce. These rules also apply to the employers of these drivers.

Definitions

Section 383.5 defines many of the terms used to describe the CDL program. You may

Figure 5-3 Drivers must meet specific knowledge and skill requirements to be licensed to drive certain vehicles and haul certain cargo.

more than one state. This is known as the Single License Requirement. This requirement became effective as of July 1, 1987, and it applies to all CMV drivers.

You may have one driver's license issued by the state where you live.

If you are found to have more than one license, you are breaking the law. You may be fined up to $5,000.

Check now to see whether you are holding more than one license. If so, return all those not issued by your home state. Use the Driver's License Return Form (Figure 5-5). If you have more than one license to return, make copies of the form. You can use a copy machine or simply write out the same words on a separate piece of paper. Fill out one form for each license you are returning. Send the form and the license together to the Department of Motor Vehicles of the state that issued the license. Addresses of Department of Motor Vehicle offices are listed in Appendix B at the back of this book.

Don't simply destroy the license or wait for it to expire. The state's records will still show that you have an active license.

Testing and Licensing

Section 383.23 of the FMCSR states that effective April 1, 1992, all drivers of commercial vehicles must have taken and passed the CDL tests. No one may drive a CMV without a Commercial Driver's License.

There are certain drivers who are exempt from the CDL requirement. Drivers whose state of domicile is in a foreign country that does not have a CDL program don't get a regular CDL. These drivers get a "non-resident CDL." This non-resident CDL must meet the requirements of the regular CDL.

(There's an exception to this exception. Canada's CDL meets the requirements of the U.S. CDL, so Canadian drivers must have a Canadian CDL. They then may not have a U.S. CDL or a non-resident CDL. This would cause them to be in violation of the single license requirement.)

People who are learning to drive a CMV obviously don't have a CDL. Yet, they must be able to drive a commercial vehicle to train properly. These people should get a learner's permit from their state. A learner's permit allows learners to drive a CMV. They must be accompanied when they are driving the CMV by someone who does hold a valid CDL for the same group type CMV. Also, these learners must have a valid automobile driver's license or at least have passed all the vision, sign/symbol, and knowledge tests they would take to get an automobile driver's license.

Notification Requirements and Employer Responsibilities

Once you have a CDL and are operating a CMV, you are subject to the notification requirements. These apply to traffic violations other than parking offenses. They apply no matter what type of motor vehicle you were driving.

Drivers who are convicted of a traffic violation in a state **other** than the one that issued their license must notify their home state. That is, they must notify the state that issued their CDL of a conviction they received for a traffic violation in any other state. This notification must be made within 30 days from the date of the conviction.

They must also notify their employer of the conviction. This also must be done within 30 days of the conviction. If they are not employed at the time, they must notify the state that gave them their CDL license.

License Return Form

I am returning my license. Please change your records to show that I no longer hold an active license in your state.

Figure 5-5 License Return Form

They must make this notification in writing. This should include:

- the driver's full name
- the driver's license number
- the date of conviction
- the specific offense or violation
- any suspension or loss of driving privileges that resulted from the violation
- whether the violation was in a CMV
- where the offense took place
- the driver's signature

The written notification must be made to both the state official and the employer.

When an employee's license is suspended, revoked, or canceled, the employee must notify the employer. This notification must be made before the end of the business day following the day the employee received notice of the suspension. This notification must be made if the license is lost due to suspension, revocation, cancellation, or disqualification.

When applying for a job as a CMV driver, an applicant must provide the future employer with certain background information. Employers must require this information at the time the applicant makes the employment application. The background information must cover the past 10 years of employment. The information that must be provided consists of:

- a list of the names and addresses of the applicant's previous employers. Only those employers who hired the applicant as a CMV driver need to be listed.
- the dates the applicant was employed by these employers and the reason for leaving such employment
- certification by the applicant that the information is true and complete
- additional information that the employer requires

Before the application is turned in, the employer must tell the applicant that these references will be checked. The future employer may contact former employers to confirm this work history.

Employers may not knowingly hire or require anyone to drive a CMV whose CDL has been suspended, revoked, or canceled and not yet restored. An employer may not knowingly hire or require anyone to drive a CMV who has more than one valid CDL.

Disqualifications and Penalties

As you might expect, there are serious penalties for violating these CDL laws. These are described in FMCSR Part 383.51.

Very simply, a driver who is disqualified may not drive a CMV. An employer may not allow a disqualified driver to operate a CMV.

What causes a driver to be disqualified? Causes are:

- driving while under the influence of alcohol
- driving while under the influence of a controlled substance
- leaving the scene of an accident involving a CMV
- a felony that involves the use of a CMV

Figure 5-6 Driving while under the influence of alcohol is grounds for disqualification.

TIP *Recall the definition of DUI? Quick, write down what you remember. Then review the earlier material on Section 383.5 or review the material in your copy of the FMCSR.*

The length of the disqualification depends on the offense. First-time offenders are disqualified for one year. This is unless hazardous materials requiring placards are involved. In that case, a first-time offender is disqualified for three years.

There is also a special penalty for drivers involved in certain felonies. This is the case of the driver who uses a CMV to commit a felony that involves the manufacture, distribution, or issue of controlled substances. This driver is disqualified for life. That's right. Such a driver can never legally drive a CMV ever again.

Some people never learn, so there are harsher penalties for repeat offenders. Repeat offenders are disqualified for life if they have already been convicted of DUI (alcohol or drugs), leaving the scene of an accident, or committing a felony. The law does provide for a second chance, though. A driver who has been disqualified for life can reduce the lifetime disqualification to 10 years. First, the driver must enroll in and successfully complete a rehabilitation program. This rehabilitation program must meet the state licensing agency's standards. After completing the program, the driver must apply to restore the CDL. Last, the driver must meet any requirements the state has for reinstating CDLs.

Having gotten the CDL restored, if the driver commits one of these offenses a third time, the driver is again disqualified for life. There are no second chances this time.

There are also no second chances for drivers disqualified for using a CMV to manufacture, distribute, or issue controlled substances. On conviction, that offense earns a lifetime disqualification the first time out. This disqualification is permanent.

There are separate penalties for CMV drivers who commit serious traffic violations. Recall the definition of serious traffic violations? If not, review that section now. Then return to this page.

There is no disqualification penalty for the first offense. (There may be other types of penalties for breaking traffic laws, such as fines or sentences.) If two offenses are committed within three years, the second conviction earns the driver a 60-day disqualification. Three violations in three years results in disqualification for 120 days.

States honor each other's disqualification penalties. That means a driver who is disqualified by one state will not likely be given a CDL by another state.

Remember, states may have additional penalties for these crimes. Disqualification as a commercial driver is simply the penalty set forth by federal law.

Before we leave this section, make note of this. The disqualification penalties are for offenses committed using a CMV. The notification requirements cover traffic violations committed using any motor vehicle. If you commit a moving violation in your personal car, you must notify your employer. Of course, you have to pay whatever price that violation brings. However, you may not be disqualified as a CDL driver because of it.

Other Testing and Licensing Requirements

The CDL law adds testing and licensing standards to qualification requirements that already exist. Applicants for a CDL who plan to drive interstate must meet the qualifications set in FMCSR Part 391. Persons who will drive intrastate must certify that they are not subject to Part 391 and must meet any state driver qualification requirements.

CDL applicants must pass a Knowledge Test and a Driving Test. (These tests will be described in greater detail later in this section.) The driving test must be taken in a vehicle that is representative of the one the CDL applicant plans to drive.

CDL applicants must supply the information required to fill out a CDL document and application. This will become the Commercial Driver's License or CDL. The license itself is described in Subpart J of FMCSR 383.

PASS Billboard

FMCSR Part 391 deals with the qualifications of drivers. Even with the CDL program, drivers still have to meet these qualifications or show they are exempt from them.

Briefly, drivers who meet the qualifications:

- are at least 21 years old
- can read and speak English well enough to talk with the general public, understand highway signs, respond to officials, and fill out reports and records
- can safely operate the vehicle
- can tell whether cargo is distributed properly
- can secure cargo
- meet physical qualifications
- have a single valid commercial motor vehicle operator's license
- have notified the employer of any violations or certified that there are none to report
- have not been disqualified to drive a motor vehicle
- have completed a road test or its equal
- have taken a written test on the FMCSR (and Hazardous Materials Regulations, if required) or its equal
- have completed an official "driver application for employment"

This section also provides for drug testing. Applicants must take and pass a drug test before they can be hired. Drivers must then take and pass a drug test at least once every two years.

Figure 5-7 Drivers must be able to secure cargo.

The application asks for such information as:

- the full name, signature, and mailing address of the person getting the license
- physical and other information describing the licensed person
- a color photograph of the driver
- the driver's state license number
- the name of the state issuing the license
- the date the license was issued and when it expires
- the CMV or CMVs the driver is licensed to operate
- any endorsements
- an air brake restriction, if it applies
- the driver's social security number, unless this is a non-resident CDL

CDL applicants must then certify that they are not disqualified from driving. They must state that they do not have any other driving licenses from any other state. If they have any non-CDL driver's licenses, they must give them over to the state.

This section of the FMCSR (Section 383.71) also tells what to do if you already have a CDL and want to transfer it, renew it, or upgrade it.

If you move your permanent residence to another state, you must transfer your license. That way your CDL will be issued by your new state of domicile. You must apply for a new CDL from your new home state no more than 30 days after you have settled in your new home.

You provide your new state with the same type of information you gave to get your original CDL. You give up your CDL from your old home state. Then you get a new CDL from your new home state. As long as your old CDL was still valid, you do not need to retake the tests.

If you had a hazardous materials endorsement, you must show that within the past two years, you passed the test to earn this endorsement. If this isn't the case, you can take and pass a hazardous materials test or pass a training course that the state accepts as a substitute.

Commercial driver's licenses do expire. If you want to go on driving, you must renew yours. The process is similar to transferring your license. You certify that you are or are not covered by FMCSR Part 391. You update the information you gave to get your CDL the first time. Renewing your hazardous materials endorsement involves the same process as transferring it.

As you progress in your driving career, you may want to upgrade your license. You may want to change the type of vehicle you are licensed to drive. You may want to add endorsements.

To upgrade your CDL, you again certify that you are or are not covered by FMCSR Part 391. You pass all the tests you took to get your original CDL. You take and pass any additional tests to earn new endorsements.

Some pages back, we introduced the nonresident CDL. This license is for drivers whose home state is a foreign country, without a CDL program. These drivers get one, and only one, non-resident CDL from any state with a CDL program. To get one, applicants must complete the same requirements for getting a regular CDL. They also must report any action their home government, or any government, may make against their driving privileges. This report must be made to the state that gave them the non-resident CDL. This report must be made within the same time limits as the regular notification requirements discussed earlier.

Implied Consent

Getting a CDL carries with it an "implied consent to alcohol testing." This is stated in FMCSR 383.72. If you are stopped on suspicion of drunkenness, you may not refuse to take a breath test or other test for drunkenness. By accepting your license, you state in advance that you agree to take such tests. If you refuse anyway, you may be disqualified from driving. This was stated in FMCSR 383.51. Reread the section on Disqualifications and Penalties to see how these two sections relate to each other.

State Procedures

Section 383.73 of the FMCSR outlines the state's role in granting CDLs. Your home state takes your application. It gives you the appropriate tests and decides whether you passed them. The state makes sure you take the test in the type of vehicle you plan to drive. It conducts the process of transferring, renewing, or updating your CDL.

The state checks your driving record. In making this check, the state uses the Commercial Driver's License Information System (CDLIS). Through CDLIS, all the states can share the records they have on drivers they have licensed. Because of CDLIS, bad drivers can no longer bury their driving violations in one state and get a license from another.

It is the state that hands out penalties to applicants who provide false information on their applications. Your CDL comes from your home state. Still, other states that have

CDL programs honor your CDL. This is known as reciprocity.

The CDL law permits states to contract with a third party to give the CDL tests. This explains why you may actually take one or all of your CDL tests at a truck driving school or motor carrier or other private company, instead of on state grounds.

Last, this section permits states to excuse some applicants from having to take the Skills Test. If you have a current, valid license and have a good driving record, your state may excuse you from taking the Skills Test. A "good driving record" means that in the past two years you have not had your license suspended, revoked, or canceled. You must not have been disqualified from driving in the past two years. Your driving record for the past two years must be free of traffic violations connected with an accident (other than parking violations). You must also prove that you are regularly employed as a CMV driver. You must show evidence that in the past, you took and passed a skills test and received a classified license.

TIP *A classified license is one that states or limits the type of vehicle you may drive.*

You must prove that the skills test you passed was behind the wheel of a vehicle representative of the one you plan to drive with your CDL. Last, you must show evidence that you have experience driving this type of vehicle. You must have had this experience in the two years that just passed before you applied for a CDL.

If you can prove all these things, your state may waive, or excuse you from taking, the CDL Skills Test.

Vehicle Groups and Endorsements

You have now seen two terms "representative vehicle" and "endorsements" used many times. FMCSR 383 Subpart F defines these two important terms.

The CDL law takes the view that different levels of skill are required to drive different types of commercial vehicles. The driver of a tractor hauling a liquid-cargo tanker needs different skills from those the driver of a straight truck needs. The CDL law puts vehicles into three groups. These groups are described in FMCSR Part 393.91. They are as follows:

"Group A" is the **combination vehicles** group. A combination vehicle is any combination of vehicles with a GCWR of 26,001 or more pounds, as long as the GVWR of the vehicle or vehicles being towed is more than 10,000 pounds.

"Group B" vehicles are the **heavy straight vehicles.** This group includes any single vehicle with a GVWR of 26,001 or more pounds or any such vehicle towing a vehicle of no more than 10,000 GVWR.

"Group C" is the **small vehicle** group. A small vehicle is any one vehicle, or combination of vehicles, that isn't a Group A vehicle or a Group B vehicle. Group C vehicles are further defined as designed to carry 16 or more passengers (including the driver) or used to haul hazardous materials (haz mat). "Hazardous materials" includes not only substances that are hazardous by themselves. It also includes materials that are hazardous when hauled in large enough amounts that placards are required. The Hazardous Materials Regulations (Title 49 CFR Part 172 Subpart F) go into more detail about when placards are required.

You must take your CDL tests in a vehicle that is representative of the one you plan to drive. This means that your test vehicle must belong to the same group, A, B or C, as your work vehicle. It doesn't mean that the two vehicles must be the same make or model. They simply must belong to the same group.

You may get your CDL to drive Group C vehicles and later want to be licensed to drive Group A vehicles. At that time, you must upgrade your CDL. Review the earlier material on Testing and Licensing where upgrading your CDL is discussed. Exceptions to these requirements are as follows.

A driver who is licensed for Group A may also drive Group B and C vehicles. This driver must simply have the added endorsements needed to drive these vehicles. For example, this driver may need to have a haz mat endorsement to drive Group C vehicles as well as Group A.

Also, drivers who have passed the knowledge and skills tests for Group B vehicles may drive Group C vehicles. These drivers simply must have the added endorsements required for Group C vehicles, such as the haz mat endorsement.

Figure 5-8 shows the three groups and some of the different vehicles that make up those groups.

Now to the **endorsements.** These are described in FMCSR 393.93. You recall that "endorsement" means authorization. Adding different endorsements to your CDL is like adding options to a car. If you don't live in an area where having air conditioning is a must, why go to the extra trouble and expense to put AC in your car? You choose which endorsements to add to your CDL based on the type of vehicle you want to drive.

The endorsements cover the following vehicle types:

- double/triple trailers
- passenger vehicles
- tank vehicles
- vehicles that require haz mat placards

For some endorsements, you need only take another knowledge test. For others, you need a knowledge **and** a skill test. Here are the endorsements again, with the type of test you must take to earn them:

- double/triple trailers: knowledge test
- passenger vehicles: knowledge **and** skill test
- tank vehicles: knowledge test
- vehicles that require haz mat placards: knowledge test

Your CDL will be coded according to the group type of vehicle you may operate and any endorsements or restrictions you have. These codes are:

- A for Combination Vehicle Group
- B for Heavy Straight Vehicle
- C for Small Vehicle
- T for Double/Triple Trailers
- P for Passenger
- N for Tank Vehicles
- H for Hazardous Materials
- X for Tank Vehicle and Hazardous Materials combined

Your state may have other codes for other combinations.

An endorsement gives authorization. A restriction does the opposite. It limits what you can do. The CDL program includes one restriction. This is the air-brake restriction described in FMCSR 393.95. If you wish to drive a CMV with an air brake system, you must take and pass a Knowledge Test on air brakes. You must take your skills tests in a vehicle with air brakes. If you fail the Knowledge Test or take the Skills Tests in a vehicle without air brakes, an air brake restriction is put on your CDL. This means you are not allowed to drive a CMV with an air brake system. This includes braking systems that rely in whole or in part on air brakes.

Last, applicants for Group A CDLs may be asked to take an additional knowledge test on combination vehicles. This is to test how much they know about coupling and uncoupling and inspecting combination vehicles. Of course, the skills test must be taken in a representative vehicle.

We're nearly finished with this chapter. What's left to cover is the knowledge and skill required to earn a CDL. We'll also give a brief preview of what may be included on the tests. We'll take a look at the test procedure.

First, let's quickly recap what we've covered this far:

- CDL background
- driver licensing
- commercial driver licensing
- how the CDL laws came to be and where they may be found
- definition of terms
- single license requirement
- notification requirements
- disqualification and penalties
- vehicle groups
- endorsement and restriction

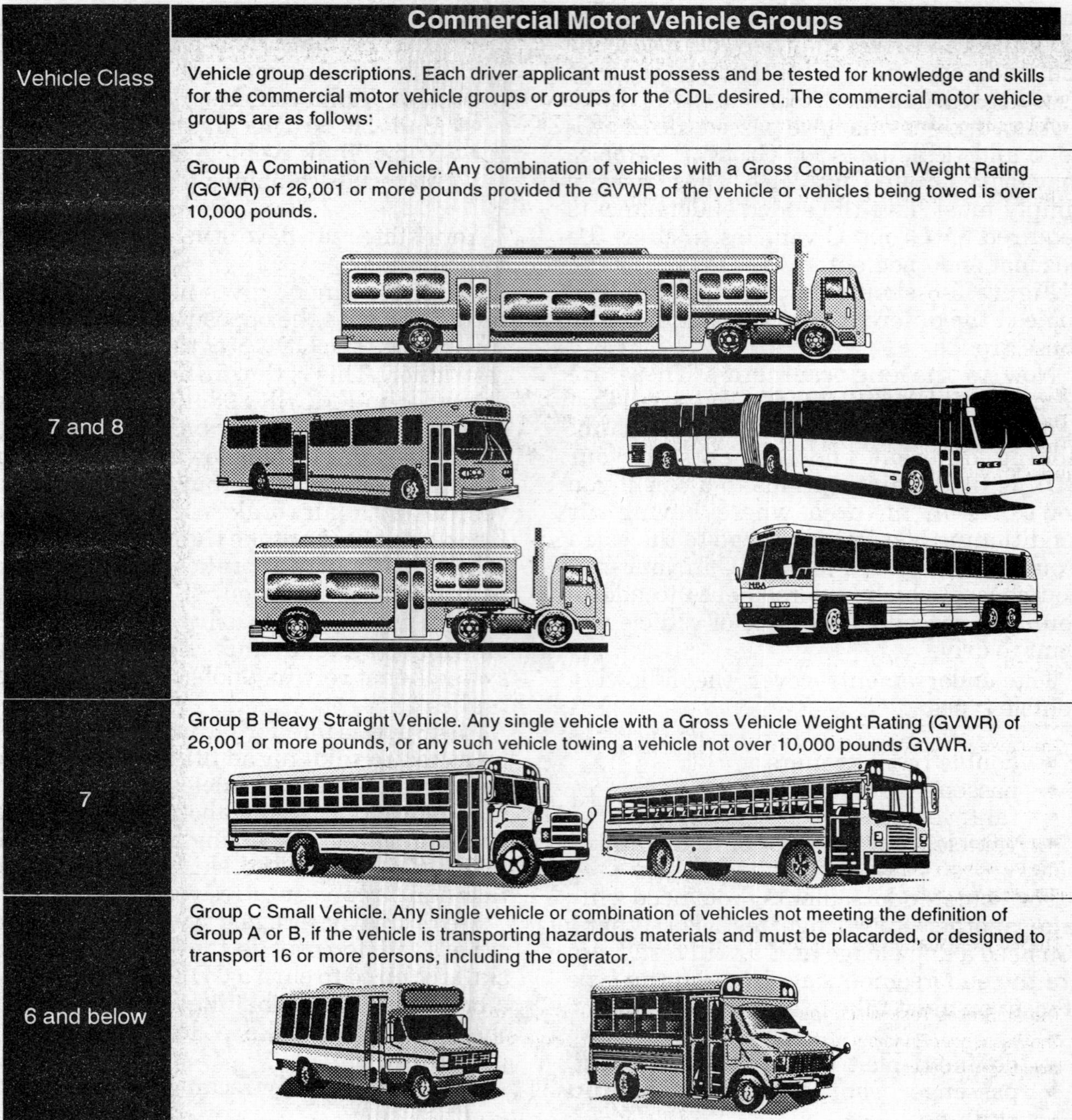

Vehicle Class	Commercial Motor Vehicle Groups
	Vehicle group descriptions. Each driver applicant must possess and be tested for knowledge and skills for the commercial motor vehicle groups or groups for the CDL desired. The commercial motor vehicle groups are as follows:
7 and 8	Group A Combination Vehicle. Any combination of vehicles with a Gross Combination Weight Rating (GCWR) of 26,001 or more pounds provided the GVWR of the vehicle or vehicles being towed is over 10,000 pounds.
7	Group B Heavy Straight Vehicle. Any single vehicle with a Gross Vehicle Weight Rating (GVWR) of 26,001 or more pounds, or any such vehicle towing a vehicle not over 10,000 pounds GVWR.
6 and below	Group C Small Vehicle. Any single vehicle or combination of vehicles not meeting the definition of Group A or B, if the vehicle is transporting hazardous materials and must be placarded, or designed to transport 16 or more persons, including the operator.

Figure 5-8 Chart of CDL tests and endorsements.

Commercial Drivers License Tests

Knowledge Tests. Each driver applicant will have to take one or more knowledge tests, depending on what group of license and what endorsements are needed. The CDL tests include:	Endorsements
The General Knowledge Test, taken by all applicants	A
The Air Brakes Test, which you must take if your vehicle has air brakes. The Combination Vehicles Test, which is required if you want to drive combination vehicles. The Passenger Endorsement Test, required for vehicles designed to carry 16 or more passenger including the driver	P
The General Knowledge Test, taken by all applicants.	B
The Air Brakes Test, which you must take if your vehicle has air brakes. The Passenger Endorsement Test, required for vehicles designed to carry 16 or more passengers including the driver.	P
The General Knowledge Test, taken by all applicants.	C
The Air Brakes Test, which you must take if your vehicle has air brakes. The Passenger Endorsement Test, required for vehicles designed to carry 16 passengers or more including the driver.	P

It wouldn't hurt to be sure you are well acquainted with the material that has been presented up to this point. We've covered a lot. You may wish to stop now and review the first part of this chapter before going on.

Required Knowledge and Skill

Subpart G of FMCSR 383 lists all the areas of knowledge and skill a CMV driver must have to drive safely. The main knowledge areas are as follows:

- safe operations regulations
- commercial motor vehicle safety control systems
- safe vehicle control
- relationship of cargo to vehicle control
- vehicle inspections
- hazardous materials knowledge
- air brake knowledge

Drivers of combination vehicles must know about coupling and uncoupling. They must also know how to inspect combination vehicles.

The main skill areas are:

- basic vehicle control
- safe driving
- air brakes
- pre-trip inspection
- driving

At least some of the skills must be tested in "on-street" conditions. Some of them may be tested off the street or with a truck simulator.

Additional areas of knowledge and skill are listed for drivers who want the different endorsements.

Does that sound like the table of contents for this book? That's with good reason. The chapters that follow will provide detailed information in all these areas.

Sections 383.111 and 383.113 of the FMCSR list the specific items of knowledge and skills required in each area. Sections 383.115, 383.117, 383.119, and 383.121 list the knowledge and skill areas required for the endorsements. The appendix to Subpart G goes into yet more detail.

We won't list those details here. Instead, we'll list them in the chapters that relate to the main knowledge and skill areas. However, if you have a current copy of the FMCSR, you can preview them now.

FMCSR 383.131 directs states to provide a study manual for CDL applicants. These driver information manuals tell how to obtain a CDL. They describe the vehicle groups and endorsements. They contain the facts that relate to the required areas of knowledge and skill.

The state driver information manual also gives details of testing procedures that apply in that state. This includes directions for taking the test and time limits, if any.

You should definitely get your state's driver information manual. You will find much of it contains the same information that this book does. However, your state's manual will also cover any special laws or requirements beyond the federal standards that your state has for CDL applicants. Read the state driver information manual thoroughly. If there are practice tests or exercises, do them.

Also, make sure to get any additional manuals or booklets your state Department of Motor Vehicles (DMV) may have on laws and requirements for commercial vehicle drivers in that state. While we're on the subject, here's another state manual you should have. Read your state's driver's manual for a regular automobile license. This is especially important for new drivers. The CDL manual and even this book will assume you have read the state automobile driver's manual. You must be familiar with general rules of the road and basic safe driving practices. These are covered in the automobile driver's manual. The automobile driver's license book will have information about road markings, right-of-way, and other subjects that all drivers must know.

FMCSR 383.133 covers testing methods. It gives states guidelines on how to construct and score their tests. The guidelines in this part help ensure that tests will be fair. Last, FMCSR 383.135 states the minimum passing scores. CDL applicants must get at least 80 percent on the Knowledge Test. How well you have to do on the skills tests to pass depends on what's being tested. In all cases, an applicant who breaks a

Figure 5-9 All drivers must know the rules of the road.

PASS Billboard

In most states, you will be able to walk into any DMV office during normal working hours and take the CDL tests. This may not be the case in all areas, however.

In some states, only certain DMV offices will be prepared to give the entire set of CDL knowledge and skill tests. Sometimes, you may have to go somewhere else to get the skill tests. You may even be required to make an appointment to take the test. In other words, you may not be able just to walk into any DMV office on the spur of the moment and test for your CDL.

When you first apply for your CDL, the state must check your record. The state will check with CDLIS and the National Driver Register (NDR). There may be a delay while this check is being made. You may not be allowed to take the test until the record check is complete. There may also be a delay before you can take skills tests. Some states may not have enough examiners or sites to test all the people who want to be tested.

These delays can throw a monkey wrench into your timetable for getting your CDL. Find out about them now.

Most applicants will be expected to bring the following items:

- photo identification or driver's license
- Social Security card
- medical card (certification of medical exam)

Know, before you go, whether there is anything else your state requires. You may need some lead time to collect any special documents the state would like to see. If your medical card has expired, get your DOT physical before you apply for your CDL. That way you will have a valid medical card.

Now's a good time to find out what the process is in your state. Start by contacting your state DMV office. The main state DMV offices are listed in Appendix B at the back of this book. You may already know the location of a DMV office near you.

Find out:

- where you may take the Knowledge Test
- where you may take the Skills Test
- where you may test for air brakes or endorsements
- whether you must make an appointment to take any part of the test
- how much the test costs and whether there are separate fees for the endorsement tests
- how long the tests take or whether there are time limits
- what, if anything, you should bring to the test

traffic law automatically fails the test. So does any applicant who causes an accident during the test.

That's it. That's all the particulars on the CDL laws. Step-by-step, we've gone through each one as it appears in the FMCSR. You should become familiar with the laws just as they are written in the FMCSR. This chapter's aim was to explain them in more detail.

After April 1, 1992, you will have to take at least the written part of the test and obtain a Commercial Driver's License to be allowed to continue to drive. As you have seen, your state may excuse you from taking the driving portion of the test if you have a good driving record. Also, different states have different schedules as to when their CDL laws go into effect. So if your current valid license expires before your state is prepared to offer a CDL test, you may be given an ordinary truck driving license. However, by April 1, 1992, all CMV drivers covered by the CMVSA 1986 must have a Commercial Driver's License issued by their home state.

The following chapters will give you the facts you need to pass the knowledge and skills tests and earn the passenger endorsements. Air brakes will be covered in detail so you can avoid the air brake restriction if that is your goal. The tank vehicle, doubles/triples, and hazardous materials endorsements are covered in our companion book, *How to Prepare for the Commercial Driver's License Truck Driver's Test.*

Before you start Chapter 6, test your knowledge of the CDL laws with this **PASS** Post-trip.

PASS POST-TRIP

Instructions: Read the statements. Decide whether each statement is true or false. If it is true, circle the letter A. If it is false, circle the letter B.

1. Federal law requires that the CDL Knowledge Test must be identical in every state.
A. True
B. False

2. The CDL knowledge test must be taken every two years.
A. True
B. False

3. If you do not have a Hazardous Materials Endorsement on your Commercial Driver's License, you can never haul hazardous materials.
A. True
B. False

4. It is legal to have a commercial driver's license from more than one state if you lived in that state when you got that license.
A. True
B. False

5. There is a national Commercial Driver's License required by federal law, but your home state may decide not to adopt the CDL.
A. True
B. False

6. A driver who fails the air brake test receives an air brake endorsement.
A. True
B. False

7. A driver with a Group A CDL may drive Group B or Group C vehicles with no further testing at all.
A. True
B. False

8. You must have an endorsement to drive a commercial vehicle if the vehicle has hydraulic brakes.
A. True
B. False

9. No one from any state can drive a commercial motor vehicle without a CDL effective April 1, 1986.
A. True
B. False

10. A CDL applicant who wants a doubles/triples endorsement must take the regular knowledge and skills test, plus an extra knowledge and an extra skills test.
A. True
B. False

CHAPTER 6

Federal Motor Carrier Safety Regulations

When you have finished this chapter, you will be able to provide the correct answers to questions about:

- the qualifications of motor vehicle drivers
- procedures for safe vehicle operations
- the effects of fatigue, poor vision, poor hearing, and general health on safe motor vehicle operation
- the hours of service of drivers
- motor vehicle inspection, repair, and maintenance
- the transportation of hazardous materials

To complete this chapter you will need:

- a dictionary
- pencil or pen
- blank paper or notebook
- colored pencils, pens, markers, or highlighters
- a CDL preparation manual from your state Department of Motor Vehicles, if one is offered
- Federal Motor Carrier Safety Regulations pocketbook (or access to U.S. Department of Transportation regulations, Parts 383 and 390–399 of Subchapter B, Chapter 3, Title 49, Code of Federal Regulations)

PASS PRE-TRIP

Instructions: Read the statements. Decide whether each statement is true or false. If it is true, circle the letter "A." If it is false, circle the letter "B."

1. If a drug or medicine you are taking was prescribed for you by your doctor, it is both safe and legal to take it while on duty.
   A. True
   B. False

2. The main reason for the post-trip inspection is to let the vehicle owner know about vehicle problems that may need repair.
   A. True
   B. False

3. No driver may drive a vehicle hauling any amount of hazardous material without a hazardous materials endorsement.
   A. True
   B. False

If you were able to answer all these questions easily, that's great. That shows you are very familiar with FMCSR Parts 391, 392, 393, 395, 396, and 397. And well you should be. These parts of the Federal Motor Carrier Safety Regulations have been in force for some time. They are regulations CMV drivers have had to live with for many years. They are not the CDL regulations. Those are fairly new by comparison.

If you were not able to answer the **PASS** Pre-trip questions easily, you have some homework to do. You've got to bone up on these sections of the safety regulations.

Why, you ask, if these are not CDL regulations? It's because the first item in the list of required knowledge and skill that all CMV drivers must have is knowledge of "safe operations regulations." This is stated in FMCSR Part 383. The "safe operations regulations" happen to be the FMCSR sections that were listed at the beginning of this chapter.

FMCSR Part 383.110 states as a general requirement that all drivers of commercial motor vehicles shall have knowledge and skills necessary to operate a commercial motor vehicle safely as contained in this subpart.

FMCSR Part 383.111 states as required knowledge that all CMV drivers must have knowledge of the following general areas:

Safe operations regulations: Driver-related elements of the regulations contained in 49 CFR Parts 391, 392, 393, 395, 396, and 397, such as:

- motor vehicle inspection, repair and maintenance requirements
- procedures for safe vehicle operations
- the effects of fatigue, poor vision, poor hearing, and general health on safe motor vehicle operation
- the types of motor vehicles covered by safe operations regulations
- the types of cargo covered by safe operations regulations
- the effects of alcohol and drug use on safe motor vehicle operations

Your CDL preparation must include a good review of these safety regulations. Has it been some time since you looked at the safety regulations? Then this should be more than a good review. It should be a close examination.

If you haven't gotten a copy of the FMCSR yet, now would be a good time to do so. We won't recreate the FMCSR in this book. In this chapter, we'll touch briefly on each of the FMCSR sections you must know for the CDL. We won't cover them in detail, though. We'll just cover the highlights. These regulations are covered in depth in the FMCSR. You should follow along in your copy of the FMCSR. You must be completely familiar with the FMCSR to drive a CMV.

We will provide extra information, charts, and pictures that will help to explain these safety regulations. In reading these rules, you may find you haven't been living up to the letter of the law. You may discover some common driver practices are actually illegal.

You may be tested on any of this by the CDL Knowledge Test. The test will be looking for the right answer according to law. You may find that some of the methods differ from what you or other drivers usually do. As far as the test is concerned, it doesn't matter that "nobody does it that way." Laws state what has been judged to be the best for everyone. The CDL test will test your knowledge of these laws.

The following are the parts of the FMCSR the CDL requires you to know:

- Part 391 — Qualifications of Drivers
- Part 392 — Driving of Motor Vehicles
- Part 393 — Parts and Accessories Necessary for Safe Operation
- Part 395 — Hours of Service of Drivers
- Part 396 — Inspection, Repair, and Maintenance
- Part 397 — Transportation of Hazardous Materials; Driving and Parking Rules

You must know the driver-related parts. As you read the FMCSR, you will find regulations that apply more to employers than to drivers. You may certainly read them for your own information. However, the CDL does not require you to know those regulations unless you are an employer as well as a driver.

In this chapter, we will focus on Group A, B, and C straight vehicles. We will give more attention to vehicle combinations in Chapter 12.

FMCSR PART 391

FMCSR Part 391 covers Qualifications of Drivers. We touched briefly on this part in Chapter 5. It came up in the section on FMCSR 383.71. FMCSR 383.71 is the CDL regulation that deals with the qualification of drivers for commercial driver licensing. There it stated that unless drivers are not covered by Part 391, they must meet the qualifications described in Part 391.

Part 391 covers the following subjects:

- Qualification and Disqualification of Drivers
- Background and Character
- Examinations and Tests
- Physical Qualifications and Examinations
- Files and Records
- Exemptions
- Controlled Substance Testing

The point of Part 391 is to set minimum qualifications for motor vehicle drivers. This is different from the minimum standards set by the CDL regulations. These minimum standards refer to knowledge and skills. Minimum qualifications have to do with age, background, physical limitations, and so forth.

General Exemptions

Let's get the exemptions out of the way first. Certain drivers are not covered by Part 391. These are drivers of vehicles involved in custom-harvesting operations. Drivers of vehicles involved in beekeeping, and certain other farm vehicles, are also exempt. FMCSR 391.2 discusses these exemptions in greater detail.

Some intracity zone drivers are exempt from some of the regulations in FMCSR 391. For example, these drivers can be younger than 21 years old. They must meet nearly all the other conditions of Part 391, though.

Qualifications

Most motor vehicle drivers, as you can see, must meet the qualifications. Briefly, these are:

- must be at least 21 years old
- must read and speak English well enough to talk with the general public, understand highway signs, respond to officials, and fill out reports and records
- must be able to operate the vehicle safely
- must be able to tell whether cargo (including passenger baggage) is distributed properly
- must be able to secure cargo in the vehicles they drive
- must meet the physical qualifications set out in Subpart E of this section
- must have a single valid commercial motor vehicle operator's license
- must have notified the motor carrier of any violations or certified that there are none to report
- must not have been disqualified to drive a motor vehicle
- must have completed a road test like the one described in Section 391.33
- must have taken a written test on the FMCSR (and Hazardous Materials Regulations, if required) or its equal
- must have completed an official "driver application for employment"

TIP *To "certify" means to confirm that something is correct and true. You usually certify in writing. A "certification" is that written statement.*

Disqualifications

Simply put, the regulations state that drivers who are disqualified shall not drive a CMV. If your license has been revoked, withdrawn, or denied or is suspended, you are disqualified. You are disqualified for the length of time you are without your license.

A driver may also be disqualified for criminal or other offenses. This would be the case under the following conditions:

- First, the driver must be convicted of the crime. Being charged with a crime and forfeiting bond ("skipping bail") before being convicted is treated the same as a conviction.
- Second, the offense must have been committed while the driver was on duty.
- Third, the driver must have been employed by a motor carrier or involved in commercial transport. If all these three conditions are met, the driver may be disqualified for criminal offenses.

What are those offenses? One is driving while under the influence of alcohol. This is defined as driving a CMV with an AC of .04 (four-tenths) percent or more. Your state may have a stricter definition. Your state may set the AC even lower than .04 percent.

If you refuse to take a test for alcohol, you may be disqualified just as if you were DUI. Remember "implied consent"? If you don't, review "implied consent" in Chapter 5.

You may be disqualified for driving a motor vehicle while under the influence of a controlled substance or "scheduled" drug. A list of controlled substances is supplied in the FMCSR. It's Appendix D.

TIP *You may find a drug your doctor prescribed for you on the list of drugs in Appendix D. Just because your doctor prescribed it doesn't mean it's safe to take it while driving. These drugs may have side effects. These side effects may make safe driving impossible. Ask your doctor about the side effects of any medicine prescribed for you. Find out whether it's safe to take it while driving. And never take drugs prescribed for someone else.*

You can also get a list of Schedule I drugs from the Office of Motor Carrier Standards or any regional office of Motor Carrier and Highway Safety of the Federal Highway Administration. You can find addresses for these agencies in Appendix D of this book.

Figure 6-1 Just because your doctor prescribed some medicine doesn't mean it's safe to take while driving.

You are also considered DUI for taking amphetamines or narcotics while driving. Amphetamines, or "speed," make you feel more alert. It may seem like a good idea to take speed in order to keep on driving when you are tired. Not only is this illegal, it's a bad idea. Speed doesn't cure your tiredness. Then the disqualification is for six months.

All other offenders are disqualified for three years.

Background and Character

When you apply for a job as a motor vehicle driver, you must fill out a driver application form. This asks for the same type of information ordinary job applications do, and then some. You must supply the following information:

- the name and address of the motor carrier employer
- your full name, mailing address, birth date, and Social Security number
- addresses you have had within the past three years
- the date the application was made
- the name of the state that issued your valid motor vehicle license or permit, plus the number and expiration date of the license or permit
- your experience in motor vehicle operation, including the type of equipment you have driven
- a list of all motor vehicle accidents you have had in the last three years. This must include the date and type of each accident. Any deaths or injuries that resulted must also be listed.
- a list of all violations of motor vehicle laws or ordinances (other than parking) for which you were convicted in the last three years. (Skipping bail counts as a conviction.)
- the details of any denial, revocation, or suspension of any motor vehicle license or permit. If you have never had a license or permit denied, revoked, or suspended, you must certify that.
- the names and addresses of employers you worked for in the last three years. You must include the dates you were employed and why you left the job or jobs.

If you wish to drive a **commercial** motor vehicle in one of the CDL vehicle groups, you must list the names and addresses of former employers for the seven years before the three years in the item above. In other words, you must give the past 10 years of your employment history. Again, you must include the dates you were employed and why you left.

Last, you date and sign the certification at the end of the form. The statement reads, "This certifies that this application was completed by me, and that all entries on it and information in it are true and complete to the best of my knowledge."

If your motor carrier asks you for yet more information, you must provide it. The law permits your motor carrier to request such information from you. The motor carrier is required to tell you that the information you provide may be used. You are also to be told that your background may be checked. Former employers may be contacted.

Every 12 months, your motor carrier must review your driving record. The motor carrier must check to see that all its drivers meet the minimum requirements for safe driving. The motor carrier must check that none has been disqualified. The motor carrier will look closely not only at accidents but also at speeding, reckless driving, and DUI. All these show the driver is not sincere about safe driving.

As a licensed CMV driver, you have notification responsibilities with regard to your motor carrier. You must report convictions for traffic law violations to your motor carrier. The motor carrier will require you to complete a form like the one in Figure 6-2.

If you have already given this information in meeting your CDL notification requirements, you don't have to give it again.

MOTOR VEHICLE DRIVER'S CERTIFICATION

I certify that the folowing is a true and complete list of traffic violations (other than parking violations) for which I have been convicted or forfeited bond or collateral during the past 12 months.

Date of conviction | Offense

Location | Type of vehicle operated

If no violations are listed above, I certify that I have not been convicted or forfeited bond or collateral on account of any violation required to be listed during the past 12 months.

(Date of certification) (Driver's signature)

(Motor carrier's name)

(Motor carrier's address)

(Reviewed by: Signature) (Title)

Figure 6-2 Motor Vehicle Driver's Certification.

Examinations and Tests

FMCSR Part 391 describes the road test CMV drivers must take. This road test is different from the CDL skills test. This road test is given to you by your motor carrier employer. The CDL skills test is given to you by the state that gives you your CDL license. You must take both.

The road test required by FMCSR Part 391 must include at least the following:

- a pre-trip inspection (described in FMCSR 392.7)
- coupling and uncoupling any combination units
- putting the vehicle in operation
- use of the vehicle's controls and emergency equipment
- operating the vehicle in traffic and while passing other vehicles
- turning the vehicle
- braking, and slowing the vehicle without using the brakes
- backing and parking the vehicle

Your motor carrier employer will give you the road test. It can also be given by someone the employer appoints to do this. (If you yourself are the motor carrier, you cannot give yourself the road test. You must assign someone else to give you the test.)

Your performance will be rated on a form. The person who gave you the test will sign the form.

When you complete the road test, you will get a copy of the Certification of Road Test. It will look like the one in Figure 6-3. You'll sign the original, and the motor carrier will keep it on file.

If you recently had a road test elsewhere and have a valid CMV license, the motor carrier may waive (excuse you from taking) another road test. The motor carrier may also waive the road test if you have a valid certificate of driver's road test that is no more than three years old.

On the other hand, even if you have such a certificate, the motor carrier may still have you take a new road test.

FMCSR Part 391 describes the written exam you must take. This test is different from the CDL Knowledge Test. The state that gives you your CDL license gives you the CDL Knowledge Test. This written test is given to you by your motor carrier employer. You must take both tests.

This written test is on the FHWA rules and regulations on commercial vehicle safety. In other words, it's a test on the FMCSR sections we're covering in this chapter.

This test is quite a bit different from the CDL Knowledge Test. For one, it's more a teaching tool than a true test. It's "open book." That is, you can have a copy of the FMCSR with you when you take the test. You can look things up in it. Of course, the test will be a lot easier to take if you are already familiar with the FMCSR.

The test has 66 questions. Questions 58 through 66 are on haz mat. If you don't plan to haul haz mat, you don't have to answer these questions.

There is no time limit. There is no pass or fail. When you finish the test, the examiner will review any questions you missed. That way you will learn the correct answers. The point of the test truly is to get you familiar with the FMCSR. If you aren't before you take the test, you will be when you are finished.

The examiner will complete a Certificate of Written Examination, like the one in Figure 6-4. You will get a copy. The original will go in your file.

You may be excused from taking this test as well as the road test. For a waiver, you must have a valid certificate of written examination that is no more than three years old. Even if you have one, the motor carrier may have you take the test again.

Physical Qualification and Examinations

CMV drivers must meet certain physical qualifications. These are described in

CERTIFICATION OF ROAD TEST

Driver's name . . . .
Social Security No. . . . .
Operator's or Chauffeur's License No. . . . .
State . . . .
Type of power unit . . . .
Type of trailer(s) . . . .
If passenger carrier, type of bus . . . .

This is to certify that the above-named driver was given a road test under my supervision on ....19.........consisting of approximately ....miles of driving.

It is my considered opinion that this driver possesses sufficient driving skill to operate safely the type of commercial motor vehicle listed above. . . . .

. . . .

. . . .
(Signature of examiner) (title)

. . . .
(Organization and address of examiner)

Figure 6-3 Certification of Road Test.

CERTIFICATION OF WRITTEN EXAMINATION

This is to certify that the person whose signature appears below has completed the written examination under my supervision in accordance with the provisions of §391.35 of the Federal Motor Carrier Safety Regulations.

. . . .
(Signature of person taking examination)

. . . .
(Date of examination)

. . . .
(Location of examination

. . . .
(Signature of examiner)

. . . .
(Title)

. . . .
(Organization and address of examiner)

Figure 6-4 Certificate of Written Examination.

FMCSR Part 391. We won't list them here. A doctor will check for these qualifications by giving you a physical. This isn't an ordinary physical. You've probably heard it called a "DOT physical." What makes this CMV driver physical special is described in this section of the FMCSR.

Among other things, your hearing, sight, and reflexes will be tested. You'll be asked about your use of drugs and alcohol. You may be tested for drug and alcohol use. It's here that the doctor will advise you about any medicines you may be taking. The doctor must assure you that such drugs are safe to use while driving. If they are not, taking them can get you disqualified, as we mentioned before. This is true even if the doctor prescribed them.

This physical must be done by a licensed doctor of medicine (M.D.) or of osteopathy (D.O.). Drug testing may be done by an outside lab, and the vision tests may be done by an eye doctor (licensed optometrist).

The physical must follow the guidelines in FMCSR Part 391. The doctor will sign and date the examination form and a medical examiner's certificate. The doctor will keep the exam form on file. Both you and your motor carrier will be given a copy of the Medical Examiner's Certificate. It will look like Figure 6-5.

You must have the physical if you have never had a so-called "DOT physical" before. If your last DOT physical was more than two years ago, you must be examined again. Exempt intracity zone drivers must get a DOT physical if their last one was more than one year ago. You must also get an exam if your ability to drive has been reduced by injury or illness.

FMCSR Part 391 tells you what to do if you disagree with the doctor's findings. Also, rules about certain physical problems that might disqualify you may be waived. The process of getting a waiver is described in this part.

MEDICAL EXAMINER'S CERTIFICATE

I certify that I have examined . . . .
(Driver's Name (Print))
in accordance with the Federal Motor Carrier Safety Regulations (49 CFR 391.41-391.49) and with knowledge of his/her duties. I find him/her qualified under the regulations.

☐ Qualified only when wearing corrective lenses.
☐ Qualified only when wearing a hearing aid.

A completed examination form for this person is on file in my office at
(Address)

(Date of examination) (Name of examining doctor (Print))

. . . .
(Signature of driver)

. . . .
(Signature of examining doctor)

. . . .
(Address of driver)

Figure 6-5 Medical Examiner's Certificate.

Files and Records

FMCSR Part 391 describes the files and records motor carriers must keep on each of their drivers. These regulations are not what you would consider driver-related. Read them enough to be familiar with them. Unless you yourself are a motor carrier, though, you don't need to be concerned about complying with them.

Limited Exemptions

FMCSR 391.61, 391.62, 391.63, 391.65, 391.67, 391.69, and 391.71 are of interest mainly to the motor carrier. These regulations list the few drivers who are exempt from FMCSR 391. There are few indeed. Some drivers who work only now and then are exempt from some of the regulations. So are drivers who usually work for one motor carrier but are doing a job for another motor carrier. Drivers of farm vehicles are exempt from some of the regulations. So are some drivers in Hawaii and some intrastate drivers hauling combustible liquids.

If you read these sections, you will see that most drivers are covered by FMCSR 391.

Controlled Substances Testing

The last part of FMCSR 391 deals with drug abuse and testing for drug abuse. The drugs covered by Part 391 are listed in 49 CFR Part 40. Briefly, they are marijuana, cocaine, opium and opium-related drugs, amphetamines, and phencyclidine (PCP or "angel dust").

A drug test can involve looking for drugs in a sample of body tissue. Commonly, a sample of urine is used.

Sad to say, drug (and alcohol) misuse are seen to be big problems in the transport industry. (They may be problems in other industries, too. But those people don't drive CMVs out on the highway.) This part of the FMCSR came about to reduce accidents that result from CMV drivers using the wrong drugs or using drugs wrongly.

FMCSR Part 391 talks about "reasonable cause." An example of reasonable cause is a motor carrier having good reason to suspect a driver of abusing drugs. The driver's actions, looks, or conduct may cause the motor carrier to have these suspicions. Reasonable cause gives carriers permission to test for drugs if they have a good reason to suspect drug abuse.

Besides testing for reasonable cause, carriers must test for drugs before they hire a driver. You cannot refuse to take this test when you apply for a driving job. It is part of the qualification process.

Carriers may use some drivers without testing them. Perhaps you usually drive for one motor carrier but are working temporarily for another. You may not have to be tested by the second motor carrier. Other exceptions are described in detail in FMCSR Part 391.103.

You may be retested at least once every two years. This is called periodic testing. Or you may be retested as part of a random testing program. Both periodic and random testing are described in FMCSR Part 391.

You must also be tested if you are involved in a reportable accident. This test must be done within 32 hours of an accident if you are cited for a moving traffic violation as a result of the accident. If you have been involved in an accident that resulted in a death, you must give a urine sample. You may be disqualified for one year for refusing to do so.

Should you return to work after having tested positive for drugs, you must continue in a program of after-care. You must stay in the program and take follow-up tests for no more than 60 months after you return to work.

Since you don't abuse drugs (you don't, do you?), you may feel insulted or offended when your employer wants to test you. You may not refuse to be tested, though. The FMCSR says a refusal must be treated just like a positive test. You'll just have to take the test. Tell yourself the hassle is worth the improved highway safety for you as well as for other people.

The FMCSR offers certain protection for the driver being tested. For one, no one except the medical review officer and your motor carrier may obtain your test results without your permission. What if you test positive and believe that must be a mistake? You may discuss the test results with the medical review officer before they are released to the motor carrier. Read the safety regulations carefully to understand your rights and responsibilities with regard to drug testing.

Part of reducing accidents due to drug abuse is teaching people about the dangers of drug abuse. FMCSR Part 391 provides for an Employee Assistance Program (EAP). All motor carriers must have one. This is an education and training program on drug abuse. It's for the motor carrier's drivers and supervisors. The EAP teaches people about the effects of drug abuse on health, safety, and work. In the EAP, you learn how to spot the signs that someone (yourself?) has a drug problem. You must get at least 60 minutes of training.

The regulations on drug testing conclude FMCSR 391.

FMCSR PART 392

The next part of the FMCSR that all drivers must know is Part 392, Driving of Motor Vehicles. This part covers:

- illness, fatigue, drugs, intoxicating beverages, driver schedules, equipment, safe loading, and other general topics
- driving of vehicles
- stopped vehicles
- use of lights and reflectors
- accidents and license revocations

- safety while fueling
- unauthorized passengers, coasting, and other prohibited practices

This part introduces the concept of "higher standard of care." The FMCSR says that drivers must obey local laws first. If the federal law is stricter, though, the federal law must be obeyed instead. This results in a "higher standard of care." Simply put, the stricter rule applies.

We've mentioned higher standard of care before, although not in so many words. It's what allows states to have a stricter definition of DUI than the federal law. Federal law considers a driver with .04 percent AC as DUI. A state could make that .03 percent, or less. That would result in a higher standard of care. If a state set the AC at .05 percent, the federal law would apply, since that would result in the higher standard of care.

Following are highlights of the other sections of FMCSR 392.

Ill or Fatigued Operator

Illness or fatigue is not to be taken lightly. A sick or tired driver is not a safe driver. It's not merely being lazy to get rest when you need it. You're not being a hero by continuing to drive. You are in fact breaking the law. FMCSR Part 392 says a driver must not drive if too tired or ill to be fully alert and in control. Only in an emergency should you continue to drive. Then, you should go on only as long as needed to handle the emergency.

Illness

Once in a while, you may become so ill that you cannot operate a motor vehicle safely. If this happens to you, you must not drive. However, in case of an emergency, you may drive to the nearest place where you can safely stop.

Fatigue

Driving a vehicle for long hours is tiring. Even the best of drivers will become less alert. To stay alert and safe, get enough sleep. Leaving on a long trip when you're already tired is dangerous. If you have a long trip scheduled, make sure that you get a good sleep before you go. Most people require seven to eight hours of sleep every 24 hours.

Be aware that your body gets used to sleeping during certain hours. If you are driving during those hours, you will be less alert. Also know that many heavy motor vehicle accidents occur between midnight and 6 a.m. You can easily fall asleep at these times, especially if you don't regularly drive at those hours.

Avoid medication. Many medicines can make you sleepy. Those that do have a label warning against operating vehicles or machinery. The most common medicine of this type is an ordinary cold pill. If you have to drive with a cold, you are better off suffering from the cold than from the effects of the medicine.

Keep cool. A hot, poorly ventilated cab can make you sleepy. Keep the window or vent cracked or use the air conditioner, if you have one.

Take breaks if you can. Short breaks can keep you alert. But the time to take them is

Figure 6-6 Most heavy motor vehicle accidents happen between midnight and 6 AM.

before you feel really drowsy or tired. Stop, walk around, and inspect your vehicle. It may help to do some physical exercises.

When you are sleepy, trying to push on is far more dangerous than you think. It is a major cause of fatal accidents. When your body needs sleep, sleep is the only thing that will work.

Avoid drugs. There are no drugs that can overcome being tired. While they may keep you awake for a while, they won't make you alert. And eventually, you'll be even more tired than if you hadn't taken them at all. Sleep is the only thing that can overcome fatigue.

Drugs and Other Substances

The misuse of drugs and alcohol while on duty is forbidden by several regulations. Some are found in FMCSR Part 393 and FMCSR Part 391. FMCSR 392.4 states that no driver shall be on duty and possess, be under the influence of, or use:

- a Schedule I or Appendix D drug
- amphetamines ("pep pills" or "bennies")
- narcotics
- any substance that keeps a driver from being able to drive safely

This part reminds you that it is OK to use drugs a doctor has prescribed for you. This is only if the doctor has assured you the drug will not affect your driving ability.

This part also clears up the definition of "possession." It is legal for CMV drivers to possess and transport these drugs as cargo. But, they must be listed on the manifest.

Intoxicating Beverages

All drivers are affected by drinking alcohol. Alcohol affects judgment, vision, coordination, and reaction time. It causes serious driving errors, such as:

- increased reaction time to hazards
- driving too fast or too slow
- driving in the wrong lane
- running over the curb
- weaving
- straddling lanes
- quick, jerky starts
- failure to signal or use lights
- failure to stop at stop signs and red lights
- improper passing

All these can mean increased chances of a crash and chances of losing your driver's license. Accident statistics show that the chance of a crash is much greater for drivers who have been drinking than for drivers who have not.

FMCSR Part 392 states that no driver shall drink an intoxicating beverage within four hours before going on duty, driving, or otherwise being in control of a motor vehicle. This means any and all intoxicating beverages. It doesn't matter how much alcohol is in them. A little or a lot, they are prohibited. Remember, alcohol is alcohol. Beer and wine are no safer than liquor.

You must not even be under the influence of such a beverage within four hours of going on duty. This may mean that if you are drinking, you must stop much sooner than four hours before going to work. It's possible to be under the influence of drinking for more than four hours. Here's why.

You have seen that drunkenness is measured as a percentage of alcohol in the blood. Three factors affect this percentage: time, the amount of alcohol, and your weight.

Alcohol, like any food or drink, is used by the body over time. After a certain amount of time, your body has used up the alcohol. There is no more in your system. It no longer affects you.

How much time must pass before you are free of the effects of alcohol? It depends on your weight and how much you drank. It takes most people about one hour to burn off one 12-ounce bottle of beer, one 1½-ounce shot of liquor, or one 5-ounce glass of wine. Smaller people feel the effects of alcohol more than larger people.

Figure 6-7 It takes most people about one hour to "burn off" one 12-ounce bottle of beer, one 1½-ounce shot of liquor, or one 5-ounce glass of wine.

Put together the facts you have just learned about the effects of alcohol and the requirements of the law. The law requires you to be free of the effects of alcohol for four hours before you go on duty. Say you have one beer at noon. You are due to go on duty at 4 P.M. Is it safe? No, it's not. You had the beer at noon. At 1 P.M., you were still affected by it. By 4 P.M., only three hours have passed. You still have an hour to go. Only then will you be free of the effects of that one beer you drank at noon.

Right away, you can see why you must stop drinking far in advance of when you plan to drive.

What if you had more than one drink? What if you are lighter or heavier than the average person? The chart in Figure 6-8 helps answer that question.

Body Weight	Blood Alcohol Content (in percents)									
100 lbs	.04	.09	.13	.17	.22	.26	.30	.35	.39	.44
125 lbs	.03	.07	.10	.14	.17	.21	.24	.28	.31	.35
150 lbs	.03	.06	.08	.12	.14	.17	.20	.23	.26	.29
175 lbs	.02	.05	.07	.10	.12	.15	.17	.20	.22	.25
200 lbs	.02	.04	.06	.09	.11	.13	.15	.17	.19	.22
225 lbs	.02	.04	.06	.08	.10	.12	.14	.16	.17	.19
250 lbs	.02	.03	.05	.07	.09	.10	.12	.14	.16	.17

Figure 6-8 Blood alcohol content and body weight.

The numbers in the chart are AC percentages. Remember the legal limit? It's .04 percent.

Read down the left side to find the row with the figure closest to your own weight. Read along the top to find the column with number of drinks you're asking about. The number found where the column and row come together is your AC at that weight, having had that many drinks.

Take, for example, a 200-pound man who has four drinks. The chart shows his AC would be .09 percent. He is clearly under the influence. As far as the law is concerned, he will be for some time.

One drink would take one hour to burn off. Four drinks would take far longer to burn off. For each hour that passes **since that last drink was consumed,** subtract .01 percent. That's a little less than the alcohol in one drink. Our 200-pound drinker will need five hours after he has that last drink to get his AC below .04 percent. (He will need nine hours to completely burn off all four drinks.) Then he needs the additional four hours required by FMCSR 392.5. This man cannot legally drive for nine hours **after he has his last drink!**

If you have many drinks spread throughout an afternoon or evening, you can easily still be affected by them the next day. You may feel fine and think you are sober. But your judgment and reflexes simply won't be up to par.

Don't think you can speed up the process of sobering up. Coffee and cold showers will make you feel more alert, but you will still be under the influence. Only the passing of enough time will return you to a normal state.

PASS Billboard

There are many beliefs about how alcohol works in the body. So many of them are not based in fact. A common one is, "I can handle it better than other people." It's simply not true.

The first thing alcohol does is affect your judgment. It also gives you a false sense of competence. All it takes is one drink. After that, you simply can't trust yourself to decide whether you are drunk or not. You must assume you are, even if you feel fine. Of course you'll feel great – you've been drinking! You won't **be** great, though. You'll be impaired. Most people are legally under the influence after having one drink.

Perhaps you wait until your reaction time slows before you decide you've had enough.

That's too late. By the time you notice your reactions have slowed, you are at about .05 percent AC. This is already over the legal limit. Maybe you decide to stop when you begin to stagger and your speech slurs. At this point you are at .2 percent AC. This is five times the .04 percent AC the law considers the limit. You could go on drinking until you pass out. For most people this will happen by the time they reach .3 percent AC. If you drink enough to reach .4 percent AC, you will definitely not be driving. At .4 AC, you will fall into a coma and likely die.

It's hard not to conclude that drinking and driving don't mix.

Certainly, you must not consume an intoxicating beverage **while** on duty, much less before.

CMV drivers may transport intoxicating beverages, of course. As with controlled substances, such cargo must be on the manifest and transported as part of a shipment to be legal.

A driver who violates these regulations is immediately put out of service for 24 hours. You have to report this to your employer within 24 hours. You also have to report this to the state that gave you your license. You must make this report within 30 days, unless you request a review.

If you want a review of the out-of-service order, you must request it within 10 days. You must write to the Director of Motor Carrier Safety for the region in which the order was issued. The addresses of the Motor Carrier Safety offices for all 10 regions are listed in Appendix B of this book. The Regional Director may overturn the order or let it stand.

Schedules and Speed Limits

You must drive within the speed limit. It's no excuse to claim you can't stay on schedule unless you drive at an illegal speed. FMCSR Part 392 states your employer must not set schedules that force you to exceed the speed limit.

Equipment Inspection and Use

Your vehicle cannot be operated safely without certain parts. Before you take a vehicle out, you must make sure these parts are in place and working. Also, you must know how to use them, and use them when needed. These parts are listed in FMCSR Part 392. They are:

- service brakes, including trailer brake connections
- parking (hand) brake
- steering mechanism
- lights
- tires
- horn
- windshield wipers
- rear-view mirrors
- coupling devices

Before you take a vehicle out, you must make sure your emergency equipment is in place and working. Also, you must know how to use:

- a fire extinguisher
- spare fuses
- warning devices for stopped vehicles (like flares or reflectors)

and use them when needed.

Safe Loading

You must not drive a vehicle unless you are certain the cargo is loaded properly and secure and the weight is evenly distributed. If the weight is unbalanced, the vehicle could overturn in curves and sharp turns. So you must know both proper cargo distribution and securement.

Doors, the spare tire, and other such items must be in good condition and in place. FMCSR Part 392 also states that nothing may block your view or your ability to move around. You must be able to reach the vehicle's controls. You and your passengers must be able to exit the vehicle easily.

Before you begin to drive, make sure all standees are behind the standee line. Aisle seats must meet the requirements stated in

FMCSR Part 393. (You'll find more details about this in the next section of this chapter.) Baggage and freight must be stowed and secure. It must not keep you from freely moving around the bus and operating its controls. There must be no danger of it falling or flying around such that you or your passengers would be injured. Also make sure that everyone in the bus, including you, can get to the exits, both the regular and emergency ones.

FMCSR Part 391 states certain minimum physical requirements for drivers. Some drivers need glasses (or contact lenses) and hearing aids to be able to see and hear well enough to meet the qualifications. FMCSR Part 392 states if you need any of these items, you must be wearing them when driving.

Slowing and Stopping

When you're transporting passengers, you must take special action when crossing railroad tracks. (These regulations also apply to drivers hauling chlorine or haz mat that requires placards and to tank vehicle drivers.) These steps must be taken at railroad crossings that are uncontrolled. "Uncontrolled crossings" are ones without signal lights, a police officer, flagman, or some other way of telling you it's safe to proceed.

FMCSR 392.10 states you must stop between 50 feet and 15 feet of the track. Look both ways and listen for oncoming trains. When it's safe, you must proceed at a speed that will let you get all the way across without changing gears. You must not change gears while crossing the track.

You don't have to follow these procedures when signs tell you the rail line has been abandoned or is exempt.

If you are driving a vehicle other than the types described in FMCSR Part 392, you must at least slow down when you approach a railroad crossing. You must not cross the track until you are sure it is safe to do so.

Similar rules apply at drawbridges. When you're transporting passengers, you must come to a complete stop not less than 50 feet from the lip of the draw. Make sure the draw is completely closed and only then proceed across. When the drawbridge is controlled (by signals, an attendant, or traffic officer), follow the stop and go instructions.

Hazardous Conditions

FMCSR Part 392 states you should slow down when hazardous conditions exist. This could be snow, ice, fog, rain, or slick roads – anything that reduces your ability to guide or control the vehicle. If conditions are bad enough, you are to stop altogether. An exception to this is if stopping will increase the hazard to your passengers. If that's the case, you may continue long enough to get to the nearest place where your passengers will be safe.

Turn Signals

You are required to use turn signals when you make a turn. FMCSR 392.15 states you must start to signal 100 feet before you make the turn. You must keep signaling until you complete the turn. You must also use turn signals when you enter traffic from a parked position or change lanes. You are not to use turn signals to show you are parked.

You are also not to use turn signals to show other drivers it is safe to pass you. If you are driving slowly enough to be a hazard to other drivers, you may use your four-way flashers to alert other drivers (unless there is a local law against this).

Seat Belts

If the driver's seat of your vehicle has seat belts, you must wear them while driving.

Hazard Warning Flashers

Usually, you shouldn't use your signal lights to direct traffic. However, if you are moving much slower than the rest of the traffic, you may turn on your four-way flashers to warn other drivers. Be advised, though, that state and local regulations sometimes forbid this use of your flashers.

Stopped Vehicles

Drivers must also take special action when their vehicles are stopped. FMCSR Part 392 states that you should not leave your vehicle unattended without setting the parking brake. Don't stop or park on the traveled part of the highway if you can safely pull off to the side. If you have no choice but to park on the road, leave as much room as possible for other vehicles to get around you. Make sure other drivers can clearly see your parked vehicle.

Emergency Signals

One way to do this is with emergency signals. Such signals and their use are described in FMCSR Part 392. You must use these signals when you stop on the traveled portion of the highway (other than traffic stops). Briefly, the rule is to turn on your four-way flashers when you first stop. Keep your flashers on until you put out your warning devices. These are the flares or reflective devices described in FMCSR Part 393. We'll cover the devices themselves later in this chapter.

You must put these devices out within 10 minutes of stopping. You must put one at the traffic side of your stopped vehicle. It must be within 10 feet of the front or rear of your vehicle.

You must put another device 100 feet from your vehicle, in the **center** of the traffic lane or shoulder occupied by your vehicle. If you put the first device at the front of your vehicle, put this second device at the front. If you put the first device at the rear, put this second device at the rear.

You put a third device 100 feet from your vehicle in the opposite direction from the other two. That is, if the first two are at the front of your vehicle, put this third device at the rear. If the first two devices are at the rear of your vehicle, put this last one at the front.

This is almost easier to show than to describe. See Figure 6-9.

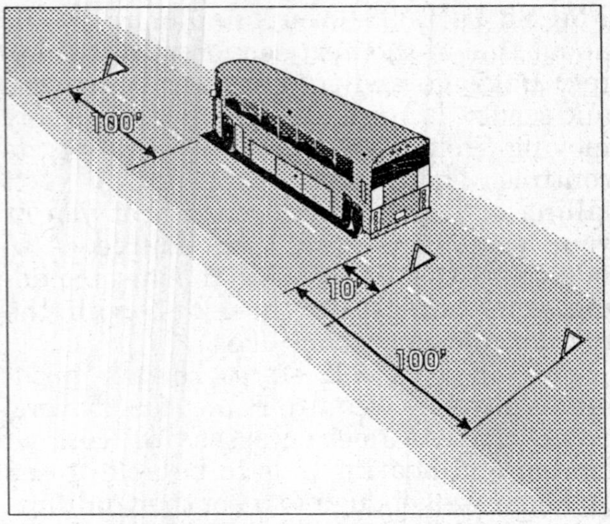

Figure 6-9 Placement of warning devices on the highway.

You place your warning devices slightly differently when you are stopped on a hill, in a curve, or on a divided or one-way road. Figures 6-10 and 6-11 show the correct placement of warning devices under these conditions.

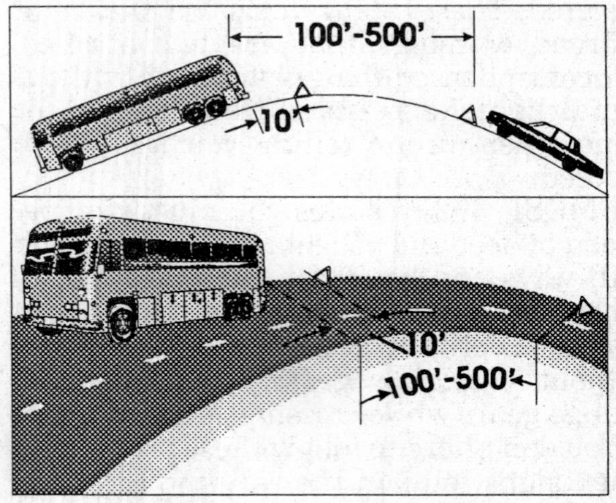

Figure 6-10 Placement of warning devices on a hill.

For older vehicles, flares and liquid-burning flares (called pot torches) may be used instead of reflective triangles. However, they may not be used when flammable liquids are leaking onto the road. That could start a fire. CMV drivers may not use them to protect vehicles hauling explosives or flammable cargo, even if the vehicles are empty. Last, you may not use pot torches to protect a vehicle fueled by compressed gas. Any of these could cause a fire or explosion.

Figure 6-11 Placement of warning devices on a one-way road.

Lights and Reflectors

FMCSR Part 393 describes the required lights and reflectors. FMCSR Part 392 describes their use. You must have these lights, and have them lit, from one-half hour after sunset, through the night, to one-half hour before sunrise. You should also put your lights on any time it is too dark to see more than 500 feet away from you.

If you are parked or stopped during these hours, FMCSR Part 392 states you must have at least one light (white or amber) lit on the traffic side of your vehicle. This light must be visible from 500 feet in front of the vehicle. You must have one red light lit. This light must be visible from 500 feet to the rear of the vehicle. Turn your headlights down or off.

FMCSR Part 392 states the rules for using your headlights. They must be on during the same hours just described. When oncoming vehicles are more than 500 feet away, use your high beams.

Otherwise, use your low beams. Use low beams in fog, when high beams would make it hard for you to see. Use low beams when you are in a city area, where street lights help you to see. Use low beams when an oncoming vehicle is within 500 feet of you.

Accidents and License Revocation

FMCSR Part 392 states that motor vehicle drivers have certain responsibilities when they are involved in accidents where there is property damage or where people are hurt or killed. "Involved" does not mean only if you caused the accident. It also means if you were any part of the accident.

These are your responsibilities. First, stop immediately. Then, protect the scene of the accident so others are kept from becoming part of it. That is, put out flares or take other action to alert others to the hazard. If your vehicle is involved in the accident, try to get it to the side of the road. This will help prevent another accident and allow traffic to move.

If you're stopping to help, park away from the accident. The area immediately around the accident will be needed for emergency vehicles.

Put on your flashers. Don't forget the rules about stopping on the highway. Put out reflective triangles to warn other traffic. Make sure the reflective triangles can be seen by other drivers in time for them to avoid the accident.

Then, help injured people. If it is safe to leave injured people where they are, they should not be moved. Moving them could increase their injuries. Move injured people only when leaving them where they are opens them up to greater danger.

If a qualified person is at the accident and helping the injured, stay out of the way unless you are asked to assist. Otherwise, do the best you can to help any injured parties. Here are some simple steps to follow in giving assistance:

- stop heavy bleeding by applying direct pressure to the wound
- keep the injured person warm

Give any witness who asks for it the following information:

- your name
- your address
- the name and address of your motor carrier

Figure 6-12 A fuel island fire just waiting to happen!

- the state tag registration number of your vehicle

If asked, show your license.

As soon as you can, report all the details of the accident to your motor carrier.

FMCSR Part 392 states what you must do if you hit an unattended vehicle while on the highway. You must stop immediately and try to find the person in charge of the vehicle. If you have tried and can't find that person, leave your name, address, and the name and address of your motor carrier with the vehicle you hit.

You must notify your motor carrier if your license is revoked. The requirements in FMCSR Part 392 are similar to FMCSR 383.33.

Fueling Procedures

The fuel your vehicle runs on can be dangerous if mishandled. The rules in FMCSR Part 392 describe how to handle fuel safely. Unless you need to run the engine to fuel your vehicle, you must not fuel your vehicle with the motor running. Do not smoke or have any open flame in the fueling area. Fueling lets off vapors you can't see. A cigarette or match could ignite those vapors.

Keep the nozzle of the fuel hose in contact with the fuel tank's intake pipe at all times. Do not allow anyone else to smoke or do anything else in the fueling area that would cause an explosion.

Do not carry any reserve fuel in your vehicle. Carry fuel only in the fuel tanks.

When you're carrying passengers, you must take special fueling measures. Don't fuel your vehicle in a closed building with passengers aboard. Also, you must aim to make the minimum number of fueling stops possible when carrying passengers.

Prohibited Practices

The last part of FMCSR 392 describes actions that are forbidden. One is "no passengers." You must not transport anyone else in your motor vehicle. There are some exceptions to this rule. One, of course, is if your vehicle is a passenger bus. Another exception is you may transport other people who have been assigned to the vehicle, such as co-drivers. You may take a passenger when your motor carrier has authorized it, in writing.

You must not allow unauthorized people to drive your vehicle. You may do this only in an emergency. Also, in an emergency, you may take passengers only as far as needed to get them to safety.

When driving your bus, don't talk or do anything else that will take your full attention from your driving.

If your bus breaks down, it cannot be towed if passengers are still on board. Nor may you tow another vehicle with your bus if you have passengers. The only exception is if the safety of your passengers is at greater risk when you follow these rules. If that's the case, you may tow or be towed only as far as it takes to get your passengers to safety.

The last few rules in this section have to do with personal safety while inside the vehicle. First, motor vehicles must have an exit. The exit must be one that can easily be operated by the person inside. Next, no one with sleeper berths in the vehicle may transfer into or out of the sleeper while the vehicle is moving, unless there is direct access between the sleeper and the cab.

Carbon monoxide can be dangerous in a closed area. If someone in the vehicle shows the effects of carbon monoxide poisoning, no one else may ride in or drive that vehicle. This is also true if carbon monoxide is found in the vehicle. No one may drive or ride in a vehicle if carbon monoxide poisoning might occur due to some mechanical defect.

Some drivers carry flame-producing heaters. They use them to melt ice from trailer doors or to warm the area when loading and unloading. This is permitted. It is, however, forbidden to use a flame-producing heater while the vehicle is moving.

FMCSR Part 392 prohibits coasting. No motor vehicle may be driven if the drive wheels don't have power.

The last regulation in this section states that only one person may be in a sleeper berth when the vehicle is moving.

That completes our overview of FMCSR 392.

FMCSR PART 393

FMCSR Part 393 describes parts and accessories needed to operate the vehicle safely. Briefly, these are:

- lights, reflectors, and electrical equipment
- brakes
- windows
- fuel systems
- coupling devices
- tires, windshield wipers, horn, and other assorted parts
- emergency equipment
- cargo securement systems
- frame and body parts, wheels, steering, and suspension systems

Some of these were referred to by earlier FMCSR sections. This part describes them in detail.

Since you are driving a CMV, not building one, you may think you don't need to know the technical specifications of lights and brakes. You must inspect these parts, though. You can't know whether something is missing or broken if you don't know what's supposed to be there in the first place.

TIP *It would be helpful to have access to a CMV while you go through FMCSR Part 393. Every time you get near that vehicle, see how many of the parts you read about you can identify. When you next hit the books, review the section. Note any parts you missed in your identification. Go over those parts again and again until you can name every part of your CMV from memory.*

We won't cover this part of the FMCSR in great detail now. That's not because the details aren't important. They are. We'll cover them in future chapters on vehicle safety control systems and vehicle inspection.

The first two rules in FMCSR Part 393 state you may have other parts and accessories on your vehicle. However, you must have at least the parts described in this section. They must meet the specifications stated in this section.

FMCSR 393.5 defines terms used throughout the rest of the section. For example, a bus is defined as "a vehicle designed to carry more than 15 passengers, including the driver." The amount you can turn your steering wheel before the front wheels also begin to move is called "steering wheel lash." Review all the definitions in this section to make sure you know the official names of the required parts.

Lights and Reflectors

FMCSR Part 393 describes the types of lights CMVs must have. It includes a table and several figures that show the color, location, and other specifications of all these required lights. Study the table and the

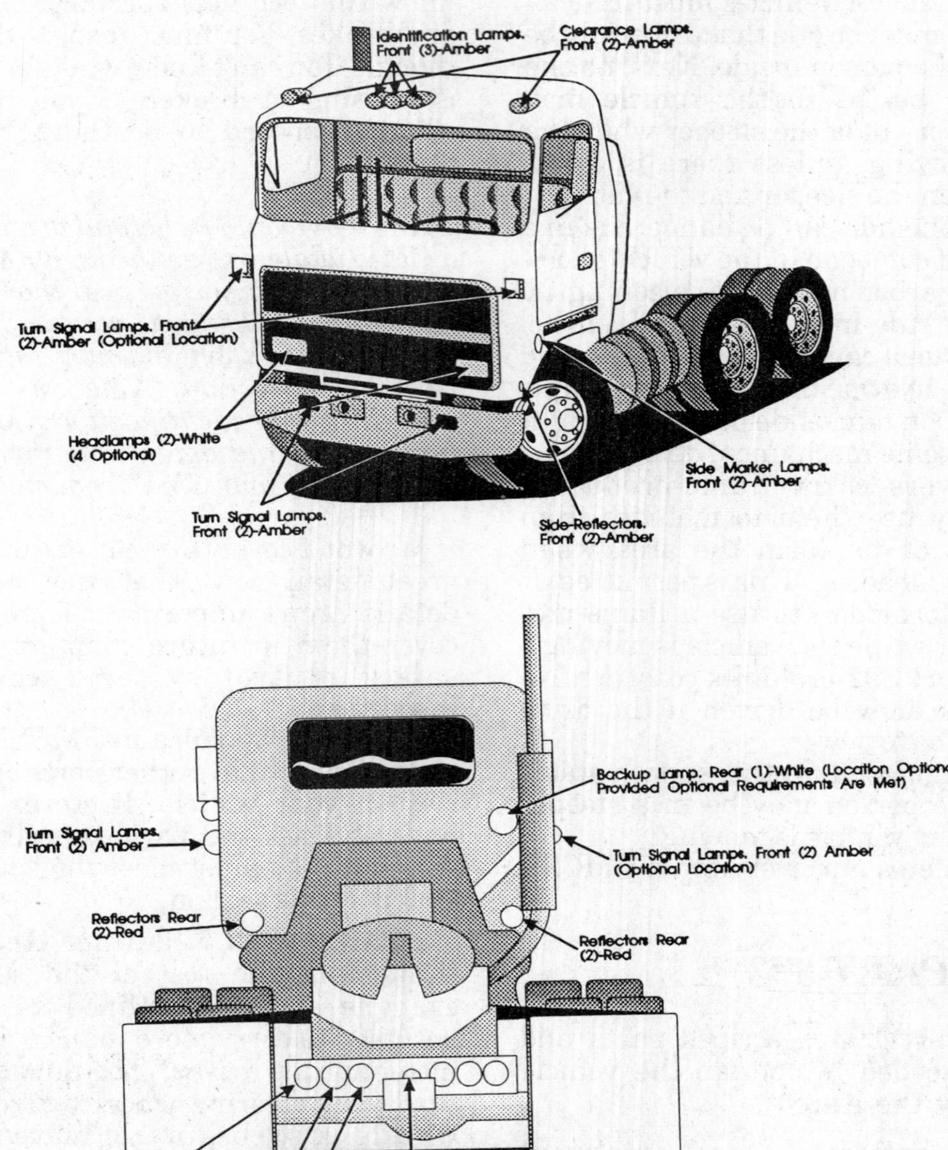

Figure 6-13A Required lights and reflectors.

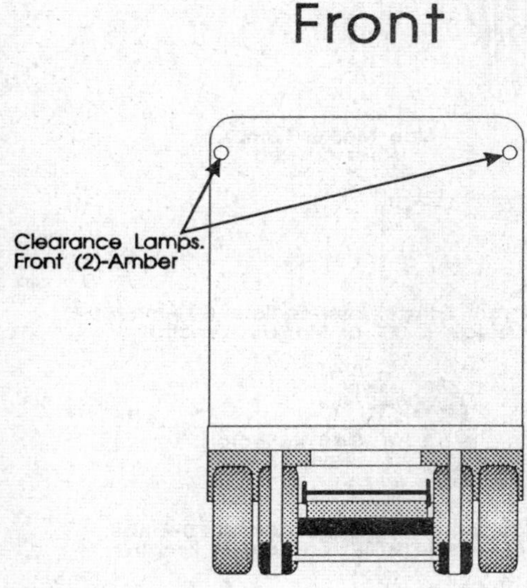

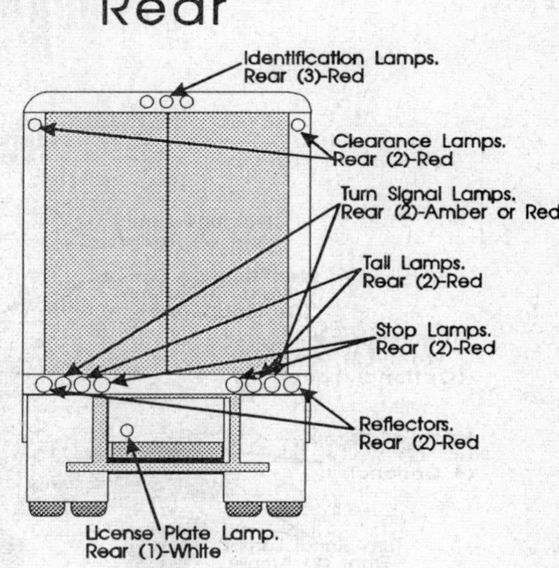

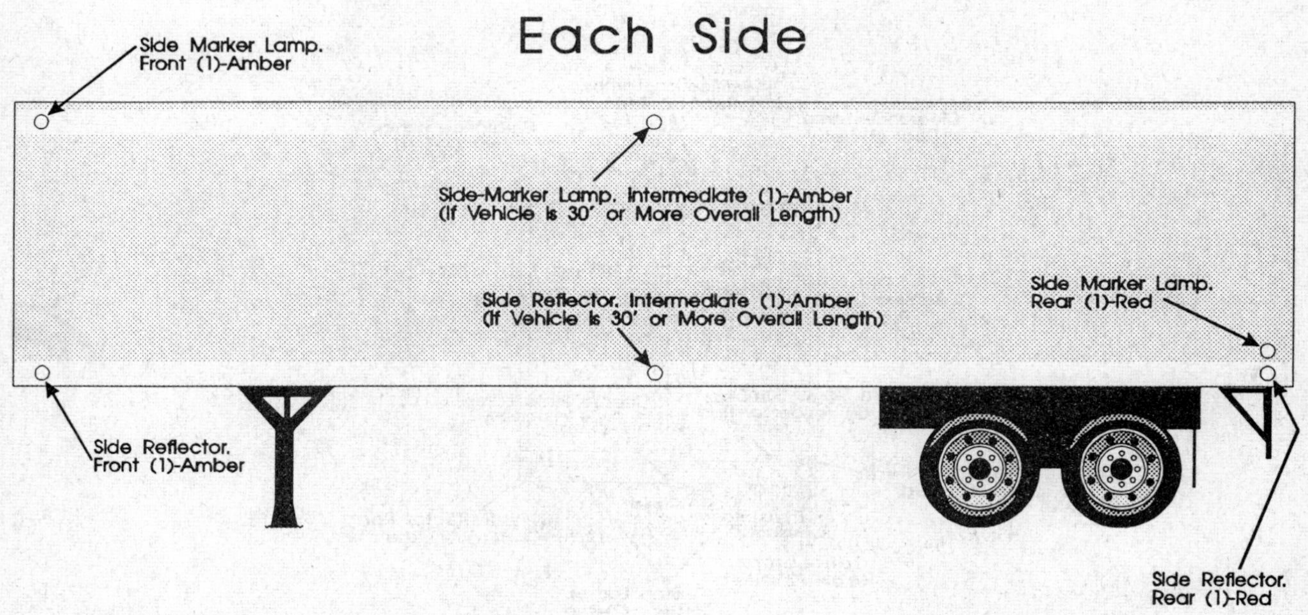

Figure 6-13B Required lights and reflectors.

Over 80 Inches

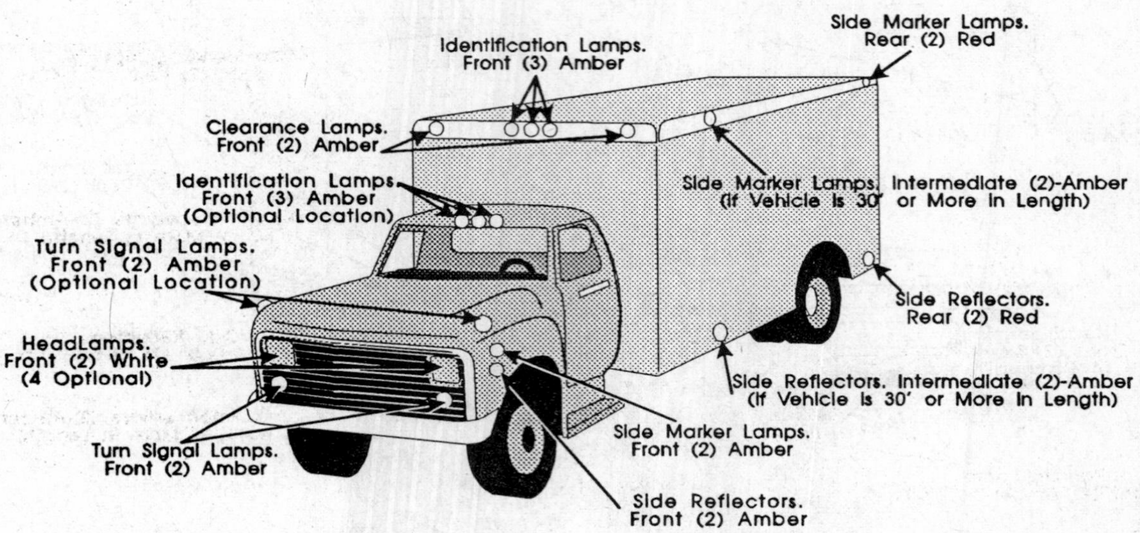

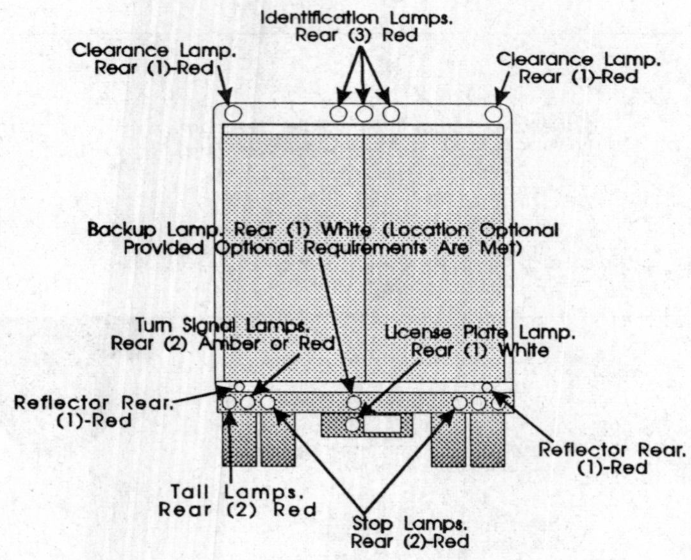

Figure 6-13C Required lights and reflectors.

Under 80 Inches

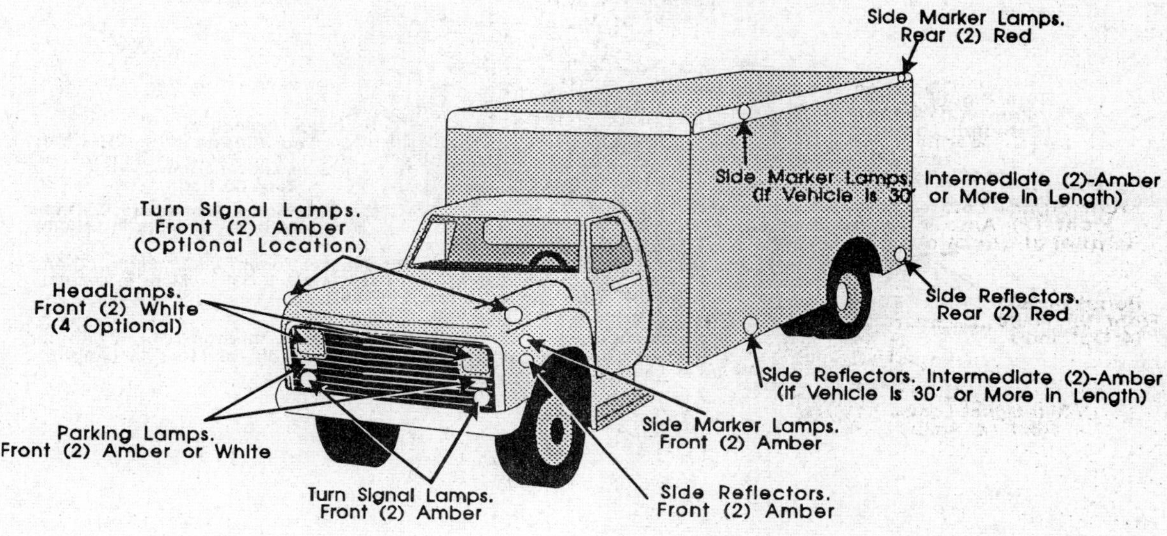

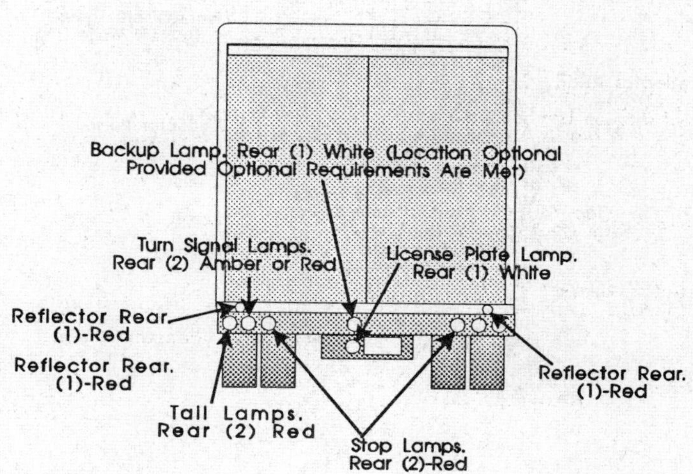

Figure 6-13D Required lights and reflectors.

Under 80 Inches

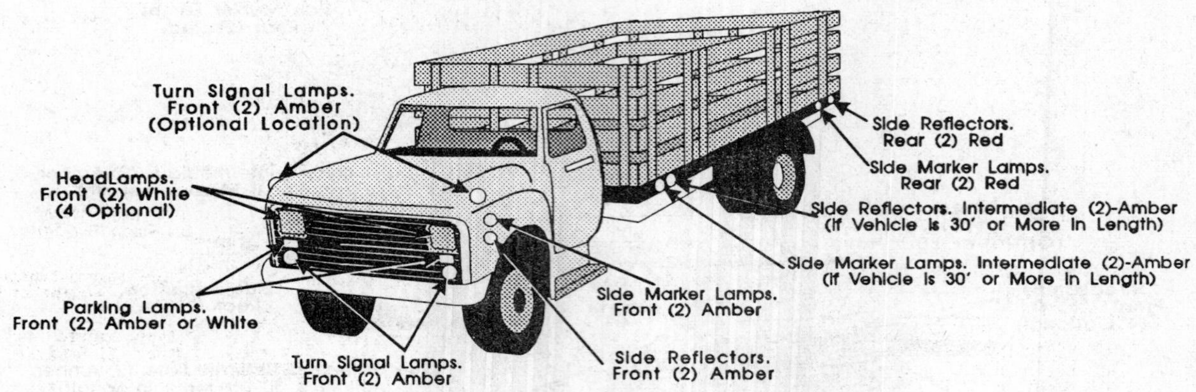

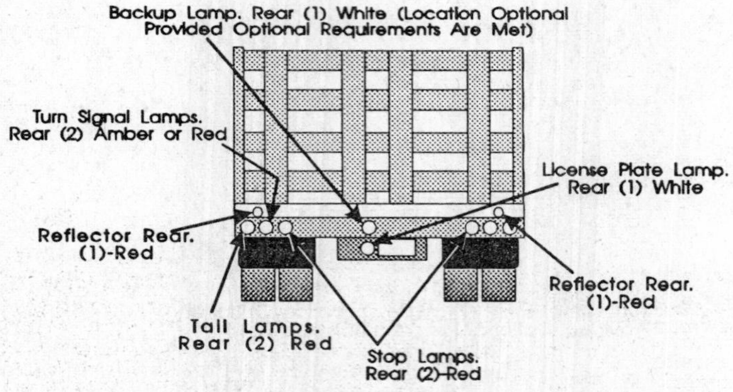

Figure 6-13E Required lights and reflectors.

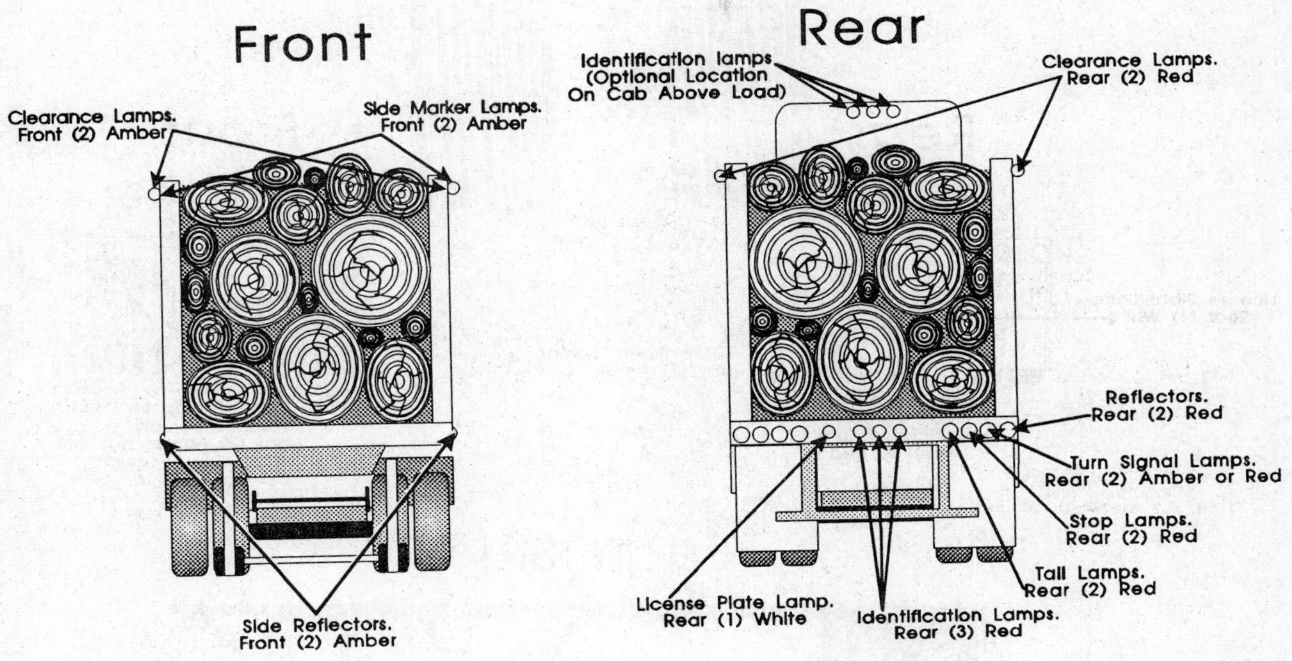

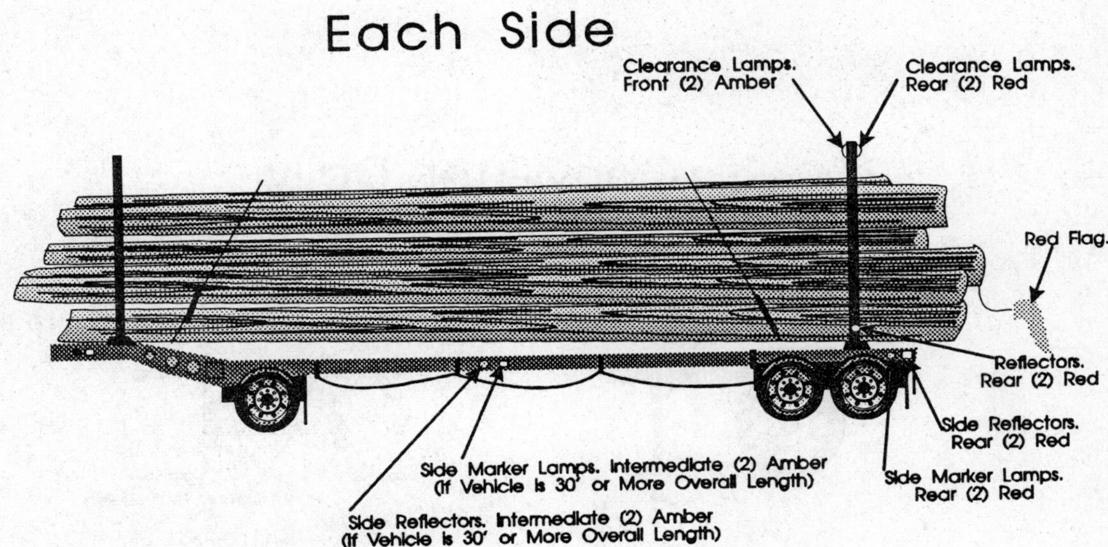

Figure 6-13F Required lights and reflectors.

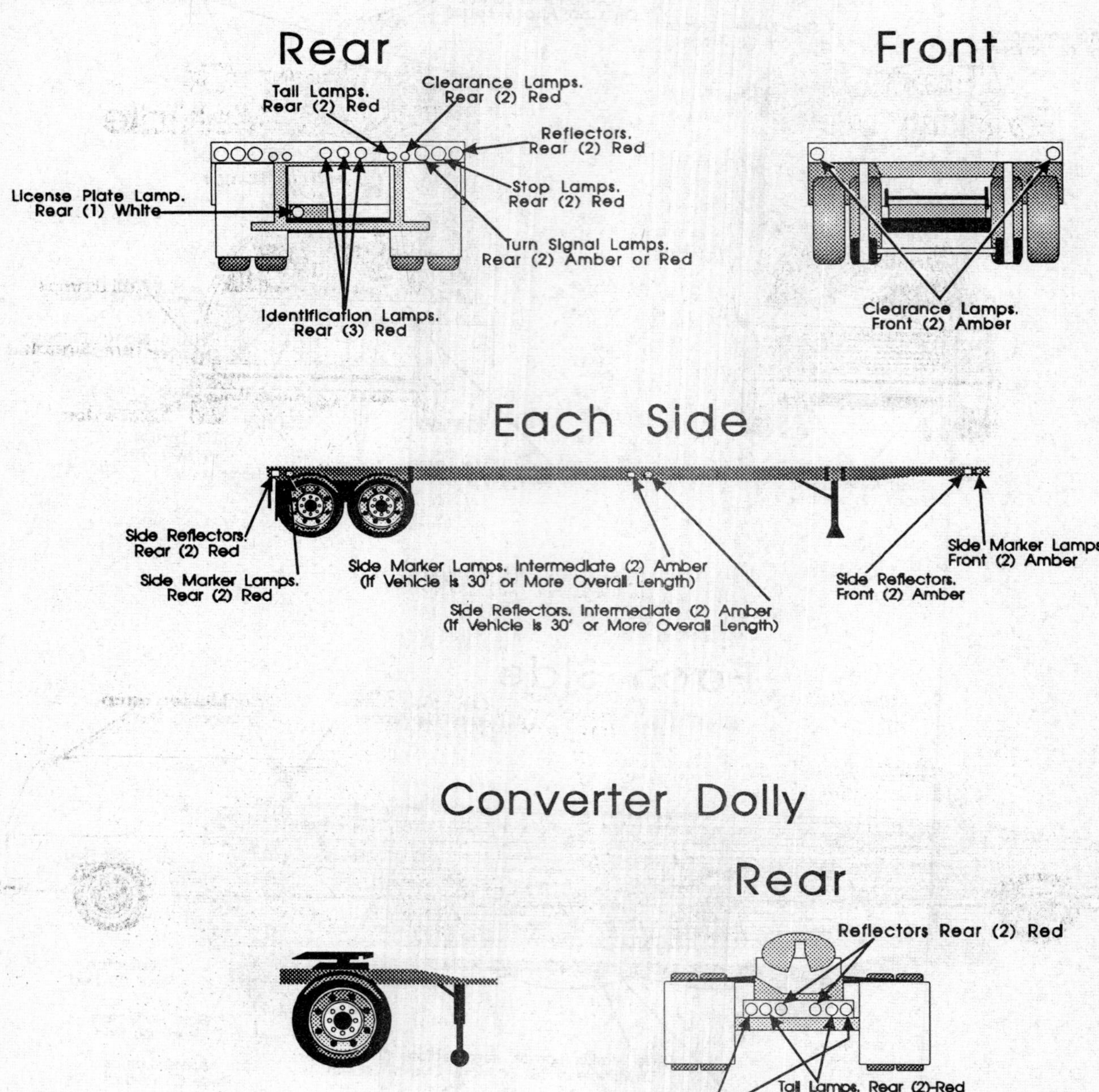

Figure 6-13G Required lights and reflectors.

Front Of
Towing Vehicle

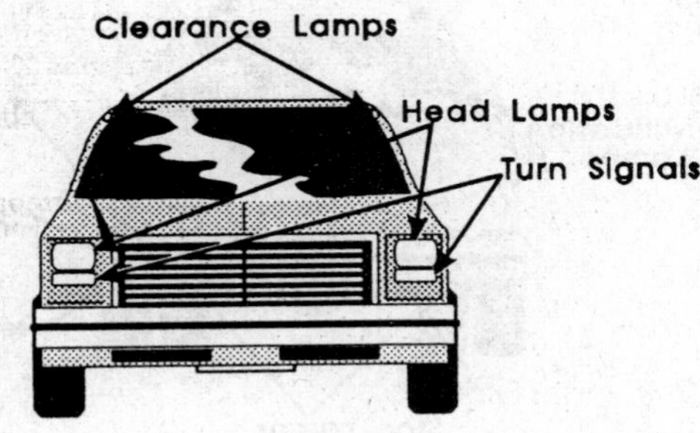

Rear Of
Towed Vehicle

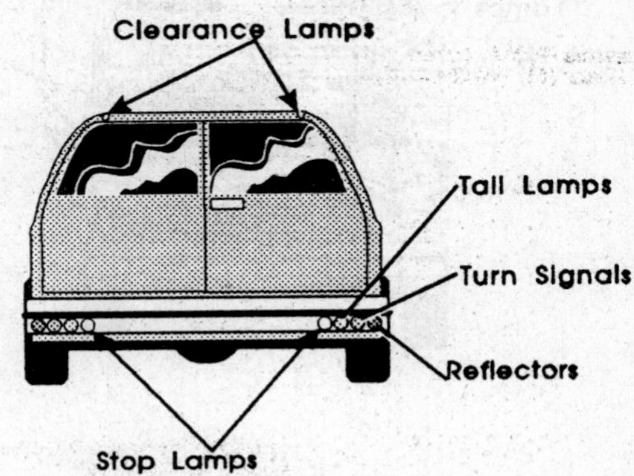

Each Side

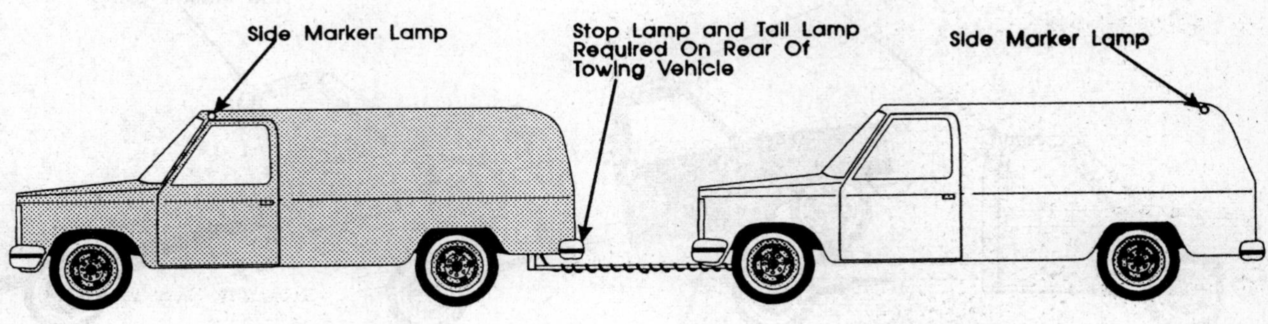

Figure 6-13H Required lights and reflectors.

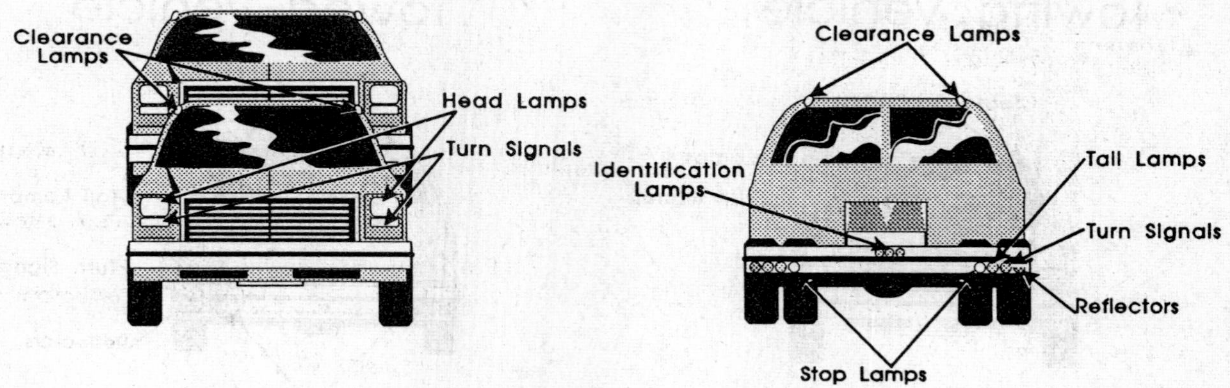

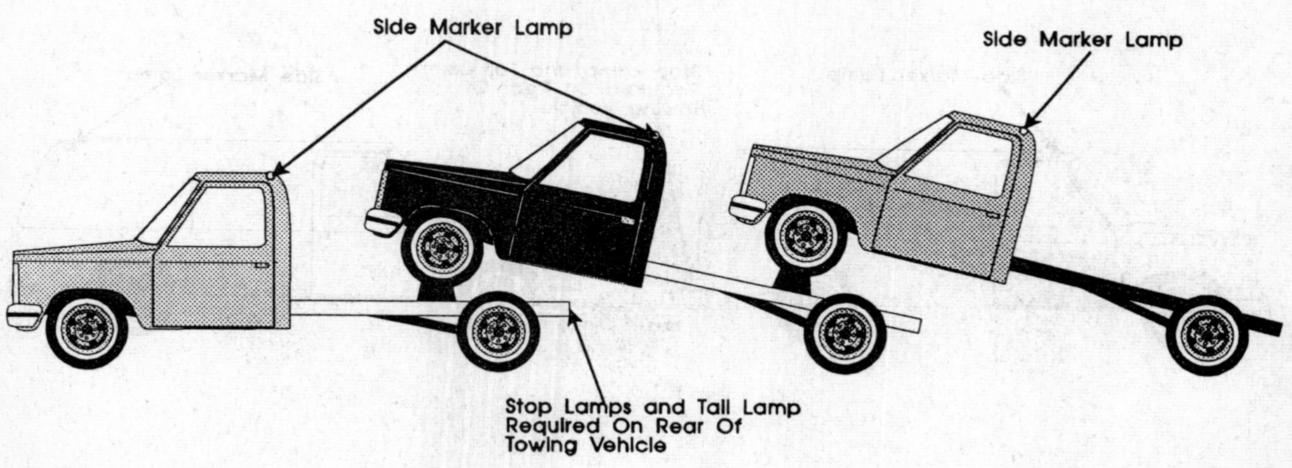

Figure 6-13I Required lights and reflectors.

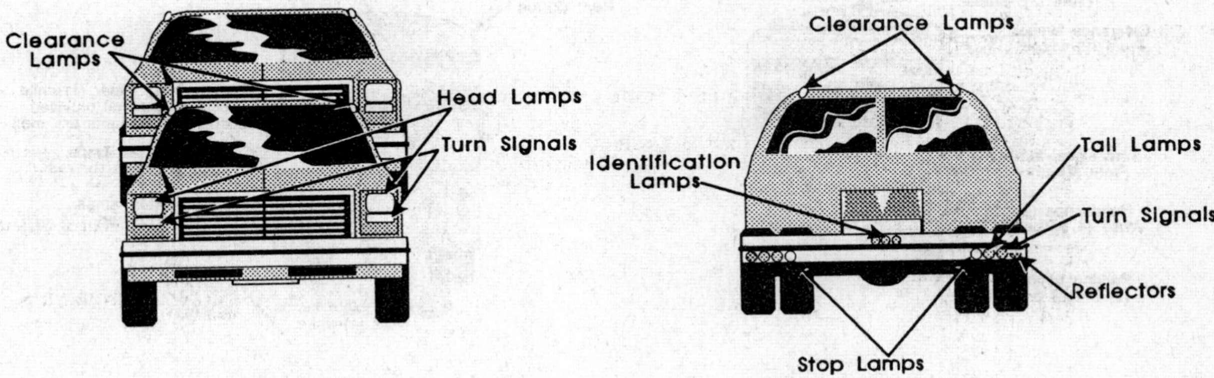

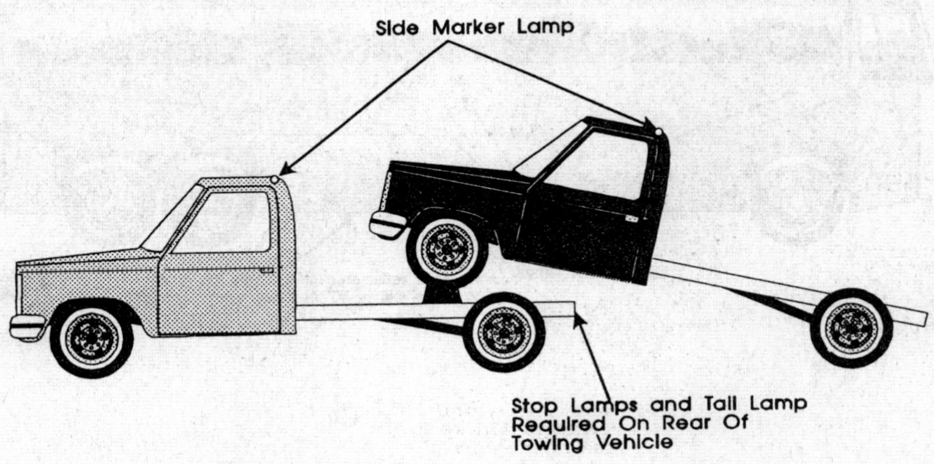

Figure 6-13J Required lights and reflectors.

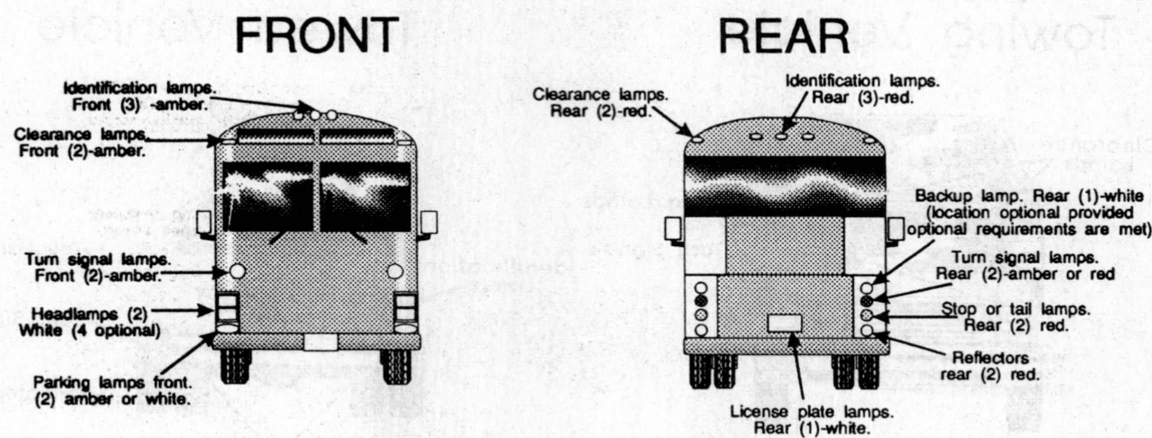

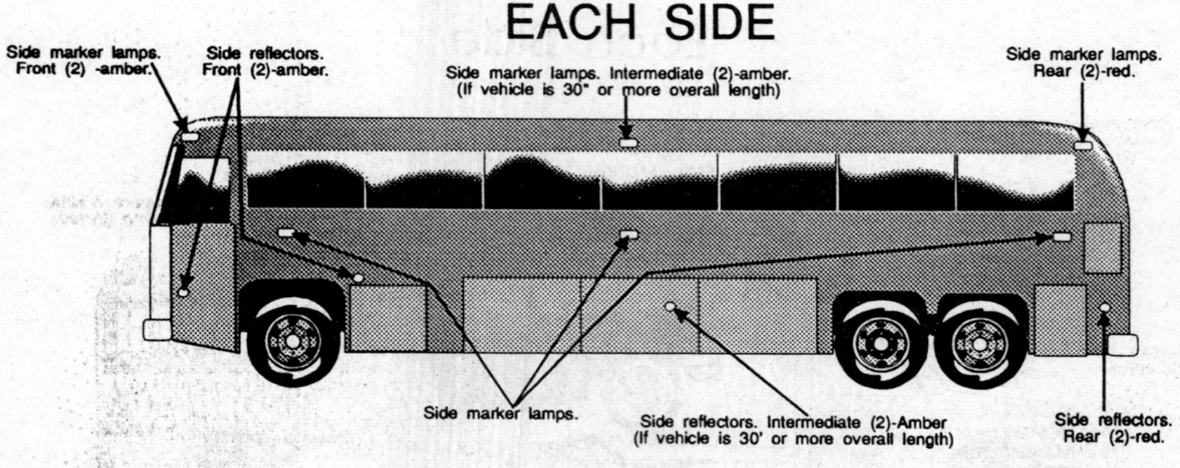

Figure 6-13K Required lights and reflectors.

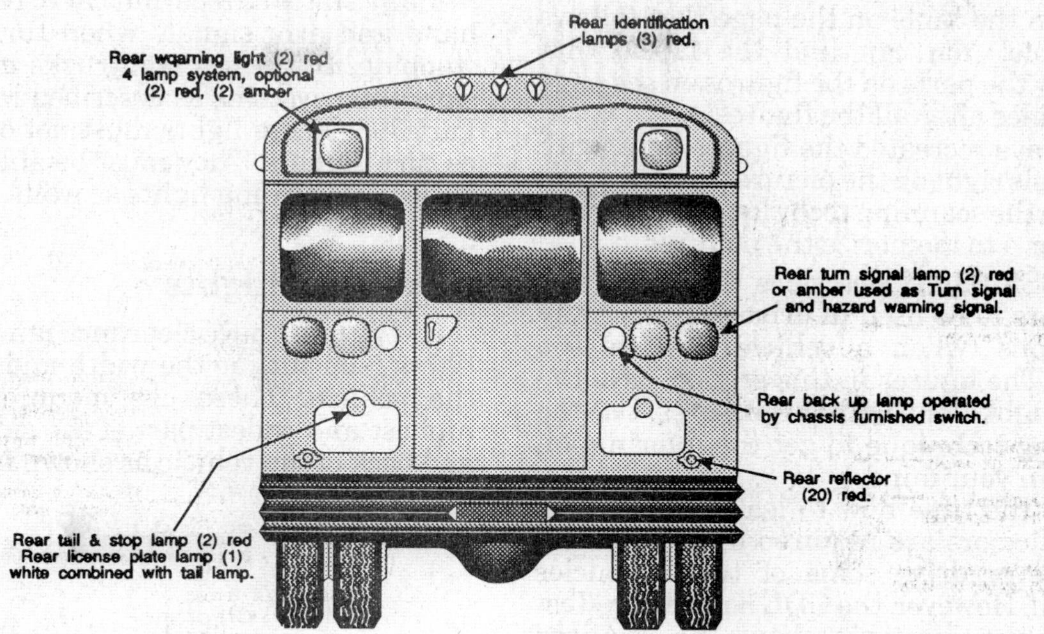

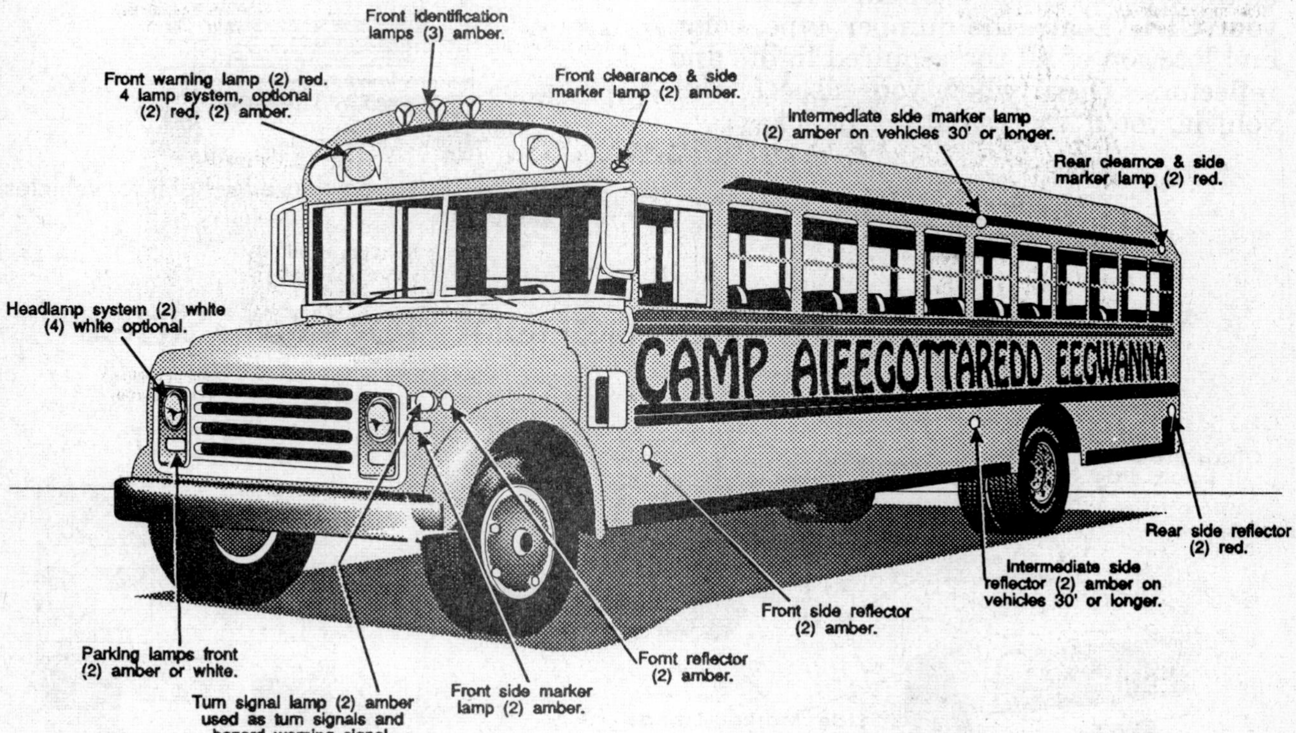

Figure 6-13L Required lights and reflectors.

figures in your copy of the FMCSR. There are footnotes that give more details about items in the table on the page that follows the table. You can find the labels that identify the parts on the figures on the page that comes after all the figures.

We have recreated the figures here, with the labels right on the picture. That way you can use the scanning technique described in Chapter 4 to memorize the pictures.

FMCSR 393.17 describes the lights and reflectors to be used in driveaway-towaway operations (when a vehicle itself is the cargo). The figures in this section have the labels right along with the pictures. Use the scanning technique to get the information firmly in your mind.

Take the time now to learn what lights and reflectors are required on CMVs. You may never drive some of these vehicles yourself. However, the CDL Knowledge Test could have questions about the required lights and reflectors for any of the vehicles pictured. So you should be familiar with all of them. Then pay special attention to those on the type of vehicle you plan to drive with your CDL. Learn the number, type, color, and location of all the required lights and reflectors. Then, when you inspect your vehicle, you'll know what to look for.

Turn Signals

Many states still permit car drivers to use hand and arm signals when turning and stopping. But buses and trucks must have signalling systems as described in FMCSR Part 393. These lights must not only serve as turn signals. They must be able to work as hazard warning lights as well.

Clearance Lights

CMVs must have clearance lamps. These lights help outline the width and height of the vehicle. These are mounted at the highest and widest part of the sides, front, and back of the vehicle as shown in Figures 6-14A and B.

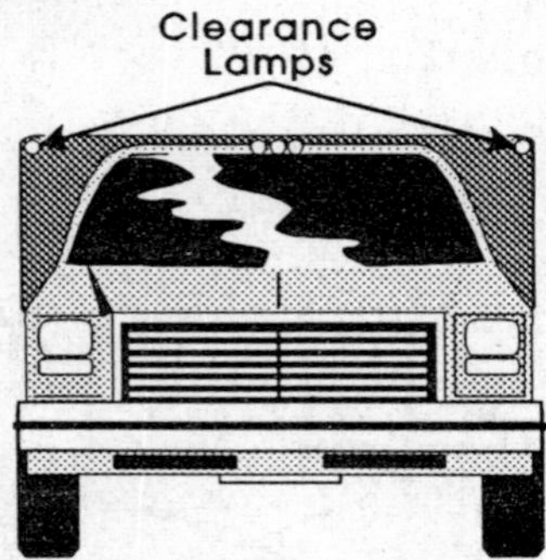

Figure 6-14A Required clearance lights for vehicles with sleepers.

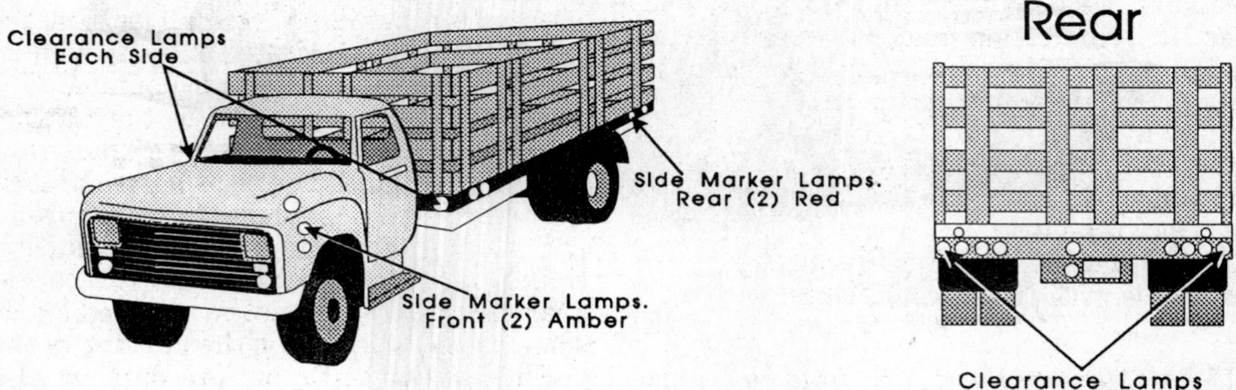

Figure 6-14B Required clearance lights for vehicles without permanent tops or sides.

Other Lights

You may have other lights and markers on your vehicle. However, they must not reduce the effectiveness of the required lights. For instance, an extra light that is brighter than the required light will make the required light hard to see. This extra light would be prohibited.

All the lights must be electric. Liquid burning lights may sometimes be used to mark the end of loads that stick out past the rear of the vehicle.

Headlights and Reflectors

FMCSR Part 393 describes the types of headlights and fog lights you must have on your vehicle and lists the requirements for all other lights. Lights must be visible from a distance of 500 feet to 50 feet away in clear weather. This part describes how reflectors should be placed so as to give the greatest visibility.

Wiring, Battery, and Fuses

FMCSR Part 393 discusses the wiring system, battery, and overload protective devices (fuses). As a driver, of course you want these to work safely and well. Still, many of the regulations in the section are not driver-related. They are chiefly of concern to manufacturers. In the chapter on inspections, we'll describe the parts of the wiring system, battery, and fuses that do concern the driver.

This part also discusses detachable connections. Detachable connections are the electrical connection made between towing and towed vehicles. You probably call this a "pigtail." This connection can't be made simply by twisting wires together. It must be special, shielded cables. You should leave some slack in the cable to allow for movement of the vehicle.

Wires and cables must be attached to terminals with proper connectors.

TIP *Many of the details in the sections you just read may seem too small to bother with. However, you are expected to be fully familiar with your equipment. When you inspect your vehicle as part of your CDL test, you may be asked questions about these parts. You must know the answers.*

Brakes

The next group of sections in FMCSR 393 deals with the brakes. Many drivers fail the CDL tests because they don't know enough about their braking systems. A faulty braking system threatens your life and the lives of everyone else around you. You must know your braking system like the back of your hand.

FMCSR Part 393 states your CMV must have service, parking, and emergency brakes. The emergency brake controls must be placed so you can reach them when you are in the driver's seat with the seat belt on. The emergency brake control may be combined with either the service or parking brakes. However, all three controls may not be combined into one.

The brake systems on your CMV must be designed so no matter what happens, one will always work.

Parking Brakes

FMCSR Part 393 describes the parking or spring brakes. All CMVs made after March 7, 1989, must have parking brakes. Certain farm vehicles and pole trailers must also have chocks.

On some vehicles, you set the parking brakes by pulling a lever or knob. This controls a cable that pulls the brakes into position mechanically. You can feel that this takes a little effort. But such systems must not require great strength to operate.

On other vehicles, setting the parking brake requires more strength than most drivers have. Then the parking brake is set with the help of air pressure. When this is the case, the air supply for the parking brake must be separate from the service brake air supply. It must be reserved for the sole purpose of applying the parking brake.

Fluid pressure or air pressure or electricity may be used to set the parking brakes. But they must not be used to keep the parking brakes applied. Also, when you release the brakes, the system must be such that you can immediately reapply them. No other system may be used. Air pressure does not meet these requirements. Air pressure takes time to build. You might use up all your air pressure to keep the parking brakes on. Then, if you release them, you might not have enough air pressure to reapply them immediately.

The parking brake systems on most vehicles meet these requirements. (You'll see how in Chapter 7 and Chapter 11.) These regulations are mostly of concern to manufacturers. As a driver, your job will be to inspect and maintain the system so your brakes are always in working order.

All wheels on a CMV must have working brakes. This is required by FMCSR 393.42, which also lists the few exceptions. Among them are vehicles manufactured before 1980. If you have disconnected or removed the front brakes, you should know that after February 26, 1988, all other CMVs must have working front brakes.

Emergency Brakes

FMCSR Part 393 covers pulling a trailer that has brakes. It requires that the service brakes on the tractor will still work if the trailer breaks away.

Vehicles with air brakes must have two ways of starting the trailer emergency brakes. One must work automatically if the tractor air supply falls to between 20 and 45 pounds per square inch (psi). The other must be a manually-controlled device. This must be within easy reach of the person in the driver's seat. The control must be clearly marked. It must be easy to see how to work the control.

Vehicles that pull trailers with vacuum brakes must have two controls. The first must be a single control that will operate all the brakes of the total combination. The second must be a trailer emergency brake control. This must be a manual control. It must be independent of brake air, hydraulic, and other pressure. It must be separate from all other controls. There's only one

PASS Billboard

Anti-lock and Front Brakes

Some drivers believe that front brakes are dangerous. They think they can lock up in emergencies and cause the driver to lose control.

Experience and tests have shown this simply isn't true. Since January, 1982, all heavy vehicles in California have been required to have working front brakes. Accident records have shown that front wheel brakes do not cause accidents or make accidents more serious.

Tests made by the National Highway Traffic Safety Administration (NHTSA) have shown that working front brakes allow drivers to handle vehicles better and stop sooner.

Locked-up brakes are more the result of panic stopping than faulty equipment. When the front brakes do lock, the vehicle can get out of control, skid, and possibly jackknife. To combat brake lock-up, the industry has, from time to time, tried anti-lock brakes. These have worked with different degrees of success. Some drivers familiar with the first tries at anti-lock brakes may think these cause more problems than they solve.

The best anti-lock prevention is probably to avoid making panic stops in the first place. If you are a careful and alert driver and keep a good following distance, you won't have to stand on your brakes to avoid an accident.

exception to this – if failure of the pressure that the second control depends on will cause the trailer brakes to come on automatically.

A trailer that is required to have brakes must have brakes that will apply automatically if the trailer breaks away from the tractor. These trailer brakes must stay on for at least 15 minutes.

The tractor-braking air supply must be protected from air back-flow if the tractor air pressure falls. If a problem with the tractor air supply develops, the system must prevent the trailer air supply from flowing back to the tractor. If that happened, both the tractor and the trailer would be left without a supply of air. A relay or check valve takes care of this. Brake valves will be discussed in more detail in the next few chapters.

These requirements don't apply to vehicles being towed as cargo.

Again, these regulations are mostly of concern to manufacturers. Your vehicle will probably have brakes designed to meet these requirements. Your job will be to inspect and maintain your brakes.

Front Brakes on Buses

Buses with air brakes must be equipped so the driver can apply brakes to the rear wheels if something happens to the front wheel brake lines. The control for this must be easily operated by a driver in the driver's seat with the seat belt on.

Brake Tubing and Hoses

FMCSR Part 393 sets the requirements for brake tubing and hoses. The brake lines on your vehicle will likely meet these manufacturing standards. Through use, however, they can become worn or damaged. As a CMV driver, you'll check to make sure your brake lines continue to meet these requirements.

Working Brakes

FMCSR Part 393 states that for the most part, all the brakes on the vehicle must work. There are a few exceptions, which are also described in this section. If you drive a vehicle manufactured before March 1, 1975, read this section of the FMCSR carefully.

Brake Reservoirs

FMCSR Part 393 describes the brake reservoirs (tanks). For air or vacuum brake systems, these tanks must be large enough to ensure a full service brake application with the engine stopped. This must not reduce the air pressure or vacuum below 70 percent of the pressure that was on the gauge just before the brakes were applied. A "full service brake application" is defined here as pushing the brake pedal to its limit.

This tank must be protected from leaks. If the connection to the air or vacuum supply is broken, some device must seal off the tank so its supply isn't lost. This device is usually called a "check valve." You'll test this valve to make sure it's working.

Some air brake systems have a wet tank and a dry tank. The check valve is found between these two tanks. In such systems, there's a manually-operated drain cock on the wet tank. This can be used to inspect the check valve.

Test the check valve operation of vacuum systems with the engine off. The vacuum gauge should show the system still holds a vacuum. If the gauge shows the pressure rising, the check valve isn't working right.

Warning Devices and Gauges

Vehicles must have warning devices that will tell you when there's a problem with the service brake system. Hydraulic and vacuum brake system warning devices can be heard and seen. Air brake warning systems must have a low-air-pressure warning device.

Braking systems must have gauges, too. Air brake gauges tell how many psi of pressure are available for braking. Vacuum gauges give this information in inches of mercury.

Warning devices can't help you if they don't work. You will check to see the warning devices are working when you do your inspection. This section of the FMCSR states that warning devices and gauges must be kept in working order.

Some hydraulic braking systems are assisted by air or by vacuum. These systems must have warning devices and gauges for the air or vacuum part as well as the hydraulic part.

Brake Performance

FMCSR 393 sets standards for brake performance. When you inspect your brakes, you will check to see that they perform to these standards.

This section of the FMCSR includes a vehicle brake performance table. It describes how service and emergency brakes should work for different vehicles. It gives braking force as a percentage of the GVWR

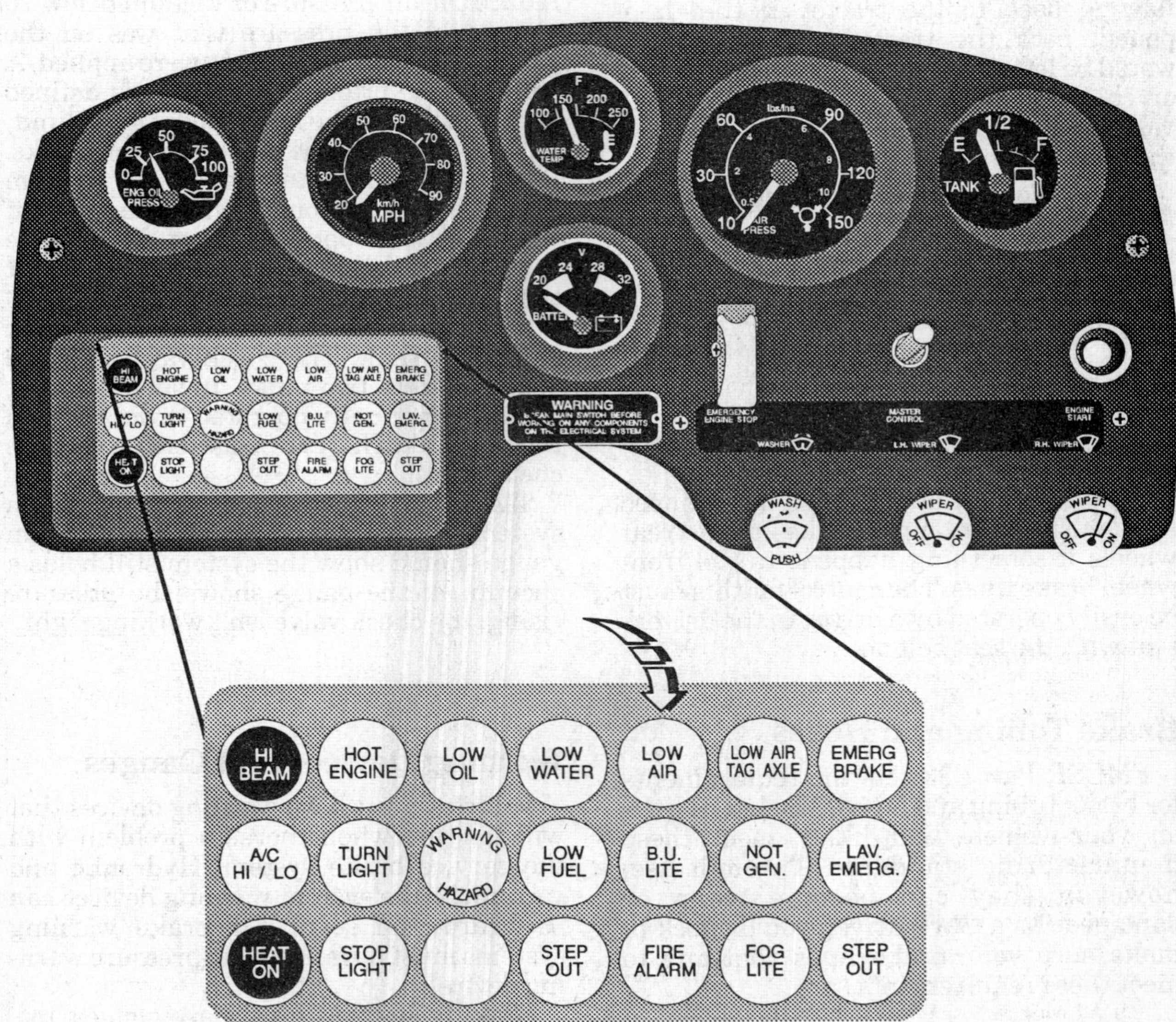

Figure 6-15 Brake systems have warning lights.

or the GCWR. This is not something the driver is expected to check. Braking force is a manufacturing specification.

The performance table also states how quickly the vehicle must slow and how far it may travel while slowing. As a driver, you could test the braking speed and distance. These are not the typical brake tests you perform in an inspection. But you could perform tests that tell you whether your vehicle's braking rate and distance meet the requirements. Here's how to read the rest of the table.

The speed and distance requirements assume you were going 20 miles per hour (mph) when you applied the brakes. The

Type of motor vehicle	Service brake systems			Emergency brake systems
	Braking force as a percentage of gross vehicle or combination weight	Deceleration in feet per second per second	Application and braking distance in feet from initial speed of 20 mph	Application and braking distance in feet from initial speed of 20 mph
A. Passenger-carrying vehicles. (1) Vehicles with a seating capacity of 10 persons or less, including driver, and built on a passenger car chassis	65.2	21.0	20.0	54.0
(2) Vehicles with a seating capacity of more than 10 persons, including driver, and built on a passenger car chassis; vehicles built on a truck or bus chassis and having a manufacturer's GVWR of 10,000 pounds or less	52.8	17.0	25.0	66.0
(3) All other passenger-carrying vehicles	43.5	14.0	35.0	85.0
B. Property-carrying vehicles. (1) Single unit vehicles having a manufacturer's GVWR of 10,000 pounds or less	52.8	17.0	25.0	66.0
(2) Single unit vehicles having a manufacturer's GVWR of more than 10,000 pounds, except truck tractors. Combinations of a 2-axle towing vehicle and trailer having a GVWR of 3,000 pounds or less. All combinations of 2 or less vehicles in driveaway or towaway operation	43.4	14.0	35.0	85.0
(3) All other property carrying vehicles and combinations of property-carrying vehicles	43.5	14.0	40.0	90.0

Figure 6-16 Braking performance.

second measure of braking performance states the braking rate in feet per second per second. "Per second per second" isn't a misprint. Here's what it means. It means you should slow at the rate of so many feet per second. Then, for every second it takes you until you are stopped, you should have slowed at that rate.

So, if it took you one second to slow to a stop, you would have gone so many feet. If it took you two seconds, you would have traveled twice as far, and so on. For example, the service brakes on a Group C bus should provide a braking force of 52.8 percent. They should slow the vehicle at a rate of 17 feet per second per second. This vehicle should slow at the rate of 17 feet per second. Then, for every second it takes until the vehicle stops, you should have slowed 17 feet. If it took you one second to slow to a stop, you would have gone 17 feet. If it took you two seconds, you would have traveled 34 feet.

The third measure of braking performance is braking distance. This is a simple measure of how far the vehicle travels before it comes to a stop. The same Group C bus must come to a stop from 20 mph in no more than 25 feet.

Required braking performance, then, is a combination of how quickly the brakes bring you to a stop and how far you travel before you stop. Performance is also measured by how much force the brakes apply.

These standards assume the vehicle is braking on a level, dry, smooth, hard surface that is free of gravel or other loose material. The vehicle starts in the center of a 12-foot wide lane and does not pull to either side when tested for this type of performance.

Figure 6-16 is the brake performance table. Find the vehicle you plan to be licensed to drive. You may be interested to note the braking performance required for that vehicle. Know that the brake system tests you will make during your inspection will not have to yield such technical information, however.

The braking systems on most vehicles, if properly installed and maintained, will provide all the functions required by FMCSR Part 393. In Chapter 7 we'll explain how brakes work. When you understand how brakes work, you will be better able to spot and correct problems. Then you'll have no trouble getting good performance from your brakes.

Windows

The next few regulations in this section of the FMCSR cover windows. There must be a certain amount of glass in your vehicle. This is so you have a good field of vision. The glass must be a certain material, for your safety and the safety of any passengers you may carry.

Your windshield must be clear, clean, and undamaged. FMCSR Part 393 sets the standards for windshield condition. You'll check for these items when you inspect your vehicle.

You may not have any labels, stickers, decals, or other decorations on your windshield or on your side windows. The only ones that are allowed are those stickers required by law. They must be placed at the bottom of the windshield. They must not extend higher than 4½ inches from the bottom of the windshield.

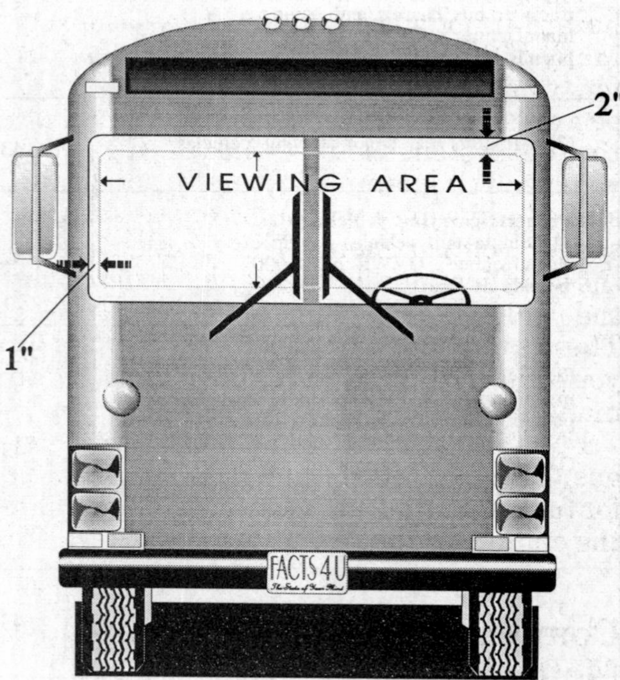

Figure 6-17 Required viewing area.

Trucks must have a windshield and a window on each side of the cab. Trucks with folding doors or doors with clear openings in place of windows don't have to be equipped with windows.

In buses, the number and size of windows (escape windows as well as the windshield) and where they are placed depends on the seat rating. That's the number of passengers the bus is designed to carry. This section of the FMCSR is very specific about how many push-out windows and emergency exits there should be, how large they should be, how they should work, and how they should be marked. Most of this information is of concern to manufacturers. We'll cover the driver's responsibilities regarding windows and exits in the chapter on inspections.

TIP *This has been a lengthy part of the FMCSR, and we're not finished with it yet. Hang in there. As these chapters get longer and longer, you're getting used to concentrating for longer and longer spans of time. This practice will help you to stay sharp when you take your CDL tests.*

Fuel Systems

The fuel that powers your vehicle can be a hazard if not stored and handled properly. Many of the regulations in this section exist for your safety and the safety of your passengers. FMCSR Part 393 specifies how the fuel system should be installed on your vehicle. For example, it must not be installed anywhere within or above the passenger compartment. This section states the specifications for fuel tanks. It describes the leakage tests fuel tanks must pass. These are not tests you can easily make by yourself. They are of greater concern to manufacturers.

FMCSR Part 393 covers liquid petroleum gas (LPG) systems. Some CMVs use LPG for fuel, or to fuel auxiliary equipment, like the engine for the reefer unit.

Coupling Devices and Towing Methods

The next section in this part concerns coupling devices. It includes important definitions and descriptions of the fifth wheel, locking jaws, and safety chains. These are parts you will definitely check when you inspect combination vehicles. These devices are covered in more detail in Chapter 12.

This section states limits on coupling and towing many vehicles together and hauling them as cargo. Your job isn't likely to involved much towing of vehicles. If it does, you should read the material in this section.

Tires

The next section of FMCSR Part 393 deals with tires. You may already know that you cannot drive on tires whose tread is so worn the belts show through. Also prohibited are tires

- that have tread or sidewall separation
- that are flat or have leaks you can hear
- that have a tread groove pattern of less than 2⁄32 of an inch (4⁄32 of an inch for front tires)

Regrooved tires may not be used on front wheels with a load carrying capacity equal to or greater than 8.25-20 8-ply tires. That is, regrooved tires may not be used on a truck or tractor which has more than an 8,000 pound front axle rating. Regrooved, recapped, or retreaded tires may not be used on the front wheels of buses at all. With few exceptions, you can't use tires to support weights heavier than what the tire is rated for. (A number of different agencies rate tires. These agencies are listed in Federal Motor Vehicle Safety Standard (FMVSS) Number 571.119.)

TIP *Federal Motor Vehicle Safety Standards not included in the FMCSR can be found in the Code of Federal Regulations Title 49.*

You must also keep the tire inflated to the pressure specified for the load being carried.

Sleeper Berths

The size, shape, and structure of the

sleeper berth is specified in FMCSR Part 393. Most of these specifications are geared to the driver's safety and comfort. They're chiefly of concern to manufacturers.

Heaters

You may carry a heater in your vehicle. FMCSR Part 393 states what type of heater you may have. Some are prohibited. An example would be a heater that gives off exhaust gases into your cab.

The heater must be securely mounted. Combustion heaters must be vented to the outside. The fuel tank for such a heater must be located outside the passenger space. The heater on a bus must be installed so that passengers can't get to the controls.

As you can see, much of the information in this section is of interest to manufacturers. You'll find the driver's responsibilities discussed in Chapter 10.

Windshield Wipers

Your CMV must have windshield wipers. In some cases, one wiper will do. It must clear your windshield to within one inch of your field of vision at either side. In a driveaway-towaway operation, only the vehicle you drive has to have wipers. The towed vehicles don't need working wipers.

Defrosting Device

If you drive in snow, ice, or frost, your vehicle must have a windshield defroster. As with windshield wipers, vehicles towed as cargo don't need defrosters.

Rear-view Mirrors

All trucks and buses made after 1980 must have rear-view mirrors, one on each side. Earlier models may have one outside mirror at the driver's side and one inside mirror, if it gives a full view of the rear. Your mirrors should show you the highway behind you and the sides of the vehicle.

Horn

FMCSR Part 393 says trucks and buses must have a horn.

Speedometer

Your vehicle must also have a speedometer. A vehicle being driven in a driveaway-towaway operation doesn't need a speedometer if there's a way to limit its speed to 45 mph. Of course, the vehicles being towed as cargo don't have to have speedometers.

Exhaust Systems

Motor vehicles must have exhaust systems. The system must be installed so hot gases or surfaces don't damage wiring, the fuel supply, or any part of the vehicle that could burn.

This section of FMCSR Part 393 specifies how exhaust gases must be discharged. Exhaust systems that are properly installed and maintained will meet these requirements. Your job will be to ensure that the system continues to work correctly.

This section also notes that the exhaust system may not be repaired with wrap or patches.

Floor

FMCSR Part 393 even considers the floor necessary for safe vehicle operations. A floor with holes or openings can allow exhaust fumes into the cab. That could harm the driver or passengers. So the floor must be sturdy and in good condition. It must also be free of oil or grease, which would make it slippery to walk on.

Rear End Protection

FMCSR Part 393 requires certain vehicles to have rear bumpers. Vehicles higher than 30 inches from the ground (when empty) must have rear bumpers. This keeps shorter vehicles from running under the taller vehicle. The clearance between the bumper and the ground must be no more than 30 inches, again measured when the vehicle is empty. These bumpers must meet other size and mounting requirements described in this section. As with many of the regulations in this part, the driver's responsibility is to maintain the equipment.

Projecting Loads

Any part of the vehicle or load that extends too far beyond the rear or sides must be marked with a red flag. An extension more than four inches from the side or four feet from the rear has to be marked. The flag must be 12 inches square and red.

Television Receivers

You are allowed to have a TV in your vehicle. But you definitely must not be watching it while driving. Therefore, FMCSR Part 393 states the TV must be set behind the driver's seat. It must be placed outside your line of vision when you are driving. The controls must be placed far enough away so you have to leave your seat to get to them.

Requirements for Buses

FMCSR Part 393 lists several requirements for buses. Some of these, such as driveshaft protection, are of concern to manufacturers.

Others are of concern to drivers who carry passengers. These involve the standee line, which sets off an area of the bus prohibited to passengers. Your vehicle must have signs telling passengers how to treat the standee line. Another item concerns aisle seats, mentioned earlier in this chapter. If your vehicle has them, they must fold up automatically to clear the aisle when they're not in use. Other seats must be securely fastened to the vehicle, and you must not operate the vehicle if they aren't. Your bus must have lights that mark the emergency exits. They must be lit during those hours when your vehicle lights must be on.

Most buses will come with the proper equipment. You, the driver, should confirm the equipment is in place when you inspect the vehicle.

Seat Belts

Nearly every bus and truck on the road today must have a seat belt for the driver. Some trucks must have seat belts for the passenger. Tractors with incomplete cabs don't have to have seat belts when they are being towed as cargo.

Noise Levels

Maximum levels for noise in your cab are set by FMCSR Part 393. Too much noise could be distracting and make you tired. As a driver, you'll be the first to notice unusually high noise levels. You're not expected to whip out a sound level meter and perform tests. You could report an unusually high level of noise to Maintenance, though. It could be a sign of some mechanical problem. Repairing that would give you relief from the noise, also.

Emergency Equipment

Most vehicles must have emergency equipment. One exception is lightweight vehicles. Another is vehicles towed as cargo. The required emergency equipment is as follows:

- fire extinguisher
- spare fuses
- warning devices for stopped vehicles

The fire extinguisher must be securely mounted and easy to get to. You must ensure that it's always filled and ready to use.

You must have at least one spare fuse. You don't need spare fuses if all your overload protective devices are circuit breakers that can be reset.

You must have warning devices to set out when you make emergency stops. Vehicles equipped with warning devices after 1974 must have three red reflective triangles. Older vehicles may have three electric lamps (or three red emergency reflectors) and two red flags instead. Another substitute can be three liquid-burning emergency flares used with three fusees and two red flags. This last choice is not an option for any vehicle hauling explosives or flammable liquids or gas. You also may not use these flares with a cargo tank, empty or full, that hauls compressed gas or uses it for fuel.

Cargo Securement

This section applies to trucks and trailers. While you're not likely to be hauling the type of cargo described in this section, you should be familiar with the rules. This is because a CDL does allow a driver to transport cargo in a truck. The information is part of the general knowledge all CMV drivers must have.

Trucks and trailers must be equipped to keep cargo from shifting or falling. FMCSR Part 393 lists four ways to do this. Vehicles must use one of these options to contain cargo.

Option A states the vehicle must have sides, sideboards or stakes, and a rear endgate, endboard, or stakes. These do not have to be solid pieces. But they must not have spaces large enough that cargo could slip out. They must be installed so they won't fall down or fall off the vehicle.

Option B states the vehicle must have tiedowns for at least every 10 feet of cargo. Sometimes, extra tiedowns are needed to contain the entire load. Only two tiedowns are needed on pole trailers, one at each end.

Option C describes the securement of metal cargo.

Option D allows other securement devices, as long as they do as good a job as Option A, B, or C.

FMCSR Part 393 describes how to secure coils of metal on a flatbed. It also covers how to tie down other metal cargo. We'll go into this in greater detail in a later chapter on cargo securement.

This part of the FMCSR also covers hauling intermodal cargo containers (fishyback, piggyback, and the like). These containers must be fastened securely to the trailer. They must not move or shift too much in response to the motion of the trailer. Containers may not move more than one-half inch forward, backwards, or sideways. They may not rise up off the trailer more than one inch. Containers must be tied down to the trailer just like any other freight unless they have their own tiedowns or locks that attach to a special frame.

FMCSR Part 393 states specifications for chains, straps, cables, binders, webbing, hardware, and other securement devices. CMV drivers must not use any securement device that doesn't meet these specifications.

The regulations state a trailer must have a "front-end structure." Most trailers have a headerboard. This keeps the cargo in place. Without such a structure, the cargo could shift and crush the tractor cab in a short stop.

When the vehicle doesn't have a headerboard, the cargo must be blocked or braced. FMCSR Part 393 describes how.

Most cargo-carrying vehicles must have a headerboard, though. Vehicles that are used only to tow other vehicles don't have to have one. If the tractor has a cab guard, the trailer doesn't have to have a headerboard.

Body Components

This is the last section in FMCSR Part 393. It lists standards and specifications for body parts such as the frame, cab, wheels, steering, and suspension. We'll cover these details in the chapters on vehicle control systems and inspections.

The next part in the FMCSR deals with reporting accidents. This is not required knowledge for your CDL license. Most of the responsibility in this area falls on the motor carrier. But as the driver, you're the one at the scene. Your employer needs your help in making the required reports. You'll probably have a routine to follow if you're involved in an accident.

If you are a motor carrier as well as a driver, you should read FMCSR Part 394 thoroughly.

That brings us to the next Part.

FMCSR PART 395

FMCSR Part 395 covers the Hours of Service of Drivers. It requires drivers to keep a Record of Duty Status. The subjects covered by this part include the following:

- maximum driving and on-duty time

- travel time
- driver's record of duty status
- adverse driving conditions
- emergency conditions
- relief from regulations
- drivers declared "out of service"

Driving is different from almost every other profession. It's not a 9-to-5 job. Instead, you work the number of hours your schedule requires, within the limits set in FMCSR Part 395. These limits are called the "hours of service regulations." The regulations state that you can work just so many hours at a time. Your legal day is the number of hours the regulations permit you to work before you must stop to rest. The number of hours you can work and the kind of work you can do on any day depends on the hours you worked the day before and up to eight days in the past.

You record the hours you worked and the kind of work you did in a log book. This log is called your "record of duty status." It helps you stay within the hours of service limits.

The first section in FMCSR Part 395 defines terms used throughout the rest of the part. They are as follows.

On-duty time. From the moment you begin your work day until the time you are relieved of your duties, you are on duty. If you are required to be ready for work, then you are on duty. Even if you are just at the terminal loading passengers, you are on duty. All of the time you spend working but not driving is called on-duty (not driving) or (ON) time. Here are some examples of on-duty not driving time:

- waiting to be dispatched
- inspecting or servicing your vehicle
- filling out reports for your employer
- loading and unloading passengers, including supervising and taking care of paper work
- accident reporting duties
- repairing, getting help for, or waiting with a disabled vehicle
- providing a service for the employer
- any other work that you are paid for by the bus line or another job

You are on duty (driving) or (D) when you are at the vehicle's controls. This is also referred to as "driving time" or simply "driving." When you are simply driving your bus from the garage to the terminal, your employer may instruct you to log this as on duty (not driving), even though you are driving.

Seven consecutive days. This is seven days, one right after the other. It can be any seven days in succession. (A "day" is any 24-hour period. A "24-hour period" is also defined in this section.)

Eight consecutive days. This is eight days, one right after the other.

Twenty-four hour period. This is a period of 24 hours, one right after the other. You start counting based on what time it was at the terminal from which you are normally dispatched. That is, you don't add or subtract hours as you cross time zones.

Sleeper berth. When this term is used, it means that area of a truck meeting the specifications in FMCSR Part 393. You'll see later that time spent in the sleeper is logged separately from ON or D (driving). You'll also see that CMV drivers can't log time as spent in the sleeper if they're napping on the seat. They must be "officially in" the "official sleeper."

Driver-salesman. Some drivers who work for private carriers are called "driver-salesmen." They sell products as well as transport them. Driver-salesmen drive within 100 miles of the terminal where they report for work. They do not spend more than 50 percent of their ON time driving.

Multiple stops. All stops made in any one village, town, or city may be counted as one stop.

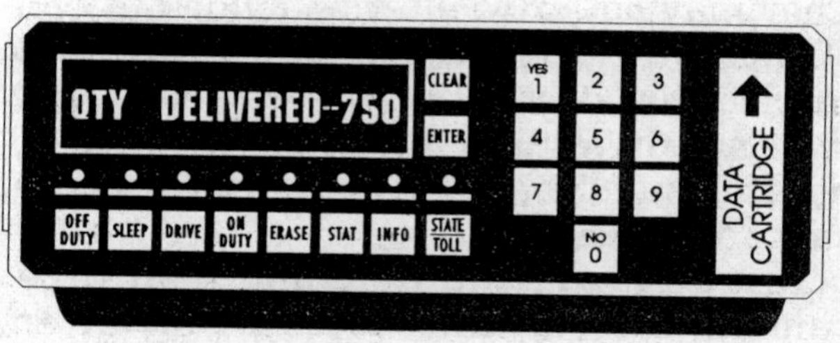

Figure 6-18 Trip recorder or on-board computer.

Automatic on-board recording device. Some vehicles have a device that completes your log for the driver. You may hear this called a "trip recorder." It must record at least engine use, road speed, miles driven, the date, and time of day.

Maximum Driving and On-duty Time

FMCSR Part 395 sets the limits for how long you may drive. These are often referred to as the "10-hour Rule" and the "15-hour Rule." After eight straight hours of off-duty time you may drive for no more than 10 hours. That's the 10-hour Rule. After eight straight hours of off-duty time you may be on duty for no more than 15 hours. Then you may not drive again until you have had some off-duty time. That's the 15-hour Rule.

As you might expect, there are exceptions.

You may get your eight hours off-duty in two separate sleeper berth periods. Each period must be at least two hours long.

The two periods must add up to eight hours. Drivers at natural gas or oil wells may rest elsewhere other than the sleeper berth.

If your company does not work every day of the week you must not drive after being on duty for 60 hours in seven straight days. This is often called the 60 hours/7 day rule. If your company does work every day of the week you must not drive after being on duty for 70 hours in a period of eight straight days. You may hear this referred to as the 70 hours/8 day rule. Drivers in Alaska are sometimes exempt from these rules. They may not drive more than 15 hours after being off duty for eight hours. They may not drive after being on duty for 20 hours or more after an eight-hour off-duty period. They may not drive after being on duty for 70 hours in seven consecutive days for a carrier that doesn't work every day. They may not drive after being on duty for 80 hours in eight consecutive days for a carrier that does work every day.

Driver-salesmen are exempt from these rules if driving time doesn't go over 40 hours in seven consecutive days.

Drivers who work only to make deliveries from retail stores to consumers are exempt from December 10 through December 25. They are limited to driving within 100 miles of where they normally report for work.

For some drivers of oil-well servicing vehicles, on-duty (ON) time does not always include waiting time. They must carefully account for all their waiting time.

Travel Time

Sometimes you may have to travel for your employer. You are not driving or doing any other kind of work. Perhaps you're just deadheading to another terminal (riding the bus as a passenger). This is still counted as on-duty time unless you take eight straight hours off when you reach the destination. If you do take the off-duty time, then you'll be considered off duty for the entire time. That's the travel time plus the eight straight hours off.

Log Books

You must keep a "record of duty status." Most people in the industry call this a "log book" or "log." A log book shows how you spent your time for each 24-hour period. You can use a handwritten log. If you do, you must make two copies. You must record the information on a form that meets the requirement of FMCSR Part 395. This is referred to as a "grid." There are examples of different types of grids in the FMCSR. You also may use Forms MCS-59, MCS-139, and 193A. These are older forms that still meet the requirements of FMCSR Part 395.

You also may record your hours with a trip recorder. If trip recorders are used on the vehicles you are to drive, your carrier will make sure you know how to use them. You should still know how to do a log by hand. Trip recorders can break down. You will have to do your log by hand until the trip recorder is repaired.

You will log four different types of duty status. They are:

- off duty or OFF
- sleeper berth or SB (but only if the sleeper berth is used)
- driving or D
- on duty (not driving) or ON

Note that sleeper berth time doesn't have to be shown on the grid if the vehicles used don't have sleepers.

Every time you change from one duty status to the other, you log it. You log where you were when this change occurred. You can show this with the highway number, the nearest milepost, the name of the nearest town, city or village, and the state abbreviation.

If you are at a terminal or service station, you can put the name of the business in place of the milepost. If you are at an intersection of two highways, put the number of the two roads instead of the milepost.

The log calls for other information besides change of duty status and location. You must also record the following:

- the date
- the total miles you drove the day you fill out the log
- the vehicle number
- the name of your employer
- the driver's signature or certification
- the starting time of this 24-hour period
- the motor carrier employer's main office address
- remarks (the information about where your change of duty status took place)
- the co-driver's name, if there's a co-driver
- total hours
- shipping document numbers, or the name of the shipper and the freight

If your work isn't properly logged, both you and your employer may be prosecuted. Your log must meet the following requirements.

Entries to be current. At all times, your log must be current to your last change of duty status.

Entries made by driver only. The log reflects the driver's duty status. If you are the driver, your handwritten log must be in your handwriting. It must be readable.

Date. Put the month, day, and year for the start of each 24-hour period.

Total mileage driven. "Total mileage driven" is NOT the total of the miles the vehicle moved. Don't include miles driven by a co-driver if there is one. (A co-driver's mileage goes on the log the co-driver completes.) Record the total miles driven by the driver.

Vehicle identification. Look for bus or tractor numbers on the front of the cab or on the door. You can find trailer numbers on the front panel or the rear doors. If you cannot find the vehicle identification numbers, use the license plate number.

Name of carrier. This is the name of the employer for whom you are making this trip. It may be different from the motor carrier for whom you usually work. You may work for more than one carrier in a 24-hour period. In that case, show both names. Follow each name with the start and finish time worked for that carrier. Don't forget to include A.M. and P.M. with these start and finish times.

Signature/certification. When you, as the driver, sign the log, you are saying everything is true and correct. You must use your legal signature, not your nickname or initials.

Twenty-four hour period. Use the time in effect at your home terminal. Don't try to account for changes in time as you cross time zones. Start the 24-hour period, seven and eight consecutive days with the time your motor carrier specifies for your home terminal.

Main office address. If your motor carrier has more than one terminal, the address of the main office is the one called for here.

Recording days off duty. You may have two or more consecutive 24-hour periods off duty. You may record all of them on one log.

Total hours. Total all the hours spent in each duty status during one 24-hour period. Record the total for each to the right of the grid. They should add up to 24. If they don't, you've made an error somewhere. Either you added wrong or you forgot to record something.

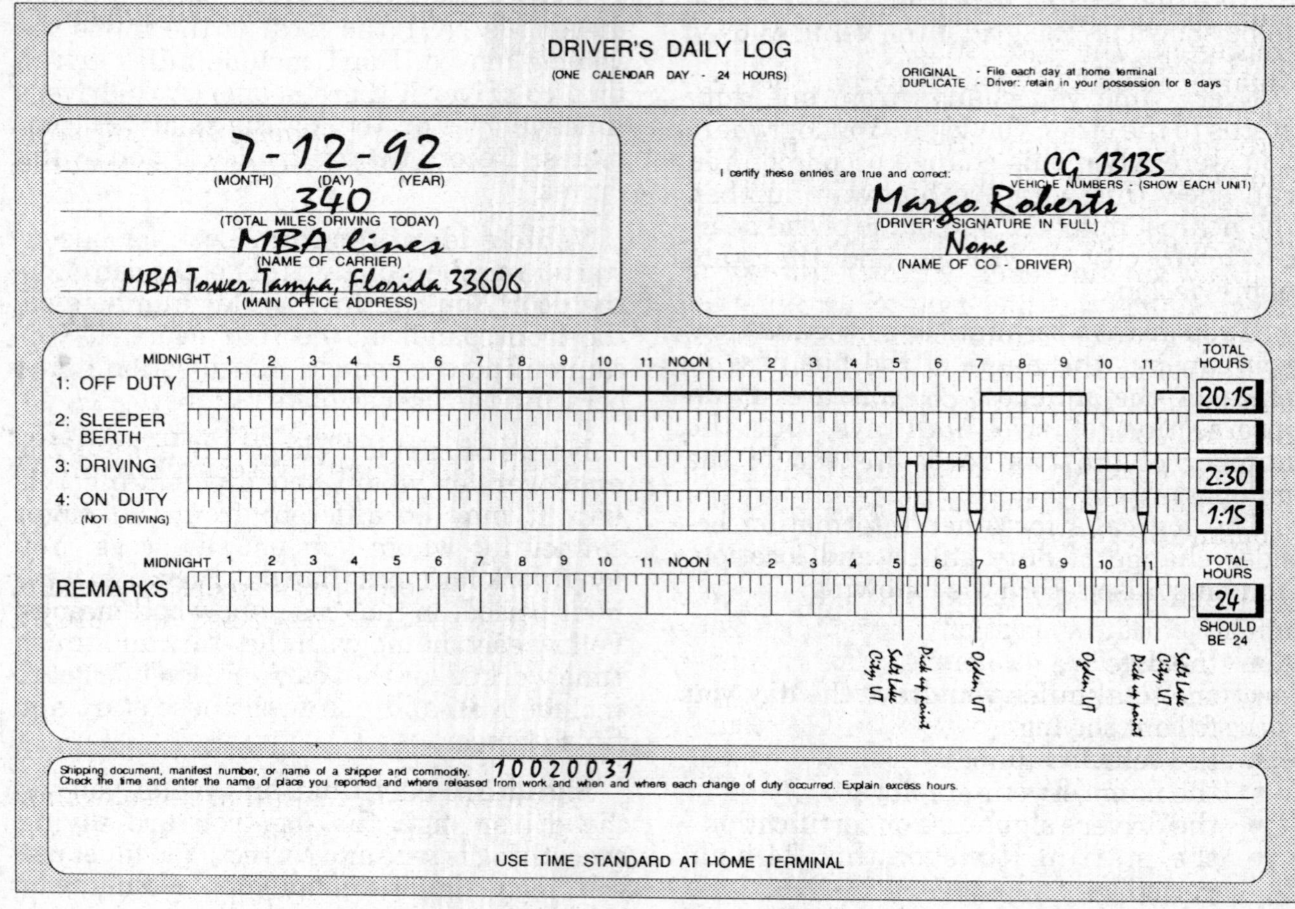

DRIVER'S DAILY LOG

(ONE CALENDAR DAY - 24 HOURS)

ORIGINAL - File each day at home terminal
DUPLICATE - Driver: retain in your possession for 8 days

7-12-92
(MONTH) (DAY) (YEAR)

340
(TOTAL MILES DRIVING TODAY)

MBA lines
(NAME OF CARRIER)

MBA Tower Tampa, Florida 33606
(MAIN OFFICE ADDRESS)

I certify these entries are true and correct:

CG 13135
VEHICLE NUMBERS - (SHOW EACH UNIT)

Margo Roberts
(DRIVER'S SIGNATURE IN FULL)

None
(NAME OF CO - DRIVER)

MIDNIGHT 1 2 3 4 5 6 7 8 9 10 11 NOON 1 2 3 4 5 6 7 8 9 10 11

	TOTAL HOURS
1: OFF DUTY	20.15
2: SLEEPER BERTH	
3: DRIVING	2:30
4: ON DUTY (NOT DRIVING)	1:15

MIDNIGHT 1 2 3 4 5 6 7 8 9 10 11 NOON 1 2 3 4 5 6 7 8 9 10 11

REMARKS

TOTAL HOURS 24 SHOULD BE 24

Salt Lake City, UT
Pick up point
Ogden, UT
Ogden, UT
Pick up point
Salt Lake City, UT

Shipping document, manifest number, or name of a shipper and commodity. 10020031
Check the time and enter the name of place you reported and where released from work and when and where each change of duty occurred. Explain excess hours.

USE TIME STANDARD AT HOME TERMINAL

Figure 6-19 A filled out log grid.

Shipping document numbers. If you are carrying freight as well as passengers and do not have a shipping document number to put here, use the name of the shipper and what's being shipped.

Grid Preparation

You must fill out the grid as described in FMCSR Part 395. You can use the form horizontally or vertically. The following description assumes you're using the form horizontally.

The four rows in the grid are for the length of time spent in each duty status. The columns mark off time segments. Each block in each row is one hour. Each long line in the middle of each block is the half hour (30 minutes). The short lines are quarter hours (15 minutes). The first one is one-fourth (15 minutes after the hour) and the second is three-fourths (45 minutes after the hour). In other words, each hour is broken into fourths. Each line within each box is one quarter of an hour. You record your duty status to the nearest quarter of an hour.

To record the length of time spent in each duty status, start at the vertical line that represents the start time, to the nearest quarter hour. Put your pencil on that vertical line in the row for the duty status you are about to begin. Draw an unbroken horizontal line. The line stops at the quarter hour marker that stands for the time when you next switch duty status.

Draw an unbroken vertical line up or down along the line that represents the time you switch status. Stop when you get to the row for the next duty status. Then start a new unbroken horizontal line in the new duty status.

This is easier to do than to describe. Figure 6-19 should clear up any confusion you have at this point.

Whenever you change duty status, you must record the location where the change took place. This is done in the Remarks section. You recall there are three ways to describe the locations where the duty status change took place.

Filing the Log

You will have to fill out an original and one copy of each log. You must send the original log to your carrier within 13 days after you complete the form. If you drive for more than one carrier, you must send each carrier a complete copy of your log.

You must keep the copies of your logs for the past seven straight days with you.

Exemptions

Most drivers have to keep logs just as we've described. Some drivers are exempt. To be exempt, they must meet all the following conditions:

- they work within a 100 air-mile radius of where they normally report for work
- they return to where they normally report for work within 12 consecutive hours
- they have eight consecutive hours off duty between each 12-hour on-duty shift
- they don't exceed 10 hours driving time after eight consecutive hours off duty
- their motor carrier keeps a record of their time as described in FMCSR Part 395

Some drivers in Hawaii are also exempt from logging requirements.

Emergencies

You may exceed the maximum driving time allowed under certain conditions. You may drive for two extra hours if you find yourself driving under adverse conditions that prevent you from completing your trip within the allowed 10 hours. Adverse driving conditions include:

- snow
- sleet
- fog
- highways covered with snow or ice

Also included are unusual road or traffic conditions if the dispatcher didn't know about them when you began your trip. If you work in Alaska and you encounter adverse driving conditions, you may continue to drive until you complete the trip. But you must take eight straight hours off at the end of the trip.

If an emergency comes up that causes a delay in your trip, you may complete your trip. This is only if the trip could have been finished within the usual time limit had there not been an emergency.

The hours of service rules are also set aside when a driver provides transportation to help in a natural disaster, like an earthquake or flood.

Penalties

If you don't keep track of your time properly or don't obey the rules about how much time you spend working, you can be declared "out of service." Any agent of the Federal Highway Administration (FHWA) may inspect your log book and declare you out of service. These agents include highway patrol officers, DOT inspectors, and weigh masters.

You may be put out of service for disobeying the hours of service regulations. This would be the case if you work more hours than FMCSR Part 395 allows. When that happens, you must go off duty immediately. You may not go back on duty until you have had all the off-duty time you are supposed to have.

You can be put out of service for not having a current record of duty status. If your log is current for the past six days, but not for the present day, you are given a chance to bring it up to date. Otherwise, you are put out of service. Then you must spend the next eight hours off duty. Your motor carrier employer cannot require or permit you to drive during this eight-hour period. You must get a copy of the out of service form to your carrier within 24 hours.

Trip Recorders

As you have seen, you may use a trip recorder to do your log. The trip recorder will show how much time you spent in each duty status. It will show your start time for that 24-hour period. Trip recorders must be able to produce a printed log (printout) for officials who want to check your hours. The driver must sign any such printouts. Trip recorders must store information for the past seven consecutive days. They must record the same information as the handwritten log. This includes not only the four duty status types. It also includes the date, total mileage today, vehicle numbers, carrier name, main office address, and so on.

If handwritten entries are needed, they must be made by the driver in the driver's own handwriting.

Should your trip recorder fail, you must make note of it. As the driver, you will have to recreate any lost or missing records for the past seven days. You will have to continue to do your log by hand until the trip recorder is repaired.

On your vehicle, you must have instructions telling you how to store information in the trip recorder. You must have instructions on how to get information out of the recorder. You must have enough blank log grids for the current trip.

As the driver, you must still get each day's log to the carrier within 13 days. With a trip recorder, there may be a way to do this electronically. Before you send your log to your carrier, you must check that all the entries the recorder has made are correct. In sending the log to the carrier you certify that it is a true and correct record of your duty status.

Even though your vehicle has a trip recorder, the FHWA may require you or your motor carrier to return to handwritten logs. One reason for this is if the carrier's drivers set a pattern of exceeding the hours of service limits. It can also be required if the motor carrier or any of the drivers tamper with the trip recorders.

That completes the overview of FMCSR Part 395. Part 396 is next.

FMCSR PART 396

FMCSR Part 396 deals with the inspection, repair, and maintenance of motor vehicles. If you look at your copy of the FMCSR, you'll see this part is quite brief. That's because this FMCSR part doesn't give you the details of what or how to inspect. It mostly states when to inspect your vehicle. It describes the forms you should fill out. It also covers:

- lubrication
- unsafe operations
- inspection of motor vehicles in operation

So how do you know what to look for in an inspection? Well, as you learned earlier, certain vehicle parts must meet certain specifications. These are described in other parts of the FMCSR. You reviewed many of them quickly when you went through Part 393. Other parts of the FMCSR name the important vehicle components. Part 396 tells you to inspect those components.

We won't go into inspections in detail in this chapter either. We'll cover that in Chapter 10. There you'll learn how to do a proper inspection.

For now, we'll just review what FMCSR Part 396 has to say about inspections.

Responsibility

FMCSR Part 396 states that vehicle inspection is the carrier's responsibility. Regulations call for carriers to have a regular system for inspecting all their vehicles. The parts to be inspected are as follows:

- parts and accessories mentioned in FMCSR Part 393
- frame and frame assemblies
- suspension system
- axles and attachments
- wheels and rims
- steering system
- pushout windows, emergency doors, and emergency door-marking lights on buses

Carriers must also keep a maintenance record on each of their vehicles. This account must include:

- vehicle identification
- type and date of inspection and maintenance
- lubrication record
- tests made of pushout windows, emergency doors, and emergency door marking lights on buses

If you have been driving for any time at all, you know that the driver, not the carrier, ends up doing the actual inspection and filling out the reports. FMCSR Part 396 states the carrier must inspect the vehicle or **cause it to be inspected.** That's how you as the driver end up with the job. So although these regulations are aimed at the carrier, we'll discuss them as if they were your responsibility. In effect, they are.

Lubrication

Motor vehicles must be lubricated. They must be free of oil and grease leaks.

No Unsafe Operations

The law prohibits you from abusing your vehicle. You may not drive it in a way that would cause it to break down or cause an accident.

In spite of your best efforts, your vehicle may develop a problem on the road. You must stop immediately if it won't cause a public hazard to do so. If stopping right where you are will create a hazard, you may continue to drive. But you may drive the vehicle only so long as it takes to get it to the nearest place where it can be repaired.

Official Highway Inspections

FMCSR Part 396 permits special agents of the Federal Highway Administration (FHWA) to stop and inspect your vehicle while you're out on the highway. This agent could be a representative of the Bureau of Motor Carrier Safety (BMCS). It could be any official, such as a highway patrol officer or weigh master, charged with enforcing transportation laws.

This agent will record the results of this inspection on a Driver-Equipment Compliance Check form.

If your vehicle doesn't pass inspection, it can be declared "out of service" by the special agent. Then you cannot drive the vehicle until it's been repaired and reinspected. If the vehicle cannot be repaired right where it is, it will have to be towed to a repair shop by a tow truck or wrecker.

If your vehicle does not pass the inspection, you must deliver the report to your carrier when you next arrive at the terminal. If you won't reach a terminal within 24 hours, you must mail the report. Once the motor carrier has received the inspection report, the carrier has 15 days to take care of the problems stated on the report.

Driver Vehicle Inspection Reports

As a driver, you will inspect your vehicle before and after your trip. FMCSR Part 396 states you should inspect your vehicle at the end of your trip and report any repairs that should be made. You probably call this a post-trip inspection.

Your report will show you inspected the following items:

- service brakes, including trailer brake connections
- parking brake
- steering
- lights and reflectors
- tires
- horn
- windshield wipers
- rear-view mirrors
- coupling devices
- wheels and rims
- emergency equipment

You'll mark the form to report anything you think would keep you from operating the vehicle safely. If nothing is wrong, you will state so on the form. In either case, you as the driver will sign the form. In the case of team operations, only one driver need sign the report. If you operate more than one vehicle in one day, you must fill out a report on each vehicle.

Any defects you noted must be repaired. The person who made the repairs signs the report. Then a copy of the report goes with the vehicle.

Before the vehicle goes out again, the driver performs another pre-trip inspection. In your pre-trip inspection, you verify repairs have in fact been made. If the post-trip inspection turned up some defects and they are certified as repaired, you sign the report. This shows you noticed there were problems after the last trip, but you found they have been repaired.

This last signature isn't needed for defects that were part of a towed unit that is no longer in combination with the towing vehicle.

Driveaway-towaway Operations

Vehicles being towed as cargo don't have to be inspected from top to bottom. But the saddle-mount or tow bar must be inspected.

In a driveaway operation, you are delivering the vehicle by driving it to its destination. Since you are actually driving the vehicle, you must make sure it's in a safe, road-worthy condition as required by law. It requires a complete inspection.

Periodic Inspections

Motor carriers must inspect their vehicles fully once every 12 months. This inspection won't usually be the driver's responsibility. However, if you are a motor carrier as well as a driver, you are charged with inspecting your vehicles every year as described in FMCSR Part 396.

That's it. That's just about all FMCSR Part 396 has to say about vehicle inspections. Of course, actually doing the inspection takes a little longer to describe. That's a subject for another chapter.

FMCSR PART 397

We're almost finished. Part 397 is the last part of the FMCSR that Part 383 requires you to know for your CDL. It covers the transportation of hazardous materials. This includes:

- attendance of motor vehicles
- parking
- routes
- fires
- smoking
- fueling
- tires
- instructions and documents

As you know, you must have placards on your vehicle if you are hauling materials that are hazardous. Some materials are not so hazardous by themselves. They become so when transported in certain amounts.

And, you now also know you need a special endorsement to drive a placarded CMV. If you don't want or need the haz mat endorsement, you may wonder what's left for a bus driver to know about haz mat.

FMCSR Part 383 states there are things you must know about hazardous materials to get your CDL. That is, you must know what hazardous materials are. You must know when you need placards to haul them. You must know what you can haul without an endorsement and when you need an endorsement to haul hazardous materials. The law wants you to be aware that it takes special training to haul haz mat in placarded loads.

A knowledge of FMCSR Part 397 will fill the bill.

What Is Hazardous?

Certain materials are hazardous in any amounts. Others become hazardous when in large enough amounts or when they are present with other materials. Title 49 CFR Parts 170 through 189 define hazardous materials.

You might find the important sections of these parts summarized in the back of your FMCSR. This summary is called a Compendium of Hazardous Materials Regulations. If you don't find it there, visit the public library. Ask the reference librarian to help you find the right section of the CFR.

We'll highlight some of the main points in 49 CFR 170–189, then return to FMCSR Part 397.

Section 171.8 of the Federal Hazardous Materials Regulations (FHMR) defines hazardous materials as those the Secretary of Transportation has judged to pose "a risk to health, safety and property when transported in commerce." This includes hazardous wastes, the dangerous by-products of many chemical processes. Hazardous materials include:

- radioactive materials
- poisonous gases or liquids
- flammable gases
- nonflammable gases
- flammable liquids
- oxidizers (cause other materials to react with oxygen, possibly with dangerous results)
- flammable solids
- corrosive materials (able to dissolve or wear away other materials)
- irritating materials
- combustible liquids
- explosives
- etiologic agents (able to cause disease)

These hazardous materials are grouped into classes. The classes are as follows.

Radioactive Material. A material, or combination of materials, that gives off radiation is radioactive.

Poisonous Gas or Liquid. Class A poisons are very dangerous. They harm or kill when even small amounts are mixed with air. Class B poisons are less dangerous, yet harmful to the skin. They should not be exposed to the body.

Flammable Compressed Gas. Flammable compressed gas is flammable gas under pressure.

Nonflammable Compressed Gas. A nonflammable compressed gas is a gas that is under pressure but will not burn.

Flammable Liquid. A flammable liquid gives off vapors that ignite. Gasoline is a good example of a flammable liquid.

Oxidizer. This is a substance that causes others to react with oxygen. This in turn causes other materials to burn.

Flammable Solid. A flammable solid is not an explosive. However, it can burn as a result of friction or a chemical change that involves heat. It also could start burning by itself due to a chemical change that occurred in processing. When some materials get wet, they can burn or give off flammable or toxic gases.

Corrosive Material. Materials are considered corrosive if they can destroy human skin tissue or eat away steel.

Irritating Material. A liquid or solid that produces dangerous fumes when it comes into contact with air or fire is considered an irritating material.

Combustible Liquid. A liquid that gives off vapors that will ignite between 100 and 200 degrees Fahrenheit is combustible.

Explosives. Explosives can be chemical compounds, mixtures, or devices that explode. Class A explosives are the most dangerous. Class B explosives are less dangerous. They don't explode but burn rapidly instead. Class C explosives pose the least danger. They are materials that contain only small amounts of Class A or B explosive. Blasting agents are explosive. They are the least dangerous because they're not likely to explode by accident.

Etiologic Agent. Materials that are able to cause human diseases are called etiologic agents.

Other Regulated Materials (ORM). Materials that in some way may risk public safety, health, or property while being transported are considered hazardous. These materials fall into five smaller categories.

Being able to recognize a hazardous materials shipment is the first step in handling it correctly and safely. All licensed CMV drivers must be able to recognize a hazardous materials shipment. This is so even if they don't plan to haul it.

As you can see, there are almost too many hazardous materials for you to remember. That's why you must take the time to review your cargo information. One way to do this is by the package labels and markings. Another is by the shipping paper and manifest listings. Also, you must be able to recognize a hazardous shipment on the road. Vehicle placards are your clue that the vehicle is hauling haz mat.

Labels

The packages holding hazardous materials must be labeled. (Only certain Department of Defense packages are exempt from this.) Special labels are used for this. An example of a haz mat label is pictured in Figure 6-20.

Haz mat package labels are diamond shaped and four inches square. The labels show the class of hazardous materials the package belongs to. Any numbers that

Figure 6-20 Hazardous materials label.

might be on the labels are part of a worldwide system used to identify hazardous materials. Each number stands for a different haz mat.

Labels are not used on compressed gas cylinders. They don't stick well to slick metal surfaces. Instead, the label is placed on a hang tag hung around the neck of the cylinder. Or a decal may be used. The cylinders themselves may be stamped as holding compressed gas. Compressed gas cylinders that are permanently mounted on a vehicle don't need labels. ORM packages don't need labels. Neither do packages of combustible liquids or those with low activity radioactive materials.

Shipping Papers

Hazardous materials must be carried with the proper shipping papers. Shipping papers tell all who might need to know that the cargo is dangerous. Also, shippers certify on the shipping paper that the haz mat has been handled and packaged according to DOT regulations.

Shipping Paper Accessibility

Drivers must carry shipping papers so they are easy to get to. They must be marked differently from shipping papers for regular cargo. The haz mat shipping papers can be placed on the top of a stack of cargo documents. They must be within easy reach of a driver wearing a seat belt. They can be kept in the holder mounted on the inside of the driver's door. They must be where they can be seen easily by someone looking into the cab.

Shipping papers are to be left in the cab, even when the driver leaves the tractor. They should be left in the holder or on the driver's seat in plain view. That is important in case of accidents. The driver may be hurt and not be able to speak. But emergency crews will know where to find the shipping papers that tell them what kind of haz mat they're dealing with.

Placards

Placards are required by regulations. A placard is similar to a label. However, a placard is attached to the outside of the vehicle to show clearly that it contains a load of hazardous materials. The placard for a certain material will be of the same color and wording as its label. Look at Figure 6-21.

Figure 6-21 Hazardous materials placard.

When more than one type of haz mat is being hauled, the vehicle must have more than one type of placard. For certain mixed loads, a placard reading "Dangerous" is enough.

Tank vehicles used to haul any hazardous materials must have placards at all times, even when empty.

Now, back to FMCSR Part 397. This part repeats the idea of "higher standard of care." Recall this from reading about FMCSR Part 392? Remember, when there are two or more sets of regulations, you should follow the stricter set. Local haz mat regulations may be stricter than the federal regulations. If so, follow the local regulations.

Attendance and Parking

With few exceptions, a vehicle hauling explosives must never be abandoned. There must always be a qualified person with the vehicle. FMCSR Part 397 refers to this as "attendance." To say you must attend the vehicle means you must stay with it at all times. You may at times see an unattended vehicle placarded for explosives. This vehicle is probably parked in a "safe haven." Safe haven is a term used for a special parking area set aside just for this purpose.

There are rules about where a vehicle with other types of haz mat may park or stop.

Routing

Vehicles hauling hazardous cargo don't always follow the easiest and fastest highways. Convenience does not determine the route. Instead, haz mat routing must avoid roads that go through heavily populated areas. The only exception to this is when there is no other possible way to get to the destination.

For Class A or B explosives, the carrier or driver must supply a written route plan. This written plan must include curfews and permits from those cities that require them. Any such permit must be applied for prior to the trip.

The written plan may list certain hours of the day during which a vehicle hauling haz mat may travel through a city. Some cities have ordinances as to what time of day hazardous materials are allowed to pass through. Other cities require permits that must be applied for in advance. More and more cities and states are passing laws that deal with hazardous materials.

Fire

Vehicles with hazardous cargo must be kept away from flames. This includes flames used to light cigarettes, so smoking is not allowed within 25 feet of a haz mat vehicle. Special care must be taken when fueling a vehicle loaded with hazardous cargo. A tire fire can be especially dangerous when you're hauling haz mat. Therefore, frequent tire inspections are required en route.

This has been a very general review of the haz mat regulations. Remember, even if you don't need or want a haz mat endorsement, you must know something about the subject. You must know what makes up a hazardous shipment so you don't haul it illegally by mistake. You should also know that not all dangerous cargo is hazardous in the legal sense.

Even without a haz mat endorsement, you may haul certain "hazardous materials." Those are, of course, dangerous materials that don't require the vehicle to have hazardous materials placards. There are also a few special times when a haz mat vehicle may be moved without placards. These are:

- when the vehicle is escorted by a state or local government representative
- when the carrier has permission from the Department of Transportation
- when the vehicle must be moved to protect property or people

We have now gone all the way through the FMCSR parts you must know to pass your CDL Tests. This was a long chapter. But it was a very brief survey of these regulations. We'll return to some of these parts in the next few chapters on vehicle control systems, inspection, and driving. That will give you another chance to become well acquainted with them.

You should also spend some time reading through the FMCSR on your own. You must know the laws that govern your job. You may have heard the saying, "Ignorance of the law is no defense." This means you cannot break a law, then claim you are innocent because you didn't know the law. It's your job to know.

PASS POST-TRIP

Instructions: For each true/false test item, read the statement. Decide whether the statement is true or false. If it is true, select the letter "A." If it is false, select the letter "B." For each multiple-choice test item, choose the answer choice – A, B, C, or D – that correctly completes the statement or answers the question. There is only one correct answer.

1. A state considers a driver with an AC of .06 percent to be DUI. A driver found to be driving with an AC of .05 percent would be_____.

A. asked for a urine sample
B. disqualified
C. allowed to continue driving
D. put "out of service"

2. When you apply for a motor vehicle driving job, you must give your employer information on all your driving jobs for at least the last_____.

A. three years
B. year
C. 10 years
D. two years

3. If a drug or medicine you are taking was prescribed for you by your doctor, it is both safe and legal to take it while on duty.

A. True
B. False

4. While on a scheduled trip, your vehicle gets a flat. You would log the time you spend getting it fixed as_____.

A. on duty
B. on duty (not driving)
C. off duty
D. on duty (maintenance)

5. You are put "out of service" for violating the hours of service regulations. You may not drive again_____.

A. for one year
B. for 10 hours
C. until you have enough off duty time to be allowed on duty
D. until your employer gives you permission

6. The main reason for the post-trip inspection is to let the vehicle owner know about vehicle problems that may need repair.
A. True
B. False

7. No driver may drive a vehicle hauling any amount of hazardous material without a hazardous materials endorsement.
A. True
B. False

Instructions: Match the letter for the description in Column B with the number of the part in Column A that fits the description.

Column A Vehicle Parts	Column B Description
8. set of three reflective triangles	A. a part necessary for safe operation
9. clearance light	B. optional equipment
10. television receiver	C. emergency equipment necessary for safe operation

CHAPTER 7

Safety Control Systems

When you have finished this chapter, you will be able to provide the correct answers to questions about:

- CMV safety control systems:
  - lights
  - horns
  - side and rear-view mirrors and their proper adjustment
  - fire extinguishers
  - instruments and gauges
- troubleshooting

To complete this chapter, you will need:

- a dictionary
- pencil or pen
- blank paper or notebook
- colored pencils, pens, markers, or highlighters
- a CDL preparation manual from your state Department of Motor Vehicles, if one is offered
- Federal Motor Carrier Safety Regulations pocketbook (or access to U.S. Department of Transportation regulations, Parts 383 and 393 of Subchapter B, Chapter 3, Title 49, Code of Federal Regulations)
- operator's or owner's manual for your vehicle

PASS PRE-TRIP

Instructions: Read the statements. Decide whether each statement is true or false. If it is true, circle the letter "A." If it is false, circle the letter "B."

1. The proper way to use a fire extinguisher is to douse the flames with the dry chemical.
 A. True
 B. False

2. A vehicle will have warning lights or warning buzzers, but not both.
 A. True
 B. False

3. Vehicles with diesel engines don't have vacuum brakes because diesel engines don't create a vacuum on the intake stroke.
 A. True
 B. False

You just finished a long "tour" of FMCSR Parts 391, 392, 393, 395, 396, and 397. It was quite an effort, but very important. Thorough knowledge of the FMCSR is vital to your success on the CDL tests.

Return now to Part 383. You'll recall this part contains the CDL laws themselves. If your copy of the FMCSR contains Subpart G, Required Knowledge and Skills, turn to it now. You'll see that item (a) states you must have knowledge of the safe operations regulations. Now that you've covered that requirement, let's tackle item (b), CMV safety control systems.

SAFETY CONTROL SYSTEMS

Know what equipment makes up your vehicle's safety control systems. Know where they are and how and when to use them.

Lights

Lights help you to communicate with other drivers. Lights help others see you and help you to see others. You use lights to signal your plans to change lanes, slow down, or stop. Remember that you must have your lights on from one half-hour after sunset until one half-hour before sunrise. Also turn on your lights any time you need more light to see clearly.

As you recall, FMCSR Part 393 describes the types of lights and reflectors CMVs must have. This part also describes the lights and reflectors needed in towaway operations. You studied tables and figures in Chapter 6 that illustrated these required devices. How much do you recall? Stop now and select from figures 7-1A through N the one that fits the vehicle you plan to test in. Use the scanning recall technique to identify the lights and reflectors. Compare your recall with the completed figure that follows. (Figures 7-2A through N).

To review, you need the following:

Headlights. Two white headlights, one at the left and one at the right on the front of the tractor. These are required on buses, trucks, and truck tractors. They must offer a high and low beam setting.

You may have fog lamps and other lights for bad weather or dark roads. These are in addition to, not instead of, headlights. Buses and trucks, semitrailers, full trailers, and pole trailers must have these.

Front side marker lamps. Two amber lights, one on each side at the front of the side of buses and trucks, tractors, semitrailers, and full trailers.

Side marker lamps. Two amber lights, one on each side at or near the center between front and rear side marker lamps of buses and trucks, semitrailers, full trailers, and pole trailers.

Front side reflectors. Two amber reflectors, one on each side towards the front of buses and trucks, tractors, semitrailers, full trailers, and pole trailers.

Side reflectors. Two amber reflectors, one on each side at or near the midpoint between the front and rear side reflectors of buses and trucks, large semitrailers, large full trailers, and pole trailers.

Front turn signals. Two amber signals, one at the left and one at the right side on the front of the tractor, above or below the headlights. These are required on buses, trucks, and truck tractors.

Front identification lamps. Three amber lights, at the center of the vehicle or cab. These are required on large buses and trucks and truck tractors.

Front clearance lamps. Two amber lamps, one on each side of the front of larger buses and trucks, truck tractors, large semitrailers and full trailers, pole trailers, and projecting loads.

Rear side marker lamps. One each at the lower left and lower right rear of the side of buses and trucks, semitrailers and full trailers, and pole trailers. These lights are red.

Rear side reflectors. Found just below the rear side marker lamps. These reflectors are red. These are required on buses and trucks, semitrailers, full trailers, and pole trailers.

Rear identification lamps. Three red lights centered at the top rear of large buses and trucks, large semitrailers and full trailers, and pole trailers. They're not required on smaller trucks and buses.

Rear clearance lamps. Two red lights, one at the top right and one at the top left of the rear of large trucks and buses, tractors, large semitrailers and full trailers, pole trailers and projecting loads. These describe the overall width. They're not required on smaller trucks and buses.

Rear reflectors. Two red reflectors, one at the lower right and one at the lower left of the rear of small and large buses and trucks, semitrailers, full trailers, and pole trailers.

Stop lamps. Two red lights, one at the lower right and one at the lower left of the rear. All vehicles must have these. Stop lamps are not required on projecting loads.

License plate lamp. One white light at the center rear, low, on buses and trucks, tractors, semitrailers and full trailers, and pole trailers.

Backup lamp. One white light at the rear of buses and trucks and truck tractors.

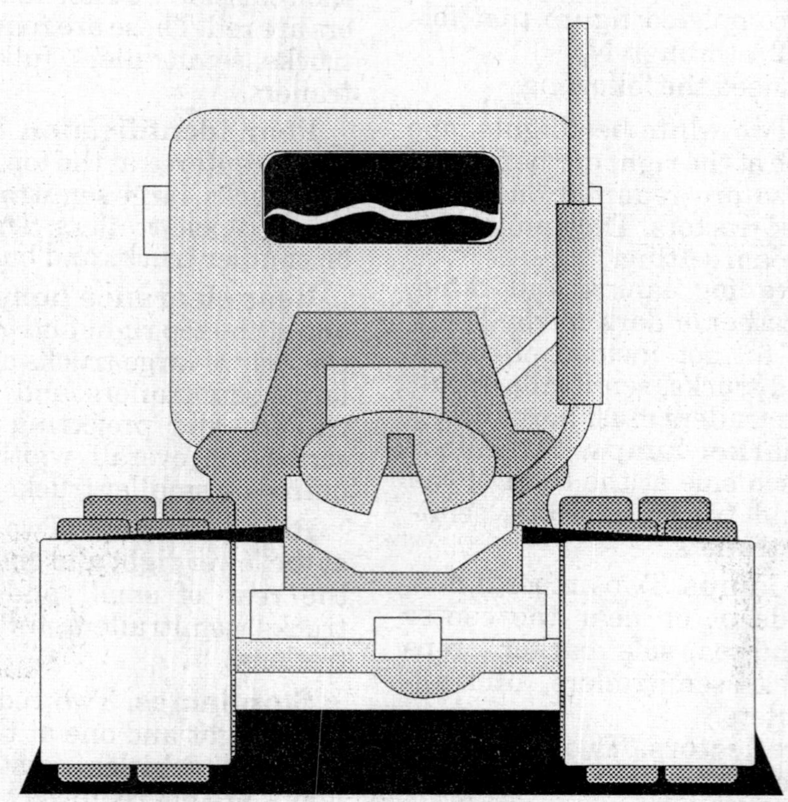

Figure 7-1A Select the figures that look most like your vehicle. Draw in the required lights and reflectors. Label them according to color and number required.

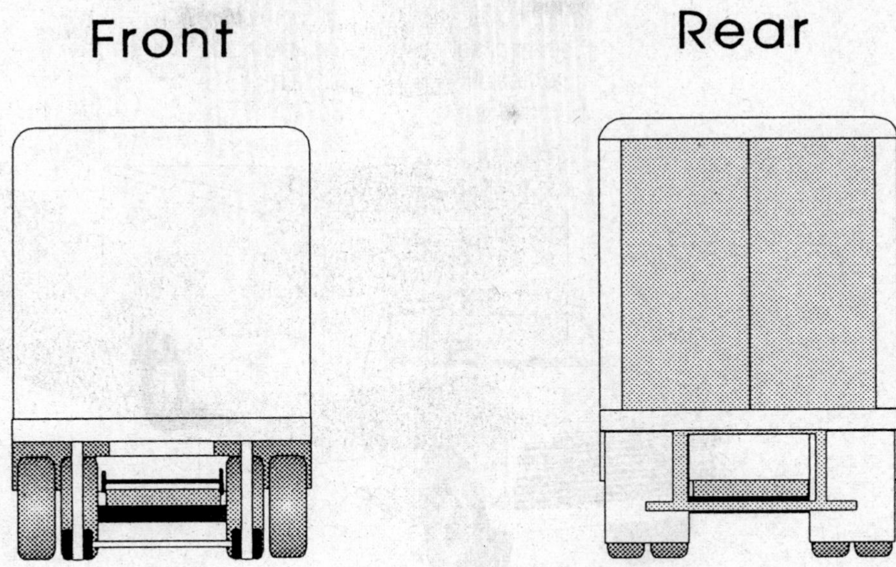

Figure 7-1B Select the figures that look most like your vehicle. Draw in the required lights and reflectors. Label them according to color and number required.

Over 80 Inches

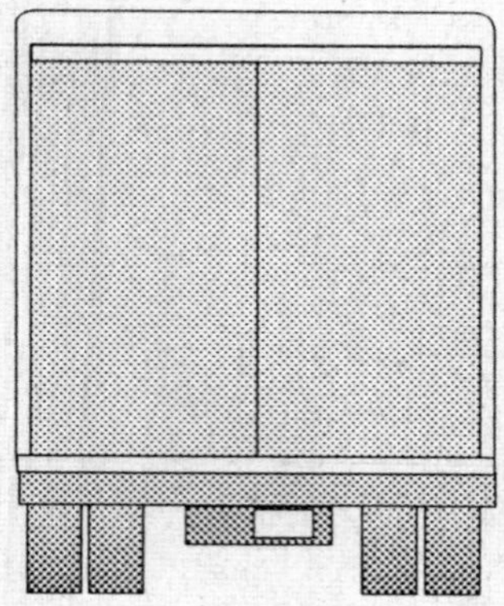

Figure 7-1C Select the figures that look most like your vehicle. Draw in the required lights and reflectors. Label them according to color and number required.

Under 80 Inches

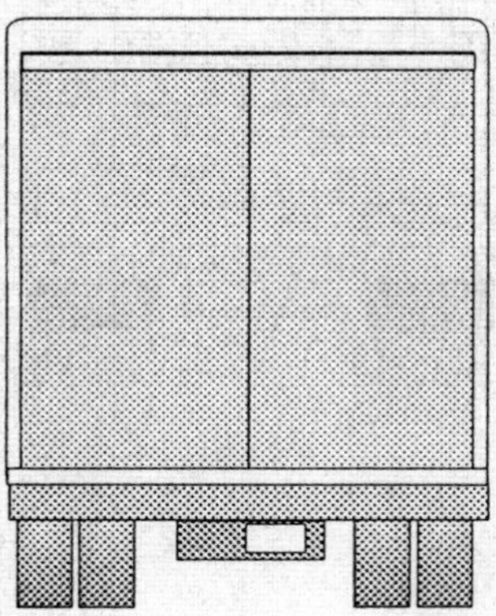

Figure 7-1D Select the figures that look most like your vehicle. Draw in the required lights and reflectors. Label them according to color and number required.

Under 80 Inches

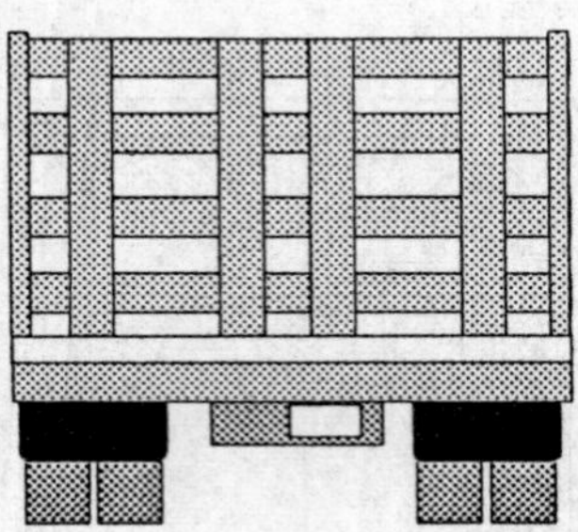

Figure 7-1E Select the figures that look most like your vehicle. Draw in the required lights and reflectors. Label them according to color and number required.

Pole Trailers - All Vehicle Widths

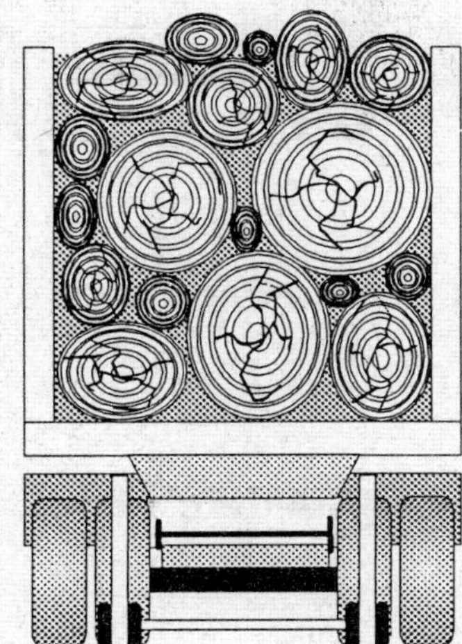

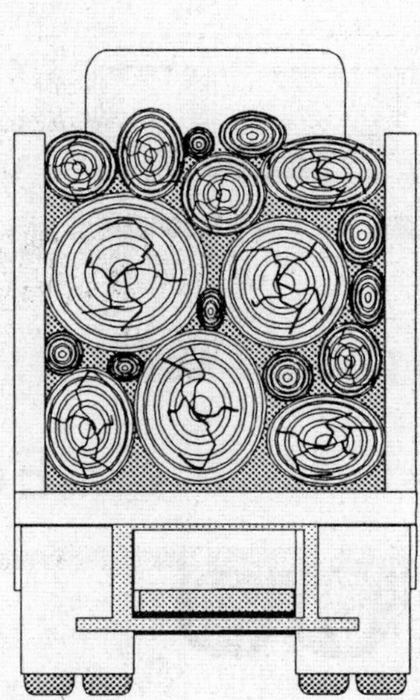

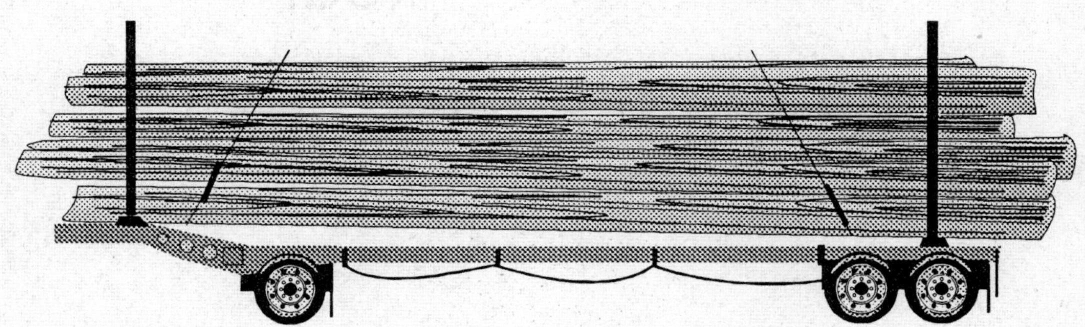

Figure 7-1F Select the figures that look most like your vehicle. Draw in the required lights and reflectors. Label them according to color and number required.

Container Chassis

Rear

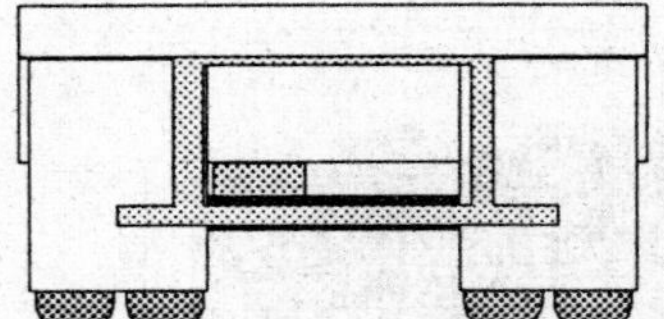

Front

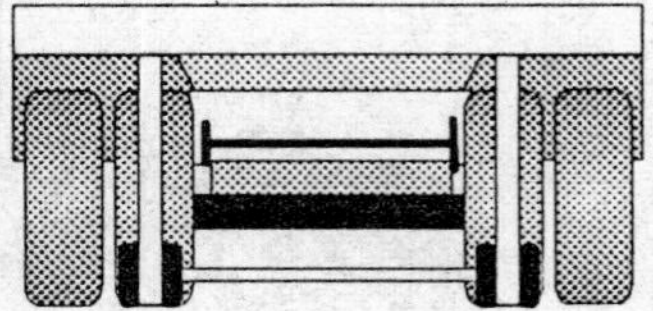

Each Side

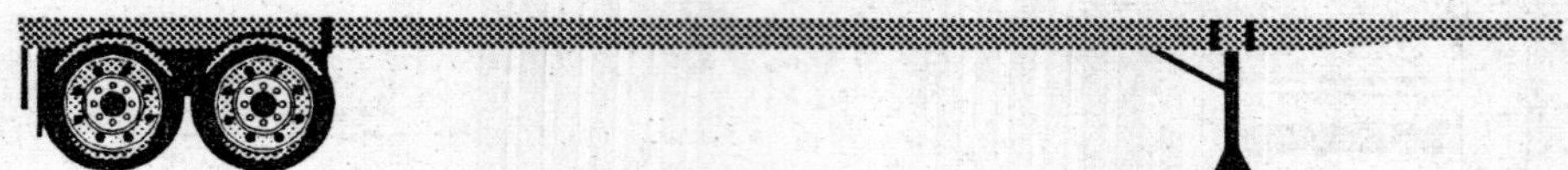

Converter Dolly

Rear

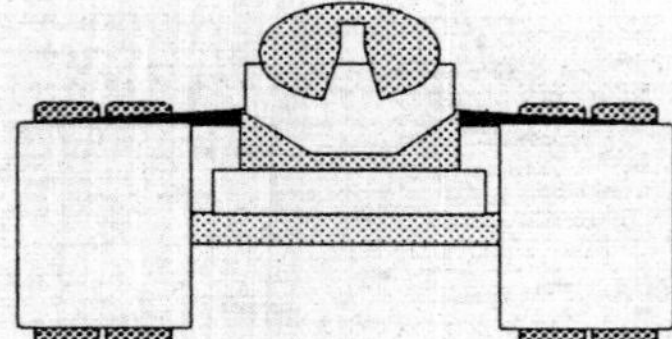

Figure 7-1G Select the figures that look most like your vehicle. Draw in the required lights and reflectors. Label them according to color and number required.

Front Of
Towing Vehicle

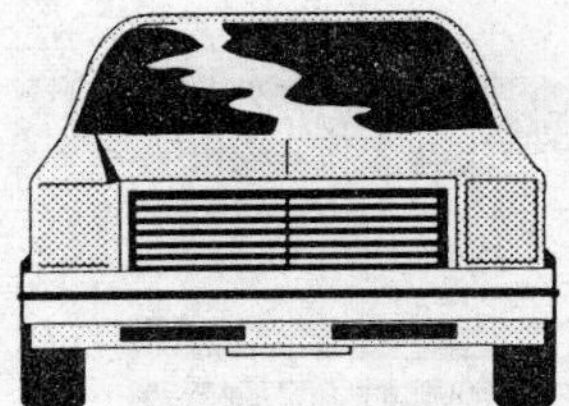

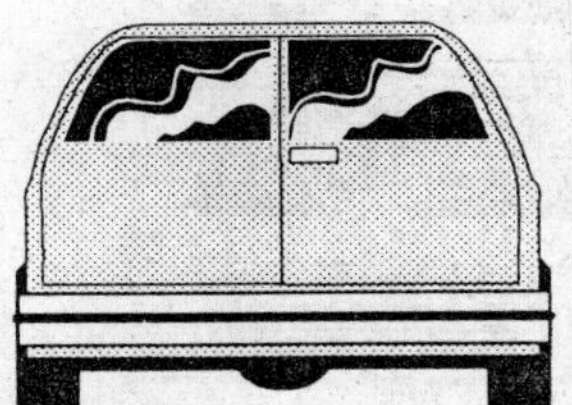

Each Side

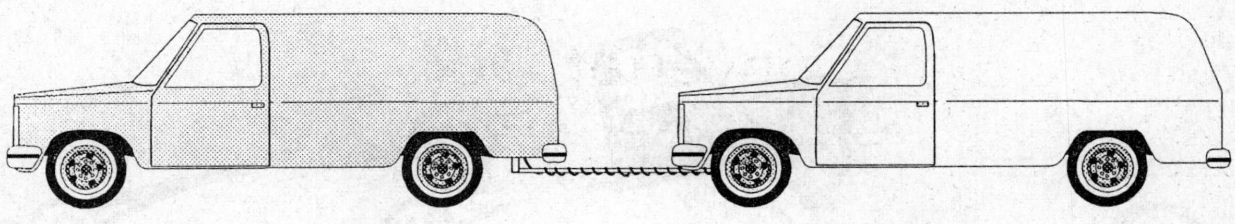

Figure 7-1H Select the figures that look most like your vehicle. Draw in the required lights and reflectors. Label them according to color and number required.

Front Of
Towing Vehicle

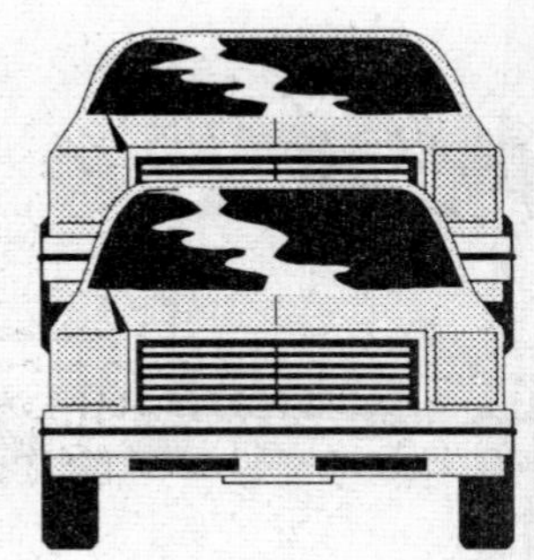

Rear Of Rearmost
Towed Vehicle

Each Side

Figure 7-11 Select the figures that look most like your vehicle. Draw in the required lights and reflectors. Label them according to color and number required.

Front Of
Towing Vehicle

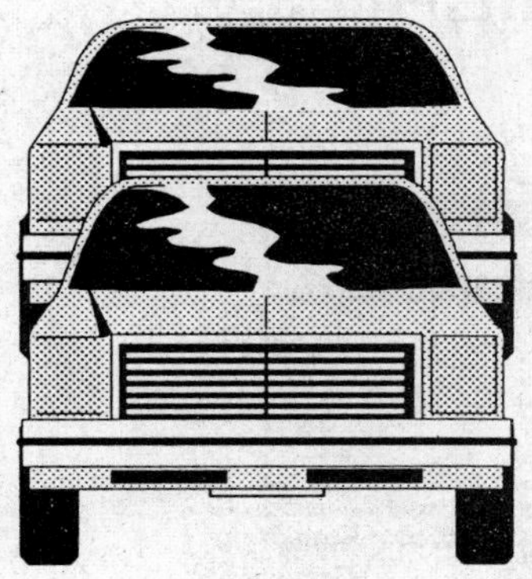

Each Side

Figure 7-1J Select the figures that look most like your vehicle. Draw in the required lights and reflectors. Label them according to color and number required.

REAR

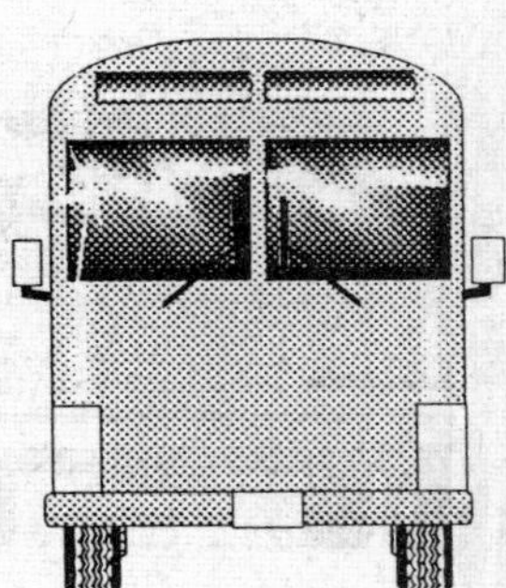

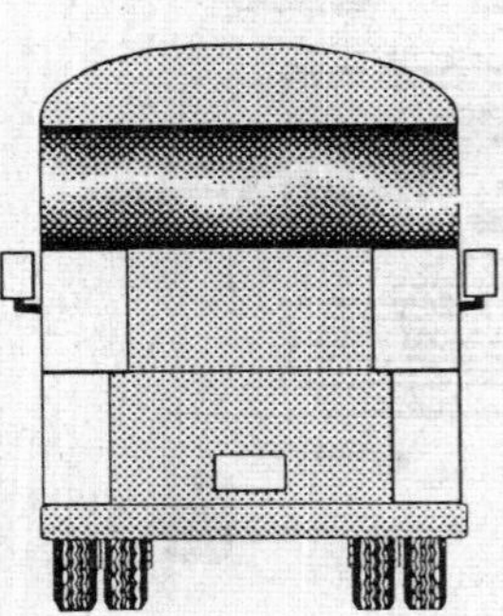

EACH SIDE

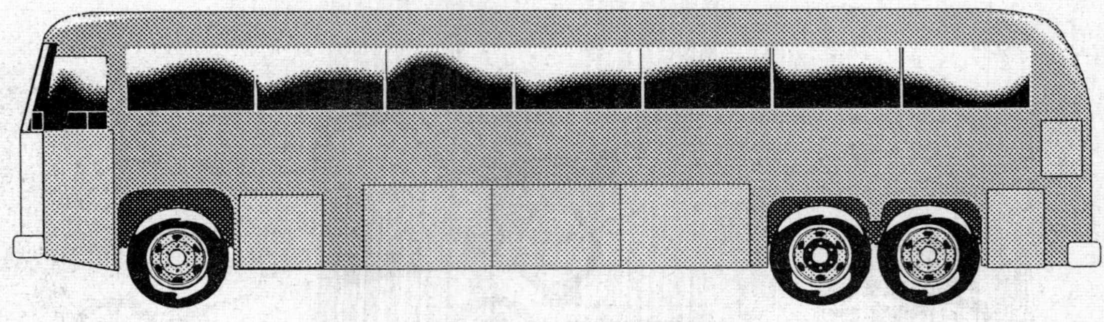

Figure 7-1K Select the figures that look most like your vehicle. Draw in the required lights and reflectors. Label them according to color and number required.

Figure 7-1L Select the figures that look most like your vehicle. Draw in the required lights and reflectors. Label them according to color and number required.

Front

Figure 7-1M Select the figures that look most like your vehicle. Draw in the required lights and reflectors. Label them according to color and number required.

Vehicle Without Permanent Top Or Sides

Rear

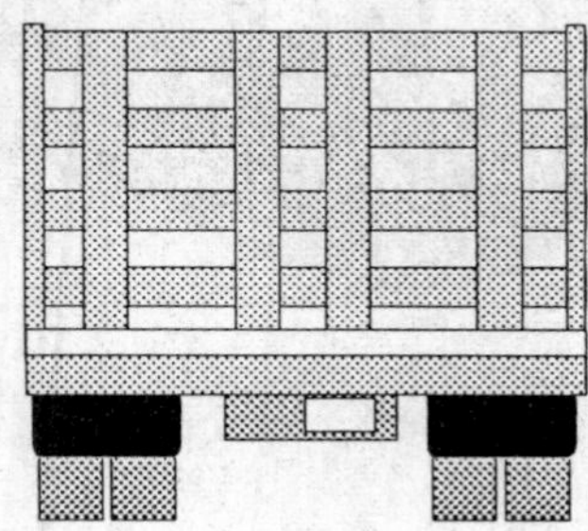

Figure 7-1N Select the figures that look most like your vehicle. Draw in the required lights and reflectors. Label them according to color and number required.

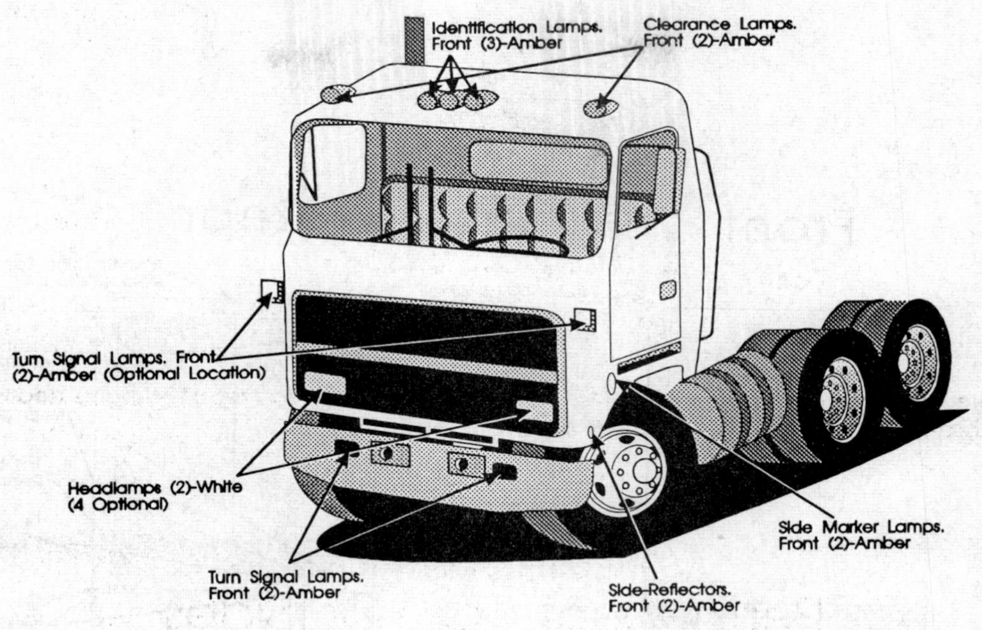

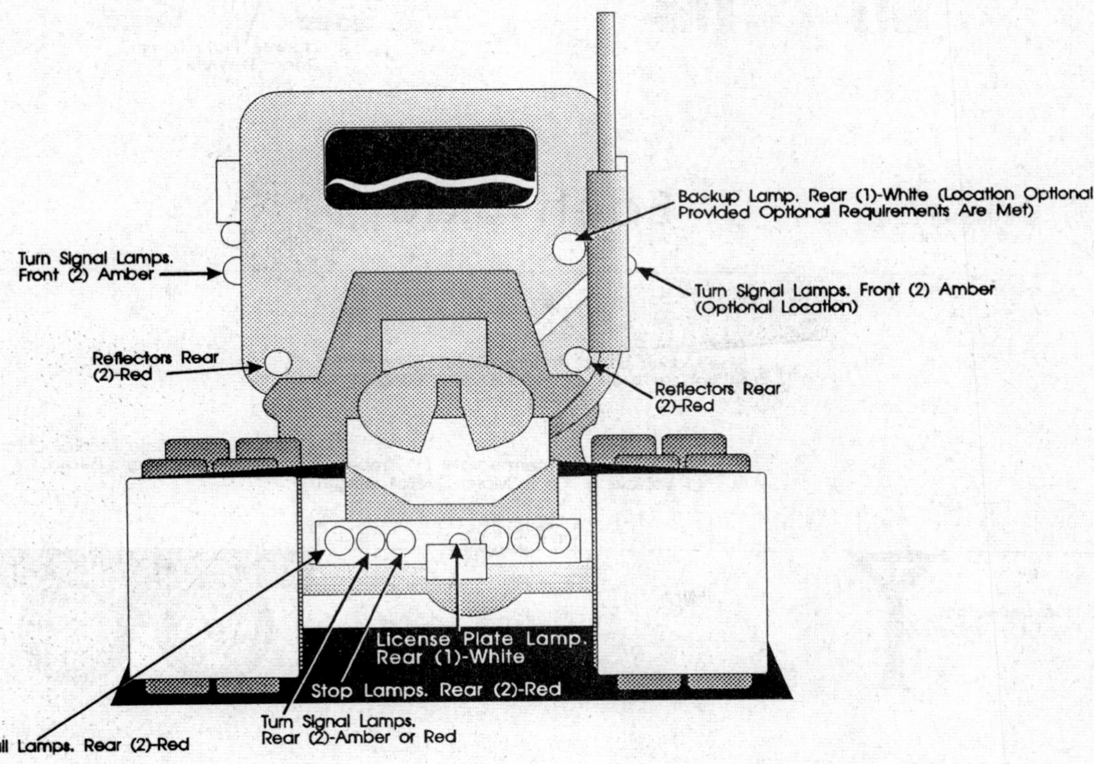

Figure 7-2A Use these figures to check your recall of the required lights and reflectors.

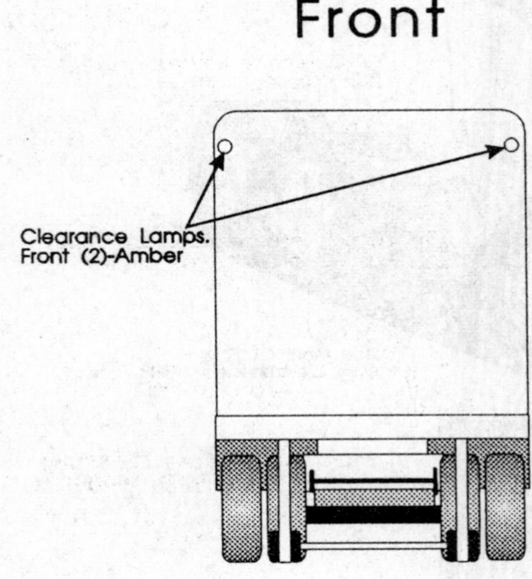

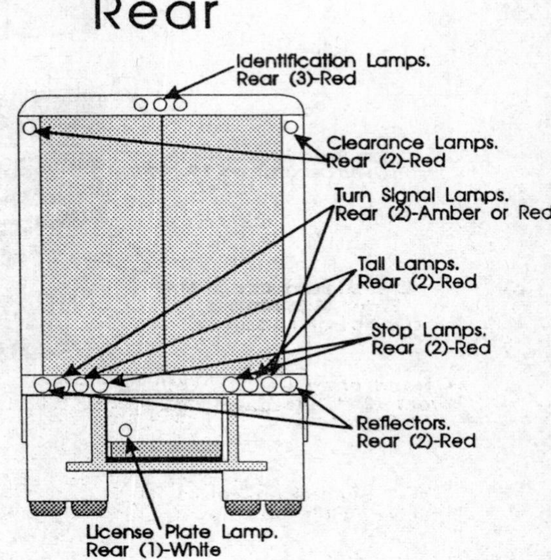

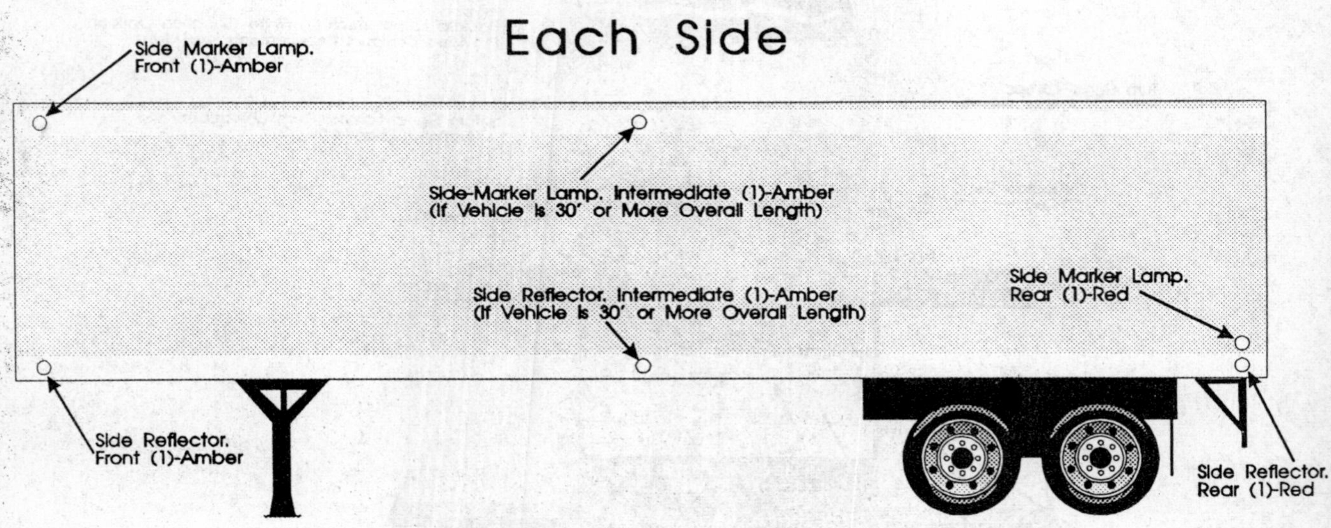

Figure 7-2B Use these figures to check your recall of the required lights and reflectors.

Over 80 Inches

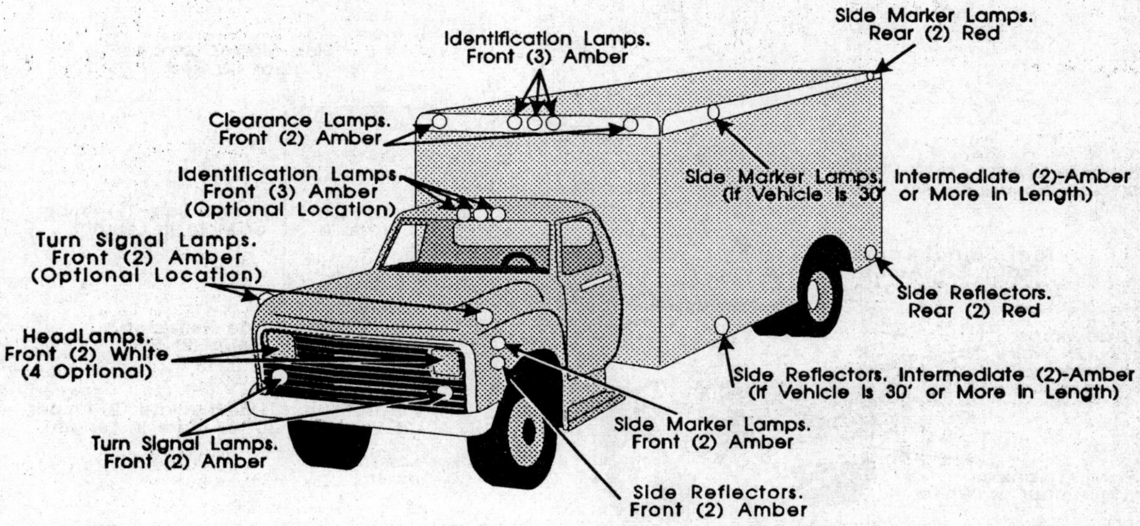

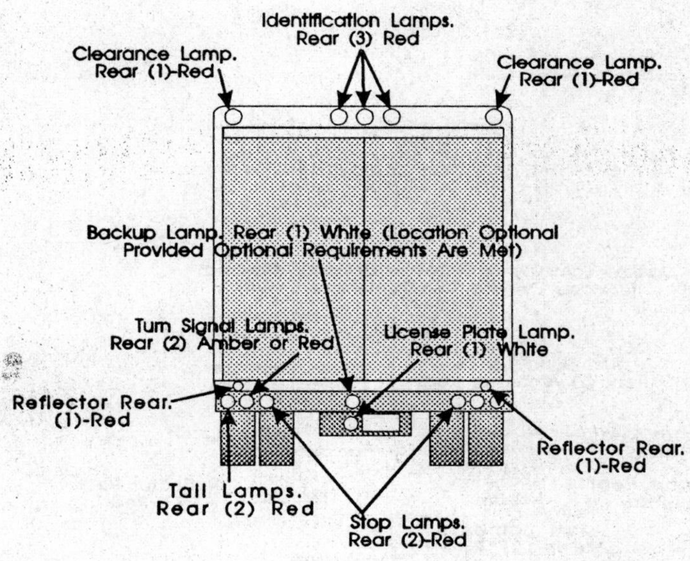

Figure 7-2C Use these figures to check your recall of the required lights and reflectors.

Under 80 Inches

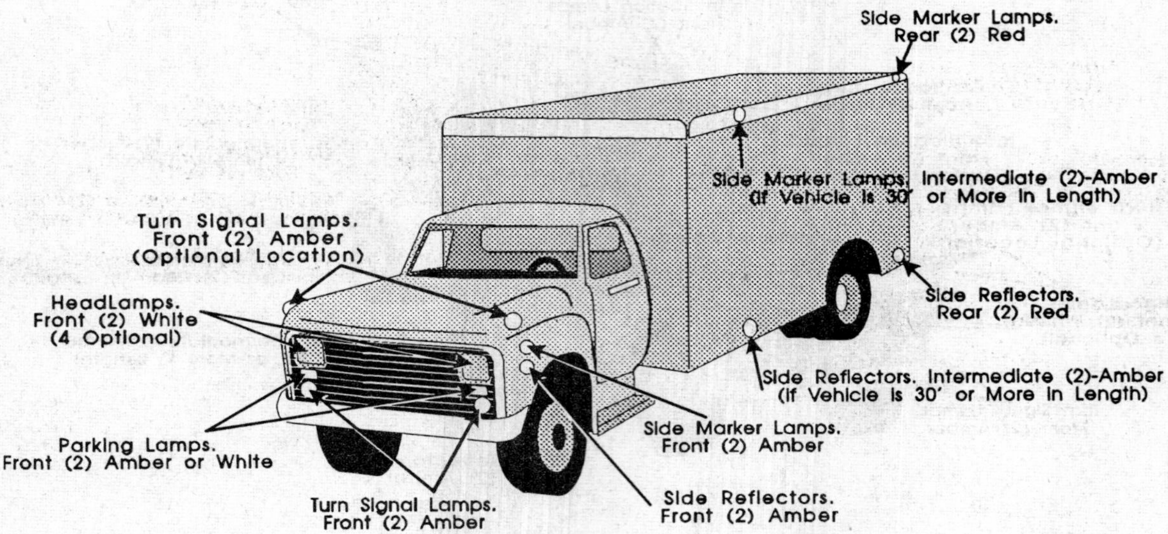

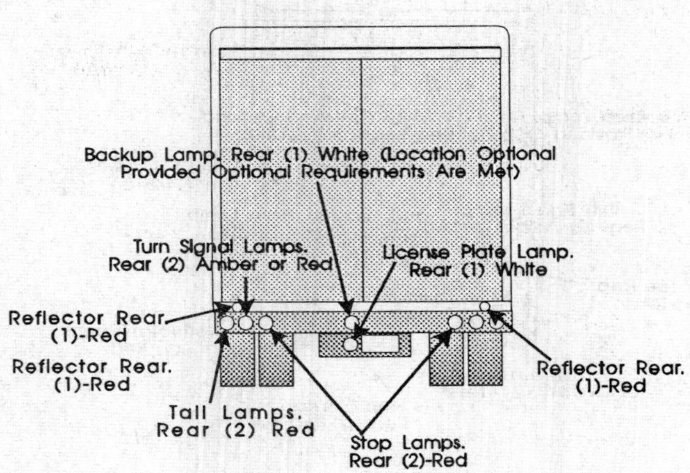

Figure 7-2D Use these figures to check your recall of the required lights and reflectors.

Under 80 Inches

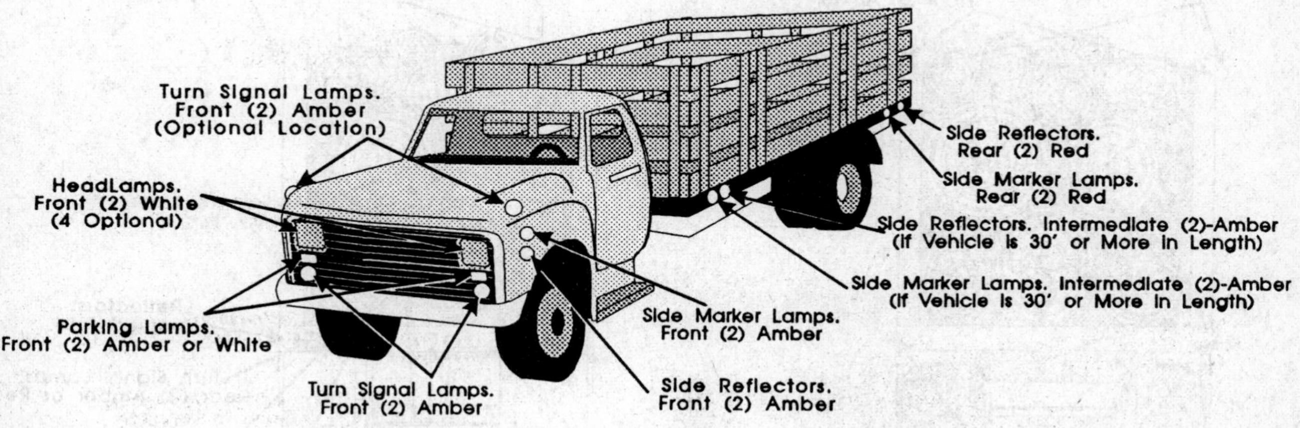

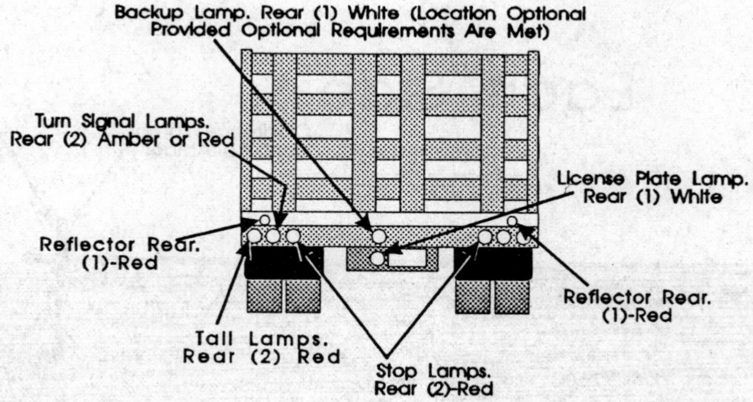

Figure 7-2E Use these figures to check your recall of the required lights and reflectors.

Pole Trailers - All Vehicle Widths

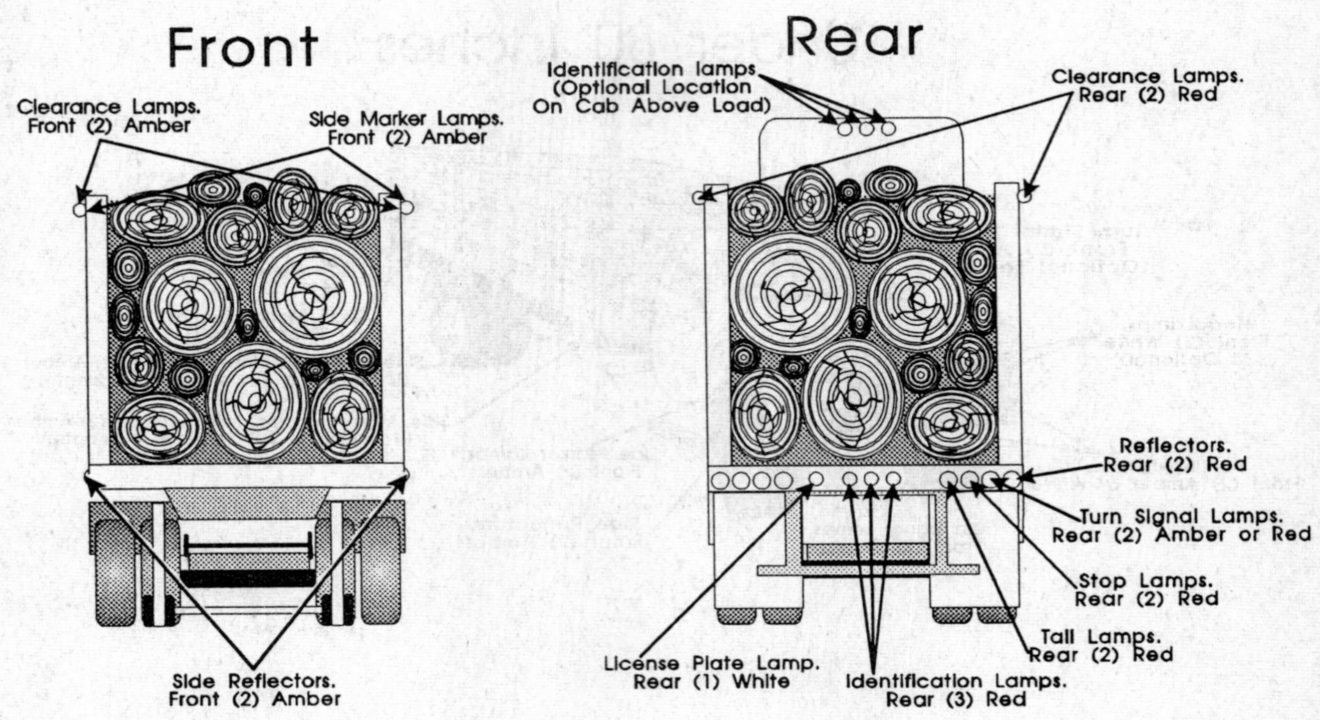

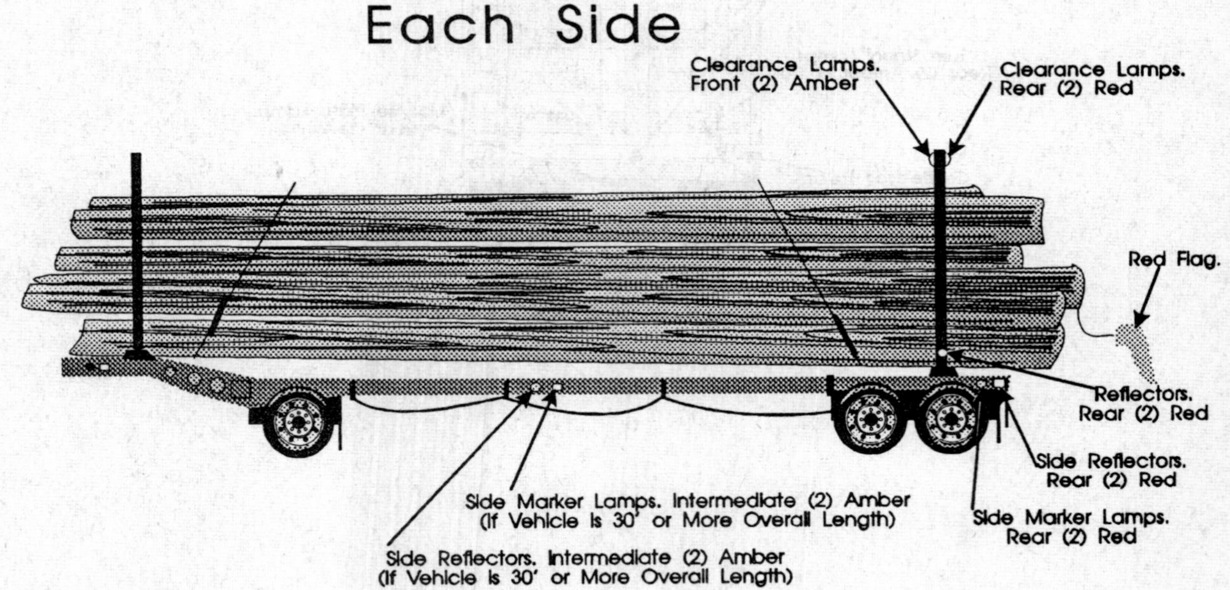

Figure 7-2F Use these figures to check your recall of the required lights and reflectors.

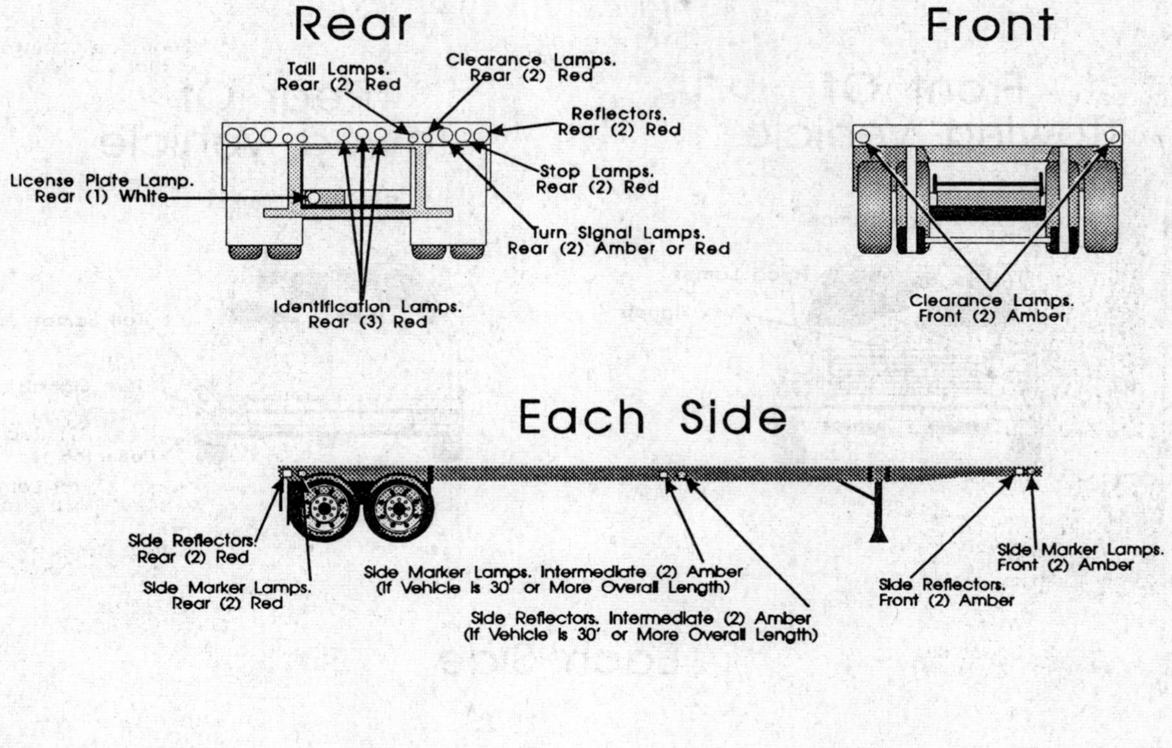

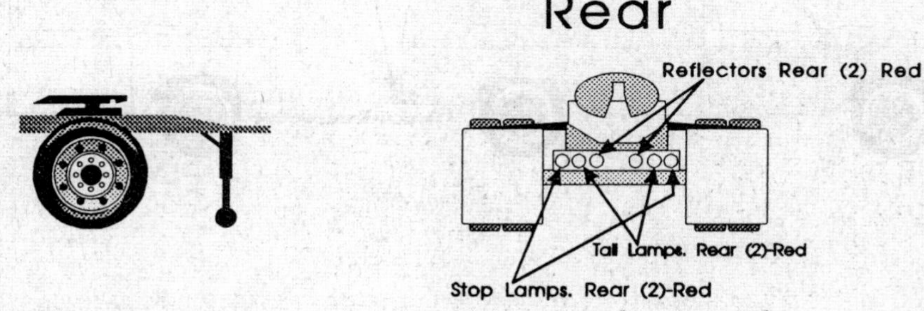

Figure 7-2G Use these figures to check your recall of the required lights and reflectors.

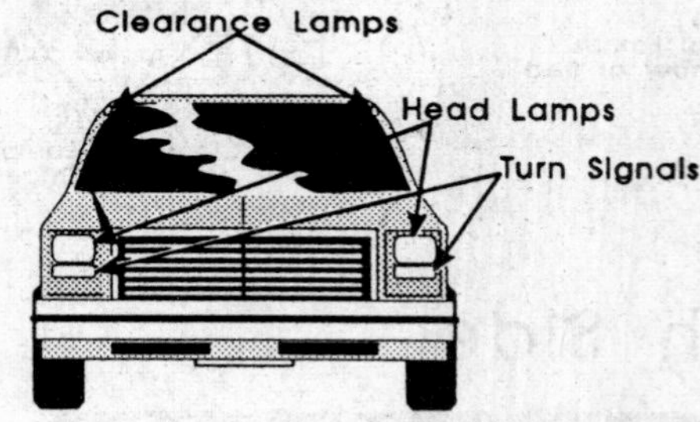

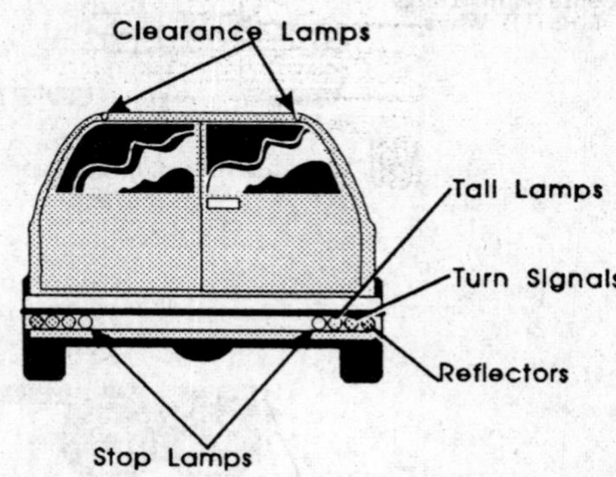

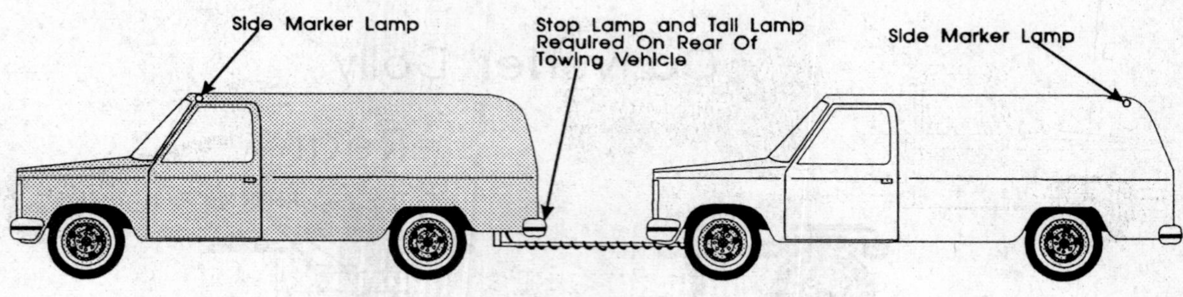

Figure 7-2H Use these figures to check your recall of the required lights and reflectors.

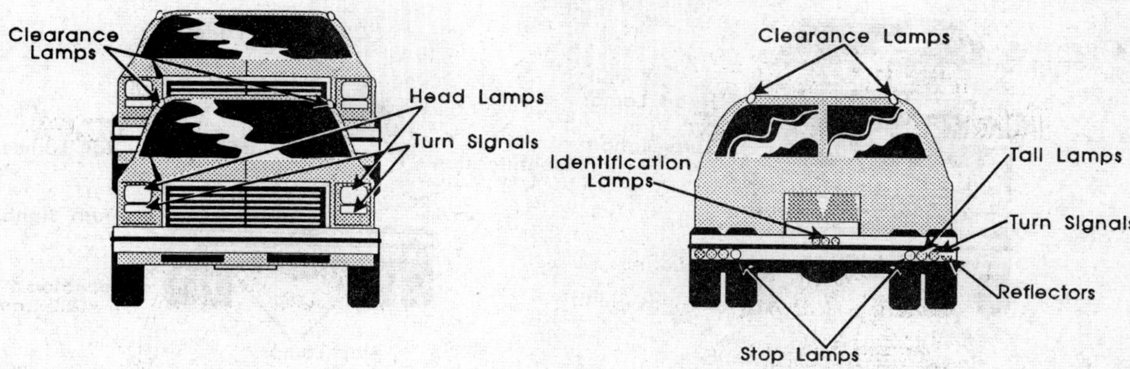

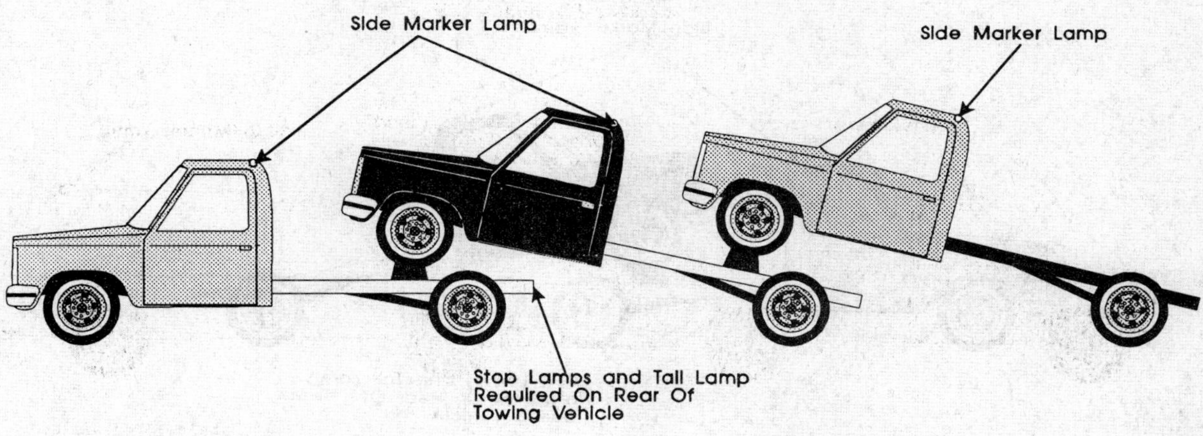

Figure 7-21 Use these figures to check your recall of the required lights and reflectors.

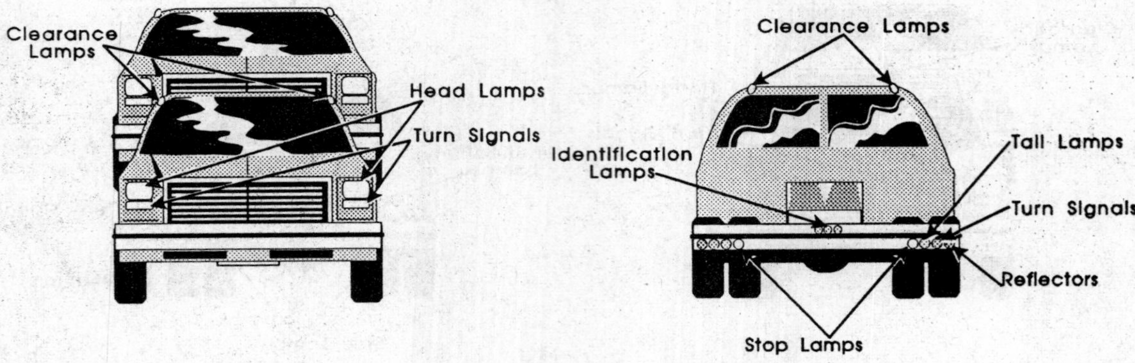

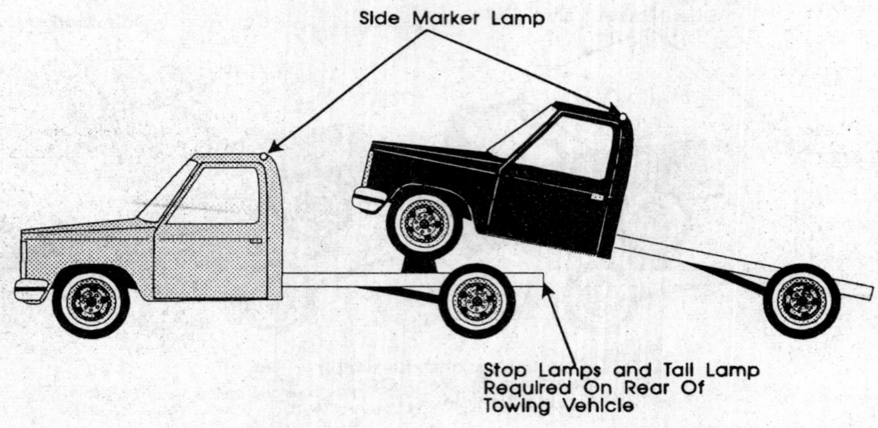

Figure 7-2J Use these figures to check your recall of the required lights and reflectors.

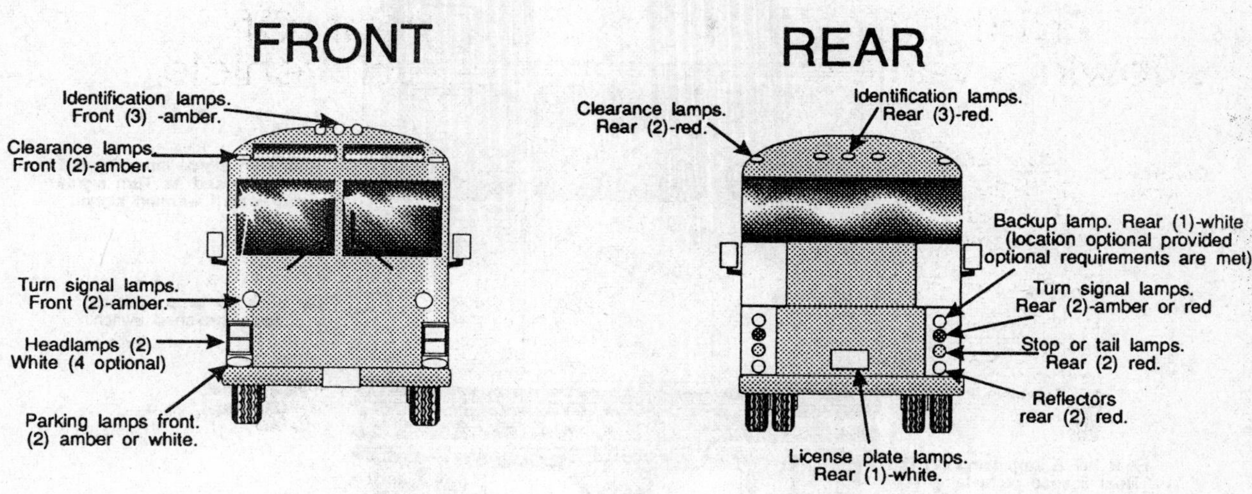

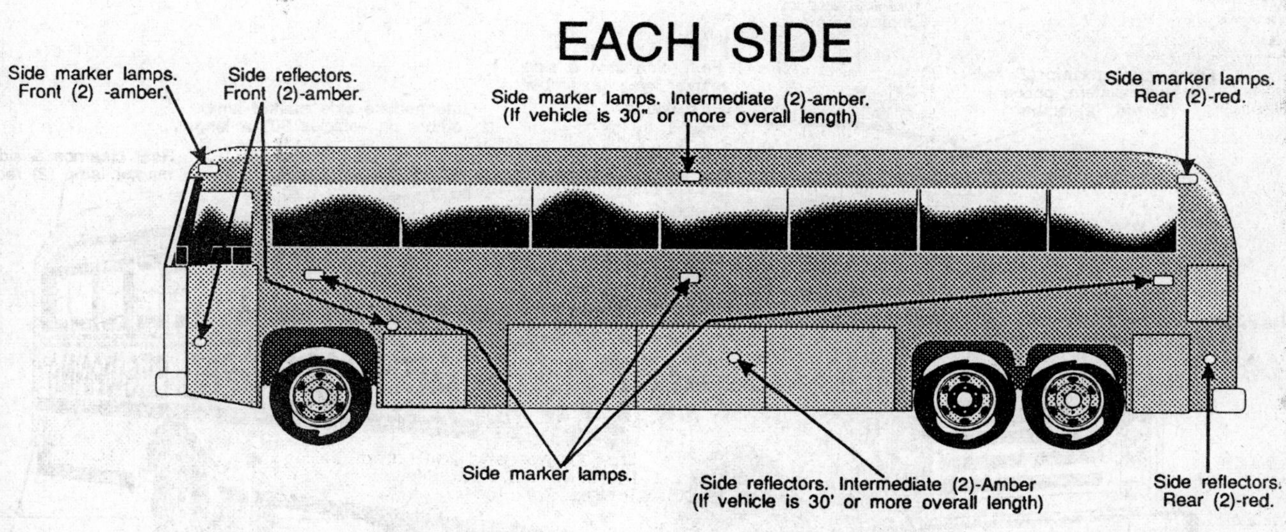

Figure 7-2K Use these figures to check your recall of the required lights and reflectors.

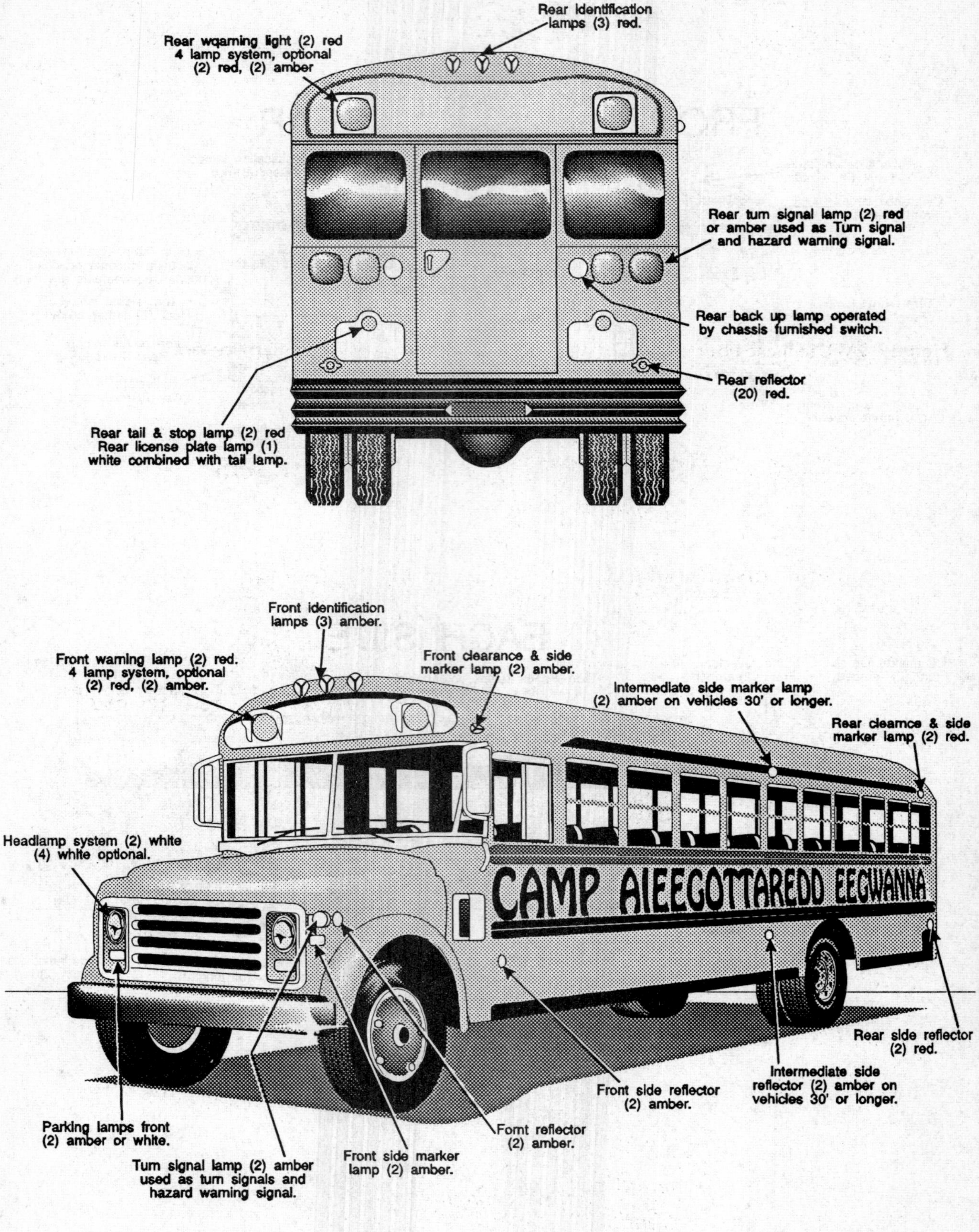

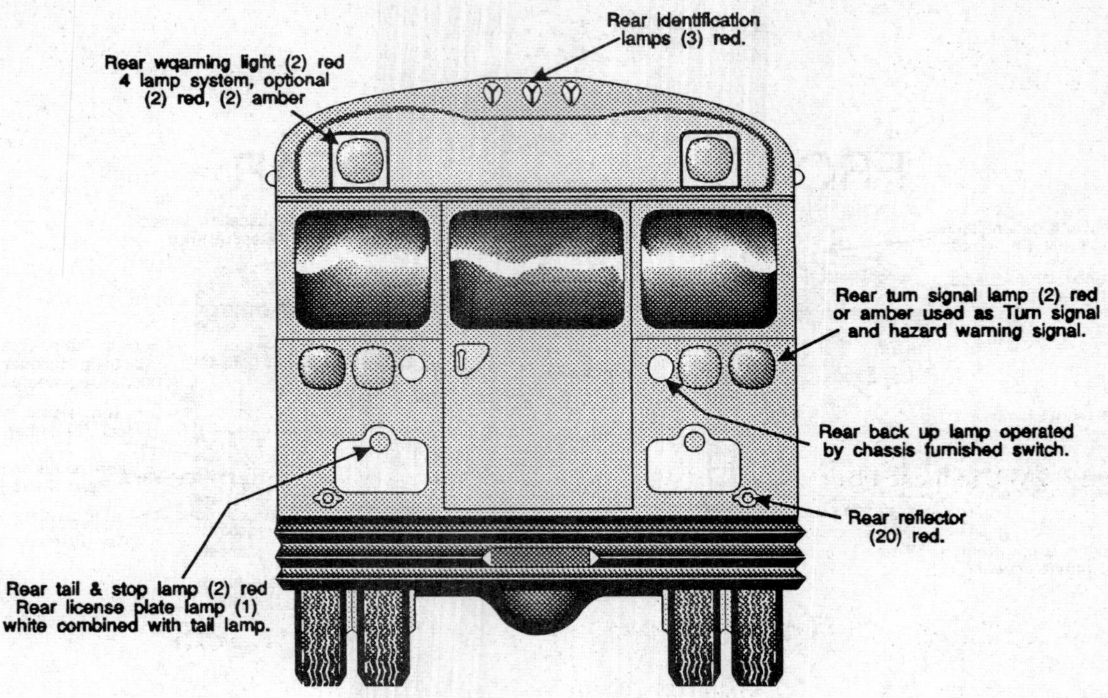

Front identification lamps (3) amber.

Front warning lamp (2) red. 4 lamp system, optional (2) red, (2) amber.

Front clearance & side marker lamp (2) amber.

Intermediate side marker lamp (2) amber on vehicles 30' or longer.

Rear clearnce & side marker lamp (2) red.

Headlamp system (2) white (4) white optional.

CAMP AIEEGOTTAREDD EEGWANNA

Rear side reflector (2) red.

Intermediate side reflector (2) amber on vehicles 30' or longer.

Front side reflector (2) amber.

Parking lamps front (2) amber or white.

Fornt reflector (2) amber.

Front side marker lamp (2) amber.

Turn signal lamp (2) amber used as turn signals and hazard warning signal.

Figure 7-2L Use these figures to check your recall of the required lights and reflectors.

Front

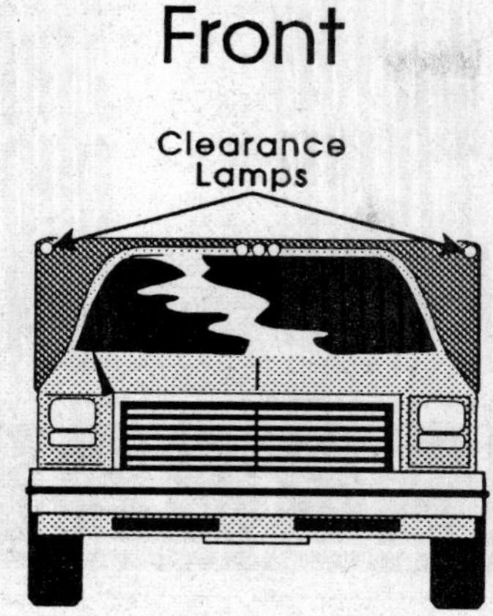

Figure 7-2M Use these figures to check your recall of the required lights and reflectors.

Vehicle Without Permanent Top Or Sides

Rear

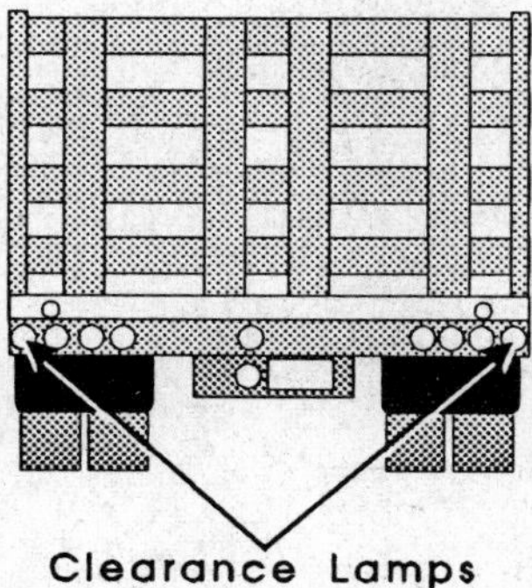

Figure 7-2N Use these figures to check your recall of the required lights and reflectors.

Figure 7-3 What your large flat mirrors let you see (A) and what your smaller convex (spot) mirrors let you see (B).

Rear turn signal lamps. Two amber or red lights, one at the lower right and one at the lower left of the rear of buses and trucks, tractors, semitrailers, full trailers, pole trailers, and converter dollies.

Rear tail lamps. Two red lights, one at the lower right and one at the lower left of all vehicles, even on projecting loads and converter dollies.

Parking lamps. Two amber or white lights, just below the headlights on small buses and trucks.

Four-way flashers. Two amber lights at the front and two amber or red lights at the rear of the vehicle. These are usually the front and rear turn signal lamps. They're equipped to do double-duty as warning lights. You can set them to flash simultaneously. They're required on buses and trucks, truck tractors, semitrailers and full trailers, pole trailers, and converter dollies.

Horn

Your vehicle must have a horn. Like lights, this is a communication tool. Use it with restraint. The horn can often alarm other drivers needlessly.

As part of your inspection, make sure your horn works. If it doesn't, there could be a blown fuse or faulty wiring.

Mirrors

Your vehicle must have a rear-view mirror at each side of the cab. (Some vehicles may have one outside mirror on the driver's side. Another mirror inside the vehicle gives a view to the rear.)

In the large, flat mirror, you should see the traffic and the sides of your vehicle and trailer if you have one. You should be able to see the road behind you from about the middle of the vehicle or trailer. Adjust the mirrors so you see the ground starting in front of the trailer wheels, all of both lanes next to your vehicle, and behind the trailer. In the small convex (spot) mirror, you should see the traffic and your drive wheels. The convex mirrors help you to see "blind spots" along the side of your vehicle.

Fire Extinguisher

As a professional driver, you have responsibilities in a vehicle fire. First, protect your life and the lives of your passengers and any bystanders. Then, try to save your vehicle and any freight. To do this, you need two things. You need to know something about fires and you need a working fire extinguisher.

Fires can start after accidents as a result of spilled fuel or the improper use of flares. You could have a tire fire. Under-inflated tires and duals that touch create enough friction to burst into flame. Electrical fires can result from short circuits caused by damaged insulation or loose connections.

Carelessness around fuel can cause fires. Smoking around the fuel island, improper fueling, and loose fuel connections can lead to fires. Flammable cargo and packages that aren't properly sealed or loaded can cause fires. So can poor ventilation in the baggage compartment. This is why it's so important to make a complete pretrip inspection of the electrical, fuel, and exhaust systems, tires, and baggage compartment.

Also, check the tires, wheels, and vehicle body for signs of heat whenever you stop during a trip. Fuel the vehicle safely as outlined later in this chapter. Be careful with any part of the vehicle that creates heat or flame. Check your instruments and gauges often for signs of overheating. Use the mirrors to look for signs of smoke from tires or the vehicle. Fix whatever is causing the overheating, smoke, or flame before you have a big problem on your hands.

Use normal caution in handling anything flammable. Knowing how to fight fires is important. Fires have been made worse by drivers who didn't know what to do. Here's what to do if a fire does start:

- First, get the vehicle off the road and stop. Park in an open area. Park away from buildings, trees, brush, other vehicles, or anything that might catch fire. Don't pull into a service station. There's too much flammable material there.

- Use your CB, if you have one, to notify the highway patrol or police of your problem and your location.
- Keep the fire from spreading. Before trying to put out the fire, make sure that it doesn't spread any farther.
- If you have an engine fire, turn off the engine as soon as you can. Don't open the hood if you can avoid it. Aim your fire extinguisher through louvers, the radiator, or from the underside of the vehicle.
- If you have a cargo fire in a van or box trailer, keep the doors shut. This is especially important if your cargo contains hazardous materials. Opening the van doors will supply the fire with oxygen. That can cause it to burn very fast.
- Use water on burning wood, paper, or cloth. Don't use water on an electrical fire. You could get shocked. Don't use water on a gasoline fire. It will just spread the flames.
- A burning tire must be cooled. You may need a lot of water. If you don't have water, try throwing sand or dirt on the tire.
- If you're not sure what to use, especially on a hazardous materials fire, wait for qualified fire fighters.
- Use the right kind of fire extinguisher for the fire.

FMCSR Part 393 states your CMV must carry a fire extinguisher. This regulation also lists which fire extinguishers are acceptable. Make sure the extinguisher in your vehicle conforms to the regulations.

Fires have been grouped according to class. When the fuel for the fire is wood, paper, cloth, trash, and other ordinary material, the fire is a Class A fire. When the fuel is gasoline, grease, oil, paint, or other flammable liquid, the fire is a Class B fire. Electrical fires are Class C fires.

Most CMVs must carry a five-pound fire extinguisher that can put out B- and C-type fires. Vehicles hauling haz mat that is placarded must have a 10 pound B:C fire extinguisher.

This type of extinguisher is filled with a dry chemical. When you squeeze the handle, a needle punctures an air pressure cartridge inside the tank. The released air pressure forces the powder out of the tank. The powder travels through the hose, through the nozzle, and onto the fire.

The dry chemical puts the fire out by smothering it. In other words, the chemical coats what's burning. That prevents air from fueling the fire. So aim the fire extinguisher at the base of the fire. You're not trying to douse the flames. You're trying to cover the burning material.

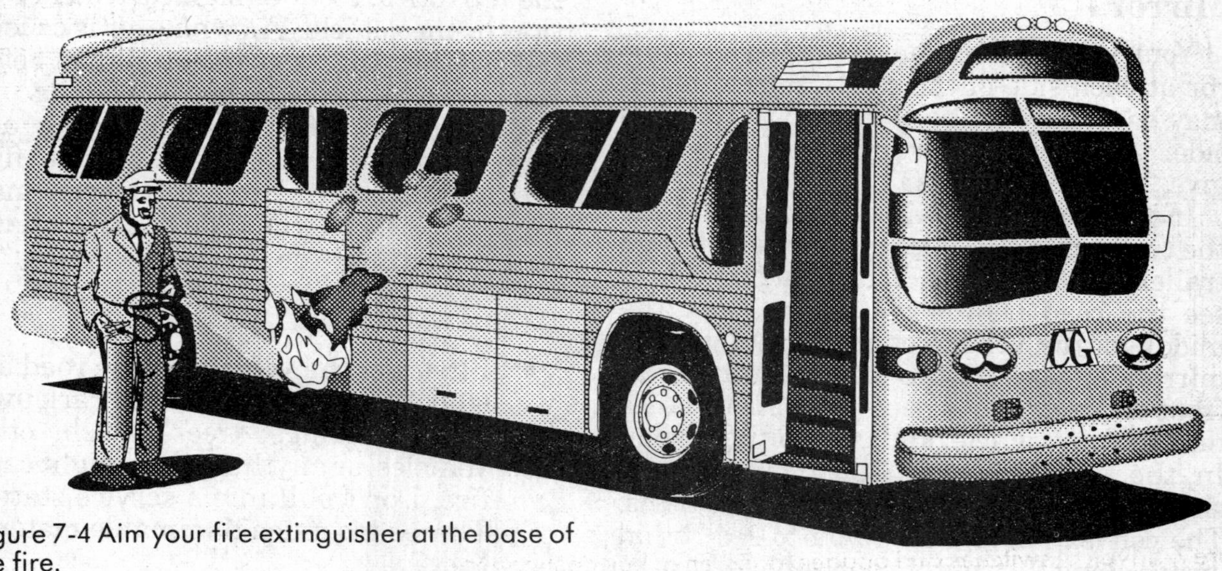

Figure 7-4 Aim your fire extinguisher at the base of the fire.

Know how the fire extinguisher works. Study the instructions printed on the extinguisher before you need it.

When using the extinguisher, stay as far away from the fire as possible. Position yourself with your back to the wind. Let the wind carry the extinguisher to the fire rather than carrying the flames to you.

Continue until whatever was burning has cooled. Just because there is no smoke or flame doesn't mean the fire is completely out or cannot restart.

Instruments and Gauges

The dashboard is also called a "dash" or "instrument panel." Figure 7-5 shows you an example of the gauges, switches, lights, and controls you'll find on a bus dashboard. Not all dashboards are the same. However, this is typical of what you'll find.

Some gauges monitor the operating condition of the engine. Others monitor the condition of systems that support the engine.

Besides gauges and warning lights, there are also switches and controls on the dash. They are used to operate the vehicle or its systems. An example is the switch for the air conditioner. When you use this switch, you turn on the air conditioner.

Start at the left of the illustration. The first thing you'll see is a panel of 12 switches. Starting at the top left, and scanning from left to right and back to the left, you'll see:

- the engine start switch
- the master control switch
- the emergency engine stop switch
- the defroster switch
- the fan speed switch

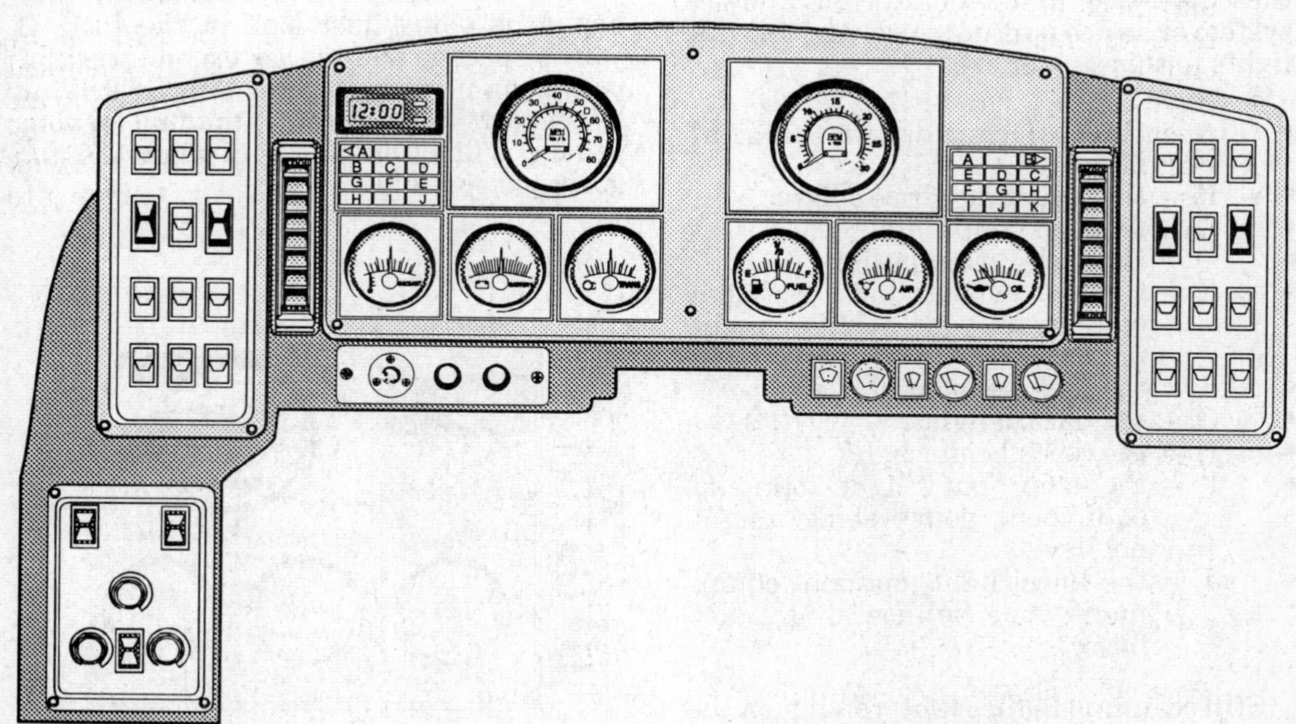

Figure 7-5 Typical switches and gauges found on a bus dashboard.

- the passenger air conditioning and heating switch
- the driver's air conditioning switch
- the trailing axle unload switch
- the fast idle switch
- the engine retarder switch (optional equipment your vehicle may not have)
- the mirror heater switch (optional equipment your vehicle may not have)
- the auxiliary passenger air conditioning switch (optional equipment your vehicle may not have)

These switches control the function of the systems or devices for which they're named. For example, the trailing axle unload switch partly unloads the trailing axle when the drive axle needs more weight for traction on slippery roads.

To the right of this panel of switches is an air conditioning vent. You can adjust the louvers to direct the flow of air to where it does you the most good. To the right of the vent is a clock, and below it, the left-hand tell-tale cluster assembly. When one of these tell-tale lights is lit, you know a system or device is on or in use. The tell-tale lights in this cluster are:

- A = the left-hand turn signal indicator
- B = the emergency brake light
- C = the stop lamps light
- D = the back-up lamps light
- E = the starter alert light (optional equipment your vehicle might not have)
- F = the high-beam light
- G = the hazard light
- H = the coach heater light
- I = the step "out" light (optional equipment your vehicle might not have)
- J = the kneel light (optional equipment your vehicle might not have)

Still scanning to the right, you'll next see the speedometer/odometer. The speedometer shows the vehicle's road speed in miles per hour (mph). It may also show a metric measurement, kilometers per hour (kph). Inside each speedometer is an odometer. The odometer keeps track of the total miles the vehicle has traveled. The mileage is shown in miles and tenths of miles.

To the right of the speedometer you'll find a tachometer. The tachometer (also called the "tach") shows engine crankshaft revolutions per minute (rpm). This tells you when to shift gears. To read the engine rpm, you multiply the number shown on the tachometer by 100. For example, 15 on the tach means 1500 rpm.

The number of revolutions per minute that an engine can make differs from engine to engine. The average high horsepower diesel goes to a maximum of only 2100 rpm. The range of the engine may go from 500 rpm (idle speed) to 2100 rpm. The typical operating range of the engine is even shorter. Stay within the operating range to achieve good engine performance. You'll find the recommended operating range in your operator's manual.

Engine speeds in most engines are governed. This means that there's a limited number of rpm the engine will make in any gear. If you want to see how many rpm your engine is doing, just look at the tach. If you've reached the top governed speed for your gear, it's time to shift. This is "driving by the tach." The operator's manual for your vehicle will often tell you what the top governed speed is.

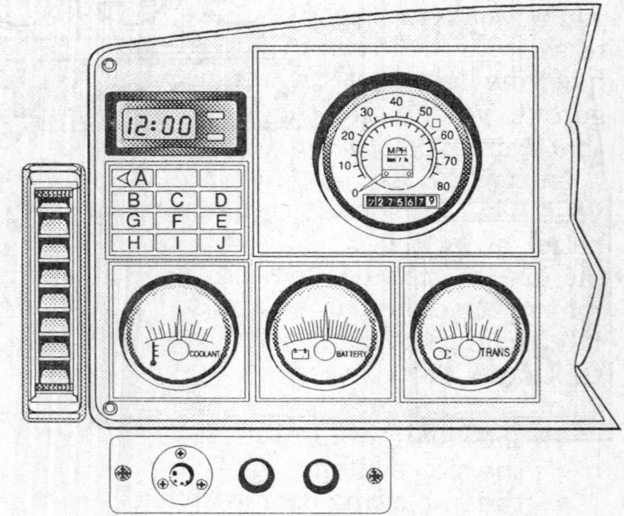

Figure 7-6 The speedometer.

In place of a tachometer, some vehicles have an oversized air gauge. The air gauge shows the amount of air pressure in an air brake system.

Next to this gauge is the right-hand tell-tale light cluster. All of these are warning lights (except for the right-hand turn signal indicator). When they're lit, you know there's a problem in the system they monitor. Sometimes there will also be warning buzzers that will sound at the same time the lights come on.

The lights in this cluster are:

- A = low air warning light
- B = right-hand turn signal indicator
- C = fire alarm (overheating in the engine compartment) light (optional equipment your vehicle might not have)
- D = lavatory emergency light (on vehicles with lavatories)
- E = air conditioning malfunction light
- F = low fuel light
- G = low water light
- H = low oil light
- I = low air/tag axle light
- J = generator not charging light
- K = engine overheated light

When you start the engine, the tell-tale lights should come on for a few moments. That shows you that they are working. If you have a light that doesn't come on, check to see whether it is in fact broken. If you have one light that stays on after the others go out, you should check for problems in that system before you drive.

Next you'll find another air conditioning vent. Then at the far right there's another panel of switches. A few of the switches pictured operate optional equipment, so you may not find these on your dashboard. From left to right and right to left, the switches in this panel are:

- the steplight and chimes switch
- the step switch
- the bi-parting door switch
- the driver's lights switch
- the galley switch
- the coach light switch
- the clearance lights switch
- the headlamp switch
- the hazard light switch
- the kneel switch
- the speaker switch
- the radio switch

Scanning back toward the left you'll see a row of gauges. These monitor the operation of different systems. From right to left they are:

- the oil pressure gauge
- a small air pressure gauge (optional equipment your vehicle may not have)
- a fuel gauge (optional equipment your vehicle may not have)
- a transmission temperature gauge (optional equipment your vehicle may not have)
- a voltmeter (optional equipment your vehicle may not have)
- the water temperature gauge

The oil pressure gauge shows how well the engine is being lubricated. Measurements are displayed in pounds per square inch (psi). This gauge shows a reading when the engine is running. When the oil is cold, the gauge shows a high reading. After the engine has warmed up, the reading should return to normal. When the engine is running at normal temperatures and the oil is hot, the normal idle pressure runs from 5 to 15 psi. The normal operating pressure runs from 50 to 75 psi. Check the operator's manual to find out what's normal for your vehicle.

Always check this instrument after starting the engine. If no pressure is shown, stop the engine at once. You can seriously damage the engine by running it with no oil pressure. A low reading may mean you're simply low on oil. This can be caused by a leak. You may also have a clogged filter.

A fuel gauge shows the fuel level in the supply tank. (Some vehicles have an auxiliary [extra] fuel supply tank.)

If you don't have a fuel gauge, you'll rely on the low fuel light. When you're down to a certain fuel level (your operator's manual will tell you what that level is), the light will come on.

A transmission temperature gauge displays measurement in degrees. A high temperature reading alerts you to problems in the transmission. If the temperature is high, you should stop the vehicle before more damage occurs. Transmission oil temperatures range from 180 to 250 degrees Fahrenheit. The normal range for axles is from 160 to 220 degrees Fahrenheit. These are only guidelines. Check your operator's manual to find out what's normal for your vehicle.

A voltmeter shows the charge condition of the battery. The voltmeter is marked by the word "Volts" on the lower portion of the gauge. There is often a picture of a battery as well as the word "Volts."

The voltmeter has three segments, each for a different battery condition. The left-hand red segment shows an undercharged battery. The middle green segment shows normal battery condition. The right-hand red segment shows an overcharge condition. The gauge pointer shows which condition the battery is in. If the voltmeter shows a continuous undercharging or overcharging condition, there is likely a problem in the charging system. The voltmeter in Figure 7-5 is in the normal range.

The water temperature gauge shows the engine cooling system temperature. The gauge displays measurements in degrees. A typical gauge has a range of about 100 to 250 degrees Fahrenheit. A normal reading is between 170 and 195 degrees Fahrenheit. (Your vehicle may be different. Check your operator's manual.) The gauge will read higher if you are running in hot weather.

Below the gauges are several controls. To the left of the steering wheel is the public address (P.A.) system panel. From left to right the P.A. system controls are:

- the microphone jack
- the tone control knob
- the volume control knob

To the right of the steering wheel you'll find windshield wiper and washer controls. When the light to the left of the panel is on, you know the washer system is in operation. The lights in the center tell you if the wiper system is on or off. The leftmost knob turns the washer on or off. The knobs to the right control the left and right wipers.

Finally, below the left hand tell-tale light panel, you'll see one more panel of switches and knobs, the fascia console switch assembly. At the top of the panel are cruise control switches (optional equipment your vehicle may not have). At the center is a potentiometer/heat control. Use this control to direct the heating system to maintain a certain temperature inside the vehicle. The knobs at the bottom of the panel are rheostat controls. The left knob dims or brightens your gauges. The right knob dims or brightens your dashboard. The last control on this panel is the passenger blowers switch at bottom center.

Your vehicle's dashboard may have different lights, gauges, and controls, such as:

- an oil temperature gauge
- a pyrometer
- a differential lock control and light
- a charging circuit warning light
- a low vacuum warning light
- a cab lock warning light
- an engine start, master control, or ignition switch
- a throttle
- a fuel filter gauge
- an air filter indicator
- a slide control

If you have an oil temperature gauge, make sure the temperature is within the normal range while you are driving.

A pyrometer tells you the engine exhaust temperature. The safe temperature range will be shown on the dashboard next to the gauge or on the gauge. High exhaust temperatures mean trouble. You might have a leak or a clog in the air intake or the exhaust system. There could be problems with the fuel ignition. Or you could simply be in the wrong gear ratio for the load, grade, or altitude.

If your vehicle has dual rear axles that have inter-axle differentials, you use the inter-axle differential control. The differential is a rear axle gear assembly. With the control in the unlocked position, each axle shaft and wheel can turn at different speeds when the vehicle makes a turn. The control should be set at "Unlocked" or "Off" unless the road surface is slippery. For slippery roads, you want equal power at all wheels. So set the control to "Locked" or "On." The differential lock light reminds you the differential lock is in the locked position.

Your vehicle may also have a charging circuit warning light. This light comes on if your battery isn't charging. The light normally lights when the starter switch is turned on. This tells you the light is working. It goes out when the engine starts, unless you have a problem.

Your vehicle may also have a low vacuum warning light. When this light comes on, it means the vacuum in the brake booster is below the safety limit. You could be dangerously low on braking power. Stop as soon as it is safe to do so. Don't drive again until the brake problem is fixed.

There may be a cab lock warning light. This light tells you the cab tilt lock is not secure.

The starter or ignition switch turns on the electricity. It turns the engine over so it can start. When the key is straight up and down, the switch is off. When you turn the key to the left, it turns on the accessory circuits. Turn the key to the right to turn on both the accessory and ignition circuits. Turn the key to the far right to engage the starter.

Release the key as soon as the engine turns over. After a false start, let the starter cool for 30 seconds before trying it again.

The throttle is a kind of accelerator on the dashboard. You pull it out to set engine speed, or rpm. You use the throttle in very cold weather to keep the engine warm when idling. You might also use it to get engine speed up and deliver more power to operate a power take-off (PTO) device.

The fuel filter gauge shows the condition of the fuel filter. It has a colored band divided into two segments. The left segment is white. The middle and right segments are red. It also has numbered markings. You have a clogged fuel filter if the needle reads in the red range.

If your vehicle doesn't have an air filter gauge, the air filter will at least have an indicator. Color-coded readings will lock into place when the air filter needs changing.

If your vehicle has air brakes, controls and gauges for this system come next. These are covered in detail in Chapter 11.

On some vehicles, the light switches are on a stalk to the left of the steering wheel. You may find all your light switches here, including the dimmer switch, turn signals, and flashers.

Tractors with sliding fifth wheels will have a slide control here. This moves the fifth wheel into different positions on the tractor frame. That allows you to put more or less of the trailer weight on the tractor. You can make the vehicle more stable. You'll learn more about weight distribution in Chapter 9.

There are more controls on the floor of the cab:

- the accelerator pedal
- the brake pedal
- the clutch pedal
- the transmission control lever

You'll find the accelerator on the floor of the cab under the steering wheel. You use your right foot to operate this pedal and control engine speed. When you depress the pedal, the speed of the vehicle increases. As you let your foot off the pedal, the speed decreases. If you take your foot off the pedal, the engine idles.

You'll find the brake pedal just to the left of the accelerator. You operate this pedal with your right foot. When you depress the brake pedal, the brakes are applied.

To the left of the brake pedal is the clutch pedal. You use your left foot to operate the clutch pedal. You disengage the clutch when you depress the clutch pedal. You engage the clutch when you release the clutch pedal.

Use the transmission control lever (shift lever) to change gears.

You may have a dimmer switch just to the left of the clutch pedal. You use your left foot. It lets you switch the headlights between high and low beams. Use low beams when driving in traffic. Use high beams on open roads when there is no oncoming traffic and no traffic closer than 500 feet in front of you.

Your vehicle may also have a power take-off (PTO) lever. This control is really two knobs. Pull up on the first knob to connect the PTO to the transmission. Pull up on the second knob to use the PTO.

There are still more controls throughout the cab:

- the auxiliary P.A. control
- the entrance door lever
- the entrance door lock overrule switch
- the driver's heater valve
- the fresh air control valve
- the driver's heater or air conditioner gasper
- the driver's fresh air gasper

The entrance door opens when you push up the entrance door control lever on the right side of the dash. To close the door, pull the handle down. This automatically operates the entrance door air lock. If the air lock fails to operate automatically, use the overrule switch under the dash.

Your vehicle provides many controls for adjusting the temperature in the cab. This is because a cab that's too warm can make you drowsy. You'll find the driver's heater valve to the driver's left just above the floor. This valve controls the flow of water to the

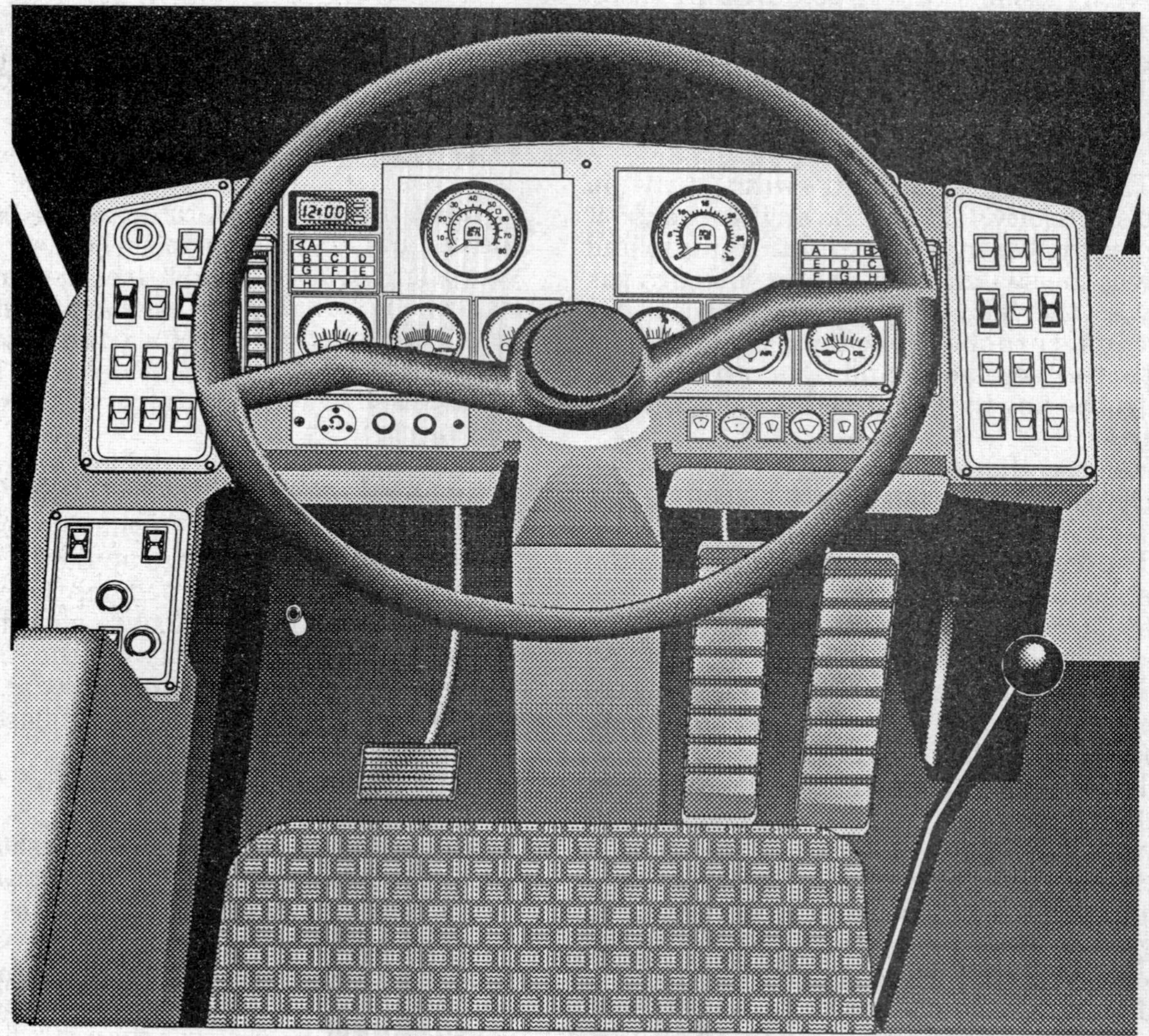

Figure 7-7 The controls on the floor under the steering wheel.

driver's heater system. Pull the handle up to open the valve and push the handle down to close it. Use the fresh air control valve (found just behind the water valve) to control the flow of fresh or recirculated air into the driver's heater system. Use the gaspers under the dashboard to control the flow of heated, cooled, and fresh air.

We'll cover the baggage compartment controls in Chapter 9.

TROUBLESHOOTING

FMCSR Part 383 says you must be able to do a certain amount of troubleshooting. Your instruments and gauges tell you something's wrong. You must know how to read them and what you should do in response. You must be able to do some problem-solving when your vehicle fails to work as expected.

Let's look at the main systems that support your vehicle. When you understand what these systems do, you'll be better able to figure out what's wrong when they fail. (Plus, inspecting your vehicle will be easier and make more sense.)

Also, you'll be better prepared for the CDL tests. During the inspection, the examiner may ask you questions about vehicle parts and systems. You must know what makes them work. You must be able to show good knowledge about mechanical systems.

The systems and parts we will cover are those required by FMCSR Part 393. You can learn a lot about these parts from the FMCSR. You can learn still more from the operator's manual for your vehicle. Ask your employer, safety supervisor, or maintenance personnel whether there is one available. Or ask at the reference desk of your local public library. Another place to try would be a vehicle dealer. Last, you could try writing to the vehicle's manufacturer.

Maybe your knowledge of mechanical systems needs some serious shoring up. Check a nearby bookstore or library for books on diesel mechanics, electricity, hydraulics, motor vehicles, and so forth. You're sure to find a few good books on the mechanics of heavy vehicles.

Wiring and Electrical Systems

The power that runs your CMV comes from the engine. The power behind that engine power is electrical power. You can't even start your vehicle without a starting circuit. You can't keep it going for long without a charging circuit. You can't run your lights without a lighting circuit and your dashboard instruments won't work without an instrument circuit.

As you can see, electricity serves many functions in vehicles. Unless you understand the electrical system, it just looks like a mess of wires. The first step in understanding the system is to understand some of the basics of electricity.

An electron is a tiny particle that carries a negative charge of electricity. Electrical flow produces electrical current. Everything contains electrons, but some things conduct electricity better than others.

A good conductor of electricity has electrons that can easily be set in motion. Copper wire is a good conductor of electricity. Rubber is not a good conductor. That's why copper wire is used to move electric charges from one place to another. Rubber is used as an insulator around copper wire, in places where you don't want to conduct electricity.

Wires

Insulated wires bring current to parts that need electricity to operate. Terminals are the connecting devices. They are found on the ends of the wires. They are on the electrical parts used to connect the wires to the components. There is also a main terminal from which the wires start and which contains all the system circuit breakers and fuses.

Measuring Electricity

Pressure gets the electrons flowing. "Voltage" is another name for this electrical pressure. Batteries and alternators or generators produce voltage. A voltmeter measures voltage. The term "amperage" or "amps" refers to the amount of electric current that is produced and carried by the wires. An ammeter measures amps. You

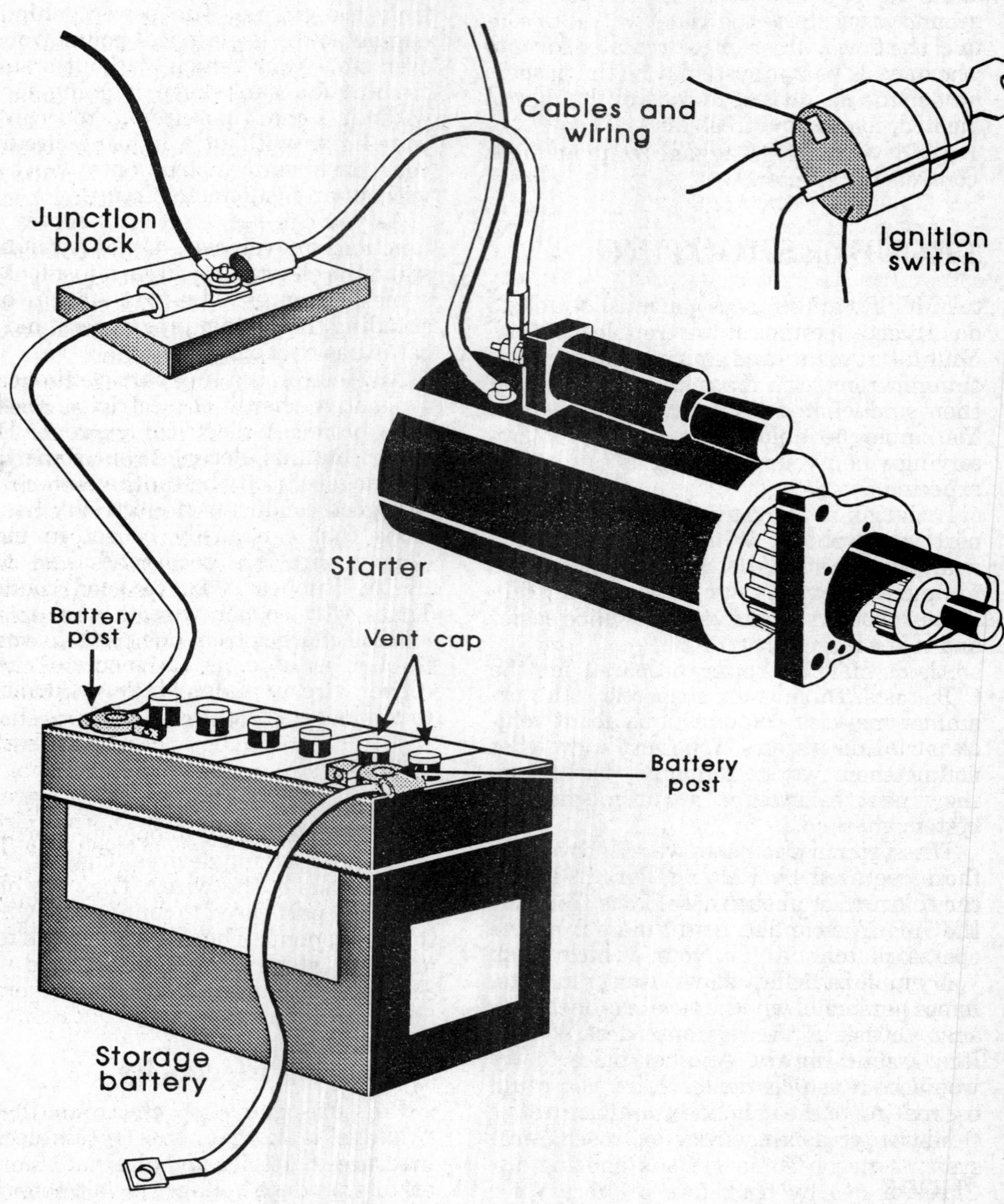

Figure 7-8 Battery and starter.

may have an ammeter on your dashboard. This gauge tells you the amount of charge or discharge the battery is getting from the generator or alternator. The NOT GEN telltale light will also alert you to alternator problems. It will come on if the alternator is not charging during normal operations. Should this happen, turn off all electrical accessories (except driving lights at night). This will reduce the load on the batteries. Get service as soon as possible.

You also have a voltmeter on your dashboard. The voltmeter tells you about the charge condition of your battery. This in turn tells you how much power the battery has to get electrons flowing. Your battery might be undercharging – not getting enough electrons flowing to crank the engine. Undercharging causes the fluid in the battery to thicken. This shortens battery life.

Your voltmeter could show the battery is overcharging. Too much pressure and too much electron activity overheat the battery and cause the battery fluids to evaporate. This shortens battery life as well.

Your battery could be cycling, a rapid series of charges and discharges. This, too, shortens the life of the battery.

The desired voltmeter reading is a normal battery charge condition. Battery problems could be serious. If the reading on your voltmeter shows the battery is overcharging, undercharging, or cycling, have the battery checked.

When you inspect your vehicle, check the fluid level in the battery. It should be up to the filler rings in each cell. If you can't see the rings, just make sure the fluid covers the cell plates.

If you must add fluid, use distilled water. Avoid underfilling or overfilling. As you know, either of these can shorten battery life. Gases form when the battery is charging. Vent caps over the cells let these gases escape. At the same time, they keep the fluid from splashing out of the battery.

Wiring

The electrons flow through electrical circuits. A circuit is a continuous path made up of a conductor (such as wire) and a source of power that drives the current around the circuit (the batteries and alternator or generator). The devices that use the electricity (your vehicle's starter and lights, for instance) are also part of the path. This type of circuit is called a "complete" or "closed" circuit. For current to flow, there must be a closed circuit. For a circuit to be closed, all the parts in that circuit must be grounded. That means there must be a wire or a conductor to bring the electrons back to where they started.

There are two other kinds of circuits: the open circuit and the short circuit. Electricity will not flow in either of these types of circuits. That usually means trouble, such as your lights not working.

An open circuit occurs when the normal flow of electrical current is stopped. A number of conditions can cause this. Corroded connections and broken wires account for most open circuits. Open circuits account for most electrical problems. You can spot, and often fix, an open circuit caused by faulty connections and wires when you inspect your vehicle. Reconnect loose wires. Broken wires must be replaced.

A short circuit occurs when the electrical current bypasses part of the normal circuit. This means that instead of flowing to a light bulb, for instance, the current stops short of its destination and flows back to the battery.

Shorts happen when the insulation has come off a section of a wire. The wire can touch something outside the normal circuit, like another wire or part of the frame. Then the current leaves the circuit. It takes the shortest route back to the source, along the other wire or frame. It never does make it to the light bulb.

Either of the following conditions can also cause a short circuit:

- the wires in an electrical coil (like the starter winding) lose their insulation and touch each other.
- a wire rubs against the frame or other metal part of the vehicle until the bare wire touches another piece of metal.

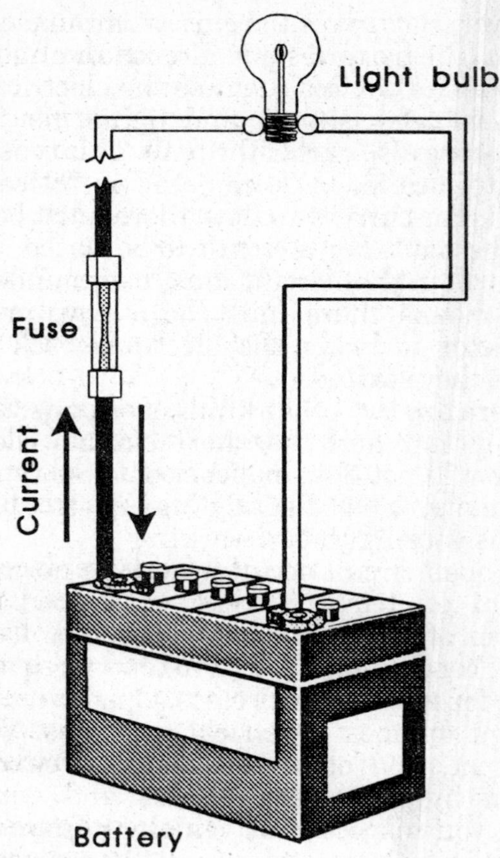

Figure 7-9 A short circuit will keep current from getting to the device it's meant to operate.

Regulations require that wiring be installed and insulated so shorts won't occur. During inspections, look for frayed, broken, loose, or hanging wires. These might result in a short circuit if not repaired. Electric power would then fail to reach the parts that need it, like your lights. A short could lead to an electrical fire. Replace any wires that have worn insulation.

Grounding

A grounding circuit provides a short-cut path for the current, much the way a short circuit does. But a grounding circuit works for your safety. Here's how.

When electrical wires burn or break, the normal path or circuit is broken. The current looks for some way to complete the circuit. If you were to grasp the broken wire ends, the current would use you to complete the circuit. Or perhaps the short is directing the current to the vehicle frame. Again, if you touch the frame, you become part of the circuit. Strong-enough current can electrocute you. A ground provides an alternate, safe path for the current if the normal path is broken.

Batteries

Batteries convert chemical energy into electrical energy. They then supply power to the rest of the electrical system. The major parts of a battery are a case, a number of individual cells, cell connectors, and two terminal posts.

The two posts on the top part of the battery are called "main battery terminals" or "battery posts." The positive (+) post is the larger one. The other is the negative (−) post. The battery cables are connected to these posts.

The vent caps are also on the top part of the battery. Gases build up when the battery charges. The vent caps let these gases escape. You remove the vent caps to check the battery. In doing so, you may see that the vents are clogged. They must be clean so the gases can escape.

Batteries are dry-charged, wet-charged, and maintenance-free. The dry-charged battery has no fluid in it when it leaves the factory. The dealer adds that to the battery when it's sold. The wet battery has fluid

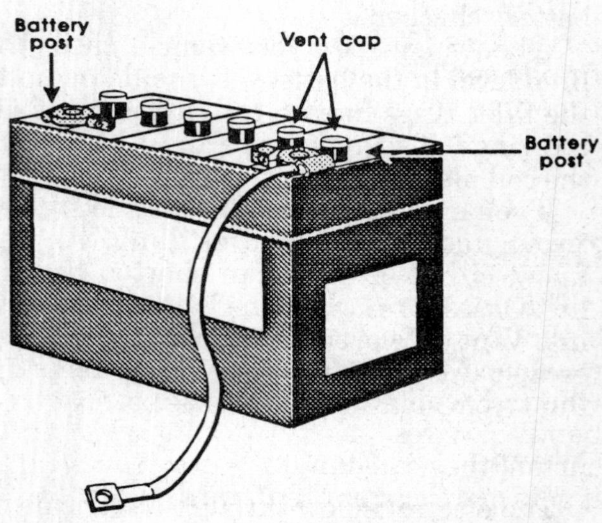

Figure 7-10 Battery.

already in it when it leaves the factory. With these types of batteries, you must check the fluid level as part of your inspection. (The maintenance-free battery does not usually require this.)

Make sure each cell has a vent cap. Check to see that the vents are not clogged.

Check the battery mount. Check the hold-down bars to make sure the battery is snug. This keeps it from being damaged by vibration. The battery box cover should be in place. The battery box itself must not be cracked or leaking.

Look for battery cables that are frayed, worn, or cracked. They must be replaced. Check to make sure the battery connections are tight.

Electricity can be dangerous if you're not careful. Here's how to work around batteries safely. Disconnect the battery ground strap before you begin any electrical or engine work. Connect the ground strap last when you install a new battery. Do not lay metal tools or other objects on the battery.

Never hook up the battery backwards. Instead, be sure to connect the positive cable to the positive terminal post. Connect the negative cable to the negative terminal post. The positive cable clamp and terminal is usually larger than the negative.

Take care around battery acid. It's corrosive. Don't lean too close to the battery when adding water. Battery fluid could splash up into your eyes.

Keep sparks and fires away from batteries. Gas from the electrolyte can catch fire. If you're a smoker, this is **not** a good time for a cigarette.

Overload Protective Devices

Circuit breakers and fuses protect the circuit from short circuits and from current overloads. A current overload happens when a circuit gets more current than it can handle. Wires are rated for how much current they can handle. Wiring can burn if it gets more current than it's designed for.

A short circuit is usually the cause of an overload. This is what happens. Turning on the lights, the starter motor, or radio "uses" (actually, slows down) the flow of the electricity. If there is a short circuit, the bulb, the motor, or the radio won't work. Nothing slows down the flow of current. This means there is more current in the wire than the wire can handle by itself. It will overheat and burn. Fuses or circuit breakers are placed in each circuit to prevent this.

Here's how they work. Like wiring, fuses are rated by their ability to handle so much current. To protect a circuit, you use a fuse rated lower than the wiring. An overload that exceeds the fuse's rating will blow the fuse. This opens or breaks the circuit. The fuse will go before the current builds to a point that exceeds the rating of the wiring. The wiring is protected.

Once a fuse is blown, it must be replaced. You see why, if your vehicle uses fuses, you must have spares. That way, you can replace any fuses that might be blown and get back the use of your lights or starter. (Of course, you'll need to fix the cause of the overload before you replace the fuse. Otherwise, you'll just blow the new fuse.)

Circuit breakers are also rated by their ability to carry current. A circuit breaker used on a circuit will have the same current-carrying capacity as the circuit. If there is more current load than the circuit breaker can carry, the circuit breaker opens. This breaks the circuit. Once a circuit breaker has opened, it can be reset. This is an advantage circuit breakers have over fuses. Again, though, give some attention to whatever caused the circuit breaker to open. If you don't, it will just open again the next time the problem occurs.

You'll probably find there are two sets of circuit breakers in your vehicle. One set protects the air conditioning condenser blower motor and heating system blower. These circuit breakers can be found at the front of the baggage compartment. If they open, you can get to them to reset them through the left front baggage door.

The second set, the main circuit breaker, is in the junction panel to the left of the operator's compartment or cab. The circuit breakers in this set reset automatically when the breaker element cools. They will continue to open and close until the electrical problem is fixed.

Detachable Electrical Connections

There's one more important electrical part on a CMV. That's the detachable electrical connection between a tractor and trailer in a combination vehicle. You probably call this a pigtail. It carries current from the tractor to the trailer, where it powers the trailer lights. Like any other circuit, this connection can short out or break. You'll make checking the electrical connection to the trailer part of your inspection.

If you're driving a straight vehicle and not pulling a trailer, you don't have detachable electrical connections.

The Electrical System

Wires, circuit breakers, fuses, terminals, and current-using parts make up the circuits in your vehicle. There is one main terminal block that contains all the circuit breakers and fuses. From this terminal block, wires run out in bunches to connectors. At the connectors the wires split and go to other connectors or to the parts that use the electricity.

Most CMVs have a basic 12-volt electrical system. Many of the parts are the same as the ones in the humble family car. The battery is the power source for your vehicle's electrical system. It supplies the power that starts the vehicle's engine. Then the alternator or generator supplies the power that keeps the battery charged and runs the vehicle's systems. Older vehicles may have generators. Newer vehicles have alternators.

While the engine is running, a belt from the engine crankshaft drives the generator. The generator then produces electricity to run all the other electrical circuits and to keep the battery charged. When the engine is not running, the stored energy in the battery provides the energy for circuits that need electricity. The lights, radio, and other instruments get their electrical power from the battery when the engine is not running.

The alternator does the same job the generator does, but it's lighter, cheaper to build, and produces more current at low speeds.

Figure 7-11 traces the path of current through a vehicle's electrical system. The path begins at the battery. When the ignition switch is turned to the start position, the current flows from the battery to the starter. The starter cranks the engine. After the engine has started running, current flows from the alternator back to the battery to replace the current used to start the engine. Current also flows to the other parts that need electrical power.

Brakes

What makes your vehicle stop? The brakes, yes. Dumb question.

Here's a better question. What makes the brakes work? Ah, that's a little tougher.

The answer is friction. In drum brakes, brake shoes move toward the brake drums. The shoes wear a lining or pad of coarse material. The shoes bring this lining into contact with the drum. This creates friction, which stops the truck. (In disc brakes, the friction pad moves into contact with a metal disc. The result is the same.) Varying the amount of pressure applied to the brakes changes the amount of force the brake shoe applies to the brake drum and the amount of friction that's created. The brake drum or disc is bolted to the wheel. If the drum (or disc) slows, so does the wheel. This is how you control the slowing and stopping of the vehicle.

In CMVs, the brake shoes and their linings or pads are brought into contact with the brake drums or discs and held there with pressure. The pressure is created in one of three ways:

- hydraulic pressure
- vacuum pressure
- air pressure

Sometimes the pressure is used to apply the brakes when you need to stop. This is the case with hydraulic and air brakes. Vacuum brakes work the opposite way. There, pressure holds the brakes back so the wheels move freely. When you need the brakes, you take away the pressure. This releases the brakes. They apply, and stop the vehicle.

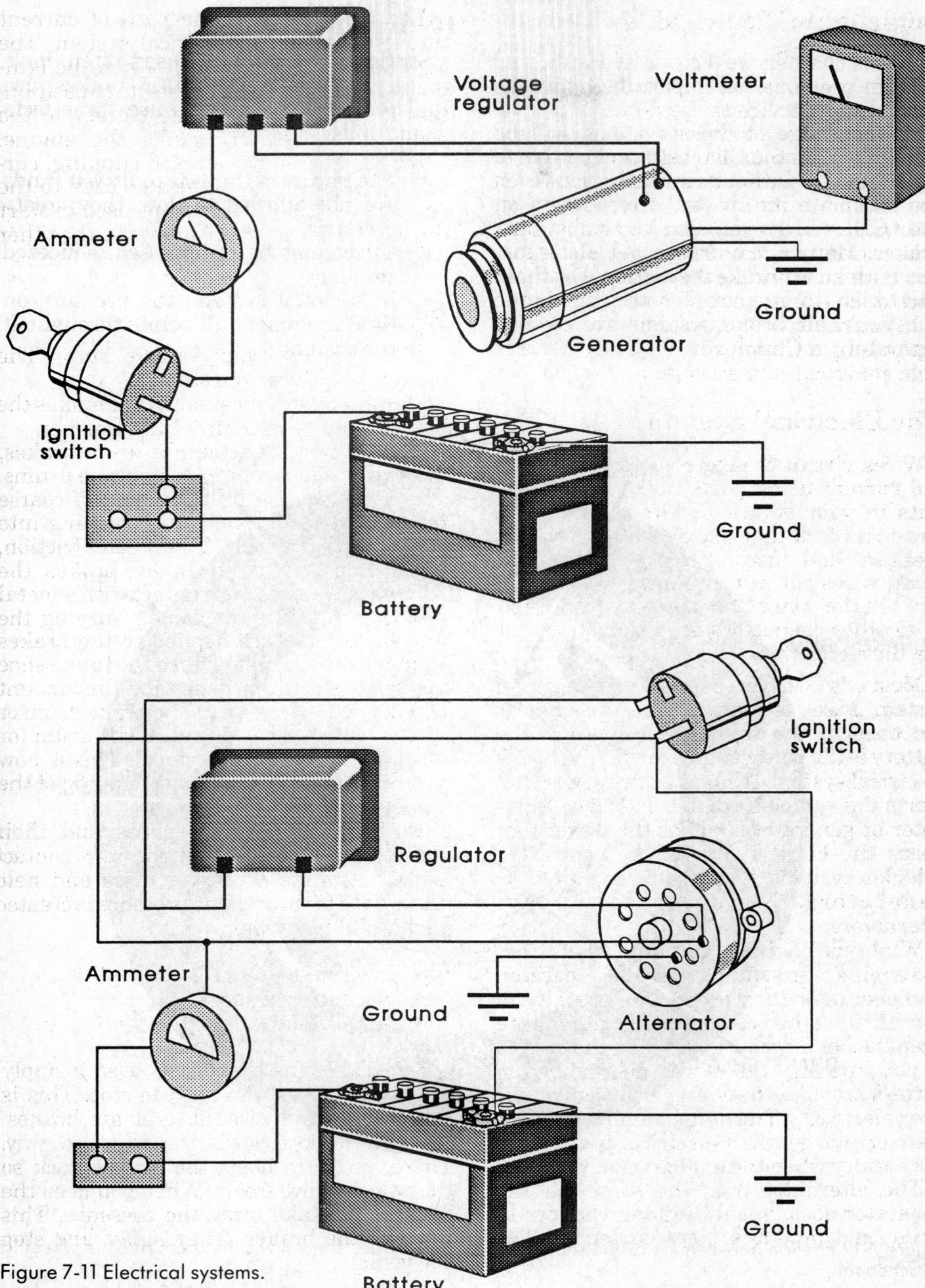

Figure 7-11 Electrical systems.

In this chapter, we'll cover hydraulic and vacuum pressure. We'll describe hydraulic and vacuum service brakes.

A knowledge of those systems will be enough to pass the CDL tests and be able to drive vehicles without air brakes. However, you will have an air brake restriction on your CDL unless you also know about air brakes. Many CMV drivers get along just fine with an air brake restriction. For those who wish to prepare for the air brake questions, air brake systems are covered separately in Chapter 11.

Hydraulic Brakes

Straight trucks and buses often have hydraulic brakes. Hydraulic brakes use fluid pressure. Hydraulics use three facts about fluids:

- The nature of fluids is to flow. If fluids are not allowed to flow, they create pressure.
- Oil cannot be compressed (squeezed smaller).
- In a closed system, the pressure on fluid is equal at all points throughout the system.

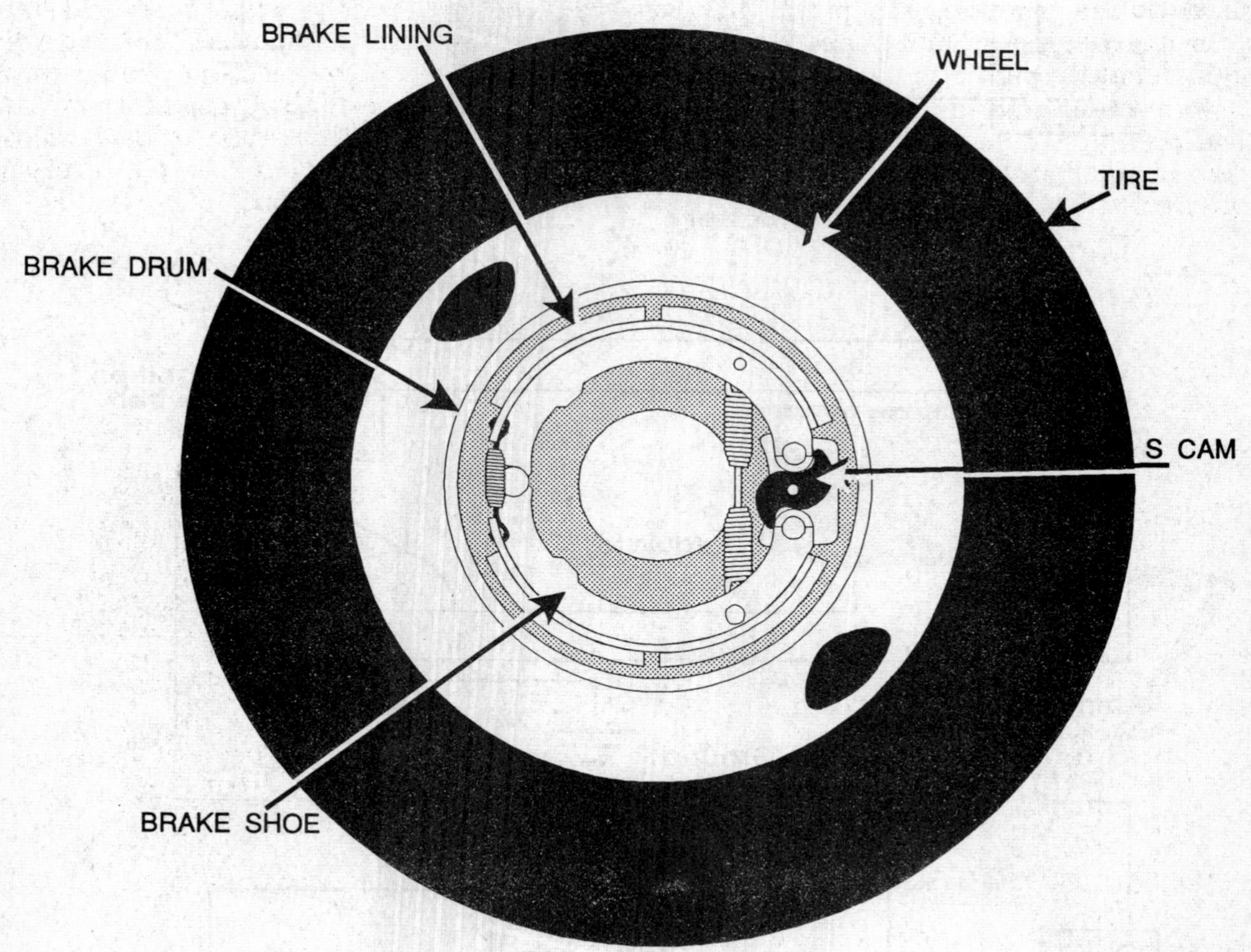

Figure 7-12 Friction between the brake shoe lining and the brake drum slows the drum and the wheel it's attached to.

Take the first point. The nature of fluids is to flow. Can you stop a fluid from flowing? The only way to do this is to put it in a container. (You may argue that you can also stop a fluid from flowing by freezing it. But then it's not liquid anymore. It's considered a solid at that point).

Take the second point. Oil cannot be compressed. You can't squeeze it into a smaller mass.

The third point is best explained by example. Look at Figure 7-13. This shows a simple closed hydraulic system. A pump or piston at the left and a cylinder supporting a weight at the right close the system. Inside the pipeline is hydraulic fluid. Pressing the handle pushes the pump or piston down. This exerts pressure on the hydraulic fluid in the pipeline. The pressure flows through the system and pushes up on the cylinder at the right.

At no point in the system is there more or less pressure. There is just as much pressure at the right, pushing the cylinder up, as there is at the left, where the piston is pushing on the fluid.

This helps explain how pressure you exert at the brake pedal in the cab is transmitted in full force to the brake down at the wheels.

A hydraulic brake system looks a lot like Figure 7-13. There are lines holding hydraulic fluid between the brake pedal and the brakes. There are cylinders at both ends. When you press the brake pedal, you move a push rod and piston in a cylinder. This cylinder is called the master cylinder. This exerts pressure on the hydraulic fluid. The pressure moves through the fluid until it meets the cylinder at the brake end (the wheel cylinder). The pressure pushes on the cylinder. The cylinder moves the brake shoe and pad into contact with the drum or disc. Friction results. The wheel slows and stops.

If oil could be compressed, this wouldn't work. Pressing the master cylinder would just squeeze the oil. But remember, oil can't be compressed. Since the system is closed, the fluid has nowhere to go. Pressure results.

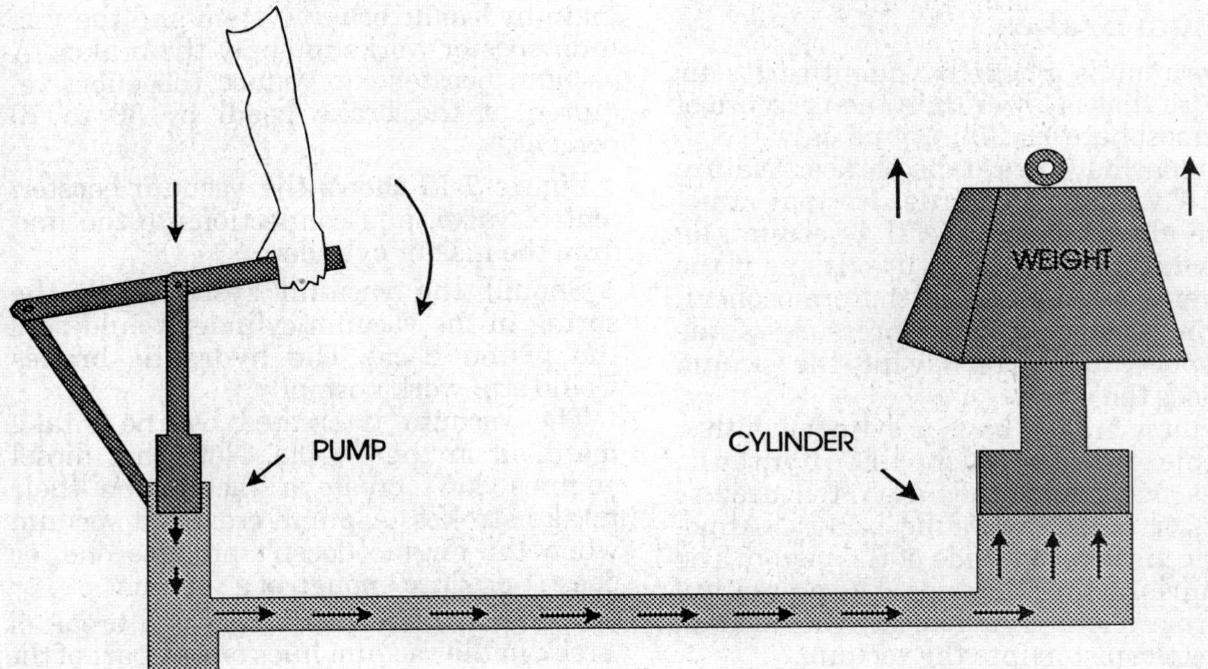

Figure 7-13 A simple hydraulic system.

Also remember, this pressure will be equal at all points in the system. When the driver presses the brake pedal, equal pressure is applied at all wheels. By making the master and wheel cylinders different sizes, you can increase the pressure applied at the brake pedal when it reaches the wheels. That way, the driver doesn't have to press very hard at all to get a lot of braking force.

What if there are breaks or leaks in the system? Right – no brakes. Since fluid must flow, it will flow out any leak it finds. If there is no fluid, there is nothing to transmit the pressure from the master cylinder to the wheel cylinders. (That's why inspecting for leaks in your braking system is so important.)

Dual brake systems help in such emergencies. They're designed with two fluid tanks and two pistons in the master cylinder. They're set up so that you will still have braking power at some wheels even if there's a leak in one of the brake lines.

Figure 7-13 showed a simple hydraulic system. A typical hydraulic brake system in a CMV would look like Figure 7-14.

Vacuum Brakes

A vacuum is a negative quantity. It's air pressure that is lower than the pressure of the atmosphere, the air around us.

You may have heard the phrase, "Nature hates a vacuum." It's true. Normal atmosphere always moves to fill a vacuum, an area with lower air pressure. It's as if the vacuum were sucking in the atmosphere, only in reverse. It's this pressure of the atmosphere forcing its way into the vacuum that does the work.

Vacuum brakes have a cylinder with a movable piston, much like hydraulic brakes. Vacuum brakes are often used to assist, or boost, hydraulic brakes. Atmospheric air is on one side of the piston. The vacuum is on the other side. The pressure of the atmosphere trying to fill the vacuum pushes the piston into the vacuum.

When the brakes are off, the piston is drawn back inside the cylinder. It's held in place by a spring. The piston has vacuum on both sides of it.

The vacuum cylinder has a control valve with four chambers. One chamber has atmospheric air. The second combines atmospheric air and vacuum to create different air pressure levels. The third chamber has a vacuum. The last chamber has hydraulic fluid.

When you press the brake pedal, hydraulic pressure from the master cylinder affects the control valve. It closes the vacuum valve and opens the atmospheric valve. This in turn allows atmospheric air to enter the second, mixing chamber. The result is lowered pressure. This closes the atmospheric valve, but you can reopen it by stepping on the brake pedal again. Letting up on the brake pedal opens the vacuum valve. You see that pressing and releasing the brake pedal changes the level of air pressure in the mixing chamber.

Pressure from the master hydraulic cylinder also affects the vacuum cylinder itself. It pushes the piston forward. The piston pushes hydraulic fluid beyond it into the brake lines. Pressure from the control valve adds to, or boosts, the pressure from the master cylinder. So pressure from both the main hydraulic brake system and the vacuum booster works to apply the brakes. A vacuum booster can reduce the effort required at the brake pedal by 30 to 70 percent.

Figure 7-15 shows the vacuum booster, control valve, and connections to the line from the master cylinder.

Should the vacuum system fail, the spring in the vacuum cylinder would hold the piston back. The hydraulic brakes would still work normally.

The vacuum is created by the intake manifold in the engine. Note that diesel engines don't create a vacuum on their intake strokes. A pump creates a vacuum when the engine doesn't produce one, or doesn't produce enough of a vacuum.

None of this works if there's a break or crack in the vacuum lines or any part of the system. Can you state why? A break allows the vacuum to leak out. Or more accurately, it allows atmosphere in, filling the vacuum. No vacuum, no brakes.

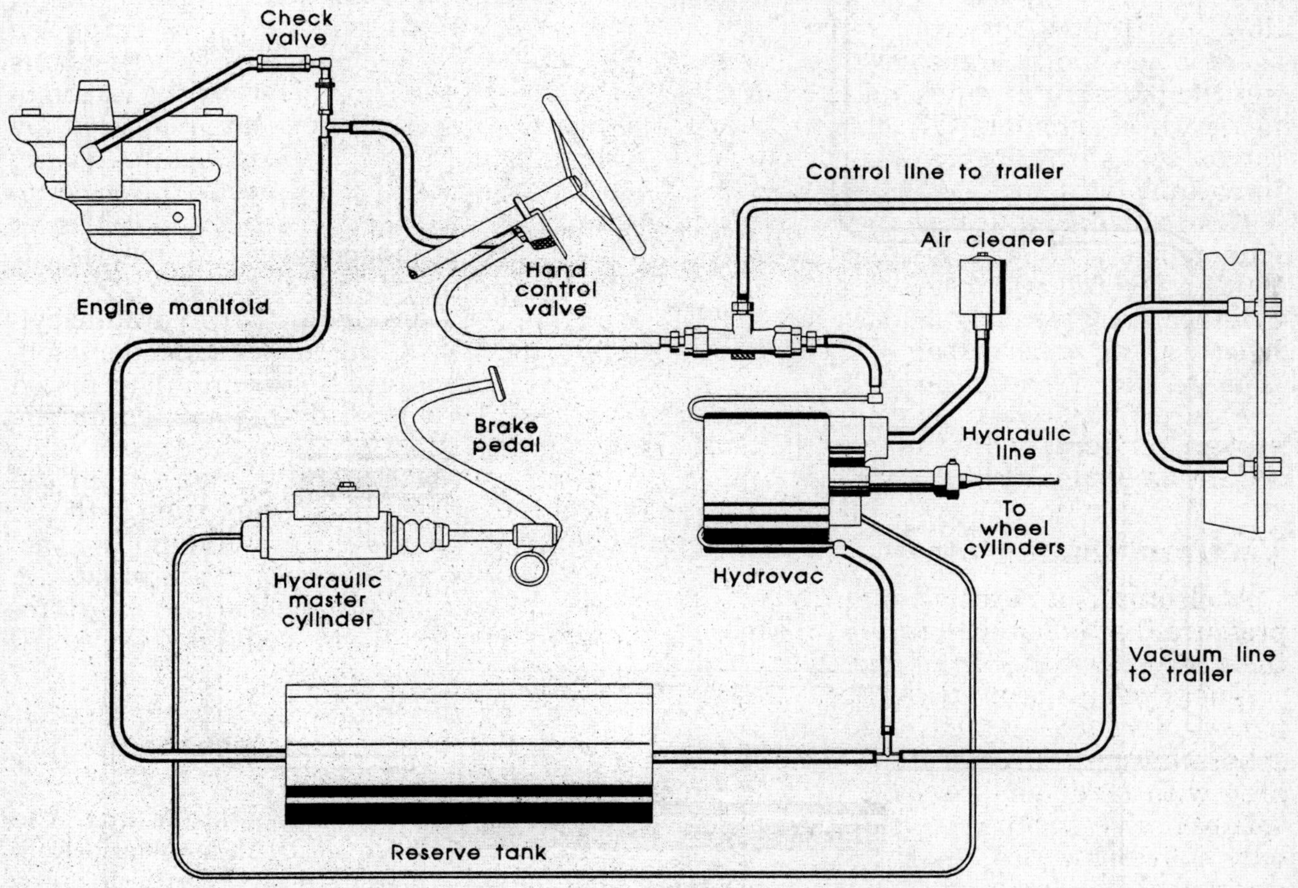

Figure 7-14 A hydraulic brake system.

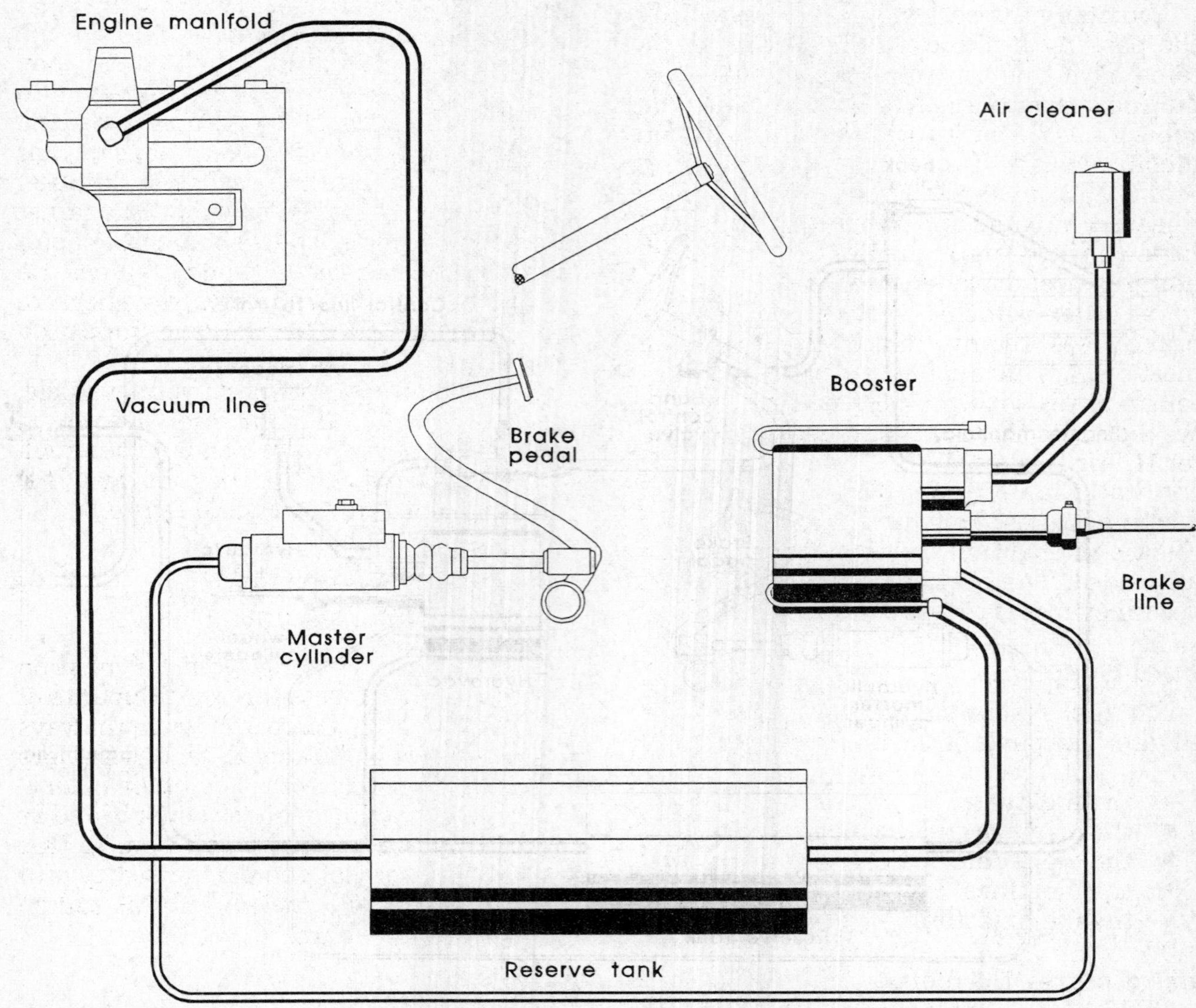

Figure 7-15 A vacuum brake system.

Parking Brakes

The parking brake system comes into play when you park. You recall nearly all CMVs made after 1989 must have parking brakes.

You apply the parking brakes by pulling the parking brake control. All brake systems have this control. On some vehicles, pulling a lever or knob controls a cable. The cable pulls the parking brakes into position mechanically. To release the parking brakes, you push the control back in. This releases the cable and the brakes. It takes a little effort to "pull" the brakes on. But it's nothing most drivers can't handle.

On other vehicles, setting the parking brake does require more strength than most drivers have. Then the parking mechanism is set with the help of air pressure. We'll discuss this system in detail in Chapter 11, Air Brakes.

Recall what FMCSR Part 393 requires of parking brakes? You must be able to set and release the manual parking brake as often as needed. The parking brake system just described meets these requirements.

Fuel Systems

The fuel system delivers the fuel to the engine. The parts of the fuel system are:

- the fuel tank
- the primary and secondary fuel filters
- the fuel pump
- the fuel lines
- the fuel injectors

and, of course, the fuel.

The fuel tank holds the fuel. Primary and secondary filters clean it before it reaches the fuel pump. The fuel pump delivers the fuel to the engine. Fuel lines carry the fuel from the pump to the cylinders. Fuel injectors spray the fuel into the combustion chambers.

Figure 7-16 traces the flow of the fuel through the fuel system. The fuel leaves the fuel tank and runs through the fuel lines to the check valve. From there, it flows through the primary and the secondary filters and into the fuel pump. The pump forces it through the fuel lines and into the fuel injectors. The injectors spray a measured amount of fuel into the cylinders.

Fuel is flammable. It can be dangerous if not handled with care. Fuel lines must not be allowed to touch hot surfaces. They must be supported so they don't drag on the ground. Keep in mind your vehicle may cross grade crossings that are higher than the regular road surface. Also, see that the fuel lines are protected from objects that can bounce up from the road. See that fuel lines are not damaged or rubbing against other vehicle parts. There should be enough slack in the lines so they won't break as the vehicle moves. You can certainly check to see that the fuel tanks are mounted securely.

Also, when you inspect your vehicle, check for leaks. If your fuel system is leaking, of course you'll lose precious fuel. But leaking fuel can also be a hazard. If it drips on a hot surface, it could ignite.

Coupling Devices and Towing Methods

Vehicles that tow other vehicles must do it in a way that meets the requirements of FMCSR Part 393. There are two main ways you will see vehicles towed. One is trailers being pulled by tractors. The other is tractors or other towing vehicles being towed as cargo. This is a towaway operation. In this section we'll look at the parts used to pull trailers. Then we'll look briefly at saddle mounts and drawbars.

Fifth Wheel

The fifth wheel allows the trailer to articulate (pivot). FMCSR Part 393 states that the towed vehicle must not trail more than three inches to either side of the tractor.

The fifth wheel also allows the trailer to oscillate (rise or drop) along with the tractor.

Of course, the fifth wheel allows you to separate the trailer from the tractor. The power unit isn't "married" to the cargo unit as it is with a straight vehicle.

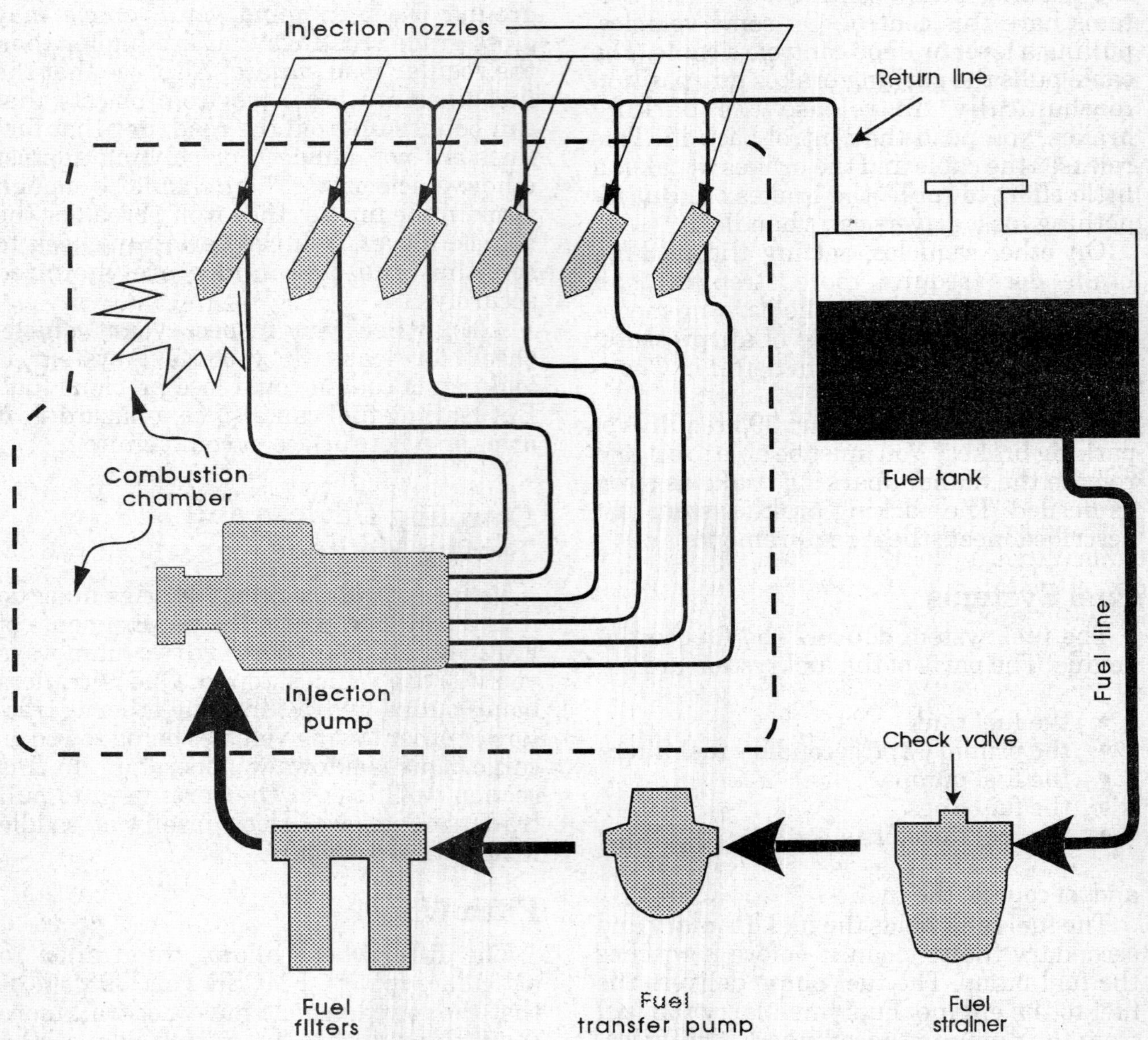

Figure 7-16 A fuel system.

The fifth wheel is mounted on the rear of the tractor frame. The proper brackets and fasteners must be used to do this. The lower half of the fifth wheel (the mounting assembly) must not shift around on the frame. There must not be any bent parts or loose bolts in the fifth wheel lower half.

The placement of the fifth wheel is important. It controls how much weight is on each axle between the front and rear of the tractor. Poor weight distribution can reduce steering control. It also causes uneven wear on tires, brakes, and wheels.

You'll find fifth wheels on converter dollies as well as on tractor frames. A converter dolly converts a semitrailer to a full trailer.

Locking Device

The fifth wheel must have a locking device. This device keeps the towed and towing vehicles together until you release them on purpose. You might refer to this locking device as the "jaws." The jaws lock around the shaft of the trailer kingpin. This makes a secure connection. Any forward or backward movement of the tractor will be transmitted to the trailer. You have to get out of the cab and manually pull a lever to open the jaws.

Tow Bars and Saddle Mounts

Tow bars and saddle mounts are used in towaway operations. When the towed vehicles have all wheels on the road, tow bars are used to connect them. A pair of safety chains or cable is used with the tow bar connection to the towing vehicle.

A saddle mount is a steel assembly used to couple a towed vehicle to the towing vehicle when only the rear wheels of the towed vehicle are on the ground.

Tires

Tires provide proper traction and reduce vibration. They absorb road shock. They transfer braking and driving force to the road. There are many different tire designs, but all tires are made about the same way.

Tires are made up of:

- plies
- bead coils and beads
- sidewalls
- tread

and the inner liner.

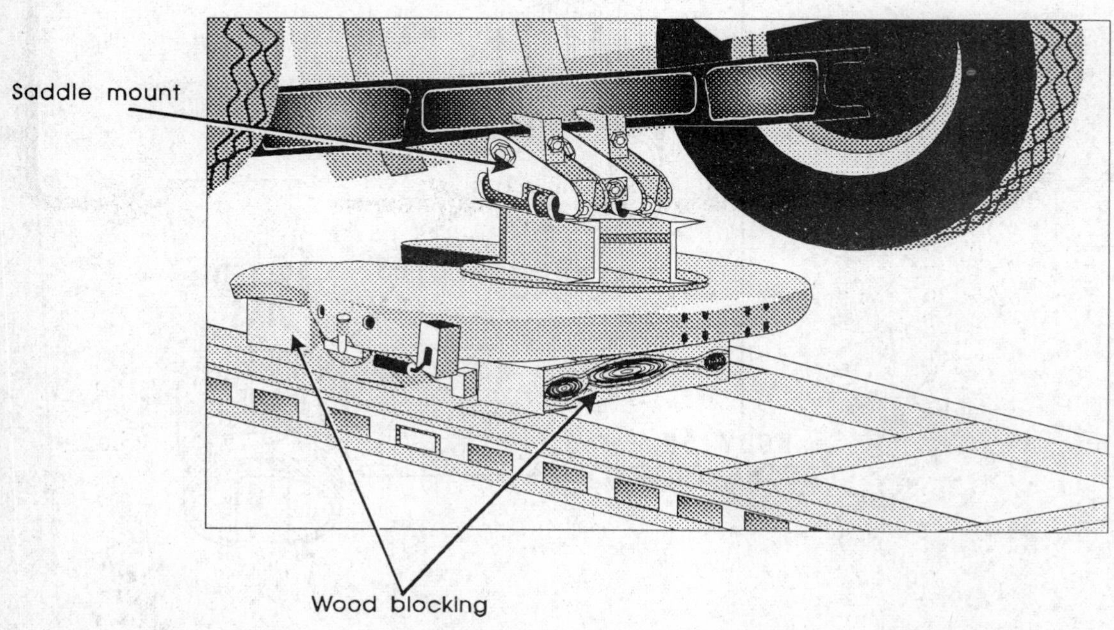

Figure 7-17 A saddle mount.

Plies consist of separate layers of rubber-cushioned cord. They make up the body of the tire. The plies are tied into bundles of wire called the bead coils.

Plies can be bias, belted bias, or radial. Bias plies are placed at a crisscross angle. This makes the sidewall and tread rigid. In a belted bias ply tire, the plies cross at an angle. There's an added layered belt of fabric between the plies and the tread. The belts make the tread of this tire more rigid than the bias ply tire. The tread lasts longer because the belts reduce tread motion when the tire is running.

In radial tires, the plies on this tire do not cross at an angle. The ply is laid from bead to bead, across the tire. Like the belted bias ply tire, the radial also has a number of belts. Radial construction supports the tread better than either the bias ply or the belted bias ply. The radial design means the sidewalls flex with less friction. That requires less horsepower and saves fuel. Radial tires also hold the road better, resist skidding better, and give a smoother ride than the bias types.

Bead coils form the bead. This is the part of the tire that fits into the rim. It secures the tire to the rim. Bead coils provide the hoop strength for the bead sections. This helps the tire hold its shape when it's being mounted on a wheel.

The sidewalls are layers of rubber covering. They connect the bead to the tread. Sidewalls protect the plies in the sidewall area.

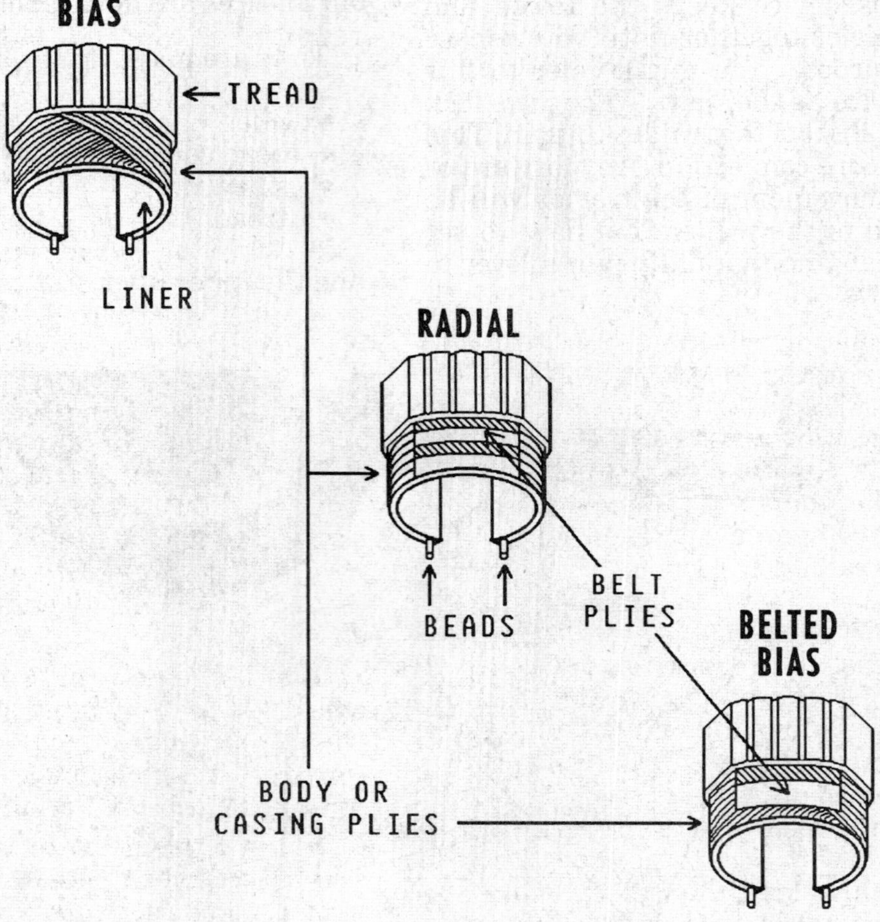

Courtesy Mike Byrnes and Associates

Figure 7-18 Cross sections of the three tire types.

The tread is the part of the tire that contacts the road. Treads are designed for specific driving jobs. Some jobs require that the tread provide extra traction. Others call for a tread designed for high-speed use. Tires on steering axles must roll well and provide good traction for cornering. Drive tires must provide good traction for both braking and acceleration. Trailer tires mostly need to roll well. Tire treads are also designed to face specific road conditions. For example, drive wheel position tires need maximum traction in rain, snow, sleet, and ice.

The inner liner is the sealing material that keeps the air in the tire.

That's the basics of tire construction.

Tire size is shown by either a number or a series design designation. You find this information on the sidewall of your tires. An example of the number designation is a 10.00 x 22 tire. The first number is the tire's width. This means the inflated tire measures 10 inches from the farthest outside point on one sidewall to the farthest outside point on the other sidewall. The second number is the rim size. Our example tire will fit a 22-inch diameter rim.

The series designation system was developed because of the low profile tire. This tire is wide in relation to its height. Once again, let's take an example to look at this. Say a tire sidewall reads 295/75 R 22.5. This means the section width is 295 millimeters. (Low profile tires are measured in millimeters rather than inches). The aspect ratio (the height compared with the width) is 75. The type is radial. The rim is 22.5 inches in diameter.

The government requires tire manufacturers to label all tires with several items of information. For example, tire labels must show the tire brand and manufacturer. Tire labels must also show the load rating and maximum load pressure.

Load rating refers to tire strength. This is rated from "A" to "Z." "Z" is the strongest. The maximum load the tire can carry in terms of weight is shown in pounds. FMCSR Part 393 states you must not use a tire that is too weak to support the load. The load rating helps you select the right tire for the load.

The maximum pressure is shown in psi. It is given for cold tires that have been driven for less than one mile. This is why you check tire pressure before you drive. Don't try to check tire pressure by hitting your tires with a stick or a billy or by kicking them. These methods will tell you a tire is not completely flat. But they will not give you an accurate tire pressure reading. Instead, use a calibrated tire gauge. It wouldn't hurt to have one and know how to use it when you inspect your vehicle for the CDL test.

All this pertains mainly to new tires. Used tires can sometimes be made like new. These are regrooved tires and recaps or retreads.

A regrooved tire is one in which the grooves in the tread have been cut deeper into the surface of a tire that is nearly worn down to the legal minimum. A retreaded, or recapped, tire has had the old tread surface removed. Then new tread is bonded to the outside layers of the belts or body plies.

The legal minimum for tire tread depth is set in FMCSR Part 393. A motor vehicle must not use tires that

- have any fabric exposed through the tread or sidewalls.
- have less than 4/32 of an inch of tread measured at any point in a major tread groove on the front axle.
- have less than 2/32 of an inch of tread measured at any point in a major tread groove on all other axles.
- have front tires that have been regrooved, if the tires have a load-carrying capacity equal to or greater than an 8.25-20 eight ply tire.

Buses must not have regrooved tires on the front wheels. Most states do not allow the front tires of any vehicle to be regrooved. You must make yourself aware of any such local regulations.

You should measure tread depth when you inspect your vehicle. When you make groove measurements, you must not make them at a tie bar, hump, or fillet. A hump is a pattern of tire wear that looks a little like a cupped hand. The hump is the edge or higher part of the cup. Tie bars and fillets are not patterns of tire wear. They are design factors. So is a sipe. Sipes are cut across the tread to improve traction on wet road surfaces.

You must take the tread depth measurement on a major tread groove. Find a spot where the way is clear all the way to the body of the tire. See Figure 7-19.

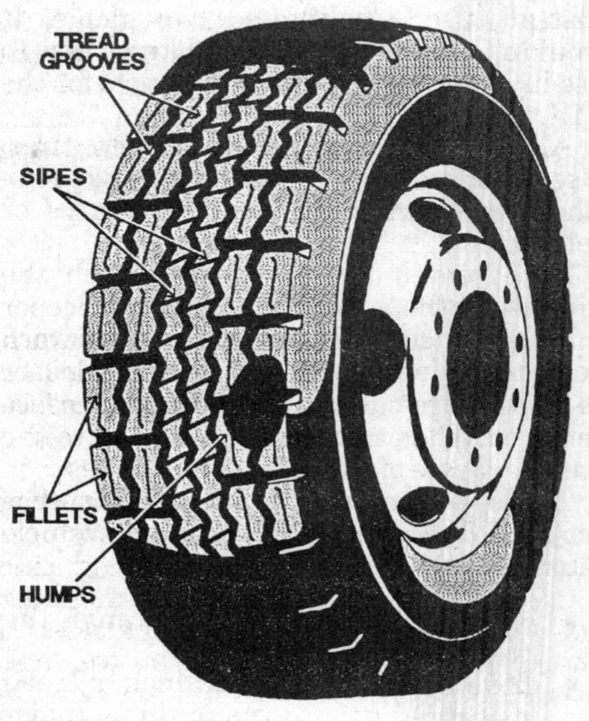

Courtesy Mike Byrnes and Associates

Figure 7-19 Measure tread depth in a major tread groove, not on a hump or in a fillet or sipe.

You can use a special tread depth gauge for this. Or you could use a common Lincoln-head penny. Insert the penny in the groove, with Lincoln's head upside down. The edge of the penny touches the body of the tire. The tread should come up to the top of Lincoln's head. That's about 2/32 of an inch. For 4/32 of an inch, the tread should come up to Lincoln's eyebrow.

Regrooved tires, recaps, and retreads, then, can be used on drive wheels and trailer wheels. They cannot be used on steering, or front, wheels on buses and most trucks.

Wheels

Wheels provide a mounting for the tires. The wheel supports and connects the tire to the vehicle axle. There are spoke wheels and disc wheels.

Spoke wheels use separate rims. They are clamped onto the wheels with wheel clamps. If the wheel clamps are not installed just right, the wheel may be out of round and wobble.

The rim and center portion of the disc wheel are one piece. The rim is part of the wheel and the wheel is bolted to the hub and brake drum assembly. No clamp is used. There is less chance of the wheel being out of round. A wheel that is out of round or wobbling is said to be not true running.

The rim's job is to support the tire bead and the lower sidewall.

Neither the wheel nor the rim should be cracked or broken. The stud or bolt holes on the wheels should be perfectly round. When you inspect your vehicle, look for holes that are egg-shaped (out-of-round). These are signs of defects. All the nuts and bolts should be in place, tightened down.

Cracked or broken wheels or rims can cause an accident. A damaged rim can cause the tire to lose pressure or come off. Missing clamps, spacers, studs, and lugs can cause problems. Mismatched, bent, or cracked lock rings are dangerous. If you see signs that the wheels or rims have been repaired by welding repairs, note that as a defect.

Rust around wheel nuts may mean the nuts are loose. Use a wrench to check tightness. You can't judge tightness well enough with just your hands. (If you have just had a tire changed, stop after you have driven on the new tire a while. Double-check to see that the nuts have not loosened.)

Make sure there is a good supply of oil in the hub. Check the oil level mark on the hub cap window. Check that there are no leaks.

Suspension System

The suspension supports the vehicle's weight. It keeps the frame from resting directly on the axles. It provides a smoother ride for the driver and the cargo. The suspension absorbs road shocks. Your vehicle may have one of the following suspension types:

- leaf spring
- coil spring
- torsion bar
- air bag

In a leaf-spring suspension, layers of flexible metal are bolted together. The axle rests on the middle of the spring. The front and rear of the spring are attached to the frame.

Courtesy Mike Byrnes and Associates

Figure 7-20 A multi-leaf front suspension.

A coil spring suspension puts a spiral of heavy-duty metal at each wheel. The top of the coil is attached to the frame, while the bottom is indirectly connected to the wheel.

Torsion bars absorb shock by twisting. They're made of special metal that returns to its original shape even after it's been twisted.

In these suspension types, the metal contracts and extends, or twists, in response to bumps or low spots in the road. This allows the wheel to move up and down with the road surface, while the frame remains level.

Your vehicle may have an air bag suspension instead of leaf springs or coils. The air bags are made of rubber fabric and are supplied with compressed air. The air supply allows the bag to expand or shrink, just as springs contract or extend.

Shock absorbers are attached to the springs. These are cylinders partly filled with hydraulic fluid. A piston moves up and down in the cylinder in response to the action of the spring. This helps to lessen the amount of springing motion that's transmitted to the driver.

Springs must always be in good condition. Suspension system defects can reduce your ability to control the vehicle.

Air bags are subject to leaks and valve problems. With air bag suspensions, the braking system should get charged with air before the air bag does. The air pressure valve on the air bag should not let air into the suspension until the braking system has at least 55 psi. The air bags should fill evenly all around. Otherwise, the vehicle will not be level. When the vehicle's air pressure gauge reads "normal," there should be no air leakage greater than 3 psi over five minutes.

Steering

The steering system enables the vehicle to change direction and get around corners. A good steering system provides precise rolling, without slipping, when you turn a corner or take a curve.

The wheel in your hands is the steering wheel. It controls the wheels on the road that are connected to the steering axle. Between the steering wheel and the steering axle are the parts that make steering possible. Figure 7-21 shows you the basic steering components. You can see how the steering action flows through the system.

The steering wheel is connected to the steering column by a nut. The steering wheel transfers the driver's movements to the steering system.

As you turn the steering wheel, the column turns in the same direction. This turning motion continues through the U-joint to the steering gear shaft. From there the motion continues through another U-joint to the steering gear box. The steering gear box is also called the steering sector. It changes the rotating motion of the steering column to the reciprocating (back and forth) motion of the Pitman arm. The Pitman arm is a lever attached to the steering gear box. The drag link joins the Pitman arm and the steering lever.

The steering lever is the first part of the steering axle. The steering, or front, axle does two jobs. First, it carries a load just like other axles. Second, it steers the vehicle.

The steering lever turns the front wheels left and right when the Pitman arm pulls it back and forth. The steering lever is connected to the steering knuckle. This is a movable connection between the axle and the wheels. It allows the wheels to turn left or right.

There is a steering knuckle at the end of each axle. The steering knuckles contain the seals, bushings, and bearings that support the vehicle's weight. The steering knuckles transfer motion to the cross steering lever and the cross steering tube.

The spindles are the parts of the steering axle knuckles that are inserted through the wheels.

The cross steering tube, or tie rod, holds both wheels in the same position. As the left wheel turns, the right wheel moves in the same direction. A kingpin in the steering knuckle allows each wheel to have its own pivot point. The wheel rotates on a spindle. The spindle is also called the stub axle. It's attached to the kingpin.

Your vehicle may have manual or power steering. Power steering systems use hydraulic pressure or air pressure to assist the mechanical linkage in making the turn. You use less of your strength to turn the steering wheel.

When hydraulic pressure is used to assist steering, a hydraulic unit replaces the steering gear box. A hydraulic pump is added to the engine to supply the pressure used to help turn the wheels. When you turn the steering wheel to the right, the hydraulic valve senses it. A valve opens. Fluid pressure helps turn the wheels to the right.

That's it – a quick tour through the major systems in most commercial motor vehicles. Now you know how wiring and electrical, braking and fuel systems, coupling devices, tires, emergency equipment, body components, and suspension and steering systems support your vehicle.

All these systems and equipment are "necessary for safe operation," according to the FMCSR. The CDL examiner may and probably will ask you questions about some or all of these. You must be able to identify the parts on your vehicle. You must be able to give a basic description of how they work. You must be able to recognize defects, and state how they affect safe operations.

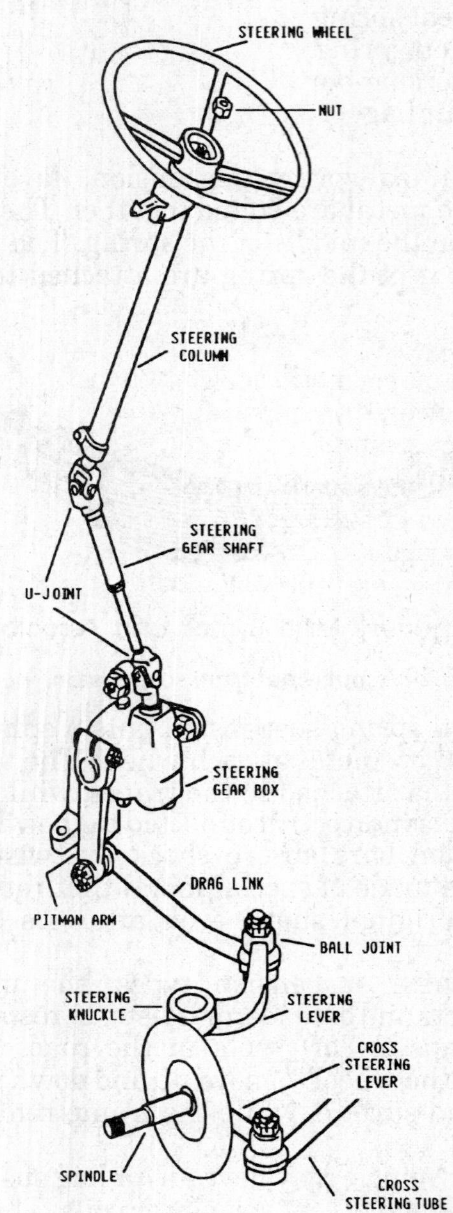

Figure 7-21 These components make up all types of steering systems, whether manual or power.

EMERGENCIES

It's not enough to know how to operate your vehicle under normal conditions. FMCSR Part 393 states you must know how to use these systems and controls in emergencies. Two examples are mentioned. They are skids and loss of brakes. Of course there are others. The next chapter, on basic vehicle control, includes emergency maneuvers.

PASS POST-TRIP

Instructions: For each true/false test item, read the statement. Decide whether the statement is true or false. If it is true, select the letter "A." If it is false, select the letter "B." For each multiple-choice test item, choose the answer choice – A, B, C, or D – that correctly completes the statement or answers the question. There is only one correct answer.

1. When you first start your engine, you should get a normal reading on the dashboard's ______ within a few seconds.
A. oil pressure gauge
B. fuel pressure gauge
C. tire pressure temperature gauge
D. all of the above

2. The proper way to use a fire extinguisher is douse the flames with the dry chemical.
A. True
B. False

3. Regrooved tires are prohibited for use on the ______.
A. rear wheels of buses, but may be used on the front wheels
B. rear wheels of trucks, but may be used on the front wheels.
C. front and rear wheels of buses
D. front wheels of buses, and often trucks as well

4. A vehicle will have either warning lights or warning buzzers, but not both.
A. True
B. False

5. Warning lights tell you ______.
A. a control is working
B. a control or gauge is **not** working
C. there is a serious problem with a part or system
D. any of the above

6. If the low vacuum warning light comes on while you are driving, you should ______.
A. note it and plan to fix it when you arrive at your destination
B. feel confident the brake system is working properly
C. stop as soon as it is safe to do so
D. look for a blown fuse or loose wire

7. ______ at the top governed speed is the proper way to operate your vehicle.
A. Driving
B. Stopping
C. Idling
D. Shifting

8. Broken wires should be ______.
A. reconnected
B. replaced
C. restripped
D. regauged

9. You can skip checking the battery fluid level during your pre-trip inspection if ______.
A. you are confident the level is at "FULL"
B. you added fluid within the past 24 hours
C. your battery is the "maintenance-free type"
D. none of the above

10. Vehicles with diesel engines don't have vacuum brakes because diesel engines don't create a vacuum on the intake stroke.
A. True
B. False

CHAPTER 8
Basic Vehicle Control

When you have finished this chapter, you will be able to provide the correct answers to questions about basic vehicle control, including:

- shifting gears
- backing
- visual awareness while driving
- communicating with other drivers
- controlling speed
- managing space
- driving at night
- driving in adverse conditions
- road hazards
- emergency maneuvers
- controlling skids
- accident procedures

To complete this chapter you will need:

- a dictionary
- pencil or pen
- blank paper or notebook
- colored pencils, pens, markers, or highlighters
- a CDL preparation manual from your state Department of Motor Vehicles, if one is offered
- Federal Motor Carrier Safety Regulations pocketbook (or access to U.S. Department of Transportation regulations, Parts 383, 393, and 396 of Subchapter B, Chapter 3, Title 49, Code of Federal Regulations)
- operator's manual for your vehicle

PASS PRE-TRIP

Instructions: Read the statements. Decide whether each statement is true or false. If it is true, circle the letter "A." If it is false, circle the letter "B."

1. Rough acceleration can not only damage the vehicle, it can cause you to lose control.
A. True
B. False

2. "Fanning the brakes" is a recommended downhill braking tactic.
A. True
B. False

3. You may hear a tire blow before you feel it.
A. True
B. False

As you know, Part Two of this book is about the knowledge and skill you must have to get your CDL. Chapters 5, 6, and 7 contained the facts you must have to have the "knowledge." This chapter, and the chapters to come, are more about "skills." As you read them, keep this in mind. You must practice to become skilled. We can describe a procedure or maneuver for you. To be skilled at that procedure or maneuver, you must practice it. The more you practice, the better you become. The goal is for the skill to become second nature to you. Practice what you read about in Chapters 8, 9, and 10.

This chapter began with a long list of skills licensed CMV drivers must have. Who says you need to know this stuff to be a good driver? If you have a copy of the FMCSR, turn to it now. Does it include Subpart G? This is a list of the required knowledge and skills CMV drivers must have to earn a CDL. It tells you that you must know:

- the importance of visual search
- techniques for controlling the space around the vehicle
- the causes and major types of skids

among other things.

Unless you're already an expert at everything in Subpart G, you'll find this chapter helpful. This chapter fleshes out the required knowledge and skill areas listed in Subpart G.

By reviewing the FMCSR in Chapter 6, you've become well acquainted (or reacquainted) with the safe operating regulations (Item a). In Chapter 7, you brushed up on CMV safety control systems. Let's continue with Subpart G and cover safe vehicle control.

SAFE VEHICLE CONTROL

To drive a vehicle safely, you must be able to control its speed and direction. Safe operation of a commercial vehicle requires skill in:

- accelerating
- steering
- shifting gears
- braking

Preparing to Drive

You must be in complete command of the vehicle, its systems and controls. If the vehicle is new to you, prepare to drive by getting to know the vehicle first. Look it over before you start it. A good driver never starts the engine without first inspecting the vehicle. We'll discuss vehicle inspections in more detail in Chapter 10.

Before you climb in, look at the handhold and the steps to make sure they are free of dirt and grease. For large vehicles, use the three-point stance to enter the cab. Use either both hands and one foot or both feet and one hand to enter the cab.

Pull yourself in behind the wheel. Adjust your seat so you're in the correct sitting position. Your left foot should rest comfortably on the floor. The seat should not be putting pressure on the underside of your leg. When your right foot is on the accelerator, your right knee should be slightly bent. Sit high up enough to have good visibility. Sit close enough to the steering wheel so you can reach the top of it by leaning forward slightly.

Some driver's seats have weight and height controls and suspension systems that allow for a smooth ride even on bumpy roads. If you are too high or too low to see and reach for the controls, look for the seat adjuster.

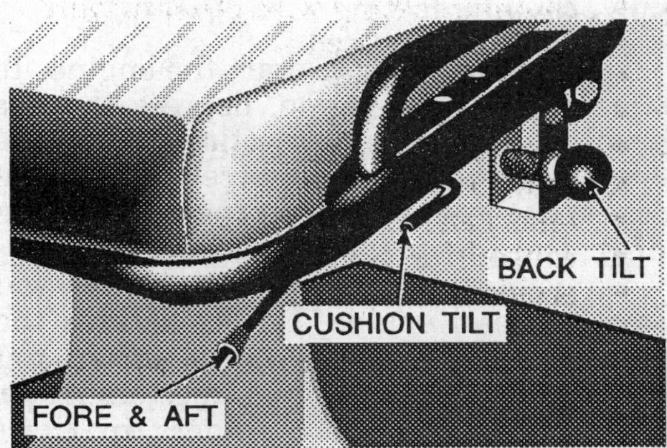

Figure 8-1 Adjust your seat so you have clear vision and your hands and feet can reach all the controls.

Adjust the rear view mirrors. Check the left mirror. You should be able to see the left side of your vehicle in the right edge. Near the bottom of the mirror you should see the rear portion of the vehicle at ground level. The horizon line should be ¾ of the way up the mirror.

When the right mirror is properly adjusted, you should see the right side of the vehicle in the left edge. Again, the horizon line should be about ¾ of the way up the mirror.

The convex mirror amplifies the right side mirror view. Keep in mind, this view is distorted. Don't use it to judge distances. Use it only to spot objects near the vehicle. If you see something in your convex mirror, you know that it is close enough to be dangerous.

Find the ignition or master switch. Put the key in the switch, but don't turn it on. Find the parking brake. Be sure it's set. Look at the transmission shift lever to see what type it is. Look for the shifting pattern. It will be posted in the cab. You'll also find a picture of the shift pattern in the operator's manual.

If you have an automatic transmission, put it in "Park." If it's manual, grab the gear shift lever, depress the clutch, and place the lever in the neutral position. Let the clutch pedal out and sit back and locate the cab controls and gauges described in Chapter 7.

Fasten your seat belt.

Starting

Now you're ready to start the engine. To start a gasoline engine, depress the gas pedal at least once to the floor. When the engine starts, press the accelerator to increase the rpm and keep the engine running. This pumps gas into the engine.

Do not depress the fuel pedal when you start a diesel engine. Do not depress the pedal when the engine starts, either. You don't need to, because fuel injectors meter diesel fuel into the cylinders in exact amounts. Instead, press the clutch pedal to the floor and hold it there.

Turn the key. This causes electricity from the batteries to flow to the starter motor. The starter motor turns the flywheel and cranks the engine. The air and fuel ignites in each cylinder in turn, driving down the pistons and turning the crankshaft. As soon as the engine fires, release the key.

The engine is now running. Before you let the clutch out smoothly and slowly, make sure the gear shift lever is in neutral position ("P" or "Park" for automatic transmissions). If the transmission is in gear when you let the clutch out, the vehicle could lurch forward or backward. You can cause an accident by thinking the transmission is in neutral or park when it isn't.

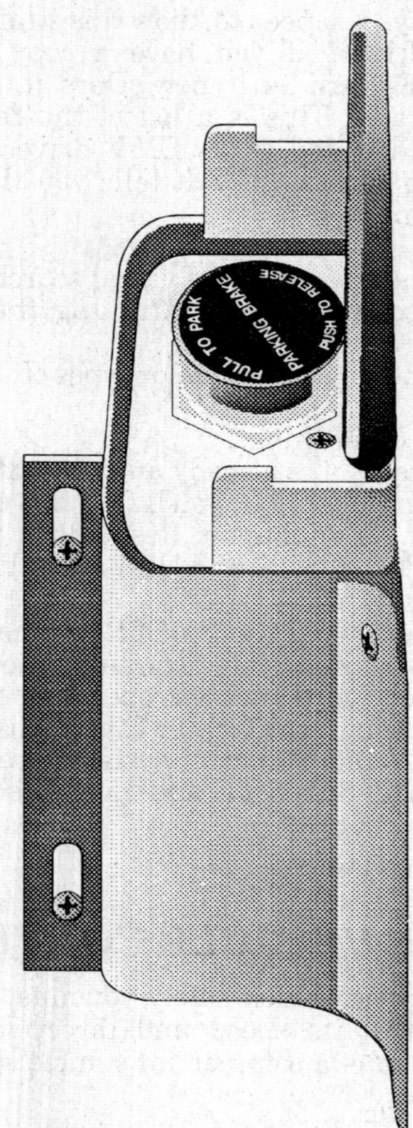

Figure 8-2 Parking brake.

Another reason you depress the clutch when you start a diesel engine is to let the starter turn as fast as it can. The transmission is filled with heavy gear oil that thickens in cold weather. If you don't depress the clutch pedal, the shaft will turn inside the transmission. This creates resistance, or drag, and slows the starter motor. If the starter motor turns the engine too slowly, the engine may not start.

The best rule is to start the engine with the clutch pedal down to the floor. Doing it every time will ensure safety and better starting.

Warm-up

Engines work best when they're warm. Give gasoline engines about five minutes for the engine to warm up before you put the vehicle into motion.

A diesel engine should warm up to at least 120 degrees Fahrenheit before you engage the clutch and start rolling. Recall the normal operating temperature? It's between 170 and 195 degrees Fahrenheit. Check your operator's manual to see what's normal for your vehicle.

The diesel fuel and air mixture ignites best at high temperatures. The lubricating oil in the engine flows best when warm. You can start the vehicle moving as soon as the air and oil pressures are up. Do not try to use full engine power until the engine has reached its operating temperature.

Your operator's manual will tell you the correct idling rpm. Automatic transmissions idle at higher rpm than manual. A warm-up or fast idle switch will cause an even higher idling rpm. If you don't have a warm-up switch, adjust engine speed with the hand throttle rather than the accelerator. Find the lowest speed at which the engine will run smoothly.

Don't roll back when you start. You might hit someone behind you. Partly engage the clutch before you take your right foot off the brake. Put on the parking brake if that helps to keep from rolling back. Release the parking brake only when you have applied enough engine power to keep from rolling back.

Accelerating

Speed up smoothly and gradually so the vehicle does not jerk. Rough acceleration can cause mechanical damage. If you're pulling a trailer, rough acceleration can damage the coupling. Speed up very gradually when traction is poor, as in rain or snow. If you use too much power, the drive wheels may spin. You can then lose control. If the drive wheels begin to spin, take your foot off the accelerator.

Steering

Hold the wheel correctly. Use both hands. Your hands should be on opposite sides of the wheel. Unless you have a firm hold, the wheel could pull away from your hands if you hit a curb or pothole.

Imagine the steering wheel is a clock. Put one hand at 10 o'clock and one hand at 2 o'clock. Rest your thumbs along the top of the wheel; don't wrap them around it. Your hand could be injured if the wheel were to turn sharply or quickly.

When turning, don't cross your arms over the steering wheel. Pick up your hands one at a time and reposition them. Your left hand should not go past 12 o'clock when you turn right. Your right hand should not go past 12 o'clock when you turn left. You'll have good control of the wheel using this method.

Shifting

It's important to shift correctly. If you can't get your vehicle into the right gear while driving, you will have less control.

If you have a tachometer, use it as a guide. Your operator's manual will tell you what the operating rpm range is for your vehicle. Engine rpm is not the same thing as road speed (mph). Still, you may hear proper shifting technique called "matching" your engine rpm to your road speed.

Watch your tachometer, and shift up when your engine reaches the top of the range. (Some newer vehicles use "progressive" shifting. The rpm at which you shift becomes higher as you move up in the gears. Find out what's right for the vehicle you will operate.)

Or you could use road speed (mph). Learn what speeds each gear is good for. Then, by using the speedometer, you'll know when to shift up.

With either method, you may learn to use engine sounds to know when to shift.

Most heavy vehicles with manual transmissions require double clutching to change gears. This is the basic upshifting method:

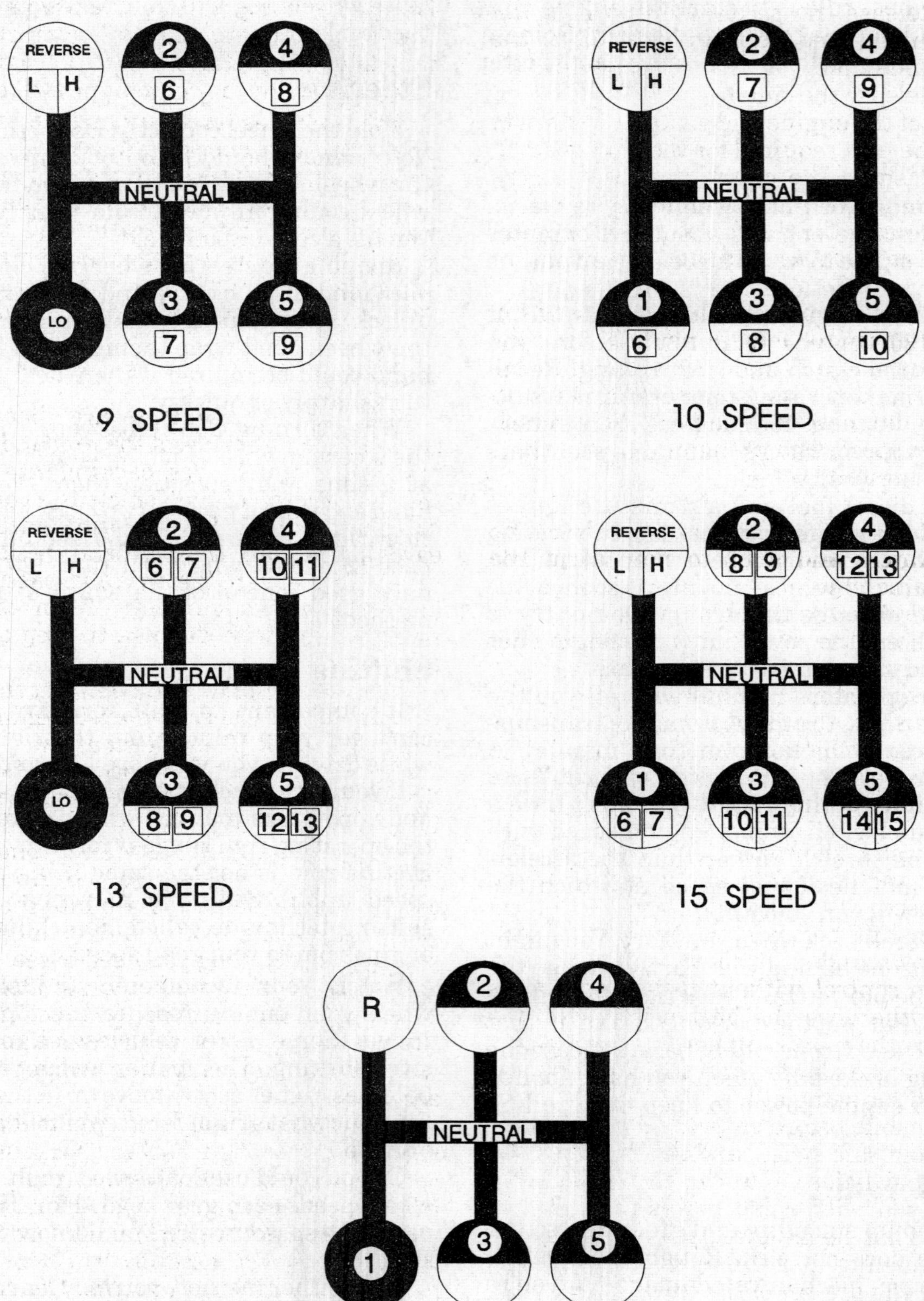

Figure 8-3 Shift patterns.

1. Release the accelerator, push in the clutch, and shift to neutral at the same time.
2. Release the clutch.
3. Let the engine and gears slow down to the rpm required for the next gear.
4. Push in the clutch and shift to the higher gear at the same time.
5. Release the clutch and press the accelerator at the same time.

Double clutching well requires practice. If you remain too long in neutral, you may find it hard to put the vehicle into the next gear. If so, don't try to force it. Remain in neutral. Increase the engine speed to match the road speed, and try again.

To downshift:

1. Release the accelerator, push in the clutch, and shift to neutral at the same time.
2. Release the clutch.
3. Press the accelerator, increase the engine and gear speed to the rpm required in the lower gear.
4. Push in the clutch and shift to lower gear at the same time.
5. Release the clutch and press the accelerator at the same time.

Again watch the tachometer or the speedometer and downshift at the right rpm or road speed.

Downshift before starting down a hill. Slow down and shift down to a speed that you can control without using the brakes hard. Otherwise the brakes can overheat and lose their braking power. Usually you shift to a gear lower than the one you used to climb the same hill.

Downshift before entering a curve. Slow down to a safe speed, and downshift to the right gear before entering the curve. This leaves you with some power through the curve. That helps keep the vehicle stable while turning. It also lets you speed up as soon as you are out of the curve.

Many vehicles have multi-speed rear axles and auxiliary transmissions. These provide extra gears. You usually control them by a selector knob or switch on the gearshift lever of the main transmission. There are many different shift patterns. Your operator's manual will picture your vehicle's shift pattern. Learn the right way to shift gears in the vehicle you will drive.

Some vehicles have automatic transmissions. You can choose a low range to get greater engine braking when going down grades. The lower ranges prevent the transmission from shifting up beyond the selected gear (unless the governor rpm is exceeded). It is very important to use this braking effect when going down grades.

Backing

Most backing accidents are those that occur on the right side, at the rear and at the top of your vehicle. Yes, backing into something at the top of the vehicle is a common backing accident. Low-hanging wires and eaves can damage the overhead area of your vehicle. Make sure the area above is clear of anything that might tear off an exhaust stack or otherwise damage the top of your cab.

Backing accidents often occur at the rear of the vehicle. Check the area behind you before you back. Then check again.

Most backing accidents occur on the right side because of the right side blind spot. The blind spot reaches from the right side door to the rearmost trailer axle and from about midway down the door to the ground. A spotter mirror helps you see into the blind spot. But even a spotter mirror might not show you everything you need to see.

Backing takes your complete attention. Turn off the radio and the CB, too. The less there is to distract you, the less likely you will be to lose concentration and get into an accident.

Always check the area you're backing into before you begin backing. Get out of the vehicle, walk behind it, and visually check the area. Even if you're just backing up in a straight line, get out and take a good look at the area. Never assume you will catch everything with your mirrors. Don't forget to look at the top and under your vehicle. Always check just before you begin backing. You may have to get out and check the area after each few feet of backing.

Use your mirrors. Watch both sides of the

vehicle. Don't open your door and lean out of it. That makes it impossible to use the right side mirror.

Never back up without putting on your emergency flashers. Your emergency flashers warn others that you are about to do something they need to watch out for. So will a couple of light taps on your horn.

Your vehicle may be equipped with a back-up alarm and back-up lights. The alarm will sound and the lights will go on automatically when you shift into reverse. A tell-tale light on the dash will tell you the back-up lights are on.

Part of the CDL Skills Test tests your backing ability. You'll be asked to perform several backing maneuvers, from straight-line backing to a backward serpentine. A backward serpentine requires you to turn to the left, then to the right, then to the left again, all while going backward. You'll find guidelines that will help you practice backing in Chapter 16.

Backing with a Trailer

Backing with a trailer requires special techniques. If you plan to take your CDL test in a tractor-trailer combination, it's vital you master these backing techniques.

Briefly, here's the idea behind backing with a trailer. When backing a straight vehicle, turn the top of the steering wheel toward the direction you want to go. When backing a trailer, turn the steering wheel in the opposite direction. This is called "jacking the trailer." Once the trailer starts to turn, you must turn the wheel the other way to follow the trailer. This is, in fact, called "following the trailer."

Slowing and Stopping

It's one thing to be able to start, shift, and steer your vehicle. It's quite another to be able to slow and stop it safely. If you can't stop a 20,000-plus pound vehicle when you want to, you cannot say you are in control.

Of course you can use the brakes to slow the vehicle. In some situations, you can downshift. There's still another way to slow the vehicle. Some vehicles have auxiliary brakes (engine retarders). By helping to slow a vehicle, they reduce the need for using your brakes. They reduce brake wear and give you another way to slow down.

There are many types of retarders (exhaust, engine, hydraulic, electric). All retarders can be turned on or off by the driver. On some the retarding power can be adjusted. When turned "on," retarders apply their braking power (to the drive wheels only) whenever you let up on the accelerator pedal all the way.

Caution. *When your drive wheels have poor traction, the retarder may cause them to skid. Therefore, you should turn the retarder off whenever the road is wet, icy, or snow-covered.*

Shutting Down

Allow the engine to idle for at least three minutes before you turn the engine off (longer if you have a turbocharger). This keeps lubrication flowing while hot engine

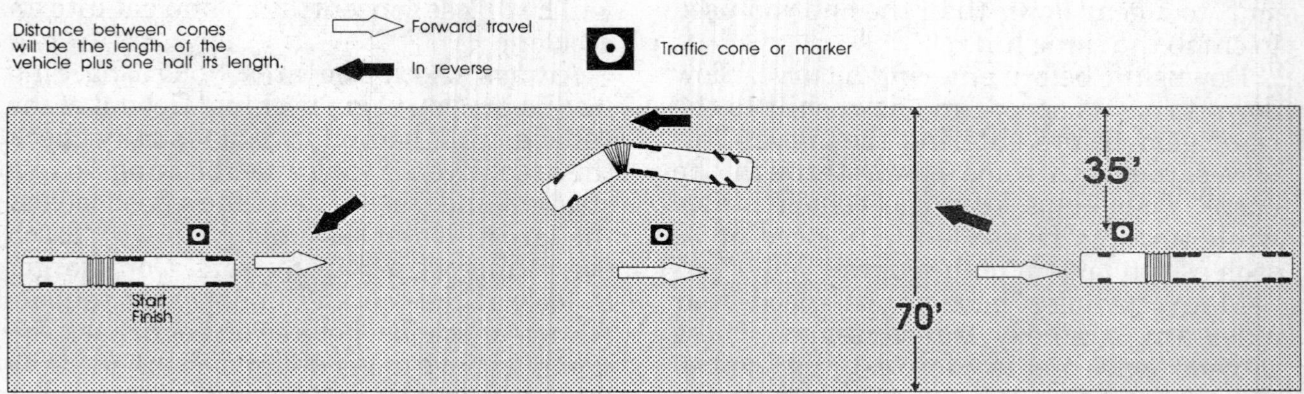

Figure 8-4 The CDL Skills Test will test your backing ability.

parts cool off. Never stop the engine with the accelerator pedal pressed. You could damage the governor. Always stop the engine from idle.

You may have an engine emergency stop. Use this only when the master switch fails to stop the engine.

Apply the parking brake when you leave your vehicle.

VISUAL ALERTNESS

To be a safe driver, you need to know what's going on all around your vehicle. Not being visually alert is a major cause of accidents.

Looking Ahead

All drivers look ahead, but many don't look far enough ahead. Stopping or changing lanes can take a lot of distance. You must know what the traffic is doing on all sides of you. Look well ahead to make sure you have room to make these moves safely.

Most good drivers look 12 to 15 seconds ahead. That means looking ahead the distance you will travel in 12 to 15 seconds. In city traffic, that's about a block and a half. At highway speeds, it's about a quarter of a mile. If you're not looking that far ahead, you may have to stop too quickly or make quick lane changes. Looking that far ahead doesn't mean not paying attention to things that are closer. Good drivers shift their attention back and forth, near and far.

What should you look for? Look for vehicles coming onto the highway or into your lane or turning. Watch for brake lights from slowing vehicles. By seeing these things far enough ahead, you can prepare to slow down or change lanes if necessary to avoid a problem.

Observe the shape and condition of the road ahead. Look for hills and curves or objects in the road. Any of these could mean you'll have to slow or change lanes. Pay attention to traffic signals and signs. If a light has been green for a long time, it will probably change before you get there. Start slowing down and be ready to stop. Traffic signs may alert you to road conditions where you may have to change speed.

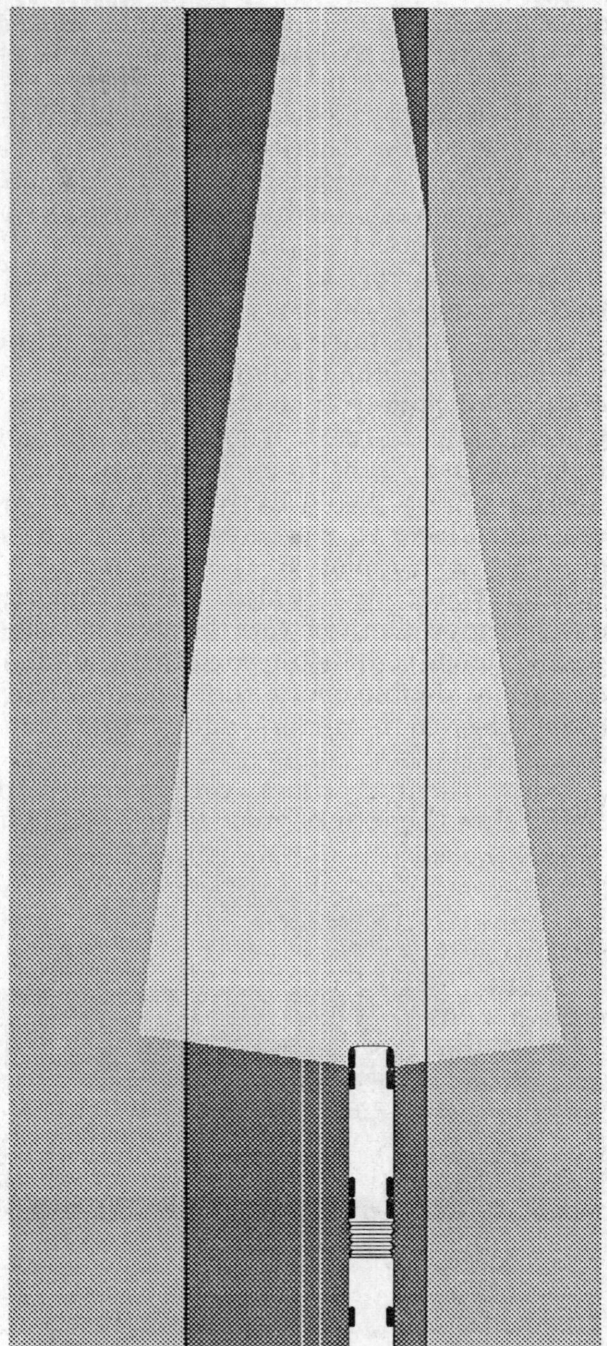

Figure 8-5 Be alert to the road ahead and to the sides.

Looking Behind and to the Sides

It's important to know what's going on behind and to the sides. Keep track of other vehicles when they enter the highway. Are they still behind you? Have they passed you or exited? In an emergency, you must know whether you can make a quick lane change. Use your mirrors to spot overtaking vehicles. There are blind spots that your mirrors cannot show you. Check your mirrors regularly to know where other vehicles are around you. Perhaps they have moved into your blind spots.

Use the mirrors to keep an eye on your tires. It's one way to spot a tire fire.

Check your mirrors even more often when making lane changes. Make sure no one is alongside you or about to pass you. Check your mirrors before you change lanes to make sure there is enough room. You have "enough" space when other drivers won't have to slow down or brake to allow you to complete the lane change.

After you have signaled, check that no one has moved out of your blind spot. Use your mirrors right after you start the lane change to double-check that your path is clear. Use your mirrors again after you complete the lane change.

When turning, check your mirrors to make sure the rear of your vehicle will not hit anything. When merging, use your mirrors to make sure the gap in traffic is large enough for you to enter safely. Other drivers shouldn't have to slow down or brake to let you in.

Proper Use of Mirrors

Use mirrors correctly by checking them quickly and understanding what you see.

When you use your mirrors while driving on the road, check quickly. Look back and forth between the mirrors and the road ahead. Don't focus on the mirrors for too long. Otherwise, you will travel quite a distance without knowing what's happening ahead.

Understand what you see. Many large vehicles have curved (convex, "fisheye," "spot," "bug-eye") mirrors that show a wider area than flat mirrors. This is often helpful. But everything appears smaller in a convex mirror than it would if you were looking at it directly. Things also seem farther away than they really are. Be aware of this and allow for it.

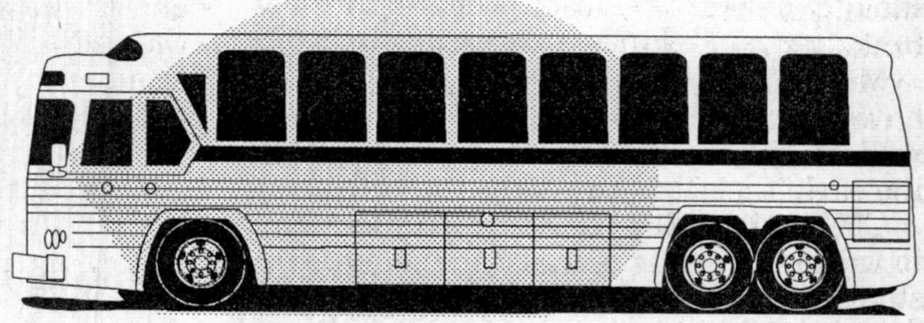

Figure 8-6 Your convex mirror will help you to see what your flat mirror doesn't.

COMMUNICATING WITH OTHER DRIVERS

Other drivers can't know what you are going to do until you tell them. You must know how to use your safety control systems to communicate with other drivers.

Turn Signals

Use your turn signals. There are three good rules for using turn signals.

Signal early. Signal well before you turn. It is the best way to keep others from trying to pass you.

Signal continuously. You need both hands on the wheel to turn safely. Don't cancel the signal until you have completed the turn.

Cancel your signal. Don't forget to turn off your turn signal after you've turned. (Some vehicles have self-canceling signals.)

Use your turn signal to show you plan to change lanes. Change lanes slowly and smoothly. That way you can cancel your plans and avoid hitting a driver you didn't see.

Brake Lights

Use the brake pedal to show you plan to slow or stop. A few light taps on the brake pedal (enough to flash the brake lights) warns other drivers that you are slowing down. Use the four-way emergency flashers when you are driving very slow or are stopped.

Warn other drivers of trouble ahead. Your large vehicle may make it hard for drivers behind you to see hazards ahead. If you see a hazard that will require slowing down, warn the drivers behind by flashing your brake lights.

Most car drivers don't know how slow you have to go to make a tight turn in a large vehicle. Warn drivers behind you by braking early and slowing gradually.

CMV drivers sometimes stop in the road to unload cargo or passengers. Some must stop at a railroad crossing. Warn following drivers by flashing your brake lights. Don't stop suddenly.

Drivers are often unaware of how quickly they are catching up to a slow vehicle until they are very close. You may be driving far below the speed limit or slower than the flow of traffic. You can alert drivers behind you by turning on your emergency flashers if it is legal. (Laws regarding the use of flashers differ from one state to another. Check the laws of the states where you will drive to make sure this is allowed.) Don't use your signals to direct traffic. You may think it's helpful to flash your lights and tell other drivers it is safe to pass. You should not do this. If it turned out **not** to be safe, you could cause an accident. You would be blamed.

Communicate Your Presence

Other drivers may not notice your vehicle even when it's in plain sight. Prevent accidents by making sure they know you're around.

When you are about to pass vehicles, pedestrians, or bicyclists, assume they don't see you. They could suddenly move in front of you. When it is legal, tap the horn lightly. At night, flash your lights from low to high beam and back. Then proceed carefully. Be prepared to avoid a crash because they may still not see or hear you.

At dawn or dusk or in rain or snow, you must make yourself easier to see. If you are having trouble seeing other vehicles, other drivers will have trouble seeing you. Turn on your lights. Use the headlights, not just the identification or clearance lights. Use the low beams. High beams can bother people in the daytime as well as at night.

Turn on your four-way flashers when you pull off the road and stop. This is important at night. Don't trust the taillights to give enough warning. Drivers have crashed into the rear of a parked vehicle because they thought it was moving normally.

Remember, if you stop on a road or the shoulder of a road, you must put out your reflective triangles within 10 minutes. Recall where to place your warning devices? Put them:

- on the traffic side of the vehicle, within 10 feet of the front or rear corners to mark the location of the vehicle

- about 100 feet behind and ahead of the vehicle, on the shoulder or in the lane you are stopped in
- back beyond any hill, curve, or other obstruction that prevents other drivers from seeing the vehicle within 500 feet

If you must stop on or by a one-way or divided highway, place warning devices 10 feet, 100 feet, and 200 feet toward the approaching traffic.

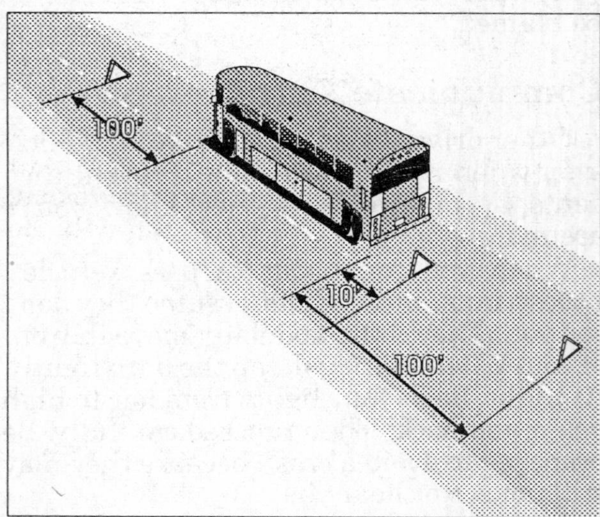

Figure 8-7 Placement of warning devices

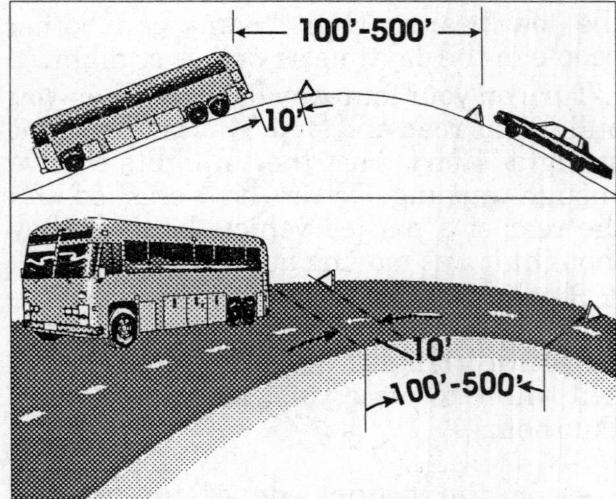

Figure 8-8 Placement of warning devices on a hill or curve.

Figure 8-9 Placement of warning devices on a one-way or divided highway.

As you are putting out the triangles, hold them between yourself and the oncoming traffic. That way other drivers can see you as you walk on the road.

You can use your horn to let others know you're there. It can help to avoid a crash. Use your horn when needed. However, it can really startle others. Use the horn only when there's no other way to get their attention. It can be dangerous when used unnecessarily.

SPEED MANAGEMENT

Driving too fast is a major cause of fatal crashes. You must base your speed on the driving conditions. These include traction, curves, visibility, traffic, and hills.

Stopping Distance

Know how much distance you need to come to a complete stop. Stopping distance is:

Perception Distance
\+ Reaction Distance
\+ Braking Distance
= Total Stopping Distance

Perception distance is the distance your vehicle travels from the time your eyes see a hazard until your brain recognizes it. The perception time for an alert driver is about ¾ second. At 55 mph, you travel 60 feet in ¾ second.

Reaction distance is the distance traveled from the time your brain tells your foot to move from the accelerator until your foot actually pushes the brake pedal. The average driver has a reaction time of 3/4 second. This accounts for an added 60 feet traveled at 55 mph.

Braking distance is the distance it takes to stop once the brakes are put on. At 55 mph on dry pavement with good brakes, it can take a heavy vehicle about 170 feet to stop. It takes about 4½ seconds.

Total stopping distance is the sum of the other three distances. At 55 mph it will take about 6 seconds to stop, and your vehicle will travel about the distance of a football field (60 + 60 + 170 = 290 feet).

Increasing the speed greatly increases the distance you need to come to a stop. Whenever you double your speed, it takes about four times as much distance to stop. Not double — four times. Your vehicle will have four times the destructive power if it crashes. By slowing down a little, you can gain a lot in reduced braking distance.

Weight also affects stopping distance. The heavier the vehicle, the more work the brakes must do to stop it. They also absorb more heat. But the brakes, tires, springs, and shock absorbers on heavy vehicles are designed to work best when the vehicle is fully loaded. Empty vehicles require greater stopping distances. That's because an empty vehicle has less traction. It can bounce and lock up its wheels. You could more easily go into a skid. This is not usually the case with buses, however. The vehicle's weight is a little bit better distributed. (You'll read more about this in Chapter 9.)

Speed and Road Conditions

You can't steer or brake a vehicle unless you have traction. Traction is friction between the tires and the road. There are some road conditions that reduce traction and call for lower speeds. Examples are slippery and curving roads.

Slippery Roads

When the road is slippery, it will take longer to stop and it will be harder to turn without skidding. You must drive slower to be able to stop in the same distance you could on a dry road. Wet roads can double stopping distance. Reduce speed by about one third on a wet road. For example, slow down from 55 to about 35 mph. On packed snow, reduce speed by half, or more. If the surface is icy, reduce speed to a crawl. In fact, stop driving as soon as you can safely do so. It's just too dangerous to go on.

Sometimes it's hard to know whether the road is slippery. Keep these facts in mind. Shady parts of the road don't get as much sun as well-lit areas. So they will remain icy and slippery long after open areas have melted. When the temperature drops, bridges will freeze before the road will. Be

Figure 8-10 In cold weather, bridges can be icy even when roads are not.

especially careful when the temperature is close to 32 degrees Fahrenheit.

An easy way to check for ice is to open the window and feel the front of the mirror, mirror support, or antenna. If there's ice on these, the road surface is probably starting to ice up.

Slight melting will make ice wet. Wet ice is much more slippery than ice that is not wet.

Black ice is a thin, clear layer. It's clear enough that you can see the road underneath it. It makes the road look wet. You might not think it is icy. Any time the temperature is below freezing and the road looks wet, watch out for black ice.

Right after it starts to rain, the water mixes with oil left on the road by vehicles. This makes the road very slippery. If the rain continues, it will wash the oil away. As you read earlier, roads are more slippery at the beginning of a rainstorm than during it.

In some weather, water or slush collects on the road. When this happens, your vehicle can hydroplane. It's like water skiing. The tires are no longer riding on the road. They are riding on top of water. As you can imagine, they have little or no traction. You may not be able to steer or brake.

You can regain control by releasing the accelerator and pushing in the clutch. This will slow your vehicle and let the wheels turn freely. If the vehicle is hydroplaning, do not use the brakes to slow down. If the drive wheels start to skid, push in the clutch to let them turn freely.

It does not take a lot of water to cause hydroplaning. Hydroplaning can occur at speeds as low as 30 mph if there is a lot of water. Hydroplaning is more likely if tire pressure is low or the tread is worn (the grooves in a tire carry away the water; if they aren't deep, they don't work well). Be especially careful driving through puddles. The water is often deep enough to cause hydroplaning.

Curving Roads

Adjust your speed for curves in the road. If you take a curve too fast, the wheels can lose their traction and continue straight ahead. You'll skid off the road. If the wheels keep their traction, the vehicle may roll over. Tests have shown that vehicles with a high center of gravity can roll over even if they are going at the posted speed limit for a curve.

Slow to a safe speed before you enter a curve. It's dangerous to apply the brakes in a curve. It's easy to lock the wheels and cause a skid. Slow down as needed. Don't ever exceed the posted speed limit for the curve. You probably need to be going much slower. Be in a gear that will let you accelerate slightly in the curve. This will help you keep control.

Figure 8-11 Don't ever exceed the posted speed limit for a curve.

Speed and Distance Ahead

You should always be able to stop within the distance you can see ahead. In fog or rain, you can't see clearly that far ahead. Slow down so you can stop within the distance you can see.

At night, you can't see as far with low beams as you can with high beams. When you must use low beams, slow down.

In heavy traffic, the safest speed is the

speed of other vehicles. Vehicles going the same direction at the same speed are not likely to run into one another. Drive at the speed of the traffic, if that is safe and legal. Keep a safe following distance. If it is safer to go slower than the other vehicles, do so.

The main reason drivers exceed speed limits is to save time. But driving faster than the speed of traffic doesn't save that much time.

Even if you do save time, the risks involved are not worth it. If you go faster than the speed of other traffic, you'll have to keep passing other vehicles. This increases the chance of a crash.

Trying to maintain the faster speed and making all those lane changes is tiring. Fatigue increases the chance of a crash.

Going with the flow of traffic is safer and easier.

Speed and Downgrades

The most important thing you can do to go down long steep hills safely is slow down. If you do not go slowly enough, your brakes can become so hot they won't slow you down. Pay attention to signs warning of long downhill grades. Check your brakes before starting down the hill. Shift your transmission to a low gear before starting down the grade.

Use your retarder if you have one. Shift to a gear that lets you go downhill at a steady, controlled speed without having to use the brakes. If you must use the brakes, use a light, steady pressure on the brake pedal. Do not "fan" them.

Going down steep hills safely is discussed more in the section on mountain driving later in this chapter. Read that section carefully.

SPACE MANAGEMENT

To be a safe driver, you need space all around your vehicle. When things go wrong, space gives you time to think and to take action.

To have space available when something goes wrong, you need to manage space. While this is true for all drivers, it is very important for drivers of large vehicles. They take up more space. They require more space for stopping and turning.

The Space Ahead

The area ahead of the vehicle (the space you're driving into) is most important. You need space ahead in case you must stop suddenly. According to accident reports, the vehicle that trucks and buses most often run into is the one in front of them. The most frequent cause is following too closely. Remember, if the vehicle ahead of you is smaller than yours, it can probably stop faster than you can. You may crash if you are following too closely.

Keep at least one second of space between you and the vehicle ahead of you for each 10 feet of vehicle length at speeds below 40 mph. What does that mean, "one second of space"? It's the distance your vehicle covers in one second. That will vary with your speed. Here's how to measure it.

Wait until the vehicle ahead passes a shadow on the road, a pavement marking, or some other clear landmark. Then count off the seconds like this: Say "one thousand-and-one, one thousand-and-two" and so on, until you reach the same spot. (It takes about a second to say "one thousand-and-one.")

		Miles Traveled				
		10	20	50	100	200
Speed	65 MPH	9 minutes	18 minutes	48 minutes	1 hour 32 minutes	3 hours 4 minutes
	60 MPH	10 minutes	20 minutes	50 minutes	1 hour 40 minutes	3 hours 20 minutes
	55 MPH	11 minutes	22 minutes	55 minutes	1 hour 49 minutes	3 hours 38 minutes

Figure 8-12 Driving faster doesn't save much time, but it does increase the chance of a crash.

Compare your count with the rule of one second for every 10 feet of length. If you are driving a 40-foot vehicle and only counted up to two seconds, you're too close. Drop back a little and count again until you have four seconds of following distance.

At speeds over 40 mph, you must add one second for safety. For example, if you are driving a 40-foot vehicle, you should leave four seconds between you and the vehicle ahead. In a 60-foot rig, you'll need six seconds. Over 40 mph, you'd need five seconds for a 40-foot vehicle and seven seconds for a 60-foot vehicle.

Add another second or two for adverse driving conditions, such as bad weather, poor lighting, or slippery roads. Add one more second for night driving. Under the worst conditions, you might need as much as seven or eight seconds of space in front of your 40-foot vehicle at highway speeds.

Space Behind

You can't stop others from following you too closely. But there are things you can do to make it safer.

Stay to the right. Heavy vehicles are often tailgated when they can't keep up with the speed of traffic. This tends to happen when you're going uphill. If a heavy load is slowing you down, stay in the right lane if you can. When going uphill, you should not pass another slow vehicle unless you can get around quickly and safely.

Many car drivers follow large vehicles closely during bad weather, especially when it is hard to see the road ahead.

It's often hard to see whether a vehicle is close behind you. It helps to be visually alert. Then you might suspect someone is behind you because you didn't see them pass you or exit.

If you find yourself being tailgated, here are some things you can do to reduce the chances of a crash. First, avoid quick changes. If you have to slow down or turn, signal early and reduce speed very gradually.

Second, increase your following distance. Opening up room in front of you will help you to avoid having to make sudden speed or direction changes. It also makes it easier for the tailgater to get around you. If in spite of all your efforts the tailgater rear-ends you, at least you won't add a front-end collision with the vehicle in front of you to the problem.

Don't speed up. The tailgater will only speed up also. It's safer to be tailgated at a low speed than a high speed. Don't turn on your taillights or flash your brake lights to shake up the tailgater.

Space at the Sides

Commercial vehicles are often wide. They take up most of a lane. Make the best use of what little space you have. Keep your vehicle centered in your lane. Try to have a little clearance on each side.

Avoid driving alongside others. There are two dangers in traveling alongside other vehicles. Another driver may change lanes suddenly and turn into you. Or you may be trapped when you need to change lanes.

Find an open spot where you aren't near other traffic. When traffic is heavy, it may be hard to find an open spot. If you must travel near other vehicles, try to keep as much space as possible between you and them. Also, drop back or pull forward so that you are sure the other driver can see you.

Strong winds make it hard to stay in lane, especially for lighter vehicles. This problem can be even worse coming out of tunnels. Don't drive alongside others if you can avoid it.

Space Overhead

Hitting overhead objects is a danger. We mentioned this in the section on backing. Make sure you always have overhead clearance.

Don't assume that the heights posted at bridges and overpasses are correct. Repaving or packed snow may have raised the height of the road since the signs were posted. This reduces the clearance.

An empty vehicle rides higher than a loaded one. Just because you got under a bridge when you were loaded doesn't mean that you can do it when you are empty.

If you doubt you have safe space to pass under an object, go slowly. If you aren't sure you can make it, take another route. Warnings are often posted on low bridges or underpasses, but sometimes they are not.

Some roads can cause a vehicle to tilt. There can be a problem clearing objects along the edge of the road, such as signs or trees. Where this is a problem, drive a little closer to the center of the road.

Before you back into an area, get out and check for overhanging branches or electric wires. It's easy to miss seeing them while you are backing. (Also check for other hazards at the same time.)

Space Below

Don't forget about the space under your vehicle. That space can be very small when a vehicle is heavily loaded. Railroad tracks can stick up several inches. This is often a problem on dirt roads and in unpaved yards where the surface around the tracks can wear away. Don't take a chance on getting hung up halfway across. Drainage channels across roads can cause the end of some vehicles to drag. Cross such depressions carefully.

Space for Turning

You need space around your CMV in order to turn safely. Large vehicles turn wide. Also, the rear wheels don't follow the same path as the front wheels. This is called "off-tracking." Because of wide turning and off-tracking, large vehicles can hit other vehicles or objects during turns.

Right turns are more difficult than left turns. You can't see what's happening at the right of your vehicle as well as you can see to the left. Turn slowly to give yourself and others more time to avoid problems. If you cannot make the right turn without swinging into another lane, turn wide as you complete the turn (see Figure 8-13). Don't turn wide to the left as you start the turn, as shown in Figure 8-14. A driver following you may think you are turning left. The driver may then try to pass you on the right. You may crash into the other vehicle as you complete your turn. Keep the rear of your vehicle no further than four feet from the curb. This will stop other drivers from passing you on the right.

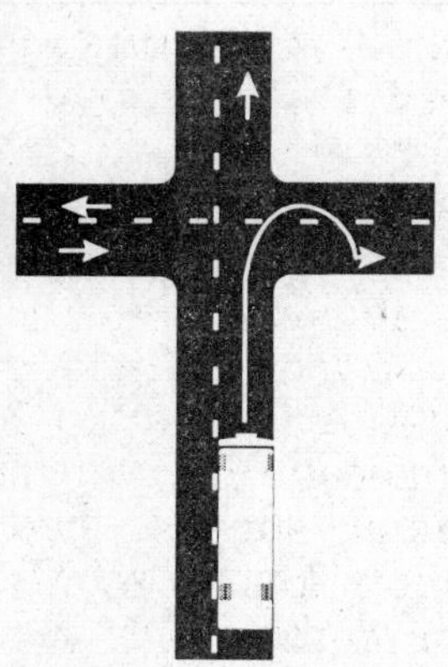

Figure 8-13 Make right turns this way.

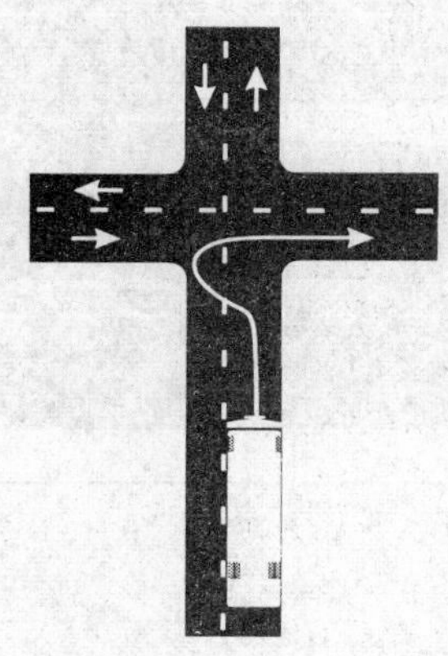

Figure 8-14 Don't make right turns this way.

If you must cross into the oncoming lane to make a turn, watch out for vehicles coming toward you. Give them room to go by or to stop. However, don't back up for them. You might hit someone behind you.

Left turns are a little easier. Make sure you have reached the center of the intersection before you start the left turn. If you turn too soon, the left side of your vehicle may hit another vehicle because of off-tracking. If there are two turning lanes, always start your left turn from the right-hand turn lane (see Figure 8-15). Don't start in the inside lane. You may just have to swing right to make the turn. Drivers on your right may be hard for you to see. You may crash into them.

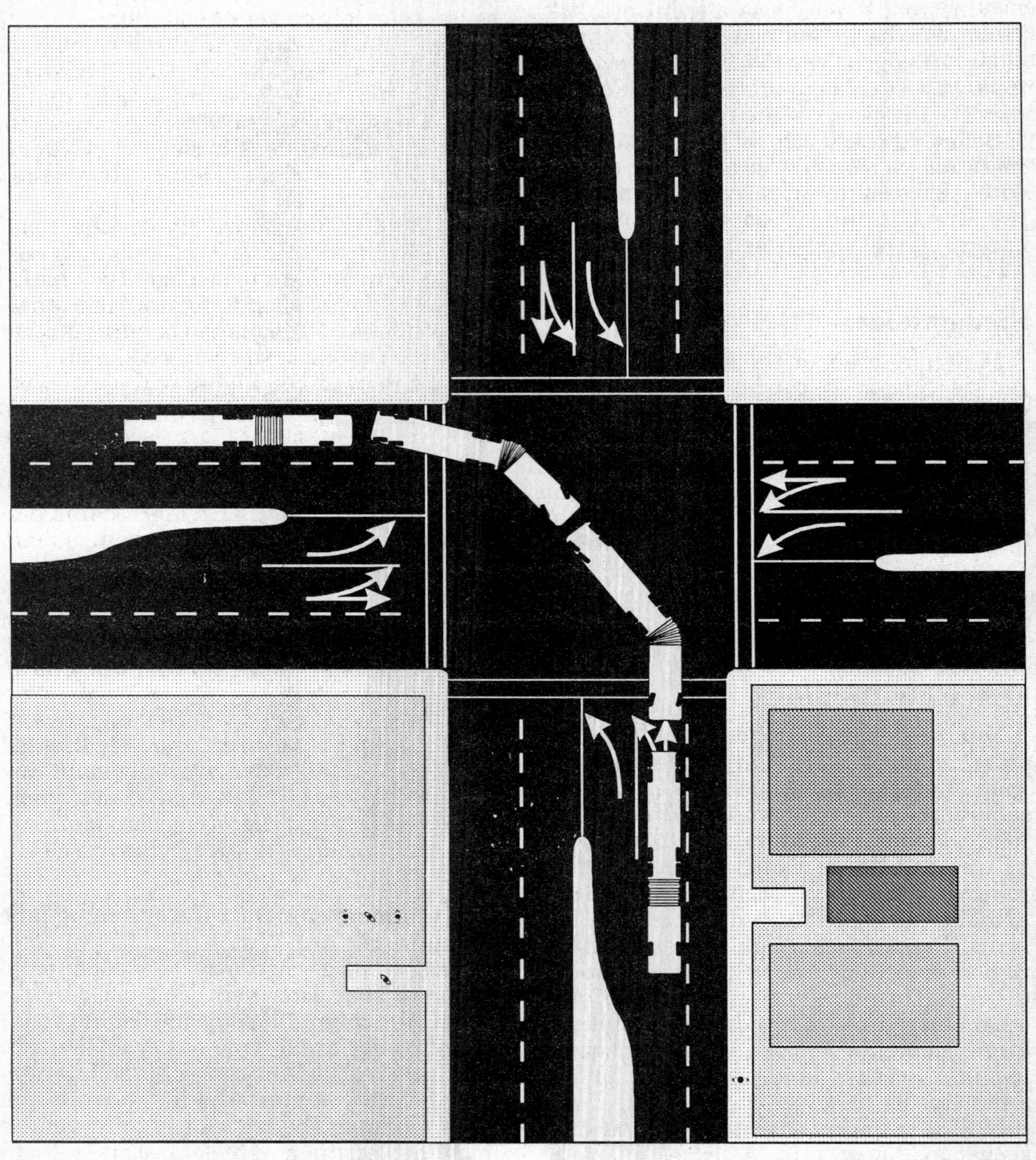

Figure 8-15 Turning left when there are two turning lanes.

Space to Enter or Cross Traffic

Be aware of the size and weight of your vehicle when you cross or enter traffic. Large vehicles accelerate slowly and need extra space. When heavily loaded, they accelerate even slower. You may need a much larger gap to enter traffic than you would in a car.

Before you start across a road, make sure you can get all the way across before traffic reaches you. Don't change lanes in an intersection.

NIGHT DRIVING

You are at greater risk when you drive at night. Drivers can't see hazards as soon as in daylight, so they have less time to respond. Drivers caught by surprise are less able to avoid a crash.

Night driving offers a number of vision problems. Also, you're simply not as alert and responsive at night. You must allow for both these handicaps.

Poor Vision

People can't see as sharply at night or in dim light. Also, the eyes need time to adjust to seeing in dim light. Think about walking into a dark movie theater. At first you can hardly see at all. After your eyes adjust to the dim light, you can see a little better. Of course, you can't see as well as you could in bright light.

Drivers can be blinded for a short time by bright light. It takes time to recover from this blindness. Older drivers are especially bothered by glare. You can probably remember being temporarily blinded by a camera flash unit or by the high beams of an oncoming vehicle.

It can take several seconds to recover from glare. Even two seconds of glare blindness can be dangerous. A vehicle going 55 mph travels more than half the distance of a football field during that time. Don't look directly at bright lights when driving. Look at the right side of the road. Watch the sidelines when someone coming toward you has very bright lights.

In the daytime there is usually enough light to see well. This is not true at night. Some areas may have bright street lights, but many areas have poor lighting. On most roads at night you will probably have to depend entirely on your headlights.

Less light means you will not be able to see hazards as well as in daytime. Pedestrians, joggers, and bicyclists don't usually have lights or reflectors. They're hard to see. There are many accidents at night involving pedestrians, joggers, bicyclists, and animals.

Even when there are lights, the road scene can be confusing. Traffic signals and hazards can be hard to see against a background of signs, shop windows, and other lights. Slow down enough to be sure you can stop in the distance you can see ahead.

At night your headlights will usually be the main source of light for you to see and for others to see you. You can't see nearly as much with your headlights as you can see in the daytime. With low beams you can see ahead about 250 feet. With high beams you can see about 350 to 500 feet. Again, adjust your speed to keep your stopping distance within your sight distance. This means going slow enough to be able to stop within the range of your headlights. Otherwise, by the time you see a hazard, you will not have time to stop.

Night driving can be more dangerous if you have problems with your headlights. Dirty headlights may give only half the light they should. This cuts down your ability to see and makes it harder for others to see you. Make sure your lights are clean and working.

Headlights can be out of adjustment. If they don't point in the right direction, they don't give you a good view and they can blind other drivers. Have a qualified person make sure they are adjusted properly.

In order for you to be seen easily, the following must be clean and working properly:

- reflectors
- marker lights
- clearance lights
- taillights
- identification lights

At night your turn signals and brake lights are vital for telling other drivers what you intend to do. Make sure you have clean, working turn signals and stop lights.

It is also vital to have clean windshields and mirrors. Bright lights at night can cause dirt on your windshield or mirrors to create a glare. This can block your view. Think about times you have driven toward the sun just as it has risen or is about to set. You really find out how clean your windshield is then. Clean your windshield on the inside and outside for safe driving at night.

Poor lighting isn't the only handicap you have at night. Fatigue (being tired) and lack of alertness are bigger problems at night than during the day. The body's need for sleep is beyond a person's control. Most people are less alert at night, especially after midnight. This is particularly true if you have been driving all day.

Drivers may not see hazards as soon or react as quickly at night, so the chance of a crash is greater. If you are sleepy, the only safe cure is to get off the road and get some sleep. If you don't, you risk your life and the lives of others.

PASS Billboard

Working the Graveyard Shift

You may think that if you usually drive at night, you'll get used to sleeping during the day. You may figure you'll get used to being awake at night. More and more, studies on what is called "circadian rhythms" are showing this just isn't so. The human body just doesn't like being awake when it's dark.

Also, you have a sort of internal clock that keeps track of how much rest you've had. When you need rest, your body is going to fight your attempts to stay up and about. This battle between your mind and your body adds to your fatigue.

These studies have become very important to drivers. You drive according to the schedule you're given. It doesn't matter if it's day or night. Because of this, you're often at a disadvantage no matter how hard you try to be a good driver.

More and more, magazines for commercial drivers are covering this subject. If you often drive through the night, pay attention to articles on circadian rhythms, inner clocks, and the need for sleep. You'll find helpful hints for overcoming this handicap.

Here's another hazard of night driving. You're more likely to run into drunk drivers. Drunk drivers and drivers under the influence of drugs are a hazard to themselves and to you. Be especially alert around the times bars close. Watch for drivers who have trouble staying in their lane or maintaining speed or who stop without reason. These are all signs of being under the influence of alcohol or drugs.

Pre-trip Inspection for Night Driving

Make special preparations for driving at night. Pre-trip your vehicle and yourself with reduced visibility in mind.

Do a complete pre-trip inspection of your vehicle. Pay special attention to checking all lights and reflectors. Clean all those you can reach.

Check your own fitness to drive. Make sure you are rested and alert. If you are drowsy, sleep before you drive! Even a nap can save your life or the lives of others.

If you wear eyeglasses, make sure they are clean and unscratched. Don't wear sunglasses at night.

Night-driving Tactics

Avoid blinding others. Glare from your headlights can cause problems for drivers coming toward you. They can also bother drivers going in the same direction you are when your lights shine in their rear view mirrors. Dim your lights before they cause glare for other drivers. Dim your lights within 500 feet of an oncoming vehicle and when following another vehicle within 500 feet.

Avoid glare from oncoming vehicles. Remember, don't look directly at lights of oncoming vehicles. Look slightly to the right at a right lane. If other drivers don't put their low beams on, don't try to get back at them by putting your own high beams on. This increases glare for oncoming drivers and increases the chance of a crash.

Use your high beams when you can. Some drivers make the mistake of always using low beams. This seriously cuts down on their ability to see ahead. Use high beams when it is safe and legal to do so. Use them when you are not within 500 feet of an oncoming vehicle.

Also, don't let the inside of your cab get too bright. This makes it harder to see outside. Keep the interior light off. Adjust your instrument lights as low as you can and still read the gauges.

Avoid a heavy meal before you drive. Definitely avoid alcohol. Keep your cab slightly on the cool side and well ventilated. Keep your eyes moving. Stop at least every two hours. Move around or get some rest.

In spite of all this, you'll eventually get sleepy. When you do, stop driving at the nearest safe place. People often don't realize how close they are to falling asleep even when their eyelids are falling shut. This is a very dangerous condition.

When you're this tired, cool air won't make you more alert. You'll just be a cold sleepy driver. Coffee and other drinks with caffeine won't make you more alert. They'll only make you a jittery, bug-eyed sleepy driver. The only sure cure for sleepiness and fatigue is sleep.

DRIVING IN ADVERSE CONDITIONS

Driving under ideal conditions is no easy job. Driving under adverse conditions takes real skill. Any of the following can make your driving job that much harder:

- winter weather
- very hot weather
- mountain terrain

You should prepare for adverse conditions with the same care you prepare for night driving. If conditions change on you from normal to adverse, you must know how to adjust.

DRIVING IN WINTER

Winter weather can present some of the worst driving challenges you'll face. Snow and ice reduce traction. Blowing snow can reduce visibility. Fighting the weather and trying to maintain control over your vehicle can wear you out. So fatigue is a problem.

Slippery Surfaces

Very simply, when the road is slippery, don't make any sudden or abrupt moves. Start gently and slowly. When first starting, get the feel of the road. Don't hurry. Drive slowly and smoothly.

Turn as gently as possible. Don't brake any harder than you need to. Give yourself lots of space and following distance. Then you can brake gently when you need to slow or stop. Don't use the engine brake or speed retarder. They can cause the driving wheels to skid on slippery surfaces.

Avoid passing slower vehicles. Go slow and watch far enough ahead to keep a steady speed. Then you won't have to keep slowing down and speeding up. Take curves at slower speeds. Don't brake while in curves. Be aware that as the temperature rises to the point where ice begins to melt, the road becomes even more slippery. Slow down more. Reduce your normal speed by half for snow, by two-thirds for ice.

Don't drive alongside other vehicles. Keep a longer following distance. When you see a traffic jam ahead, slow down or stop to wait for it to clear. Try hard to anticipate stops early, and slow down gradually.

If it is very slippery, you shouldn't drive at all. Stop at the first safe place.

Pre-trip Inspection for Winter Driving

Before driving in winter weather, make your regular pre-trip inspection. Pay extra attention to the items that are important in cold weather.

Make sure the cooling system is full. There must be enough antifreeze in the system to protect against freezing. You can check this with a special coolant tester.

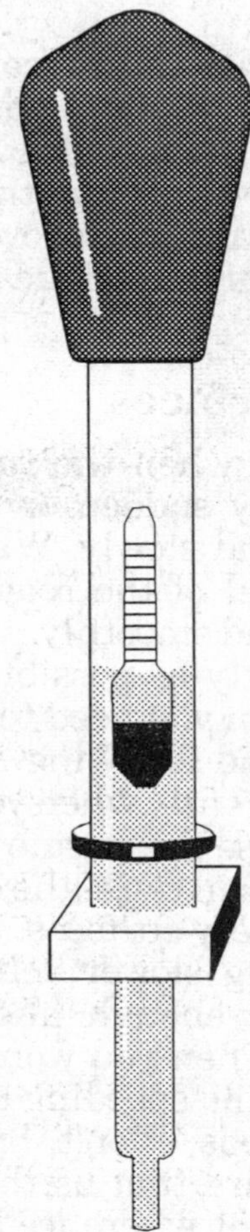

Figure 8-17 A coolant tester.

Make sure the defrosters work. They are needed for safe driving. Make sure the heater is working and that you know how to operate it. You may have other heaters, such as mirror heaters, battery box heaters, or fuel tank heaters on your vehicle. If you plan to use them, make sure they work.

Make sure the windshield wiper blades are in good condition. The wiper blades should press against the window hard enough to wipe the windshield clean. Otherwise they may not sweep off snow properly. Make sure the windshield washer works and there is washing fluid in the washer reservoir. Use windshield washer antifreeze to keep the washer liquid from freezing.

If you can't see well enough while driving (for example, if your wipers fail), find a place to stop safely. Fix the problem before you go on.

Don't take chances with your tires. Make sure they have enough tread. The drive tires must provide traction to push the vehicle over wet pavement and through snow. The steering tires must have traction to steer the vehicle. Enough tread is especially important in winter conditions. You should have at least a 4/32-inch tread depth in every major groove on front wheels and at least a 2/32-inch tread depth on other wheels. More would be better. Use a gauge to determine whether you have enough tread for safe driving.

You may find yourself in conditions where you can't drive without snow chains, even to get to a place of safety. Carry the right number of chains and extra cross links. Make sure they will fit your drive tires. Check the chains for broken hooks, worn or broken cross links, and bent or broken side chains. Learn how to put on the chains before you need to do it in snow and ice.

PASS Billboard

How to Mount Snow Chains

Check the condition of your chains. Look for broken links and fasteners.

Straighten out the chain. Drape the chain over the tire, with the open ends of the cross-chain hooks facing away from the tire. Fasteners are to be on the outside of the tire.

Tuck the first cross-chain under the front of the tire. Drive the vehicle forward until the fasteners are at hub-level. Be careful not to drive over the fasteners.

Get out and straighten and center the chain. There should be an equal amount on either side of the tire. Hook the inside side chains first. Then fasten the fasteners on

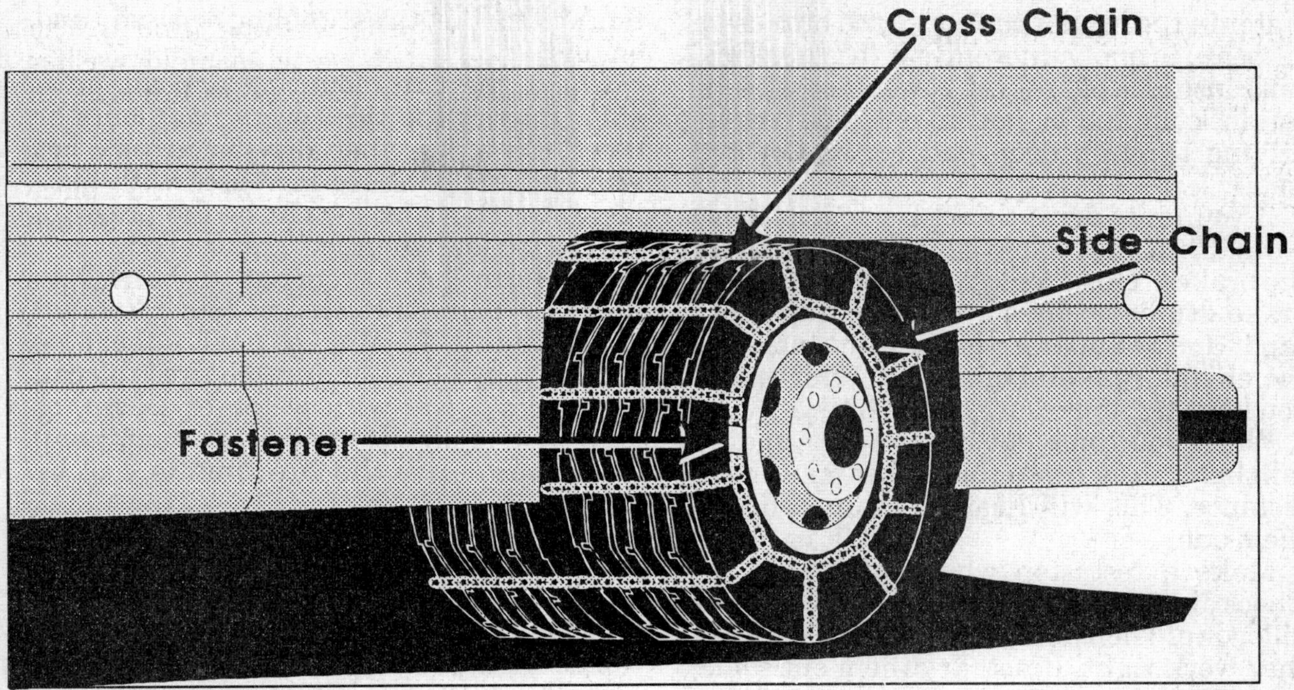

Figure 8-18 Snow chains mounted on a dual tire.

the outside side chains. Take up all the excess slack you can while fastening the outside side chains.

If you are chaining duals, use the same procedure. If it's safe to do so, stop after driving about five miles with the chains on to check for excess slack in the chains. If the chains are too loose around the tire or tires, unhook the outside fastener, remove the slack, and rehook the fastener.

To remove snow chains, unhook the fasteners on the outside. Unhook the inside chains next. Spread the chains on the ground. Drive the vehicle off the chains. Be careful not to run over the fasteners.

Make sure the lights and reflectors are clean. Lights and reflectors are especially important during bad weather. Check from time to time during bad weather to make sure they are clean and working right. Remove any ice, snow, and dirt from the lights, reflectors, windshield, windows, and mirrors before starting. You may need to use a windshield scraper, snow brush, or windshield defroster.

Remove all ice and snow from handholds, steps, and deck plates that you use to enter or to move about the vehicle. This reduces the chance of slipping.

Remove ice from radiator shutters. If you have a winterfront, make sure it's not closed too tightly. If the shutters freeze shut or the winterfront is closed too much, the engine may overheat and stop.

Exhaust system leaks are especially dangerous when you have your vehicle tightly buttoned up against winter's cold. Loose connections could allow poisonous carbon monoxide to leak into your vehicle. Carbon monoxide gas will make you sleepy. In large enough amounts it can kill you. Check the exhaust system closely for loose parts and for sounds and signs of leaks.

DRIVING IN THE RAIN

Remember that roads are more slippery at the start of a rainstorm than during it. That's because the rain mixes with oil and grease on the road. If the rain continues, it washes the oil away. So be most careful when it first starts raining.

When you drive in heavy rain or deep standing water, your brakes will get wet.

Water in the brakes can cause the brakes to be weak, to apply unevenly, or to grab. This can cause lack of braking power. The wheels can lock up and or pull to one side. Avoid driving through deep puddles or flowing water.

If you must drive through puddles, slow down. Shift into a low gear. Gently put on the brakes. This presses the linings against brake drums or discs and keeps mud, silt, sand, and water from getting in. Increase the engine rpm and cross the water while you keep light pressure on the brakes.

When you come out of the water, maintain light pressure on the brakes for a short distance. This will heat them up and dry them out.

Make a test stop when safe to do so. Check behind to make sure no one is following. Then apply the brakes to be sure they work right. If not, dry them out some more. Do not apply too much brake pressure and accelerate at the same time or you can overheat brake drums and linings.

When it's raining, reduce your normal speed by about one fourth.

DRIVING IN HOT WEATHER

Hot weather taxes your cooling system, engine, and tires. You can't lower the temperature outside. But you can keep from making it worse. Slow down enough to prevent overheating. High speeds create more heat for tires and the engine. In desert conditions the heat may build up to the point where it is dangerous. The heat increases chances of tire failure, or even fire and engine failure.

Slippery Surfaces

Watch for bleeding tar. Tar in the road pavement often rises to the surface in very hot weather. Spots where tar bleeds to the surface are very slippery.

Pre-trip Inspection for Hot Weather

If you'll be driving in hot weather, do a normal pre-trip inspection. Pay special attention to the tires, cooling system, and engine.

Check the tire mounting and air pressure. Inspect the tires every two hours or every 100 miles when driving in very hot weather. Air pressure increases with temperature. Don't let air out or the pressure will be too low when the tires cool off.

Tires can get hot enough to burst into flame. If a tire is too hot to touch, remain stopped until the tire cools off. Otherwise the tire may blow out or catch fire. You can cool down a tire with water, of course, or even sand or dirt. If you have neither, you'll just have to give the tire time to cool by itself.

Pay special attention to recapped or retreaded tires. Under high temperatures the tread may separate from the body of the tire.

The engine oil helps keep the engine cool, as well as lubricating it. Make sure there is enough engine oil. If you have an oil temperature gauge, make sure the temperature is within the proper range while you are driving.

Before starting out, make sure the engine cooling system has enough water and antifreeze. Your operator's manual should have some information for you on this. (Antifreeze helps the engine under hot conditions as well as cold conditions.)

While you're driving, check the water temperature or coolant temperature gauge from time to time. Make sure that it remains in the normal range. If the gauge goes above the highest safe temperature, there may be something wrong that could lead to engine failure and possibly fire. Stop driving as soon as safely possible and try to find out what is wrong.

The coolant in your vehicle is held under pressure. Never remove the radiator cap or any part of the pressurized system until the system has cooled. Taking the cap off releases the pressure. Steam and boiling water can spray out and burn you. If you can touch the radiator cap with your bare hand, it is probably cool enough to open.

Some vehicles have sight glasses or see-through coolant overflow containers or coolant recovery containers. These allow you to check the coolant level even while the engine is hot. If the container is not part of the pressurized system, you can safely remove the cap and add coolant even when the engine is at operating temperature.

If you have to add coolant to a system without a recovery tank or overflow tank, follow these steps.

- shut the engine off
- wait until the engine has cooled
- protect your hands (use gloves or a thick cloth)
- turn the radiator cap slowly to the first stop (that releases the pressure seal)
- step back while pressure is released from the cooling system
- when all the pressure has been released, press down on the cap and turn it farther to remove it
- visually check the coolant level
- add more coolant if the level is below "Add" or "Low"
- replace the cap and turn it all the way to the closed position

Learn how to check V-belt tightness on your vehicle by pressing on the belts. Your operator's manual will tell you how slack they should be. Belts that are too loose will not turn the water pump or fan properly. If the fan doesn't cool the water, it will overheat, and so will the engine. Also check belts for cracking or other signs of wear. Heat just puts more stress on them. That's why they always seem to break when you need them the most.

Make sure coolant hoses are in good condition. Heat can turn a little break into a big one. If a hose breaks while you're driving, it can lead to engine failure and even fire.

MOUNTAIN DRIVING

Gravity plays a major role in mountain driving. In a heavy vehicle, you will have to use lower gears and go slower to climb hills. When you head down, gravity will tend to speed you up. You must go slowly enough that your brakes can hold you back without getting too hot. When brakes become too hot, they may start to fade. This means that you have to apply them harder and harder to get the same stopping power. If you continue to use the brakes hard, they can continue to fade until you can't slow down or stop at all.

Pre-trip for Mountain Driving

If you'll be driving in the mountains, do a normal pre-trip inspection. Inspect your braking system thoroughly. If your vehicle has an engine retarder, make sure it's working.

When you're driving, highway signs will give you plenty of warning that a long downgrade is coming up. You'll usually find a "pull out" at the top of the hill. This is an

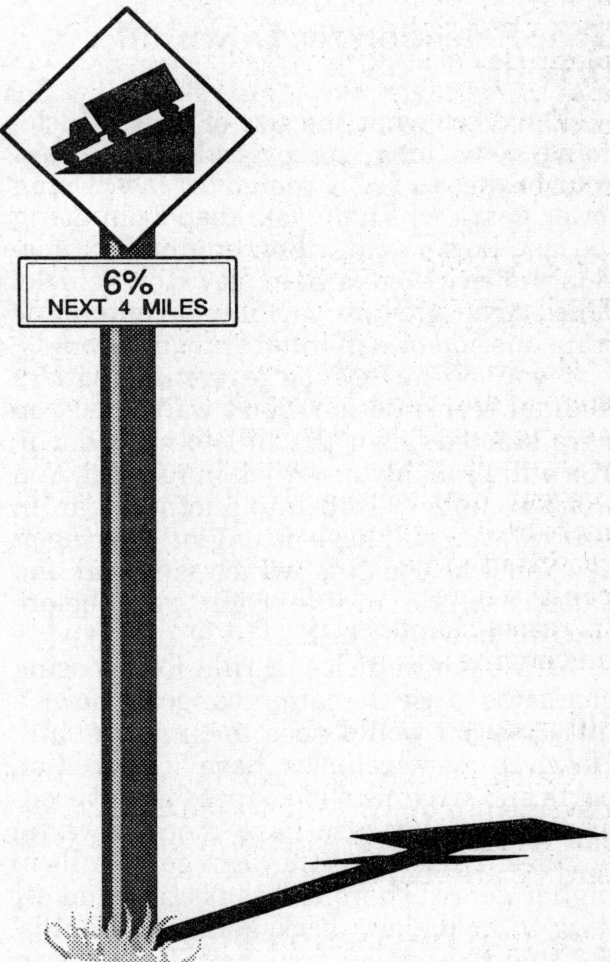

Figure 8-19 Watch for highway signs that warn you of downgrades.

area to the side of the road where you can safely leave the vehicle and check the brakes. Do it. Don't just stomp on the brake pedal and decide the brakes work. Do a complete brake check, as you would during a pre-trip.

Your vehicle may have manually-adjusted brakes. Check the travel of the slack adjusters. If the distance is too great, you'll lose braking power. Tighten the slack before you continue. Slack adjustment is discussed in greater detail in Chapter 12.

Downhill Tactics

These dangers can be avoided by going downhill slowly. Use the gear (and retarder, if you have it) that allows you to descend safely while using the brakes very little or not at all.

Gear Selection for Downhill Driving

No matter what the size of your vehicle, going down long, steep grades can cause your brakes to fail if you go too fast. Using lower gears will help you keep from going too fast. Lower gears allow engine compression and friction to help slow the vehicle. This is true whether you have an automatic transmission or a manual transmission.

If you do have a large vehicle with a manual transmission, don't wait until you have started down the hill to shift down. You will probably get stuck in neutral. You won't be able to shift into another gear. In neutral, you will have no engine braking at all. You'll be coasting, which is illegal and dangerous. Be in the right gear before starting down the hill.

With older vehicles, a rule for choosing gears was to use the same gear going down a hill that you would need to climb the hill. However, new vehicles have low friction parts and streamlined shapes for fuel economy. They may also have more powerful engines. This means they can go up hills in higher gears. There is less friction and air drag to hold them back going down hills. For that reason, you may have to use lower gears going down a hill than would be required to go up the hill. Find out what is right for your vehicle. If you don't know, try this. Stop at the top of the hill. As you restart, upshift to a gear that will set the vehicle's speed at 20 mph while keeping the rpm just under the rated engine speed. Then stay in that gear until you reach the bottom of the hill.

Braking on Downgrades

When you are going downhill, brakes always heat up. As you know, the reason brakes work is that the brake shoes or pads rub against the brake drum or discs to slow the vehicle. This creates heat. Brakes are designed to take a lot of heat.

However, brakes eventually fail from too much heat. Excessive heat results from trying to slow down from too high a speed too many times or too quickly. Brakes fade (have less stopping power) when they get very hot. They can get to the point where they will no longer slow the vehicle.

The right way to use your brakes for long downhill grades is to go slow enough that a fairly light use of the brakes will keep your speed from increasing. If you go slowly enough, the brakes will be able to get rid of the heat without getting too hot.

Don't fan the brake. You may think that applying and releasing the brakes repeatedly will allow them to cool enough so they don't become overheated. Tests have proven this is not true. Brake drums cool very slowly. The amount of cooling between applications is not enough to prevent overheating. This type of braking requires heavier brake pressures than steady application does. Heavy pressure on the brakes from time to time builds up more heat than light continuous pressure does.

So select the right gear, go slowly enough, and maintain a light, steady use of the brakes.

Loss of Braking Power

What if, in spite of your best efforts, you lose your brakes? Knowing what to do will not only help you earn your CDL. It will save your life.

Escape ramps have been built on many steep mountain grades. Escape ramps are made to stop runaway vehicles safely without injuring drivers and passengers. Escape ramps lead your vehicle into a long bed of loose soft material, such as pea gravel. The gravel offers enough extra friction to slow a runaway vehicle.

Escape ramps are sometimes built on an upgrade. Your vehicle then has to overcome gravity as well as friction. The two forces together are enough to stop your vehicle.

Know where the escape ramps are on your route. Maps for professional drivers pinpoint escape ramp locations. While you're driving, note the highway signs that tell you a ramp is coming up. If there is no escape ramp available, take the least hazardous escape route you can. Head for an open field or a side road that flattens out or turns uphill. Make the move as soon as you know your brakes don't work. The longer you wait, the faster the vehicle will go and the harder it will be to stop.

ROAD HAZARDS

You can't avoid road hazards if you don't see them in the first place. What is a hazard? A hazard is anything or anyone on the road that could be a danger.

Picture this. A car in front of you is headed toward the freeway exit. You think he's going to leave the freeway. Instead, his brake lights come on and he begins braking hard. This could mean that the driver is uncertain about taking the off ramp. He might suddenly return to the highway. He may come to a complete stop. This car is a hazard. If the driver of the car cuts in front of you or stops, it is no longer just a hazard. It is an emergency. If you had speeded up, thinking he was going to leave the freeway, you might be in big trouble.

Be Prepared

Seeing hazards before they become accidents helps you prepare. You have more time to act. In the example above, you should have slowed down, not speeded up. Then you could change lanes or slow down even more to avoid a crash. Seeing this hazard would give you time to check your mirrors and signal a lane change. Being prepared reduces the danger.

If you did not see the hazard until the slow car pulled back on the highway in front of you, you would have to do something quickly. Sudden braking or an abrupt lane change is much more likely to lead to a crash. If you have not been managing your space, you may have no room to move at all.

Recognize the Clues

There are often clues that will help you see hazards. The more you drive, the better you get at seeing hazards. Slow down and be very careful if you see any of the following road hazards:

- work zones
- pavement drop-off
- objects in the road
- off-ramps and on-ramps
- dangerous drivers
- dangerous nondrivers

Work Zones

Road work can present many hazards. There may be narrower lanes, sharp turns, or uneven surfaces. Other drivers stop paying attention to their driving so they can watch the work. Workers and construction vehicles may get in the way. Drive slowly and carefully near work zones. Use your four-way flashers or brake lights to warn drivers behind you that you are slowing.

Drop-off

Sometimes the pavement drops off sharply near the edge of the road. If you are driving too near the edge, your vehicle can tilt toward the side of the road. It can hit signs, tree limbs, and other objects along the side of the road. Also, it can be hard to steer as you cross the drop-off, go off the road, or come back on.

Objects in the Road

Things that have fallen on the road can be hazards. They can damage your tires and wheel rims. They can damage electrical and brake lines. They can get caught between dual tires and cause severe damage.

Some obstacles that appear to be harmless can be very dangerous. For example, cardboard boxes may be empty. They could also contain some solid or heavy material that could cause damage. The same is true of paper and cloth sacks.

Be alert for objects of all sorts. If you see them early enough, you can avoid them without making sudden, unsafe moves.

Off-ramps and On-ramps

Freeway and turnpike exits can be particularly dangerous for commercial vehicles. Off-ramps and on-ramps often have speed limit signs posted. Remember, these speeds may be safe for automobiles but not for larger vehicles or heavily loaded vehicles. The safest speed is not the posted one. It's the one that gives you the most control over your vehicle.

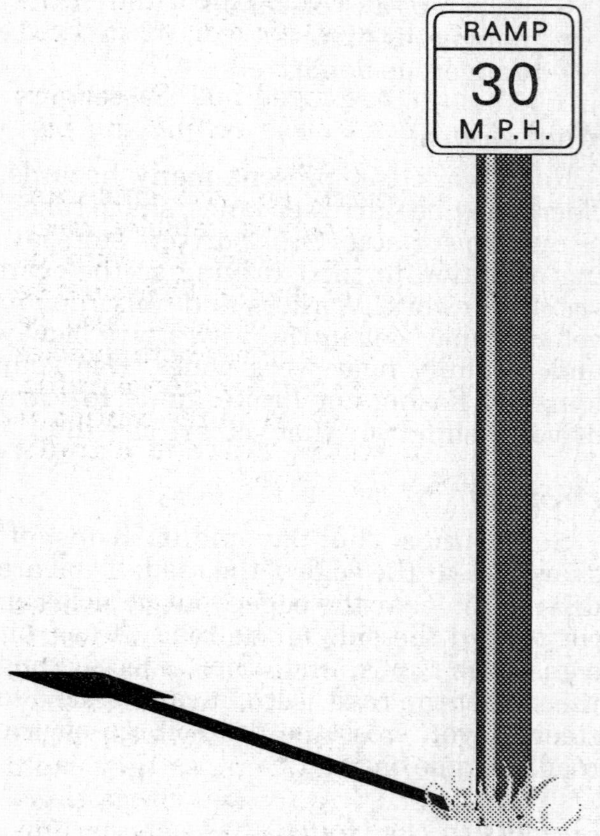

Figure 8-20 The speed posted for the off-ramps may be too high for your CMV.

Exits that go downhill and turn at the same time can be especially dangerous. The downgrade makes it hard to reduce speed. Braking and turning at the same time can be a dangerous practice. Make sure you are going slowly enough before you get on the curved part of an off-ramp or on-ramp.

As you saw earlier, off-ramps can be dangerous for other reasons. Drivers ahead of you may slow in order to exit. They may decide suddenly to move for the exit. Or they may start to exit and change their mind.

On-ramps mean drivers will be entering the highway. They may not always be very skilled at doing this. They'll probably assume you can slow to make room for them. If you can't, a crash can result. If you're in the merge lane, manage your space and speed very carefully.

Dangerous Drivers

Other drivers can present still more hazards. Learn how to read the clues. Confused drivers often change direction suddenly or stop without warning. Confusion is common near freeway or turnpike interchanges and major intersections. Stopping in the middle of a block, changing lanes for no apparent reason, and putting on backup lights suddenly are all clues to confusion. Hesitation is another clue. So is driving very slowly, using brakes often, or stopping in the middle of an intersection. You may also see drivers who are looking at street signs, maps, and house numbers. These drivers may not be paying attention to you.

Tourists unfamiliar with the area can be very hazardous. Clues to tourists include car-top luggage and out-of-state license plates.

Slow drivers are hazards. Seeing slow-moving vehicles early can prevent a crash. Some vehicles (mopeds, farm machinery, construction machinery, tractors, etc.) by their nature are slow. Some of these will have the "slow-moving vehicle" symbol to warn you. This is a red triangle with an orange center. Watch for it. Proceed with caution around slow-moving vehicles.

Drivers signaling a turn may be a hazard. They may slow more than expected or stop. If they are making a tight turn into an alley or driveway, they may go very slowly. If they are blocked by pedestrians or other vehicles they may have to stop on the roadway.

Vehicles turning left may have to stop for oncoming vehicles.

Drivers in a hurry may think your CMV is keeping them from getting where they want to go on time. Such drivers may pass you without a safe gap in the oncoming traffic, cutting too close in front of you. Drivers entering the road may pull in front of you in order to avoid being stuck behind you. Be careful around drivers who are going faster than the flow of traffic and making many lane changes.

Drivers who are sleepy, have had too much to drink, are on drugs, or are ill are hazards. Be suspicious of drivers who are:

- weaving across the road or drifting from side to side
- leaving the road (dropping right wheels onto the shoulder or bumping across a curb in a turn)
- stopping at the wrong time (stopping at a green light or waiting for too long at a stop)
- driving with the window open in cold weather
- speeding up or slowing down suddenly, driving too fast or too slow

As you learned earlier, you should be especially alert for drunk and sleepy drivers late at night.

Learn to read the body movements of other drivers. Drivers look in the direction they are going to turn. You may sometimes get a clue from a driver's head and body movements that this driver may be going to make a turn even though the turn signals aren't on. Drivers making over-the-shoulder checks may be going to change lanes. These clues are most easily seen in motorcyclists and bicyclists. Watch other road users and try to tell whether they might do something hazardous.

Be alert for drivers whose vision is blocked. Vans, loaded station wagons, and cars with the rear window blocked are examples. Rental trucks should be watched carefully. The driver's vision to the sides and rear of the truck is limited. In winter, vehicles with frosted, ice-covered, or snow-covered windows are hazards.

Vehicles may be partly hidden by blind intersections or alleys. If you can see only the rear or front end of a vehicle but not the driver, then he or she can't see you. Be alert because the driver may back out or enter your lane. Always be prepared to stop.

Delivery trucks can present a hazard. The driver's vision is often blocked by packages or vehicle doors. Drivers of step vans, postal vehicles, and local delivery vehicles often are in a hurry. They may suddenly step out of their vehicles or drive their vehicles into the traffic lane.

Parked vehicles can be hazards when the people start to get out. Or their drivers may suddenly start up and drive into your way. Watch for movement inside the vehicle or movement of the vehicle itself that shows people are inside. Brake or backup lights and exhaust are clues that a driver is about to move.

Be careful of a stopped bus. Passengers may cross in front of or behind the bus. Often, they can't see you.

Some situations are just accidents waiting to happen. Anywhere vehicles meet, there is a chance of danger. Be cautious where lanes of traffic merge. This could be at an on-ramp, as you've seen. Also be cautious at the end of a lane, where vehicles are forced to move to another lane of traffic. Another situation that requires caution is slow-moving or stalled traffic in a traffic lane and at accident scenes.

Dangerous Nondrivers

There can be others on the road besides drivers, and they can be hazards. Pedestrians, joggers, and bicyclists may be on the road with their back to the traffic, so they can't see you. Sometimes, they wear portable stereos with head sets, so they can't hear you, either. On rainy days, pedestrians may not see you because of hats or umbrellas. They may be hurrying to get out of the rain and may not pay attention to the traffic.

People who are distracted are hazards. Watch for where they are looking. If they are looking elsewhere, they can't see you. Be alert to what's distracting them.

Be alert to others even when they are looking right at you. They may believe that they have the right of way.

Children tend to act quickly without checking traffic. Children playing with one another may not look for traffic and are a serious hazard. Look for clues that children are in the area. For example, someone selling ice cream is a hazard clue. Children may be nearby and may not see you.

Drivers changing a tire or fixing an engine often do not pay attention to the danger that roadway traffic is to them. They are often careless. Jacked-up wheels or raised hoods are hazard clues.

Accidents are particularly hazardous. People involved in the accident may not look for traffic. Passing drivers tend to look at the accident. People often run across the road without looking. Vehicles may slow or stop suddenly.

People in and around shopping areas are often not watching traffic because they are looking for stores or looking into store windows.

You should always be looking for hazards. They may turn into emergencies. Look for the hazards in order to have time to plan a way out of any emergency. When you see a hazard, think about the emergencies that could develop. Figure out what you would do. Always be prepared to take action based on your plans. That makes you a prepared, defensive driver. You will improve not only your own safety but the safety of all road users.

EMERGENCY MANEUVERS

In spite of your best efforts, you may be faced with an emergency. Traffic emergencies occur when two vehicles are about to collide. Vehicle emergencies occur when tires, brakes, or other critical parts fail. Your chances of avoiding a crash depend upon how well you take action.

Don't Stop

Stopping is not always the safest thing to do in an emergency. When you don't have

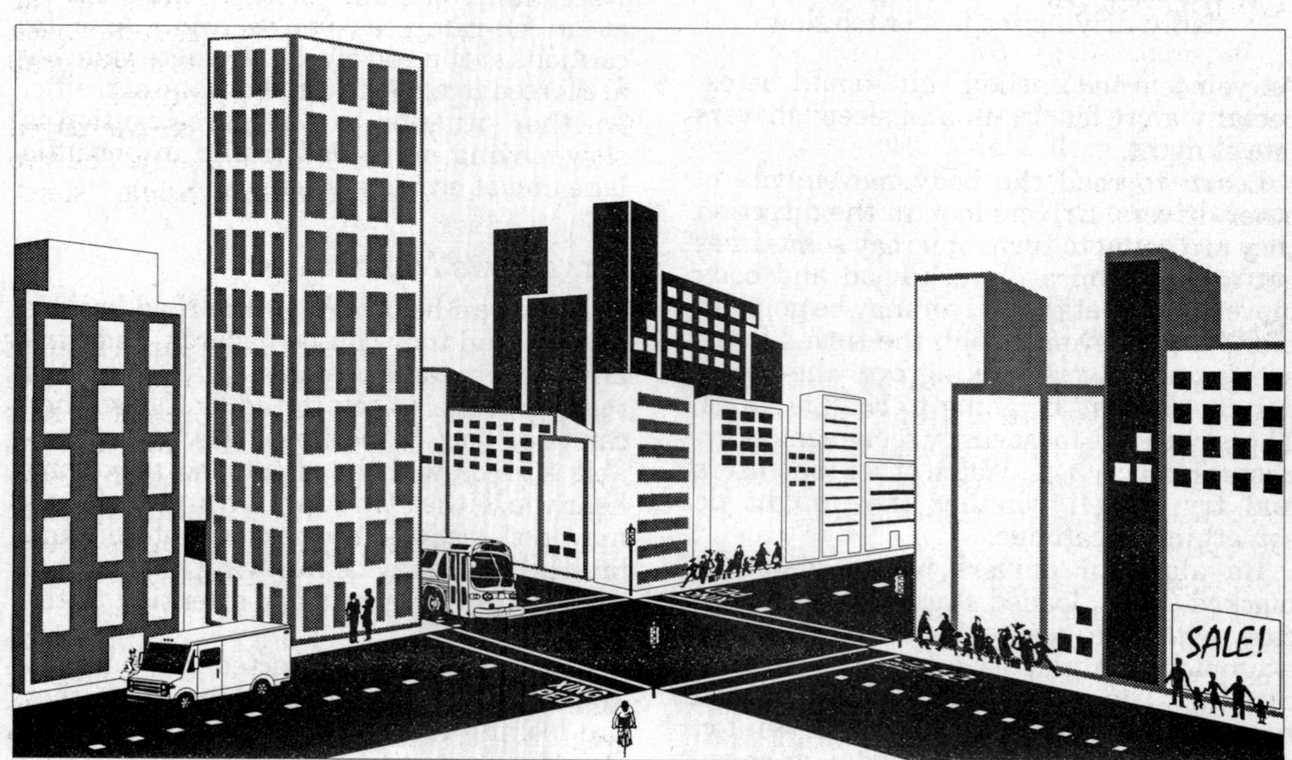

Figure 8-21 How many possible hazards can you spot in this picture?

enough room to stop, you may have to steer away from what's ahead. You can almost always turn to miss an obstacle more quickly than you can stop. Keep in mind, though, that top-heavy vehicles may flip over.

Turn Quickly and Safely

To turn quickly, you must have a firm grip on the steering wheel with both hands. The best way to have both hands on the wheel if there is an emergency is to keep them there all the time. Use the grip described at the beginning of this chapter.

A quick turn can be made safely, if it's done the right way. Don't apply the brake while you are turning. It's very easy to lock your wheels while turning. If that happens, you may skid out of control. If you have been managing your speed, you should be going slowly enough to control the vehicle without braking. Don't turn any more than needed to clear whatever is in your way. The more sharply you turn, the greater the chances of a skid or rollover.

Countersteer

Be prepared to "countersteer." Countersteering is turning the wheel back in the other direction once you've passed whatever was in your path. Unless you are prepared to countersteer, you won't be able to do it quickly enough. Think of emergency steering and countersteering as two parts of one driving action.

Steer to the Right

In most cases, steer to the right. If an oncoming driver has drifted into your lane, a move to your right is best. If that driver realizes what has happened, the natural response will be to return to his or her own lane.

If something is blocking your path, the best direction to steer will depend on the situation. If the shoulder is clear, going right may be best. No one is likely to be driving on the shoulder but someone may be passing you on the left. You will know if you have been using your mirrors.

If you are blocked on both sides, a move to the right may be best. At least you won't force anyone into an opposing traffic lane and a possible head-on collision.

If you have been using your mirrors, you'll know which lane is empty and can be safely used.

Leaving the Road

In some emergencies, you may have to drive off the road. It may be better than colliding with another vehicle. Most shoulders are strong enough to support the weight of a large vehicle.

If you do leave the road, avoid using the brakes until your speed has dropped to about 20 mph. Then brake very gently to prevent skidding on a loose surface. Keep one set of wheels on the pavement if possible. This helps to maintain control.

Stay on the shoulder. If the shoulder is clear, stay on it until your vehicle has come to a stop. Signal and check your mirrors before pulling back onto the road.

If you are forced to return to the road before you can stop, use the following procedure. Hold the wheel tightly and turn sharply enough to get right back on the road safely. Don't try to edge gradually back on the road. If you do, your tires might grab unexpectedly. You could lose control.

When both front tires are on the paved surface, countersteer immediately. The two turns should be made as a single "steer-countersteer" move.

Stop Quickly and Safely

If somebody suddenly pulls out in front of you, your natural response is to hit the brakes. This is a good response if there's enough distance to stop and you use the brakes correctly. You should brake in a way that will keep your vehicle in a straight line and allow you to turn if it becomes necessary. You can use the "controlled braking" method or the "stab braking" method.

In controlled braking, you apply the brakes as hard as you can without locking the wheels. Keep steering wheel movements very small while doing this. If you need to make a larger steering adjustment or if the wheels lock, release the brakes. Reapply the brakes as soon as you can.

In stab braking, you apply your brakes all the way. Release the brakes when the wheels lock up. As soon as the wheels start rolling, apply the brakes fully again. It can take up to one second for the wheels to start rolling after you release the brakes. If you reapply the brakes before the wheels start rolling, the vehicle won't straighten out.

Don't jam on the brakes. Emergency braking does not mean pushing down on the brake pedal as hard as you can. That will only cause the wheels to lock up and skid. If the wheels are skidding, you cannot control the vehicle.

Brake Failure

We've looked at loss of braking power on downgrades. There, a runaway ramp is your escape route. But what if your brakes fail and there is no escape ramp?

First, remember that brakes kept in good condition rarely fail. That's why brake inspection and maintenance is so important.

Most hydraulic brake failures occur for one of two reasons.

- loss of hydraulic pressure
- brake fade on long hills

When the system won't build up pressure, the brake pedal will feel spongy or go to the floor. If this happens, downshift. Putting the vehicle into a lower gear helps to slow the vehicle. You can also pump the brakes. Sometimes pumping the brake pedal will create enough hydraulic pressure to stop the vehicle.

The parking or emergency brake is separate from the hydraulic brake system. Therefore, it can be used to slow the vehicle. However, be sure to press the release button or pull the release lever at the same time you use the emergency brake. That way you can adjust the brake pressure and keep the wheels from locking up.

Find an escape route. While slowing the vehicle, look for an escape route. This could be an open field or side street as well as a designated escape ramp. Turning uphill is a good way to slow and stop the vehicle. Make sure the vehicle does not start rolling backward after you stop. Put it in low gear and apply the parking brake. You may have to roll back into some obstacle that will stop the vehicle.

When your brakes fail on a downgrade, use the tactics described in the "Mountain Driving" section of this chapter.

Tire Failure

There are four important things that safe drivers do to handle a tire failure safely:

- Be aware that a tire has failed.
- Hold the steering wheel firmly.
- Stay off the brake.
- After stopping, check all the tires.

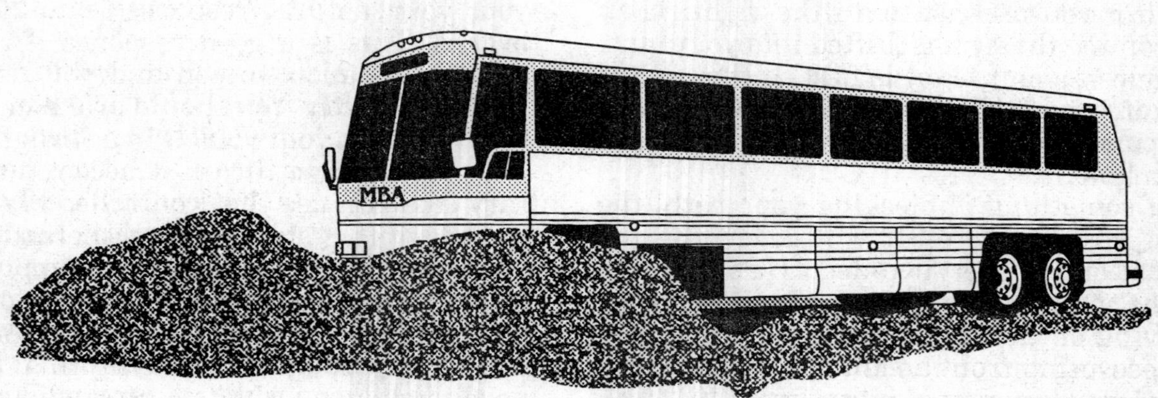

Figure 8-22 A hill of soft gravel will help stop your vehicle if you lose your brakes.

The sooner you realize you have a tire failure, the more time you will have to react. Having just a few seconds to remember what it is you're supposed to do can help you. Recognize the major signs of tire failure.

Sound is your first clue. The loud "bang" of a blowout is an easily recognized sign. Because it can take a few seconds for your vehicle to react to the tire failure, you might think the sound is coming from some other vehicle. To be safe, any time you hear a tire blow, assume it's yours.

If the vehicle thumps or vibrates heavily, it may be a sign that one of the tires has gone flat. With a rear tire, that may be the only sign you get.

If the steering feels heavy, it is probably a sign that one of the front tires has failed. Sometimes, failure of a rear tire causes the vehicle to slide back and forth or fishtail. However, dual rear tires usually prevent this.

Any of these signs is a warning of possible tire failure. To maintain control of the vehicle, hold the steering wheel firmly. If a front tire fails and you're holding the wheel loosely, the force can twist the steering wheel out of your hand. You must have a firm grip on the steering wheel with both hands at all times.

Stay off the brake. It's natural to want to brake in an emergency. However, braking when a tire has failed could cause you to lose control of the vehicle. Unless you're about to run into something, stay off the brake until the vehicle has slowed down. Then brake very gently, pull off the road, and stop.

After you've come to a stop, get out and check all the tires. Do this even if the vehicle seems to be handling all right. If one of your dual tires goes, the only way you may know it is by getting out and looking at it.

SKID CONTROL AND RECOVERY

Recovering from a skid can really challenge your emergency maneuvering skills.

A skid happens whenever the tires lose their grip on the road. A skid can result from over-braking, that is, braking too hard and locking up the wheels. Skids also can occur if you use the engine retarder when the road is slippery.

Oversteering can lead to skidding. Don't turn the wheels more sharply than the vehicle can turn.

Supplying too much power to the drive wheels can cause them to spin. That can lead to a skid.

Driving too fast is a common cause of skidding. Most serious skids result from driving too fast for road conditions. If you manage your speed, you don't have to speed up suddenly, brake hard, or oversteer to avoid a collision.

Drive-wheel Skids

By far the most common skid is one in which the rear wheels lose traction. This can result from over-braking or over-acceleration.

Skids caused by acceleration usually happen on ice or snow. They can easily be stopped by taking your foot off the accelerator. If it is very slippery, push the clutch in. Otherwise the engine can keep the wheels from rolling freely and regaining traction.

Rear-wheel braking skids occur when the rear drive wheels lock. Because locked wheels have less traction than rolling wheels, the rear wheels usually slide sideways in an attempt to catch up with the front wheels. In a straight vehicle, the vehicle will slide sideways in a "spin-out." When you're towing a trailer, a drive-wheel skid can let the trailer push the towing vehicle sideways, causing a sudden jackknife.

To correct a drive-wheel braking skid, first let off the brake. This lets the rear wheels roll again and keeps them from sliding any farther. If you are on ice, push in the clutch to let the wheels turn freely.

Turn quickly. When a vehicle begins to slide sideways, quickly steer in the direction you want the vehicle to go – down the road. You must turn the wheel quickly.

As a vehicle turns back on course, it has a tendency to keep right on turning. Unless you turn the steering wheel quickly the other way, you may find yourself skidding in the opposite direction. Your quick turn must be followed by countersteering.

Learning to stay off the brake, turn the steering wheel quickly, push in the clutch, and countersteer in a skid takes a lot of practice. You don't often get to practice skid recovery. Usually, when you're trying to get out of a skid, it's the real thing. About the only place to get this practice is on a large driving range or "skid pad."

Front-wheel Skids

Most front-wheel skids are caused by driving too fast for conditions. They can also result from worn front tires. If your cargo is loaded so that not enough weight is on the front axle, you may skid.

In a front-wheel skid, the front end tends to go in a straight line no matter how much you turn the steering wheel. On a very slippery surface, you may not be able to steer around a curve or turn.

When a front-wheel skid occurs, the only way to stop the skid is to let the vehicle slow down. Stop turning or braking so hard. Slow down as quickly as possible without skidding.

COUPLING AND UNCOUPLING

We're almost to the end of the skills CDL drivers are required to have. As you saw in Chapter 5, you must have some knowledge about hazardous materials. Even if you don't plan to haul them, you must be able to recognize a hazardous materials shipment when you see one. The basic information about hazardous materials was included in the FMCSR summary in Chapter 6 and is presented in FMCSR Part 397. Make sure you have all the information under your belt.

CDL drivers must also show they know how to inspect their vehicles and why it's important to do so. Vehicle inspections are covered in detail in Chapter 10.

There's one last area of information to mention before we leave this chapter. That's the coupling and uncoupling of tractors and trailers. If you drive a straight vehicle and plan never to pull a trailer, you may not need these skills. But you will have to take your CDL Skills Test in a Group B or C vehicle, without a trailer. If you drive a Group A vehicle or pull a trailer, you will be tested on your knowledge of coupling and uncoupling a tractor and semitrailer. You'll have to know how to inspect this vehicle combination.

Coupling and uncoupling and inspecting vehicle combinations are covered in Chapter 12. Don't skip that chapter if you are going for a Group A CDL.

We've covered a lot of ground in this chapter. The list of vital skills is long and detailed. You may already have many of these skills. Or you may have found quite a few new ones to master. To be a safe, skilled, licensed commercial driver, you must be in command of them all.

You may need several sessions with this chapter and quite a bit of practice with the tactics and techniques described here. Keep at it until safe vehicle control comes naturally to you.

PASS POST-TRIP

Instructions: For each true/false test item, read the statement. Decide whether the statement is true or false. If it is true, select the letter "A." If it is false, select the letter "B." For each multiple-choice test item, choose the answer choice – A, B, C, or D – that correctly completes the statement or answers the question. There is only one correct answer.

1. Rough acceleration can not only damage the vehicle, it can cause you to lose control.

A. True
B. False

2. How far ahead of the vehicle should a driver look while driving?

A. nine to 12 seconds
B. 18 to 21 seconds
C. 12 to 15 seconds
D. 12 to 15 feet

3. When driving 55 mph on dry pavement, allow ______ to bring the vehicle to a stop.

A. the length of a football field
B. twice the length of the vehicle
C. half the length of a football field
D. the length of the vehicle

4. Hydroplaning ______.

A. occurs only when there is a lot of water
B. occurs only at speeds above 55 mph
C. is more likely if tire pressure is low
D. is more likely if the road is banked

5. You're driving a 50-foot vehicle at night. Although you are on the highway, a bad rainstorm is forcing you to creep along at 40 mph. You should keep ______ seconds of distance between you and the vehicle ahead.

A. four
B. five
C. six
D. seven

6. When there are two turning lanes, you should start a left-hand turn from the right or outer lane.

A. True
B. False

7. When you are dead tired, the best way to refresh yourself and get ready to drive again is to ______.

A. have a drink
B. go for a brisk walk
C. drink some coffee
D. get some sleep

8. Roads are most slippery and dangerous during ______ a rainstorm.

A. the first 15 minutes of
B. the last 15 minutes of
C. the heaviest part of
D. a pause in

9. "Fanning the brakes" is a recommended downhill braking tactic.

A. True
B. False

10. You may hear a tire blow before you feel it.

A. True
B. False

CHAPTER 9

Cargo and Vehicle Control

When you have finished this chapter, you will be able to provide the correct answers to questions about:

- how natural forces affect loaded vehicles
- size and distribution regulations
- load securement and cargo inspection
- the challenge of driving a loaded vehicle

To complete this chapter you will need:

- a dictionary
- pencil or pen
- blank paper or notebook
- colored pencils, pens, markers, or highlighters
- a CDL preparation manual from your state Department of Motor Vehicles, if one is offered
- Federal Motor Carrier Safety Regulations pocketbook (or access to U.S. Department of Transportation regulations, Parts 383, 391–393 of Subchapter B, Chapter 3, Title 49, Code of Federal Regulations)
- operator's manual for your vehicle

PASS PRE-TRIP

Instructions: Read the statements. Decide whether each statement is true or false. If it is true, circle the letter "A." If it is false, circle the letter "B."

1. Axle weight is how much an axle weighs.
  A. True
  B. False

2. For stability, the center of gravity should always be in the middle of the cargo area.
  A. True
  B. False

3. If you always operate at the legal size limits set by states, you can be certain you will be operating safely.
  A. True
  B. False

Chapters 7 and 8 contained a lot of information about vehicle safety control systems and safe driving. If you don't handle it properly, your CMV can be dangerous to you and to others on the roadway and alongside it. So those chapters, and the skills described in them, are very important.

In a way, though, Chapter 9 is what the CMV driver's job is all about. After all, why drive a CMV in the first place? It's to transport something. An empty vehicle isn't earning anyone any money. You will rarely drive an empty vehicle.

Like almost everything else in CMV driving, there's a right way and a wrong way to transport cargo. As you might expect, the wrong way usually means damage, and sometimes injury and death.

FMCSR Part 383 states that CMV drivers must understand the relationship of cargo to vehicle control. This includes the principles and procedures for proper cargo handling. FMCSR Part 391 says you must be able to tell whether cargo is distributed properly and be able to secure cargo. This is so even if you don't intend to drive a cargo-carrying vehicle. That's because once you have a CDL, you are allowed to transport cargo in a truck. So the government feels you should know something about the subject.

FMCSR Part 393 gives some rules about transporting cargo. It describes how to equip trucks and trailers to keep cargo from shifting or falling. This part also describes how to secure coils of metal on a flatbed and how to tie down other metal cargo. This part of the FMCSR also covers hauling intermodal cargo containers. It states specifications for securement devices.

But there is far more to know about driving a loaded vehicle than what's in those few pages. This chapter will give you the information you need to comply with the regulations. This will help you earn and keep your CDL. This chapter will tell you what you need to drive a loaded vehicle safely. Some of the information will be useful to you no matter what the load. Some of it won't seem to have much to do with the job of driving a bus. But all of it will be on your CDL tests.

As a bus driver, your cargo is people. To transport people, you will need a Passenger Endorsement. To get it, you'll need special knowledge and skill besides what's in this chapter. You'll find what you need to know for the Passenger Endorsement in Chapter 13.

Note that to haul cargo using double or triple trailers, you'll need a Doubles/Triples Endorsement. In other driving jobs, the cargo is bulk liquids. You need a Tank Vehicle Endorsement for this. The last special type of cargo is hazardous materials. As you know, you need a Hazardous Materials Endorsement to haul placard loads. Pulling doubles and triples, hauling bulk liquids and hazardous materials are covered in our other CDL preparation book, *How to Prepare for the Commercial Driver's License Truck Driver's Test.*

FORCES OF NATURE

If you have been driving for any length of time at all, you may have noticed something about driving a loaded vehicle compared with driving an empty one. Whether it's people or package freight, cargo affects the way your vehicle handles. Sometimes the vehicle pulls to one side. It may feel top-heavy. It may feel as if it's going to tip over. It may be harder to get it rolling. You may have a hard time stopping the vehicle.

This is because, as solid and stable as it may seem, your vehicle is subject to the forces of nature. These forces are:

- friction
- gravity
- inertia

Knowing how the forces of nature affect a loaded vehicle will help you control that vehicle. This is true no matter what your vehicle is loaded with.

Friction

Simply put, friction is one surface rubbing against another. You've run into this term before. We mentioned friction in terms of how brakes work. Friction between your tires and the road is what gives you traction and the ability to move. Friction also comes into play in loading and securement.

Gravity

Gravity has to do with the natural attraction between two masses. Like friction, gravity helps to hold your vehicle on the road. Too much gravity will keep your vehicle from moving. Gravity helps keep cargo securely in place. It can also move cargo out of place. The pull of gravity on your vehicle and the load in it can make the vehicle hard to handle.

Inertia

Inertia is the tendency of an object that is in motion to stay in motion. Objects that are standing still tend to stay that way. For example, if your vehicle is moving, it will tend to continue to move. It will take a greater force, like a lot of friction, to overcome the inertia and make the vehicle stop. If it is standing still, the vehicle will tend to remain standing still. You will have to overcome inertia to get the vehicle to move.

Inertia affects cargo the same way. When you place baggage or freight in your vehicle, it's standing still. It will stay that way until a force makes it move. Once it's in motion, it takes another force to get it to stop.

Cargo and the Forces of Nature

The three forces often act on cargo together.

Picture your passengers sitting on their seats. There is friction between them and the seat surface. This friction keeps them from sliding off their seats. There is also gravity pulling on your passengers. If there were no gravity, they would simply float around weightlessly. Inertia is also working to keep the passengers in place.

This is all fine, as long as the forces are present in the right amounts. As you have seen, some friction helps keep people from sliding off their seats. A smooth seat such as a plastic or vinyl one offers little friction. People may actually slide around quite a bit. A rougher cloth seat offers more friction. When the vehicle moves, it's less likely people will slide off their seats.

Now imagine you're driving up a steep hill. Gravity works in a different way from the way it did on level ground. Without enough friction (or seat backs) to hold the passengers in place, they will all slide off their seats to the back of the bus. Once they are in motion, inertia works so they continue to move around. Once you had people sitting securely in their seats. Now you have helpless passengers rolling around on the floor.

Cargo securement devices help the forces of nature to work for you, not against you. But they help only if they are in good condition and you use them correctly. Proper loading and driving techniques also make the job of handling a loaded vehicle easier and safer. Later in this chapter, we discuss how to do just that.

SIZE AND BALANCE

The size and balance of the vehicle and its load are important for two reasons. One is that states, counties, and even cities have laws about vehicle size limits. Laws regu-

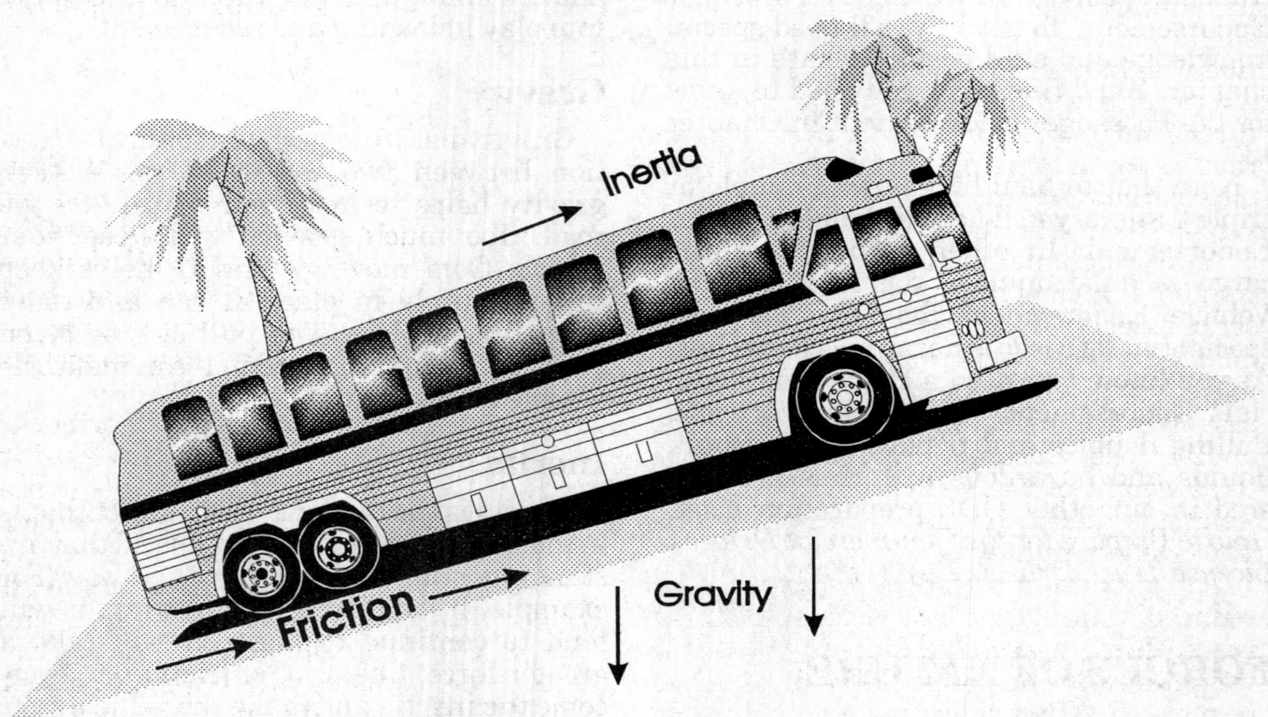

Figure 9-1 The forces of nature can work for or against you, your vehicle, and your load.

late how heavy your vehicle and load can be. They also regulate height, width, and length.

Other laws state how the weight should be distributed in the vehicle. The idea is to keep from having too much weight on any one portion of the vehicle. Why? An overloaded or poorly loaded vehicle can damage the road surface. Poor loading affects how the vehicle handles, as we have said. It affects steering, braking, and speed control. If you lose control of your vehicle, you could have an accident. Safety is the second reason size and balance are important.

Size and Balance Terms

The laws use certain terms in specific ways. Let's define those terms first.

Gross vehicle weight (GVW) is the total weight of a single vehicle plus its load. Gross combination weight (GCW) is the total weight of the power unit or tractor, plus any trailers, plus the cargo. (This also applies to a vehicle towing another vehicle as cargo.) Gross vehicle weight rating (GVWR) is a rating given to the vehicle by its manufacturer. It is the top GVW for that single vehicle plus its load. Gross combination weight rating (GCWR) is – that's right – a rating given the vehicle by its manufacturer. And it's the top GCW for the combination of power unit plus trailer or trailers plus cargo. (Again, the cargo could be a vehicle, as in a towaway operation.)

Axle weight is not how much the axle weighs. It is how much weight the axle (or set of axles) transmits to the ground. Axles hold the wheels, which enable the vehicle to move. That's true. Axles also hold the brake assembly. But axles also support the vehicle and its load. Each axle carries part of the total weight of the vehicle and load. That weight is then transmitted to the ground. That's axle weight.

The maximum legal axle weight may be reduced still further by a bridge law. Like roads, bridges can handle just so much weight at any one point. There must never be more than that at any point or the bridge will break. Many states have laws to prevent this. These are called bridge laws. A bridge formula is used to determine how much weight is put on any point by any group of axles. A tandem axle is an example of a group of axles. If there is more than one set of tandems, the formula takes into account how close the tandems are to each other. The result could be an even lower maximum axle weight for each axle in the group.

Tires, wheels, and suspensions all support the vehicle. They all carry weight. You learned in Chapter 6 that tires, wheels, and suspensions are rated. The manufacturer states how much weight these parts can carry. The most weight a tire can carry safely is called "tire load." As you learned, the rating is taken at a stated inflation pressure. If the tire is underinflated or overinflated, this rating may no longer apply. An underinflated or overinflated tire may not be able to carry safely the same load it can carry at the proper inflation pressure.

The same idea applies to other parts that have a load or weight rating. One example is coupling devices, such as saddle mounts, tow bars, and chains. Securement devices also have load or weight ratings. Loading a device beyond its rating is illegal and unsafe.

Weight Limits

There are specific laws on weight. States have limits for GVWs, GCWs, and axle weights. Some states have bridge laws. You must know the limits set by each state you run in. Professional driver's map books often have details on specific state size limits and bridge laws. You must stay within those limits.

There are laws about weight distribution, too. As mentioned, the weight must be balanced. That is, it must be spread throughout the vehicle so each axle bears an equal amount of the load.

Before you can understand weight distribution, you have to know something about "the center of gravity." The center of gravity is the point where weight acts as a force. That is, weight itself becomes something to be concerned about. The center of gravity affects the vehicle's stability. When all the axles equally support the center of gravity the vehicle is stable. The best place for the center of gravity will not always be the center of the vehicle.

It's easier to understand this by looking at an example. A cargo-carrying truck makes a better example than a bus. That's because we can examine the results of different ways of distributing the weight. So picture a flatbed straight truck.

First of all, remember that the vehicle's axles provide the support. Not the cargo floor – the axles. This includes the front axles. Imagine the empty vehicle on level ground. Picture all the wheels touching the road. Draw a line from wheel to wheel, making a rectangle. (See Figure 9-2 A.) When the vehicle's center of gravity is over the center of this rectangle, each axle supports an equal amount of weight. The vehicle is most stable.

But where is the center of gravity? Think about this vehicle. Right now it's empty. Where is the heaviest part of it? It's probably in the engine compartment. Where is the support rectangle? It's mostly under the cargo floor. The center of gravity is not well supported. (See Figure 9-2 B.) The front axles are bearing most of the weight. That's why an empty vehicle can be unstable. If you lose traction under the rear wheels while driving this vehicle, you can easily go into a rear-wheel skid.

Let's load some heavy boxes on the flatbed. Where is the center of gravity now? Remember to include the entire vehicle: cab, engine, load, and all. The load is probably as heavy as the engine. Taken as a whole, the center of gravity is somewhere around the front half of the cargo area. Picture a vertical line drawn through the center of gravity. It would drop right through the center of the rectangle, to the center of the earth. Each axle is supporting an equal amount of weight. The vehicle is stable. (See Figure 9-2 C.)

Now let's load the truck with something really heavy, like gold bars. The engine is heavy, but the cargo is heavier. The center of gravity of the vehicle, cargo and all, is now more toward the rear of the vehicle. It's no longer centered over the support rectangle. The vehicle is no longer stable. Most of the weight is being supported by the rear axles. (See Figure 9-2 D.)

You may not notice this on dry, level ground. So let's hit a slippery spot in the road. Remember, the front wheels do not have much of a load on them. The rear wheels are providing the support. You now lose what little friction there was between your front tires and the road. You go into a front-wheel skid.

This would not have happened had the load been better balanced. This truck may have even been within weight limits. But it would have been better to load the heavy cargo a little differently. The load should have been placed a little more toward the front of the cargo area. That would have moved the center of gravity. The front axles would have received their fair share of the weight.

Of course, when you load passengers in a bus, you don't take pains to distribute them evenly around the bus. (Can you just see it? "Heavy people, please sit over the wheels. Lighter people, sit in the middle of the bus.") You don't really have to. Buses are a little more stable than trucks, because of the way they're made. They're built closer to the ground. And the seats and other structures inside add weight that's evenly distributed throughout the vehicle body. The center of gravity is fairly well-supported, even in an empty bus.

Height Limits

States have height as well as weight limits. Again, there are two reasons. Overhead structures, like overpasses, can be damaged by too-tall vehicles or loads trying to go under them. Also, vehicles or loads that are too tall are unstable. Height limits ensure safety.

You saw that you could be carrying the legal amount of weight and still be unsafe. That was a center of gravity problem. You can be within the legal height limits and have a center of gravity problem with height, also. Here's how.

Let's take the load of gold bars again. We'll load into a van and spread them over the support rectangle in three even layers. Where is the center of gravity? It's centered over the rectangle, yes. It's also **low**. It's not

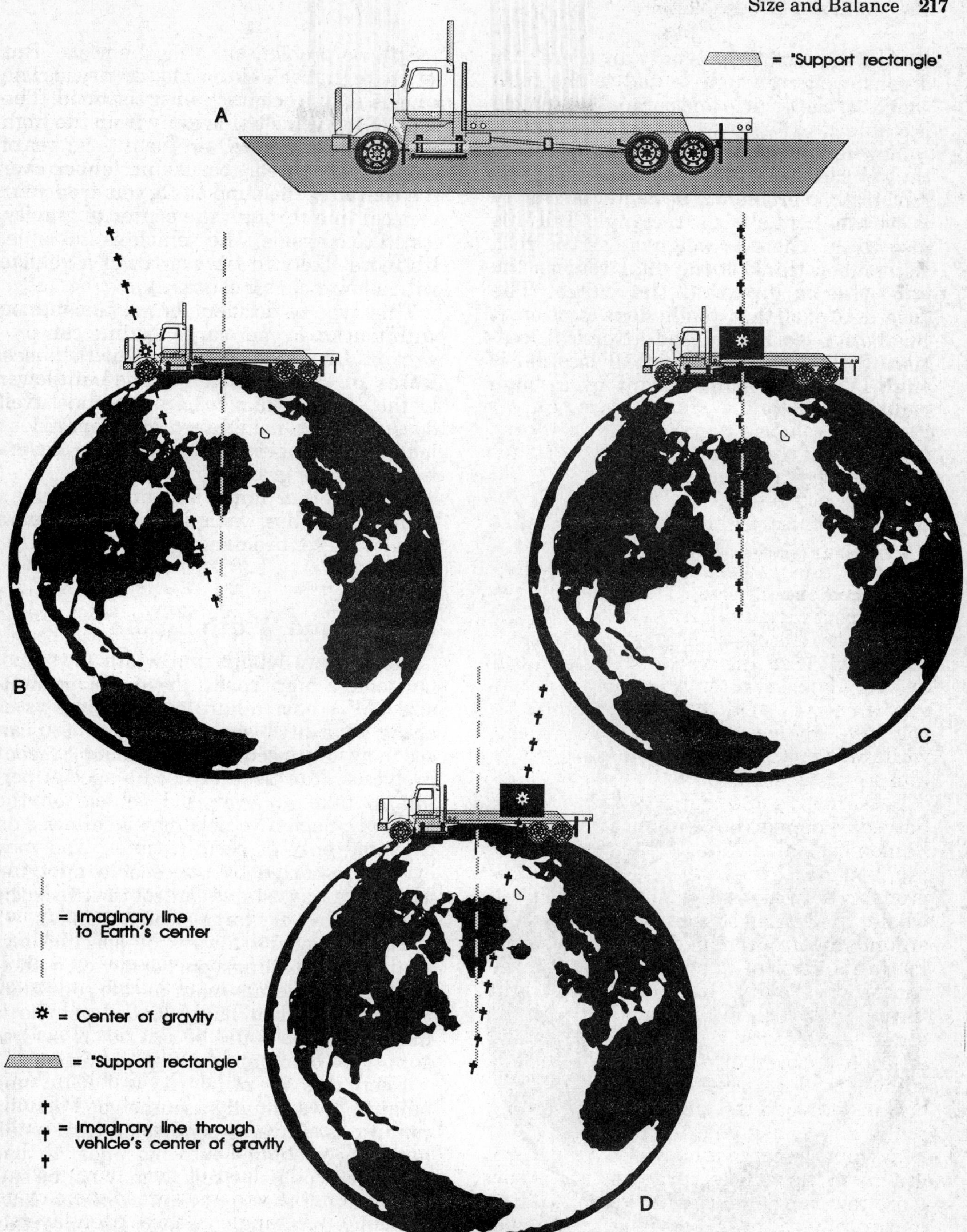

Figure 9-2 A, B, C, D. A vehicle is most stable when each axle supports an equal amount of weight.

toward the roof. There's only air there. Air doesn't weigh enough to add to the total weight of the vehicle and cargo. The vehicle is stable.

Now let's stack the bars in the center of the vehicle. Load them in stacks up to the roof. Still no problem. The center of gravity is over the center of the rectangle. But it is also **high**. There is weight near the roof. Remember, think of the total vehicle: the cab, the cargo area, the cargo. The "average" of all that weight has a location. It has both a horizontal and a vertical location. In this case, the vertical location is **high**. This is what is meant by a "high center of gravity."

= Imaginary line to Earth's center

✲ = Center of gravity

† = Imaginary line through load's center of gravity

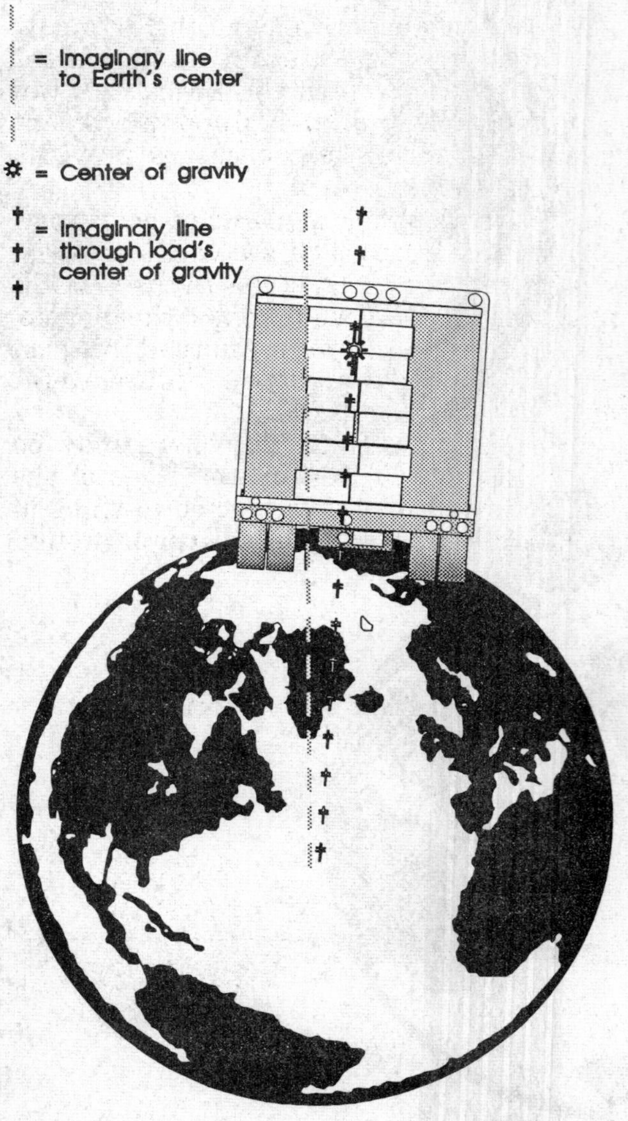

Figure 9-3 A high center of gravity can cause the vehicle to tip over.

Still no problem on a level surface. But let's take that vehicle on a banked road. The wheels stay in contact with the road. The body of the vehicle tilts away from the high side of the bank. Where is the center of gravity? It's tilted, too. It's no longer over the center of the support. If you drop your vertical line through the center of gravity, it's off to one side. The vehicle is unstable. It's more likely to tip over than a vehicle with a lower center of gravity.

This type of accident is not uncommon with trucks. Proper cargo loading can prevent it. It's less of a problem with buses. Buses are shorter in height and built lower to the ground than trucks. The bus itself does not have a high center of gravity. A load of passengers is not likely to have a high center of gravity, either.

On the other hand, you now see why a double-deck bus with its high center of gravity presents a driving challenge.

Length and Width Limits

States have length and width laws, too. On today's busy roads, drivers of normal-size CMVs have a hard enough time managing what little space they have. You can see how oversized vehicles could present problems. You usually need a special permit to take an oversized vehicle on the highway. Such a vehicle may be allowed on the road only at certain times. You may even be escorted by police or a pilot car. These are ways states control the use of the roadways by very large or heavy CMVs.

There may not always be specific laws against overloading a part or device. Still, it is illegal to operate in an unsafe condition. An overloaded or badly loaded vehicle is unsafe. So you could be put out of service simply for being in an unsafe condition.

Keep this in mind as well. Size and balance laws usually assume good driving conditions. Adverse conditions turn small handling problems into big ones. In bad weather or on bad roads, it may not be safe to operate at the legal limit. You may have to reduce the size of your load. It's for certain you should lower your speed, increase your following distances, and drive with care.

LOAD SECUREMENT AND CARGO INSPECTION

In your driving experience, you may have noticed something about baggage and package freight. It doesn't always stay where you put it. Friction, gravity, and inertia all act on cargo and can cause it to shift. The result may be damaged cargo. A severe shift in the load can make the vehicle unstable. It could even tip over. Or, cargo could spill out of the vehicle and become a highway hazard.

Proper loading isn't always enough to keep your load in place. You may need to use cargo securement devices. You may also have to take steps to protect the load. Then, you must check the load from time to time to make sure it's still safe.

Load Securement

FMCSR Part 392 has rules about securing baggage and freight on a bus. You must make sure cargo doesn't get in the way of your moving freely around the vehicle. Cargo must not block your access to the vehicle's controls. See that baggage and packages are not blocking any exits. Everyone on the bus, including the driver, must have easy access to the exits. Last, see that articles carried in the bus are safely stowed away. You must protect your passengers from falling or shifting cargo.

In Part 393 of the FMCSR, you'll find some general rules for protection against shifting or falling cargo. This information may not seem very useful to you as a bus driver. However, it is part of the general knowledge all CMV drivers must have. Therefore, you should be familiar with these rules.

Use tiedowns that are strong enough to do the job. The combined strength of all cargo tiedowns must be 1½ times the weight of the cargo being tied down.

Use enough tiedowns for the amount of cargo. There should be one tiedown for each 10 feet of cargo and no fewer than two tiedowns. Even the smallest load should have two tiedowns.

The whole purpose of chaining is to hold the load down and prevent its movement sideways or forward or backward. As you can see from Figure 9-4, proper placement and the direction of the chains prevents such movement.

FMCSR Part 393 explains in detail how coils of metal must be secured to restrict movement. The instructions in the FMCSR are quite clear. We won't repeat the instructions here. So make sure you read this part of the FMCSR thoroughly. Figures 9-5A and B illustrate these rules.

The steel hooks on the chain may be hooked to a steel rail on the sides of the trailer. Or they may be hooked to rings in the floor. The chain is placed over or around

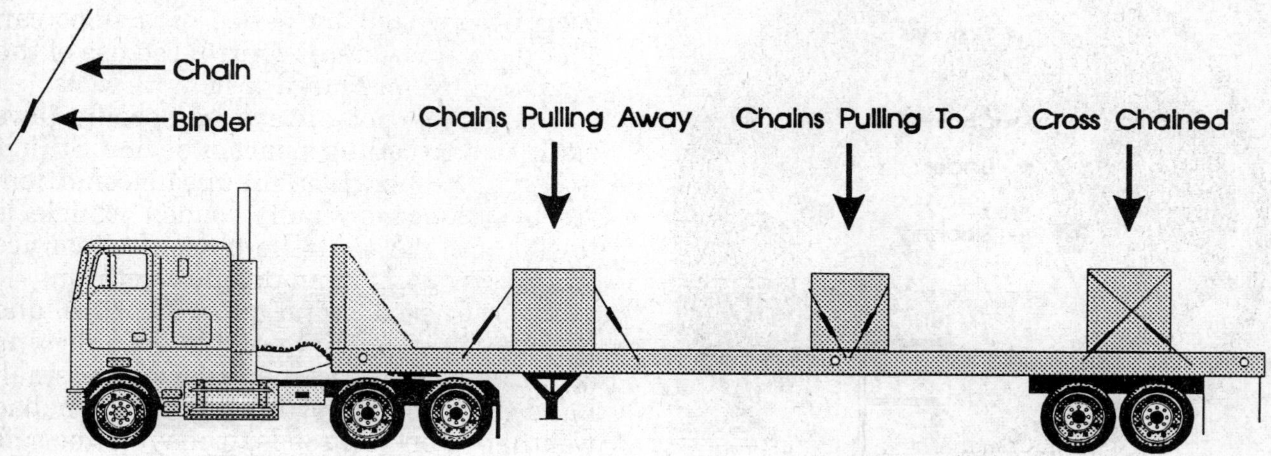

Figure 9-4 Securing a load with chains.

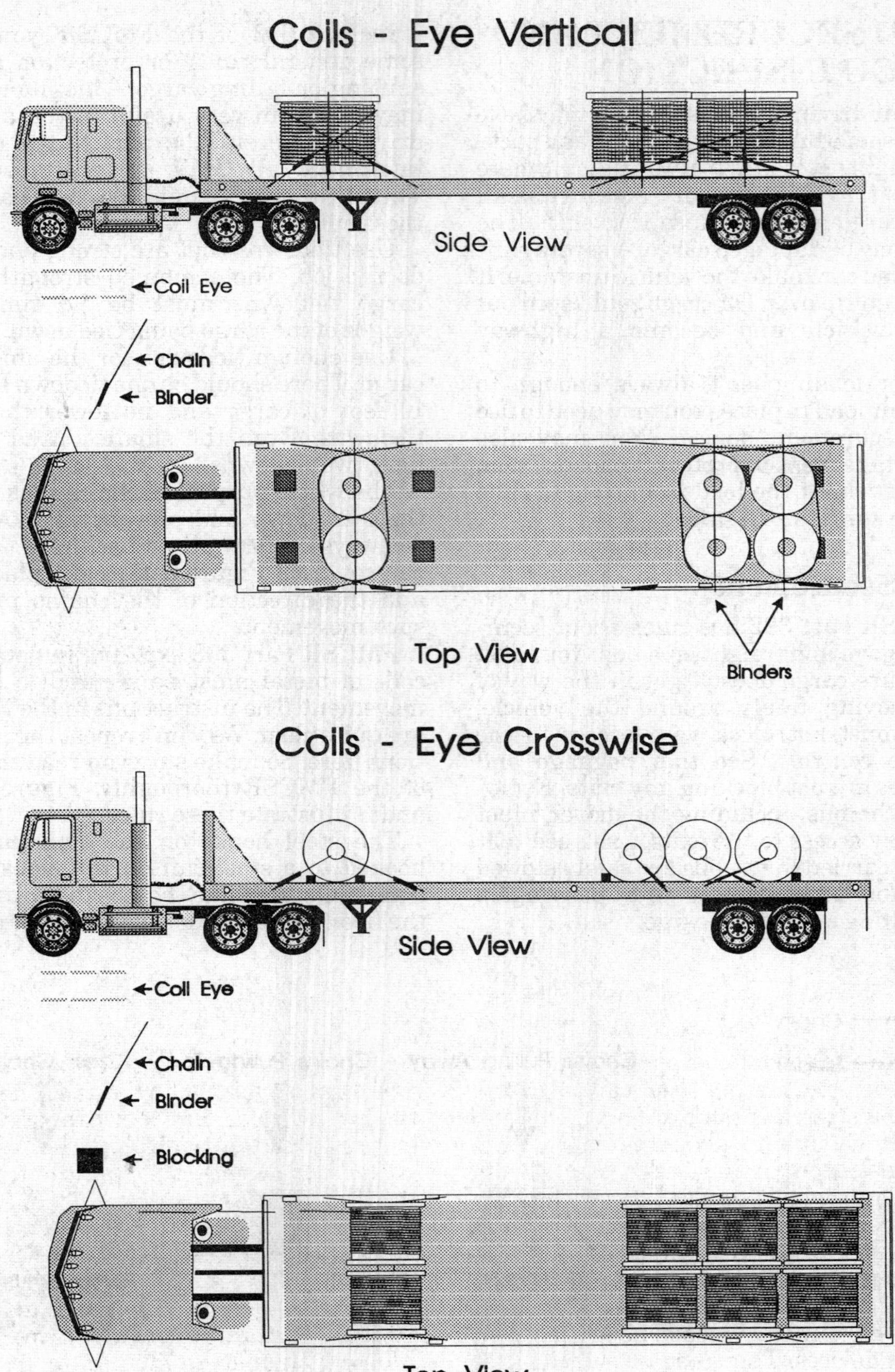

Figure 9-5A Metal coils chained on a flatbed with eyes vertical and eyes crosswise.

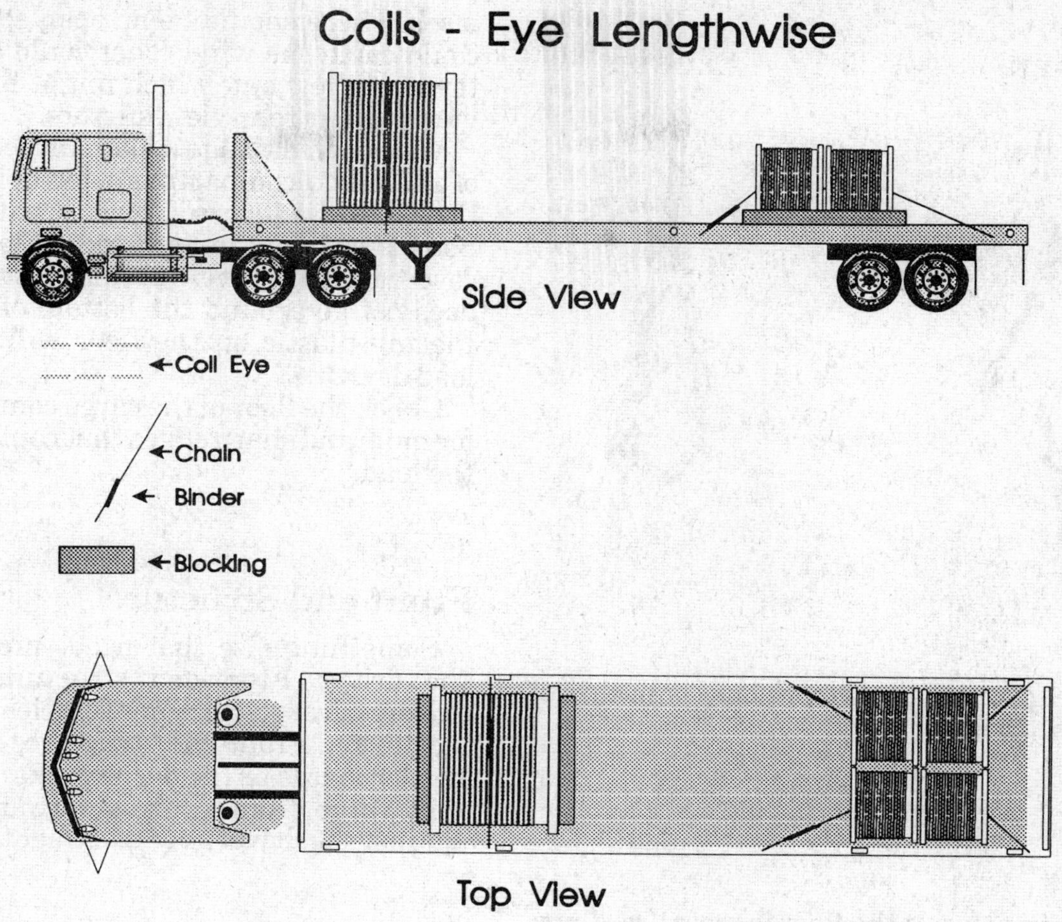

Figure 9-5B Metal coils chained on a flatbed with eyes lengthwise.

the cargo and stretched tight by hand.

However, no matter how hard you try, when you stretch chain by hand, it will not be tight enough to keep the cargo from shifting. The chain must be tightened even more. That's what a binder is for. You attach the binder end hooks to the chain with the binder lever open. Then you pull the binder lever to the closed position to tighten the chain.

Some containerized loads have their own tiedown devices. They may have locks that attach directly to a special frame. If they don't, they must be loaded onto flatbeds and tied down just like any other large cargo.

Cables, straps, and chains all help keep the load in place. But they can crush, bend, or cut the load. Wooden blocks or "V boards" between the cable, strap, or chain protect the edge of the load.

Blocking or bracing keeps the cargo in place. You can use blocking on the front, back, or sides – or all around. Bracing goes from the upper part of the cargo to the floor or walls of the cargo compartment.

Blocks should be shaped to fit snugly against the cargo. Then secure them to the floor. If the floor is wood, you can nail the

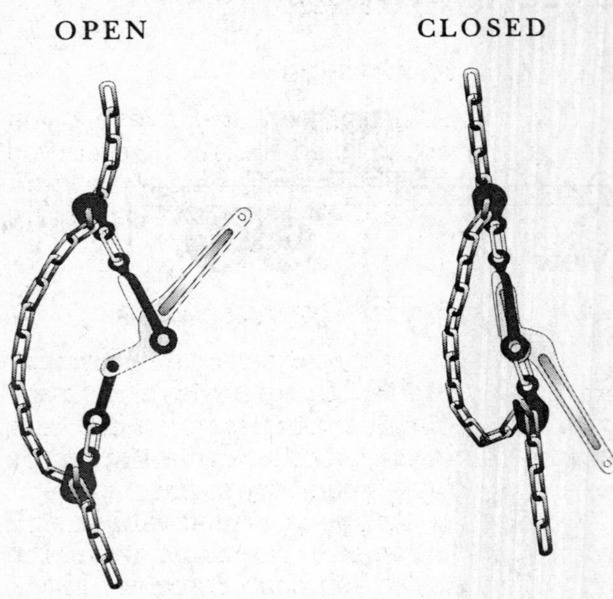

Figure 9-6 A chain binder in the open position and the closed position.

blocks in place. If the floor is metal, you can use chains to hold the bracing in place against the load.

Lumber used for the brace should be free of knots and cracks. Make sure the nails used are at least twice as long as the thickness of the board they are being driven through. They should be nailed straight down or at an angle against the movement of the cargo.

You should protect the cargo so it arrives in good condition. You may have to tarp your load. ("Tarp" is short for tarpaulin.) It covers and protects exposed cargo. It also protects others on or alongside the road from cargo that flies off or spills from the vehicle. Some states have laws that require covering any flatbed or open-top vehicle.

Tarps are tied down with rope, fabric webbing, or elastic cords with hooks. To tarp a load, lift the rolled up tarp to the top of the front and unroll it across to the back of the vehicle. The tarp must be even and tight so it will not flap at normal highway speed. That could block your view or someone else's. There should be no open spaces that could catch the wind. That could cause the tarp to billow out, which might block your view in your rear-view mirrors.

Water can damage a load. Inspect the bed of the cargo compartment for holes. If the floor is not waterproof, cover it with plastic. Sometimes the top and sides of loads come covered with plastic, but this plastic usually does not go around the bottom of the load. Placing plastic on the floor will keep the load dry.

Check the floor of the cargo compartment for nails and sharp edges that could damage the load.

Front-end Structure

Something else that needs protection is the driver. Front-end structures protect drivers of cargo-carrying vehicles if there is a collision. Front-end structures are called headerboards or headache racks. They prevent cargo from shifting forward into or against the driver's compartment.

Cargo Inspection

Regulations require that truck and truck-tractor drivers inspect cargo, including tarped loads. The only exception is sealed cargo. Of course you can't inspect sealed cargo. Drivers are still responsible if such cargo exceeds gross weight or axle limits, though.

Drivers of these cargo-carrying vehicles must check the cargo as part of the pre-trip inspection. Once they're on the road, they must check the load often. The first inspection comes within the first 25 miles. They also make a cargo inspection:

- at every change of duty status, including stops for fuel, meals, or rest or at a port of entry, or
- after the vehicle has been driven for three hours or 150 miles, whichever comes first.

This inspection should include tiedowns, blocking, bracing, and tarping. Make sure none of the nails are pulling away. Pull at each chain. Lightly tapping the chains with a tire hammer will tell you whether they are tight or loose. A tight chain will cause the hammer to bounce back. If there is any slack, open the binder and adjust it.

DRIVING WITH A LOAD

You have seen in general how the forces of nature and the center of gravity affect how a vehicle handles. Here are some specific handling problems you may run into when carrying a load.

Starting and Stopping

Adding weight increases the effects of gravity. When you are hauling a light load, the effect of gravity is small. You can move easily.

When you are hauling a heavy load, gravity pulls harder on the vehicle. The engine has to work harder to overcome the pull of gravity. It takes more effort to put the vehicle in motion.

The load, and the pull of gravity, affects the vehicle's stopping ability. A heavy load increases the effect of gravity. That gives you more traction. That means the vehicle will stop better, in less time, and in a shorter distance. A light load does not increase the pull of gravity. Since you're moving faster and more easily, it takes more time and distance to stop the vehicle. In short, when your vehicle is empty or lightly loaded, you need more stopping distance.

Poor weight distribution can make axles too light. They lose contact with the road. As you have seen, this makes it easy to skid. Although this is less of a problem with buses than with trucks, it's something you should be aware of.

Turning

Loading the vehicle puts extra weight on the axles. This includes the steering axle. The more weight on the steering axle, the harder it is to steer. Too much weight on the rear axles makes the steering axle too light. This also decreases steering control.

Banks and Curves

If you have a high center of gravity, you will really notice it on banked and curved roads. The vehicle could tip over if the bank is steep enough or the load is badly unbalanced.

Upgrades and Downgrades

A loaded vehicle will perform differently from an empty one on upgrades and downgrades. Overloaded vehicles pull a hill very slowly. Be aware that other drivers are more prone to tailgate you or try to pass.

On the downgrade, a loaded vehicle will really pick up speed. You must be in the right gear before you head downhill. If you are going too fast, you will have to use your brakes. Trying to slow or stop a heavily loaded vehicle going downhill at high speed sets the stage for brake failure. This is a type of accident that is all too common, and easily prevented.

Special Vehicle Control Problems

Some vehicles and loads present drivers of cargo-carrying vehicles with serious vehicle control problems. These vehicles and loads are:

- refrigerated vans carrying "swinging meat"
- trailers carrying livestock
- oversize loads
- tank vehicles carrying bulk loads

Today, most meat is hauled in tubs. But you'll sometimes see it transported as sides of meat hung from rails in the cargo compartment. This is called "swinging meat," and with good reason. The motion of the truck can cause the sides of meat to swing back and forth. Once they start, they can really build up some momentum. This can result in a very unstable vehicle, especially on curves and ramps.

If the animals in a livestock trailer are not held in place, they can move around. Their movements can make the vehicle very unstable.

Loads that are over legal length, width, or weight may sometimes be transported. But you will often need a special permit from the state or states you'll travel through. You may be limited to driving during certain hours. Your vehicle may have to have extra equipment, such as "wide load" signs, flashing lights, and flags. You may be required to have a police escort or pilot car. And as you might expect, an oversize load requires special driving care.

Dry bulk tanks often have a high center of gravity. The load can shift inside the tank. This calls for extreme caution on banked and curved roads.

Bulk liquids in a partly-filled liquid tank vehicle can surge back and forth. In a smooth-bore tank, there is nothing to slow down the flow of the liquid. The liquid can continue to move even when the vehicle has come to a stop. This surge can be a powerful force. When the wave hits the end of the tank, it can shove the vehicle in the direction of the wave. If the vehicle is on a slippery surface like ice, the wave can push a stopped vehicle out into an intersection. Shifting, stopping, and turning just make this vehicle control problem worse. Because of liquid surge, tank vehicle drivers must avoid abrupt vehicle movements.

TIP *Tank vehicles carry both dry and liquid loads. However for CDL purposes, the term "tank vehicle" is defined as any CMV designed to transport any liquid or gaseous materials with a tank. The tank can be either permanently or temporarily attached to the vehicle or the chassis. This includes cargo tanks, and portable tanks having a rated capacity of 1,000 gallons or more.*

Some tanks have bulkheads, while others have baffles. Bulkheads divide the tank into separate compartments. Completely different liquid cargos can be hauled side-by-side in the same tank. Bulkheads inside liquid tankers also help prevent surge. Tank vehicle drivers must take care not to overload any one compartment. That would put too much weight on one axle. As you have seen, that creates steering problems.

Baffles are like bulkheads, with a hole in the middle. Only one type of liquid cargo may be hauled at one time, since it will flow through the holes. Like bulkheads, baffles help control front-to-back surge. Side-to-side surge can still be a problem, though. Also, bulkheads form compartments inside the tank.

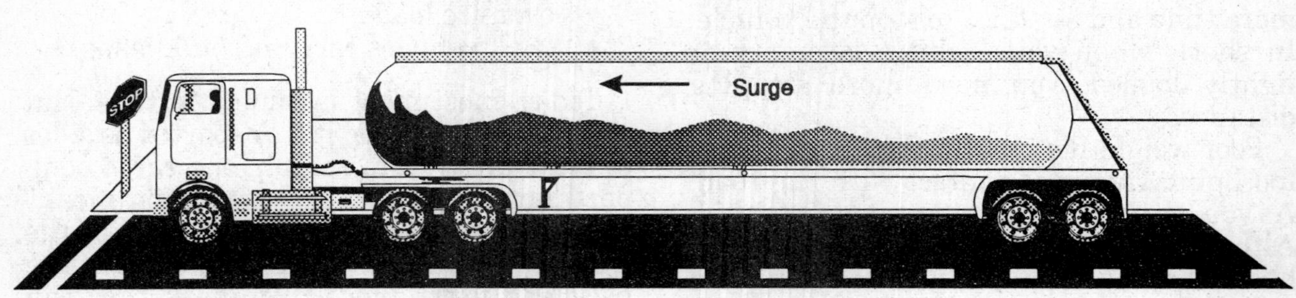

Figure 9-7 The surging of liquid loads makes a tank vehicle a driving challenge.

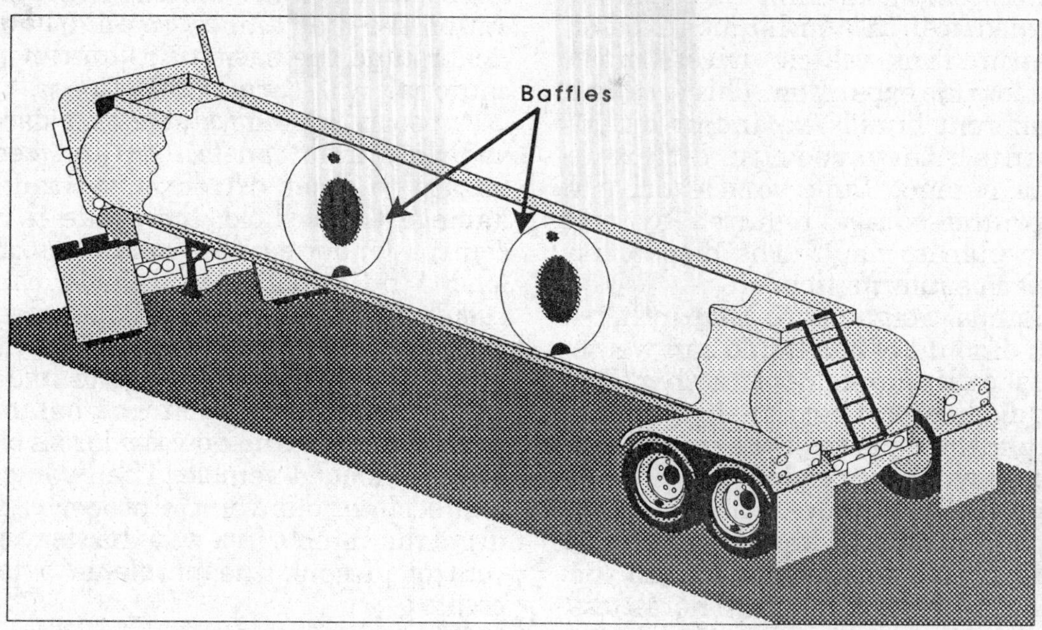

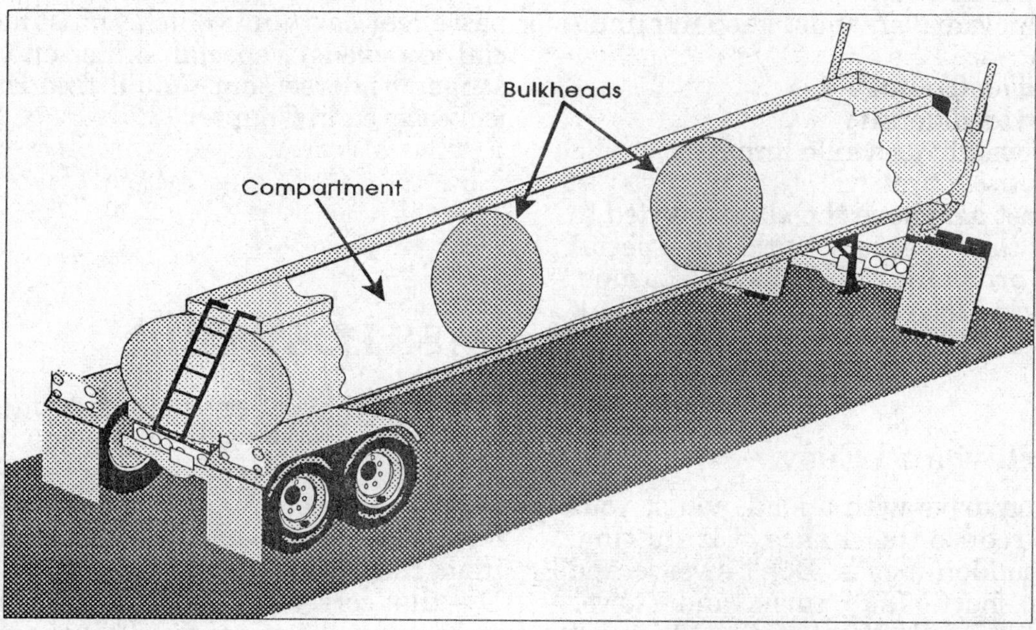

Figure 9-8 Baffles in a tank control the movement of liquid cargo. Bulkheads make completely separate compartments inside the tank.

Liquids won't surge much at all if the tank is filled completely full. But tankers can't be loaded up to the top. Liquids expand as they warm. Tank vehicle drivers must leave room for this expansion. This is called outage. Different liquids expand by different amounts. They require different amounts of outage. Tank vehicle drivers must know the outage required by the liquid they plan to haul. (The dispatcher usually has this information.)

Some liquids weigh more than others. That is, an amount of one liquid can weigh more than the same amount of another. The heavier liquid has a higher density.

The higher the density of the liquid, the less the surge will be. A high density liquid will be less likely to move. Also, a small amount of a high density liquid can be very heavy. You can't load much of it into the tank without being overweight. There's less risk of loading the tank so full it creates a high center of gravity.

Tank vehicle drivers must keep in mind:

- liquid load outage
- liquid load density
- legal weight and axle limits

They must also have the skills needed to control a tank vehicle with its special handling problems. (For these reasons, tank vehicle drivers must have a Tank Vehicle Endorsement on their CDL.)

Take It Slow and Easy

When you drive with a load, adjust your driving to reduce the chance of it shifting. Make no sudden moves. Don't swerve and don't stop short. Take turns and curves slowly and carefully. While safe under most conditions, the posted speed limits may be too high for your loaded vehicle.

Keep a safe following distance. You must carefully manage the space around your vehicle. Give yourself time, space, and distance to maneuver.

Do not pull off the roadway onto an uneven surface. Drive more slowly than usual on off-ramps and on-ramps. Avoid parking areas that have sharp inclines.

Most drivers will haul some kind of cargo almost all the time. Vehicles are rarely sent out on the road empty. So all drivers must understand the basic rules of transporting cargo safely to earn a CDL license.

A poorly loaded vehicle is a dangerous vehicle. Cargo can fall off and become a hazard to other drivers. Overloading can damage the vehicle and make it hard to control. Under adverse conditions, an overloaded or unbalanced vehicle can be a rushing missile that can't be steered or stopped.

To prevent this, you have to understand the principles of weight and balance. You have to understand how the forces of nature act on a loaded vehicle. Then you can load and secure your vehicle properly. You can drive the vehicle in a way that leaves you in control, despite the problems a load can create.

When you're carrying passengers, your cargo is very precious indeed. Drivers of passenger-carrying vehicles must have special knowledge, special skills, and a Passenger Endorsement. You'll find this subject covered in Chapter 13.

PASS POST-TRIP

Instructions: For each true/false test item, read the statement. Decide whether the statement is true or false. If it is true, select the letter "A." If it is false, select the letter "B." For each multiple-choice test item, choose the answer choice – A, B, C, or D – that correctly completes the statement or answers the question. There is only one correct answer.

1. A vehicle that is in motion will tend to stay in motion because of ______.

A. friction
B. gravity
C. inertia
D. state regulations

2. Loading the vehicle incorrectly can ___.
- A. result in damage to the road surface
- B. make the vehicle hard to steer
- C. make the vehicle hard to stop
- D. all of the above

3. The gross combination weight (GCW) of a vehicle includes ______.
- A. the weight of the entire vehicle but not the cargo
- B. the weight of the entire vehicle and the cargo
- C. the weight of the cargo but not the vehicle
- D. the weight of the power unit only

4. The gross combination weight rating (GCWR) of a vehicle is ______.
- A. the weight of the entire vehicle plus its load
- B. the manufacturer's stated weight for the vehicle
- C. the total maximum axle weight allowed by the state
- D. the maximum weight stated by the manufacturer for a specific vehicle plus the load

5. Axle weight is how much an axle weighs.
- A. True
- B. False

6. Vehicles are rated for the weight they can carry. So are ______.
- A. tires, suspension systems, and coupling devices
- B. engines, brakes, and drive shafts
- C. hoses, belts, and wires
- D. switches, lubricants, and controls

7. For stability, the center of gravity should always be in the middle of the cargo compartment.
- A. True
- B. False

8. If you always operate at the legal size limits set by states, you can be certain you will be operating safely.
- A. True
- B. False

9. Cargo securement devices can help the forces of nature work for you, not against you, if ______.
- A. you use them correctly
- B. they are in good condition
- C. they are rated for the load
- D. all of the above

10. During a trip, drivers must inspect cargo at least once each ______, whichever comes first.
- A. hour or 50 miles
- B. two hours or 200 miles
- C. three hours or 150 miles
- D. 10 hours or 500 miles

CHAPTER 10
Vehicle Inspection

When you have finished this chapter, you will be able to provide the correct answers to questions about:

- commercial motor vehicle inspection

To complete this chapter you will need:

- a dictionary
- pencil or pen
- blank paper or notebook
- colored pencils, pens, markers, or highlighters
- a CDL preparation manual from your state Department of Motor Vehicles, if one is offered
- Federal Motor Carrier Safety Regulations pocketbook (or access to U.S. Department of Transportation regulations, Parts 383, 393, and 396 of Subchapter B, Chapter 3, Title 49, Code of Federal Regulations)
- operator's manual for your vehicle

PASS PRE-TRIP

Instructions: Read the statements. Decide whether each statement is true or false. If it is true, circle the letter "A." If it is false, circle the letter "B."

1. You can be put out of service in one state for a vehicle condition that was acceptable in another state.
A. True
B. False

2. Steering wheel free play should not be more than 10 degrees on a 20-inch steering wheel.
A. True
B. False

3. A windshield is considered defective if it has even one tiny crack.
A. True
B. False

The vehicle inspection is an important part of the CDL Test. FMCSR Part 383 states that CMV drivers must be familiar with FMCSR Part 396. As you now know, that includes vehicle inspection.

Look also at the appendix to Subpart G, if that's included in your copy of the FMCSR. That's the Required Knowledge and Skills Sample Guidelines. Many states use these guidelines to develop their CDL tests. Item (e) in the guidelines suggests CMV drivers should show they can do a proper inspection. It states that drivers should be able to make certain repairs and do some maintenance. CMV drivers should also know how to tell when problems develop during operation.

Most states have you perform an inspection as part of the Skills Test. During that time, you may also be asked to describe in some detail the different parts and systems on your vehicle as you inspect them. Or the examiner may have you stop your inspection from time to time to answer questions about your equipment.

Chapters 5 through 9, which you just finished, should help prepare you for this part of the CDL tests. You know what is required to be on your vehicle. You know how these systems work. You can understand how certain defects keep you from operating your vehicle safely. You know about proper cargo loading and securement. You understand how you, as the driver, are responsible for the safety of your vehicle, your passengers, and freight.

There's one more thing that will help you

pass the inspection part of the CDL tests. That's to have an inspection routine. If you have a routine, you won't fail to check the same things every time. You'll be less likely to forget or overlook something. You won't have to stop and make decisions. You won't have to ask yourself, "Should I check this?," or "Can I skip it this time?," or "Did I already inspect that?"

In this chapter we'll focus on straight trucks and buses. Drivers of passenger buses must make sure the vehicle is safe for passengers, as well as roadworthy. They must include some extra steps in their inspection. We'll cover the steps you should take to ensure passenger safety.

We'll cover inspecting combination vehicles in Chapter 12. You should practice that inspection if you plan to get a Group A CDL.

Perhaps you already have an inspection routine. If so, compare it to the routine described in this chapter that fits your vehicle. Make sure your routine includes all the required steps. If you don't have a routine, this chapter will help you develop one.

This chapter goes hand-in-hand with Chapters 6 and 7. Chapter 6 described the parts motor vehicles must have. Chapter 7 described how they work. It described some defects you should be on the lookout for. We will not repeat that information. So you should have a good grasp of Chapters 6 and 7 before you begin Chapter 10.

As you practice your inspection routine, also practice explaining what you are inspecting and why. State what defects you're looking for. State why such defects are problems. People may wonder why you are walking around your vehicle talking to yourself. But you will be well prepared for this part of the CDL tests.

WHY INSPECT?

One of the first things to know about vehicle inspection is why you do it. Inspecting your vehicle helps you to know your vehicle is safe. As you know, federal laws require inspection. Your state may also have laws on vehicle inspection.

WHO INSPECTS?

The motor carrier has the main inspection responsibility. You may recall that motor carriers must perform a periodic inspection of their vehicles. This is often referred to as the "annual inspection."

Motor carriers usually assign the routine inspections (pre-trip and post-trip) to the CMV drivers.

Federal and state inspectors also inspect commercial vehicles. These inspections may be performed while the vehicle is on the road, in operation. An unsafe vehicle can be put "out of service" at this time.

Figure 10-1 State police may inspect your vehicle while on the road.

Do you recall how long the vehicle remains out of service? It's until the driver or owner fixes it.

WHEN TO INSPECT

You'll also recall that you do a pre-trip inspection before each trip. You look for problems that could cause a crash or breakdown. These must be repaired before you can take the vehicle out.

You do a post-trip inspection at the end of the trip, day, or duty shift on each vehicle you operated. This may include filling out a vehicle condition report. In this report you list any problems you find. The inspection report helps the vehicle owner know when to fix something.

You should also ensure your safety and the safety of others by inspecting your vehicle during a trip. You should:

- watch gauges for signs of trouble
- use your senses (look, listen, smell, and feel) to check for problems

Check critical items when you stop. Critical items are those necessary for safe operation. Remember what they are? The list includes:

- lights and wiring
- brakes
- windows
- fuel and fuel system
- coupling devices on combination vehicles
- tires
- windshield wipers
- defrosters
- rear-view mirrors
- horn
- speedometer
- floor
- rear bumper
- flags on projecting loads
- seat belts
- emergency equipment
- cargo securement devices
- frame
- cab
- wheels and rims
- steering
- suspension

Most vehicles have at least those parts and systems.

State laws may require vehicles to have still more equipment. We will cover some of the items commonly required by state regulations. You should inform yourself about the requirements of your home state and of every state you will pass through. You can be put out of service in one state for a vehicle condition that was acceptable in another state.

WHAT TO LOOK FOR

Lights and Reflectors

In your inspection, make sure you have all the required lights and reflectors. (Review Chapter 7 to refresh your memory about the requirements.) Make sure they all work. Make sure they are clean. Dirt on the lights and reflectors can cut down the amount of light they give. You can't see, or be seen, well with dirty lights and reflectors.

Electrical System

Look for wiring problems. Open and short circuits could result from the following:

- broken or loose wires
- worn insulation that exposes the wire
- bare wires that touch each other
- corroded connections

Loose wires can be reattached. Wires that are broken should be replaced. So should wires with worn insulation. Corrosion can be cleaned off with a wire brush.

If your vehicle uses fuses, check them. Replace any that have blown.

Inspect the battery. (Review Chapter 7 for a description of a complete battery check.)

You may have one or two gauges on your dashboard, the ammeter and the voltmeter, that help you judge the battery's condition. Readings outside the normal range should

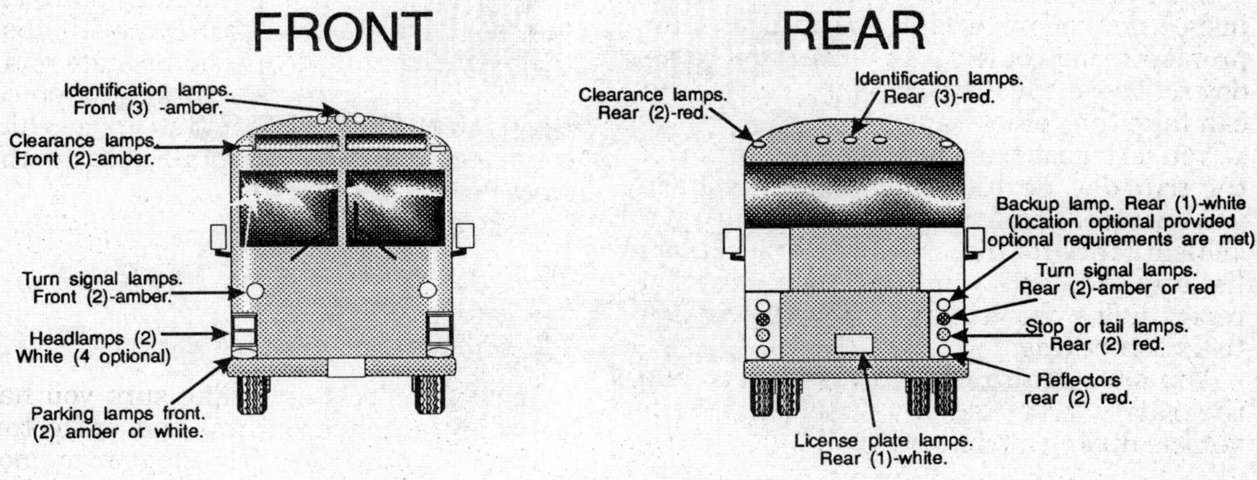

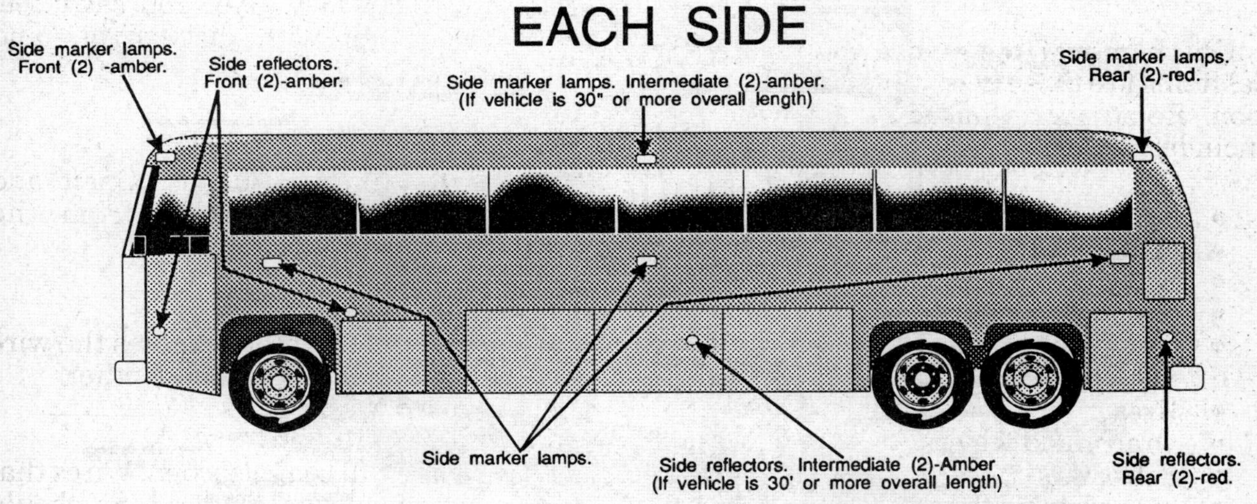

Figure 10-2A Look at the drawings in figures 10-2A and B to find the lights and reflectors required on the type of vehicle you drive.

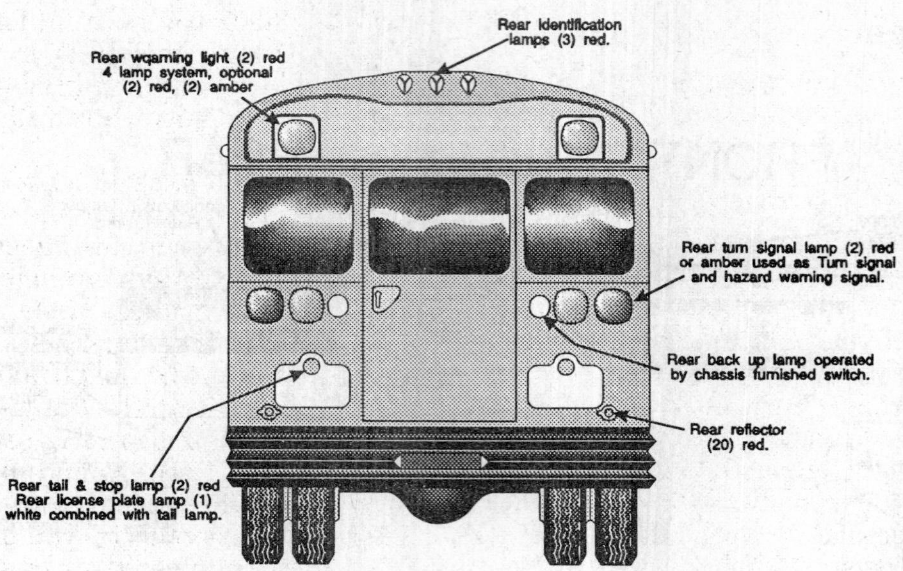

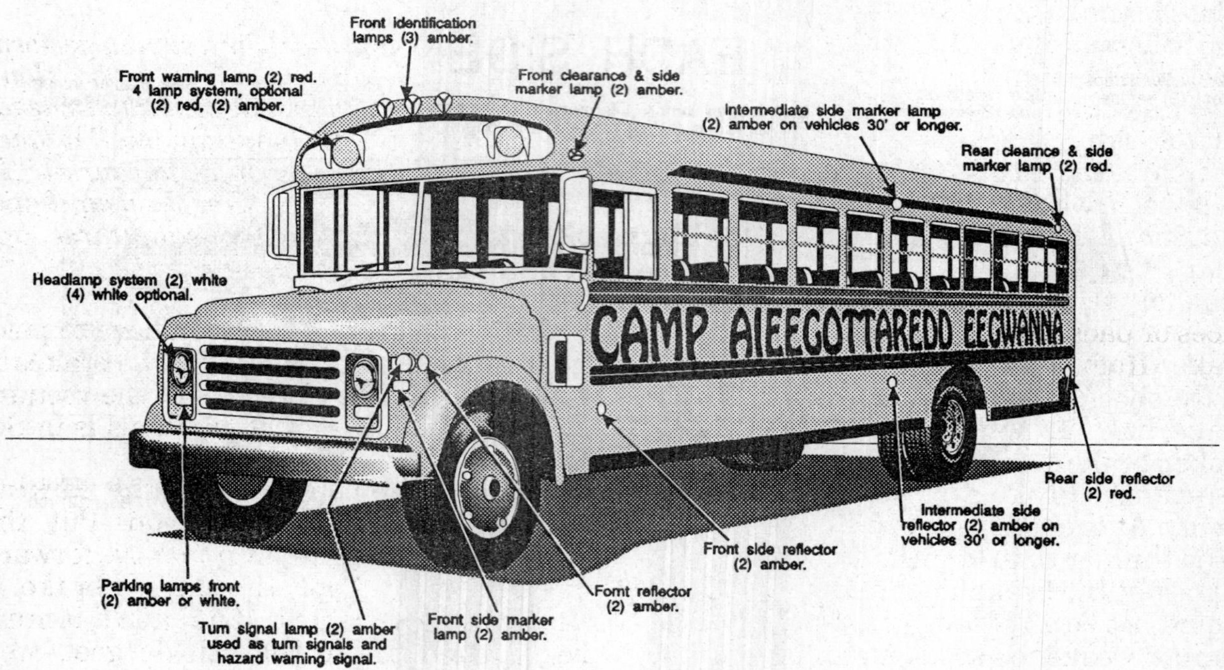

Figure 10-2B Look at the drawings in figures 10-2A and B to find the lights and reflectors required on the type of vehicle you drive.

alert you to defects. Your vehicle may also have a charging circuit warning light. This light comes on if your battery isn't charging during operation.

Brake System

Your vehicle may have hydraulic or vacuum brakes, or you may have air brakes. If you have air brakes, you must make a special inspection of that system. We'll cover the special steps in Chapter 11. Here we'll cover inspecting brake parts that all vehicles have. Plus, we'll look at inspecting hydraulic and vacuum brake system parts.

Remember, if you plan to drive a vehicle with air brakes, you must answer special air brake questions on the CDL Knowledge Test. You'll have to show you can inspect the air brake system, too. Be sure to read Chapter 11 if you don't want an air brake restriction on your CDL license.

Most brake systems have brake shoes and brake drums. Some have disc brakes on the front axle. For the most part, you have to remove the wheel to inspect a disc brake. That's beyond the scope of a pre-trip inspection. Short of doing that, check the hub for cracks and leaking fluid. Some disc brakes have a device that warns you when the pads get too thin. You hear a squealing noise when braking if this is the case.

At each wheel, check the brake drums and shoes. Look for cracks in the brake drum. Cracked drums must be replaced. Look for oil, grease, and brake fluid on the shoes or pads. Any of these will prevent the brakes from working properly. Brake fluid on the shoes or pads signals problems in the brake lines as well. Look for missing or broken brake shoes. These must be replaced or repaired. Brake pads don't usually wear evenly. At their thinnest point, they should be no thinner than ¼ inch.

Look at the brake lines and hoses. There should not be any leaks or breaks. Look for worn or weakened spots. Make sure all the lines and hoses are connected properly. There shouldn't be any kinks or twists in the lines.

Check each wheel cylinder. Leaks and loose connections are signs of trouble.

You should check the level of hydraulic fluid in the master cylinder. You do this when you inspect the engine area. Different manufacturers provide different means for doing this. In some cases, you can see through the tank. Or a sight glass may be provided. Check the manual for your vehicle to see what's available to you. In all cases, there will be some kind of fluid level marking. Make sure the fluid level comes up to that mark.

As you might expect, leaks around the master cylinder mean trouble.

When you're in the cab, check the operation of the brake system. Here's how to check hydraulic brakes. The engine should be on, and the transmission should be in neutral. Pump the brake pedal three times. Then press firmly on the brake pedal. Keep pressing for no less than five seconds (some manufacturers recommend 30 seconds). The pedal should not move.

If the pedal is not firm, you may have air in the lines. If the pedal sinks slowly to the floor, that's a sign there's a leak. These problems must be fixed before the vehicle may be driven.

Tip *Time is critical for tests you perform during vehicle inspection. But you don't need a stopwatch to count seconds. Instead, say to yourself: "One thousand one." It takes about one second to say that to yourself. To count five seconds, say "One thousand one, one thousand two, one thousand three, one thousand four, one thousand five."*

Test vacuum brakes. If you have to push hard on the brake pedal to get the brakes to work, you may have defects in the vacuum system. Another sign of problems is brake fade.

While in the cab, also test the parking brakes. Put your seat belt on. Put the vehicle in gear and allow it to move forward at a slow speed. Apply the parking brake. It should stop the vehicle. If it doesn't, it must be repaired before the vehicle goes anywhere.

To test the service brake, go forward at about five mph. Push the brake pedal firmly. If the vehicle pulls to the left or the right, you could have brake troubles. Any pause before the brakes catch is another sign of brake problems. You may also "feel" the brake pedal doesn't work right. Perhaps it travels too far before the brakes apply or takes it too much effort. This too could mean brake problems. Have the service brake checked and any problems repaired before driving.

Windows and Glass

Inspect the window glass and windshield. You must have a clear view in order to drive safely. The glass must not be dirty or discolored. Glass that has been factory-tinted to reduce glare is allowed (but sun screen film you apply yourself is not).

A certain area of your windshield must be free of decals and stickers (see Figure 10-3). You should not have stickers at all on the cab side windows. The only stickers allowed are those required by law. Place these at the bottom of the windshield. They should extend upwards no further than 4 ½ inches into the viewing area.

The glass may have some minor cracks and "dings." Single cracks no larger than ¼ inch are permitted, as long as they don't connect with other cracks. A whole spider web of cracks is not allowed.

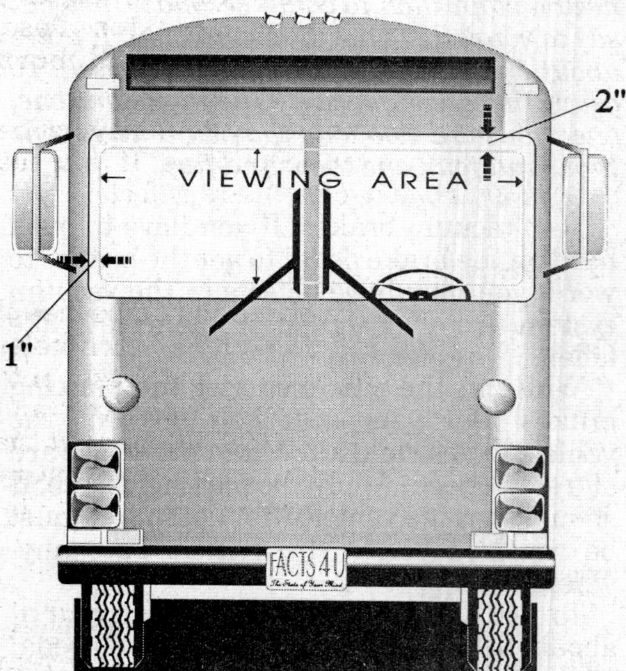

Figure 10-3 Your viewing area must be clean and free of illegal stickers.

Fuel System

If your vehicle has an external fuel tank or tanks, see that they are securely mounted and not damaged or leaking. Make sure the fuel crossover line is secure. It should not be hanging so low that it would be exposed to high grade crossings or objects bouncing up from the road. The filler caps must be on firmly. Of course, see that the tanks contain enough fuel. Tanks should not be more than 95 percent full. Fuel expands as it warms up. Filling your tanks slightly less than full leaves some room for this expansion.

Coupling Devices

If you are following along in your FMCSR, you'll see the next item of required equipment covered is coupling devices. We'll cover coupling devices and their inspection in detail in Chapter 12.

Tires

It is simply dangerous to drive with bad tires. Look for problems such as body ply or belt material showing through the tread or sidewall. Neither the tread nor the sidewall should be separating from the tire body. Look for cuts that are so deep the ply or belt shows through. Look for cut or cracked valve stems or missing valve stem caps. Naturally, a very low or flat tire has to be repaired. Don't drive on tires with any of these problems.

Listen for air leaks that could result in a flat. Look for bulges in the rubber that could lead to blowouts. Check the inflation pressure. Some drivers become expert enough to do this accurately by just thumping the tire with a tire billy. You'll never go wrong using a tire gauge, though. It is not a bad idea to use a tire gauge during the CDL test inspection. Simply kicking the tires is definitely not good enough.

Check the tires for wear. You need at least a 4/32 inch tread depth in every major groove on front wheels. You need a 2/32 inch tread depth on other wheels.

Other problems are dual tires that come in contact with each other or parts of the vehicle. You should not have two tires of different sizes on the same axle. Radial and bias-ply tires should not be used together on the same axle, either.

Figure 10-4 Don't mix tire sizes on the same axle.

Last, remember that regrooved, recapped, or retreaded tires may not be used on the front wheels of a bus. You may not have regrooved tires on the front wheel of a truck or truck-tractor which has more than an 8,000 pound front axle rating.

Wipers and Defrosters

Your vehicle must have two windshield wiper blades, one on each side of the centerline of the windshield. They must work automatically. They must clean the windshield of rain, snow, and other moisture so you have clear vision. As part of your inspection, make sure the wipers work. Make sure the rubber blades do a good job of cleaning. Blades that are stiff, crumbly, or loose can't clear your windshield well.

If your vehicle has a windshield, it must also have a windshield defroster. Turn the defroster on and off as part of your inspection. Put your hand over the vents to confirm that the defroster is putting out warm air.

Windshield washers are optional. If you have them, test them to make sure they work. If they don't, you could simply be lacking fluid in the washer reservoir. Or the fluid lines could be kinked, broken, or leaking.

Rear-view Mirrors

Your vehicle must have a rear-view mirror at each side of the cab. (Some vehicles may have one outside mirror on the driver's side. Another mirror inside the vehicle gives a view to the rear.) Make sure the mirrors are clean and undamaged. Adjust them so that when you are in the driver's seat, you have a view of the highway to the rear along both sides of the vehicle.

Horn

All vehicles must have a horn. As you inspect the vehicle, make sure your horn is working.

Exhaust System

A broken exhaust system can let poisonous gases into the cab. You should check for loose, broken, blocked, or missing exhaust pipes, mufflers, tailpipes, or stacks. Loose, broken, or missing mounting brackets, clamps, bolts, or nuts can lead to problems. Look for exhaust system parts which rub against fuel system parts, tires or other moving parts of the vehicle. Look for hoses, lines, and wires that are so close to exhaust system parts that they could be damaged by the heat.

Check for exhaust system parts that are leaking. Hold your hand close to the exhaust manifold. You'll be able to feel any leaks. (Don't put your hand too close, though. It's hot, and you could burn yourself.)

Defects in the exhaust system may not be repaired with wrap or patches. If you see such repair work, note it as a defect.

Floor

The floor of your vehicle should be free of holes and openings. Remember, such holes could allow fumes and exhaust gases into your vehicle, which could make you and your passengers ill. Also make sure that the floor is clean, free of oil or grease. Slippery floors could lead to accidents.

Rear Bumper

Vehicles that are higher than 30 inches off the ground (when empty) must have rear bumpers. If your vehicle requires or has such a bumper, check to see that it is securely attached.

Flags on Projecting Loads

Any part of the vehicle or load that extends more than four inches from the side or four feet from the rear must be marked with a red flag. If you have an oversized load or vehicle, make sure it's marked with a red flag, 12 inches square.

Requirements for Buses

There should be no seats in the aisles, unless they are of the special kind permitted by FMCSR Section 393.91. Seats must be safe for riders and must be securely fastened to the bus.

If the emergency exits are marked with red lights, make sure the lights work. The lights must be on from one-half hour after sunset to one-half hour before sunrise, or whenever it's too dark to see without them.

Seat Belts

Most trucks and buses must have a seat belt for the driver. When you inspect your vehicle make sure the seat belt is firmly attached and in good condition.

Don't forget to put the seat belt on when you take the driving portion of the CDL tests. Nearly all states require the driver (and often the passenger) to wear seat belts.

Emergency Equipment

You must carry a fire extinguisher in all but lightweight vehicles. Most vehicles are required to have one with a 10 B:C rating. (Fire extinguishers on older vehicles may be rated at 4 B:C.) Include the fire extinguisher in your inspection. Check the gauge that tells you the fire extinguisher is fully charged. Check the nozzle to make sure it's clear. Check the ring pin to make sure the tip is intact. Check the pressure gauge. The needle should be in the green area. The extinguisher must be securely mounted to the vehicle, not rolling around loose. It must be stored where you can get to it easily.

Know how to use the fire extinguisher (covered in more detail in Chapter 7).

If your vehicle was made on or after January 1, 1974, you must carry three emergency triangles that reflect from both sides. There are other devices you may carry to supplement the triangles, but you must carry the triangles. (If you're driving a vehicle that was built in 1973 or earlier, there are other warning devices you may use instead of the triangles. If your vehicle is this old, check Section 393.95 of the FMCSR for a full description of those devices.)

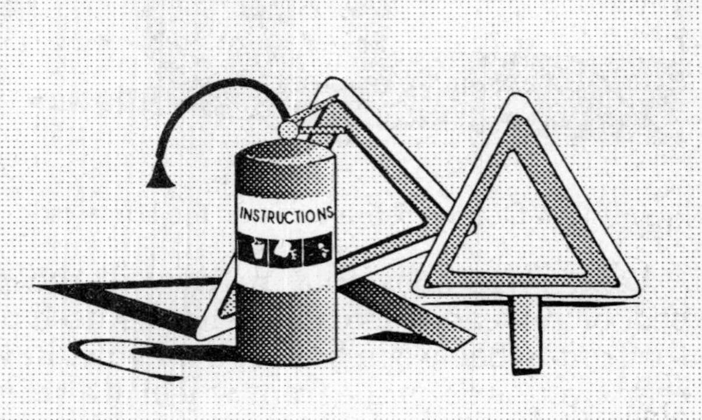

Figure 10-5 Make sure you have the required warning devices and emergency equipment.

Unless your vehicle uses circuit breakers, make sure you have spare fuses. You should know how to install them.

Cargo Securement

Cargo must be safely and securely loaded. We covered cargo loading in more detail in Chapter 9. Briefly, though, if your vehicle has any of the following parts, include them in your inspection:

- tailgate
- doors
- tarps
- spare tire
- binders
- chains
- winches
- braces and supports

All must be in good working order. Nothing should be flapping or hanging loose.

Tarps must be tied down so they don't flap or billow. If they are too slack, they could fill with air and balloon out. This could block your view in your rear-view mirrors.

Cargo must be loaded so it won't shift or fall off the vehicle. Check the security of passenger baggage in baggage compartments and overhead racks. Check that package express is securely loaded. Make sure the baggage compartment access panels are closed before driving.

Cargo must not block the view you have while driving. It must not block you in so that you can't move your arms or legs freely. You must be able to get around cargo easily so you can reach emergency equipment or exit the vehicle in an emergency.

Curbside doors should be securely closed, latched, and locked. Otherwise they may swing open and hit someone on the sidewalk.

If you're hauling a sealed load, you should have security seals in place on the doors.

If you are hauling hazardous materials, you must have the correct papers and placards to go with them. You might also need a Hazardous Materials Endorsement. Review Chapter 6 if you don't exactly recall the rules about hauling haz mat.

Frame

As you inspect your vehicle, check the condition of the frame. Look for loose, cracked, sagging, bent, or broken parts. The frame should not be missing any bolts. Make sure all bolts are in good condition and tightened down. Anything attached to the frame must be bolted or riveted. Check these fastenings to make sure they are tight.

Driver's Compartment (Cab)

Check the condition of the doors. They should open easily and close securely. Doors may not be wired shut or held closed in a way that makes them hard to open again. Look for any loose, cracked, sagging, bent, or broken parts. The hood must be securely fastened. The seats must not be loose and wobbly.

Your vehicle must have a front bumper. It must be firmly attached to the vehicle. It must not stick out so far that it becomes a hazard.

The driver's compartment should be clean and neat. Papers, cups, and other loose items could become hazards. If you stop short or turn sharply, they could fly around and hit you or get in your way.

Wheel and Rim Problems

Look for cracked or broken wheels or rims. Missing clamps, spacers, studs, and lugs could cause problems. Mismatched, bent, or cracked lock rings are dangerous. Wheels or rims should not have been repaired by welding.

Rust around wheel nuts may mean the nuts are loose. Use a wrench to check tightness. Examine the stud or bolt holes on the rims. If they are egg-shaped (out of round), that signals a problem. Check the supply of oil in the hub. See that there are no leaks.

Suspension System

Broken suspension parts can be extremely dangerous. Look for cracked or broken spring hangers. Note as defects torque rod or arm, U-bolts, spring hangers, or other axle positioning parts that are cracked, damaged, or missing. Loose or bent spring hangers will allow the axle to move out of its proper position that could result in problems with the steering or driveline. The axle must be in the proper alignment and secure. Power axles should not be leaking lube or gear oil.

Another problem to look for is missing or broken leaves in a leaf spring. If one-fourth or more are missing, it will put the vehicle out of service. However, any defect could be dangerous. Leaves that have shifted might hit and damage a tire or other vehicle part. If your vehicle has coil springs, check the coils for cracks or breaks.

Look for leaking shock absorbers. Air suspension systems that are damaged or leaking are considered defects. Make sure the air pressure regulator valve works properly. First check to see that the vehicle's air pressure gauge shows normal operating pressure. Then check to see that the air suspension doesn't leak any more than three psi in five minutes, if at all.

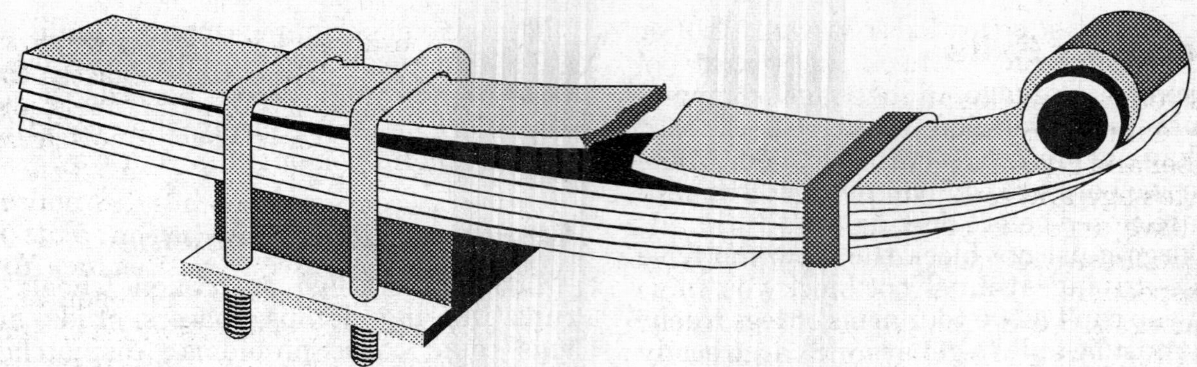

Figure 10-6 Check the suspension for broken parts.

Steering System

You'll include the steering system in your vehicle inspection. The steering wheel must not be loose. It must not have any missing or cracked spokes.

Remember what steering wheel lash is? That's the number of turns the steering wheel must make before the wheels begin to move. Another term for this is "steering wheel free play." FMCSR Part 393 sets limits on steering wheel lash. It should be no more than 10 degrees. That's about two inches at the rim of a 20-inch steering wheel. For example, a 16-inch steering wheel must not turn more than two inches before the wheels start to move (4 ½ inches if there is power steering). Anything more than that can make it hard to steer. The steering wheel should move easily both to the right and the left.

Look at Figure 10-7. Note the steering wheel lash limit for the steering wheel in your vehicle.

The steering column should be securely fastened.

Check the U-joints for signs of wear, flaws, or welding. (Damaged U-joints may not be repaired by welding.) There should be no cracks in the steering gear box. All its bolts and brackets should be secure. The Pitman arm must not be loose.

If your vehicle has power steering, all the parts must be in good working order. Look for loose or broken parts. Frayed, cracked, or slipping belts will have to be replaced or adjusted. Look for leaks in the power steering fluid tank and lines. Make sure there is enough power steering fluid. Check for missing nuts, bolts, cotter keys, or other parts. A bent, loose, or broken steering column, steering gear box, or tie rod is a defect.

Steering wheel diameter	Manual steering system	Power steering system
16" or less	2" +	4 1/2" +
18"	2 1/4" +	4 3/4" +
20"	2 1/2" +	5 1/4" +
22"	2 3/4" +	5 3/4" +

Figure 10-7 Steering wheel lash limits.

Emergency Exits

As you read in Chapter 6, your bus must have emergency escape windows. The number and type of windows depends on the vehicle's age and seat rating. You probably also have an emergency door. You should include these emergency exits in your vehicle inspection.

Emergency windows should be marked as such. There should also be labels or stickers showing people how to use them. Make sure these markings are in place and are clean and easy to read.

Emergency doors should also be marked with a decal or sign. There should be a red electric light that may be easily seen by all the passengers. This light should be lit at all times lights must be lit, as stated in the regulations.

Test the operation of emergency windows and doors. They should work exactly the way it says they should on the labels and signs. Then make sure they're closed securely before driving.

Some buses have roof hatches that may be locked in a partly open position. This is meant for emergency ventilation. You shouldn't drive with the hatch open as a normal practice. If conditions are such that you are driving with the hatch open, remember this changes the vehicle height. Pay strict attention to overhead clearances.

STATE AND LOCAL REQUIREMENTS

There may be state and local vehicle laws on top of the federal ones we just covered.

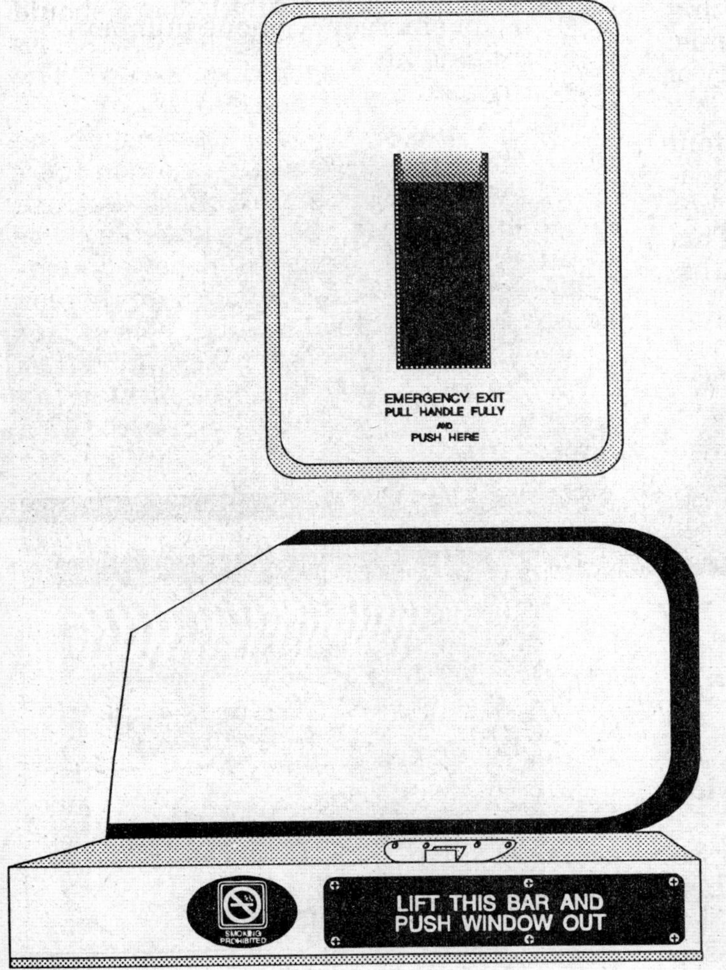

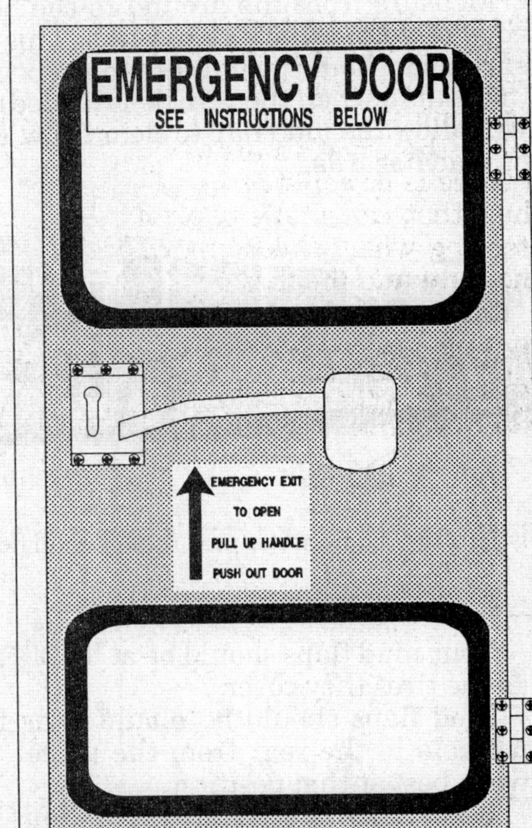

Figure 10-8 Emergency hatch, window, and door.

These may require vehicles to have still more equipment. Remember, you should inform yourself about the requirements of your home state and every state you will pass through. You can be put out of service in one state for a vehicle condition that was acceptable in another state.

Here are some common state requirements you should know about. You may have to check for these items during your vehicle inspection as well as those we already covered.

Mud Flaps

Federal law does not require you to have mud flaps on your vehicle. However, some states do. They may have mounting guidelines you must comply with. It's your responsibility to find out what those guidelines are.

If there are no regulations on mounting mud flaps, use the following as a guide. These suggestions come from the Society of Automotive Engineers.

Measure from the ground to the bottom edge of your vehicle's mud flap. This measurement should be no more than six inches (measured when the vehicle is loaded). This will allow the mud flap to clear snow, curbs, or road hazards.

Figure 10-9 Some states may require mud flaps.

Your mud flaps should be at least as wide as the tires they cover.

Mud flaps should be mounted as far as possible to the rear from the wheel. They work best at that position.

Remember, check state regulations to see whether mud flaps are required and how they should be mounted.

Tire Chains

Many states require tire chains during snowy weather. This is especially true in the West. Often, you'll see highway signs telling you to put chains on.

Again, check the regulations of your home state and every state you will pass through. Include tire chains in your stock of equipment. Practice mounting and removing them. That way you'll be prepared if you're asked how to put them on during your CDL tests.

Other Equipment

Your vehicle may have some or all of the following emergency equipment, in addition to flares and reflectors:

- tire changing kit
- accident notification kit
- list of emergency phone numbers
- first aid kit
- fire axe

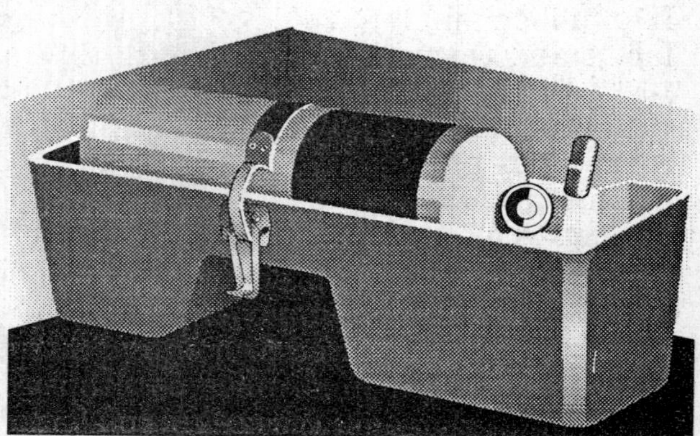

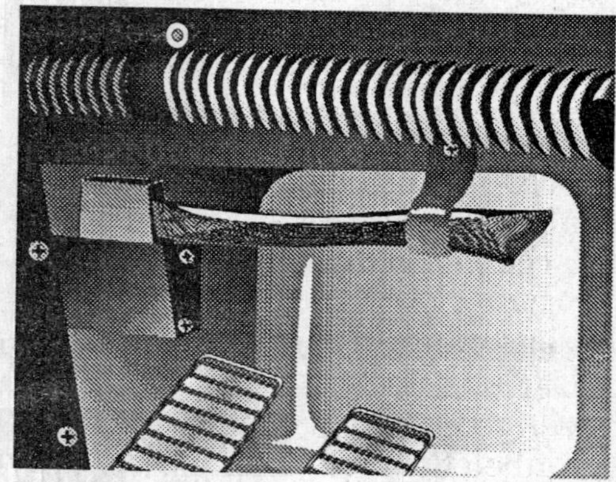

Figure 10-10 Required and optional emergency equipment you might have on your vehicle.

Read the CDL manual your state offers carefully. It may mention these items and others besides. You may see them referred to as "suggested" or "recommended." Take that as a very strong recommendation. Have those items on your vehicle when you take your CDL tests. Know what they are for and how to use them.

Hazardous Materials and Buses

You'll find most hazardous materials can't be carried on a bus. It's against regulations to have many kinds of haz mat near people or near food or items people or animals will use. Also, many hazardous materials cannot be transported without placards. Some may not be transported at all.

The Federal Hazardous Materials Table shows which materials are hazardous. You should remember from Chapter 6 that these pose a risk to health, safety, and property during transport. Regulations state that shippers must mark containers of hazardous materials with the material's name, ID number, and hazard label. The haz mat labels and placards are pictured in Figure 10-11. Don't transport any package marked with these labels unless you are certain regulations permit it. Check with the dispatcher if you're not sure.

Buses may carry small-arms ammunition labeled ORM-D, emergency hospital supplies, and drugs. You can carry small amounts of some other hazardous materials if the shipper cannot send them any other way. Class A poison, Class B poisonous liquid, tear gas, and irritating materials should never be carried on a bus. Neither should more than 100 pounds of Class B poisonous solid. Never carry explosives other than small arms ammunition in the space occupied by people. Never carry packages labeled "Radioactive Materials" in the space occupied by people. Never transport more than 500 pounds total of allowed hazardous materials, and no more than 100 pounds of any one class.

Passengers may sometimes board with an unlabeled hazardous material. They may not know it's unsafe. Don't allow people to carry on common hazards such as car batteries or gasoline.

TIP *As you can see, all licensed CMV drivers must have some knowledge of hazardous materials. That part of Chapter 6 dealing with FMCSR Part 397 covers this aspect of transporting hazardous materials.*

INSPECTION ROUTINES

Now you know what equipment you must have on your vehicle. You know what condition is considered safe. You know what defects to look for. You know why they threaten your safety, your passengers' safety, and the safety of others on the road.

All you need now is a system for checking these items. Follow the routine outlined below. This routine is more or less for most straight vehicles. Pair the checklist with the illustration that matches your vehicle. Stop and perform the check described in the list at the location marked on the diagram.

Usually, you may have the checklist with you when you take your test. Check with your state to see if for some reason this is not permitted. Otherwise, feel free to use the checklist. You'll be less likely to overlook something if you check off items as you go.

As you inspect your vehicle, tell the examiner what you are looking for. Describe what you find. You're not likely to take a defective vehicle to the test. However, the examiner will want to know that you would recognize a defect if you saw one. So as you inspect your vehicle, mention the defects typically found at the different sites. Explain how those defects impair safety.

There are seven main steps in this inspection routine. They are:

- approach the vehicle
- raise the hood or tilt the cab and check the engine compartment
- start the engine and inspect inside the driver's and passengers' compartments
- check the lights
- walk all around the vehicle, inspecting as you go
- check the signal lights
- check the brakes

DOMESTIC LABELING

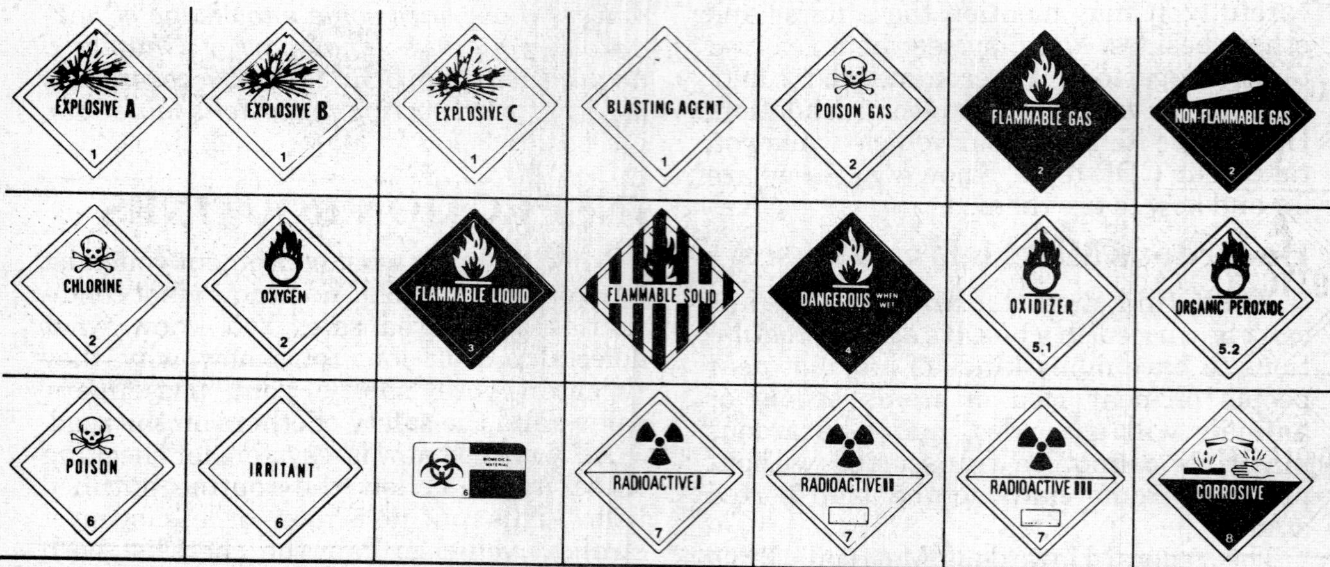

General Guidelines on Use of Labels

(CFR, Title 49, Transportation, Parts 100-177)

- Labels illustrated above are normally for *domestic shipments.* However, some air carriers *may* require the use of International Civil Aviation Organization (ICAO) labels.
- Domestic Warning Labels *may* display UN Class Number, Division Number (and Compatibility Group for Explosives only) [Sec. 172.407(g)].
- Any person who offers a hazardous material for transportation MUST label the package, if required [Sec. 172.400(a)].
- The Hazardous Materials Tables, Sec. 172.101 and 172.102, identify the proper label(s) for the hazardous materials listed.
- Label(s), when required, must be printed on or affixed to the surface of the package near the proper shipping name [Sec. 172.406(a)].
- When two or more different labels are required, display them next to each other [Sec. 172.406(c)].
- Labels may be affixed to packages (even when not required by regulations) provided each label represents a hazard of the material in the package [Sec. 172.401].

Check the Appropriate Regulations
Domestic or International Shipment

Additional Markings and Labels

HANDLING LABELS

Cargo Aircraft Only
172.402(b)

172.316

172.312(a)(c)

Package Orientation Markings

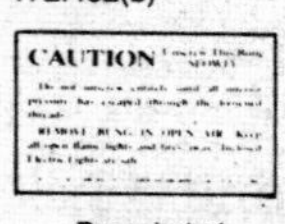

Bung Label
172.402(e)

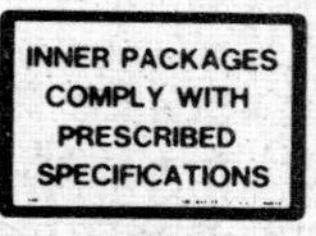

173.25(a)(4)

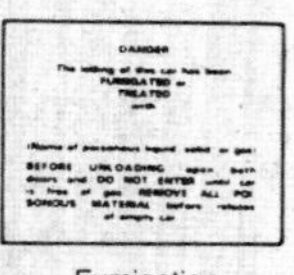

Fumigation
173.9

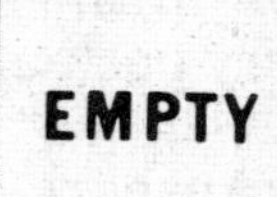

173.427

Here are a few additional markings and labels pertaining to the transport of hazardous materials. The section number shown with each item refers to the appropriate section in the HMR. The Hazardous Materials Tables, Section 172.101 and 172.102, identify the proper shipping name, hazard class, identification number, required label(s) and packaging sections.

Poisonous Materials

172.505 172.301

Materials which meet the inhalation toxicity criteria specified in Section 173.3a(b)(2), have additional "communication standards" prescribed by the HMR. First, the words "Poison-Inhalation Hazard" must be entered on the shipping paper, as required by Section 172.203(k)(4), for any primary capacity units with a capacity greater than one liter. Second, packages of 110 gallons or less capacity must be marked "Inhalation Hazard" in accordance with Section 172.301(a). Lastly, transport vehicles, freight containers and portable tanks subject to the shipping paper requirements contained in Section 172.203(k)(4) must be placarded with POISON placards in addition to the placards required by Section 172.504. For additional information and exceptions to these communication requirements, see the referenced sections in the HMR.

Keep a copy of the DOT Emergency Response Guidebook handy!

Figure 10-11 Hazardous materials labels and placards.

DOMESTIC PLACARDING

Illustration numbers in each square refer to Tables 1 and 2 below.

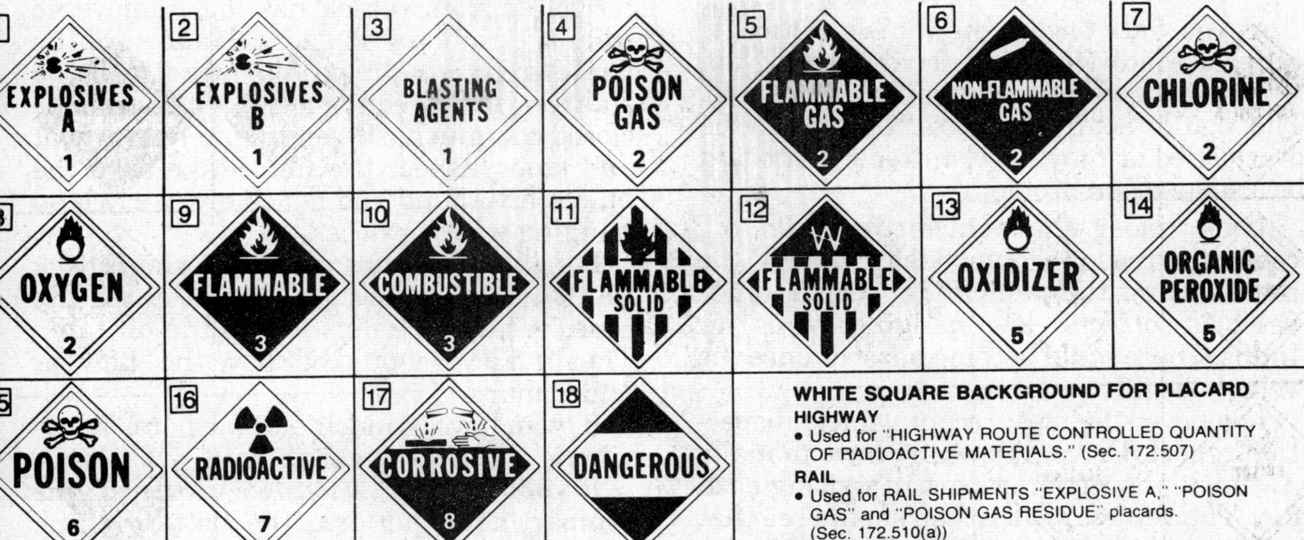

WHITE SQUARE BACKGROUND FOR PLACARD

HIGHWAY

- Used for "HIGHWAY ROUTE CONTROLLED QUANTITY OF RADIOACTIVE MATERIALS." (Sec. 172.507)

RAIL

- Used for RAIL SHIPMENTS "EXPLOSIVE A," "POISON GAS" and "POISON GAS RESIDUE" placards. (Sec. 172.510(a))

Guidelines

(CFR, Title 49, Transportation, Parts 100-177)

- Placard any transport vehicle, freight container, or rail car containing any quantity of material listed in Table 1.
- Materials which are shipped in portable tanks, cargo tanks, or tank cars must be placarded when they contain any quantity of Table 1 and/or Table 2 material.
- Motor vehicles or freight containers containing packages which are subject to the "Poison-Inhalation Hazard" shipping paper description of Section 172.203(k)(4), must be placarded POISON in addition to the placards required by Section 172.504 (see Section 172.505).
- When the gross weight of all hazardous material covered in TABLE 2 is less than 1000 pounds, no placard is required on a transport vehicle or freight container.
- Placard freight containers 640 cubic feet or more containing any quantity of hazardous material classes listed in TABLES 1 and/or 2 when offered for transportation by air or water (see Section 172.512(a)). Under 640 cubic feet see Section 172.512(b).

TABLE 1

Hazard Classes	No.
Class A explosives	1
Class B explosives	2
Poison A	4
Flammable solid (DANGEROUS WHEN WET label only)	12
Radioactive material (YELLOW III label)	16
Radioactive material:	
Uranium hexafluoride fissile (Containing more than 1.0% U^{235})	16 & 17
Uranium hexafluoride, low-specific activity (Containing 1.0% or less U^{235})	16 & 17

Note: For details on the use of Tables 1 and 2, see Sec. 172.504 (see footnotes at bottom of tables.)

TABLE 2

Hazard Classes	No.
Class C explosives	18
Blasting agent	3
Nonflammable gas	6
Nonflammable gas (Chlorine)	7
Nonflammable gas (Fluorine)	15
Nonflammable gas (Oxygen, cryogenic liquid)	8
Flammable gas	5
Combustible liquid	10
Flammable liquid	9
Flammable solid	11
Oxidizer	13
Organic peroxide	14
Poison B	15
Corrosive material	17
Irritating material	18

UN or NA Identification Numbers

MUST BE DISPLAYED ON TANK CARS, CARGO TANKS, PORTABLE TANKS AND BULK PACKAGINGS

PLACARDS OR ORANGE PANELS

1090 and FLAMMABLE 3 — 1090 3 — 1017 2 — 1993 3

Appropriate Placard must be used.

- When hazardous materials are transported in Tank Cars (Section 172.330), Cargo Tanks (Section 172.328), Portable Tanks (Section 172.326) or Bulk Packagings (Section 172.331), UN or NA numbers must be displayed on placards, orange panels or, when authorized, plain white square-on-point configuration.
- UN (United Nations) or NA (North American) numbers are found in the Hazardous Materials Tables, Sections 172.101 and 172.102.
- Identification numbers may not be displayed on "POISON GAS," "RADIOACTIVE," or "EXPLOSIVE A," "EXPLOSIVE B," "BLASTING AGENTS," or "DANGEROUS" placards. (See Section 172.334.)
- In lieu of the orange panel, identification numbers may be placed on plain white square-on-point configuration when there is no placard specified for the hazard class (*e.g.*, ORM-A, B, C, D, or E) or where the identification number may not be displayed on the placard. See Section 172.336(b) for additional provisions and specifications.
- When the identification number is displayed on a placard the UN hazard class number must be displayed in the lower corner of each placard (see Section 172.332 (c)(3)).
- Specifications of size and color of the Orange Panel can be found in Section 172.332(b).
- NA numbers are used only in the USA and Canada.

Additional Placarding Guidelines

A transport vehicle or freight container containing two or more classes of material requiring different placards specified in Table 2 may be placarded DANGEROUS in place of the separate placards specified for each of those classes of material specified in Table 2. However, when 5000 pounds or more of one class of material is loaded therein at one loading facility, the placard specified for that class must be applied. This exception, provided in Section 172.504(b), does not apply to portable tanks, tank cars, or cargo tanks.

CAUTION: Check each shipment for compliance with the appropriate hazardous materials regulations — Proper Classification, Packaging, Marking, Labeling, Placarding, Documentation — prior to offering for shipment.

In an emergency, call Chemtrec, 1-800-424-9300

Step One: Vehicle Overview

As you walk toward the vehicle, notice its general condition. Look for damage. Note whether the vehicle is leaning to one side. This could mean a flat tire. Cargo may be overloaded or may have shifted. Or it could be a suspension problem.

Look under the vehicle for fresh oil, coolant, grease, or fuel leaks. Check the area around the vehicle for people, other vehicles, objects, low hanging wires, or limbs. These could become hazards once the vehicle begins to move.

Look over the most recent vehicle inspection report. Drivers typically have to make a vehicle inspection report in writing each day. The vehicle owner then should see that any items in the report that affect safety are repaired. If the mechanic repaired the defects or determined no repairs were needed, there will be a certification to that on the form.

You should look at the last report to find out what was the matter, if anything. Inspect the vehicle to find out whether problems were fixed or whether repairs were not needed.

Step Two: Engine Compartment Check

Check that the parking brakes are on and/or wheels chocked. You may have to raise the hood or open the engine compartment door. If you have a tilt cab, secure loose items in the cab before you tilt it. Then they won't fall and break something.

You may have to go to the side or rear of the vehicle to complete the engine check. For example, the engine oil dipstick may be in the rear engine service area on your vehicle. The battery may be on the side. Be sure you inspect all the items mentioned in Step Two, wherever they are on your vehicle.

Check the engine oil level. The oil should be above the "Low" or "Add" mark on the dipstick. See that the level of coolant is above the "Low" level line on the reservoir. Check the condition of coolant-carrying hoses.

Check the radiator shutters and winterfront, if your vehicle has one. Remove ice from the radiator shutters. Make sure the winterfront is not closed too tightly. If the shutters freeze shut or the winterfront is closed too much, the engine may overheat and stop. Inspect the fan. Make sure the blades are sound and not likely to catch on hanging wires or hoses.

If your vehicle has power steering, check the fluid level and the condition of the hoses. Check the dipstick on the oil tank. The fluid level should be above the "Low" or "Add" mark.

If you have windshield washers, here's where you check the fluid level.

If your battery is located in the engine compartment, perform the battery check described earlier here.

If you have an automatic transmission, check the fluid level. You may have to do this with the engine running. Your operator's manual will tell you if that is the case.

Check drive belts for tightness and excessive wear. Press down on the center of the belt. Your operator's manual will tell you how much slack there should be. If you can easily slide a belt over a pulley, it is definitely too loose or too worn.

Look for leaks in the engine compartment. These could be fuel, coolant, oil, power-steering fluid, hydraulic fluid, or battery fluid.

Look for cracked or worn insulation on electrical wiring.

Lower and secure the hood, cab, or engine compartment door.

Next, check any handholds, steps, or deck plates. Remove all water, ice, snow, or grease from handholds, steps, and deck plates used to enter or to move about the vehicle. This will reduce the danger of slipping.

Step Three: Inside the Vehicle

Get in the vehicle. Inspect inside the driver's compartment. Make sure the parking brake is on. Shift into neutral, or Park if your transmission is automatic. Start the engine and listen for unusual noises.

BUS DRIVER'S VEHICLE INSPECTION REPORT

COMPANY ____________________ BUS NO. ____________

ODOMETER READING ____________________

END MILEAGE: ____________ DATE: ____________

START MILEAGE: ____________ TIME: ____________ ❑ AM ❑ PM

TOTAL MILEAGE: ____________ LOCATION: ____________

INSPECT ITEMS LISTED - IF DEFECTIVE, NUMBER AND DESCRIBE IN "REMARKS"

- ❑ FLUID LEAKS UNDER BUS
- ❑ LOOSE WIRES, HOSE CONNECTIONS OR
- ❑ BELTS IN ENGINE COMPARTMENT
- ❑ OIL LEVEL
- ❑ RADIATOR COOLANT LEVEL
- ❑ BATTERY
- ❑ TRANSMISSION
- ❑ UNUSUAL ENGINE NOISE
- ❑ GAUGES AND WARNING LIGHTS
- ❑ SWITCHES
- ❑ HORN
- ❑ FANS & DEFROSTERS
- ❑ WIPERS AND WASHERS
- ❑ STOP ARM CONTROL (WARNING CONTROL)
- ❑ INSIDE & OUTSIDE MIRRORS
- ❑ BRAKE PEDAL & WARNING LIGHT
- ❑ OPERATION OF SERVICE DOOR
- ❑ EMERGENCY EQUIPMENT
- ❑ FIRST AID KIT
- ❑ ENTRANCE STEPS
- ❑ CLEANLINESS OF INTERIOR
- ❑ CONDITION OF FLOOR
- ❑ EMERGENCY DOOR & BUZZER
- ❑ HEADLIGHTS, FLASHERS & 4-WAY FLASHERS
- ❑ RIGHT FRONT TIRE & WHEEL
- ❑ FRONT OF BUS - WINDSHIELD
- ❑ LEFT FRONT TIRE & WHEEL
- ❑ STOP ARM (SCHOOL BUS)
- ❑ EXHAUST SYSTEM
- ❑ LEFT SIDE OF BUS - WINDOWS & LIGHTS
- ❑ LEFT REAR TIRES & WHEELS
- ❑ REAR OF BUS - WINDOWS & LIGHTS
- ❑ TAIL PIPE
- ❑ RIGHT REAR TIRES & WHEELS
- ❑ RIGHT SIDE OF BUS - WINDOWS & LIGHTS
- ❑ DRIVERS SEAT & BELT
- ❑ DIRECTIONAL LIGHTS
- ❑ PARKING BRAKE OR SERVICE BRAKE
- ❑ CLUTCH
- ❑ STEERING
- ❑ ____________
- ❑ ____________
- ❑ ____________
- ❑ ____________

REMARKS ____________________

CONDITION OF VEHICLE ABOVE IS: ❑ **SATISFACTORY** ❑ **UNSATISFACTORY**

DRIVER'S SIGNATURE: ____________

❑ ABOVE DEFECTS CORRECTED

❑ ABOVE DEFECTS NEED NOT BE CORRECTED FOR SAFE OPERATION OF VEHICLE

MECHANIC'S SIGNATURE: ____________ DATE: ____________

DRIVER REVIEWING REPAIRS: SIGNATURE: ____________ DATE: ____________

Figure 10-12 Typical Driver's Inspection Report Form.

Check the gauge readings. The oil pressure should come up to normal within seconds after the engine is started. The ammeter and/or voltmeter should give normal readings. Coolant temperature should start at "Cold" (the low end of the temperature range). It should rise gradually until it reaches normal operating range. The temperature of the engine oil should also rise slowly to normal operating range.

Oil, coolant, and charging circuit warning lights will come on at first. That tells you the lights are working. They should go out right away unless there's a problem.

Make sure your controls work. Check all of the following for looseness, sticking, damage, or improper setting:

- steering wheel
- accelerator ("gas pedal")
- foot brake
- parking brake
- transmission controls
- horn(s)
- windshield wipers and washers if you have them
- headlights
- dimmer switch
- turn signal
- four-way flashers
- clearance, identification, and marker light switch or switches

Check other important equipment your vehicle may have, such as:

- door lock
- fresh air vent
- retractable step
- retarder controls
- interaxle differential lock (if your vehicle has one)

If your vehicle has a clutch, test it now. Depress the clutch until you feel a slight resistance. One to two inches of travel before you feel resistance is normal. More or less than that signals a problem.

Check your mirrors and windshield for the defects described earlier.

Check that you have the required emergency equipment and that it is in good operating condition.

Check for optional items, such as a tire changing kit, and for items required by state and local laws, such as mud flaps.

Check the interior of the bus. Aisles and stairwells must be clear. See that handholds and railings are securely attached to the vehicle. Clean them of any water, dirt, or grease. Inspect the floor. Look for slippery spots, snags, or protrusions that could be hazards. Look for holes in the floor. These could allow dangerous exhaust fumes to enter the bus.

Make sure the seats are clean and firmly attached to the vehicle.

See all the interior lights and signals work. Signs that direct passengers to the emergency exits and explain the standee line should be clean and easy to see. Test the emergency exits to make sure they work. Then close them securely.

If your vehicle has a lavatory (restroom), inspect it. Make sure it's clean and has enough supplies. Check to see that the door lock, lights, and "occupied" light work. Make sure the emergency buzzer and the telltale light that goes with it work.

Check any overhead parcel racks. See that nothing will shift and break or fall on the passengers when the bus is moving. Secure baggage in ways that allow the driver to move freely and easily and allow passengers to exit by any window or door in an emergency. Passengers should not leave carry-on baggage in a doorway or aisle. There should be nothing in the aisle that would trip other passengers.

Step Four: Check Lights

Next, check to see the lights are working. Make sure the parking brake is set, turn off the engine, and take the key with you. Turn on the headlights (on low beams) and the four-way flashers, and get out. Go to the front of the vehicle. Check that the low beams are on and both of the four-way flashers are working. Push the dimmer switch and check that the high beams work. Turn off the headlights and four-way hazard warning flashers. Turn on the parking, clearance, side-marker, and identification lights. Turn on the right turn signal, and start the "walk-around" part of the inspection.

Step Five: Walk-around Inspection

Walk all around the vehicle, inspecting as you go. Start at the driver's compartment on the driver's side. Cover the front of the vehicle. Work down the passenger side to the rear. Cover the rear of the vehicle. Work up the driver's side back to the starting position. Do it this way every time.

Clean all the lights, reflectors, and glass as you go along. Close any open emergency exits. Close any open access panels (baggage, lavatory service, engine, condenser, battery, and so forth).

Left Front Side

The driver's side glass should be clean. Door latches or locks should work properly.

Perform a tire, wheel, and rim check at the left front wheel. Perform a suspension system and braking system check. Check the steering parts.

Front

Check the condition of the front axle. Perform a check of the steering system parts. You should actually take hold of steering system parts and shake them to be sure that they are not loose.

Check the windshield. Pull on the windshield wiper arms to check for proper spring tension. Check the wiper blades for the defects described earlier.

Check the lights and reflectors (parking, clearance, and identification and turn signal lights) at this site. Make sure you have all the required ones as described earlier. They should be clean and working.

Right Front Side

The right front has parts similar to the left front. Perform the same checks. The passenger door glass should be clean. Door latches or locks should work properly. Check the tire, wheel, and rim at the right

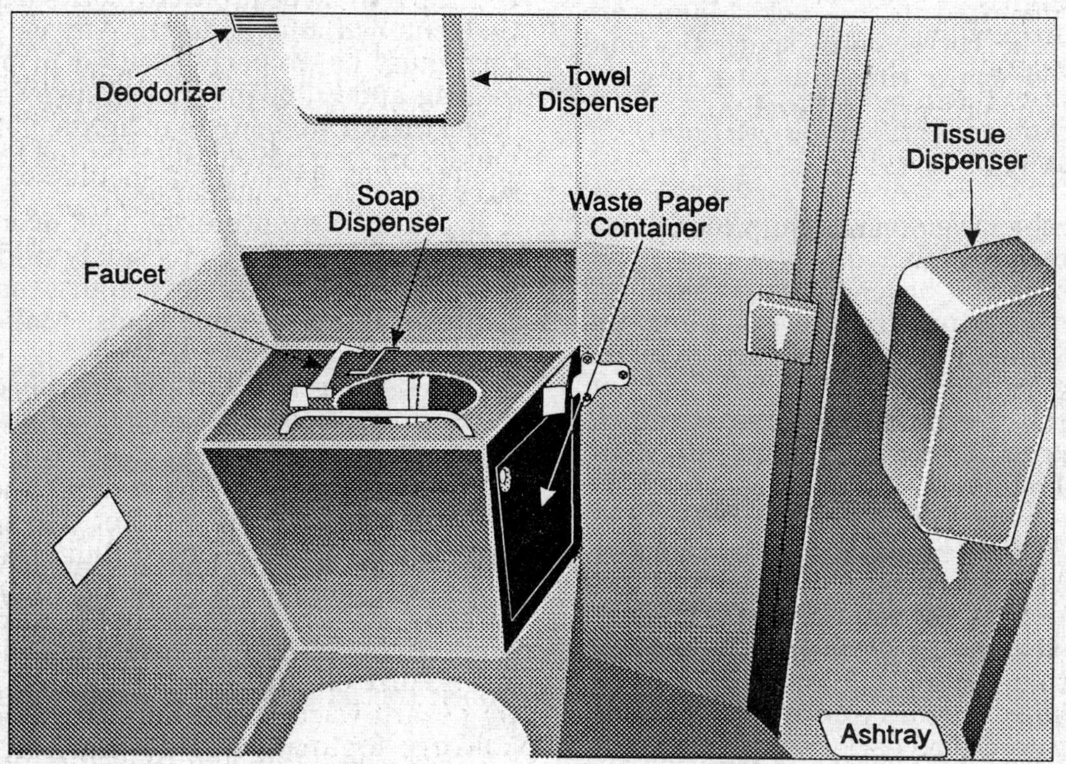

Figure 10-13 Lavatory on an intercity coach.

front wheel. Perform a suspension system and braking system check. Check the steering parts.

For cabover (COE) tractors, check the primary and safety cab locks here.

Right Side

If you have an external fuel tank, it may be located here. Check to see it is mounted securely, not damaged or leaking. The fuel crossover line must be secure and not hanging so low that it would be exposed to road hazards. The filler caps must be on firmly. Check the fuel supply. Perform these checks for each fuel tank your vehicle has.

Check all parts you can see at this site. See that the rear of the engine is not leaking. Check for leaks from the transmission. Check the exhaust system parts for defects as described earlier.

Inspect the frame and cross members for bends and cracks. Electrical wiring should be secured against snagging, rubbing, and wearing.

If your vehicle has a spare tire carrier or rack, check it for damage. It should be securely mounted in the rack. Make sure you have the correct size spare tire and wheel. The spare tire must be in good condition and properly inflated.

Cargo Check

Watch for cargo or baggage containing hazardous materials.

Make sure you haven't created handling problems for yourself by overloading the front axles. Any canvas or tarp must be properly secured to prevent tearing and billowing. If you have an oversized vehicle or load, have the necessary signs safely and properly mounted. Make sure you have the permits you need.

Check that the curbside cargo compartment doors are securely closed, latched, and locked. See that any required security seals are in place.

Right Rear

At this location, check the wheels, rim, tires, brake system, and suspension parts for the defects described in the first part of this chapter. Check that all parts are sound, properly mounted and secure, and not leaking. Check the axle. Powered axles should not leak.

Check the lights and reflectors required at this location. They should be clean and working.

Rear

Make sure you have a license plate. It should be clean and securely mounted.

If mud flaps are required, check them now. They should be free of damage and fastened according to whatever regulations apply. If there are no legal guidelines, make sure they are at least well-fastened, not dragging on the ground or rubbing the tires.

Check the lights and reflectors required at this location. They should be clean and working.

Cargo Securement

If it applies to your vehicle, check the cargo securement at the right rear of the vehicle. It must be properly blocked, braced, tied, chained, and so forth. Any canvas or tarp must be properly secured to prevent tearing and billowing. Make sure the tarp doesn't cover up your rear lights. Check to make sure you haven't distributed the load so as to overload the rear axles.

If you have an oversized load or vehicle, have the necessary signs safely and properly mounted. Have any lights or flags required for projecting loads. Make sure you have the permits you need.

Check that rear doors are securely closed, latched, and locked.

Left Rear and Front Side

At this location, check the wheels, rim, tires, brake system, and suspension parts just as you did for the right rear and front side. Check that all parts are sound, properly mounted and secure, and not leaking. Check the axle. Powered axles should not leak.

Check the lights and reflectors required at this location. They should be clean and working.

☐ Step 1 Vehicle overview
General condition

☐ Step 2 Engine compartment checks
Fluid levels and leaks
Hoses and belts
Battery
Windshield washer
Wiring

☐ Step 3 Inside the cab checks
Parking brake on
Gauge readings
Warning lights
Controls
Emergency equipment
Optional equipment

☐ Step 4 Check lights
Headlights (low and high beams)
Four-way flashers
Parking lights
Clearance lights
Side marker lights
Identification lights
Right turn signal

☐ Step 5 Walk-around inspection
A Left front side: wheel and tire, suspension, brakes, axle, side marker lamp and reflector, glass, and mirrors

B Front of cab: axle, steering system, windshield, lights and reflectors

C Right front side: Door glass, latches and locks, wheel and tire, suspension, brakes, axle, steering, side marker lamp and reflector

D Right side: fuel tank, exhaust system, frame and cross members, wiring, lights and reflectors, mirrors

E Right rear: wheels and tires, suspension, brakes, axle, lights and reflectors

F Rear: lights and reflectors, license plate, mud flaps, spare tire, exhaust and doors

G Left rear and left front: wheels and tires, suspension, brakes, steering, axle, lights and reflectors, battery

☐ Step 6 Check signal lights

☐ Step 7 Brake check

Cut Here

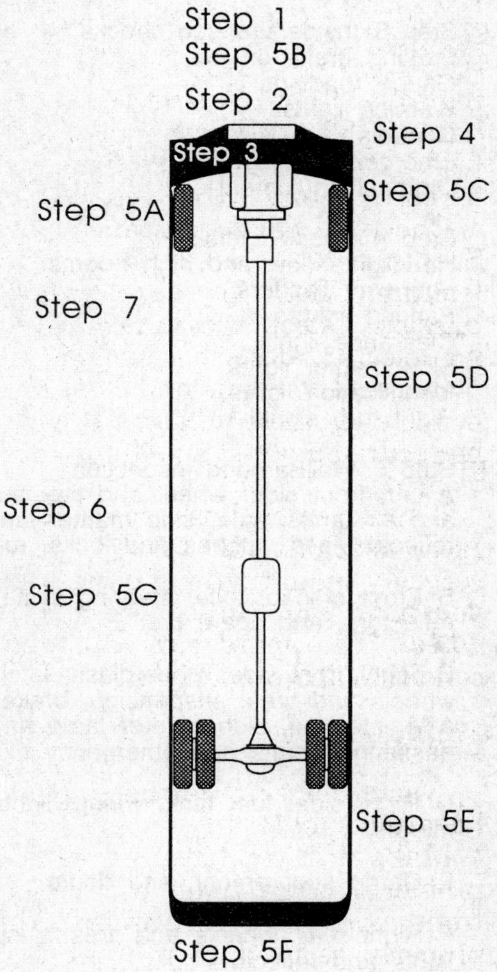

Figure 10-14 School Bus Inspection Aid.

☐ Step 1 Vehicle overview
General condition

☐ Step 2 Engine compartment checks
Fluid levels and leaks
Hoses and belts
Battery
Compressor
Windshield washer
Wiring

☐ Step 3 Inside the cab checks
Parking brake on
Gauge readings
Warning lights
Controls
Emergency equipment
Optional equipment

☐ Step 4 Check lights
Headlights (low and high beams)
Four-way flashers
Parking lights
Clearance lights
Side marker lights
Identification lights
Right turn signal

☐ Step 5 Walk-around inspection
A Left front side: wheel and tire, suspension, brakes and air tanks, axle, side marker lamp and reflector,glass, latches and locks, mirrors

B Front of cab: axle, steering system, windshield, lights, reflectors, and spare tire

C Right front side: Door glass, latches and locks, wheels and tires, suspension, brakes and air tanks, axle, steering, side marker lamp and reflectors, passenger items and emergency exits

D Right side: fuel tank, wiring, lights and reflectors, mirrors

E Cargo securement, and doors

F Right rear: wheels and tires, suspension, brakes, axle, lights and reflectors

G Rear: lights and reflectors, license plate, mud flaps, doors and exhaust system

H Cargo securement and doors

I Left rear and left front: wheels and tires, suspension, brakes and air tanks, steering, axle, lights and reflectors, battery

☐ Step 6 Check signal lights

☐ Step 7 Brake check

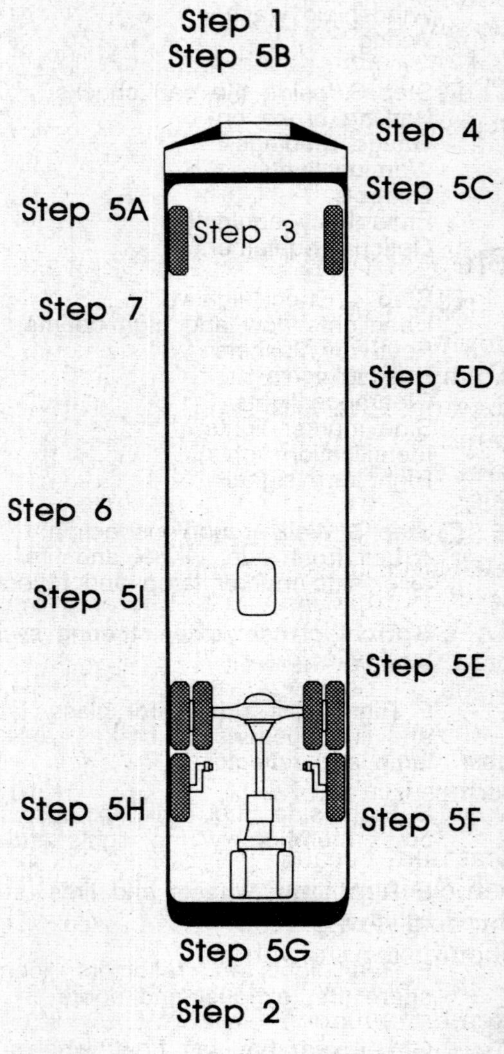

Figure 10-15 Intercity Coach/Transit Bus Inspection Aid.

Your vehicle's battery may be mounted here, rather than in the front engine compartment. If so, perform the battery check now.

Step Six: Check Signal Lights

Get in the vehicle and turn off all the lights. Then turn on the stop lights. Or have a helper step on the brake pedal while you watch to see whether the light goes on.

Now turn on the left-turn signal lights. Then get out and check the left side lights, rear and front.

Step Seven: Check Brakes

Now you'll perform some tests with the engine running. Get back in the vehicle. Turn off any lights you don't need for driving. Check to see that you have all the required papers, trip manifests, permits, and so forth. Secure all loose articles in the cab.

Start the engine. Test for leaks in the hydraulic brake system. Do you recall the test? Pump the brake pedal three times. Then apply firm pressure to the pedal and hold for five seconds. The pedal should not move.

If your vehicle has air brakes, test them now. We'll outline the air brake test procedure in Chapter 11.

Test the parking brake. First, fasten your seat belt, because you are about to put the vehicle in motion. Allow the vehicle to move forward slowly. Apply the parking brake. It should stop the vehicle.

Test how well the service brake works. Remember how? Go about five mph. Push the brake pedal firmly. The brakes should apply evenly all around the vehicle. They should not pull to one side or the other. The brake pedal should not travel all the way to the floor before the brakes apply. Nor should the pedal give you a lot of resistance or take great effort to apply.

This completes the pre-trip inspection. But this is not the end of your vehicle inspection responsibilities. You should check your vehicle regularly. You should check your instruments and gauges often. Every time you leave or return to your vehicle, take the long way around. Check the mirrors, tires, lights, and cargo as you go. If you see, hear, smell, or feel anything that might mean trouble, look into it.

As you know, you may have to make a written report each day on the condition of the vehicle you drove. Report anything that could affect safety or lead to a breakdown.

The vehicle inspection report tells the vehicle owner about problems that may need fixing. Keep a copy of your report in the vehicle for one day. That way, the next driver can learn about any problems you have found.

Different driving conditions call for special preparation. Examples are night driving, hot weather, cold weather, and mountain driving. You'll add some steps to your vehicle inspection to make sure you are prepared for these special conditions. Special preparations for driving at night, in extreme temperatures, and in the mountains were detailed in Chapter 8. You may want to go over those sections one more time before going on to the next chapter.

That completes our multi-chapter summary of the knowledge and skills you need to get a "basic" CDL with an air brake restriction and no endorsements. The next two chapters are for those who want to drive vehicles with air brakes and combination vehicles. Chapter 13 contains the information you need for the Passenger Endorsement Knowledge Test. Drivers who plan to haul liquid loads or hazardous materials requiring placards will also need endorsements. Information on the Tank Vehicle and Hazardous Materials endorsements can be found in *How To Prepare for the Commercial Driver's License Truck Driver's Test.*

PASS POST-TRIP

Instructions: For each true/false test item, read the statement. Decide if the statement is true or false. If it is true, select the letter "A." If it is false, select the letter "B." For each multiple-choice test item, choose the answer choice – A, B, C, or D – that correctly completes the statement or answers the question. There is only one correct answer.

1. You can be put out of service in one state for a vehicle condition that was acceptable in another state.

A. True
B. False

2. Which of these defects can prevent the brakes from working properly?

A. cracks in the brake drum
B. oil, grease, and brake fluid on the shoes or pads
C. brake pads that are ⅛ inch thick
D. all of the above

3. A windshield is considered defective if it has even one tiny crack.

A. True
B. False

4. Your vehicle's fuel system will not pass inspection if ______.

A. the fuel tanks are not completely full
B. the fuel tanks are external
C. there are no leaks
D. crossover lines are hanging low

5. The best way to check tire inflation pressure is ______.

A. use a tire billy
B. kick the tire
C. visually inspect the tire to see if it is low
D. use a tire gauge

6. Hoses and wires that hang close to exhaust system parts don't burn because they are protected by insulation.

A. True
B. False

7. The lights that mark emergency exits in buses must be lit ______ .

A. from sunset to sunrise
B. from one-half hour after sunset to one-half hour before sunrise
C. from one-half hour before sunset to one-half hour after sunrise
D. only in an emergency

8. Your emergency equipment must include three reflective devices and ______, if your vehicle uses them.

A. circuit breakers
B. spare fuses
C. pot torches
D. three accident notification kits

9. Suspension system defects ______.

A. can allow the axle to move out of its proper position
B. are too complex to spot during a pre-trip inspection
C. are present only on older trucks
D. do not occur on vehicles with air suspensions

10. Steering wheel free play should not be more than 10 degrees on a 20-inch steering wheel.

A. True
B. False

CHAPTER 11

Air Brakes

When you have finished this chapter, you will be able to provide the correct answers to questions about:

- how air brakes work
- the parts of the air brake system
- the causes of air brake failure
- how to respond to loss of service brakes
- how to inspect and maintain air brakes
- driving with air brakes

To complete this chapter you will need:

- a dictionary
- pencil or pen
- blank paper or notebook
- colored pencils, pens, markers, or highlighters
- a CDL preparation manual from your state Department of Motor Vehicles, if one is offered
- Federal Motor Carrier Safety Regulations pocketbook (or access to U.S. Department of Transportation regulations, Parts 383, 393, and 396 of Subchapter B, Chapter 3, Title 49, Code of Federal Regulations)
- operator's manual for your vehicle

PASS PRE-TRIP

Instructions: Read the statements. Decide whether each statement is true or false. If it is true, circle the letter "A." If it is false, circle the letter "B."

1. The compressed air in the brake chamber transmits the force exerted by the driver's foot on the brake pedal to the foundation brakes.

A. True
B. False

2. The emergency brake system is a completely separate system and is completely under the driver's control.

A. True
B. False

3. If you have an alcohol evaporator, you do not have to drain the air tanks.

A. True
B. False

Many large CMVs have air brakes. Air brakes are a safe way of stopping large vehicles, but only if the brakes are well maintained and used right.

If you want to drive a vehicle with air brakes, you have to show you know how they work. You must show you understand what causes them to fail. You must show you recognize problems and defects in the air brake system. You must show you know how to operate air brakes. You'll show you have this knowledge and skill by taking two tests just on air brakes. You'll take a special Knowledge Test and a special Skills Test.

If you don't pass these tests, you can still get a CDL. But it will be a restricted license. You will be restricted to driving vehicles without air brakes.

BRAKING WITH COMPRESSED AIR

Recall the discussion of hydraulic fluid in Chapter 7? There you learned that hydraulic fluid transmits braking force to the mechanical parts in the brake chambers. Stepping harder on the brake pedal puts more pressure on the fluid. That puts more pressure on the mechanical parts.

The air in air brakes works differently. Unlike fluid, air can be compressed. It can be made more compact and stored in a small space. Compressing air creates energy. Keeping air under pressure stores that energy. Releasing the compressed air releases energy. Compressed air actually exerts force on the mechanical parts in the brake chamber.

Air is compressed by the compressor. Stepping on the brake pedal simply opens a valve. This allows the compressed air to leave the reservoir where it's stored. Stepping on the brake pedal harder or repeatedly does not increase the pressure.

Put another way, you can press the pedal down part way. This partially opens the valve. That allows some air pressure to flow to the brake chamber. The result is light braking. Putting the pedal to the floor opens the valve all the way. That allows a full application of air pressure to flow to the brake chamber. Pressing the pedal again gives you another application, but it does not give you greater pressure.

You'll understand this idea better after we have traced the flow of air through the system. It's an important idea to understand. The idea explains why pumping or fanning air brakes results in a decrease, rather than an increase, in braking power.

We'll look at how compressed air works in the brake chambers. Then we'll track how the compressed air gets to the brake chambers.

THE BRAKE CHAMBER

Air pressure moves the brake shoes and brake pads into contact with the brake drums. This creates friction. The friction ultimately causes the wheels to stop turning.

Brake Drums

Brake drums are made of iron or steel. They are bolted to the wheels, so the wheel and the drum rotate together. The inside surface of a brake drum must be smooth and uniform. If there are scores or ridges cut into the surface, the brake shoes may not make complete contact with the drum. That could result in poor brake performance.

The braking mechanism, which consists of the brake shoes, the brake linings, and the foundation brakes, is found inside the drum. It is the action of the brake shoes pushing the brake lining against the brake drum surface that produces friction and stops the vehicle.

Brake Shoes and Lining

Each brake drum contains two brake shoes with attached linings that are made of metallic mineral fiber.

Foundation Brakes

Foundation brakes are used at each wheel. Foundation brakes are the parts of the brake that don't rotate. The most common type is the S-cam drum brake. There are also wedge brakes and disc brakes. Wedge brakes and disc brakes are less common than S-cam brakes.

S-cam Brakes

When you push the brake pedal, air is let into each brake chamber. Air pressure pushes against a diaphragm attached to the push rod. This pushes the push rod out. This moves the slack adjuster, which twists the brake camshaft. This turns the S-cam (so called because it is shaped like the letter "S"). The S-cam forces the brake shoes away from one another and presses them against the inside of the brake drum.

When you release the brake pedal, the S-cam twists back. The return spring pulls the brake shoes away from the drum. That lets the wheels roll freely again.

Locate all the parts we've mentioned so far in Figure 11-1.

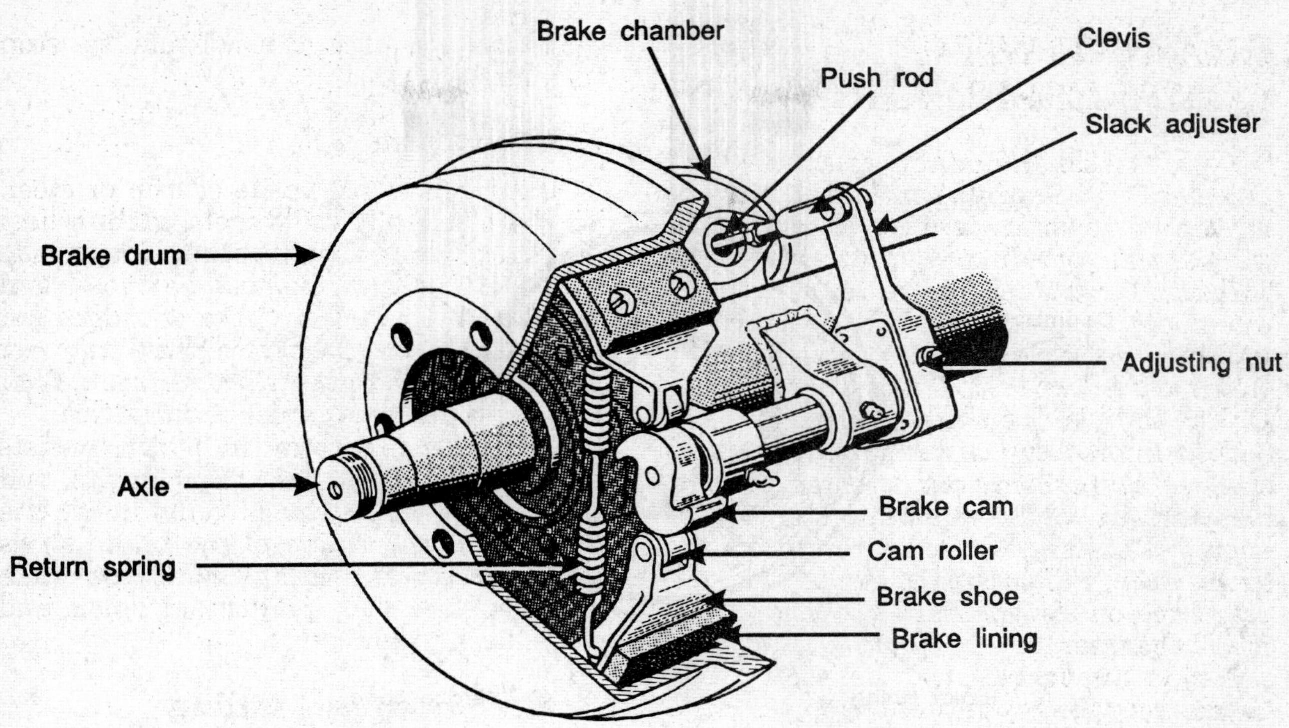

Figure 11-1 S-cam air brake.

Wedge Brakes

In wedge brakes, the brake chamber push rod pushes a wedge directly between the ends of two brake shoes. This shoves them apart and against the inside of the brake drum. Wedge brakes may have a single brake chamber, or two brake chambers, pushing wedges in at both ends of the brake shoes. Wedge type brakes may be self-adjusting or may require manual adjustment.

Figure 11-2 shows a wedge brake.

Disc Brakes

In air-operated disc brakes, air pressure acts on a brake chamber and slack adjuster, like S-cam brakes. But instead of the S-cam, a "power screw" is used. The pressure of the brake chamber on the slack adjuster turns the power screw. The power screw clamps the disc or rotor between the brake lining pads of a caliper, similar to a large C-clamp.

Figure 11-3 pictures a disc brake assembly.

All three types of foundation brakes have brake drums, linings, and shoes. (Disc brakes have discs, not shoes. But they work about the same way as shoes.)

You'll find brake drums on each end of the vehicle's axles. The wheels are bolted to the drums. As you have seen, the braking mechanism is inside the drum. When you brake, the brake shoes and linings are pushed against the inside of the drum. This causes friction, which slows the vehicle (and creates heat). The heat a drum can take without damage depends on how hard and how long the brakes are used.

Brake Fade

Too much heat can make the brakes stop working. The drum expands. The brake shoes with their linings have to travel farther to contact the drum. They don't contact the drum with as much force. This is called "brake fade."

The more you use the brakes, the more the heat will build up. Individual brakes in the system which are doing the work will

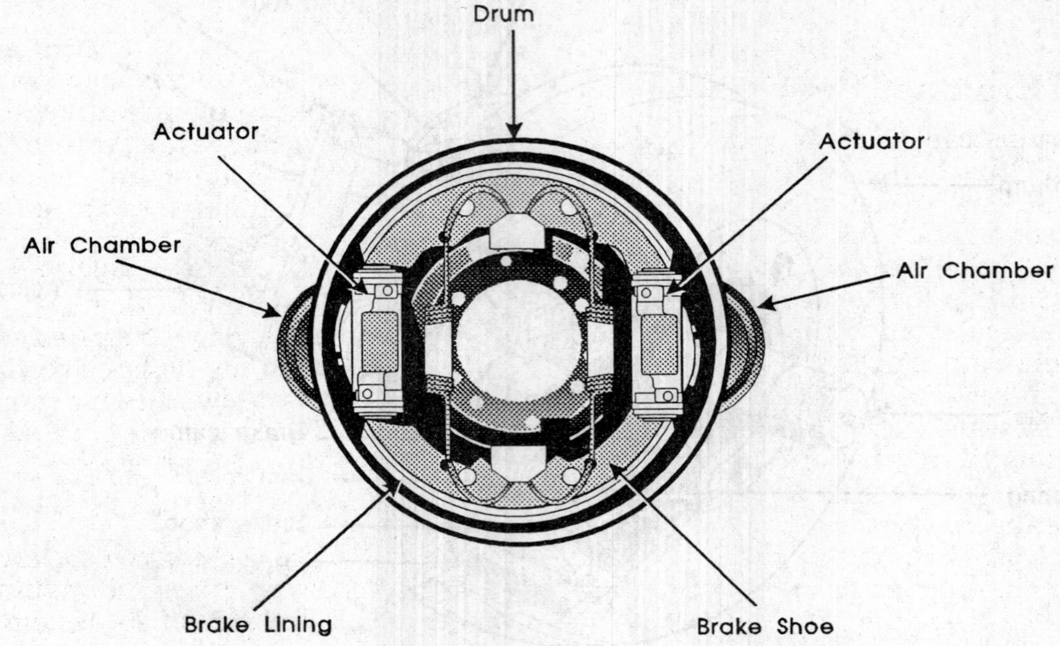

Figure 11-2 Wedge brake.

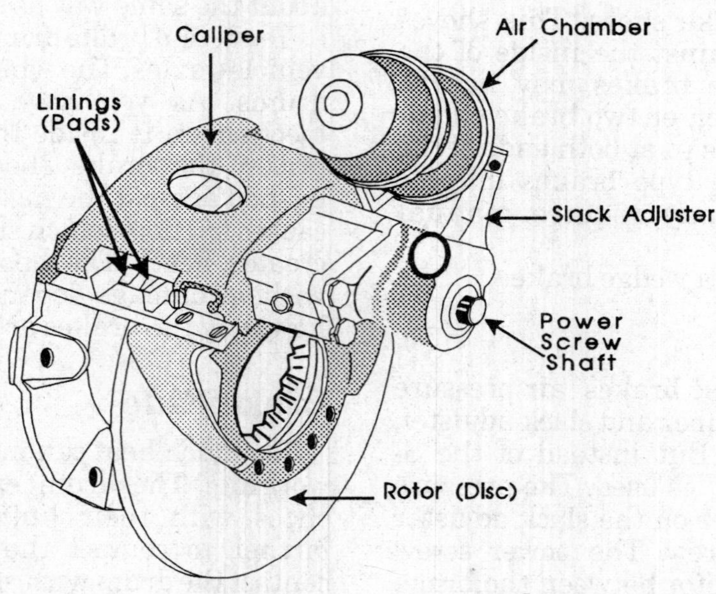

Figure 11-3 Disc brake.

develop the most heat. They'll lose stopping power first. That will affect vehicle handling.

Loss of Braking Power

The drums can heat up and expand so much that the brake shoes can't contact them at all. That's a complete loss of service braking power.

Continued abuse of the brakes can cause the metal to crack. The brake linings can burn. The seals can soften, expand, and allow grease to leak out. Create enough heat, and the grease itself can ignite.

Brake fade and loss of braking power due to overheated brakes is a common brake problem. But there are other ways in which the air brake system can fail. Since it's air pressure that works the brakes, problems with the air supply can mean brake failure, too.

Next we'll look at the other parts of the air brake system. We'll trace the flow of air from the compressor to the brake chamber. Then we'll identify places in the system where problems can occur.

THE BRAKE SYSTEM

Compressor

The compressor is a machine that draws in the air around it. It pumps that air into a smaller space to increase its pressure. Then it pumps the air into the air reservoir system where it is stored in air tanks until it is needed. The engine provides the power for the compressor, so it is usually mounted on the side of the engine.

The compressor may be air-cooled. Or it may be cooled by the engine's cooling system. It may have its own oil supply, or it may be lubricated by engine oil.

Air Governor

Located on the compressor, the air governor controls the compressor. It regulates the amount of air pressure in the system. When air tank pressure rises to the "cut-out" level, the governor stops the compressor from pumping air. The cut-out level is around 125 psi. When the tank pressure falls to the "cut-in" pressure, the governor

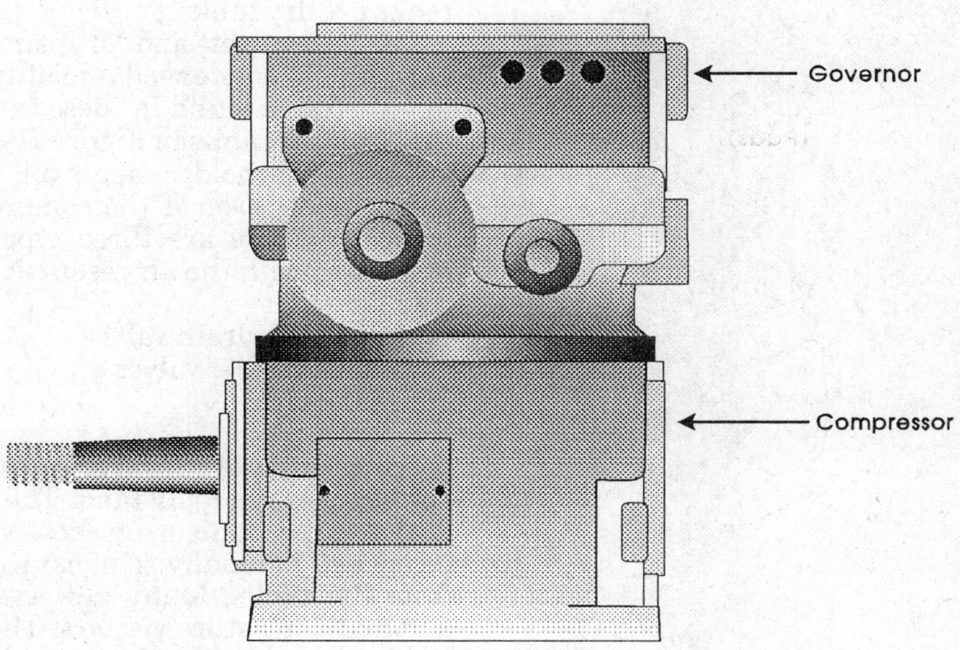

Figure 11-4 Air compressor and governor.

allows the compressor to start pumping again. Cut-in pressure is around 100 psi.

Air Dryer

Compressing air heats it. As it cools off, any moisture in it condenses out. Also, small amounts of oil from the compressor are vaporized and travel out of the compressor with the air. When the compressed air cools, this oil also condenses. The result will be a sludge. This can clog and corrode valves if it's not removed from the system.

In freezing weather, sludge can freeze in the lines and the valves. An alcohol evaporator can help prevent this.

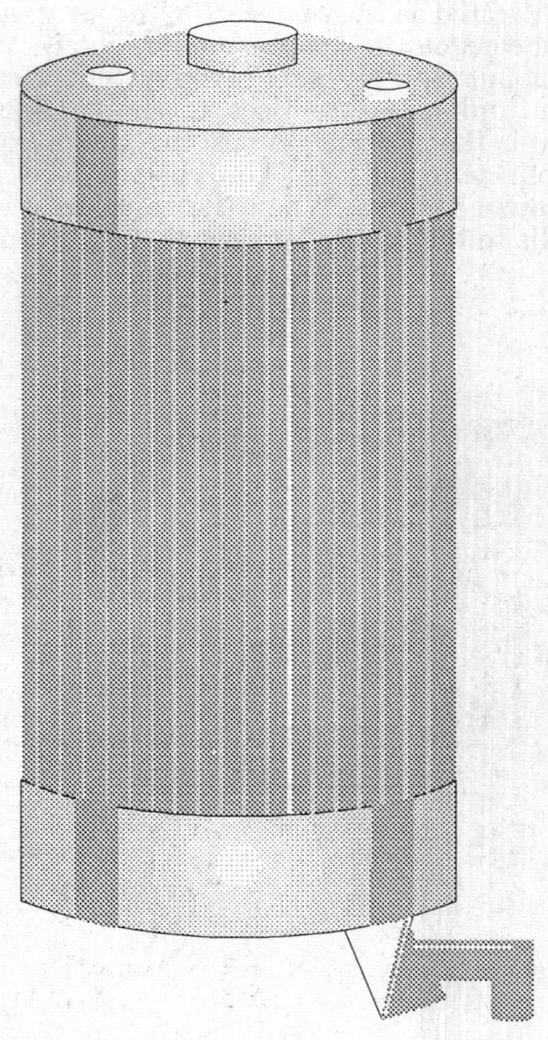

Figure 11-5 Air dryer.

When the air leaves the compressor, it flows through the air dryer. This cleans and removes moisture and vaporized oil from the compressed air. The air dryer does a pretty good job of removing the oil and moisture. But the dryer doesn't get it all. You'll need to finish the job yourself. We'll tell you how in the Inspection and Maintenance section.

The Air Reservoir System

From the air dryer, the compressed air goes to the reservoir system. Reservoirs (or tanks) store the compressed air until it is needed. Three types of tanks are used in air reservoir systems: single compartment, baffled, and multi-compartment.

The number and size of tanks varies with the vehicle. Figure 11-6A pictures a dual circuit air brake system with three tanks. A dual circuit system features separate air tanks for the front and rear axles. The first reservoir tank in a dual circuit air brake system is called the main supply tank or the wet tank. A second tank holds compressed air for the rear axle supply. This supplies air to the service brakes on the trailer, if you're pulling one. A third tank holds compressed air for the front axle supply. Both these tanks are dry tanks.

The terms "wet" and "dry" simply refer to how much condensed moisture and oil might still be found in these tanks. Locate the three air tanks in Figure 11-6A.

The tanks hold enough air for several applications, even if the compressor stops working. There are three types of valves associated with the air reservoir system:

- air tank drain valves
- safety relief valves
- check valves

An air tank drain valve is located at the bottom of each supply tank. The petcock, or draining mechanism, on these valves must be opened manually so moisture can drain from the tanks. Many new systems have automatic moisture ejectors. They can also be opened manually. Air tank drain valves help get rid of any moisture and oil the dryer doesn't take care of. Later in this

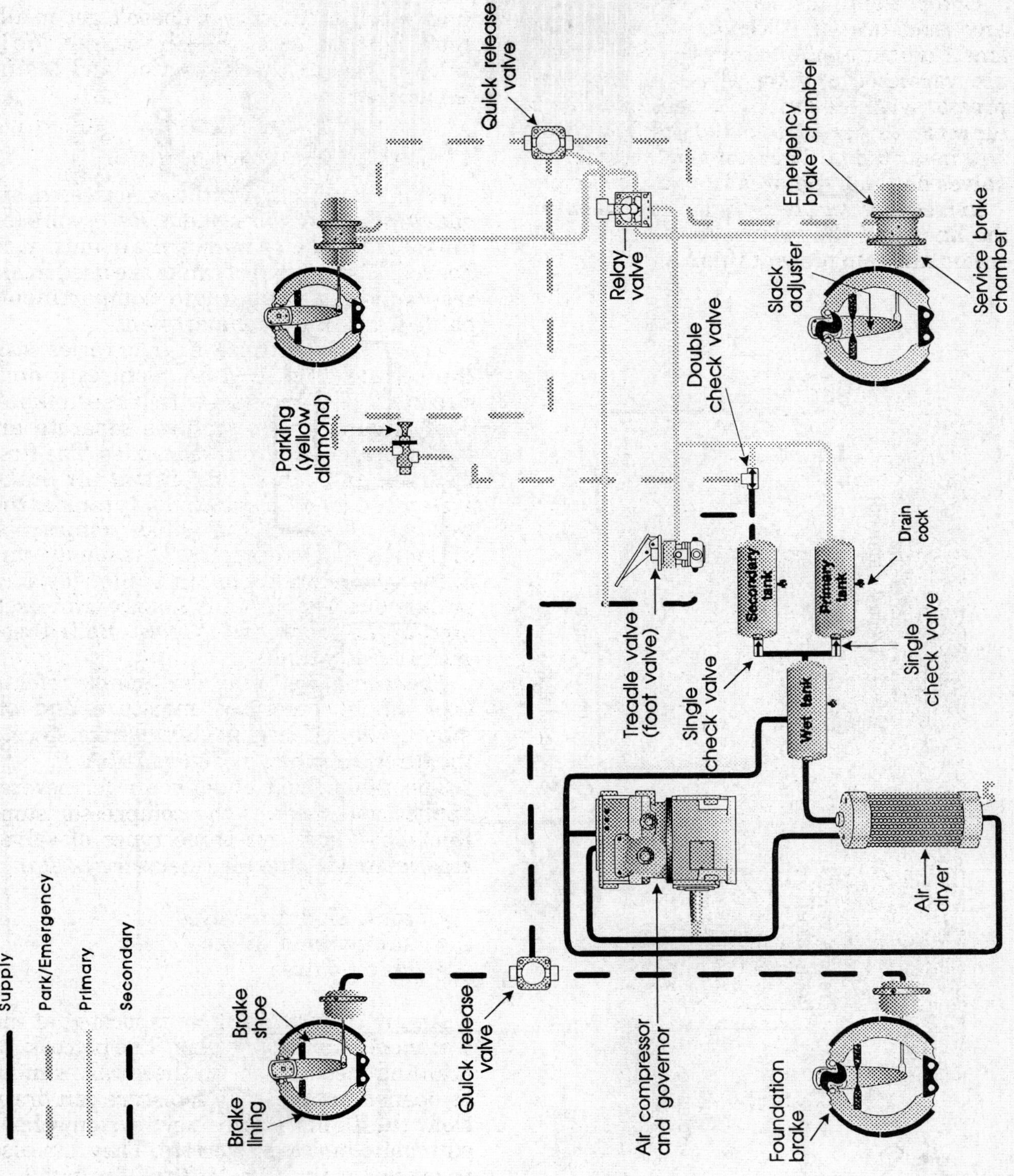

Figure 11-6A Dual circuit air brake system.

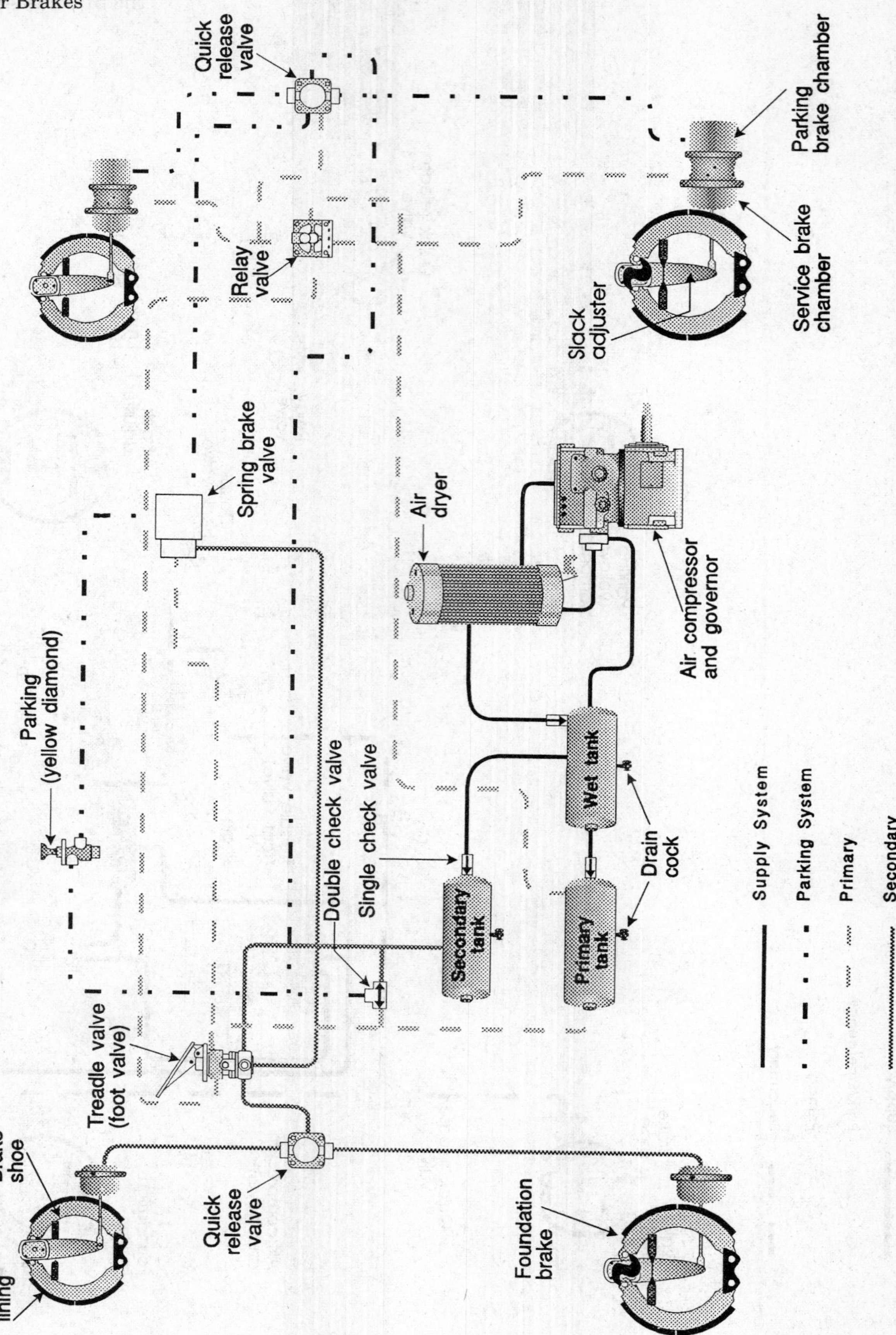

Figure 11-6B A dual circuit air brake system for a coach bus.

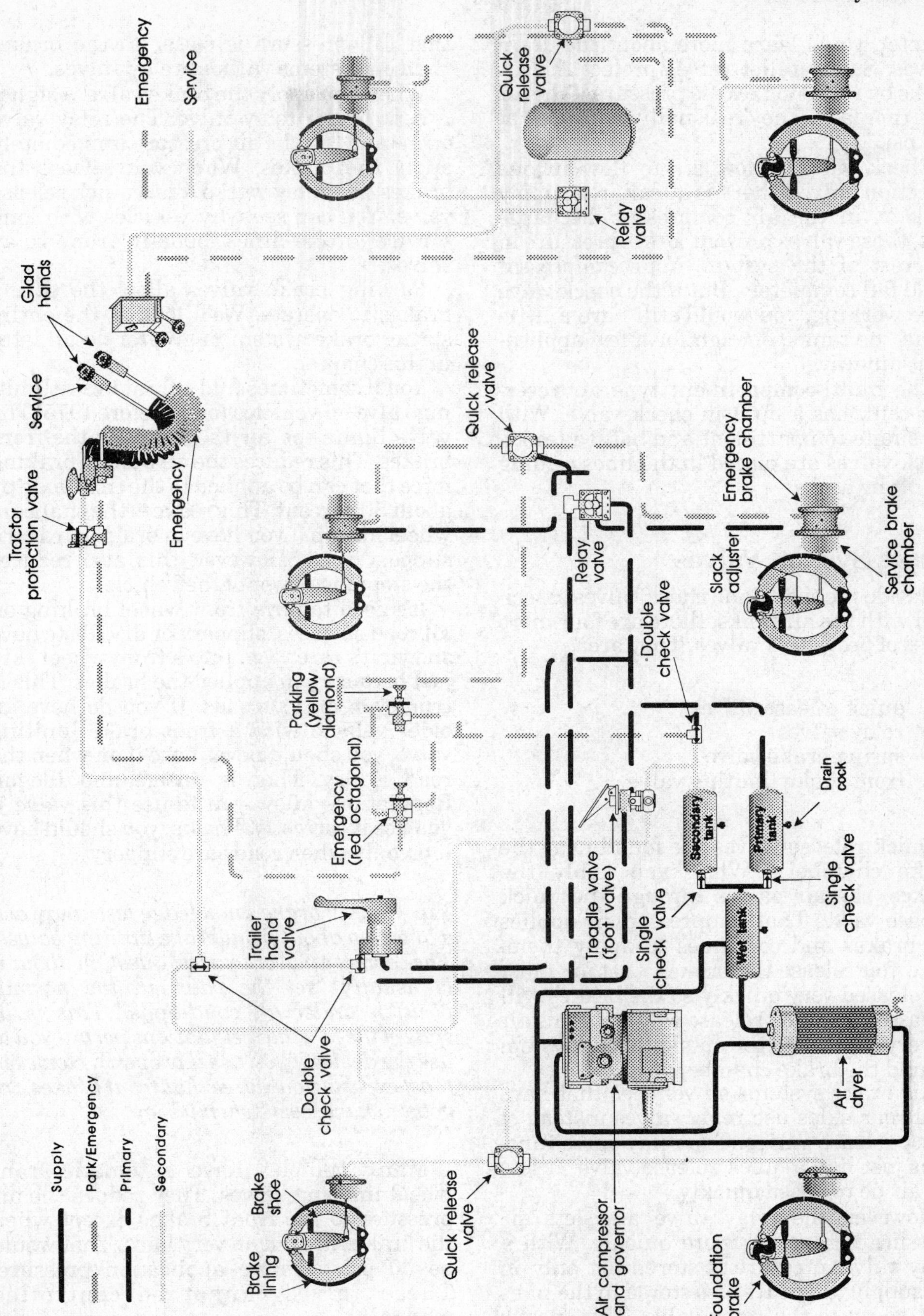

Figure 11-6C Dual circuit air brake system for a tractor-trailer bus.

chapter, you'll learn more about the drain valves. Safety relief valves protect the air tanks by releasing excess pressure if the air governor fails. They're usually set to open at 150 psi.

Check valves allow air to flow in one direction only. If there is a leak in a supply tank or in the air compressor discharge line, these valves prevent loss of pressure in the rest of the system. Your compressor could fail completely. But if the check valve were working, you would still have a little air in the tanks, enough for a few applications anyway.

The multi-compartment type air reservoir tank has a built-in check valve. With the single compartment and baffled tanks, check valves are placed in the lines coming out of the tanks.

Brake System Valves

Beside the safety and check valves associated with the air tanks, there are four more types of protective valves. They are:

- quick release valves
- relay valves
- spring brake valve
- front brake limiting valve

Quick release valves are found near the brake chambers. When you apply the brakes, the air passes through the quick release valve. That compressed air applies the brakes and continues to apply them. Once you release the brakes, that air must be released very quickly so the brakes will release. The quick release valve lets this air go very quickly to the outside of the system around the brake chamber.

Air brake systems on vehicles that have dual rear axles use relay valves instead of quick release valves. The relay valve functions just like a quick release valve. It lets the air be released quickly.

However, the relay valve also lets air pressure be applied more quickly. With a relay valve, pressure is stored not only in the supply tanks. It's also stored in the lines that go up to the relay valve. This means that full pressure is closer to the brakes than on systems without relay valves.

When you apply the brake valve, a signal is sent to the relay valve. The relay valve opens and lets the air pressure immediately apply the brakes. When you release the brakes, the relay works like a quick release valve. You can see why vehicles with long service brake lines benefit from relay valves.

Parking brake valves allow the spring brakes to operate. We'll look at the entire spring brake system in greater detail later in this chapter.

You'll sometimes find a front brake limiting valve on vehicles made before 1975. The valve limits the air that reaches the front brakes. This reduces the amount of braking force that can be applied to the front axle by about 50 percent. This reduces the chance of wheel lockup if you have to brake hard on a slippery road. However, this also reduces the stopping power of the vehicle.

It's good to have front wheel braking on all road surfaces, slippery or dry. Tests have shown it's rare to go into a front wheel skid just because you applied the brakes. This is true even on icy roads. If you do have an older vehicle with a front brake limiting valve, you should never have it on when the road is dry. That is unsafe and illegal. Regulations allow you to use this valve if you use it correctly. That is, you should have it on only when roads are slippery.

Tip *Air brake knowledge tests may ask a question about front brake limiting valves. The correct answer to a test question about it is usually "set the valve in the normal position under all conditions." This is in spite of the fact that regulations permit you to use the device if you use it properly. However, most experts now agree that front brakes are good to have, even when it's icy.*

Many vehicles have automatic front wheel limiting valves. They reduce the air pressure to the front brakes except when the brakes are put on very hard. That would be 60 psi or more application pressure. These valves cannot be controlled manually.

AIR BRAKE SYSTEM OPERATION

Now you know enough to take a close look at how the service brakes work. The compressor draws in surrounding air, compresses it, and pumps it to the air dryer. The air dryer removes moisture from the compressed air, which then flows into the air reservoir system.

You press on the treadle or foot valve. This sends a signal to the relay valve, if your vehicle has one. The relay valve opens, and air enters the brake chamber through the air inlet. The pressurized air pushes the diaphragm. The diaphragm pushes the push rod. The push rod pushes the slack adjuster. The slack adjuster twists. This twisting action turns the brake camshaft. The brake camshaft moves the S-cam, wedge, or disc. This pushes the brake shoes and linings against the brake drum. This creates friction which slows and stops the turning of the brake drum. Because the brake drum is attached to the wheel, the wheel also stops turning.

When you release the treadle, the signal to the relay valve stops. The relay valve closes the air inlet and quickly releases the air inside the brake chamber.

Figure 11-7 Treadle or foot valve.

Air brake systems are really three braking systems combined:

- the service brake system
- the parking brake system
- the emergency brake system

The service brake system applies and releases the brakes when you use the brake pedal during normal driving. The parking brake system applies and releases the parking brakes when you use the parking brake control. The emergency brake system uses parts of the service and parking brake systems to stop the vehicle in the event of a brake system failure.

The spring brake provides parking and emergency braking. When you apply the spring brake to park, it's the parking brake. When the spring brake comes on automatically in response to a loss of air pressure in the service brake system, it's the emergency brake.

You've seen how compressed air works in the service brake. Now let's see how compressed air works in the spring brake.

COMPRESSED AIR IN THE SPRING BRAKE

The spring brake chamber "piggybacks" on the service brake chamber. A heavy duty spring in the spring brake chamber is held in a compressed (released) position by air pressure. When the air pressure drops, the spring expands. This allows a piston in the spring brake chamber to move. The piston drives the diaphragm and push rod in the service brake chamber. That puts the foundation brakes into operation. The brakes are applied.

This heavy-duty spring will stay in this expanded position by itself. To push the spring back and release the brakes, you have to recharge the spring brake chamber with compressed air. When the system recharges, the spring is pushed back and held back from the brakes. The brakes are released, and you can move the vehicle again.

Recall what FMCSR Part 393 requires of parking brakes? Air pressure may be used

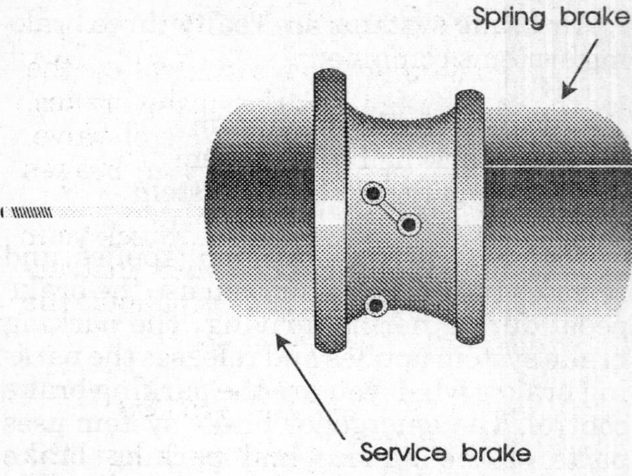

Figure 11-8 Service and spring brake chambers.

to set the parking brakes. But it must not be used to keep the parking brakes applied. Also, when you release the brakes, the system must be such that you can immediately reapply them.

The Parking Brake

When you operate this spring brake system on purpose, it's a parking brake. You operate the parking brake control in the cab. On most vehicles this control is a yellow, diamond-shaped knob. Pull it out to apply the brakes; push it in to release them. This works a valve which exhausts the compressed air from the spring brake chamber. The spring brakes go into action. The brakes remain on until you recharge the spring brake chamber. You do this by pushing the control knob back in.

See how the parking brake system we just described fills the bill? The air-pressure assisted spring brake uses air only to keep the brakes off. Once on, the strength of the spring itself keeps the brakes on. You cannot take them "off" again unless you have enough air pressure to keep them off.

Don't use the parking brakes if the brakes are very hot. (They probably are if you've just come down a steep grade.) You can damage them. Let hot brakes cool before you use them.

If you use them in cold, wet weather, they can freeze. Then you won't be able to move the vehicle. Use wheel chocks instead.

If the brakes are wet, you can dry them while driving. Apply the brakes gently while you are in low gear. The heat that's created will dry the brakes.

Never push the brake pedal down when the spring brakes are on. The combined forces of air pressure and the springs could damage the brakes. Some vehicles are designed to prevent this. You may not be sure whether yours is or not. Also, the system may not always work. So it's still a good idea to remember never to push the brake pedal down while the spring brakes are on.

Above all, never leave your vehicle unattended without either putting the parking brakes on or chocking the wheels. Your vehicle could roll away. You can imagine the damage that would do.

Some urban mass transit coaches have a brake and accelerator interlock system. The interlock applies the brakes and holds the throttle in the idle position when the rear door is open. The interlock releases when the rear door is closed. Do not use this safety feature as a parking brake.

Emergency Brakes

As you know, your vehicle must have emergency brakes. The spring brake serves as an emergency brake as well as a parking brake. You've seen how reducing the air pressure in the spring brake chamber makes the spring brakes come on.

What could cause a problem with your service brakes? A loss of pressure in the system is one cause. If you lose air pressure in the system, the spring brake chamber will be affected. Lose enough pressure, and there is no longer enough to hold the spring back. The spring brakes come on.

"Enough" in this case is a drop of air pressure to a range of 20 to 45 psi. Should your vehicle's air pressure drop this low, the emergency brakes will come on.

This meets FMCSR requirements very well. The emergency brakes work in response to a loss of service brake air pressure. They will stay applied in spite of a loss of air pressure, because they work mechanically.

You don't have to wait for the emergency brakes to come on. You should have some warning there's a problem long before it gets that bad. Your warning devices should alert you when your air pressure drops below normal. That's the time to stop, while you still have some braking power. Get the problem fixed immediately.

How well the spring brakes work depends on how well the brakes are adjusted. You've seen how the service brakes can fail if they are out of adjustment. All the spring brakes do is apply the service brakes. So if the service brakes are out of adjustment, you won't have good emergency or parking braking power, either.

OPERATIONAL CONTROL VALVES

In the cab are different pedals and knobs you use to control the many operations of the brake system. These are often called valves. Some of them truly are valves. Others are really controls that operate a valve elsewhere in the system.

One of these controls is the brake pedal.

Brake Pedal

The brake pedal is also called a foot or treadle valve. It operates a valve that supplies air pressure to the braking system. When you press on the treadle, air pressure is sent through the air lines to the brake chambers.

If your vehicle uses relay valves, then the air is already at the brake chambers being held back by the relay valves. When you press on the treadle, the relay valve opens. When you release the treadle, the air exhausts through the quick release valve and the brakes are off.

Parking Brake Valve

Another control is the parking brake valve. On late model vehicles, this is a yellow, diamond-shaped, push-pull knob. You pull the knob out to apply the spring brakes for parking. You push it in to release them. (On older vehicles, the parking brakes may be controlled by a lever. On still other vehicles, the parking brake is a round, blue knob.)

Modulating Control Valve

Your vehicle may have a control on the dashboard that regulates the spring brakes. This is called a modulating control valve. You use it to apply the spring brakes gradually, instead of all at once.

If your vehicle is so equipped, check your operator's manual for operating instructions. Or ask your supervisor about the proper use of this control.

Dual Parking Control Valves

When the main air pressure is lost, the spring brakes come on automatically. To move the vehicle again, you have to release the spring brakes. For this, you need a fresh supply of air pressure. Some vehicles have a separate air tank for the spring brakes. It has a supply of air large enough to release the spring brakes. Then you can move the vehicle off the roadway, out of danger, or to someplace where you can repair the problem in the service braking system that caused the emergency brakes to come on.

This dual control consist of two knobs. One is a push-pull type you use to apply the spring brakes for parking. The other valve is spring loaded in the "Out" position. When you push the control in, air from the separate air tank releases the spring brakes. Then you can move the vehicle. When you release the button, the spring brakes come on again.

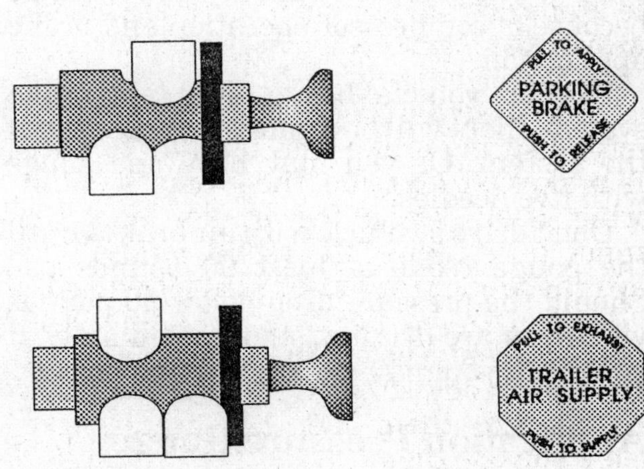

Figure 11-9 Parking and emergency cab control valves.

There is only enough air in the separate tank to do this a few times. So you must plan your next move carefully. You clearly can't rely on this system to complete your run. It's just enough to move the vehicle away from danger or to a service station.

If you have an older vehicle with a front brake limiting valve, you will find a control for it in the cab. The control is usually marked "Normal" and "Slippery." Switching it to "Slippery" reduces the air pressure at the front wheels. The "Normal" setting gives you full braking power. As you read earlier, front wheel braking has been shown to be good for all road conditions. Most experts now recommend you leave the front brake limiting valve on "Normal" at all times.

GAUGES AND WARNING DEVICES

Your vehicle has instruments that inform you of the braking system's operating condition. Warning devices alert you to problems that have occurred.

Air Pressure Gauge

The air pressure gauge is marked with the word "Air" on the lower portion of its face. The air gauge shows a reading in pounds per square inch (psi). It indicates psi available in the reservoirs for braking power. The normal gauge reading is 85 to 105 psi. The pressure will vary in this range because of compressor operation and brake application.

If your vehicle has a dual air brake system, there will be a gauge for each half of the system. Or you may have one gauge with two needles.

Don't drive a vehicle with air brakes until the gauge reads at least 90 pounds psi. Should the pressure drop below 90 pounds when you are driving, stop immediately. If you don't, you may lose all braking power.

Application Pressure Gauge

Some vehicles have an application pressure gauge. This gauge shows the amount of pressure applied to the brakes. Naturally, a heavy brake application will cause a higher reading than a light brake application. When the brakes are released, the gauge pointer should return to "zero."

When going down steep grades, you may see the brake pressure going up, while your speed remains the same. This is a sign of brake fade. It can also mean your brakes are out of adjustment, or are leaking, or have other mechanical problems.

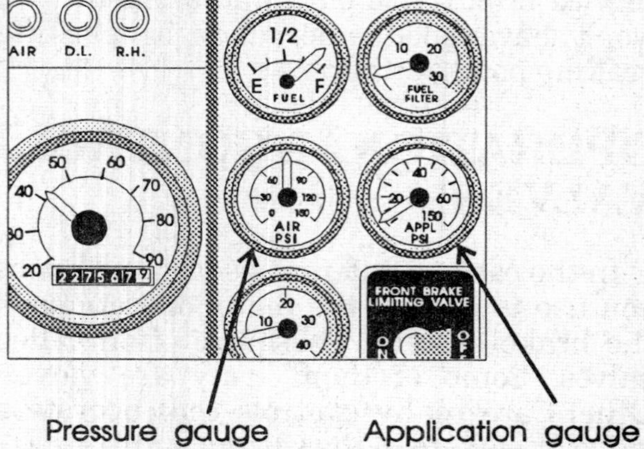

Figure 11-10 Air pressure gauge.

Warning Devices

Two devices warn you of low air pressure: the warning light and warning buzzer. If you have air brakes, your vehicle must have at least one of them. They are located in the cab. If the pressure in any one of your service air tanks drops below 60 psi while the ignition is on, these devices will alert you.

TIP *On large buses, the warning devices may come on if air pressure drops below 70, 80, or even 85 psi. Check your operator's manual to see what to expect for your vehicle.*

If a low air pressure warning device comes on, pull off the road immediately. Do not resume driving until the air pressure problem has been corrected.

Some vehicles with air brakes also use a wigwag low pressure indicator. This is mounted above the windshield. If the air pressure falls to the danger level, the signal arm will drop down across the windshield. You can't reset it (push it back out of view) until air pressure is brought above 60 psi. Don't operate the vehicle with the signal arm lever down.

One last device connected with the air brake system is the stop light. In an air brake system, air pressure operates an electric switch. This switch turns on the brake lights when you put on the brakes. This tells drivers behind you that you are slowing or stopping.

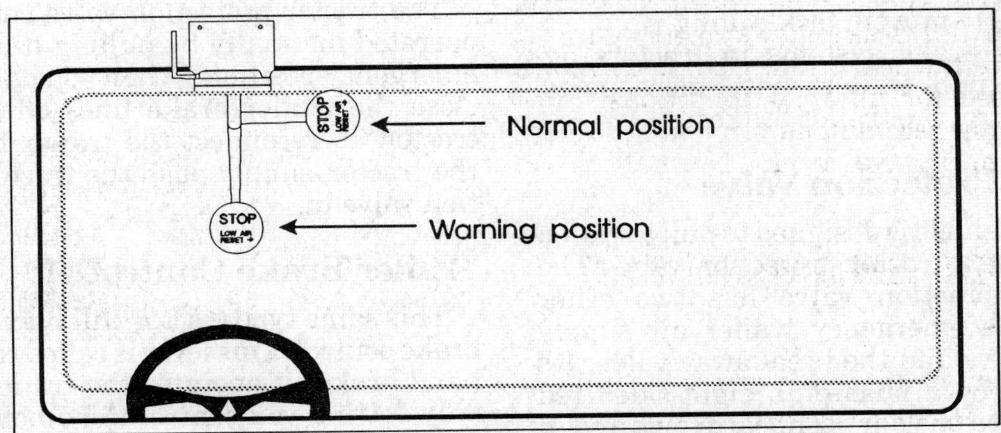

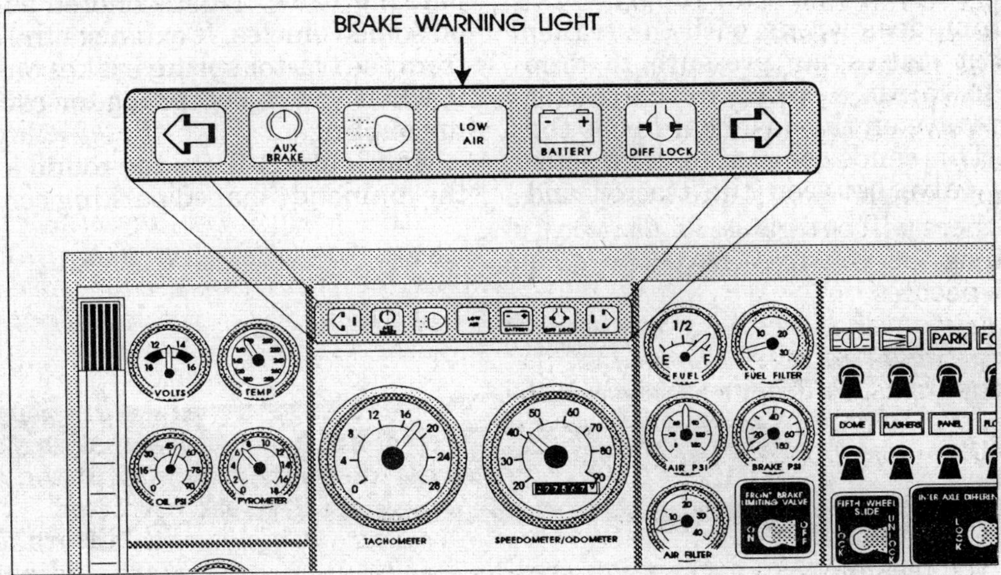

Figure 11-11 Low air warning devices.

AIR BRAKES IN TRACTOR-TRAILER COMBINATIONS

Your bus may actually be a tractor-trailer vehicle combination, rather than a straight vehicle. When you are pulling a trailer, some of the air supply must go to the trailer service brakes. The foot valve sends 60 percent to the trailer's system and 40 percent to the tractor's system. So when you brake, the trailer pulls back on the tractor. That helps to prevent jackknifing.

The air brake systems in tractors designed to pull trailers have more parts. These control the trailer brakes.

Tractor Protection Valve

If your vehicle is designed to pull a trailer, it will have a tractor protection valve. The tractor protection valve has two other names: the emergency trailer air supply control valve and the breakaway valve. It's controlled by a push-pull, eight-sided red knob located on your dashboard (pictured in Figure 11-9). Like the spring brake valve, this valve works automatically.

This valve's job is to protect the tractor air tanks in case of air pressure loss. The valve itself is located at the point where the flexible air lines that go to the trailer are connected. The valve separates the tractor air supply from the trailer air supply.

If anything goes wrong with the trailer system that causes air pressure to drop below 20 to 45 psi, a spring in the tractor protection valve on the dashboard pops the valve out. This sends a signal to the tractor protection valve between the tractor and trailer. It then closes off the air supply to the trailer.

This has two effects. One, it protects the tractor air supply from loss, so the tractor's service brakes will work. Two, because the trailer is losing air pressure and no more is coming from the tractor, the trailer spring brakes apply. So, the trailer spring brakes are on and you have control over the tractor service brakes. This lets you bring your tractor-trailer to a controlled, safe stop.

The tractor protection valve can also be operated manually by pulling it out to the emergency position. When you do that, you close the trailer brake lines off from the tractor. To reconnect the trailer brakes to the tractor, simply push the tractor protection valve in.

Trailer Brake Control

This same type tractor will have a trailer brake control. This lever is called the trailer hand brake. It operates the trailer brakes only, letting you control the amount of air directed to the trailer brakes. This brake must never be used as a parking brake. It can be used to lock the trailer brakes when coupling or uncoupling.

Tractor Parking Valve

Your vehicle may have a tractor-only parking valve. This is offered as an option on some vehicles. It exhausts the air supply from the tractor spring brakes only. You use it when you're bobtailing, or coupling and uncoupling.

(In Figure 11-9, it's the round knob above the diamond- shaped parking control.)

Figure 11-12 Trailer hand brake.

Gladhands

Gladhands (also called hose couplers) are the coupling devices on the ends of the air hoses on the back of your tractor and on the front of your trailer. These hoses connect the service and emergency brakes of your trailer to the tractor air supply system. They must be connected properly. Often they are color-coded. In that case, the service brake gladhands are colored blue and the emergency brake gladhands are colored red. The coupling device is a push, snap-lock type, similar to a radiator cap.

When you're bobtailing, you can connect the gladhands to special couplers on the back of the cab. These couplers are often called "dummy couplers." They protect the lines and keep water and dirt out. If your tractor doesn't have dummy couplers, just connect the lines together and secure them to the back of the tractor.

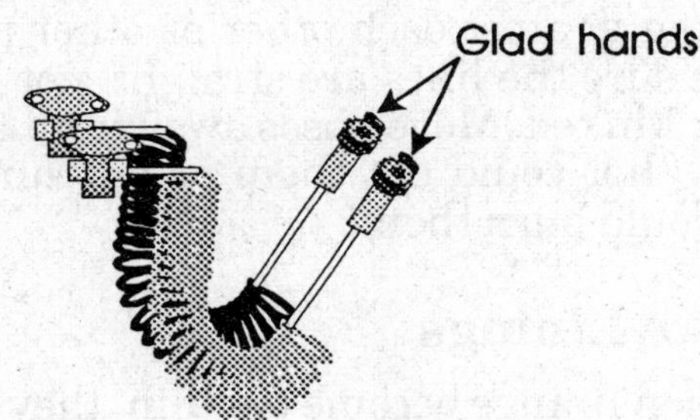

Figure 11-13 Service and emergency brake connections (glad hands).

BRAKE SYSTEM PROBLEMS

Air brake systems do a good job of stopping large vehicles, when the system is well-maintained and used correctly. If it's not, problems can develop.

Problems almost always come up because of a drop in or loss of air pressure. Let's look at how this can happen.

Compressor

The compressor could break down. What looks like a compressor problem could also be a faulty governor. If your compressor is belt-driven, though, the belt might need attention. It might be broken or too loose. Any of these problems could leave you with too little or no air pressure.

Air Lines and Hoses

What is more likely is that there is a leak or break in the air lines. The normal vibration of the vehicle can loosen air hoses. Heat can cause the rubber to dry out and crack. Hoses that are too close to hot exhaust parts can burn. Hoses that rub up against other parts can get cut.

If a service brake air line breaks, the air will escape from the service line. This will cause a rapid pressure drop. When the pressure falls below about 45 psi, the emergency brakes automatically apply and bring the vehicle to a stop. If an emergency

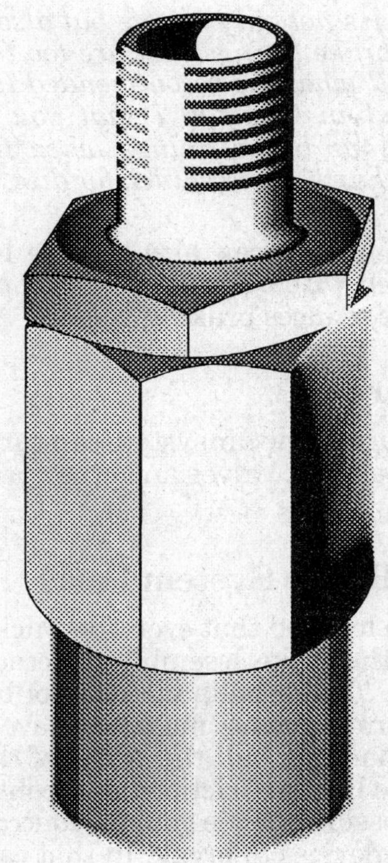

Figure 11-14 One-way check valve.

brake air line ruptures, there will be an immediate and rapid loss of pressure in the emergency brake lines.

If the line from the compressor to the main supply tank ruptures, there will be a loss of air from this tank. The one-way check valve between the main tank and the dry tanks will prevent the loss of air from those tanks. When the main air tank air pressure drops below 60 psi, one of the warning devices will come on. There should be enough air pressure left in the tank to bring the vehicle to a stop. There will be enough for a limited number of brake applications.

Brake Linings

Over time, friction causes the brake linings to wear and become thinner. This results in reduced contact with the brake drums, and reduced braking power.

TIP *It's not only unsafe but also illegal to have brake linings that are too thin. Do you recall what the recommended limit is? We stated in Chapter 7 that you should replace your brake linings when they get thinner than 1/4 inch (1/8 inch for disc brakes).*

Brake linings can also become loose or get soaked with oil or grease. Any of these problems reduces braking power.

Moisture

Moisture in the air system can turn to ice in cold weather. Valves and other parts can freeze.

Other Brake System Parts

You've learned that even the thick metal parts in the brake assembly can crack from the heat. That results in a loss of braking power. Brake drums must not have cracks longer than one half the width of the area the brake linings (friction pads) contact.

It is possible for the gauges, controls, and warning devices to break. In that case, you would not know the true condition of the braking system or get proper warning of system failure.

MAINTAINING AND INSPECTING AIR BRAKES

Fortunately, most air brake problems can be prevented with a little maintenance. Problems, large and small, can be spotted in time if you do your pre-trip inspection thoroughly.

Compressor

If the compressor has its own oil supply, making sure it has a good supply of oil will prevent problems. Some compressors are belt-driven. Make sure the belt is in good condition and tightened properly.

Lines and Hoses

Prevent little brake problems from becoming big ones by repairing or replacing brake lines and hoses that look worn or cracked. Check to see that they're not rubbing against each other or other parts. Make sure the lines are straight, not knotted or kinked. Move hoses away from sharp edges that could cut them or hot surfaces that could burn them.

Brake Linings

When linings become too thin, they must be replaced. Up until the time you replace them, you can make up for lining wear with a slack adjustment.

Slack Adjustment

Slack adjusters adjust the brakes to make up for brake lining wear. A slack adjuster is a lever arm attached to the push rod of the brake chamber at the clevis assembly. You can see the slack adjuster in Figures 11-1 and 11-6. Its job is to adjust the position of the S-cam, which then adjusts the distance of the brake shoe from the brake drum.

Slack adjusters can be manually adjusted or automatic. Here's how to adjust the slack manually.

Make sure you are parked on level ground. Chock the wheels so the vehicle won't move. Turn off the service and parking brake. Otherwise, you won't be able to move the slack adjuster. Wear gloves to protect your hands.

Pull hard on the slack adjuster. It should not move more than about one inch where the push rod attaches to it. If it does, it needs adjustment.

Locate the adjusting nut. Turn the nut clockwise until it is tight. This pushes the brake shoe tight against the drum. Then turn the nut counterclockwise one-fourth turn. This puts the brake shoe the proper distance from the drum.

Automatic slack adjusters make an adjustment whenever the brakes are applied. They sense the distance the push rod travels each time and keep the brakes in constant adjustment. They can be manually adjusted, if necessary.

Moisture

An air dryer can help remove some moisture. Even the best air drying system won't get rid of all the water and oil that condenses out of the compressed air. It tends to collect on the bottom of the air tank. Therefore, each air tank has a drain valve in the bottom. There are three types:

- manual
- automatic
- spit valve

You can open a manual drain valve by turning it one quarter turn. You may also be able to open it by pulling a cable. You should drain this type of tank at the end of each driving day or shift.

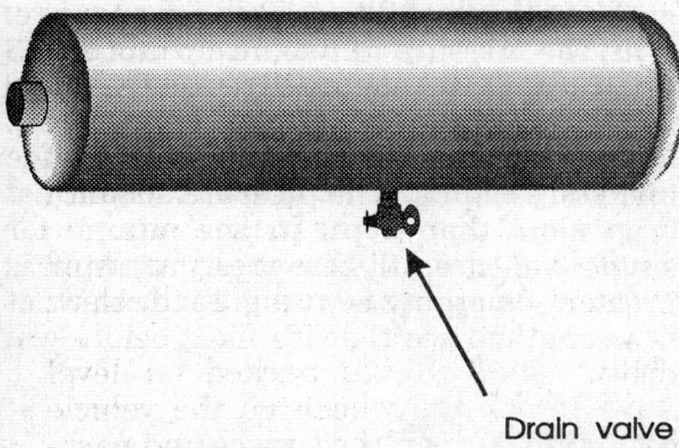

Figure 11-15. Air tank with drain valve.

An automatic drain valve automatically expels oil and water from the tank. These valves can be opened manually as well. You may have to do this if the automatic system fails.

A spit valve is also automatic. It expels water and oil from the tank each time the governor cycles.

Both automatic valves have electric heaters. The heater keeps the valve from freezing in cold weather.

If your vehicle does not drain automatically, daily manual draining is a must. An alcohol evaporator will help prevent moisture in the system from freezing. Make sure the container has a good supply of alcohol.

Safety relief valves protect the air tanks by releasing excess pressure if the air governor fails. They're usually set to open at 150 psi. If the safety valve releases air, something is wrong. It should be fixed by a mechanic.

Other Brake System Parts

When you first start the electrical system, you should get some response from your gauges and warning devices. This tells you the devices themselves are working. Warning lights should come on for a moment, then go out. The needles on gauges should move, then establish a reading.

If you don't get a response, there could be a defect in the electrical system. You may have a blown fuse, a broken or loose wire, or some other electrical problem. If you can't find and fix the problem, have a mechanic look into it. You must be able to rely on your gauges, controls, and warning devices in order to operate safely.

Bent, cracked, or worn metal parts must be repaired or replaced. If you can't do it yourself, get someone who can to give your brake system some attention. You should not drive off with any part of your brake system in less than top condition. It's simply not safe.

AIR BRAKE SYSTEM INSPECTION

If your vehicle has air brakes, you must add some steps to your normal vehicle inspection routine. We'll describe those steps in detail first. Then we'll outline the entire seven-step pre-trip inspection, including the air brake checks. This seven-step routine was first described in Chapter 10 but did not include inspecting the air brakes. We repeat it here, with the air brake inspection steps included, for your convenience.

Air Brake System Inspection

When you are at the engine compartment, you should check the compressor. Check the oil supply and belt as discussed in the Maintenance section beginning on page 270.

During the "walk-around" part of the inspection, check the hoses for leaks and breaks. At each wheel, check the brake assembly. Look for parts that need replacement or repair. You might find a cracked drum, a loose or worn brake lining. Check the slack adjuster. Adjust it if necessary.

Drain all air tanks that must be drained manually. You may find air tanks at the right front, left front, or center of the vehicle. It depends on the manufacturer. Don't forget any air tanks on the trailer, if you're pulling one.

When you're in the vehicle, your brake system check should include the following tests. Some of them are performed with the parking brakes off. Make sure the vehicle wheels are chocked so the vehicle doesn't roll while you perform these tests with the parking brakes off.

Test One: Air Pressure Build-up

This procedure tests pressure build-up time, the low pressure warning indicator, and the air governor.

Open the petcock. Drain the wet and dry air tanks until the gauges read zero. Then close the petcock. Start the engine and run it at a fast idle (600 to 900 rpm). The compressor will start to fill the tanks.

When the pressure reaches 50 psi, start timing. Also watch the warning mechanism. It should come on and stay on until the pressure builds to more than 60 psi.

In a vehicle with a single air system, the pressure should go from 50 psi to 90 psi within three minutes. In dual air systems, pressure should build from 85 to 100 psi within 45 seconds. If the build-up takes longer, the compressor needs attention.

Some vehicles with larger air tanks can take longer. Your operator's manual gives the best advice on this.

Keep filling the tanks until the governor stops the compressor. If it stops below 100 psi or starts above 125 psi, the governor needs to be adjusted. Your operator's manual may give slightly different upper and lower limits.

Run the engine at a fast idle. The air governor should cut-out the air compressor at the psi stated in the manual. The air pressure should stop rising. With the engine still idling, step on and off the brake, reducing the air pressure. The compressor should cut-in at the psi stated in the manual. The air pressure should begin to rise. If the governor cuts in or out too early or too late, it requires adjustment.

If the warning light doesn't go out once you have reached 60 psi, there could be a problem with the light. More seriously, it could be that one part of the dual braking system isn't working.

Test Two: Air Leakage Rate

With these simple steps, you can test the brake system's ability to hold air pressure. With the pressure fully built up (about 125 psi), turn off the engine. Release the parking brakes. Press the service brake pedal. Watch the reading on the pressure gauge and start timing. The pressure should not drop more than 2 psi in one minute for single vehicles. If the pressure drop is greater, something is wrong. Find out what is wrong and see that it's fixed before you drive.

Test Three: Air Leakage Rate

Here's another way to test the combination system's ability to hold air pressure. With the engine turned off, press on the brake pedal. Bring the pressure to 90 psi on the application gauge. Watch the air pressure gauge. The pressure drop should not be more than 3 psi per minute.

Test Four: Warning Device and Emergency Brake

These two steps test your warning device and your spring brake emergency application. Bring the air pressure to 90 pounds on the air pressure gauge and shut the engine off. Push and release the foot brake, reducing the air tank pressure, until the low air pressure warning indicator comes on. If the warning indicator comes on above 70 psi or below 50 psi, get it adjusted before you drive. (Your operator's manual may give different upper or lower limits.) The warning device should come on before the spring brakes are automatically applied.

TIP *Remember the air pressure at which the spring brakes will automatically come on? It's usually in the range between 20 and 40 psi.*

Allow the air pressure to build back up so you can release the parking brakes. Next, turn the engine off. Then push and release the foot brake, reducing the air pressure, until the spring brakes apply automatically. If they apply above 45 psi or not until 20 psi, something is wrong.

Test Five: Parking Brake

Begin the test from a dead standstill. You'll be moving the vehicle, so remove any wheel chocks you may have put in place. Get in the vehicle. Put the parking brake on. Put the vehicle in a low gear and try to move forward. The parking brake should hold you back. If it doesn't, it needs attention.

Test Six: Service Brake

Again, you'll be moving the vehicle. If you have wheel chocks in place, move them.

Build the air pressure to normal. Release the parking brake. Move the vehicle forward at about five mph. Apply the brakes firmly with the brake pedal. The vehicle should not pull to one side or the other. It should stop firmly, promptly, and evenly. If it doesn't, the brakes need adjustment.

Seven-Step Pre-trip Inspection

As you recall, there are seven main steps in this inspection routine. They are:

- approach the vehicle
- raise the hood or tilt the cab and check the engine compartment
- start the engine and inspect inside the driver's and passengers' compartments
- check the lights
- walk all around the vehicle, inspecting as you go
- check the signal lights
- check the brakes

Step One: Vehicle Overview

As you walk toward the vehicle, notice its general condition. Look for damage. Note whether the vehicle is leaning to one side. This could mean a flat tire. Cargo may be overloaded or may have shifted. Or it could be a suspension problem.

Look under the vehicle for fresh oil, coolant, grease, or fuel leaks. Check the area around the vehicle for people, other vehicles, objects, low hanging wires, or limbs. These could become hazards once the vehicle begins to move.

Look over the most recent vehicle inspection report. Drivers typically have to make a vehicle inspection report in writing each day. The vehicle owner then should see that any items in the report that affect safety are repaired. If the mechanic repaired the defects, or determined no repairs were needed, there will be a certification to that on the form.

You should look at the last report to find out what was the matter, if anything. Inspect the vehicle to find out whether problems were fixed or whether repairs were not needed.

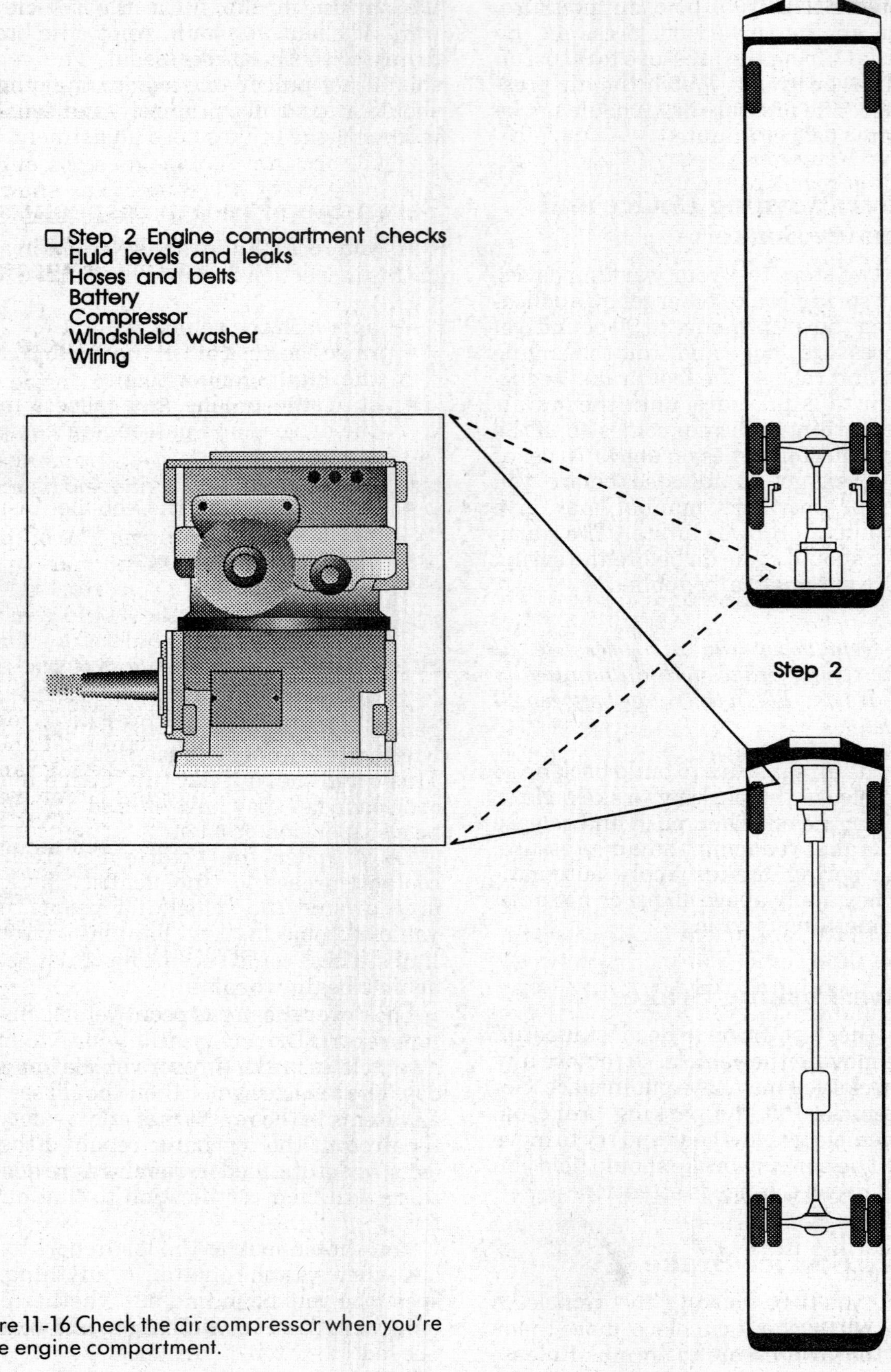

Figure 11-16 Check the air compressor when you're at the engine compartment.

Step Two: Engine Compartment Check

Check that the parking brakes are on and/or wheels chocked. You may have to raise the hood or open the engine compartment door. Remember, you may have to go to the side or rear of the vehicle to inspect all the items in Step Two. If you have a tilt cab, secure loose items in the cab before you tilt it. Then they won't fall and break something.

Check the engine oil level. The oil should be above the "Low" or "Add" mark on the dipstick. See that the level of coolant is above the "Low" level line on the reservoir. Check the condition of coolant-carrying hoses.

Check the radiator shutters and winterfront, if your vehicle has one. In cold weather, remove ice from the radiator shutters. Make sure the winterfront is not closed too tightly. If the shutters freeze shut or the winterfront is closed too much, the engine may overheat and stop. Inspect the fan. Make sure the blades are sound and not likely to catch on hanging wires or hoses.

If your vehicle has power steering, check the fluid level and the condition of the hoses. Check the dipstick on the oil tank. The fluid level should be above the "Low" or "Add" mark.

If you have windshield washers, here's where you check the fluid level. If your battery is located in the engine compartment, perform the battery check now.

If you have automatic transmission, check the fluid level. You may have to do this with the engine running. Your operator's manual will tell you if that is the case.

Check drive belts for tightness and excessive wear. Press down on the center of the belt. Your operator's manual will tell you how much slack there should be. If you can easily slide a belt over a pulley, it is definitely too loose or too worn.

Look for leaks in the engine compartment. These could be fuel, coolant, oil, power-steering fluid, hydraulic fluid, or battery fluid.

Look for cracked or worn insulation on electrical wiring.

Check the compressor for the air brakes. Check the oil supply. If it's belt-driven, check the belt. It should be in good condition. Check belt tightness.

Lower and secure the hood, cab, or engine compartment door. Close maintenance hatch doors.

Next, check any handholds, steps, or deck plates. Remove all water, ice, snow, or grease from handholds, steps, and deck plates used to enter or move about the vehicle. This will reduce the danger of slipping.

Step Three: Inside the Vehicle

Get in the vehicle. Inspect inside the driver's compartment. Start the engine. Make sure the parking brake is on. Shift into neutral, or "Park" if your transmission is automatic. Start the engine and listen for unusual noises.

Check the gauge readings. The oil pressure should come up to normal within seconds after the engine is started. The ammeter and/or voltmeter should give normal readings. Coolant temperature should start at "Cold" (the low end of the temperature range). It should rise gradually until it reaches normal operating range. The temperature of the engine oil should also rise slowly to normal operating range.

Oil, coolant, and charging circuit warning lights will come on at first. That tells you the lights are working. They should go out right away unless there's a problem.

Make sure your controls work. Check all of the following for looseness, sticking, damage, or improper setting:

- steering wheel
- accelerator ("gas pedal")
- foot brake
- trailer brake (if your vehicle has one)
- parking brake
- transmission controls
- horn(s)
- windshield wipers and washers if you have them
- headlights
- dimmer switch
- turn signal
- four-way flashers
- clearance, identification, and marker light switch or switches

Check other important equipment your vehicle may have, such as:

- door lock
- fresh air vent
- retractable step
- retarder controls
- interaxle differential lock

If your vehicle has a clutch, test it now. Depress the clutch until you feel a slight resistance. One to two inches of travel before you feel resistance is normal. More or less than that signals a problem.

Check your mirrors and windshield for defects.

Check that you have the required emergency equipment and that it is in good operating condition.

Check for optional items, such as a tire changing kit, and items required by state and local laws, such as mud flaps.

Check the interior of the bus. Aisles and stairwells must be clear. See that handholds and railings are securely attached to the vehicle. Clean them of any water, dirt, or grease. Inspect the floor. Look for slippery spots, snags, or protrusions that could be hazards. Look for holes in the floor. These could allow dangerous exhaust fumes to enter the bus.

Make sure the seats are clean and firmly attached to the vehicle.

See all the interior lights and signals work. Signs that direct passengers to the emergency exits and explain the standee line should be clean and easy to see. Test the emergency exits to make sure they work. Then close them securely.

If your vehicle has a lavatory (restroom), inspect it. Make sure it's clean and has enough supplies. Check to see that the door lock, lights, and "occupied" light work. Make sure the emergency buzzer and the telltale light that goes with it work.

Check any overhead parcel racks. See that nothing will shift and break or fall on the passengers when the bus is moving. Secure baggage in ways that allow the driver to move freely and easily and allow passengers to exit by any window or door in an emergency. Passengers should not leave carry-on baggage in a doorway or aisle. There should be nothing in the aisles that could trip other passengers.

Step Four: Check Lights

Next, check to see the lights are working. Make sure the parking brake is set, turn off the engine, and take the key with you. Turn on the headlights (on low beams) and the four-way flashers, and get out. Go to the front of the vehicle. Check that the low beams are on and both of the four-way flashers are working. Push the dimmer switch and check that the high beams work. Turn off the headlights and four-way hazard warning flashers. Turn on the parking, clearance, side-marker, and identification lights. Turn on the right turn signal, and start the "walk-around" part of the inspection.

Step Five: Walk-around Inspection

Walk all around the vehicle, inspecting as you go. Start at the driver's compartment on the driver's side. Cover the front of the vehicle. Work down the passenger side to the rear. Cover the rear of the vehicle. Work up the driver's side back to the starting position. Do it this way every time.

Clean all the lights, reflectors, and glass as you go along. Close any open emergency exits. Close any open access panels (baggage, lavatory service, engine, condenser, battery, and so forth).

Left Front Side

The driver's side glass should be clean. Door latches or locks should work properly.

Perform a tire, wheel, and rim check at the left front wheel. Perform a suspension system and braking system check. Check the steering parts. Check the air hoses for leaks and breaks. Check the brake assembly. Look for parts that need replacement or repair: a cracked drum, a loose or worn brake lining. Check the slack adjuster. Adjust it if necessary. Drain air tanks if necessary.

Step 5 Walk-around inspection
A Left front side: wheel and tire, suspension, brakes and air tanks, axle, side marker lamp and reflector,glass, latches and locks, mirrors

B Front of cab: axle, steering system, windshield, lights, reflectors, and spare tire

C Right front side: Door glass, latches and locks, wheels and tires, suspension, brakes and air tanks, axle, steering, side marker lamp and reflectors, passenger items and emergency exits

D Right side: fuel tank, wiring, lights and reflectors, mirrors

E Cargo securement, and doors

F Right rear: wheels and tires, suspension, brakes, axle, lights and reflectors

G Rear: lights and reflectors, license plate, mud flaps, doors and exhaust system

H Cargo securement and doors

I Left rear and left front: wheels and tires, suspension, brakes and air tanks, steering, axle, lights and reflectors, battery

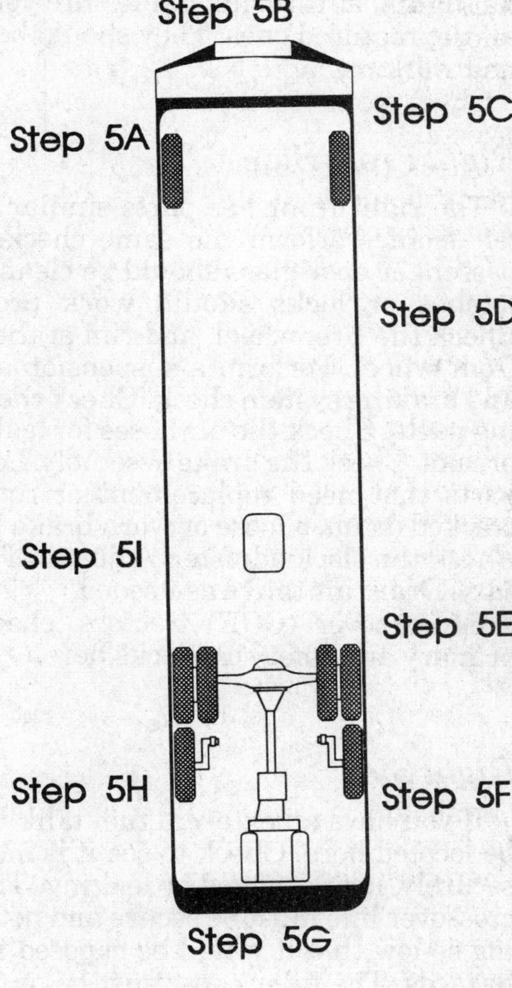

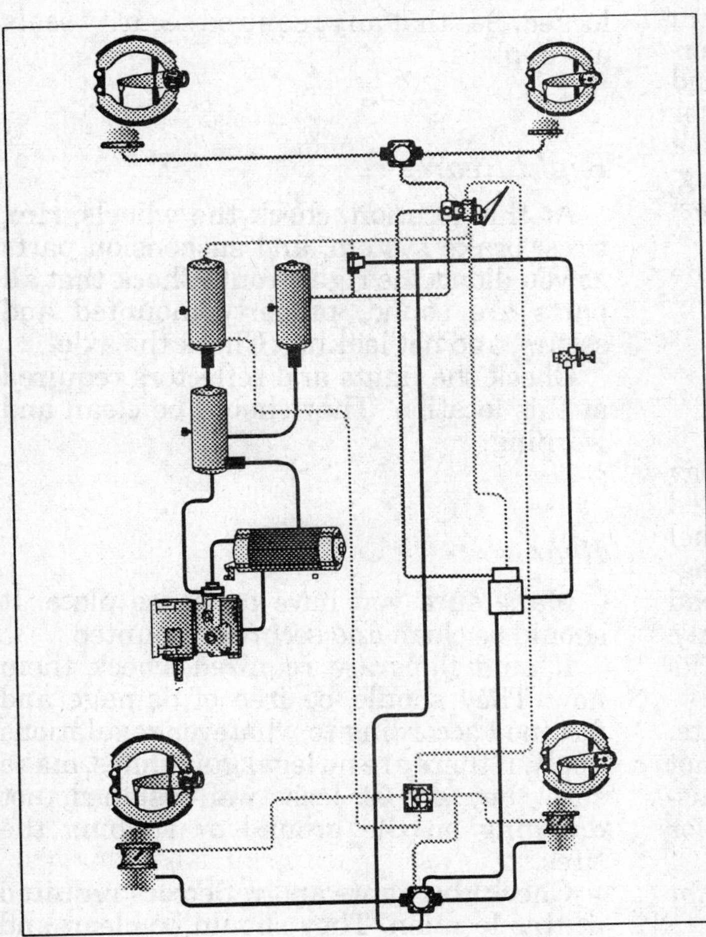

Figure 11-17 Check the air brake assembly when you inspect the wheel area.

Front

Check the condition of the front axle. Perform a check of the steering system parts. You should actually take hold of steering system parts and shake them to be sure that they are not loose.

Check the windshield. Pull on the windshield wiper arms to check for proper spring tension. Check the wiper blades for defects.

Check the lights and reflectors (parking, clearance and identification, and turn signal lights) at this site. Make sure you have all the required ones. They should be clean and working.

Right Front Side

The right front has parts similar to the left front. Perform the same checks. The passenger door glass should be clean. Door latches or locks should work properly. Check the tire, wheel, and rim at the right front wheel. Perform a suspension system and braking system check. Check the steering parts. Check the air hoses for leaks and breaks. Check the brake assembly. Look for parts that need replacement or repair: a cracked drum, a loose or worn brake lining. Check the slack adjuster. Adjust it if necessary. Drain air tanks as needed.

For cabover (COE) tractors, check the primary and safety cab locks here.

Right Side

If you have an external fuel tank, it may be located here. Check to see it is mounted securely, not damaged or leaking. The fuel crossover line must be secure and not hanging so low that it would be exposed to road hazards. The filler caps must be on firmly. Check the fuel supply. Perform these checks for each fuel tank your vehicle has.

Check all parts you can see at this site. See that the rear of the engine is not leaking. Check for leaks from the transmission. Check the exhaust system parts for defects.

Inspect the frame and cross members for bends and cracks.

Electrical wiring should be secured against snagging, rubbing, and wearing.

If your vehicle has a spare tire carrier or rack, check it for damage. It should be securely mounted in the rack. Make sure you have the correct size spare tire and wheel. The spare tire must be in good condition and properly inflated.

Cargo Check

Watch for cargo or baggage containing hazardous materials.

Make sure you haven't created handling problems for yourself by overloading the front axles. Any canvas or tarp must be properly secured to prevent tearing and billowing. If you have an oversized vehicle or load, have the necessary signs safely and properly mounted. Make sure you have the permits you need.

Check that the curbside cargo compartment doors are securely closed, latched, and locked. See that any required security seals are in place.

Right Rear

At this location, check the wheels, rim, tires, brake system, and suspension parts as you did at the right front. Check that all parts are sound, properly mounted and secure, and not leaking. Check the axle.

Check the lights and reflectors required at this location. They should be clean and working.

Rear

Make sure you have a license plate. It should be clean and securely mounted.

If mud flaps are required, check them now. They should be free of damage and fastened according to whatever regulations apply. If there are no legal guidelines, make sure they are at least well-fastened, not dragging on the ground or rubbing the tires.

Check the lights and reflectors required at this location. They should be clean and working.

Cut Here

☐ Step 1 Vehicle overview
General condition

☐ Step 2 Engine compartment checks
Fluid levels and leaks
Hoses and belts
Battery
Compressor
Windshield washer
Wiring

☐ Step 3 Inside the cab checks
Parking brake on
Gauge readings
Warning lights
Controls
Emergency equipment
Optional equipment

☐ Step 4 Check lights
Headlights (low and high beams)
Four-way flashers
Parking lights
Clearance lights
Side marker lights
Identification lights
Right turn signal

☐ Step 5 Walk-around inspection
A Left front side: wheel and tire, suspension, brakes and air tanks, axle, side marker lamp and reflector, glass, and, mirrors

B Front of cab: axle, steering system, windshield, lights and reflectors

C Right front side: Door glass, latches and locks, wheel and tire, suspension, brakes and air tanks, axle, steering, side marker lamp and reflector

D Right side: fuel tank, exhaust system, frame and cross members, wiring, lights and reflectors, mirrors

E Right rear: wheels and tires, suspension, brakes, axle, sliders, lights and reflectors

F Rear: lights and reflectors, license plate, mud flaps, spare tire, exhaust and doors

G Left rear and left front: wheels and tires, suspension, brakes and air tanks, steering, axle, lights and reflectors, battery

☐ Step 6 Check signal lights

☐ Step 7 Brake check

Figure 11-18 Vehicle Inspection Aid for straight vehicles with air brakes.

Cargo Securement

If it applies to your vehicle, check the cargo securement at the right rear of the vehicle. It must be properly blocked, braced, tied, chained, and so forth. Any canvas or tarp must be properly secured to prevent tearing and billowing. Make sure the tarp doesn't cover up your rear lights.

Check to make sure you haven't distributed the load so as to overload the rear axles.

If you have an oversized load or vehicle, have the necessary signs safely and properly mounted. Have any lights or flags required for projecting loads. Make sure you have the permits you need to haul this load.

Check that rear doors are securely closed, latched, and locked.

Left Rear and Front Side

At this location, check the wheels, rims, tires, brake system, and suspension parts just as you did for the right rear and front side. Check that all parts are sound, properly mounted and secure, and not leaking. Check the axle.

Check the lights and reflectors required at this location. They should be clean and working.

Your vehicle's battery may be mounted here, rather than in the front engine compartment. If so, perform the battery check now.

Step Six: Check Signal Lights

Get in the vehicle and turn off all the lights. Then turn on the stop lights. Or have a helper step on the brake pedal while you watch to see whether the light goes on.

Now turn on the left-turn signal lights. Then get out and check the left side lights, rear and front.

Step Seven: Check Brakes

Now you'll perform some tests with the engine running and the parking brakes off. Make sure you're on a level surface. Chock the wheels.

Get back in the vehicle. Turn off any lights you don't need for driving. Check to see that you have all the required papers, trip manifests, permits, and so forth. Secure all loose articles in the vehicle. If they are free to roll around, they could hinder your operation of the controls or hit you in a crash. Start the engine. Perform air brake tests numbers one through four. Then stop the vehicle. Remove the chocks. Perform brake tests five and six.

DRIVING WITH AIR BRAKES

Your air brakes will be there to serve you if you treat them right. You've seen how to maintain and inspect them. It's important that you also know the right way to use them.

Normal Stops

For normal stops, simply push the brake pedal down. Control the pressure so the vehicle comes to a smooth, safe stop. If you have a manual transmission, don't push the clutch in until the engine rpm is close to idle. Once you have stopped you can select a starting gear.

Don't "ride" the brakes. That just draws down your air pressure and heats up your brakes. The only time you might want to do this is if your brakes get very wet. Then ride the brakes only for as long as it takes to dry the brakes.

Emergency Stops

Good speed and space management will keep the need for panic stops to a minimum. But if you do have to brake suddenly, try to maintain steering control. Keep the vehicle in a straight line. You can do this by using "controlled" or "stab" braking. These braking techniques were described in Chapter 8. Remember them?

In controlled braking, you apply the brakes as hard as you can without locking the wheels. Don't turn the steering wheel while you do this. If you need to make a larger steering adjustment or if the wheels lock, release the brakes. Reapply the brakes as soon as you have traction again.

In stab braking, you apply your brakes all the way. Release the brakes when the wheels lock up. As soon as the wheels start rolling, apply the brakes fully again. It can take up to one second for the wheels to start rolling after you release the brakes. If you reapply the brakes before the wheels start rolling, the vehicle won't straighten out.

Air Brakes and Stopping Distance

You need increased stopping distance with air brakes. It takes time for air to flow to the brakes after you have stepped on the pedal. The braking response is not as immediate as it is with hydraulic brakes.

Remember the stopping distance formula? It's:

perception distance
\+ reaction distance
\+ braking distance
= total stopping distance

You must add the distance taken up by "brake lag" to this formula. At 55 mph on a dry surface, you can travel about 32 feet before the brakes respond to your stepping on the pedal. That makes your total stopping distance over 300 feet longer than a football field.

Braking on a Downgrade

Brake fade and brake loss are real dangers on a downgrade. It's easy to lose your brakes on a hill, and that's when you really need them, so it's vital you use them correctly. Start down the hill in a low gear that will give you a lot of engine braking. That way you can use your brakes lightly instead of standing on them. They'll be able to stay cool enough to give you braking power all the way to the bottom.

Above all, don't fan the brakes. Using them hard builds up tremendous heat. Releasing them briefly does not give them enough time to cool off. When you apply them again, you just increase the heat. Brakes won't take too much of this treatment before they expand beyond usefulness or even burn up.

So again, use a low gear and light steady pressure.

If your brakes are out of adjustment, you'll really notice it on a downgrade. Most long grades offer a "pull-out" at the top of the hill. This is a safe area to the side of the road. Stop, check, and adjust your brakes before heading down. Don't just step on the brakes and decide they're OK. Get out of the vehicle and check them thoroughly.

Low Air Pressure

Heed your low air pressure warning. It means you still have a little air pressure left and can probably still make a safe stop. Stop and park the vehicle the first chance you get to do so safely. Don't wait until the emergency brakes come on. It's harder to control the vehicle when the spring brakes come on.

As you can see, the idea behind air brakes is not a complicated one. Air brakes are fairly easy to use, maintain, and inspect. The system as a whole is not that complex. But it is large and has many parts. So there are many chances for problems to develop. A single problem can cause the whole system to fail. So if you plan to drive a vehicle with air brakes, you must understand each and every part. You must commit yourself to proper maintenance and thorough inspection. If you do, your air brakes should work dependably and reliably.

PASS POST-TRIP

Instructions: For each true/false test item, read the statement. Decide whether the statement is true or false. If it is true, select the letter "A." If it is false, select the letter "B." For each multiple-choice test item, choose the answer choice – A, B, C, or D – that correctly completes the statement or answers the question. There is only one correct answer.

1. The compressed air in the brake chamber transmits the force exerted by the driver's foot on the brake pedal to the foundation brakes.

A. True
B. False

2. When you use brakes hard, the first thing that happens is ______.

A. the linings become worn
B. they get out of adjustment
C. they get hot
D. they crack

3. If you have an alcohol evaporator, you do not have to drain the air tanks.

A. True
B. False

4. If your air compressor fails, ______.

A. you will have no brakes
B. the brakes will immediately lock up
C. gradually decreasing air pressure will continue to be available from the air tanks for a while
D. air pressure will not be affected at all

5. Front wheel braking is good to have on ______.

A. dry roads
B. wet roads
C. icy roads
D. all of the above

6. Pushing the brake pedal down when the spring brakes are on will ______.

A. set the parking brakes
B. release the parking brakes
C. damage the brakes
D. adjust the slack

7. The emergency brake system is a completely separate system and is completely under the driver's control.

A. True
B. False

8. The low air pressure warning device should come on when air pressure drops below ______.

A. 20 psi
B. 45 psi
C. 60 psi
D. 125 psi

9. At 55 mph on a dry surface, the average driver needs more than ______ feet to stop a CMV with air brakes.

A. 100
B. 200
C. 300
D. 400

10. The best braking technique to use on a downgrade is ______.

A. light braking
B. controlled braking
C. stab braking
D. hard braking

CHAPTER 12

Tractor-Trailer Buses

When you have finished this chapter, you will be able to provide the correct answers to questions about:

- coupling and uncoupling a single semitrailer
- inspecting tractor-trailers
- pulling trailers safely

To complete this chapter you will need:

- a dictionary
- pencil or pen
- blank paper or notebook
- colored pencils, pens, markers, or highlighters
- a CDL preparation manual from your state Department of Motor Vehicles, if one is offered
- Federal Motor Carrier Safety Regulations pocketbook (or access to U.S. Department of Transportation regulations, Parts 383, 393, and 396 of Subchapter B, Chapter 3, Title 49, Code of Federal Regulations)
- operator's manual for your vehicle

PASS PRE-TRIP

Instructions: Read the statements. Decide whether each statement is true or false. If it is true, circle the letter "A." If it is false, circle the letter "B."

1. A trailer jackknife is more likely when you are pulling a fully loaded trailer than an empty one.
  A. True
  B. False

2. The trailer landing gear should not contact the tractor during turns.
  A. True
  B. False

3. A fully-loaded tractor-trailer is ten times more likely to roll over in a crash than an empty one.
  A. True
  B. False

If you plan to pull a trailer with your vehicle, you will have to take your CDL test in a vehicle with a trailer. You'll be tested on your knowledge of coupling and uncoupling. You'll have to show you can inspect the combination.

You'll have to pass the Knowledge Test all CDL applicants must take. You must show you have additional knowledge on combination vehicles. Then, once you pass the Skills Test in a "representative vehicle," you'll have a CDL with an "A" code. You'll be licensed to drive Group A ("combination") vehicles.

In this chapter, we'll cover the material you need to get a CDL for driving a tractor-trailer bus. If you plan to pull only a single trailer, this chapter has the information you will need for the knowledge test.

If you want to pull doubles and triples, you'll need a Doubles/Triples Endorsement. You'll not only have to answer additional knowledge questions about pulling doubles and triples. You'll also have to take the Skills Test while pulling those trailers. If you want the Doubles/Triples Endorsement, you should read *How to Prepare for the Commercial Driver's License Truck Driver's Test.*

Remember, FMCSR Part 383 states that drivers of tractor- semitrailer combinations must know the correct way to couple and uncouple a tractor and semitrailer. They must know why and how to inspect the vehicle combination.

We'll begin this chapter with coupling and uncoupling a single tractor and trailer. Toward the end of this you'll find the inspection routine for this type of bus.

COUPLING A SINGLE TRACTOR AND SEMITRAILER

Coupling and uncoupling aren't hard procedures, but for safety's sake, they must be done right. In this chapter we'll outline steps that will ensure a safe coupling every time.

What's involved in coupling? To put it very simply, you're going to back the tractor up to the trailer so the coupling assemblies connect. Then you must supply electricity to the trailer so the lights will work. If you have air brakes, you must supply the trailer with air. And you must make sure you can control the trailer from the tractor.

Slow and steady wins the race here. Follow the procedures step by step every time. Use the rear-view mirrors. Know your equipment. You have to know the width of the tractor as compared to the width of the trailer. Then remember that the center of the fifth wheel is always in the center of the tractor frame and the kingpin is always in the center of the front of the trailer.

Inspect Area

Before you begin any coupling procedure, walk the area around the trailer and tractor. Look for anything in your path that could damage the tractor or trailer. Boards lying on the ground can fly up when popped from the ground by a tire. Nails, glass, or other objects can damage a tire. Make sure the way is clear before you begin the first stages of alignment.

Inspect Vehicles

Check the coupling devices on the tractor and the trailer. Look for damaged or missing parts. Inspect the tractor frame and the fifth wheel mounting. There should be no cracked or bent parts. The mounting should be secure. Make sure the trailer kingpin isn't bent or broken.

Lubricate the fifth wheel. Lubrication reduces friction between the fifth wheel and the trailer. That gives you better steering control.

Pre-position the fifth wheel. It should be tilted down (toward the rear of the tractor). The locking jaws should be open.

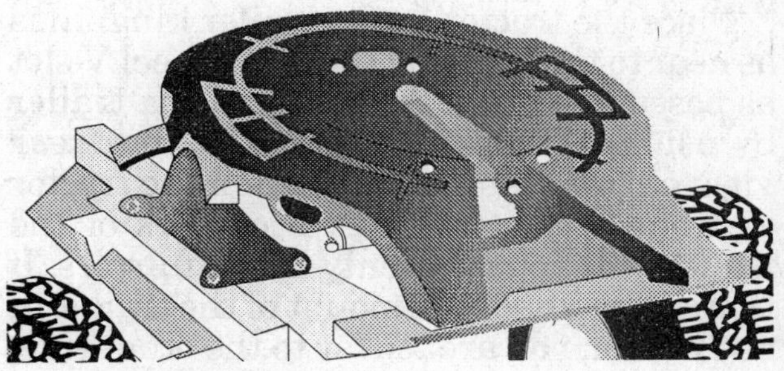

Figure 12-1 Fifth wheel.

Stabilize Vehicles

Work on the most level ground you can find if you have a choice about it. Uneven ground will make your task just that much harder. Put the spring brakes on. As you move the tractor under the trailer, it can move the trailer. Having the brakes on will keep the trailer from rolling backward.

Some older trailers don't have spring brakes. If yours doesn't, put chocks at the rear of your trailer tires. Perhaps you're not sure whether you have spring brakes. You can tell just by looking at the brakes. Find the service brake chamber. Look for the

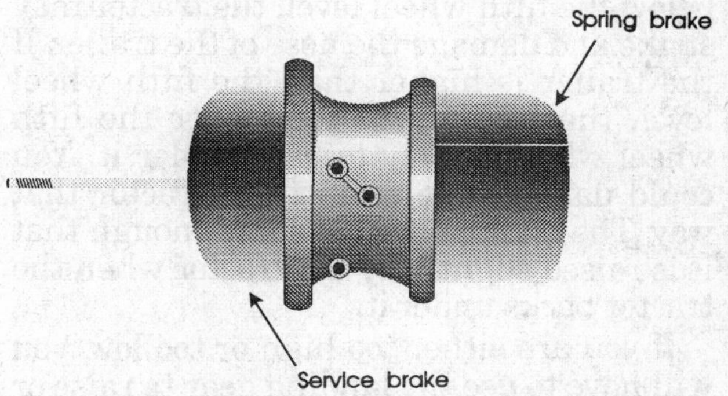

Figure 12-2 Look for the spring brake chamber mounted on the service brake chamber.

spring brake chamber "piggybacking" on the service brake chamber. If you don't find it, use chocks to keep your vehicle from moving.

Align the Tractor

A proper coupling requires you to center the kingpin in the fifth wheel within a small margin of error. Before you back, you must align the tractor and trailer precisely. If you don't, you'll have to move the tractor or trailer before you can complete the coupling.

Place the tractor so the trailer kingpin is as near to the center of the fifth wheel V-slot as possible. Locate the center of the trailer by using its sides as a gauge in your rear view mirrors. As you straighten the tractor in front of the trailer, the corners of the trailer will appear evenly in the mirrors. If there is an unequal amount of the trailer in one mirror, you are too far to the other side.

Don't try to back under the trailer at an angle. You could damage the landing gear or push the trailer sideways.

Back Slowly

If you back slowly, you can steer the tractor in the desired direction to align the fifth wheel with the kingpin. Keep backing until the fifth wheel just touches the trailer. Don't hit the trailer.

Align the Trailer

Put on the parking brake and put the transmission in neutral. Go out and compare the level of the fifth wheel with the height of the kingpin. If the trailer is too far below the fifth wheel level, the tractor may strike and damage the nose of the trailer. If the trailer is higher than the fifth wheel level, the trailer will come over the fifth wheel when you try to back under it. You could damage the rear of the tractor that way. The trailer should be low enough that it is raised slightly by the tractor when the tractor backs under it.

If you are either too high or too low, you will have to use the landing gear to raise or lower the trailer to the fifth wheel level. It isn't all that easy to roll up a loaded trailer.

The landing gear crank is hinged and swings under the trailer to a latch. The latch secures it to the frame while the trailer is in motion. If the crank handle were allowed to swing freely while the trailer is moving, it could damage a nearby vehicle or passing pedestrian. Always secure the crank handle when you've finished using it.

Connect Air Lines

The first step of actual coupling of the tractor and trailer is to connect the air supply lines. First, check the rubber seals on both connections. If one is worn or cracked, have it replaced immediately. Otherwise, you might end up with a service line air leak you wouldn't notice until you put the brakes on.

There are two air supply lines, the service brake line and the emergency brake line. These are almost always colored red for emergency and blue for service. The connections at the front of the trailer will usually be painted the color of the air hose that should be connected to them. Secure each air supply line to the matching colored trailer connection.

If you cross the air lines on a new trailer with spring brakes, you will not be able to release the trailer brakes. If you cross the air lines on an old trailer without spring brakes, you could drive off and not have any braking power on the trailer.

Lock the Trailer Brakes

After you return to the tractor, apply the trailer parking brakes by pulling the trailer brake knob. This puts on the trailer brakes to keep the trailer from moving. Release the tractor brakes by pushing in the tractor brake knob.

Back Under the Trailer

Put the transmission in the lowest reverse gear and back... slowly. Keep backing until the tractor comes into contact with the trailer. You will feel a definite bump. Don't bump the kingpin too hard. Continue backing slowly until progress is stopped by the kingpin locking into the fifth wheel.

Check Connection

Raise the landing gear slightly. Check the connection by pulling forward very slowly. If the tractor does not move, the connection is complete. If it does move, stop immediately and back again.

Put the transmission in neutral. Put the parking brakes on. Shut off the engine. Take the key with you so someone else can't move the truck while you are under it.

Get out of the tractor and check to see that the fifth wheel locking jaw is closed around the trailer kingpin. To do this, you must look under the front of the trailer at the fifth wheel. Use a flashlight if it's too dark to see clearly. If the jaw is closed you will see it locked securely around the back of the kingpin. There should be no space between the upper and lower fifth wheel. If there is space, the kingpin may be on top of the closed fifth wheel jaws. The trailer could come loose very easily.

If the connection is good, check that the locking lever is in the "Lock" position. Make sure the safety catch is in position over the locking lever. You may have to put it in place by hand.

If the connection is poor, don't drive the coupled unit. Get it fixed.

Connect Electrical Power and Check Air Supply

Connect the light supply cable to the trailer. Fasten the safety catch. Inspect the air and electrical lines for signs of damage. Make sure air and electrical lines will not hit any of the vehicle's moving parts.

Return to the tractor, and turn on the emergency flashers and trailer lights. Walk around the trailer to make sure the lights are working. Check the clearance lights and side marker lights. Walk to the back of the trailer and check the turn signals. Turning on the emergency flashers at the tractor will make the turn signals flash.

While you're checking out the trailer tires, gauge the tire inflation if you didn't do this in your routine inspection. Also check for worn hoses or loose connections on the trailer's brake system. The hiss of escaping air may be heard coming from these areas. Rusty connections should be closely inspected for cracks. Should any leaks exist, have them repaired immediately. A ruptured air hose or broken connection is sure trouble while the vehicle is in motion.

Raise Landing Gear

The trailer is finally connected to the tractor and ready to roll. But you must first remove any tire chocks. If they are yours, put them in the tractor storage compartment. If they belong in the yard, find out where they should be stored and put them there. Roll up the landing gear. Use low gear to begin raising the landing gear. Once

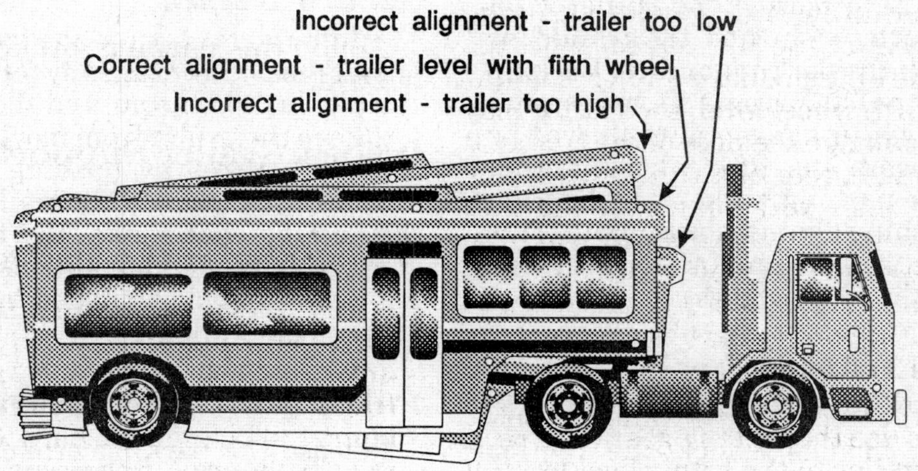

Figure 12-3 Aim for a good vertical alignment.

the weight is fully supported by the tractor, you can switch to high gear.

Roll the gear as high as it will go. Never drive with the landing gear only part way up. It may catch on railroad tracks and objects in the road.

Check for clearance between the rear of the tractor frame and the landing gear. When the tractor turns sharply, it must not hit the landing gear.

Check that there is enough clearance between the top of the tractor tires and the nose of the trailer.

UNCOUPLING A SINGLE TRACTOR AND SEMITRAILER

Before you start, make sure the surface that the landing gear will be sitting on when lowered can support the trailer. A heavy trailer could sink into hot asphalt or loose dirt. On such surfaces you should always place something, a wide plank or pad, under the landing gear plate.

Position Vehicles

Straighten out so the tractor and trailer are in a straight line. If you park with the trailer at an angle, you can damage the landing gear during uncoupling.

Ease Pressure on Locking Jaws

Once you have parked the trailer on a firm, level surface, shut off the trailer air supply to lock the parking brakes. Back up slightly. This will take some of the pressure off the fifth wheel locking jaws. It will be easier to release the fifth wheel locking lever. Put the parking brakes on while the tractor is pushing against the kingpin. This will hold the vehicle combination with the pressure off the locking jaws.

Chock the Trailer Wheels

Get out of the tractor. If the trailer doesn't have spring brakes, chock the trailer wheels. Once the trailer tires are chocked, lower the landing gear.

Lower Landing Gear

Next, lower the landing gear until it touches the ground.

Disconnect Air Lines and Electrical Cable

The next step is to remove the air supply lines and electrical cable from the trailer. Stow each in its proper position at the rear of the tractor. Connect the air line glad-hands to the dummy couplers at the back of the cab or couple them together. Hang the electrical cable with the plug end down. This prevents moisture from getting into the cable. Secure the lines so they won't be damaged by moving the tractor.

Unlock Fifth Wheel

Raise the release handle lock. Pull the release handle to the "open" position. Keep your legs and feet clear of the rear tractor wheels. If the vehicle were to move, you could be injured.

Pull Tractor Partially Clear of Trailer

Pull the tractor forward until the fifth wheel comes out from under the trailer. Stop with the tractor frame under trailer. This prevents the trailer from falling to the ground if the landing gear collapses or sinks.

Secure Tractor

Apply the parking brake. Shift into neutral.

Inspect Trailer Supports

Before you put all the trailer weight on the landing gear, make sure the ground is supporting the trailer. Make sure the landing gear is not damaged and can still support the trailer.

Pull Tractor Clear of Trailer

Release the parking brakes. Check the area and drive the tractor clear.

Once the tractor is completely uncoupled

from the trailer, pull away from the trailer slowly. You will know when you are free of the trailer. The rear of the tractor will rise as the shock absorbers extend with the release of the trailer weight.

That covers coupling and uncoupling a semitrailer. To get a CDL for combination vehicles, you also need to know why and how to inspect this combination.

INSPECTING A TRACTOR-SEMITRAILER COMBINATION

Use the seven-step inspection procedure first described in Chapter 10 to inspect your vehicle combination. There are more things to inspect on a vehicle combination than on a single vehicle. Many of these are just more of what are on a single vehicle (for example, tires, wheels, lights, and reflectors).

However, there are also some new things to check. We'll describe those steps in detail first. Then we'll outline the entire seven-step pre-trip inspection and include stopping to check the coupling and trailer brakes. As first described in Chapter 10, this seven-step routine was suited more to inspecting straight trucks or buses. We'll repeat it here and include the steps for inspecting a tractor with air brakes coupled to a semitrailer.

Lower Fifth Wheel

Check that the lower fifth wheel is securely mounted to the frame. Look for missing or damaged parts. There should be no visible space between the upper and lower fifth wheel.

The locking jaws should be around the shank, not the head of the kingpin. The release arm should be properly seated and the safety latch or lock engaged.

Upper Fifth Wheel

See that the glide plate is securely mounted to the trailer frame. Check the kingpin for damage.

Air Lines to Trailer

The air lines should be properly connected to the gladhands, with enough slack for turns. All lines must be free from damage and air leaks.

Sliding Fifth Wheel

Check the slide for damaged or missing parts. See that all the locking pins are present and locked in place.

If the slider is air-powered, check for air leaks.

Check that the fifth wheel is not so far forward that the tractor frame will hit the landing gear, or the cab will hit the trailer, during turns.

Landing Gear

The landing gear should be fully raised. Check for missing parts and damage. The crank handle should be in place and secured. If the landing gear is power-operated, check for air or hydraulic leaks.

Detachable Electrical Connections

Detachable electrical connections carry current from the tractor to the trailer, where it powers the trailer lights. You probably call this a pigtail. Like any other circuit, this connection can short out or break. Make sure the electrical cord is firmly plugged in and secure. Check the electrical lines for damage.

Brakes

Perform the following checks in addition to the other brake checks you do as part of your inspection.

Test Tractor Protection Valve

Charge the trailer air brake system. (That is, build up normal air pressure and push the "Air Supply" knob in.) Shut the engine off. Step on and off the brake pedal several times to reduce the air pressure in the tanks. The tractor protection valve control should pop out (or go from "Normal" to "Emergency" position) when the air pressure falls into the pressure range spec-

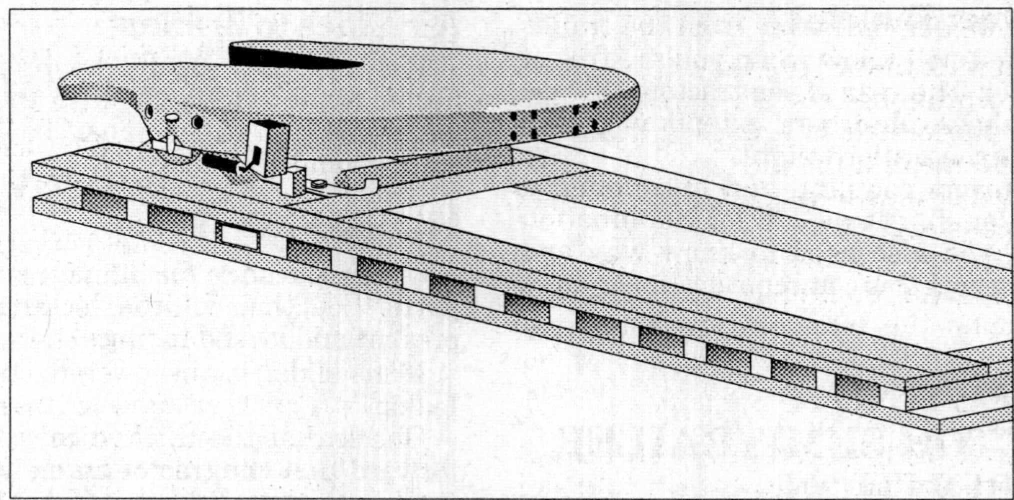

Figure 12-4 Sliding fifth wheel.

ified by the manufacturer (usually 20 to 45 psi).

TIP *Remember, the tractor protection valve is an eight-sided, red, push-pull knob.*

If the tractor protection valve doesn't work right, an air hose or trailer brake leak could drain all the air from the tractor. This would cause the emergency brakes to come on, and you could lose control of the vehicle.

Test Trailer Emergency Brakes

Charge the trailer air brake system and check that the trailer rolls freely. Then stop and pull out the tractor protection valve control (or trailer emergency valve) or place it in the "Emergency" position. Pull gently on the trailer with the tractor to check that the trailer emergency brakes are on.

Test Trailer Service Brakes

Check for normal air pressure and release the parking brakes. Move the vehicle forward slowly, and apply the trailer brakes with the hand control (trolley valve or Johnson bar), if so equipped. You should feel the brakes come on. This tells you the trailer brakes are connected and working. (The trailer brakes should be tested with the hand valve but controlled in normal operation with the foot pedal, which applies air to the service brakes at all wheels.)

It's a good idea to check the brakes after several moments of charging the air system. Look under the trailer at the brakes. You should be able to see if the brake lining is against the drum. If not, allow the compressor to continue charging the system for a little longer. Even a trailer brake system that has lost all of its air supply from sitting will be fully charged by the time you have completed all your safety checks and made all the connections, if the air supply hoses were connected early in the coupling procedure.

To test the brake system for crossed air lines, turn the tractor engine off. Apply and release the trailer brakes with the hand valve. Listen for brake movement and air release.

SEVEN-STEP VEHICLE COMBINATION INSPECTION

As a reminder, the seven main steps in this inspection routine are:

- approach the vehicle
- raise the hood or tilt the cab and check the engine compartment
- check the lights
- walk all around the vehicle, inspecting as you go
- check the signal lights
- check the brakes

Step One: Vehicle Overview

As you walk toward the vehicle, notice its general condition. Look for damage. Note whether the vehicle is leaning to one side. This could mean a flat tire. Cargo may be overloaded or may have shifted. Or it could be a suspension problem.

Look under the vehicle for fresh oil, coolant, grease, or fuel leaks. Check the area around the vehicle for people, other vehicles, objects, low hanging wires, or limbs. These could become hazards once the vehicle begins to move.

Look over the most recent vehicle inspection report. Drivers typically have to make a vehicle inspection report in writing each day. The vehicle owner then should see that any items in the report that affect safety are repaired. If the mechanic repaired the defects or determined no repairs were needed, there will be a certification to that on the form.

You should look at the last report to find out what was the matter, if anything. Inspect the vehicle to find out whether problems were fixed, or whether repairs were not needed.

Step Two: Engine Compartment Check

Check that the parking brakes are on and/or wheels chocked. You may have to raise the hood, open the engine compartment door, or open maintenance hatches on the side or rear of the vehicle to check everything in this step. If you have a tilt cab, secure loose items in the vehicle before you tilt it. Then they won't fall and break something.

The engine oil level should be above the "Low" or "Add" mark on the dipstick. See that the level of coolant is above the "Low" level line on the reservoir. Check the condition of coolant-carrying hoses.

Check the radiator shutters and winterfront, if your vehicle has one. In cold weather, remove ice from the radiator shutters. Make sure the winterfront is not closed too tightly. If the shutters freeze shut or the winterfront is closed too much, the engine may overheat and stop. Inspect the fan. Make sure the blades are sound and not likely to catch on hanging wires or hoses.

If your vehicle has power steering, check the fluid level and the condition of the hoses. Check the dipstick on the oil tank. The fluid level should be above the "Low" or "Add" mark.

If you have windshield washers, here's where you check the fluid level. If your battery is located in the engine compartment, perform the battery check described in Chapter 10.

If you have automatic transmission, check the fluid level. You may have to do this with the engine running. Your operator's manual will tell you if that is the case.

Check drive belts for tightness and excessive wear. Press down on the center of the belt. Your operator's manual will tell you how much slack there should be. If you can easily slide a belt over a pulley, it is definitely too loose or too worn.

Look for leaks in the engine compartment. These could be fuel, coolant, oil, hydraulic fluid, or battery fluid.

Look for cracked or worn insulation on electrical wiring.

Check the compressor for the air brakes. Check the oil supply. If it's belt-driven, check the belt. It should be in good condition. Check belt tightness.

Lower and secure the hood, cab, or engine compartment door.

Next, check any handholds, steps, or deck plates. Remove all water, ice, and snow or grease from handholds, steps, and deck plates used to enter or move about the vehicle. This will reduce the danger of slipping.

Step Three: Inside the Vehicle

Get in the vehicle. Inspect inside the driver's compartment. Start the engine. Make sure the parking brake is on. Shift into neutral, or "Park" if your transmission is automatic. Start the engine and listen for unusual noises.

Check the gauge readings. The oil pressure should come up to normal within seconds after the engine is started. The ammeter and/or voltmeter should give normal readings. Coolant temperature should start at "Cold" and rise gradually to normal operating range. The engine oil temperature should also rise slowly to normal operating range.

Oil, coolant, and charging circuit warning lights will come on at first. That tells you the lights are working. They should go out right away unless there's a problem.

Make sure your controls work. Check all of the following for looseness, sticking, damage, or improper setting:

- steering wheel
- accelerator
- foot brake
- trailer brake
- parking brake
- transmission controls
- horn or horns
- windshield wipers and washers (if your vehicle has them)
- headlights
- dimmer switch
- turn signal
- four-way flashers
- clearance, identification, and marker light switch or switches

Check other important equipment your vehicle may have, such as:

- door lock
- fresh air vent
- retractable step
- retarder controls
- interaxle differential lock

If your vehicle has a clutch, test it now. Depress the clutch until you feel a slight resistance. One to two inches of travel before you feel resistance is normal. More or less than that signals a problem.

Check your mirrors and windshield for defects.

Check that you have the required emergency equipment and that it is in good operating condition.

Check for optional items, such as a tire changing kit, and items required by state and local laws, such as mud flaps.

Check the interior. Aisles and stairwells must be clear. See that handholds and railings are securely attached to the vehicle. Clean them of any water, dirt, or grease. Inspect the floor. Look for slippery spots, snags, or protrusions that could be hazards. Look for holes in the floor. These could allow dangerous exhaust fumes to enter the bus.

Make sure the seats are clean and firmly attached to the vehicle.

See all the interior lights and signals work. Signs that direct passengers to the emergency exits and explain the standee line should be clean and easy to see. Test the emergency exits to make sure they work. Then close them securely.

If your vehicle has a lavatory (restroom), inspect it. Make sure it's clean and has enough supplies. Check to see that the door lock, lights, and "occupied" light work. Make sure the emergency buzzer and the telltale light that goes with it work.

Check any overhead parcel racks. See that nothing will shift and break or fall on the passengers when the vehicle is moving. Secure baggage in ways that allow you to move freely and easily and allow passengers to exit by any window or door in an emergency. Passengers should not leave carry-on baggage in a doorway or aisle. There should be nothing in the aisles that could trip other passengers.

Step Four: Check Lights

Next, check to see the lights are working. Make sure the parking brake is set, turn off the engine, and take the key with you. Turn on the headlights (on low beams) and the four-way flashers, and get out. Go to the front of the vehicle. Check that the low beams are on and both of the four-way flashers are working. Push the dimmer switch and check that the high beams work. Turn off the headlights and four-way hazard warning flashers. Turn on the parking, clearance, side-marker, and identification lights. Turn on the right turn signal, and start the "walk-around" part of the inspection.

Step Five: Walk-around Inspection

Walk all around the vehicle, inspecting as you go. Start at the driver's compartment on the driver's side. Cover the front of the vehicle. Work down the passenger side to the rear. Cover the rear of the vehicle. Work up the driver's side, back to the starting position. Do it this way every time.

Clean all the lights, reflectors, and glass as you go along. Close any open emergency exits. Close any open access panels (baggage, lavatory service, engine, condenser, battery, and so forth).

Left Front Side

The driver's door glass should be clean. Door latches or locks should work properly.

Perform a tire, wheel, and rim check at the left front wheel. Perform a suspension system and braking system check. Check the steering parts. Check the air hoses for leaks and breaks. Check the brake assembly. Look for parts that need replacement or repair: a cracked drum, a loose or worn brake lining. Check the slack adjuster. Adjust it if necessary. Drain air tanks if necessary.

Front

Check the condition of the front axle. Perform a check of the steering system parts. You should actually take hold of steering system parts and shake them to see for sure that they are not loose.

Check the windshield. Pull on the windshield wiper arms to check for proper spring tension. Check the wiper blades for defects.

Check the lights and reflectors (parking, clearance and identification, and turn signal lights) at this site. Make sure you have all the required ones. They should be clean and working.

Right Front Side

The right front has parts similar to the left front. Perform the same checks. The passenger door glass should be clean. Door latches or locks should work properly. Check the tire, wheel, and rim at the right front wheel. Perform a suspension system and braking system check. Check the steering parts. Check the air hoses for leaks and breaks. Check the brake assembly. Look for parts that need replacement or repair: a cracked drum, a loose or worn brake lining. Check the slack adjuster. Adjust it if necessary. Drain air tanks as needed.

For COE tractors, check the primary and safety cab locks here.

Check the coupling to the trailer: the fifth wheel and locking jaw, the air and electrical connections, the landing gear, and other parts. Check for damaged and broken parts. Make sure the connection is secure. The lights and brakes should work.

Right Side

If you have an external fuel tank, it may be located here. Check to see it is mounted securely, not damaged or leaking. The fuel crossover line must be secure and not hanging so low that it would be exposed to road hazards. The filler caps must be on firmly. Check the fuel supply. Perform these checks for each fuel tank your vehicle has.

Check all parts you can see at this site. See that the rear of the engine is not leaking. Check for leaks from the transmission. Check the exhaust system parts for defects.

Inspect the frame and cross members for bends and cracks.

Electrical wiring should be secured against snagging, rubbing, and wearing.

If your vehicle has a spare tire carrier or rack, check it for damage. It should be securely mounted in the rack. Make sure you have the correct size spare tire and wheel. The spare tire must be in good condition and properly inflated.

Cargo Check

Watch for freight or baggage containing hazardous materials. Make sure you haven't created handling problems for yourself by overloading the front axles. Any canvas or tarp must be properly secured to prevent tearing and billowing. If you have an oversized vehicle or load, have the necessary signs safely and properly mounted. Make sure you have the permits you need.

Right Rear

At this location, check the wheels, rim, tires, brake system, and suspension parts for defects. Check that all parts are sound, properly mounted and secure, and not leaking. Check the axle.

Check the lights and reflectors required at this location. They should be clean and working.

Rear

Make sure you have a license plate. It should be clean and securely mounted.

If mud flaps are required, check them now. They should be free of damage and fastened according to whatever regulations apply. If there are no legal guidelines, make sure they are at least well-fastened, not dragging on the ground or rubbing the tires.

Check the lights and reflectors required at this location. They should be clean and working.

If you have an oversized load or vehicle, have the necessary signs safely and properly mounted. Have any lights or flags required for projecting loads. Make sure you have the permits you need to haul this load.

Check that rear doors are securely closed, latched, and locked.

Left Rear and Front Side

At this location, check the wheels, rim, tires, brake system, and suspension parts just as you did for the right rear and front side. Check that all parts are sound, properly mounted and secure, and not leaking. Check the axle.

Check the lights and reflectors required at this location. They should be clean and working.

Your vehicle's battery may be mounted here, rather than in the front engine compartment. If so, perform the battery check now.

Check the coupling to the trailer: the fifth wheel and locking jaw, the air and electrical connections, the landing gear, and other parts. Check for damaged and broken parts. Make sure the connection is secure. The lights and brakes should work.

Step Six: Check Signal Lights

Get in the vehicle and turn off all the lights. Then turn on the stop lights by applying the trailer hand brake. Or have a helper step on the brake pedal while you watch to see whether the light goes on.

Now turn on the left-turn signal lights. Then get out and check the left side lights, rear and front.

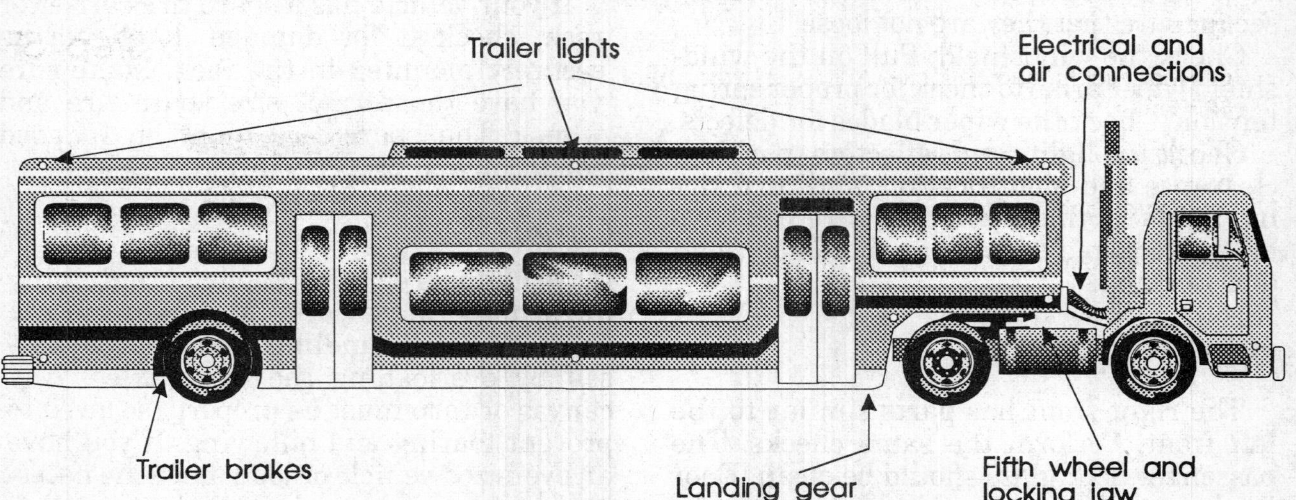

Figure 12-5 Include checking the coupling to the trailer in your inspection.

- ☐ Step 1 Vehicle overview
  General condition

- ☐ Step 2 Engine compartment checks
  Fluid levels and leaks
  Hoses and belts
  Battery
  Compressor
  Windshield washer
  Wiring

- ☐ Step 3 Inside the cab checks
  Parking brake on
  Gauge readings
  Warning lights
  Controls
  Emergency equipment
  Optional equipment

- ☐ Step 4 Check lights
  Headlights (low and high beams)
  Four-way flashers
  Parking lights
  Clearance lights
  Side marker lights
  Identification lights
  Right turn signal

- ☐ Step 5 Walk-around inspection
  A Left front side: wheel and tire, suspension, brakes and air tanks, axle, side marker lamp and reflector, door glass, latches and locks, mirrors

  B Front of cab: axle, steering system, windshield, lights and reflectors

  C Right front side: Door glass, latches and locks, wheels and tires, suspension, brakes and air tanks, axle, steering, coupling to trailer, landing gear, side marker lamp and reflector

  D Right side: fuel tank, exhaust system, frame and cross members, wiring, lights and reflectors, mirrors

  E Seating, overhead compartments

  F Right rear: wheels and tires, suspension, brakes, axle, lights and reflectors

  G Rear: lights and reflectors, license plate, mud flaps, spare tire

  H Left rear and left front: wheels and tires, suspension, brakes and air tanks, steering, axle, lights and reflectors, battery, coupling to trailer

- ☐ Step 6 Check signal lights

- ☐ Step 7 Brake check

Figure 12-6 Combination Vehicle Inspection Aid.

Step Seven: Check Brakes

Turn off any lights you don't need for driving. Check to see that you have all the required papers, trip manifests, permits, and so forth. Secure all loose articles. If they are free to roll around, they could hinder your operation of the controls or hit you in a crash.

Start the engine. Perform air brake tests numbers one through four. (Review Chapter 11 if you don't recall the tests.) Remove the chocks. Perform brake tests five and six as described in Chapter 11. Test the trailer brakes.

PULLING A TRAILER SAFELY

A tractor-trailer is usually longer and heavier and requires more driving skill than a straight truck or bus. If you're pulling a trailer, you need more knowledge and skill than drivers of straight vehicles.

You should understand such effects as

- off-tracking
- response to steering
- response to braking
- rollover risks

Off-tracking

When a vehicle goes around a corner, the rear wheels follow a different path from the front wheels. This is called off-tracking or "cheating." Figure 12-7 shows how off-tracking causes the path followed by a tractor-semitrailer to be wider than the vehicle combination itself.

Longer vehicles will off-track more. The rear wheels of the power unit (truck or tractor) will off-track some. The rear wheels of the trailer will off-track even more. (If there were more than one trailer, the rear wheels of the last trailer would off-track the most.)

In a right turn, for example, the rear trailer wheels will tend to pass closer to the curb than the tractor wheels. You must steer the front end wide enough around a corner so the rear end does not run over the curb, pedestrians, other vehicles, and so forth. At the same time, keep the rear of your vehicle close to the curb. This will stop other drivers from passing you on the right.

If you cannot complete your turn without entering another traffic lane, turn wide as

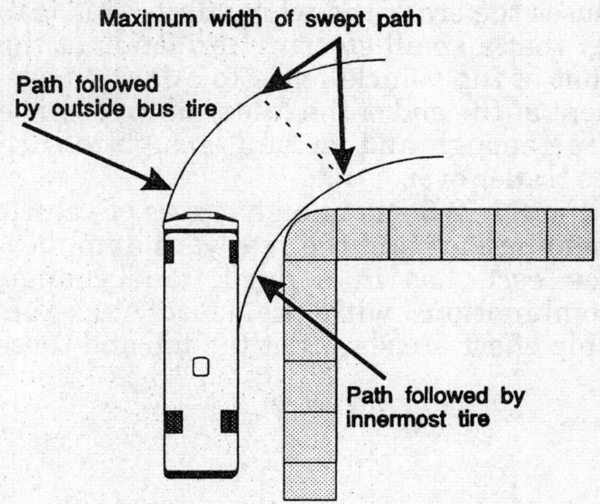

Figure 12-7 Off-tracking.

you complete the turn (Figure 12-8). This is better than swinging wide to the left before starting the turn. It will keep other drivers from passing you on the right. If drivers pass on the right, you might crash into them when you turn.

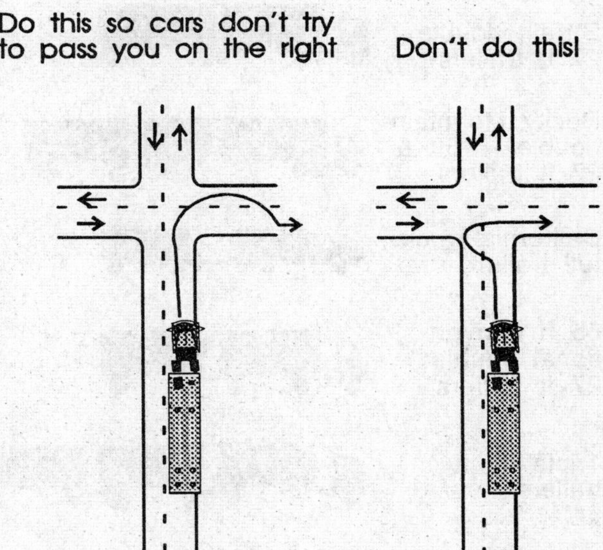

Figure 12-8 Turning right while pulling a trailer.

Response to Steering

Tractors with trailers have a dangerous "crack-the-whip" effect. When you make a quick lane change, the crack-the-whip effect can turn the trailer over. There are many accidents where only the trailer has overturned. "Rearward amplification" causes the crack-the-whip effect. This is to say that a small steering correction at the front of the vehicle leads to a large movement at the end of the last trailer. It can be large enough and forceful enough to turn the trailer over.

Figure 12-9 shows eight types of vehicle combinations and the rearward amplification each has in a quick lane change. Combinations with the least crack-the-whip effect are shown at the top and those with the most at the bottom. Rearward amplification of 2.0 in the chart means that the rear trailer is twice as likely to turn over as the tractor. You can see that triples have a rearward amplification of 3.5. This means you can roll the last trailer of triples 3.5 times as easily as a five-axle tractor-semitrailer.

More than half of CMV driver deaths in crashes are from rollovers.

Remember, even small steering movements have big results at the end of your tractor-trailer. You must steer gently. Avoid sudden changes in direction. If you make a sudden movement with your steering wheel, you could tip over a trailer. Follow far enough behind other vehicles. Follow at least one second for each ten feet of your vehicle length, plus another second for

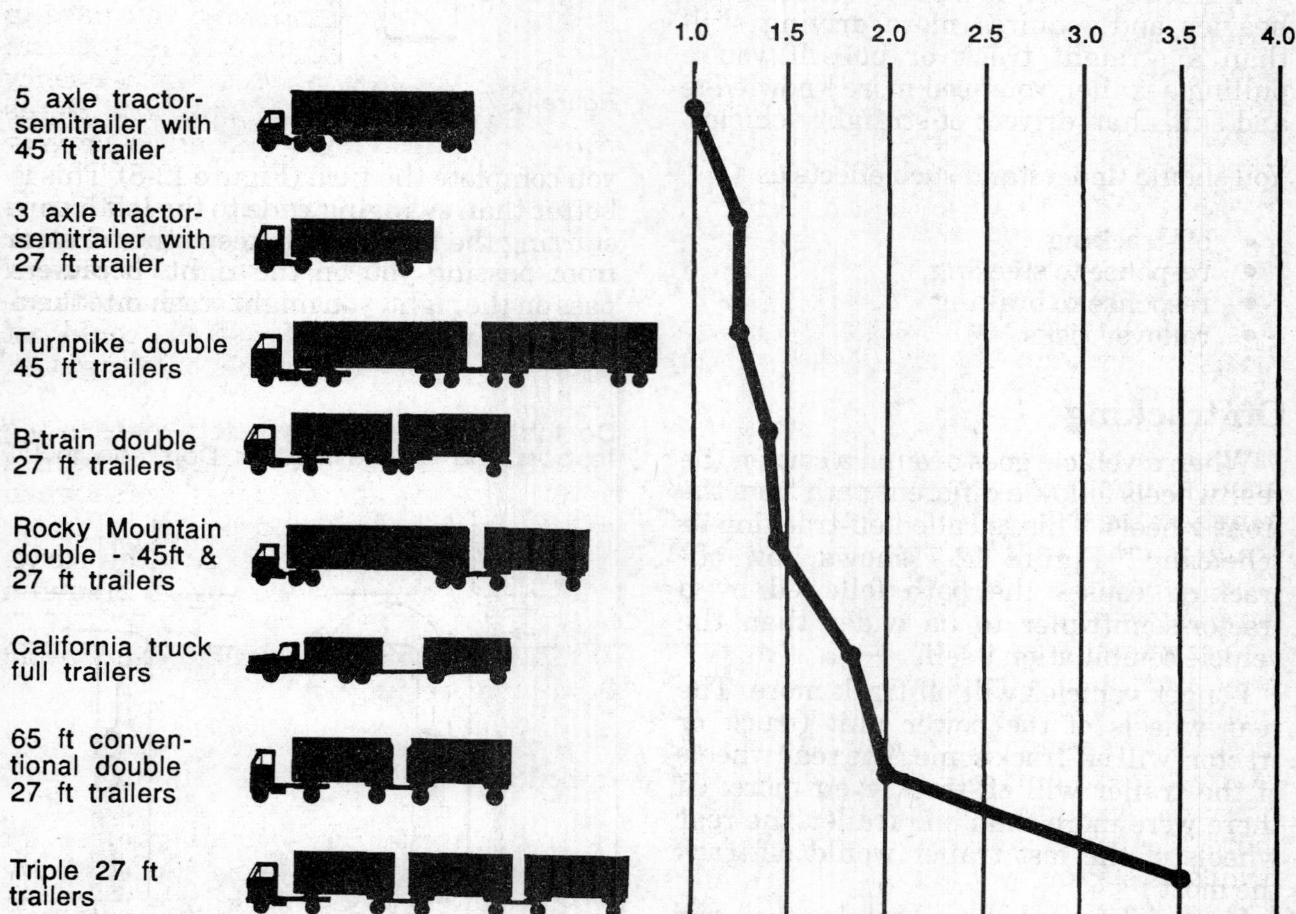

Figure 12-9 Rearward amplification of different vehicle combinations.

speeds over 40 mph. Look far enough down the road to avoid being surprised and having to make a sudden lane change. At night, drive slowly enough to see obstacles with your headlights before it's too late to change lanes or stop gently. Slow down to a safe speed before going into a turn.

Braking

Control your speed, whether the CMV is fully loaded or empty. Large tractor-trailers that are empty take longer to stop than when they are fully loaded. When lightly loaded, the very stiff suspension springs and strong brakes give poor traction. That makes it very easy to lock up the wheels. Your trailer can swing out and strike other vehicles. Your tractor can jackknife very quickly.

You also must be very careful about driving "bobtail" tractors (tractors without semitrailers). Tests have shown that bobtails can be very hard to stop smoothly. It takes them longer to stop than a tractor-semitrailer loaded to maximum gross weight.

In any vehicle combination, allow lots of following distance. Look far ahead, so you can brake early. Don't be caught by surprise and have to make a panic stop. You're more likely to lock up the wheels when you stop short.

When the wheels of a trailer lock up, the trailer will tend to swing around. This is more likely to happen when the trailer is empty or lightly loaded. This type of jackknife is often called a "trailer jackknife." This is similar to a rear-wheel skid on a straight vehicle.

You stop a trailer skid much the same way you stop a rear-wheel skid. First, realize you've lost traction. The earliest and best way to recognize that the trailer has started to skid is by seeing it in your mirrors. Anytime you apply the brakes hard, check the mirrors to make sure the trailer is staying where it should be. Once the trailer swings out of your lane, it's very difficult to prevent a jackknife.

If you have started to skid, stop using the brake. Release the brakes to get traction back. Do not use the trailer hand brake (if you have one) to "straighten out the rig." This is the wrong thing to do. It's the brakes on the trailer wheels that caused the skid in the first place. Once the trailer wheels grip the road again, the trailer will start to follow the tractor and straighten out.

Rollover Risks

Because of a high center of gravity, fully loaded tractor-trailers are 10 times more likely to roll over in a crash than empty vehicles. Tractor-trailer buses are built lower to the ground than cargo tractor-trailers. They have a lower center of gravity and present a smaller rollover risk. But you still have to drive carefully.

Entering a steady turn at cruising speed sets up the conditions which can result in a rollover. To understand why, you have to know something about another natural force: centrifugal force. This is the tendency of objects to move in one direction. Here's how it works when you take an on-ramp or an off-ramp.

You have been driving forward in a straight line. You enter a ramp and steer the vehicle around the curve. But because of centrifugal force, the vehicle tends to continue in a straight line. If you could not control the vehicle, it would drive right off the curve.

Straight vehicles don't have quite as big a problem fighting centrifugal force in a curve. The problem becomes worse when you're driving a tractor-trailer.

Slow down before you enter the curve. Keep going slowly when you go around a curve.

Go slowly around corners, and avoid abrupt lane changes.

Sharing the Road

Tractor-trailers cause extra problems for other motorists. Vehicle combinations are slower on upgrades. They take longer to pass, and it takes longer to pass them.

When you're in the right-most or merging lane with your tractor-trailer, you make it hard for other motorists to enter or exit. You could easily block the entrance and exit ramp.

The splash and spray from your vehicle combination can make it difficult for other motorists to see. Also be aware that as your vehicle cuts through the wind, it creates drafts. For small vehicles coming up alongside yours, it can be like getting hit by a crosswind.

Last, tractor-trailers take longer to change lanes. The steer-countersteer involved in changing lanes can cause the vehicle combination to become unstable, as you have seen. You must drive very smoothly to avoid rolling over or jackknifing. To avoid accidents, you must look far ahead so you can slow down or change lanes gradually when necessary.

Good space management is vital. Tractor-trailers take up more space than straight vehicles. They are longer and need more space because they can't be turned or stopped suddenly.

Allow more following distance. Make sure you have large enough gaps before entering or crossing traffic. Be certain you are clear at the sides before changing lanes.

Be more careful in adverse conditions. In bad weather, slippery conditions, and mountain driving, you must be especially careful if you drive a tractor-trailer. You will have greater length and more dead axles to pull with your drive axles than other drivers. There is more chance for skids and loss of traction.

An 18-wheeler, a three-axle tractor pulling a two-axle semitrailer, is the most popular heavy over-the-road vehicle used in the trucking industry. So, many CDL applicants (including you?) need a Group A type license. You know this means you must pass the basic knowledge and skills tests. You must take your skills test in an 18-wheeler. Then you must answer special knowledge questions about pulling a trailer.

Your 18-wheeler will probably have air brakes. In that case, you can't afford an air brake restriction on your CDL. Be sure to master Chapter 11 so you can pass the air brake tests.

PASS POST-TRIP

Instructions: For each true/false test item, read the statement. Decide if the statement is true or false. If it is true, select the letter "A." If it is false, select the letter "B." For each multiple-choice test item, choose the answer choice – A, B, C, or D – that correctly completes the statement or answers the question. There is only one correct answer.

1. Before coupling, trailer height should be _____.

A. about three inches higher than the tractor fifth wheel
B. just higher than the center of the tractor fifth wheel
C. just low enough to be raised slightly as the tractor is backed under it
D. just below the top of the tractor frame rails

2. When the coupling is complete, there should be _____ between the upper and lower fifth wheel.

A. about two inches
B. no more than an inch
C. no space
D. just enough space to see through

3. Air lines should be connected to the trailer during _____.

A. coupling
B. uncoupling
C. coupling and uncoupling
D. at no time during coupling or uncoupling

4. When uncoupling, you should pull the tractor partly clear of the trailer and stop because _____.

A. the air lines are still connected at this time
B. the electrical cable is still connected
C. the support of the tractor frame will keep the trailer from falling if the landing gear collapses or sinks
D. you need to know if the trailer will need to have chocks

5. A trailer jackknife is more likely when you are pulling a fully loaded trailer than an empty one.

A. True
B. False

6. The trailer landing gear should not contact the tractor during turns.

A. True
B. False

7. The emergency air line to the trailer _____.

A. supplies air to the trailer air tanks and controls the emergency brakes on vehicle combinations
B. is usually color-coded red
C. will cause serious problems if it fails or comes loose on the highway
D. all of the above

8. A fully-loaded tractor-trailer is 10 times more likely to roll over in a crash than an empty one.

A. True
B. False

9. When a tractor-trailer makes a right turn, _____.

A. the trailer wheels will pass closer to the curb than the tractor wheels
B. the tractor wheels will pass closer to the curb than the trailer wheels
C. the trailer wheels will track the tractor wheels exactly
D. it's accepted that the trailer wheels will run up over the curb

10. On a curved off-ramp, centrifugal force _____.

A. gives you more traction
B. helps you stay in the curve
C. tends to force you out of the curve
D. decreases the effects of rearward amplification

CHAPTER 13

Transporting Passengers

When you have finished this chapter, you will be able to provide the correct answers to questions about:

- bus inspections
- how to load and unload passengers properly
- proper use of emergency exits, including push-out windows
- emergency situation response
- what to do at railroad crossings and drawbridges
- proper braking procedures
- other safe driving practices for bus drivers

To complete this chapter you will need:

- a dictionary
- pencil or pen
- blank paper or notebook
- colored pencils, pens, markers, or highlighters
- a CDL preparation manual from your state Department of Motor Vehicles, if one is offered
- Federal Motor Carrier Safety Regulations pocketbook (or access to U.S. Department of Transportation regulations, Parts 383, 392, 393, and 398 of Subchapter B, Chapter 3, Title 49, Code of Federal Regulations)
- operator's manual for your vehicle

PASS PRE-TRIP

Instructions: Read the statements. Decide whether each statement is true or false. If it is true, circle the letter "A." If it is false, circle the letter "B."

1. A drunk or disruptive passenger should be discharged immediately.
  A. True
  B. False

2. You don't have to bring your bus to a complete stop at a drawbridge if there is a green light traffic signal.
  A. True
  B. False

3. You should talk with passengers while driving your bus to keep them entertained.
  A. True
  B. False

At last we come to the point of driving a bus, that is, to transport passengers. While all CMV drivers' jobs are challenging and important, yours is perhaps the riskiest. After all, your "cargo" doesn't come in a protective carton. It can't be tied down, blocked, and braced to keep it from shifting during transport. As you now know, you must have a commercial driver's license if you drive a vehicle designed to seat 16 or more persons, including the driver. This is stated in FMCSR Part 383. You must pass a written test on the general knowledge required of all commercial drivers.

You must also have a passenger endorsement on your commercial driver's license. To get the endorsement, you have to pass another knowledge test. Federal regulations require CMV drivers who transport passengers to know:

- how to load and unload passengers properly
- the proper use of emergency exits, including push-out windows

- emergency situation response
- what to do at railroad crossings and drawbridges
- proper braking procedures

We'll cover those items in this chapter. We'll also review vehicle inspections and safe driving.

If your bus has air brakes, you must pass a written test on air brakes. Also, if your bus is a tractor-trailer, you may have to answer additional knowledge questions on combination vehicles. These questions are on coupling, uncoupling, and inspecting combination vehicles. This was covered in Chapter 12.

Last, you must pass the skills tests required for the class of vehicle you drive. You must take the skills test in a bus that represents the one you drive. This could be a straight vehicle or tractor-trailer.

Note that you are not considered a bus driver (and don't need a CDL) if you carry only family members for personal reasons. This exception to Part 383 is stated in Part 390.

Another exception is made for school bus drivers. Federal regulations do not require school bus drivers to have a CDL. This is also stated in Part 390. But – and it's a very big but – state regulations may. In fact, most states do include school bus drivers in their CDL program. Some even have a special CDL code, like "S," for school bus drivers (instead of "P," for drivers of other types of buses). States may give school bus drivers a special CDL test. Or they may test all passenger endorsement applicants on school bus driving.

You can see it's very important that you find out what your state's policy is. Ask your employer. Or contact your Department of Motor Vehicles, the State Police – whatever agency in your state licenses drivers. (In some states even the Department of Education is involved in licensing school bus drivers.) Make sure you know what the state regulations are. Get a CDL preparation manual from your state. Pay close attention to information about school bus driving.

If you're still not certain you understand the requirements, call your state's Department of Transportation. Most state DOTs have a CDL Coordinator. Ask the CDL Coordinator for more details on school bus driver licensing in your state.

PASS Billboard

Transporting Migrant Workers

If your job is transporting migrant workers, you may wonder whether you need a CDL and a passenger endorsement. Two factors that determine whether CDL regulations apply to you are the group your vehicle belongs to (based on its weight) and the seat rating. Clearly, if you drive a Group A or B vehicle, you need a CDL.

But what if you drive a light-duty vehicle that doesn't meet the definition of Group A or B? Your vehicle is a Group C vehicle if it's designed to transport 16 or more passengers including the driver. Then you need a CDL and a passenger endorsement.

Unsure about whether your vehicle is "designed to transport 16 or more passengers"? Ask your employer, or contact your state's CDL Coordinator.

Figure 13-1 Drivers of vehicles like these need a CDL and a passenger endorsement.

This chapter has information you must know to answer the knowledge test questions if you drive an urban mass transit bus, an intercity bus, suburban (commuter) bus, or a tractor-trailer bus ("people mover"). We'll cover the skills these bus drivers need in Chapter 15, which deals with the range and road tests.

At the end of this chapter, we'll include some of the special knowledge school bus drivers must have. As you have seen, the knowledge requirements for school bus drivers vary greatly from state to state. A state that does license school bus drivers won't always test the same knowledge and skills as another state. We won't try to include every state requirement. We will, however, cover some of the more common requirements.

VEHICLE INSPECTIONS

The first step in transporting passengers safely is making sure your vehicle is roadworthy and safe for passengers. You'll do this in your pre-trip inspection.

PASS Billboard

A Bomb in the Bus

(Stop us if you've heard this tale about what could happen if you don't do a thorough pre-trip.)

An intercity bus driver was running a little late getting his vehicle ready for its scheduled trip upstate. In the terminal, he did a "quick and dirty" pre-trip. He gave the outside of the bus a once-over. He saw no flat tires, no drips or leaks, nothing dragging on the pavement. So he figured all was OK. He got up in the cab and sighted down the length of the interior. Everything seemed to be in place. He signed off on his pre-trip, got his passengers on board, and off they went.

An hour or so into the trip, he happened to be looking in his rear view mirror. He saw one of his passengers opening the restroom door. The passenger stood and looked into the restroom for a moment. Then he closed the door and went back to his seat without using the restroom.

The driver worried about that for a moment, because he hadn't checked the restroom. He had been pretty sure there were plenty of supplies from the last trip. There wasn't anything he could do about it now, though. He turned his attention back to the road and forgot about it.

A few minutes passed, and the driver began to notice something. The passengers at the back of the bus seemed upset. They were whispering among themselves, worried looks on their faces. The driver kept shifting his attention from the road to his rear view mirror. Each time he looked, a passenger would be whispering something to the person seated in the next row up. Some message was being passed from the back of the bus to the front.

Finally, the whispers got close enough for the driver to hear. "There's a bomb in the restroom!" he heard someone say.

A bomb in the restroom? Oh, no!

The driver signalled he was pulling over, slowed the bus, and brought it to a stop at the side of the road. He put on his four-ways and the parking brake. He jumped up and ran to the back of the bus. Flinging open the restroom door, he found, lying on the floor, a shabby vagrant, fast asleep with an empty bottle of Old Rotgut in his hand.

There was no BOMB in the restroom. It was a BUM in the restroom – one the driver would have found if he'd done a thorough pre-trip. And one he was going to have a tough time explaining on his post-trip.

We've covered vehicle inspection in detail in other chapters. Before going on, you may wish to review the chapter or chapters that deal with the type of bus you operate:

- straight vehicle without air brakes: Chapter 10
- straight vehicle with air brakes: Chapter 11
- tractor-trailer bus with air brakes: Chapter 12

Here's a brief summary of the major points of bus pre-trip inspections.

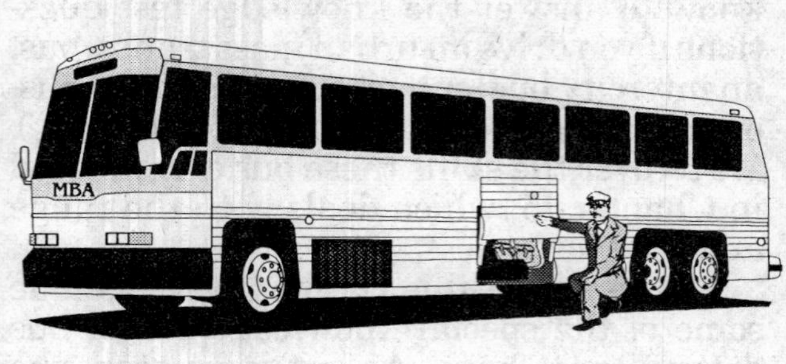

Figure 13-2 Close any open access panels before driving.

Bus Pre-trip Inspection

Before driving your bus, make sure it is safe. During the pre-trip inspection, check defects reported by previous drivers. Only if defects reported earlier have been fixed should you sign the previous driver's report. This is your certification that the defects reported earlier have been fixed.

Make sure these things are in good working order before driving:

- service brakes, including air hose couplings (if your bus has a trailer or semitrailer)
- parking brake
- steering mechanism
- lights and reflectors
- tires (front wheels must not have recapped or regrooved tires)
- horn
- windshield wiper or wipers
- rear-vision mirror or mirrors
- coupling devices
- wheels and rims

As you check the outside of the bus, close any open emergency exits. Also close any open access panels (for baggage, restroom service, engine, and so on) before driving.

People sometimes damage unattended buses. Always check the inside of the bus before driving to make sure it's safe for your passengers. Aisles and stairwells must always be clear.

The following parts of your bus must be in safe working condition:

- each handhold and railing
- floor covering
- signaling devices, including the restroom emergency buzzer, if the bus has a restroom
- emergency exit handles

The seats must be safe for riders. All seats must be securely fastened to the bus.

TIP *You may read elsewhere that there's an exception to this rule. Federal regulations used to permit a charter bus carrying agricultural workers to have up to eight temporary folding seats in the aisle. This exception is no longer made. You won't find it in your FMCSR. However, the exception was in force when CDL laws and materials were written. So you may see this exception mentioned in your state's CDL preparation materials and on the CDL tests. You might find that the only right answer to a question about bus seats is one that mentions this exception. If that's the case, and all the other answer choices are clearly wrong, select that answer choice. Your answer will be scored correct, even though this exception is no longer made.*

Never drive with an open emergency exit door or window. The "Emergency Exit" sign on an emergency door must be easy to see. If there is a red emergency door light, it must work. Turn it on at night or any other time you use your outside lights.

TIP *Remember what hours outside lights are required to be lit? They must be on from one-half hour after sunset to one-half hour before sunrise. You should also have them on anytime you need more light to see clearly.*

You may lock some emergency roof hatches in a partly open position for fresh air. Do not leave them open as a regular practice. Keep in mind the bus will be taller if you're driving with them open. Pay close attention to overhead clearance.

Make sure your bus has the fire extinguisher and emergency reflectors required by law. The bus must also have spare electrical fuses unless it uses circuit breakers.

The driver's seat should have a seat belt. Always use it for safety. You will find many states require drivers to wear seat belts.

Bus Post-trip Inspection

Inspect your bus at the end of each shift. If you work for an interstate carrier, you must complete a written inspection report for each bus driven. The report must specify each bus. List any defect that would affect safety or result in a breakdown. If there are no defects, state so on the report.

Passengers sometimes damage safety-related parts such as handholds, seats, emergency exits, and windows. If you report this damage at the end of a shift, mechanics can make repairs before the bus goes out again. Mass transit bus drivers should also make sure passenger signaling devices and brake-door interlocks work properly.

LOADING AND UNLOADING PASSENGERS

Drivers of cargo-carrying trucks must load their cargo so the weight is properly distributed. They must secure cargo so it will arrive undamaged. As a bus driver, you have a different task when it comes to loading. You'll ensure that passengers get on board without tripping. Make sure that parcels stowed in overhead racks won't shift or fall. Baggage in the cargo bins must be secured against damage.

Passengers can be injured at the end of the trip, too, if you don't follow careful unloading procedures.

Here are some other important points about loading and unloading passengers that bus drivers should know. There are often even stricter rules for school bus loading and unloading. You can read examples of these rules at the end of this chapter. Also, be sure to check your state's CDL preparation manual.

Loading Passengers

People can stumble when getting on the bus. Helping people to board will prevent injuries.

Figure 13-3 Helping passengers board the bus will prevent injuries.

Wait for passengers to sit down or brace themselves before starting. Starting should be as smooth as possible. Otherwise, people could be jarred, even knocked off their feet if they're standing.

Charter bus drivers should not allow riders on the bus until departure time. This will help prevent theft or vandalism of the bus.

Many charter and intercity carriers have passenger comfort and safety rules. Explain the rules about smoking, drinking, or using radios and tape players at the start of the trip. Explaining the rules at the start will help to avoid trouble later on.

Standee Line

Don't allow anyone to stand forward of the rear of the driver's seat. Buses designed to allow standing must have a two-inch line on the floor or some other means of showing riders where they cannot stand. This is called the standee line. All standing passengers must stay behind it.

Unloading Passengers

Stopping smoothly is as important as starting smoothly, especially if you have standees. Later in this chapter, in the section on braking, we'll explain how to bring the bus to a smooth, safe stop.

When you arrive at the destination or stops in between announce the following:

- the location
- the reason for stopping
- the next departure time
- the bus number

Remind passengers to take carry-ons with them if they get off the bus. If the aisle is on a lower level than the seats, remind riders of the step-down. It is best to tell them before coming to a complete stop.

Caution your passengers to watch their step when leaving the bus. Offer to help if they appear to need assistance.

Loading Baggage and Package Express

A little care in loading baggage and package freight will ensure a safe trip for you and your passengers. Baggage and packages will also arrive at the destination in good condition.

Do not allow passengers to leave carry-on baggage in a doorway or aisle. There should be nothing in the aisle that might trip others. Secure baggage and freight in ways that avoid damage and:

- allow you, the driver, to move freely and easily
- allow passengers to exit by any window or door in an emergency
- protect passengers from injury if carry-ons fall or shift

Load packages in bus bins or cargo bays with care. They should arrive at their destination undamaged. If you have to leave a bus with packages still on it, make sure you've secured them against theft.

Hazardous Materials

Watch for cargo or baggage containing hazardous materials. Most hazardous materials cannot be carried on a bus. Buses may carry small-arms ammunition labeled ORM-D, emergency hospital supplies, and drugs. You can carry small amounts of some other hazardous materials if the shipper cannot send them any other way. Remember that buses must never carry:

- Class A poison, Class B poisonous liquids, tear gas, irritating material
- more than 100 pounds of Class B poisonous solids
- explosives in the space occupied by people, except small arms ammunition
- labeled radioactive materials in the space occupied by people
- more than 500 pounds total of allowed hazardous materials, and no more than 100 pounds of any one class

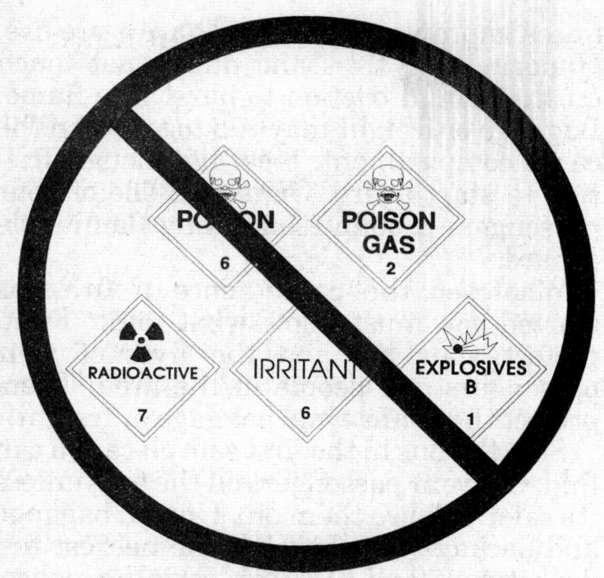

Figure 13-4 Certain cargo must never be transported on a bus.

Be alert to the items passengers carry on board. They may not know it's unsafe. Don't allow passengers to bring common hazards such as car batteries or gasoline on the bus. Don't take on items that are very fragile, like television sets. Avoid taking on items you can't protect or care for properly, such as animals.

Sometimes you may have to leave a bus unattended with passenger baggage or personal items still on board. When you do, secure the bus so these items aren't stolen.

EMERGENCY EXITS

Emergency exits are fairly simple to use. They have to be. After all, they wouldn't be of much help if your passengers needed special training to operate them. Signs, stickers, and decals on or near the exits give instructions for use. Since your passengers will rely on these instructions, it's important that the signs be in place, clean, and easy to read. You'll make sure of this in your pre-trip inspection. You'll also confirm that the exits work properly.

Two types of exits you're likely to find on a transit, commuter, or coach bus are the side sash push-out window and the emergency exit hatch.

Side Sash

All side passenger windows can be opened from the inside for emergency escape. The window sash is hinged at the top. To open it, pull out and up on the release bar. Then push the window sash out.

Emergency Exit Hatch

Emergency escape hatches are located in the roof. To open the hatch, pull the handle all the way out. Then push the hatch open. (To reclose the hatch, pull it down with the handle in the open position. Then push the handle in to lock it.)

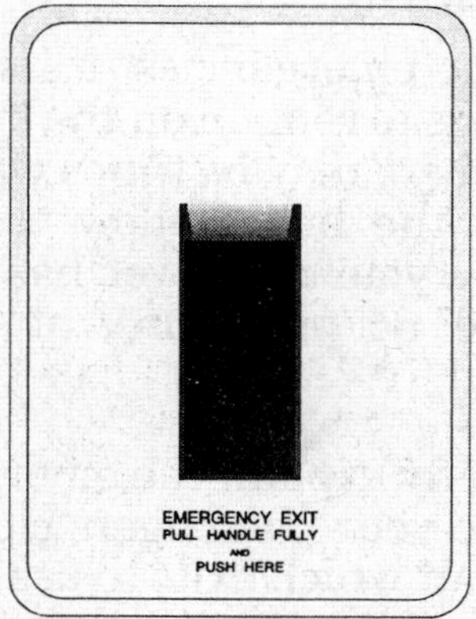

Figure 13-5 Side sash emergency escape and emergency exit hatch.

EMERGENCY SITUATIONS

Do a thorough job of pre-tripping your vehicle, drive safely and defensively, and you should rarely be faced with an emergency. If, in spite of your best efforts, an emergency arises, you must know how to respond. In general, when faced with an emergency:

- stay calm
- protect your passengers and yourself
- assist your passengers if they become ill or injured

- get help
- protect your vehicle, the baggage, and any freight

Of course, follow the accident response procedures you read about in Chapter 6.

Delays

When something happens that will cause a delay in the trip, tell the passengers. Give them a brief reason for the delay. Estimate how long the bus will be delayed. Keeping passengers informed will keep them calm.

Evacuation

In some emergencies, it's safer for your passengers to remain on the bus than to get off. But there may be times when you must evacuate the bus. Follow the evacuation procedure your employer has given you. If you have no procedure, at least do the following:

- briefly explain the emergency
- give your passengers clear directions about which exits to use
- tell passengers where to go once they're off the vehicle
- make sure the exits are open
- keep your passengers in a group
- direct them as far away from the bus and traffic as possible

Railroad Crossings

If your bus stalls on a railroad track with a train approaching, evacuate the passengers immediately. Direct them to move away from the tracks. They should head in the same direction as the approaching train. That way they'll be less likely to be injured by flying debris when the train collides with the bus.

Fires

As you read in earlier chapters, there are several reasons why a fire might start in your vehicle. A fire could start after an accident as a result of spilled fuel or using flares improperly. You could have a tire fire. Underinflated tires and duals that touch create enough friction to burst into flame. Baggage or freight may rub together in the cargo compartment, creating enough friction to start a fire. Or maybe one of your passengers brought something flammable aboard.

Whatever the cause, once a fire has started you must know what to do. First, protect your life and the lives of your passengers and people in the area. Then, protect the vehicle and baggage or freight.

Stop the bus in the first safe place you can find. Get your passengers off the bus (unless it's safer to leave them on). Unload baggage and package freight. Call the nearest fire department and highway patrol or police. Keep the fire from spreading farther. Then try to put out the fire. Last, contact your employer.

We covered fire fighting and fire extinguishers in general in Chapter 7. To review:

- If you have an engine fire, turn off the engine as soon as you can. Don't open the hood if you can avoid it. Aim your fire extinguisher through louvers, the radiator, or from the underside of the vehicle.
- If you have a fire in a cargo bay, keep the doors shut.
- Use water on burning wood, paper, or cloth. Don't use water on an electrical or gasoline fire.
- Cool a burning tire with water. If you don't have water, try throwing sand or dirt on the tire.
- If you're not sure what to use, wait for qualified fire fighters.
- Use the right kind of fire extinguisher for the fire.

Unruly Passengers

Once in a while, you may have a drunk or disruptive passenger. Many carriers have guidelines for handling disruptive passengers. Here's one carrier's policy for dealing with disorderly passengers:

- First, look for clues that tell you why the person is upset. Then you can deal with the problem, rather than the person. That keeps the situation from getting personal.
- Second, if the person turns angry or offensive, don't take it personally. Although the person may seem to be angry with you, that's probably not the case. But if you get personally and emotionally involved, that adds fuel to the fire.
- Third, look for a way to solve the problem. You may have to go the extra mile to reach a solution.

Sometimes, no matter how hard you try, you may not be able to solve the problem. You may have to discharge the passenger. This is especially true if the passenger puts the other riders at risk. When you do have to discharge a passenger, you must ensure this person's safety as you would the others. Don't discharge unruly passengers where it would be unsafe for them. It may be safer at the next scheduled stop or at a well-lit area where there are other people. Make sure there is shelter, a telephone, and other transportation available.

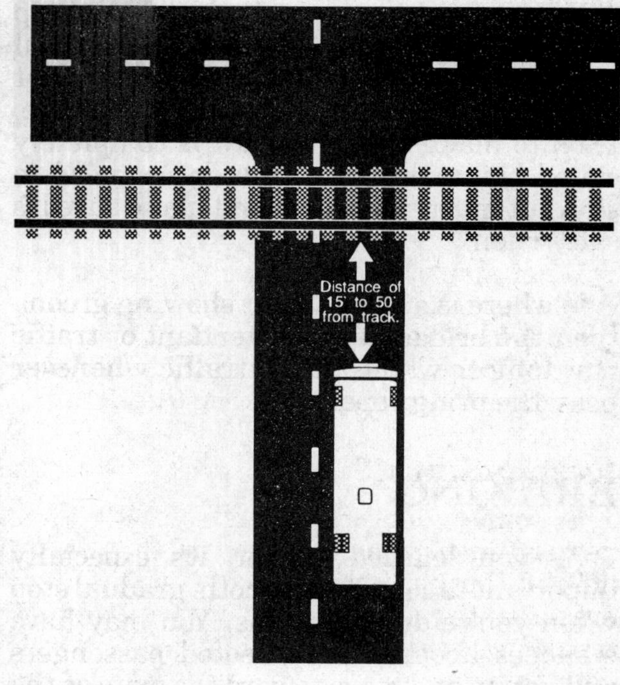

Figure 13-6 Bus drivers must stop at railroad crossings.

RAILROAD CROSSINGS AND DRAWBRIDGES

At a railroad crossing or drawbridge, bus drivers must follow different rules than drivers of common cargo-carrying vehicles do.

Railroad Crossings

You must stop at railroad crossings. Stop your bus between 15 and 50 feet before railroad crossings. Listen and look in both directions for trains. You should open your forward door if it improves your ability to see or hear an approaching train. Once the train has passed, before you proceed across, make sure there isn't another train coming in the other direction on other tracks. If your bus has a manual transmission, don't change gears while crossing the tracks.

At certain crossings, you do not have to stop but must slow down and carefully check for other vehicles. These crossings are:

- street car crossings
- railroad tracks used only for industrial switching within a business district
- where a policeman or flagman is directing traffic
- where a traffic signal shows green

You also don't have to stop (but should proceed with caution) if the crossing is marked "Exempt."

Your employer may give you further instructions, such as turning off the radio, turning on your four-ways (unless state laws prohibit this), and pulling far to the right.

Drawbridges

You must also stop at drawbridges. Stop at drawbridges that do not have a signal light or traffic control attendant. Stop at least 50 feet before the draw of the bridge. Look to make sure the draw is completely closed before crossing. You do not need to stop but must slow down and make sure it's safe, when:

- there is a traffic light showing green
- the bridge has an attendant or traffic officer who controls traffic whenever the bridge opens

BRAKING

As you learned earlier, it's especially important to come to a smooth, gradual stop when you're driving a bus. You may have standees aboard. Even seated passengers will get up and move toward the exits as the bus approaches a stop. Passengers who are standing could be jolted or even knocked off their feet if you stop short. That could result in injuries which could have been prevented.

Planned Stops

Here's how to bring the bus to a smooth, safe stop. Apply brake pressure steadily at the beginning of a stop. Then ease off as the vehicle slows down. Just before the bus comes to a complete stop, gently release the brake, keeping only enough pressure to hold the vehicle when stopped. That will keep the bus from jerking when you stop.

That's fine for planned stops. But what about unplanned stops? Can you make a panic stop smoothly?

Sudden Stops

Recall the discussion of stopping distance in Chapter 8? If you do, you remember that total stopping distance equals perception distance plus reaction distance plus braking distance. All told, you could travel a total of 290 feet before you come to a complete stop.

A way to make the stop more smoothly is to begin braking sooner. Keep perception time to a minimum by being especially alert. Learn to expect hazards and be on the lookout for them. Be aware that most accidents in the city happen within 45 minutes of the terminal. Also be aware that bus crashes often happen at intersections. Review the section in Chapter 8 on "Seeing Hazards."

Next, try to decrease reaction distance. Reaction distance is the distance your vehicle travels from the time your brain tells your foot to move from the accelerator until your foot actually presses the brake pedal. Reaction time for most drivers is ¾ of a second. If you're moving at highway speeds, you could travel 60 feet in that time. You can decrease reaction distance by "covering the brake." That means keeping your foot poised over the brake, ready to apply it if need be. Cover your brake as you approach an intersection, alley, driveway, or anywhere else you can expect to have to brake suddenly.

Stopping on the Highway

If you have to stop suddenly on the highway, use emergency braking techniques. These were discussed in Chapter 8. Remember them? They are the stab braking and controlled braking methods. Either will help keep your vehicle in a straight line while braking. You'll avoid locking up the wheels, and you'll keep control of the vehicle.

Above all, don't jam on the brakes. That will only lock up the wheels, not to mention tossing your passengers about.

Using the Brake-door Interlock

If you drive an urban mass transit coach, you may have a brake-door and accelerator interlock system. The interlock applies the brakes and holds the throttle in idle position when the rear door is open. The interlock releases when you close the rear door. Do not use this safety feature in place of the parking brake.

SAFE DRIVING PRACTICES

While it's important to know the proper way to respond in emergencies, it's best to avoid them altogether.

While driving, scan the interior of your bus as well as the road ahead, to the sides, and to the rear. You may have to remind passengers about rules, or to keep their arms and heads inside the bus.

Look ahead and keep a safe following distance. Look ahead about 12 to 15 seconds. That's about ¼ mile at highway speed. Leave at least one second following distance for each 10 feet of vehicle length. Add a second for speeds over 40 mph. Add at least another second each for adverse conditions and driving at night or in fog.

Be on guard as you approach intersections. Use caution, even if a signal or stop sign controls other traffic. Mass transit buses tend to hit fixed objects, scrape off mirrors, or hit passing vehicles when pulling out from a bus stop. Remember the clearance your bus needs, and watch for poles and tree limbs at stops. Know the size of the gap your bus needs to accelerate and merge with traffic. Wait for the gap to open before leaving the stop. Never assume other drivers will brake to give you room when you signal or start to pull out.

Crashes on curves kill people and destroy buses. They result from going too fast for conditions, such as when rain or snow has made the road slippery. Every banked curve has a safe "design speed." In good weather, the posted speed is safe for cars, but it may be too high for many buses. If your bus leans toward the outside on a banked curve, you are driving too fast. By taking a turn too fast, you risk injuring your passengers. Passenger seats on buses don't usually have seat belts. So it's not hard for your passengers to get tossed around. At high speeds in a curve, with good traction, the bus may roll over. With poor traction it might slide off the curve.

Reduce your speed for curves. Slow down before you enter the curve. Then accelerate slightly as you go through it.

Prohibited Practices

Don't fuel your bus with people on board unless absolutely necessary. Never refuel in a closed building with passengers on board.

Don't talk with passengers or allow yourself to be distracted while driving. It's too dangerous. Your employer probably has rules against using radios, tape players, and the like while driving.

Do not tow or push a disabled bus with people aboard either vehicle, unless putting them off would be unsafe. Tow or push the bus only to the nearest safe spot to discharge passengers. Follow your employer's guidelines on towing or pushing disabled buses.

SCHOOL BUS DRIVERS

As you learned at the beginning of this chapter, school bus drivers are exempt from the federal regulations we've been discussing. But most states do regulate school bus driving. Most require school bus drivers to have a CDL and a passenger endorsement. Some have a special school bus endorsement. To get such an endorsement, you must meet knowledge and skill requirements that are different from or in addition to those for a passenger endorsement.

If you haven't checked your state CDL preparation manual yet, it's very important that you do so now. That's the best way to find out about the unique requirements your state might have for school bus drivers.

When you're a school bus driver, you have a bigger job of ensuring your passengers' safety than the bus driver who transports adults. Children are not mature enough to be held fully responsible for their own safety. You have to do it for them. Many of the rules for school bus drivers have to do with added safeguards for young riders. The following rules for school bus drivers are from several states. They'll give you an idea of the types of requirements you may run into. Remember, though, your state's requirements may be different. Check with the CDL agency in your state.

Emergency Door

If your bus has a rear emergency door, it should be marked by an "Emergency Exit" sign. Like emergency exit windows, it should have a sign or sticker with instructions nearby. To open the door, usually you pull out the handle. Then you push out the door. Become familiar with how the emergency door works on your vehicle.

Remember, if there is a red emergency door light, it must work. Turn it on at night or any other time you use your outside lights.

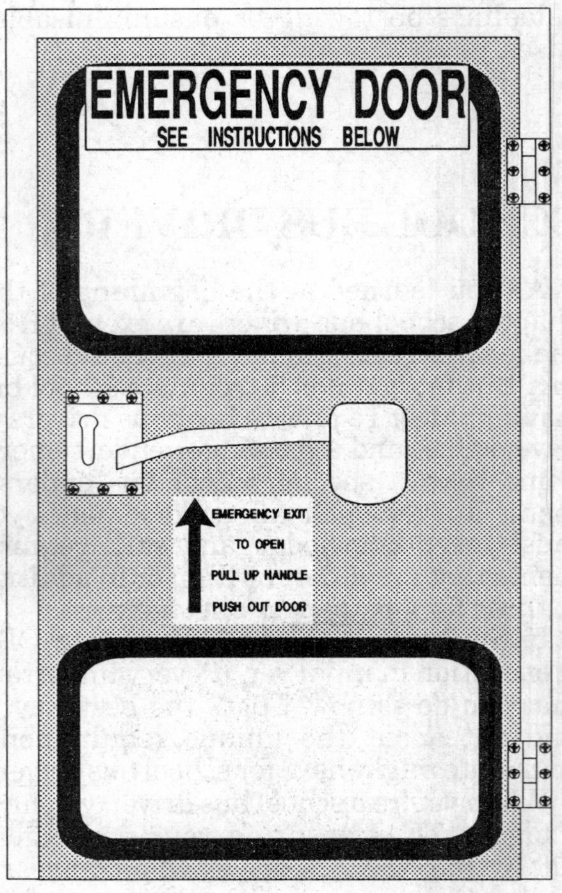

Figure 13-7 Rear emergency door.

Warning Light Systems

Control the traffic at school bus stops with warning lights and a stop sign that extends from the left side of the bus. Two types of warning light systems are the four-light system and the eight-light system.

In the four-light system, there are four red lights that flash alternately. There are two on the front and two on the rear of the bus near the roof line. Use the red lights at a bus stop to keep traffic from approaching the bus from the front or the rear.

In the eight-light system, you also have four alternately flashing red lights. There are also four amber alternately flashing lights alongside the red ones. The amber lights warn other drivers that the bus is preparing to stop at a bus stop. The amber light signal prepares them for the red lights which follow.

Turn the amber lights on:

- no less than 100 feet and no more than 300 feet from the bus stop where the posted speed limit is 35 mph or less
- no less than 300 feet and no more than 500 feet where the posted speed limit is more than 35 mph

When you pre-trip your bus, make sure that traffic warning light systems work. All lights should operate in the correct order.

School Bus Stop Procedures

Student passengers must enter and leave the school bus only at regular stops (unless school district policy directs otherwise).

School bus stops must be chosen with care. It's best if students don't have to cross a road. They should be loaded and unloaded on the side of the street they live on.

If students have to cross the road or if you can't pull the bus completely off the street, you should have at least 500 feet of visibility to the front and rear. Let the school, state police, or state traffic department know if there's a school bus stop on your route that doesn't meet these requirements. Signs will be put up to make the stop safer or the stop will be moved to a safer spot.

As you approach a school bus stop, slow gradually to a stop. When you're stopped at the bus stop, extend the stop sign. This turns on the red lights. Wait for all traffic to stop. When the roadway is clear, signal your passengers to cross. Students must cross six to 12 feet in front of the bus. They must

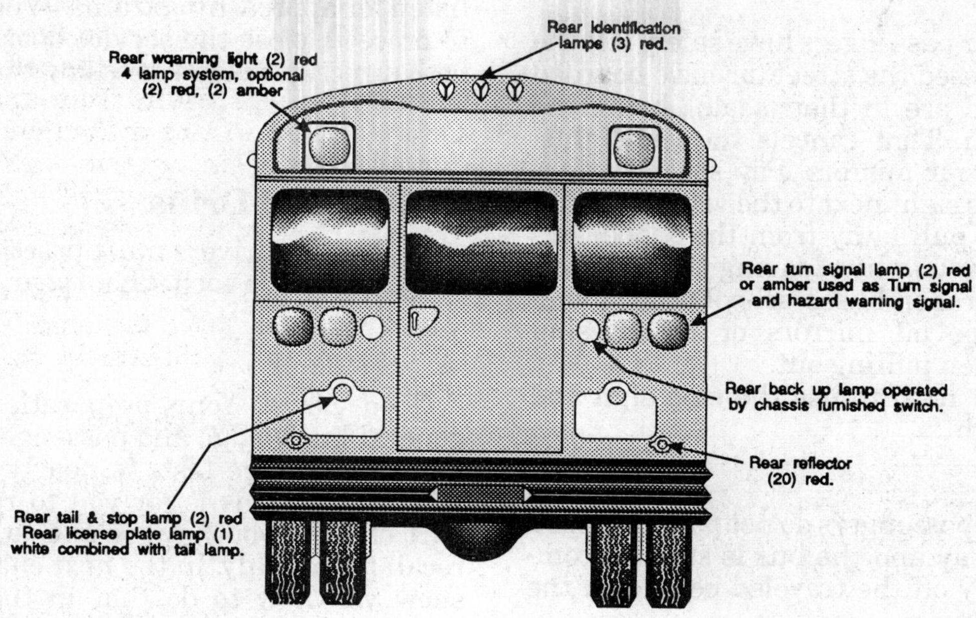

Figure 13-8 School bus warning lights.

never cross the street from behind the vehicle.

After your passengers have safely left the bus and crossed the street (or have boarded the bus and are in their seats), bring the stop sign in. That cancels the red lights. Check all your mirrors. Pay special attention to areas right next to the vehicle. When all is clear, pull away from the school bus stop. Be careful when leaving the bus stop. Like mass transit buses, school buses sometimes scrape off mirrors or hit passing vehicles when pulling out.

You don't need to use the stop sign and warning light:

- when passengers do not have to cross a roadway and the bus is stopped completely off the traveled portion of the roadway
- when a school bus is stopped at an intersection or place where traffic is controlled by a traffic officer or official traffic signal
- when a school bus is stopped on school grounds in order to receive or discharge passengers, and passengers don't have to cross the roadway

Standee Line

Your school bus may have a standee line. But you should never allow students to stand while riding. Students must remain seated while the bus is moving.

Unattended Vehicle

School bus drivers should never leave students unattended in a school bus.

Railroad Crossings

School bus drivers must stop at railroad crossings just as drivers with adult passengers must. In addition, they must open the service door and the driver's window before crossing. Then look both ways and listen for approaching trains. When it's safe to proceed, close the service doors. Look in both directions before crossing the tracks.

Evacuation Drills

School bus drivers must practice evacuation drills twice each school year.

Good news! Your preparation for the general knowledge and passenger endorsement knowledge tests is nearly complete. All that remains is for you to review any part of what you have read that you don't recall thoroughly. In the next chapter, we'll show you how to do that in the shortest amount of time and with the least amount of effort.

PASS POST-TRIP

Instructions: For each true/false test item, read the statement. Decide whether the statement is true or false. If it is true, select the letter "A." If it is false, select the letter "B." For each multiple choice test item, choose the answer choice – A, B, C, or D – that correctly completes the statement or answers the question. There is only one correct answer.

1. Which of the following statements about emergency roof hatches is false?

A. You may leave the emergency roof hatch partly open for fresh air.

B. A partly-open emergency escape hatch increases the vertical clearance you need.

C. You should drive with the escape roof hatch open to allow for speedier exits in an emergency.

D. Emergency roof hatches are designed so it is easy to operate them.

2. Which of the following statements about emergency exits is true?

A. You must keep emergency exit lights off at night because the glare makes it hard for you to see.
B. You must drive with emergency window exits open if you have an air conditioning failure.
C. There must be a functioning red light for each emergency exit.
D. Emergency exit lights must be lit when outside lights are required to be lit.

3. A drunk or disruptive passenger should be discharged immediately.

A. True
B. False

4. Do not allow passengers to store carry-on baggage _____.

A. under seats
B. in a doorway or aisle
C. in overhead bins or racks
D. in the main baggage compartment

5. Hazardous materials may be transported on a bus _____.

A. if a passenger brings them on board
B. if the shipper insists on it
C. if they're stowed in the under-floor baggage compartment
D. only in very rare instances

6. Don't change gears _____.

A. if your bus has a manual transmission
B. on a railroad track
C. coming out of a curve
D. if your bus has an automatic transmission

7. At a drawbridge, stop the bus at least _____ before the draw.

A. 15
B. 25
C. 50
D. 100

8. You don't have to bring your bus to a complete stop at a drawbridge if there is a green light traffic signal.

A. True
B. False

9. You should talk with passengers while driving your bus to keep them informed and entertained.

A. True
B. False

10. Do not push or tow a disabled bus with passengers on board _____.

A. unless the road is level or an upgrade
B. unless it's more dangerous to evacuate them
C. unless a professional commercial towing company is doing the towing
D. under any conditions

PART THREE

CHAPTER 14

Review

When you have finished this chapter, you will be able to provide the correct answers to questions about:

- how to review what you've read
- general knowledge needed to get a CDL with no endorsements and the air brake restriction
- air brakes
- tractor-trailer vehicle combinations
- transporting passengers

To complete this chapter you will need:

- pencil or pen
- book of notes

You're almost at the end of this book. Just three more chapters to go! They'll help you put the finishing touches on the job of preparing to take the CDL tests.

You've read through a lot of pages and covered a lot of ground. What follows are questions on both the general and the endorsement knowledge areas. Answering the questions will help you measure how much you remember.

In this chapter, you'll also find tips on how to review what you've read if you find that necessary.

You can use this chapter in the way you think will work best for you. Take the tests first. Then use your test results to guide your review. Or you can review your reading first, then take the tests.

HOW TO REVIEW

Quick – what was Chapter 5 about? What was the subject of Chapter 11?

You may recall Chapter 11 quite well, especially if you finished it just a few **PASS** sessions ago. On the other hand, you may hardly be able to remember the subject of Chapter 5. If that's the case, it's not really that surprising. It may be some time since you read Chapter 5. You've worked to absorb a lot of information since then. Before you take your CDL Knowledge Test, though, the information from Chapter 5 should be as fresh in your mind as that from Chapter 11. You may need to review.

You could read each chapter again from the start. You probably don't have time to do that, though. Anyway, it's not necessary. Why review what you know? All you need to review is what you don't know as well.

How do you identify what you need to review? Try the systematic approach. Just as having a system helped you get through the material the first time, a system will help you do a quick and thorough review. Follow these steps:

- retake the **PASS** Pre-trip
- reread the chapter objectives
- scan the chapter
- read your notes
- retake the **PASS** Post-trip
- retake the Sample Test in Chapter 2
- take the Review Tests in this chapter

Retake PASS Pre-trip

Take another look at the three questions that began each chapter in Part Two. If you know the material well, you should be able to answer each question correctly. If you can't, you should review the information tested by any question you missed.

Reread Chapter Objectives

The chapter objectives list the major areas of information in the subject covered by the chapter. How confident do you feel in your knowledge of that area? Use your feelings to guide you to the part of the chapter you need to review.

Scan the Chapter

Mark for review any chapter that covers information you're still in doubt about. Look over the chapter main headings and subheadings. Pause to take stock of how familiar the words seem. Can't quite remember what a topic was about? Then plan to go over that part of the chapter in detail.

Pay special attention to any areas you marked with your highlighter. Those were areas that were new or hard for you at first. Make sure you feel confident about them now.

Take the time to reread thoroughly the parts of chapters that answer any test questions you may have missed.

If you have quite a lot of time left before you take your CDL Knowledge Test, scan Chapters 5 through 12 all the way through one more time. Start with the chapter that's the least fresh in your mind.

Read Your Notes

As you read, you made notes of words that were new or ideas you wanted to remember. You wrote yourself a brief summary of each chapter. Use these notes to refresh your memory.

Retake PASS Post-trip

Look at your answer sheets from the **PASS** Post-trip questions at the end of each chapter in Part Two. If you missed any the first time, review the part of the chapter covered by those questions. Then take the Post-trip again. You should be able to answer all of them easily and correctly. Try for a perfect score on the **PASS** Post-trips this time.

Retake Sample Test

Chapter 2 had a Sample CDL Knowledge Test. Take the test again. Compare your score with the first time you took the test. Note which questions you missed, if any. They may be the same, or they may be different. Either way, they point to areas of information you could be stronger in before you take the CDL Knowledge Test.

Take Review Test

You can use the review tests in this chapter before or after you review the other chapters. The results will pinpoint any areas of information you're still weak in.

Take the review tests under "actual" test conditions. Turn off the radio. Don't smoke, eat, or drink while taking the test. Put your books and dictionary away. You won't be able to use them when you take the CDL Knowledge Test.

Follow the instructions given.

You'll find Answer and Self-Scoring Forms starting on page 382.

GENERAL KNOWLEDGE QUESTIONS

For each true/false test item, read the statement. Decide whether the statement is true or false. If it is true, select the letter "A." If it is false, select the letter "B." For each multiple-choice test item, choose the answer choice – A, B, C, or D – that correctly completes the statement or answers the question. There is only one correct answer.

1. One purpose of Commercial Driver Licensing is to disqualify drivers who operate commercial motor vehicles in an unsafe manner.

A. True
B. False

2. All drivers who need a CDL must take the _____.

A. air brakes test
B. combination vehicles test
C. chauffeur's license test
D. general knowledge test

3. All CDL skill tests must be taken in _____.

A. a representative vehicle
B. a company vehicle
C. a vehicle with air brakes
D. a rented vehicle

4. A driver who meets the requirements of the CDL laws does not have to meet the qualifications set in FMCSR Part 391.

A. True
B. False

5. If you are an experienced driver, your state may issue your CDL without having you take _____.

A. a written test, if you have never failed a written driver test
B. a skill test, if you have a safe driving record
C. a skill test, if you have over 500,000 miles worth of driving experience
D. a written or skill test if you have three points or less

6. If you are convicted of a traffic violation in a state other than the one that issued your CDL, _____.

A. you must notify your home state of the conviction
B. that state will notify your home state
C. it's nobody's business but your own
D. it doesn't go on your record

7. If you are convicted of a traffic violation in a state other than your home state, you must make notification _____.

A. to your employer
B. within 30 days of the date of conviction
C. in writing
D. all of the above

8. Your application for a CMV driving job must list the names and addresses of all employers who ever hired you.

A. True
B. False

9. A driver who is disqualified _____.

A. must always receive a jail sentence
B. has forfeited bond
C. may not drive a CMV
D. may not drive a motor vehicle

10. Which of the following are "serious driving violations"?

A. driving with an expired or suspended CDL
B. excessive speeding, reckless driving, or any traffic offense made while driving a CMV that causes a fatality
C. DUI, DWI, and driving while on drugs
D. driving with a load of hazardous materials that are not properly secured

11. Which of the following will result in the loss of your CDL for one year?

A. driving with an expired or suspended CDL
B. excessive speeding, reckless driving, or any traffic offense made while driving a CMV that causes a fatality
C. DUI, DWI, and driving while on drugs
D. driving with a load of hazardous materials that is not properly secured

12. Which of the following will result in the loss of your CDL for more than one year?

A. leaving the scene of an accident involving a CMV you were driving
B. using a CMV to commit a felony involving controlled substances
C. driving any vehicle under the influence of alcohol or an illegal drug
D. driving a CMV under the influence of alcohol or an illegal drug

13. Once you get your CDL for a specific vehicle group, you may never change it to another group.
A. True
B. False

14. You are pulled over for weaving between lanes. If you refuse to take a test for alcohol, you may be disqualified just as if you were DUI. This is because of the ____.
A. higher standard of care law
B. reasonable cause law
C. implied consent law
D. none of the above

15. The only sure cure for fatigue is ____.
A. narcotics
B. amphetamines
C. real sleep
D. caffeine

16. If your employer gives you a road test and you pass it, you don't have to take the CDL Skills Test.
A. True
B. False

17. Medical certificates must be renewed every ____.
A. year
B. six months
C. three years
D. time a serious illness affects your ability to drive

18. Carriers ____ test for drugs before they hire a driver.
A. may choose to
B. should
C. are not allowed to
D. must

19. If you refuse to allow your employer to test you for drugs, it's the same as if you had taken the test and tested positive.
A. True
B. False

20. Which of these statements about alcohol is true?
A. Some people aren't affected by drinking.
B. A few beers have the same effect on driving ability as a few shots of whiskey.
C. Coffee and fresh air can sober up a person.
D. Exercise can help you burn off alcohol faster.

21. When making a turn, you must start to signal ____ feet before you make the turn.
A. 10
B. 50
C. 100
D. 1000

22. When making an emergency stop on the highway, you must put on your four-way flashers and ____.
A. keep them on until you are underway again
B. keep them on until you get your warning devices out
C. hang a red flag from the rear of your vehicle
D. blow your horn

23. The law requires CMVs to have ____.
A. service brakes
B. emergency brakes
C. parking brakes
D. all of the above

24. Locked-up brakes are more often the result of panic stopping than faulty equipment.
A. True
B. False

25. You may not use tires that ____ on your vehicle.
A. are belted
B. are flat or have leaks
C. have a tread depth of more than 2/32 of an inch
D. are treaded

26. If you're required to keep a log of your time, ____.
A. you may bring it up to date once a week
B. any FHWA agent may inspect it
C. you may ask the dispatcher to fill it out and sign it for you

D. you should add an hour when you cross a time zone

27. To drive your vehicle in a way that would cause it to break down or cause an accident is not only unsafe, it's illegal.
A. True
B. False

28. If your vehicle doesn't pass a roadside inspection _____.
A. it can be declared "out of service"
B. you cannot drive the vehicle, even to a repair station
C. you may repair it on the spot, then resume your trip
D. all of the above

29. Which of the following is a hazardous materials class?
A. "Requires Placards"
B. "Other Regulated Materials"
C. "Dangerous"
D. none of the above

30. By law, you must have your vehicle lights on _____.
A. one half hour after sunset until one half hour before sunrise
B. unless street lights are lit
C. only when there's not enough natural light for you to see clearly
D. none of the above

31. The color of the turn signals facing forward must be _____.
A. amber only
B. white
C. white or amber
D. whatever the manufacturer selected

32. Vehicles must carry a five-pound B:C fire extinguisher, unless they are placarded for hazardous materials.
A. True
B. False

33. Normal engine temperature ranges from _____.
A. 180 to 250 degrees Fahrenheit
B. 100 to 250 degrees Fahrenheit
C. 170 to 195 degrees Fahrenheit
D. 20 to 45 psi

34. Normal oil pressure while idling is _____.
A. 165 to 185 degrees Fahrenheit
B. 20 to 24 psi
C. 30 to 75 psi
D. 5 to 15 psi

35. When you first start your vehicle, the warning lights should come on.
A. True
B. False

36. Overcharging in a vehicle battery _____.
A. means there isn't enough power to crank the engine
B. leads to thickened battery fluid
C. shortens battery life
D. all of the above

37. Your vehicle's battery box must have _____.
A. at least two batteries
B. enough fluid to work properly
C. at least one loose ground wire
D. a secure cover

38. Once a circuit breaker has opened, it must be replaced.
A. True
B. False

39. Which of the following creates the braking force in a braking system?
A. air pressure
B. hydraulic pressure
C. vacuum pressure
D. friction

40. Tire inflation pressure should be checked _____.
A. after the tire has warmed up
B. when the tire is cold
C. after the first 25 miles of a run
D. every two hours or 100 miles of travel

41. Rust around wheel nuts often means that _____.
A. the nuts are loose
B. the nuts are broken
C. the nuts are about to break
D. the vehicle needs painting

42. Progressive shifting means _____.
A. downshifting at lower rpm as you reach the lower gears
B. downshifting at higher rpm as you reach the lower gears
C. upshifting at lower rpm as you reach the higher gears
D. upshifting at higher rpm as you reach the higher gears

43. The engine speed that you use for shifting should be based on _____.
A. information in your operator's manual
B. the vehicle's GVWR
C. the vehicle's mpg
D. what feels right for the situation

44. You should downshift _____.
A. when the tachometer or speedometer indicates it's necessary
B. before starting down a steep hill
C. before entering a sharp curve
D. all of the above

45. When roads are wet, icy, or covered with snow, you should _____.
A. use your retarder for braking as much as possible
B. turn the retarder off
C. use the maximum setting if the retarder has power adjustment settings
D. be ready to turn the retarder on the minute you start to skid

46. Maintain good visual alertness by _____.
A. always looking as far ahead as you can see
B. fixing your eyes on the road right in front of you
C. keeping a close watch on the road behind you at all times
D. shifting your attention between the mirrors and the road ahead

47. Lane changes, turns, merges, and tight maneuvers require _____.
A. lots of luck to perform without accident
B. frequent checking and rechecking, using your mirrors
C. maintaining a constant speed
D. power steering

48. Signaling other drivers when it is safe to pass is _____.
A. a great aid to highway safety
B. a courtesy professional drivers should extend to others
C. an unsafe practice
D. required

49. Total stopping distance is _____ plus reaction distance plus braking distance.
A. visual distance
B. perception distance
C. vehicle length
D. trip distance

50. Traveling in the lane alongside other vehicles _____.
A. is a good idea since they can always see you that way
B. can cause you to be trapped when you need to change lanes
C. will make traffic flow more smoothly
D. will keep people from cutting in front of you

51. Dirty headlights give about _____ as much light as clean ones.
A. 100 percent
B. 90 percent
C. 75 percent
D. 50 percent

52. If another driver approaches you at night with high beams on, _____.
A. get them to turn them off by flashing yours
B. watching the approaching lights closely will show you where the vehicle is
C. look slightly right in the right lane or at the right edge marking if there is one

D. keep your high beams on until the other vehicle passes.

53. To prepare for winter driving, check that your antifreeze will do the job _____.
- A. by inspecting the color
- B. by checking the level in the reservoir
- C. using a special coolant tester
- D. by draining the system and replacing the antifreeze

54. Ice on your radiator shutters or winterfront _____.
- A. will melt off after the engine warms up
- B. can cause the engine to overheat
- C. will help insulate the engine compartment
- D. is a minor winter inconvenience

55. In hot weather, tire inflation pressures can be higher than normal. You should _____.
- A. inspect the tires less often
- B. let air out of your tires when the pressure exceeds 105 psi
- C. not let air out of the tires when they are hot
- D. spin the tires to cool them off

56. In hot weather, bleeding tar can _____.
- A. damage your tires
- B. damage the road
- C. give your vehicle more traction
- D. make parts of the road very slippery

57. If you try to downshift while coming down a mountain, you might _____.
- A. damage the clutch
- B. damage the engine
- C. get stuck in neutral
- D. lose traction

58. Which gear to select to go down a long grade in the latest fuel-efficient vehicles is affected by _____.
- A. their streamlined shapes that reduce air drag
- B. their low friction parts
- C. their more powerful engines that allow you to climb hills in higher gears
- D. all of the above

59. A vehicle marked at the rear with a red triangle having an orange center _____.
- A. is hauling hazardous materials
- B. is moving slowly
- C. is a farm vehicle
- D. makes frequent stops

60. Impaired drivers often _____.
- A. drive too fast or too slow or change speed for no reason
- B. drive especially well because they are trying so hard
- C. are safer because they tend to drive slowly
- D. none of the above

61. When steering to avoid a crash _____.
- A. keep one hand on the steering wheel and the other hand free for shifting
- B. turn and apply the brake at the same time for more control
- C. use both hands on the steering wheel and don't brake while turning
- D. none of the above

62. You have to leave the road to avoid another vehicle. What should you **not** do?
- A. keep one set of wheels on the pavement
- B. stay on the shoulder until you can come to a stop
- C. turn widely to be sure of avoiding the other vehicle
- D. stay off the brake

63. The most common skid is _____.
- A. rear wheels losing traction due to excessive braking or acceleration
- B. steering tires sliding due to front-brake lock-up
- C. trailer wheels sliding out on curves
- D. caused by a front tire blow-out

64. The best way to stop a front-wheel skid is to _____.
- A. let the vehicle slow down

B. brake hard
C. turn sharply
D. shift into neutral

65. The first step in correcting a drive-wheel braking skid is to let off the brake.
A. True
B. False

66. Cargo that isn't properly secured can shift. This can _____.
A. result in damaged cargo
B. overturn the whole vehicle
C. cause the cargo to spill out, resulting in a major highway hazard
D. all of the above

67. Poorly distributed cargo can _____.
A. cause the vehicle to pull to one side
B. make the vehicle feel like it's going to tip over
C. make the vehicle harder to put into motion and stop
D. all of the above

68. State laws can regulate _____.
A. the weight of your vehicle, but not the cargo
B. the weight of your cargo, but not your vehicle
C. both your vehicle and cargo weight
D. neither vehicle nor cargo weight. Only the federal government can regulate these.

69. Bridge laws _____.
A. are the same as the maximum legal axle weight
B. control traffic on a bridge
C. apply only to drawbridges
D. can lower the maximum axle weight limit

70. Tire load is _____.
A. the most weight a tire can carry safely
B. the same as inflation pressure
C. a measure of whether a tire is underinflated
D. how much weight a tire puts on the road

71. Loading a device beyond its rating is _____.
A. illegal and unsafe
B. impossible
C. the smart way to increase a payload
D. a good way to test your equipment

72. An empty vehicle is _____.
A. very stable
B. likely to tip over
C. likely to go into a jackknife
D. likely to go into a rear-wheel skid

73. A vehicle that is overloaded to the rear is _____.
A. very stable
B. likely to tip over
C. likely to go into a jackknife
D. likely to go into a front-wheel skid

74. A vehicle with a high center of gravity is _____.
A. very stable
B. likely to tip over
C. likely to go into a jackknife
D. likely to go into a front-wheel skid

75. The legal size and weight distribution limits _____.
A. should be your guide under all conditions
B. are not changed by adverse conditions
C. may not ensure safe operations in bad weather
D. are often changed by states from season to season

76. When securing cargo, drivers should use _____.
A. no fewer than three tiedowns, even for the smallest load
B. one tiedown for every ten feet of cargo
C. as few tiedowns as possible, since they only increase the overall weight

D. tiedowns that have half the strength of the weight of the cargo

77. Blocking used to prevent cargo movement _____.
- A. is secured to the cargo compartment floor
- B. is secured to the cargo itself
- C. is secured to the cargo and the walls
- D. must be placed every 2½ feet

78. Tarping a load protects the cargo and _____.
- A. the driver
- B. others on the road
- C. the vehicle
- D. the shipper

79. Drivers of cargo-carrying vehicles must inspect cargo within _____ miles after starting a trip.
- A. 10
- B. 25
- C. 50
- D. 100

80. If a load is sealed, the driver _____.
- A. is not responsible for its weight
- B. should break the seal, inspect the load, and reseal it every three hours or 150 miles
- C. should break the seal and inspect the load within 25 miles of the destination
- D. is still responsible for exceeding gross weight or axle limits

81. The lighter the load, _____.
- A. the less traction the vehicle has
- B. the longer the stopping distance
- C. the longer the stopping time
- D. all of the above

82. Dry bulk tanks _____.
- A. are designed to control the shifting of the load
- B. are stable in curves and turns
- C. tend to have a high center of gravity
- D. present the fewest driving problems of all vehicles

83. You inspect your vehicle because _____.
- A. it's important for safety
- B. it's required by federal regulations
- C. it's required by state law
- D. all of the above

84. If a state official conducts a roadside inspection and finds your vehicle to be unsafe, _____.
- A. the official will offer to repair it for you
- B. your vehicle will be put "out of service"
- C. your vehicle will be taken away from you
- D. your license to drive will be taken away from you

85. You should do a post-trip inspection _____.
- A. at the end of each run for each vehicle you operate
- B. on the last vehicle you operate each day
- C. on whichever vehicle the dispatcher selects
- D. on the same vehicle every day

86. When you stop during a trip, you should check _____.
- A. engine oil and coolant
- B. the post-trip inspection report made by the vehicle's last driver
- C. your cargo securement devices
- D. your disc brakes

87. Drive tires must have at least _____ of tread, and no less.
- A. ¼ inch
- B. 2/32 inch
- C. ½ inch
- D. 4/32 inch

88. Steering axle tires must have at least _____ of tread, and no less.
- A. ¼ inch
- B. 2/32 inch
- C. ½ inch
- D. 4/32 inch

89. A serious hazard of exhaust system leaks is _____.

A. excess smoke can enter the cab
B. exhaust smoke can damage the cargo
C. poisonous fumes can enter the cab
D. excess smoke can damage the vehicle

90. Your vehicle will be placed "out of service" if there are _____ broken or missing springs in your leaf spring suspension.

A. more than one-tenth
B. more than one-fifth
C. more than one-fourth
D. any

91. An air suspension _____.

A. should not fill evenly all the way around
B. should fill before the air brake system reaches normal pressure
C. should allow the vehicle to tilt with the load
D. should not leak more than three psi in five minutes at normal pressure

92. A bent _____ is a steering system defect.

A. torque rod
B. tie rod
C. spring hanger
D. shock absorber

93. Mud flaps _____.

A. should touch the ground
B. should have advertising on them
C. must be made of high-grade rubber
D. may be required by state law

94. Snow chains _____.

A. are required by federal regulations
B. may be required by states during the winter
C. are standard equipment on heavy vehicles
D. are so sturdy they never break

95. During the pre-trip inspection, approach the vehicle and _____.

A. note the vehicle's general condition
B. check for body damage and major leaks
C. see if the vehicle leans to one side
D. all of the above

96. When you start your vehicle's engine, the _____ should come up to normal within a few seconds.

A. oil pressure
B. fuel pressure
C. coolant temperature
D. all of the above

97. Normal clutch travel is _____.

A. less than one or two inches
B. about one or two inches
C. more than two inches
D. not something the driver can measure

98. During the pre-trip inspection, check the brake (stop) lights by _____.

A. applying the trailer hand brake, if your vehicle has one, or by getting someone to apply the treadle valve
B. bleeding the air out of the system so the tractor protection valve will act
C. fanning off air pressure so that the brakes will apply
D. pulling the red knob

99. During the walk-around part of the pre-trip inspection, you should _____.

A. leave the vehicle key in the switch so you won't lose it
B. pull the key out of the switch and put it on the dash so you'll know where it is
C. leave the vehicle key in the switch so it will be handy for the engine test
D. put the key in your pocket so no one can move the vehicle while you are under it

100. Regardless of the vehicle you have, the seven-step vehicle inspection is all you need to do.

A. True
B. False

Matching

Instructions: Match the letter for the vehicle system condition in Column B with the number of the gauge reading in Column A.

Column A Gauge Reading	Column B System Condition
101. 180 to 250 Fahrenheit	A. normal cooling system temperature
102. 175 to 195 Fahrenheit	B. normal transmission oil temperature
103. 50 to 75 psi	C. normal operating oil pressure
104. 5 to 15 psi	D. normal idle oil pressure

Instructions: Match the letter for the description in Column B with the number of the term in Column A that fits the description.

Column A Weight Term	Column B Definition
105. GVW	A. a rating given a vehicle by its manufacturer, which is the top GCW for the combination of power unit plus trailer or trailers plus cargo
106. GCW	B. a rating given to the vehicle by its manufacturer. It is the top GVW for that single vehicle plus its load
107. GVWR	C. the total weight of a single vehicle, plus its load
108. GCWR	D. the total weight of the power unit or tractor, plus any trailers, plus the cargo

AIR BRAKE QUESTIONS

1. Fanning air brakes _____.
A. cools them off
B. increases the air pressure
C. increases the braking power
D. decreases the air pressure

2. When some brakes in the system are doing more work than others, _____.
A. those brakes will develop more heat
B. vehicle handling will be affected
C. those brakes will lose stopping power first
D. all of the above

3. If your air compressor stops working, _____.
A. you will lose your brakes immediately
B. the brakes will immediately lock up
C. you'll have some air pressure left stored in the air tanks
D. your brakes won't be affected at all

4. An air brake system safety relief valve opens at about _____.
A. 20 to 45 psi
B. 60 psi
C. 120 psi
D. 150 psi

5. Your air brake safety relief valve has opened several times. This means _____.
   - A. the system is working normally
   - B. your air pressure is probably low
   - C. the air compressor has failed
   - D. you should have the system repaired

6. If your vehicle has a front brake limiting valve control, it should be in the _____.
   - A. "slippery" position on wet roads
   - B. "normal" position only on dry roads
   - C. "normal" position under all road conditions
   - D. "slippery" position under all road conditions

7. The service brake system _____.
   - A. is an inspection done by the company maintenance staff
   - B. applies and releases the brakes when you use the brake pedal during normal driving
   - C. is the pump and check valves that keep the air tank pressure serviced
   - D. is only on vehicles with hydraulic brakes

8. Spring brakes _____.
   - A. are applied by air pressure
   - B. are held in the released position by air pressure
   - C. are not affected by air pressure
   - D. have nothing to do with the emergency brake system

9. Most large vehicles with air brakes have spring brakes which _____.
   - A. are parking brakes
   - B. are emergency brakes
   - C. are part of the parking and emergency brake systems
   - D. will stop the vehicle in a shorter distance than the service brakes

10. You should avoid setting the parking brakes _____.
   - A. on a steep grade
   - B. if the air pressure is low
   - C. if the brakes are hot
   - D. in hot weather if the brakes are wet

11. Spring brakes should come on automatically when you pump air pressure down to _____ psi.
   - A. zero
   - B. 20 to 45
   - C. 60
   - D. 90

12. If your brakes are out of adjustment, you won't have good _____ braking power.
   - A. service
   - B. emergency
   - C. parking
   - D. all of the above

13. On newer vehicles with air brakes, the parking brake control is _____.
   - A. a lever
   - B. a square, red push-pull control knob
   - C. a diamond-shaped, yellow push-pull control
   - D. a round, blue push-pull control knob

14. If a low air pressure warning device comes on, _____.
   - A. pull off the road as soon as it's safe to do so
   - B. you can safely continue until you get to a service station
   - C. you may complete your trip, but remember to make note of it later on your post-trip inspection report
   - D. turn it off so it won't distract you while driving

15. The tractor protection valve _____.
   - A. works automatically
   - B. protects the tractor air tanks in case of air pressure loss
   - C. separates the tractor air supply from the trailer air supply
   - D. all of the above

16. The tractor protection valve _____.
   - A. cannot be operated manually
   - B. is the same thing as the trailer brake control

C. is also called the breakaway valve
D. all of the above

17. The trailer hand brake ____.
A. lets you control the amount of air to the trailer brakes
B. may be used as a parking brake
C. exhausts the air supply from the trailer brakes
D. exhausts the air supply from the tractor brakes

18. Which of the following statements about the gladhands is true?
A. The service brake gladhands are color-coded red.
B. The service brake gladhands are color-coded blue.
C. The emergency brake gladhands are color-coded blue.
D. The emergency brake gladhands are color-coded yellow.

19. If the service air line breaks, ____ (unless you have a dual air system).
A. the air pressure will drop slowly
B. you should apply the spring brakes
C. the spring brakes will come on
D. the check valve will prevent the dry tank from losing its air supply

20. If an emergency brake line ruptures, ____ (unless you have a dual air system).
A. the air pressure will drop slowly
B. you should apply the spring brakes
C. the spring brakes will come on
D. the check valve will prevent the dry tank from losing its air supply

21. If the line from the compressor to the main supply tank ruptures, ____.
A. the air pressure will drop slowly
B. you should apply the spring brakes
C. the spring brakes will come on when the service pressure drops below 45 psi
D. the check valve will prevent the dry tanks from losing their air supply

22. Brake drums or discs ____.
A. must not have cracks
B. must have linings that fit loosely on the shoes
C. must not have cracks longer than half the width of the friction area
D. should be well-greased between the drum or disk and the lining

23. Slack adjusters ____.
A. never need adjustment themselves
B. should be adjusted only by a qualified mechanic
C. should travel at least two inches from where the push rod is attached
D. can be adjusted manually or automatically

24. Air tanks should be drained ____.
A. at the end of each day or shift
B. to keep sludge from clogging brake system valves
C. manually when automatic devices fail
D. all of the above

25. To adjust the slack, ____.
A. apply the service brakes and release the parking brakes
B. apply both the service and parking brakes
C. pull out the automatic slack adjustment control knob
D. release both the service and parking brakes

26. To test the brakes on a single air system, run the engine at a fast idle to charge the air system. Your gauge should show you ____.
A. pressure building from 50 to 90 psi within three minutes
B. pressure building from 85 to 100 psi within 45 seconds
C. the compressor cutting out below 50 psi or above 70 psi
D. the governor stopping below 100 psi or above 125 psi

27. To test the brakes on a dual air system, run the engine at a fast idle to charge the air system. Your gauge should show you _____.

A. pressure building from 50 to 90 psi within three minutes
B. pressure building from 85 to 100 psi within 45 seconds
C. the compressor cutting out below 50 psi or above 70 psi
D. the governor stopping below 100 psi or above 125 psi

28. Your vehicle's single brake system needs adjustment if _____.

A. pressure builds from 50 to 90 psi within three minutes
B. pressure builds from 85 to 100 psi within 45 seconds
C. the compressor cuts out below 100 psi or keeps pumping air above 125 psi
D. the governor stops between 100 and 125 psi

29. In a single vehicle with a fully charged air system, air pressure loss (after an initial drop) should be less than _____ per minute.

A. 2 psi
B. 3 psi
C. 4 psi
D. 5 psi

30. When checking a single vehicle for air leaks with the brakes on, air pressure loss (after an initial drop) should be less than _____ per minute.

A. 2 psi
B. 3 psi
C. 4 psi
D. 5 psi

TRACTOR-TRAILER BUS QUESTIONS

1. Before you begin coupling, _____.

A. pre-position the fifth wheel
B. check your path for hazards
C. check the condition of the tractor frame
D. put the spring brakes on

2. You can damage the landing gear by _____.

A. aligning the tractor and trailer
B. backing under the trailer at an angle
C. positioning the trailer kingpin in the center of the fifth wheel V-slot.
D. backing under the trailer in a straight line

3. The trailer should be lowered so _____.

A. the tractor strikes the nose of the trailer
B. the trailer is well above the fifth wheel
C. you can use the landing gear to make major adjustments
D. it is raised slightly when the tractor is backed under it

4. Which of the following coupling steps comes first?

A. apply the trailer brakes
B. raise the landing gear
C. put the transmission in reverse
D. connect the air supply lines

5. When rolling up the landing gear to complete the coupling process, _____.

A. begin in high gear to make the job go faster
B. use low gear until the tractor is supporting the trailer
C. leave the landing gear half-way down to speed the uncoupling process later
D. use plenty of grease to make the job easier

6. If one of the gladhands on your blue air line is missing a seal, _____.

A. it's a minor problem and you can proceed with the coupling
B. you might end up with a service line air leak
C. you might end up with an emergency line air leak
D. you can take one off the red line and use that as a replacement

7. When uncoupling, if you park the trailer at an angle, _____.
A. you'll save space in the yard
B. you won't have to walk so far to get around the vehicle
C. your job will be easier
D. you could damage the landing gear

8. When uncoupling, it's a good practice to _____.
A. couple the gladhands together
B. couple the gladhands to dummy couplers
C. hang the electrical cable with the plug end down
D. all of the above

9. When you inspect the coupling, check to make sure that _____.
A. there's a little slack in the air lines
B. the landing gear handle is hanging freely
C. there's no slack in the air lines
D. the electrical cable is unplugged

10. Most rollovers could be avoided by making turns and _____ slowly.
A. backing maneuvers
B. speed reductions
C. lane changes
D. going down grades

11. The "crack the whip" effect is a strong force that is most likely to turn over the tractor of tractor-trailer combination.
A. True
B. False

12. If you cross your air lines on a new trailer with spring brakes, _____.
A. you won't be able to release the trailer brakes
B. you won't be able to release the tractor brakes
C. you won't have any brakes at all
D. you will have no way of knowing there's a problem

13. If you cross the air lines on an old trailer, you won't _____.
A. be able to release the trailer spring brakes
B. be able to release the tractor brakes
C. have any brakes at all
D. have any trailer brakes

14. To test the tractor protection valve, reduce the air pressure to _____. The valve should close automatically.
A. zero
B. 20 to 45 psi
C. 60 psi
D. 100 psi

15. To test the trailer emergency brake system, charge the trailer brakes. Then _____.
A. press the treadle valve
B. push in the blue round knob
C. pull the diamond-shaped yellow knob
D. pull the red, eight-sided knob

16. To test the trailer service brakes, _____.
A. press the treadle valve
B. use the trailer brake hand valve
C. push in the blue round knob
D. pull the red, eight-sided knob

17. To test for crossed air lines, _____.
A. pull the red, eight-sided knob, then push it in and listen for brake movement air release
B. pull the yellow knob out and push it in while listening for air flow
C. turn the engine off, apply and release the brake pedal, and look for an air pressure drop
D. turn the engine off, apply and release the trailer brakes with the hand valve, and listen for brake movement and air release

18. When you turn a corner, your trailer wheels follow a different path from your tractor wheels. This is _____.
   A. an alignment problem
   B. a steering problem
   C. a sign of a poorly coupled tractor-trailer
   D. normal

19. Tractors with trailers _____.
   A. have a dangerous "crack-the-whip" effect
   B. present a rearward amplification hazard
   C. can turn over in response to abrupt steering movements
   D. all of the above

20. If your vehicle starts to skid and you think it may jackknife, _____.
   A. put the tractor brakes on hard
   B. release the tractor brakes
   C. put on the trailer brakes
   D. turn the steering wheel sharply to the left, then back to the right

21. Which of the following is true?
   A. a large tractor-trailer can stop in a shorter distance when empty than when loaded
   B. stiff springs and strong brakes make it easy to lock up wheels on tractor with an empty trailer
   C. bobtail tractors are easy to stop smoothly
   D. there is no danger of the trailer swinging out when braking on a straight road

22. The trailer hand valve should be used while driving _____.
   A. for all normal stops to keep the tractor brakes from coming on before the trailer brakes
   B. to stop a trailer jackknife
   C. to prevent a trailer jackknife
   D. none of the above

23. If you don't lubricate the fifth wheel, you will have _____.
   A. less control of the braking system
   B. better steering control
   C. less steering control
   D. an easier job of uncoupling

24. When you inspect the fifth wheel after coupling, the safety catch should be _____ the locking lever.
   A. over
   B. under
   C. through
   D. around

25. To make a right turn when pulling a trailer, _____.
   A. swing to the left as you begin the turn
   B. use all the lanes you need before and during the turn
   C. guard against other vehicles trying to pass you on the left
   D. if you must use another lane to avoid running over the curb, swing wide as you complete the turn

---

TRANSPORTING PASSENGERS QUESTIONS

1. If your bus has a restroom, it must also have
   A. an "occupied" sign
   B. a double-locking door
   C. a restroom emergency buzzer
   D. a seat belt in the restroom

2. You should sign the last driver's post-trip bus inspection report only if _____.
   A. you were the last driver
   B. all the defects were repaired or there were no defects reported
   C. you are a mechanic
   D. you find defects

3. All aisles and stairwells on a bus must be _____.

A. equipped with folding seats
B. kept clear
C. lit with red lights
D. marked with signs

4. A bus must have spare electrical fuses unless _____.

A. it's equipped with circuit breakers
B. it was manufactured after 1986
C. it's used only intracity
D. it's used only for charter

5. Baggage and freight in a bus should be secured so that _____.

A. the driver can move freely
B. passengers can exit by any door or window in an emergency
C. it won't fall from overhead racks and injure someone
D. all of the above

6. Hazardous materials that buses may carry include _____.

A. small arms ammunition, emergency hospital supplies and drugs
B. radioactive material, if it's transported up front behind the driver's seat so it can be seen at all times
C. up to 500 pounds of dynamite
D. auto batteries and gasoline, as long as they belong to a passenger

7. A standee line is a marking that _____.

A. shows where bus riders must stand if they're not seated
B. keeps standing bus riders from standing too far to the front of the bus
C. shows bus passengers where to stand at a bus stop
D. shows a bus driver where to place baggage

8. Charter bus drivers should not allow passengers on the bus until _____.

A. departure time
B. the driver is on board with seat belt fastened
C. the tour guide is present
D. after the dispatcher has given the signal

9. When approaching a bus stop, a driver should announce _____.

A. the next departure time
B. the miles traveled since the last stop
C. the average speed the bus traveled
D. the location of restrooms

10. When a trip is going to be delayed, a bus driver should _____.

A. give passengers a brief explanation
B. pretend nothing is wrong so as not to alarm the passenger
C. blame it on the dispatcher
D. increase speed to try to make up time

11. If an evacuation is necessary, a bus driver should _____.

A. keep passengers on the bus where it's safer
B. tell passengers to scatter once they're off the bus
C. direct passengers where to go once they leave the bus
D. be the first one off the bus so as to obtain help the fastest

12. You may slow your bus and check for trains without coming to a full stop at a railroad crossing _____.

A. on a country gravel road
B. with double tracks
C. with an "Exempt" sign
D. if you're running behind schedule

13. When slowing for a stop at a bus stop, you should _____.

A. apply steady brake pressure, then ease off as the vehicle slows
B. use stab braking
C. use controlled braking
D. none of the above

14. A brake-door and accelerator interlock system _____.
- A. applies the brake and holds the throttle in idle when the rear bus door is open
- B. gives longer brake life by releasing the brake unless the throttle is in idle
- C. saves fuel by preventing throttle application when the brakes are on
- D. should be used for parking

15. While driving your bus, scan _____.
- A. the road ahead
- B. the road to the sides of the bus
- C. the interior of the bus
- D. all of the above

16. Mass transit buses often hit fixed objects _____.
- A. because of a lower center of gravity
- B. due to parking brake failure
- C. when pulling out from a bus stop
- D. while making turns

17. If you're going too fast on a curve in a bus, _____.
- A. your tires will squeal
- B. your vehicle will lean toward the outside of a banked curve
- C. the back wheels will begin to slide
- D. you're most likely going below the posted speed limit

18. Bus crashes often occur _____.
- A. at an intersection
- B. in the terminal
- C. out on the highway
- D. while passing

19. Never refuel a bus _____.
- A. in a closed building with passengers on board
- B. if it's more than half-full already
- C. unless the brake-door interlock is on
- D. unless the passengers are on board

20. Talking with passengers while you are driving a bus _____.
- A. is an important part of public relations
- B. makes the trip more enjoyable for you and the passengers
- C. is unavoidable
- D. is distracting and dangerous

By now you should feel well-prepared for the knowledge part of your CDL test. If you've tackled every question in this book, you've had a lot of practice answering test questions. You can think of the CDL Knowledge Test as just another set of questions about material you're familiar with. And you can feel proud of the job you've done in this self-guided training course.

You know that you must take a Skills Test as well as a Knowledge Test to get your CDL. The next chapter will help you practice so you'll be ready for a typical CDL Skills Test.

CHAPTER 15

CDL Skills Tests

When you have finished this chapter, you will be able to provide the correct answers to questions about:

- what the CDL Skills Tests cover
- how the CDL Skills Tests test your ability to inspect your vehicle
- how the CDL Skills Tests test your basic ability to control your vehicle
- how the CDL Skills Tests test your safe driving ability

To complete this chapter you will need:

- operator's manual for your vehicle
- Federal Motor Carrier Safety Regulations pocketbook (or access to U.S. Department of Transportation regulations, Parts 383, 393, and 396 of Subchapter B, Chapter 3, Title 49, Code of Federal Regulations)
- a CDL preparation manual from your state Department of Motor Vehicles, if one is offered
- driver's manual from your state Department of Motor Vehicles

By now you should feel well prepared for the CDL Knowledge Test. You've seen many sample, pre-trip, post-trip, and review test questions. Did you answer every one of them? Then you should feel less anxious about this type of test-taking.

But, as you know, that's not all there is to CDL testing. You'll have to take one or more Skills Test as well. The main skill areas tested are:

- pre-trip inspection
- basic vehicle control
- safe driving
- air brakes (to avoid the Air Brake Restriction)

At least some of the skills must be tested in "on-street" conditions. Some of them may be tested off the street or with a vehicle simulator.

You must take your CDL tests in a vehicle that is "representative" of the one you plan to drive. This means that your test vehicle must belong to the same group, A, B, or C, as your work vehicle. It doesn't mean that the two vehicles must be the same make or model. They simply must belong to the same group.

The representative vehicle may have to be equipped with air brakes. If you wish to drive a bus with an air brake system, you must take your Skills Tests in a vehicle with air brakes. If you take the Skills Tests in a bus without air brakes, an air brake restriction is put on your CDL. This is also the case if you don't pass the air brake part of the Skills Tests. This means you are not allowed to drive a CMV with an air brake system. This includes braking systems that rely in whole or in part on air brakes.

"Passing" on the Skills Tests depends on what's being tested. In all cases, anyone who breaks a traffic law automatically fails the test. So does anyone who causes an accident during the test.

Your state may excuse you from having to take the Skills Test. You must meet certain conditions, though. You must show that you had only one license in the two years just before applying for a CDL. You must have a current, valid license and have a good driving record. A "good driving record" means that, in the past two years, you have not had your license suspended, revoked, or canceled. You must not have been disqualified from driving in the past two years. Your driving record for the past two years must be free of traffic violations connected with an accident (other than parking violations).

You must also prove that you are regularly employed as a CMV driver. You must prove that, in the past, you took and passed a skills test and received a classified license. A classified license is one that states or limits the type of vehicle you may drive.

You must prove that skills test was behind the wheel of a vehicle representative of the one you plan to drive with your CDL. Last, you must prove that you have experience driving this type of vehicle. You must have had this experience in the two years that passed just before you applied for a CDL.

If you can prove all these things, your state may "waive," or excuse you from taking, the CDL Skills Test or Tests.

Let's assume, though, that you plan to take the Skills Tests. In this chapter, we'll give you an idea of what the Tests will be like. You'll learn what the examiners will be looking for. And, we'll give you some tips on how to "practice" and prepare for the Skills Tests.

PRE-TRIP INSPECTION

As part of the Skills Tests, many states test your ability to inspect your vehicle. When you take the Knowledge Test, you'll answer questions about vehicle inspection. When you take a Skills Tests that includes vehicle inspection, you will actually do one.

Having read Chapter 10, you know what a "basic" inspection involves. Keep this in mind as well. You must take your Skills Tests in, and therefore inspect, a representative vehicle. If you don't want the air brake restriction, your vehicle must have air brakes. You'll have to show you know how to inspect the air brake system. If your bus is a tractor-trailer, you'll have to show you can inspect a tractor with a trailer. These extra steps are covered in Chapters 11 and 12. Be sure to read those chapters thoroughly if they apply to your driving job.

Many states will have you do a complete inspection. The purpose is to see if you know whether the vehicle is safe to drive. Or you may actually only do certain parts of a complete inspection. But you will usually have to describe anything you would do if you were inspecting your vehicle completely.

During the Inspection Test, you may also be asked to describe in some detail the different parts and systems on your vehicle. Or the examiner may have you stop your inspection from time to time and ask you questions about your equipment.

As you inspect your vehicle, tell the examiner what you are looking for. Describe what you find. You're not likely to take a defective vehicle to the test. However, the examiner will want to know you would recognize a defect if you saw one. So as you inspect your vehicle, mention the defects likely to be found at the different sites. Explain how those defects impair safety.

The examiner may ask you for more details. For example, you might say, "The hoses are not cracked or rubbing." The examiner may tell you to point out just which hoses you are talking about. You may be asked to state the function of the hoses.

Or you might point to the battery and state that it's in good shape. The examiner might ask you to name the part and say how you know it's in good shape. You'll have to respond something like this: "This is the battery. It's securely mounted, and it's not cracked. There's no corrosion. The cables are securely attached to the correct posts," and so on.

The examiner will not prompt you or give

you hints. If you forget a step, the examiner will just assume you don't know how to do a complete inspection. For this reason, you may want to have an Inspection Aid with you. Usually, you may have a checklist with you when you take the Inspection Test. Check with your state to see if for some reason this is not allowed. Otherwise, feel free to use the checklist. You'll be less likely to overlook something if you check off items as you go.

You'll usually find just such Inspection Aids in the CDL manual your state provides. There will likely be one for straight vehicles like transit buses and coaches and another for tractor-trailer buses. You'll also find Inspection Aids at the end of this section. Your state may allow you to use the aids it provides, but not the ones in this book. You can ask about this when you arrange to take your Skills Tests or bring both with you just in case.

Inspection Test Site

You'll usually take the Inspection Test in a flat parking area or open lot. Examiners will avoid using a parking space on a street, or any place where traffic passes close by. If you do have to take the test in a busy area, don't get so involved taking the test that you forget to check for traffic and other hazards.

Safety Tips

Do keep your own safety in mind while you take the test. Never get under, in front of, or behind a vehicle when there's any chance at all the vehicle might move. Don't brace your foot on top of the bumper when you pull the engine hood open.

Use care getting in and out of the vehicle. Know where the steps or cab footholds are on your vehicle. Make sure they're free of dirt and grease. Then use them. Use the Three-point Stance to get out of a tractor.

TIP *The Three-point Stance means you use the steps or footholds and the handhold. Use either both hands and one foot or both feet and one hand. That is, use three limbs to enter the cab.*

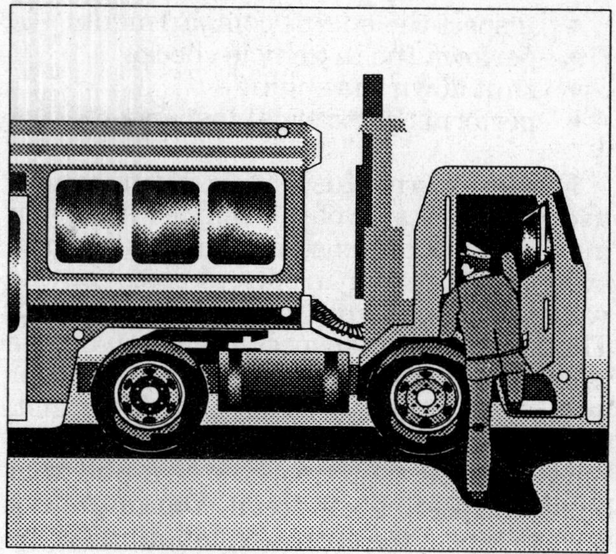

Figure 15-1 The Three-point Stance.

When you get out of a tractor, climb out backwards, as if you were using a ladder. Never jump out of the cab.

If you are about to do something really dangerous, the examiner may stop you. For the most part, though, your safety is your responsibility, not the examiner's.

Test Instructions

The examiner may give you instructions for taking the Inspection Test. They could go something like this:

"Please conduct a thorough inspection of your vehicle. As you do the inspection, point to or touch the things you are inspecting. Explain what you are looking for.

"Start by inspecting the engine compartment. Then start the engine. After you have done the start-up checks, turn off the engine. Do the rest of the inspection.

"Start whenever you are ready."

Make sure you understand the instructions. Ask questions if you don't. The examiner will be prepared to answer them.

General Procedure

As a general procedure, you'll be expected to follow these main steps:

- inspect the engine compartment
- perform the in-vehicle checks
- shut down the engine
- perform the external inspection

For the external inspection, you may have to do only one side of the vehicle. Also, you may have to explain some things only once, even if they appear in several places on the vehicle. For example, each tire has tread. The first time you inspect a tire, you'll have to explain correctly what you are looking for as far as the tread is concerned. After that, the examiner may tell you that you only have to state that this is a tire and that you're inspecting the tread. You might not have to repeat the entire explanation. (If the examiner doesn't mention this, ask. Don't assume this will be the accepted procedure. Check and make sure.)

Usually you can go about the inspection however you prefer. Just make sure you follow the main steps just listed. Of course, if the examiner gives you specific or different instructions, follow them to the letter.

TIP *Inspecting a cabover tractor? You may not have to raise the cab to inspect the engine compartment. Most of the engine items can be checked without raising the cab. Ask the examiner if you should raise the cab. You may be told you don't have to. Of course, you must tell the examiner about any items that can't be checked without raising the cab. Remember, the examiner won't prompt you for this information.*

The Inspection Test isn't timed. You can work at your own pace. You won't get any extra points for speed. In fact, if you rush, you might overlook something. Take whatever time you need to be thorough.

"Examining" the Examiner

As we've mentioned, the examiner will not prompt you or give you hints. The examiner may remind you about the main steps. But you won't hear anything like, "You forgot the brakes," or "What about the tires?"

All the same, the examiner might give you hints without meaning to. The examiner might start walking toward the next area to inspect. Or the examiner might look at a vehicle part you should inspect next.

During the inspection, if you go blank for a minute, examine the examiner. See where the examiner is standing or looking. That could be enough to jog your memory and enable you to go on.

Pre-trip Inspection Standards

In this section, we'll list the main items you should inspect and describe how to inspect them. We'll take them in the order they appear in the Inspection Test, then in their place in the seven-step inspection. You'll see what the examiner will be expecting. Don't forget, you may be asked to give far more detail about parts and systems than what we mention here. You may have to state what this part does and why you are inspecting it. You may have to explain how a defect impairs safety.

You'll find those details in Chapters 6 through 10, plus the chapters on air brakes and endorsements.

Inspect the engine compartment. Remember, you may have to go around to the sides or back of the vehicle to check everything described here.

Check the oil level, using the dipstick. The dipstick measures the amount of oil that lubricates the engine. The level should be above the "Add" mark. Check the level of coolant, which cools the engine. If your vehicle has a sight glass, use it to view the coolant level. Otherwise, take off the radiator cap. The coolant level should be above "Low." Note that if your vehicle does have a sight glass, you'll be marked wrong for failing to use it.

TIP *If the engine is hot, don't open the radiator. That could be dangerous. Instead, describe the process of checking the coolant level.*

If you have power steering, check the fluid. The fluid is part of the hydraulic system that assists steering action to the front wheels. With the engine off, pull the dipstick. The level should be above the "Add" mark.

If you have an automatic transmission, check the fluid level. (You may have to do this with the engine running. Your operator's manual will tell you if that is the case.)

You may not actually have to open reservoirs and pull dipsticks. The examiner may just have you describe the process. Your description must be thorough.

Check these belts for tightness and excessive wear:

- generator
- air compressor
- fan
- power steering
- water pump

Press down on the center of the belt. There should be no more than ¾ inch slack. Belts should not be frayed or cracked. They shouldn't have loose fibers.

Check the fluid level in the battery. It should be up to the filler rings in each cell. Make sure each cell has a vent cap. Check to see that the vents are not clogged. Check the battery mount. Check the hold-down bars to make sure the battery is snug. The battery box cover should be in place. The battery box itself must not be cracked or leaking. Look for battery cables that are frayed, worn, or cracked. Check to make sure the battery connections are tight.

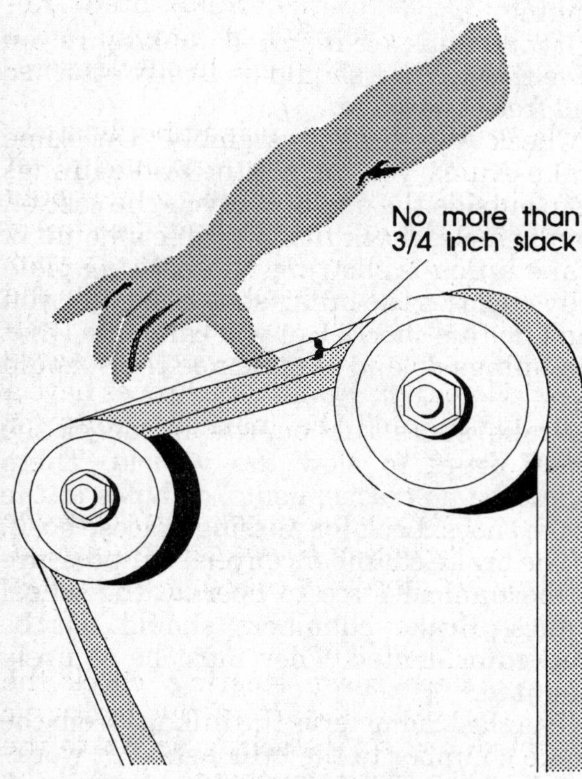

Figure 15-2 Check belts for snugness.

Look for leaks in the engine compartment. Look for fluid puddles on the ground under the engine or drips on the engine's underside.

In-vehicle checks. Make sure the parking brake is on. The clutch and gearshift disengage the engine from the drive train. This keeps the vehicle from moving and reduces the load on the starting motor. Depress the clutch before turning on the starter. Keep it there until the engine reaches idling speed. Shift into "Park" if your transmission is automatic.

Adjust the seat and mirrors. You need a clear view of the traffic to the rear. The mirrors should not be cracked, loose, or dirty.

Turn on the starter. Release it as soon as it starts. Listen for any unusual engine noises.

Watch the gauges. The oil pressure should come up to normal within seconds after the engine is started. The warning light should go off. Engine oil temperature should show a gradual rise to normal. The ammeter and/or voltmeter should show the generator or alternator is working. The warning light should go off. The needle should flutter, then give normal readings.

Check for looseness in the steering linkages. Move the steering wheel back and forth. Free play should be about two inches for a 20-inch steering wheel. Test power steering with the engine on. Note the degree of free play that occurs before the front left wheel just barely moves. It should be less than five to 10 degrees.

If you have a manual transmission, test for excessive clutch pedal travel. Depress the clutch until you feel a slight resistance. One to two inches of travel before you feel resistance is normal.

The horn warns other drivers or pedestrians of danger. Test it to make sure it works.

Check the windshield for cracks, dirt, and stickers that obscure your view. Make sure the windshield wipers work. The blades should be secure on the wiper arm, and the rubber should not be worn.

You must have emergency equipment for use during a breakdown or at the scene of an accident. You should have:

- spare fuses, if your vehicle uses them
- three red reflective triangles
- a properly charged and rated fire extinguisher

Your emergency equipment may also include these items:

- snow chains
- tire-changing equipment
- spare lamps and bulbs
- electrical tape and tools
- flashlight
- pliers
- screwdriver
- wire
- tire pressure gauge

The heater/defroster warms the cab and prevents frost and mist from forming on the windshield. Make sure it works.

Shut down the engine. Put the transmission in the lowest forward gear.

Check to see the lights are working. Make sure the parking brake is set. Turn on the headlights (on low beams) and the four-way flashers, and get out. Take the key with you. Go to the front of the vehicle.

Check that low beams are on and both of the four-way flashers are working. Push the dimmer switch and check that high beams work. Turn off the headlights and four-way hazard warning flashers. Turn on the parking, clearance, side-marker, and identification lights.

Don't forget to check the dashboard lighting indicators for signals, flashers, and headlight high beams. They should go on when the lights are on.

Check to see that seats are firmly attached to the floor. Seat frames should not be broken.

Turn on the right turn signal, and start the "walk-around" part of the inspection.

External inspection. Check the tires. Tread depth should be 4/32 inch on front tires, 2/32 inch on the other tires. Use a tire pressure gauge to check inflation. You can use a tire billy or mallet to check that the tire isn't flat. You'll be marked wrong if you simply kick the tire.

The wheel rims keep the tires on the wheel. Check the wheel for damaged or bent rims. Rims shouldn't have welding repairs. Rust trails suggest that the rim is loose on the wheel.

Lug nuts hold the wheel on the axle. Check for missing or loose lug nuts. Rust trails suggest the nuts might be loose. Bolt holes should not be out-of-round or cracked.

Spacers or axle collars between dual wheels keep the wheels evenly separated. For duals, make sure the wheels are evenly separated and that the tires don't touch each other.

Check that the wheel hub oil seal isn't leaking. If your hub has a sight glass, use it to check the oil level.

Check the axle seals. Wheel/axle mountings should not be cracked, distorted, or leaking.

If mud flaps are required, make sure you have them. They should be firmly attached and free of damage.

Check the brake assembly. On some brake drums, you can see the brake linings from outside the drum. If this is the case on your vehicle, check that a visible amount of brake lining is showing. If a backing plate fully encloses the brake shoe assembly, you can't do this check. But you can state what the linings do and what shape they should be in.

Brake shoes rub on the inside of the brake drum to slow the vehicle. There should be no cracks, dents, or holes in the brake shoes. Look for missing or loose bolts.

The brake chamber converts air pressure to mechanical force to operate the wheel brakes. Brake chambers should not be cracked or dented. They must be securely mounted.

The slack adjuster is the linkage from the brake chamber to the brake shoe. It works the brakes. Check for broken, loose, or missing parts. The angle between the push rod and the adjuster arm should be a little over 90 degrees when the brakes are released. It should be not less than 90 degrees when the brakes are applied. When you pull it by hand, the push rod should not move more than about an inch.

Brake hoses carry air or hydraulic fluid to the wheel brake assembly. Check for worn, cracked, or frayed hoses.

Check the suspension. Check all the brackets, bolts, and bushings used to attach the spring to the axle and the vehicle frame. Look for cracked or broken spring hangers. There should be no broken, missing, or loose bolts on axle mounting parts. Look for missing or damaged bushings.

Leaf or coil springs dampen wheel vibration from rolling on the road. Look for leaves that have broken or shifted. They should not contact tires, rims, brake drums, frame, or body. Look for missing or broken leaves in the leaf spring. If you have coil springs, the coil should not be broken or bent out of shape.

You may have a torsion bar suspension on some rear tractor wheels. Here, a steel bar, rod, or arm assembly acts as a spring instead of a leaf or coil spring. Make sure the bar or arm is not cracked, broken, or missing.

Check for loose, broken, or leaking shock absorbers.

Check the steering linkage. This assembly transmits steering action from the steering box to the wheel. Connecting links, arms, and rods should not be worn or cracked. Joints and sockets must not be worn or loose. There should be no loose or missing bolts.

The steering box holds the parts that transform steering column action into wheel turning action. Look for missing nuts, bolts, and cotter keys. If you have power steering, check for leaks. Inspect the power steering hose for damage.

Check the fuel tank. It should be secure, free of leaks and damage. The cap should be on tight.

The frame supports the vehicle body or trailer platform over the wheels. It should not be cracked or bent. Look for loose, cracked, bent, broken, or missing cross members. There should be no cracks in the floor.

The headerboard prevents cargo from shifting forward and hurting the driver during a panic stop. If you're required to have one, it should be securely mounted and free of damage. It must be strong enough to hold back the cargo. If you have a canvas or tarp carrier, it must be securely mounted and lashed down.

The drive shaft transmits the power from the transmission to the drive axle. It must not be bent or cracked. Shaft couplings must look secure.

The exhaust system conducts combustion gases from the engine. All the outside parts should be securely mounted. Check for cracks, holes, or bad dents.

Make sure emergency exits are secure and in good working condition. Check to see that all doors open right. Make sure locks are closed.

Entry steps should be clear and the tread should not be worn. Windows and door mirrors should be clean, not cracked or broken.

Make sure baggage doors close securely. Check to see that you have all the required emergency equipment.

Check the lights and reflectors (parking, clearance, identification, and turn signal lights). You should have all the required lights and reflectors, and they should be clean. Reflectors and clearance lights should be red at the rear, amber elsewhere. You shouldn't have any broken or missing reflectors or lights.

Running lights should be red at the rear. You must check them separately from signal, flasher, and brake lights.

Check that both brake lights come on when the brakes are applied. Each signal light should flash, and the four-way flashers must work.

Check the braking system. Test for leaks in the hydraulic brake system. Pump the brake pedal three times. Then apply firm pressure to the pedal and hold for five seconds. The pedal should not move.

Test how well the service brake works. Go about five mph. Push the brake pedal firmly. The brakes should apply evenly all around the vehicle. They should not pull to one side or the other. The brake pedal should not travel all the way to the floor before the brakes apply. Nor should the pedal give you a lot of resistance or take great effort to apply.

The parking brake should keep the vehicle from rolling when parked. Set the brake, then try to pull forward. The brakes should hold the vehicle back.

Air brake checks. If the air pressure is low, the low air pressure warning will sound immediately after the engine starts but before the air compressor has built up pressure. Test this by letting air pressure build to governed cut-out pressure (between 100 and 125 psi). The low air pressure warning should stop when the air pressure gets to 60 psi or more.

The air compressor maintains air pressure in the air brake system. With the engine off, you'll have to point to, touch, or press the belt to test for tension. Press it at the center. It should not move more than ¾ inch. Note that the belt is not frayed or cracked. There should be no loose fibers or signs of wear.

Your compressor may not be belt-driven. If that's the case, tell the examiner. Note that the compressor drive appears to be working and is not leaking.

Your air system should have no leaks.

Perform these brake system checks. Let air pressure build to governed cut-out pressure. That should occur between 100 and 125 psi. With the engine still idling, step on and off the brake, reducing the air pressure. The compressor should cut in at about 85 psi. The air pressure should begin to rise.

With the engine off, the wheels chocked, and the parking brake released, apply the foot brake. Air pressure should not drop more than three pounds in one minute on a single vehicle. The drop should be no more than four pounds in one minute for combination units.

Fan off the air pressure by rapidly applying and releasing the foot brake. The low pressure warning alarm should come on before air pressure drops below 60 psi.

Continue to fan off the air pressure. At about 40 psi on a tractor-trailer, the tractor protection valve should close (pop out). On other vehicles, the spring brake push-pull valve should pop.

Tractor-trailer bus checks. The catwalk is a platform at the rear of the cab for the driver to stand on when connecting or disconnecting trailer lines. It should be solid, securely bolted to the tractor frame, and clear of loose objects.

Air and electrical lines carry air and power to the trailer. Check that the air hoses are not cut, cracked, chafed, or worn. Steel braid should not show through. Listen for leaks. The lines must not be tangled, crimped, or pinched. They should not drag against tractor parts. Electrical line insulation must not be cut, cracked, chafed, or worn. Electrical conductor must not be showing through. Neither the air nor electrical lines should be spliced or taped.

Air and electrical connectors connect air supplies and electrical power to the trailer. Make sure trailer air connectors are sealed and in good condition. Gladhands should be locked in place and free of damage. There must not be any air leaks you can hear. The trailer electrical plug must be firmly seated and locked in place.

The fifth wheel platform holds the fifth wheel skid plate and the locking jaws mechanism. Check for cracks or breaks.

Locking pins hold a sliding fifth wheel in place on the slider rails. Look for loose or missing pins in the slide mechanism. If the slider is air-powered, there should be no leaks. Check that the fifth wheel is not so far forward that the tractor frame strikes the landing gear during turns.

The release arm releases the fifth wheel locking jaws. Then the trailer can be uncoupled. The release arm should be in the engaged position. The safety latch locks the locking jaws closed. It should be engaged.

The kingpin attaches the trailer to the tractor. The apron provides a surface for resting the trailer on the fifth wheel. The kingpin must not be bent. The apron should lie flat on the fifth wheel skid plate. Check that the part of the apron you can see is not bent, cracked, or broken.

The landing gear supports the front end of the trailer when the trailer is not coupled to the tractor. The landing gear should be fully raised. Look for missing parts. The support frame should not be bent or damaged. You must have a crank handle, and it must be secured. If the landing gear is power-operated, there must be no air or hydraulic leaks.

Inspection Test Scoring

The examiner uses a form to score the Inspection Test. Most states, when scoring an Inspection Test, give you a point for every item you inspect correctly. Of course, larger vehicles have more items that must be inspected. So you'll need more points to pass. The lowest "passing" score is 39 items correctly inspected. This applies to inspecting a straight vehicle with two axles but without air brakes. If you're inspecting a three-axle tractor coupled to a two-axle trailer, with air brakes, you need 84 points to pass.

Speaking of air brakes, if you don't perform the air brakes check during the engine start procedure, you automatically fail this part of the Inspection Test.

States do have the option to score the Inspection Test differently from the way we've just described. You may certainly ask how your Inspection Test will be scored. But try not to worry about the scoring. Focus instead on doing a thorough inspection.

You may fail the Inspection Test and be allowed to take the rest of the Skills Tests. The examiner would decide if the vehicle is safe to operate. Then the examiner could choose to continue with the skills testing. If you pass these other tests, you will have to retake the Inspection Test some other time before getting your CDL.

Some states test your knowledge of inspections in the Knowledge Test only. You can find out if this is the case in your state by looking in the state's CDL preparation manual.

COUPLING AND UNCOUPLING

If you drive a tractor-trailer bus, you may be tested on coupling and uncoupling. States may give you an extra Knowledge Test. They may also test you on the process during the Skills Test. Here's an example of the type of performance some examiners will be looking for.

Uncoupling

Set the tractor/truck and trailer parking brakes. Chock the wheels. Make sure you're working on solid ground. Lower the landing gear.

Release the locking jaws. Release the tractor brakes. Pull ahead until the fifth wheel clears the apron. Set the tractor/truck parking brakes.

Disconnect and secure the air and electrical lines. Pull forward about 16 feet.

Coupling

Back up and align the fifth wheel jaws with the kingpin. Back slowly, until the fifth wheel touches the trailer apron without flattening. Secure the tractor.

Check that the fifth wheel coupler (locking jaws) is open. Compare the height of the fifth wheel with the trailer.

Connect the air and electrical lines. Apply and release them several times. Check to see if air is releasing from the quick release valve.

Apply the tractor brakes. Back under the trailer until the fifth wheel coupler engages and locks.

Check the coupler. Pull against the trailer with the trailer brakes on. Raise the landing gear. Secure in low range.

Scoring the Coupling and Uncoupling Skills Test

There are some mistakes you could make in coupling and uncoupling that could result in immediate failure on this part of the Skills Test. Here's what some states consider serious uncoupling mistakes:

- not setting the trailer brakes before leaving the cab to lower the landing gear
- not chocking the wheels when your vehicle doesn't have spring brakes
- failing to lower the landing gear before unlocking the fifth wheel
- failing to shut off the air lines and setting the tractor parking brakes before disconnecting the air lines
- not disconnecting the air and elec-

trical lines before separating the tractor and trailers

The following coupling mistakes may cause immediate failure in some states:

- flattened fifth wheel when coupling the units
- not setting the tractor parking brake before getting out of the cab to connect the air and electrical lines
- not setting the trailer brakes before backing under the trailer to engage the fifth wheel coupler
- failing to chock the wheels before backing under the trailer to engage the fifth wheel coupler when the vehicle doesn't have spring brakes
- not checking the coupling by pulling forward with the trailer brakes on or the wheels chocked
- failing to raise the landing gear before moving

BASIC CONTROLS SKILLS TEST

The next part of the test covers your basic vehicle control skills and your safe driving ability. FMCSR Part 393 says CDL applicants must have (and be able to show they have) these skills:

- ability to start, warm up, and shut down the engine
- ability to put the motor vehicle in motion and accelerate smoothly, forward and backward
- ability to bring the vehicle to a smooth stop
- ability to back the vehicle in a straight line and check the path and clearance while backing
- ability to position the vehicle to make left and right turns, then make the turn
- ability to shift as needed and choose the right gear for speed and highway conditions
- ability to back along a curved path
- ability to observe the road and the behavior of other vehicles, especially before changing speed and direction

Most states test these abilities with a "skills test." They may test all these skills in one driving test. Or they may divide the test into two parts. One is often called the "road test" because you're driving in traffic. The other is usually called the "range test" or "static test." A test like this involves going through a series of exercises on a course laid out just for this purpose.

In this section, we'll look at how a range test examines your basic control skills.

Range Test

Typical exercises in a range test are:

- forward stop/straight line backing
- alley dock
- measured right turn
- parallel parking
- backward serpentine

Often, you'll be asked to do four of these. The easier exercises will likely be given first. Then you'll do the harder ones.

Three factors are scored as errors. They are:

- pullup
- encroachment
- wrong final vehicle position

Pullup. Anytime you stop and reverse direction to get a better position, it's scored as a pullup. A pullup is an error. Stopping without changing direction does not count as a pullup.

Encroachment. Touching or crossing an exercise boundary or cone with any part of the vehicle is an encroachment. Think of the boundaries or cones as walls. If your vehicle would touch or punch a hole in the "wall," that's an encroachment.

You're scored for an encroachment when you cross a boundary from the right side over to the wrong side. This is different from how pullups are scored. A pullup is a pullup no matter which side you're on.

Like pullups, encroachments are errors.

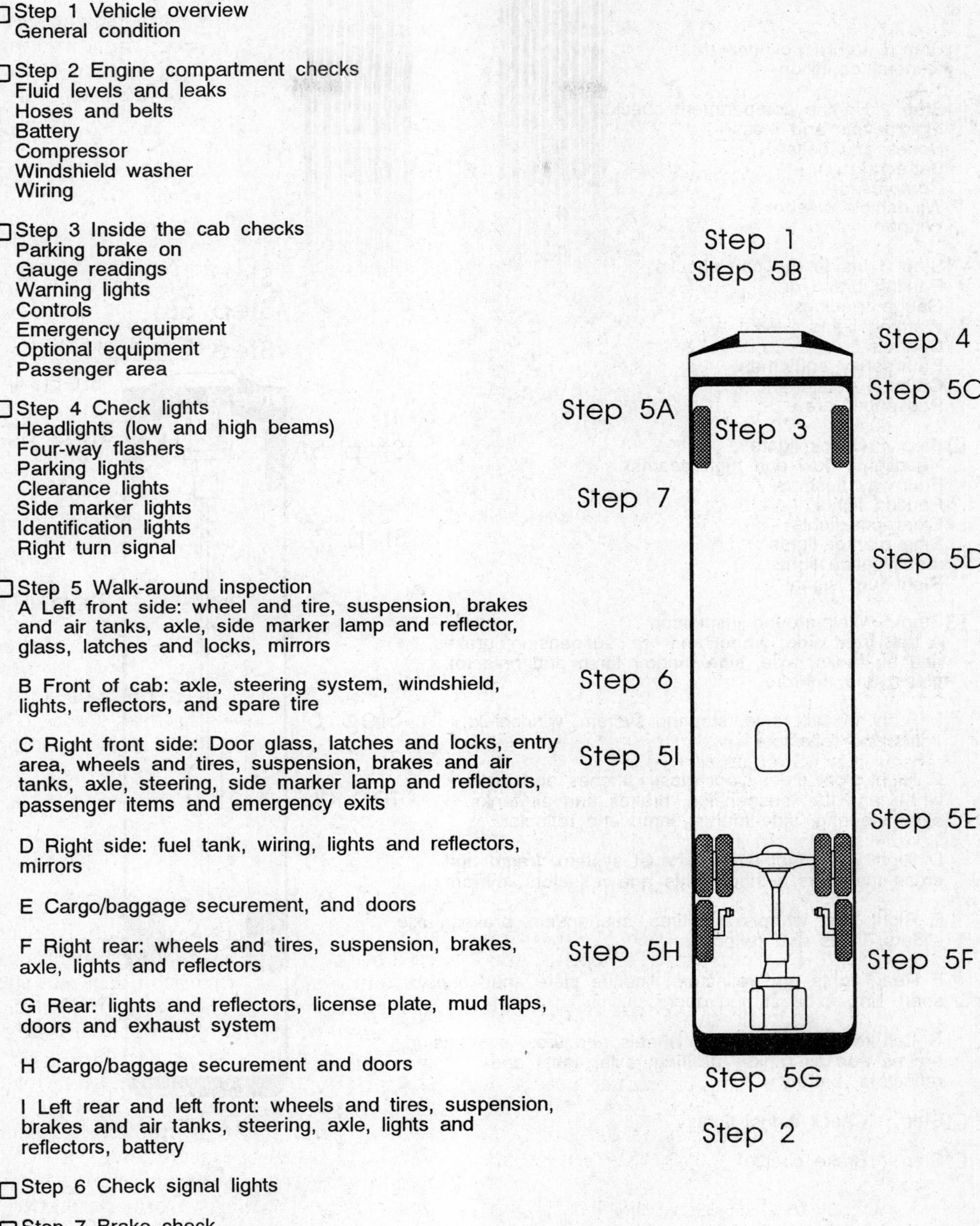

Figure 15-3A Vehicle Inspection Aid for Transit Buses.

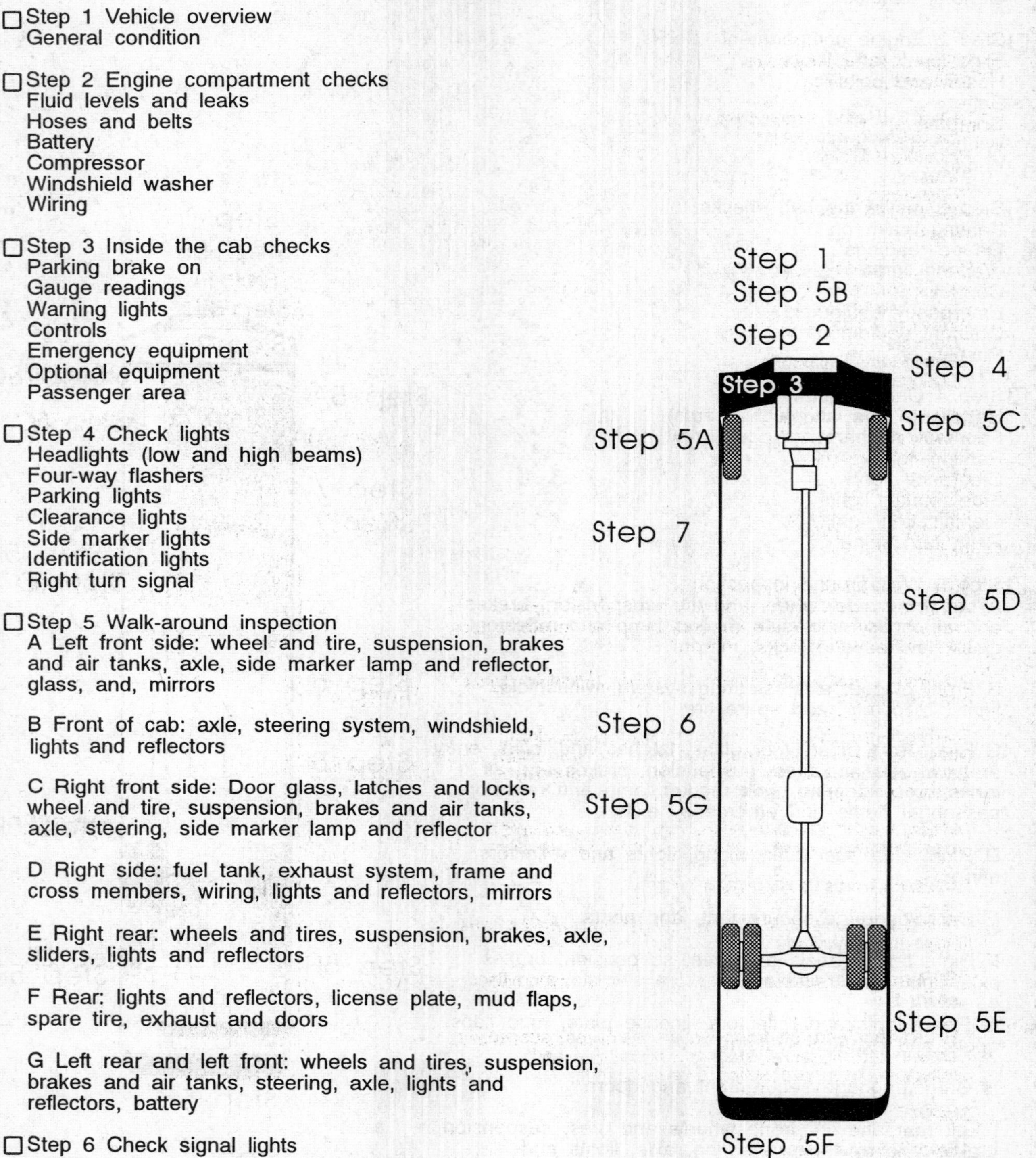

Figure 15-3B Vehicle Inspection Aid for School Buses.

☐ Step 1 Vehicle overview
General condition

☐ Step 2 Engine compartment checks
Fluid levels and leaks
Hoses and belts
Battery
Compressor
Windshield washer
Wiring

☐ Step 3 Inside the cab checks
Parking brake on
Gauge readings
Warning lights
Controls
Emergency equipment
Optional equipment

☐ Step 4 Check lights
Headlights (low and high beams)
Four-way flashers
Parking lights
Clearance lights
Side marker lights
Identification lights
Right turn signal

☐ Step 5 Walk-around inspection
A Left front side: wheel and tire, suspension, brakes and air tanks, axle, side marker lamp and reflector, door glass, latches and locks, mirrors

B Front of cab: axle, steering system, windshield, lights and reflectors

C Right front side: Door glass, latches and locks, wheels and tires, suspension, brakes and air tanks, axle, steering, coupling to trailer, landing gear, side marker lamp and reflector

D Right side: fuel tank, exhaust system, frame and cross members, wiring, lights and reflectors, mirrors

E Seating, overhead compartments

F Right rear: wheels and tires, suspension, brakes, axle, lights and reflectors

G Rear: lights and reflectors, license plate, mud flaps, spare tire

H Left rear and left front: wheels and tires, suspension, brakes and air tanks, steering, axle, lights and reflectors, battery, coupling to trailer

☐ Step 6 Check signal lights

☐ Step 7 Brake check

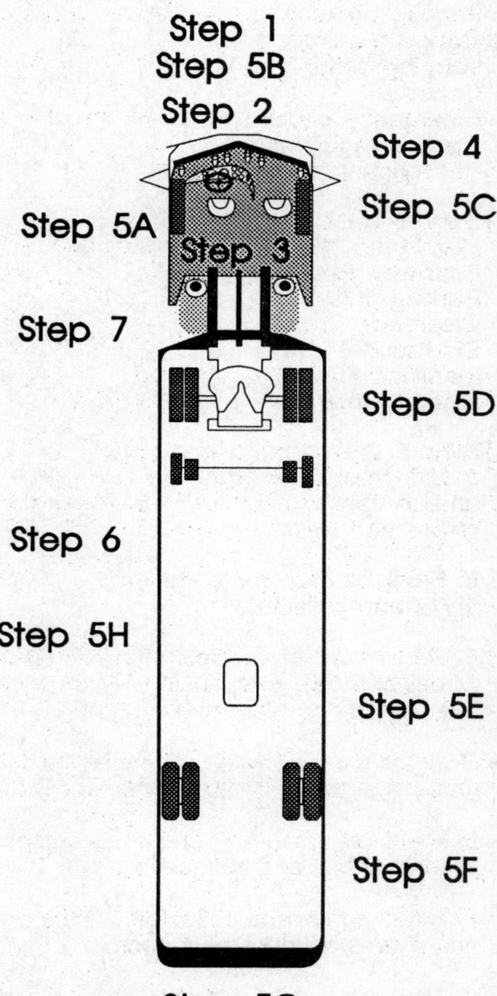

Cut Here

Figure 15-4 Vehicle Inspection Aid for Tractor-trailer Buses.

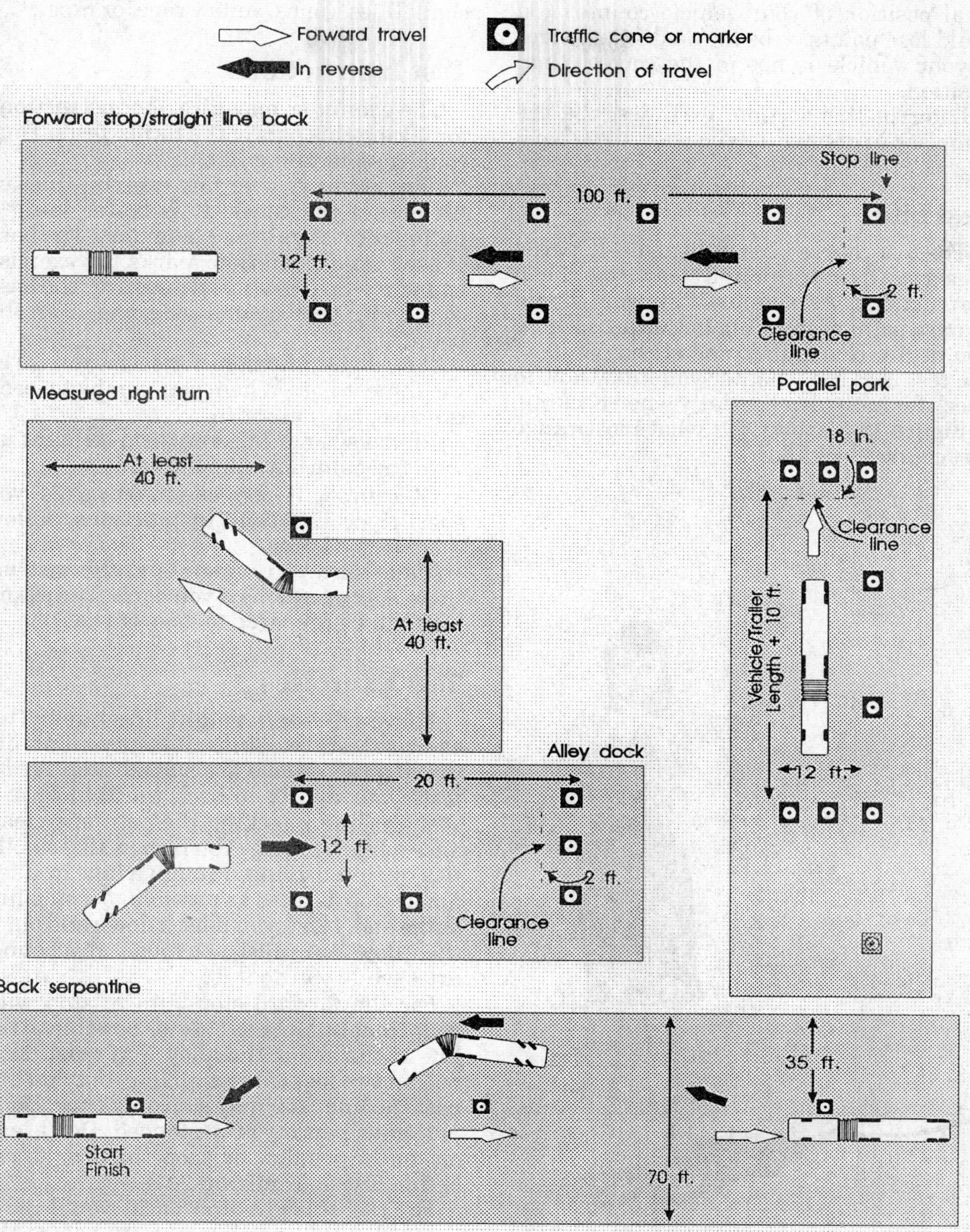

Figure 15-5 Basic Controls Skills Test Course.

Final position. For some exercises, the final position of your vehicle counts. You could lose points or be marked for an error if your vehicle is not in the correct final position.

Later in this section, we'll describe the exercises in greater detail.

Test Site

The test course is usually an open, paved area away from traffic and clear of overhead obstructions. As safe as it is, you should make a point of checking for hazards before you begin. Remember, one of the points of the test is to see whether you know how to check for hazards, especially when backing.

Figure 15-5 shows you what most range test courses look like.

Figure 15-6 Examiner giving Skills Test "STOP" signal.

Boundaries may be marked with paint or chalk lines, cones, yellow rope, or tape.

Test Instructions

The examiner may give you instructions for taking this part of the Skills Tests. They could go something like this:

"Try not to go over any exercise lines or hit any of the cones. It is better to do a pullup than to go over a boundary. The base of each cone or marker marks the exercise boundary. So if a wheel passes over the base of a cone, that counts as going over the boundary.

"You'll get directions for each exercise as we come to it. When you complete each exercise, tap your horn.

"If you see me raise my arm straight up with the palm out, stop the vehicle."

Of course, if the examiner gives you specific or different instructions, follow them to the letter.

Make sure you understand the instructions. Ask questions if you don't. The examiner will be prepared to answer them.

Test Exercises

Forward stop/straight line back. This exercise tests two skills. It tests your ability to bring the vehicle to a smooth stop. And it tests your ability to back the vehicle in a straight line, checking the path and clearance while backing. You'll show these abilities by first driving through a lane or alley. You'll stop as close as possible to a stop line at the end. Next, you'll back down and out of the alley. You must not touch any boundaries while you do this.

For the forward stop, aim to stop with your front bumper as close as possible to the line at the end of the alley. You must come within two feet of the stop line, but don't go past the line. You may stop only once. Don't pull ahead once you've stopped. Don't lean out of the window or open the door to see better. Use your mirrors.

For the straight line back, you'll drive forward. You'll position the vehicle so the rear of the vehicle is about even with the stop line. The examiner will usually signal when you're in the right position to begin.

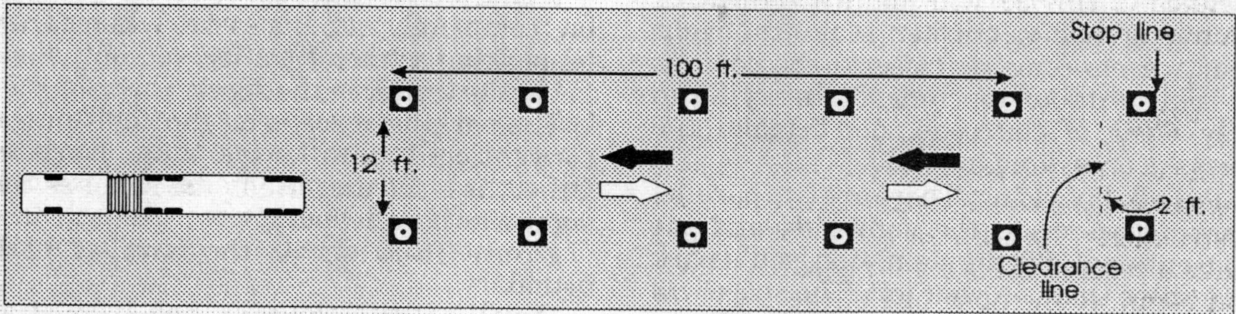

Figure 15-7 Typical forward stop/straight line back exercise layout.

Then you'll back straight down the alley.

Don't touch either side boundary. Stop with your front bumper about even with the end of the alley.

Figure 15-7 shows a typical forward stop/straight line back exercise layout.

Alley dock. This exercise tests your ability to back along a curved path. You'll drive by the alley so the entrance is on your left. Then you will try to back into the alley. You must stop within two feet of the rear of the alley without going past the end boundary. Don't cross any boundary lines while you're backing.

You may not make a 90-degree turn in front of the alley and then back straight in. In fact, you can't set up at more than a 45 degree angle. Pretend that there's a curb across from the alley that prevents you from doing this.

Figure 15-8 pictures the alley dock exercise.

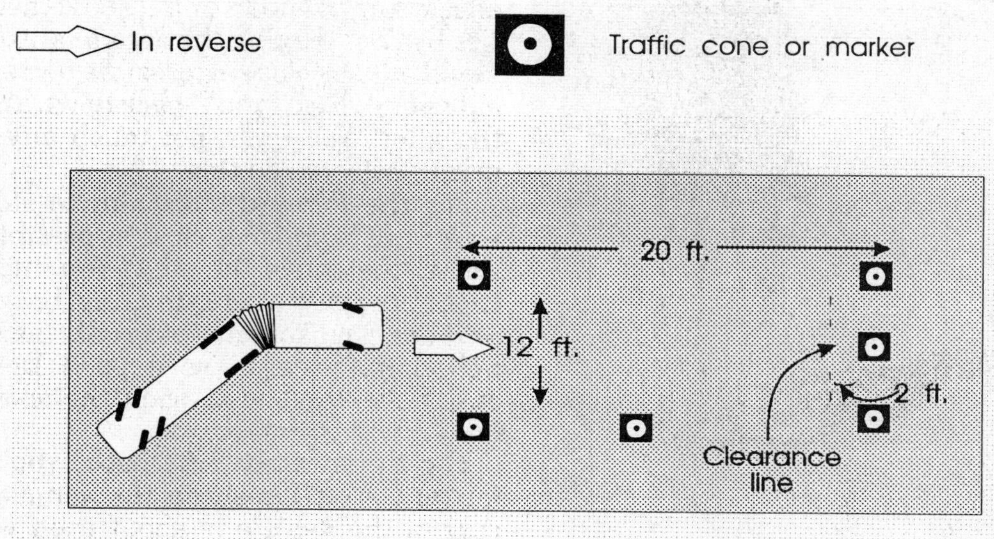

Figure 15-8 Typical alley dock course layout.

Measured right turn. This measures your ability to position the vehicle for, then make a right turn. You will start about 30 to 50 feet from a marker, as if you were approaching an intersection. You will drive forward. Then you will make a right turn around a cone or marker. Make the right rear wheels come as close to the cone as possible without touching it. In trying to stay clear of the cone, don't make the mistake of turning too wide.

Parallel parking. There are two parallel parking exercises, the sight-side and the conventional. For the sight-side, you'll park in a space that's on your left. The space will be 10 feet longer than the length of your straight vehicle (or 10 feet longer than your trailer if your vehicle is a tractor-semi-trailer). You will drive past the space, as if it were a parking space on the street. Then you'll back into it.

Try to get as close as possible to the rear and the "curb" of the space. Get within 18 inches of the rear boundary, but don't go over it. Don't cross any lines or hit any markers. Be careful while parallel-parking with a trailer. When you jack the trailer, you can easily put the rear of the tractor over the "curb" boundary. This would be marked as an encroachment.

If your bus is a straight vehicle, get your bus completely into the space. When parallel-parking a tractor-trailer, you only have to get the trailer in the space.

The parking space is on the right in the conventional parallel parking exercise. Otherwise, the exercise is the same as the sight-side parallel park.

Figure 15-10 shows the parallel park layout.

Backward serpentine. This measures your ability to back along a curved path. You'll start at the head of a row of three cones (see Figure 15-11). You'll line up near the first cone and drive forward along the right side of the line of cones. In other words, the cones will be on your left. Drive forward and stop when the rear of your vehicle is past the third cone.

Then you will back up so your vehicle will

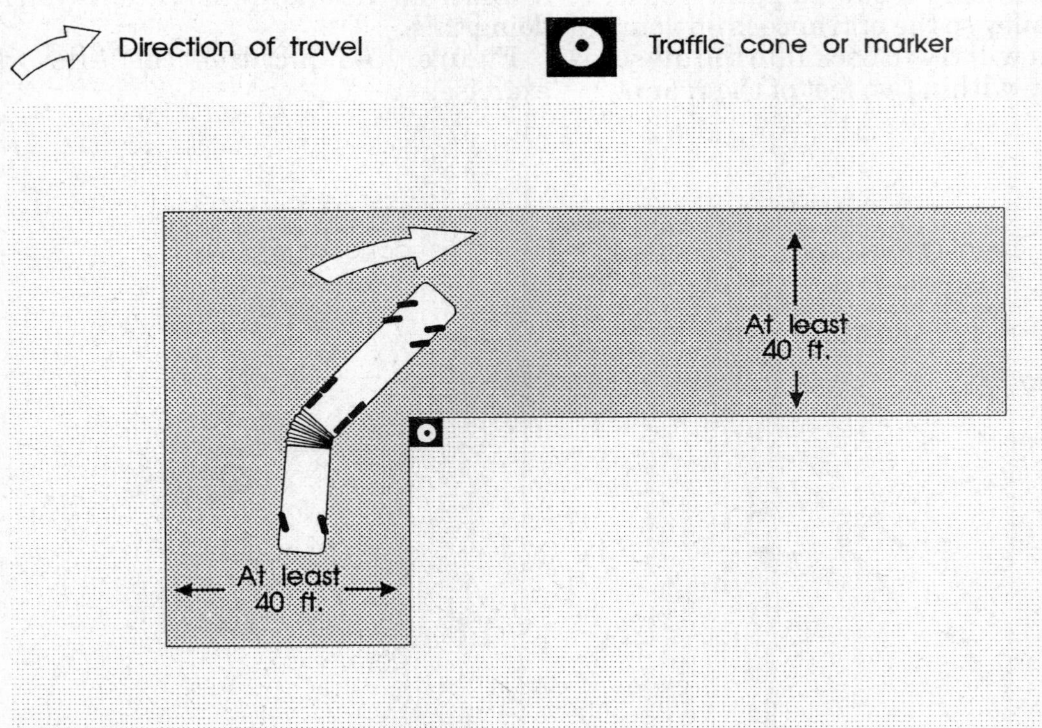

Figure 15-9 Measured right turn.

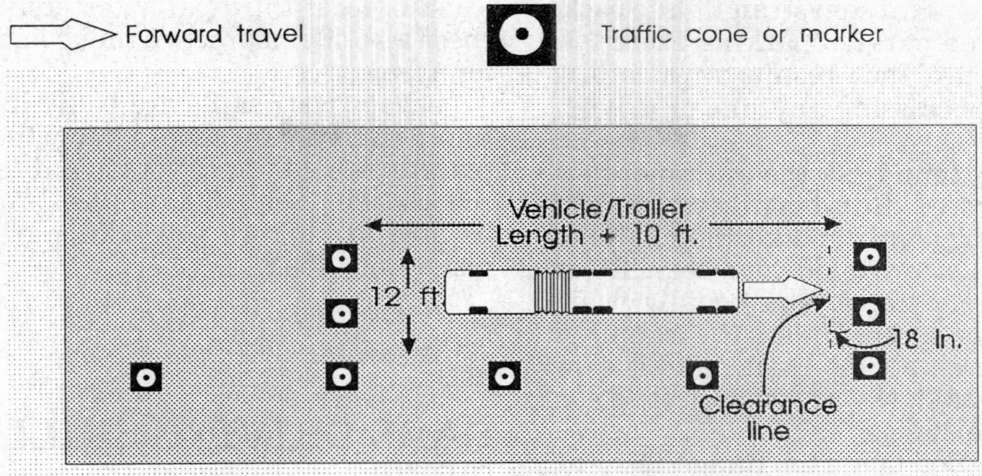

Figure 15-10 Typical parallel park exercise layout.

wind around the three cones. You'll pass the third cone so the cone is on your left. Then pass the second cone so the cone is on your right. Pass the first cone so the cone is on your left. End up in the position you started from.

As with the other exercises, don't cross any boundaries or touch any markers. You are allowed one pullup. Any more than one will be marked as errors.

You can see that some of the exercises test the same skill. In some states, you will only do some, not all of the exercises.

Range Test Scoring

Most states count each pullup and each encroachment as an error. You also lose points for an incorrect final position. For example, stopping too short of or over the end line is an error. Depending on which tests you take, you can make a total of 12 to 16 errors and still pass.

Other states start you out with 100 points. You lose a point for every error. After the Skills Test and the Road Test, you must end up with 75 points to pass.

In still other states, you are allowed three

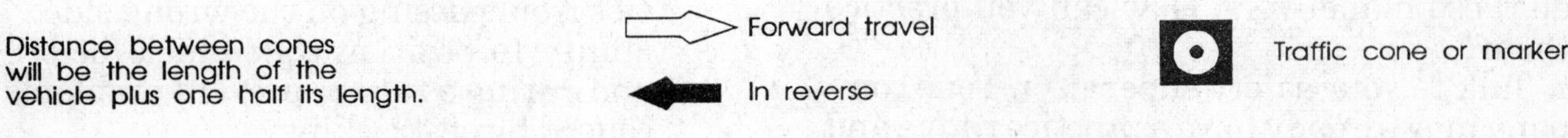

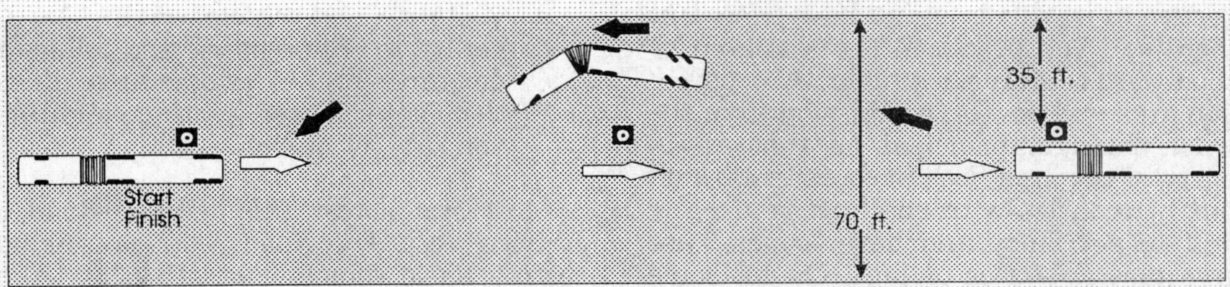

Figure 15-11 Typical backward serpentine course layout.

tries for the forward stop/straight line back, alley dock, and parallel parking exercises. Any more than that results in a failing score. So does crossing any line or driving over a flag.

You can certainly ask the examiner how the test is scored. But don't drive yourself crazy counting points and keeping score in your head. Just try to do your best. These tests are rarely timed. You usually won't gain points for speed. Unless the examiner tells you there's a time limit, take it slow and easy. Go as slowly as you need to so you don't make mistakes.

Even if you don't pass the Range Test, the examiner may decide to give you the Road Test. If you pass the Inspection Test and the Road Test, you'll have to repeat and pass the Range Test to get your CDL.

Basic Control Skills Practice

Practice these basic vehicle control skills as you go about your normal routine. Perhaps you haven't paid much attention to your backing or turning lately. Maybe you've gotten a little sloppy. Start tightening up. As you back or turn, try just a little harder to meet the standards the Range Tests will use. When you've completed the maneuver, take a moment to assess your own performance.

Has it been some time since you parallel parked or backed through a curving path? You may be concerned about your ability to do these maneuvers. How can you practice them?

Talk to your safety supervisor. Your company may already have a practice range and vehicle available for CDL applicants.

If you own your own vehicle, you can practice in it whenever you have time. But where can you practice? Try a church or school yard or store parking lot. Any paved, open area will do. Get permission from the owner, manager, principal, or whoever's in charge of the area first, of course. Mark off your boundaries with chalk. If you really want to get fancy and have "cones," use large plastic bottles or jugs. Or get some lengths of plastic pipe.

Here's another option. Ask your DMV for a list of local third-party testers. Many of these also offer a practice range and vehicle for a fee.

Perhaps your skills are badly in need of improvement. You should know that many private schools and vocational/technical schools offer "refresher courses." You might be able to improve your skills greatly for just a small fee.

SAFE DRIVING SKILLS TEST

The last part of the test covers your ability to drive safely in traffic.

FMCSR Part 393 states that CDL applicants must have (and be able to show they have) these skills:

- ability to use proper visual search methods
- ability to give the right signals when changing speed or direction
- ability to adjust speed to the shape and condition of the road, the weather and visibility, the traffic, the cargo, and the driver's own condition
- ability to choose a safe gap for changing lanes, passing, and crossing and entering traffic
- ability to position the vehicle before and during a turn to keep other vehicles from passing on the wrong side
- ability to position the vehicle before and during a turn to prevent problems caused by off-tracking
- ability to maintain a safe following distance based on road conditions, visibility, and vehicle weight
- ability to adjust speed and following distance, brake, and change directions based on the weather conditions and stay in control

Most states test this with a Road or Driving Test. The Road Test may include testing basic vehicle control skills. Or, as you have already seen, those may be tested off the road in a Range Test.

CDL Basic Control Skills Practice Test Performance Record

Instructions: Have an observer rate your performance by checking a box each time you make a pullup or encroachment. An incorrect final position counts as 1 error. The observer should mark NO ERRORS if your performance was error-free.

Test Item	No Errors	Errors				
		1	2	3	4	5
Measured Right Turn						
Pullups						
Encroachments						
Clearance						
Alley Dock						
Pullups						
Encroachments						
Final Position						
Forward Stop/Straight Line Backing						
Pullups						
Encroachments						
Final Position						
Serpentine						
Pullups						
Encroachments						
Parallel Park						
Pullups						
Encroachments						
Final Position						
Parallel Park						
Pullups						
Encroachments						
Final Position						

Cut Here

Figure 15-12 Sample Skills Test Form.

CDL Basic Control Skills Practice Test Self-Scoring Form

Instructions: Use the information from the Performance Record to score how well you did on the Basic Skills Practice Test.

Test Item	Self - Scoring Pass	Self - Scoring No Pass
Measured Right Turn		
Pullups (Failing = more than 4)	❑	❑
Encroachments (Failing = driving over marker or cone)	❑	❑
Clearance (Failing = wheel less than 1 ft. or more than 3 ft. from marker)	❑	❑
Alley Dock		
Pullups (Failing = more than 4)	❑	❑
Encroachments (Failing = backing over marker or curb)	❑	❑
Final Position (Failing = more than 2 ft. from, or over rear dock)	❑	❑
Forward Stop/Straight Line Backing		
Pullups (Failing = more than 3; more than 4 for tractor and trailer)	❑	❑
Encroachments (Failing = jackknife)	❑	❑
Final Position (Failing = more than 2 ft. from , or over stop line)	❑	❑
Serpentine		
Pullups (Failing = more than 5)	❑	❑
Encroachments (Failing = backing over marker or curb)	❑	❑
Parallel Park (Conventional)		
Pullups (Failing = more than 3)	❑	❑
Encroachments (Failing = backing over marker or curb)	❑	❑
Final Position (Failing = further than 18 in. from curb)	❑	❑
Parallel Park (Sight Side)		
Pullups (Failing = more than 3)	❑	❑
Encroachments (Failing = backing over marker or curb)	❑	❑
Final Position (Failing = further than 18 in. from curb)	❑	❑

✂ Cut Here ✂

Test Site

You'll drive a pre-set route. This will usually include:

- four left and four right turns
- traffic lights, stop signs, and uncontrolled intersections
- a straight section of a city business street
- two intersections where you must stop
- a through intersection
- a multi-lane section of roadway
- moderate traffic
- one uncontrolled railroad crossing
- a curve to the left or right
- a section of expressway or two-lane rural or semi-rural road
- a downgrade and an upgrade
- parking on an upgrade and a downgrade
- an underpass, low clearance, or bridge

Later in this section, we'll look at the skills such a route tests.

Test Instructions

The examiner may give you instructions for taking the Road Test. They could go something like this:

"I will give you instructions as we go along. I'll always give directions for turns and so forth as far in advance as possible.

"Along the way I will point out a location. I'll ask you to pretend it is the top of a steep hill that you will be going down. I'll ask you to go through the motions of what you would do if it were a real hill. Tell me what you are doing as you do it. The fact that there is this pretend hill doesn't mean there won't be real hills on the route we'll take."

(The examiner will likely ask you to pretend there's a railroad crossing on the route. At the pretend crossing, you should do whatever you would do at a real crossing. You should tell the examiner what you are doing and why.)

"There will be no trick directions to get you to do something illegal or unsafe."

Of course, if the examiner gives you specific or different instructions, follow them to the letter.

Make sure you understand the instructions. Ask questions if you don't. The examiner will be prepared to answer them.

Along the way, the examiner will mark the test form. This doesn't mean you have done something wrong. It could mean you did something right. The examiner will probably tell you not to worry about this. That's good advice. Don't let the examiner distract you. Pay attention to your driving.

Test Exercises

Each feature of the test route is designed to challenge one or more safe driving skills. Let's look at some of the challenges this route presents.

Left and right turns. Turns test your ability to give the right signals when changing speed or direction. They also test your ability to position the vehicle before and during a turn to keep other vehicles from passing on the wrong side. You must also prevent problems caused by off-tracking in the turn.

PASS Billboard

Reference Point Driving

Reference point driving is a method bus drivers use to make turns safely. To use this method, you must first know your vehicle's turning radius and tracking.

With experience, you can determine two reference points. One is on the vehicle, and the other is on the street. For example, a vehicle reference point could be the entrance door, or driver's side window. A street reference point could be the corner.

You approach an intersection or other turning point. You drive toward it until your two reference points line up. Then you turn the wheel 100 percent in the direction you want to turn.

You might find using reference point

driving especially helpful on right turns. Position your vehicle three to five feet from the curb. Approach the intersection, and line up your reference points. Then turn the wheel 100 percent to the right. You should complete the turn without scraping the curb, or turning too wide.

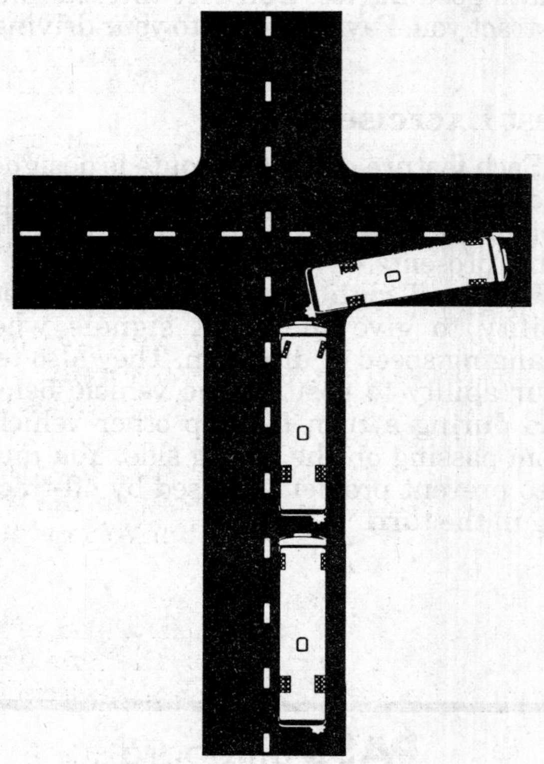

Figure 15-13 Using reference point driving to turn right.

The examiner will watch you approach the turn, stop if necessary, enter the turn and complete the turn. Slow far enough in advance as you approach a turn. You should slow to 15 mph when you approach a blind intersection. Downshift if necessary.

Don't forget to signal that you are slowing down. Start signalling that you intend to turn when you are 100 feet from making the turn.

Don't pull up too close to the vehicle in front of you. You should be able to see that vehicle's rear wheels.

When there's a stop light, stop sign, or yield sign, you will be marked wrong if you fail to stop. (Stopping because a vehicle blocks you partway through the turn isn't marked.) If you must stop, stop at the stop line or within five feet of it. Don't stop out in the intersection, over the stop line, or past the sidewalk. Don't stop past the stop sign or other intersection marker. If there's a vehicle in front of you, don't pull up too close to it. You should be able to see that vehicle's rear wheels.

If you do stop, come to a full stop. Don't roll or coast through the intersection. Your wheels should be straight ahead, not turned to the left or right.

Check for traffic. Look to the right, to the left, and to the rear. Use your mirrors. Make eye contact with other drivers and pedestrians.

Yield to vehicles having the right of way. Yield whenever it results in greater safety. But don't stop unnecessarily. That just confuses other drivers.

Start the turn from the proper lane. For a right turn, start from the right-most lane, but not over the marking on the left side of the lane unless it's necessary. Try to keep vehicles from coming up on your right. Turn without going over the curb or swinging too wide.

Start a left turn from the left-most lane, but not over the lane markings.

Turn left and right properly (review Chapter 8 if you don't recall the correct way to turn). Proceed at a smooth, even speed that allows you to maintain control over the vehicle. Don't stop in the middle of the turn (unless you have to for safety's sake), and don't change gears. (You may downshift if you need to before you start to turn. And you may change gears again to get started up from a full stop.)

Keep both hands firmly on the wheel. Don't turn the wheel with your palms.

Complete the turn by turning into the proper lane. For a right turn, you'll lose points if your rear wheels touch or come up over the curb. You'll also lose points if you turn too wide and end up in the lane of oncoming traffic. An unnecessary buttonhook will also be marked as an error. You should complete a right turn in the right-most lane.

For a left turn, you'll lose points if you end up in the right lane or in the lane of oncoming traffic.

You'll be marked for an error if you cause traffic to back up behind you on any turn.

Cancel your turn signal. Accelerate smoothly. If you've made a left turn and are in the left lane, move to the right lane as soon as it's clear.

Traffic lights, stop signs, and uncontrolled intersections. Obey all traffic signs. When signs tell you to stop, come to a full stop. Don't roll or coast through the stop.

At uncontrolled intersections, check for traffic. Look to the right, to the left, and to the rear. Use your mirrors. Make eye contact with pedestrians and other drivers.

Yield to vehicles having the right of way. Yield whenever it results in greater safety. But don't stop unnecessarily. That just confuses other drivers.

A straight section of a city business street. Watch for hazards at the side of the road and from entrances onto the street.

Figure 15-14 An unnecessary buttonhook on a right turn will be marked as an error.

Slow for hazards as soon as you see them. Plan at least seven to 15 seconds ahead for lane changes.

Travel in the right lane if it's clear. Choose the center lane if the right lane is obstructed by tree branches, utility poles, and so forth. Also choose the center lane if the traffic in the right lane causes you continually to change out of it. If there is a lot of traffic entering and exiting the right lane, choose the center lane so you can travel at a safe speed without a lot of braking and shifting.

Center your vehicle in the lane. Don't drift to the right or left.

Keep up with the flow of traffic. Choose a speed that lets you travel without lots of slowing, stopping, and speeding up.

Keep a following distance of one second for every 10 feet of vehicle length at 40 mph. Add a second for speeds over 40 mph.

Avoid riding behind larger vehicles that might block your view.

The examiner may tell you to change lanes. First, check the traffic to the front and rear. Give extra attention to your blind spot.

Signal for the lane change.

Don't tailgate the vehicle ahead of you while you wait for a gap in the lane. Don't change lanes until you have a large enough gap to do so safely.

Blend smoothly with the traffic in the new lane. Don't turn sharply or abruptly. Maintain your speed. Move to the center of the lane. Regain your following distance in the new lane of traffic. Keep a traffic gap to the front and the rear.

Cancel the signal when you complete the lane change.

Two intersections where you must stop. Check for traffic to the right, to the left, and to the rear. Use your mirrors. Make eye contact with pedestrians and other drivers. Take your foot off the accelerator. Slow far enough in advance as you approach a turn. You should slow to 15 mph when you approach a blind intersection. Downshift if necessary. Don't forget to signal that you are slowing down.

Don't pull up too closely to the vehicle in front of you. You should be able to see that vehicle's rear wheels.

Stop at the stop line or within five feet of it. Don't stop out in the intersection, over the stop line, or past the sidewalk. Don't stop past the stop sign or other intersection marker. If there's a vehicle stopped in front of you, don't pull up too close to it. You should be able to see that vehicle's rear wheels.

Come to a full stop. Don't roll or coast through the intersection.

A through intersection. Check for traffic to the right, to the left, and to the rear. Use your mirrors. Make eye contact with pedestrians.

Yield to pedestrians and other vehicles in the intersection.

Don't change lanes, or gears, in the intersection. Be in the right gear so you can proceed slowly enough without stalling. Don't allow the vehicle to drift back. Don't lug or rev the engine. Don't disrupt the flow of traffic.

A multi-lane section of roadway. This tests your ability to choose a safe gap for changing lanes, passing, and crossing and entering traffic. Check traffic to the front and rear, especially your blind spot. Signal your intent to change lanes. Don't tailgate while you're waiting to change lanes. Wait for enough of a gap before you make your move.

Blend smoothly with the traffic in the new lane. Don't turn sharply or abruptly. Maintain your speed. Move to the center of the lane. Regain your following distance in the new lane of traffic. Keep a traffic gap to the front and the rear.

Cancel the signal when you complete the lane change.

Moderate traffic. Don't drive faster than needed to stay with the flow of traffic. Driving too slowly isn't any safer than driving too fast. Keep the proper following distance for your vehicle, speed, and driving conditions.

Be visually alert. Scan "the big picture," and check your mirrors often. Anticipate problems other drivers might present.

One uncontrolled railroad crossing. Your test route may have a real railroad crossing or a pretend one. When there's no signal, you must stop and check for trains. Stop within 50 feet and no closer than 15 feet. Look to the left and right. Roll down the window and listen for a train.

Don't change gears, stop, or brake while on the track. Don't pass or change lanes. Travel at the posted speed limit or slower if that would be safer.

Of course, if the test route includes a controlled railroad crossing, you should obey the signals.

TIP *Review the regulations that cover railroad crossings. This is covered in Chapter 6.*

A curve to the left or right. Reduce your speed before you enter the curve. Maintain your speed in the curve. Stay in your lane. Don't let any wheels cross into the next lane. Make continual traffic checks. Make an extra effort to keep track of following vehicles when coming out of the curve.

A section of expressway or two-lane rural or semi-rural road. This tests your ability to merge, change lanes, and exit. When you enter the expressway, check the traffic. Check to the front and the rear. Pay special attention to your blind spot.

Signal as soon as the traffic on the expressway can see your signal.

Don't tailgate, and don't slow up traffic following you. Merge without stopping. Don't exceed the ramp speed.

Accelerate to the flow of traffic in the acceleration lane. Don't turn sharply onto the expressway lane. Don't lug or rev the engine. Move to the center of the right-most driving lane.

Cancel your signal.

When you change lanes, check traffic to the front and rear, especially your blind spot. Signal your intent to change lanes. Don't tailgate while you're waiting to change lanes. Wait for enough of a gap before you make your move.

Blend smoothly with the traffic in the new lane. Don't turn sharply or abruptly. Maintain your speed. Move to the center of the lane. Establish your following distance in the new lane of traffic. Keep a traffic gap to the front and the rear.

Cancel the signal when you complete the lane change.

To exit the expressway, start with a traffic check. Pay special attention to the right blind spot. Turn on your right turn signal.

Make a smooth change into the exit (deceleration) lane. Don't make a sharp turn. Enter the exit lane at its beginning.

Slow down in the deceleration lane. When you're on the ramp, travel at or below the posted speed. Don't accelerate in the curve. Use the correct downgrade or upgrade shifting and braking procedure for graded curves.

Don't tailgate on the ramp. Cancel your signal when you've finished exiting.

A downgrade and an upgrade. The upgrade on your route will challenge your ability to change gears to maintain your speed. Don't lug the engine. Stay in the right-most lane. Put on your four-way flashers if you are going much slower than the flow of traffic. Check the traffic to the left and the rear often. Use your mirrors.

The downgrade will test your ability to select a safe speed for going down the hill. It will test your use of the brakes.

Select a lower gear before you start down the grade. Use a gear that will require little if any braking to control the vehicle. Don't rev the engine. You should absolutely not be in neutral.

Check your brakes before you head down the grade. Press on the treadle. Feel the brakes apply. Listen for a release of air.

Use a steady, light braking. Don't fan, pump, or ride the brakes. Maintain an even speed.

Increase your following distance. Stay in the right-most lane. Keep both hands on the wheel. Check the traffic to the left and the rear often. Use your mirrors.

Parking on an upgrade and a downgrade. As you approach the grade, check the traffic to the sides and the rear, using your mirrors. Turn on your right-turn signal. Get into the right-most or curb lane. Don't block any driveways or fire hydrants.

Take your foot off the accelerator. Use steady braking as you slow down. Downshift smoothly. Do not coast.

The challenge is to park so the vehicle doesn't roll. Block the wheel against the curb. When you get going again, on the upgrade you'll have to start up against the pull of gravity.

To park, bring the vehicle parallel to the curb. Turn off the turn signal. Turn on the four-way flashers. Put the parking brake on. Put the transmission in neutral. Release the foot brake. Don't rest your foot on the clutch.

To start up again, check the traffic to the left and right. Pay special attention to the left side. Make eye contact with other drivers and pedestrians. Turn off the four-way flashers, and turn on the left turn signal.

Release the parking brake. Put the vehicle in gear. Don't turn the wheel before the vehicle moves. Don't stall the engine as you start up the grade.

Check the traffic to the left. Don't stall the engine as you accelerate. Blend smoothly with the traffic. Don't turn sharply into the traffic. Match your rpm to the road speed.

An underpass, low clearance, or bridge. An underpass or low clearance will test your ability to judge if it's safe to continue. You should be able to determine what the clearance is from the signs. You should know your vehicle height and be able to decide if you can make it under the underpass.

Before you cross a bridge, you'll have to decide whether it can support your vehicle's weight. You'll have to know your vehicle's weight. Then you'll have to determine the bridge's weight limit from the signs.

General driving behavior. Throughout the test, you should demonstrate safe driving practices in general. Downshift and upshift smoothly, without grinding the gears. You'll have to double-clutch if your vehicle doesn't have synchromesh gears. Don't over-rev or lug the engine. Don't coast with the clutch in. Don't ride the clutch to control your speed. Don't "snap" the clutch.

Use the brakes correctly. Don't ride them, pump them, or fan them. Brake smoothly with steady pressure.

Use the correct steering techniques. Keep both hands on the wheel. Grip the wheel properly. Don't turn the wheel with your palms. Don't understeer or oversteer.

Obey all traffic signals. Pull over to the right and stop if you hear a siren or see the flashing lights of emergency vehicles. Drive within the speed limit or below it if conditions demand it. Don't drive any slower than safety requires. Don't make any unnecessary stops.

Obey all traffic signs. Be alert for and obey signs that ban heavy vehicles from certain roads or bridges.

Be alert for, and avoid, traffic hazards. When you check for traffic, move your head right or left. That way the examiner can clearly see you are checking. Avoid bumping other vehicles, objects, pedestrians, animals, and so on. Never put the vehicle up on a curb or sidewalk.

Stay centered in the correct lane. Don't wander across lane lines. Don't stop over the stop line.

If you're taking your test at night, turn on your lights as soon as the law, or need for additional lighting, requires them. Use your high beams only to improve visibility. Be careful not to blind other drivers. Use the windshield washers and wipers and the heater/defroster if the weather calls for them.

Wear your seat belt.

Finally, obey the basic rules of the road that all drivers must follow. It would be a good idea to read your state's manual for automobile drivers. Review the rules about signs, road markings, right of way, and so forth. These rules apply to all road users, from the little compact car driver to the driver of an 18-wheeler. It is expected you know and will obey these rules.

Also remember that states may have added requirements for CMV drivers beyond the federal regulations. It's your responsibility to inform yourself of these and fulfill them when you take your tests.

Road Test Scoring

Different states score the Road Test different ways. You may start out with a certain number of points, say, 100. You lose a point for every error. To pass, you must end up with enough points left, such as 75.

Or you may earn a point for each mistake. If you earn too many points, 25 for example, you fail the test.

As we've already mentioned, your Road Test score may be combined with your Skills Test score.

You may earn an error point for making a mistake on a particular route test feature. Or you may earn an error point for a general driving mistake, like grinding the gears. As you know, disobeying a traffic law and causing an accident are two mistakes that result in immediate failure. You may also fail the Test if you get into a near accident, even if you manage to maneuver your way out of it.

If you're concerned about how the test will be scored, ask the examiner. Then put it out of your mind and concentrate on your driving.

Safe Driving Skills Practice

Practice these basic safe driving skills as you go about your normal routine. Perhaps you've gotten in the habit of stopping over the stop line or crowding the vehicle ahead of you. Do you neglect to signal when you change lanes? If your driving has gotten a little sloppy, start tightening up. Start driving according to the standards the Road Test will use. When you've finished a run, take a moment to assess your own performance.

Start now to get in the habit of doing things by the book. Then it will come naturally to you when you take the test. You won't have to think about it.

Well, that's it. There's not much left to do now but take the CDL tests. Have you met all your **PASS** mini-goals? Did you take all the sample, pre-trip, and post-trip tests? Have you worked on doing a thorough vehicle inspection? Are you practicing your basic vehicle control and safe driving skills?

If so, you've done a lot of work to prepare for your CDL tests. And, you did it on your own. No one stood over your shoulder and told you what to do. You can feel good about that. (Not everyone has that stick-to-it-iveness!) At this point, taking the actual CDL Tests should be a piece of cake!

Chapter 16 is the last chapter in this book. In it you'll find tips to make your Test Day go smoothly.

CDL Practice Road Test Performance Record And Self-Scoring Form

Instructions: Have an observer rate your performance by checking a box each time you make an error. The observer should mark NO ERRORS if your performance was error free.

Left Turn Errors	Turns	Right Turn Errors
1 2 3 4	**Approach**	1 2 3 4
	Traffic check	
	Signal, Decel, Coast, Lane	
1 2 3 4	**If Stop Necessary, Gap, Stop Line**	1 2 3 4
	Full Stop, Wheels Straight	
1 2 3 4	**Turning**	1 2 3 4
	Traffic check	
	Both Hands, Gears	
	Speed, Wide/Short	
1 2 3 4	**Complete Turn**	1 2 3 4
	Traffic check	
	Correct Lane	
	Signal, Accelerate, Right	
	No Errors	

Expressway

Merge On Traffic check, Signal, Spacing, No Stop, Merge, Cancel signal	1	
Lane Changes Traffic check, Signal, Spacing, Smooth Change, Cancel signal	To Left 1	To Right 1
Exit Traffic check, Signal		
Smooth merge to exit lane		
Decelerate in exit lane		
Ramp speed, Spacing, Cancel signal		
No Errors		

Intersections

	Legal Stop	Legal Stop	Through Intersections	Railroad Crossing
Stopping				
Traffic check				
Deceleration, Coast				
Gap, Stop line, Full stop				
Driving Through				
Traffic check				
Yield, Lane, Gear				
Accelerate				
No Errors				

Urban/Rural Sections	Urban	Rural
Regular traffic checks		
Selects proper lane		
Keeps vehicle in lane		
Speed, Follow distance		
Lane changes: Traffic check, Signal, Space, Smooth change		
Left		
Right		
No Errors		

Drive Up Grade		
Proper gear		
Keep right, 4-ways if slow		
Traffic checks		
No Errors		

Drive Down Grade	Actual	Simulated
In proper gear		
Brake, Clutch		
Steady speed		
Traffic checks		
No Errors		

Curve	
Speed: Enter, Through, Stay in lane	
Traffic checks	
No Errors	

Railroad Crossing	
Traffic check	
Law, Gears, Stop	
No Errors	

Bridge/Underpass	
Knew weight/clearance	
No Errors	

Start/Stop on Grade	Upgrade	Downgrade
Approach		
Traffic check		
Signal on, Correct lane, Deceleration		
Not coasting		
Stop		
Parallel, Not rolling		
Signal off/4-ways on		
Parking brake on		
Resume		
Traffic check, 4-ways off, Signal, Parking brake, Doesn't stall		
Traffic check, Accelerate		
No Errors		

Scoring

Pass = 25 or fewer errors

Pass ☐ No Pass ☐

General Driving	Errors
Used clutch properly (shifting, doble-clutched, didn't ride)	
Used gears properly (didn't over-rev or lug, clash gears or coast)	
Used brakes properly (smooth braking, no riding or pumping)	
Prper steering (both hands on wheel, didn't over or under steer)	
Obeyed all traffic signs and signals	
Drove without an accident	
Never put vehicle over sidewalks, lanes, stop lines, etc.	

Figure 15-15 Sample Road Test Form.

CHAPTER 16
Taking the Tests

When you have finished this chapter, you will be able to provide the correct answers to questions about:

- how to prepare your vehicle for the CDL tests
- how to arrange to take the CDL tests
- tips for taking the CDL tests
- retaking the CDL tests

To complete this chapter you will need:

- operator's manual for your vehicle
- Federal Motor Carrier Safety Regulations pocketbook (or access to U.S. Department of Transportation regulations, Parts 383, 393, and 396 of Subchapter B, Chapter 3, Title 49, Code of Federal Regulations)
- a CDL preparation manual from your state Department of Motor Vehicles, if one is offered
- driver's manual from your state Department of Motor Vehicles

Before we go any further, we'd like to congratulate you on getting this far. This was not the shortest or most entertaining book you could have read in your spare time. You probably didn't become a bus driver because you thought it would give you the chance to do lots of reading!

But you did it. Now all that's left to do is take the tests. Here are some final tips that should make Test Day a little easier for you.

PREPARING YOUR VEHICLE

There are a few things you can do with your vehicle that will help you during the test. These are:

- have the right vehicle
- have the vehicle in good working order
- be familiar with the vehicle

Have the Right Vehicle

This is just a reminder. You must take your CDL Skills Test or Tests in a "representative vehicle." So, if you want a Group A CDL, you must take the tests in a Group A Vehicle. If you don't want an air brake restriction, you must have air brakes on your bus.

States do not provide a vehicle for you to test in. You must bring your own.

Have the Vehicle in Good Working Order

You know you may inspect your vehicle as part of the CDL tests. But that would be a bad time to find out it had some safety defect. Better to take plenty of time, well in advance, to have your vehicle thoroughly checked out. Get your vehicle in as close-to-perfect working order as possible. That way you won't have to worry about the condition of your vehicle while you're taking the tests.

It wouldn't hurt to spruce up your vehicle, either. Tighten up loose fixtures. Repair minor flaws. Wash the vehicle. No, you won't be scored on whether your bus is clean or not. But a clean vehicle will be easier to inspect. It will reflect well on you. Also, it will give you a feeling of confidence.

Inspection Equipment

Equip yourself with the following items to use during the Vehicle Inspection Test:

- flashlight
- tire pressure gauge
- tire tread depth gauge

A flashlight will help you see into the dark corners of your engine compartment. You'll be better able to see under the vehicle and in the baggage compartment. The pressure and tread depth gauges will give you the best tire measurements. Your state may not require that you inspect your tires this accurately. But it isn't wrong to do so. And it is more professional.

Be Familiar with the Vehicle

You want to be completely familiar with the vehicle you'll take your tests in. If it's a new vehicle, or one you don't drive often, try to get some time with it before Test Day. Learn where all the controls are. Get the feel of how they respond. Know which of the vehicle's noises are normal and which are signs of trouble. Get used to how the vehicle handles.

Are there some controls you don't use often, or at all? At least find out what they do and how to work them. The examiner could ask you to explain every lever and switch in the cab. "I don't know what that does. I never use it," is not a good response.

Read the operator's manual. You'll find many useful facts about what's normal for your vehicle and how best to operate it.

ARRANGING FOR THE CDL TESTS

The process of taking the CDL tests differs from state to state. You can get the most current details from your local state DMV office. You can find the addresses of the main state DMV offices listed in the back of this book. Or check your city telephone listings.

The following is an example of what happens in some states.

License Fees

Yes, it does cost money to apply for and test for a CDL License. Here's what one state charges:

License	First CDL or Renewal with Written Exam	Renewal (No Written Exam)	Road Test
Class A	$25.00	$15.00	$25.00
Class B	$25.00	$15.00	$25.00
Class C	$12.50	$10.00	$12.50

Endorsement	First CDL Endorsement or Renewal With Written Exam	Renewal (No Written Exam)	Road Test
H*	$10.00	$10.00	*None Required
(M)	$ 7.00	No Charge	No Charge
(N)	$10.00	No Charge	None Required
(P)	$10.00	No Charge	$5.00
(T)	$10.00	No Charge	None Required
(X)	$20.00	$10.00	None Required

*A hazardous materials endorsement always requires a written examination.

Testing Sites

The Knowledge Test is almost always given at driver license stations. But not all such stations are large enough or well enough equipped for the Skills Test. These may sometimes be given at another site. Or a third-party may be authorized to give the Skills Tests.

Your local DMV can tell you where the Skills Tests may be taken. If you don't know the area, you may want to drive out there in advance of Test Day. At least find it on a map. No point in getting lost on the way to the test!

If you're curious and want to check out the test site ahead of time, call the DMV first. Make sure there's no problem with simply visiting the test site.

Testing Appointments

You can almost always take the Knowledge Test on a walk-in basis. Many states, however, give the Skills Test by appointment only. Be sure to find out if this is the case in your state.

Age Limits

Most states require CDL applicants to be at least 21 years old. Drivers between 18 and 21 years of age may sometimes apply for a Restricted CDL. This limits them to intrastate driving.

Instruction Permits

Instruction permits are often available. This lets you drive a vehicle from the group for which you want the CDL for six months. Whenever you drive your CMV during this period you must have with you someone with a CDL license for the same or higher vehicle group. This person must sit beside you as you drive.

To get a permit, you must first pass a vision test. You must also pass the Knowledge Test for the type of CDL and endorsements you want.

The fee for instruction permits is often the same as for a first-time CDL or Renewal with Written Exam.

Time Limits

The CDL Tests are rarely timed tests. Check with your DMV to see if this is the case in your state.

It does take more than a few minutes to complete the tests, though. It's not a great idea to show up at a driver license station at 4:55 p.m., wanting to take the CDL tests. That only forces the DMV staff to work overtime. Not a good use of your tax dollars.

Keep the length of the testing sessions in mind when planning for Test Day. Will you need time off from work? A baby sitter? If so, arrange to have enough time so you don't feel rushed while taking the tests.

Other Necessary Documents

Don't forget, there are a few other tests you must take besides those for your CDL. You must get a DOT physical if your current medical card has expired. Many states require you to have this when you apply for your CDL.

Most applicants are expected to bring photo identification or driver's license and a Social Security card.

States may require you to have other documents, licenses, and certificates as well, such as vehicle registration or your old license. Check with your local DMV.

Special Services

Some states offer an oral Knowledge Test, instead of a written one. If you're interested in this option, be sure to ask about it ahead of time. You may need an appointment to take an oral rather than a written Knowledge Test.

TAKING THE TESTS

Once you're in your seat with your pencil (or wheel) in hand, preparation time is over. Now's the time for the proof. The best thing you can do is relax and stay focused on the tests. Here are just a few more tips that may come in handy.

The Knowledge Test

Read the instructions. If there are no instructions and you're unsure of how to proceed, ask the examiner.

Scan the entire test once. Answer immediately all the questions you're 100 percent certain about. Then go back and tackle the harder ones.

Sometimes you may find the answer to one question in another question. If you get stuck, look for other questions on the same subject. That may be just enough to jog your memory.

Once you've answered a question, don't change your answer. Your first impulse is probably correct. Change an answer only if you are positive your first answer was wrong.

If you change an answer, erase the old one cleanly. Mark the new answer clearly. Sometimes tests are scored by machines. Such machines can read even faint pencil marks. If it appears you selected two answer choices, you'll be marked wrong. This is true even if one of your choices was correct.

Be careful marking the answer form. Don't put the "right" answer in the "wrong" space. Just before you hand in the test, check and recheck your answers.

Don't leave any blanks. If you're not sure of an answer, use intelligent guessing to narrow your choices. When you absolutely don't know the answer, use wild guessing. There's still a slim chance you'll choose the right one. But a question left blank can only be marked wrong.

Relax, and let your thoughts come. When you feel yourself tensing up or getting tired, try these stress-relievers:

Neck rolls. Slowly, allow your head to droop forward, as if you were going to rest your chin on your chest. Then, just as slowly, raise your head back up. Slowly, tilt your head to the right, as if you could touch your right ear to your right shoulder. Raise your head back up. Slowly, drop your head back and look up at the ceiling. Bring your head back to the face-forward position. Last, tilt your head to the left. Repeat the whole series five times.

Next, keeping your neck straight, swivel just your head to the right and look along the line of your right shoulder. Swivel slowly back and to the left. Return to the face-forward position. Then repeat the movement, beginning at the left this time. Do this five times also.

Deep breathing. When people concentrate hard, they often hold their breath. That cuts off the supply of oxygen to the brain. Do that for too long and you'll become fatigued. You'll find it hard to think clearly.

Every now and then, make it a point to take a deep breath. Breathe in slowly and deeply through your nose. Breathe out just as slowly through your mouth.

Muscle relaxer. Some people hunch their shoulders when they're working hard. This is fatiguing. Here's how to break the tension. Take a deep breath. Shrug your shoulders up tight, as if you were trying to touch your ears with them. Hold that position for a count of five. Then release it all at once. Feel the tension flow out of your shoulders as you exhale.

If you've tensed up your whole body, you can do something similar. Take a deep breath. Try clenching and tensing all your muscles. Clench your jaw. Hunch up your shoulders. Squeeze the muscles in your buttocks, thighs, and calves. Curl up your toes.

Hold the tension for a few seconds, then release all the tension. Feel yourself relax as you breathe out.

Try any of these stress-relievers any time you feel tense, tired, or distracted.

Skills Test

Listen carefully to the instructions. Make sure you understand them. If you don't, ask the examiner for more details. Doing so will not cost you any points. Not understanding what you're being asked to do might.

If you get the chance, squeeze in some stress-relieving exercises between the Inspection, Range, and Road Test. And don't forget to breathe!

RETAKING THE TESTS

Although you likely will pass the CDL tests the first time, you may be wondering what happens if you don't.

You can't take the Skills Tests until you pass the Knowledge Test. Some states allow you to take other parts of the Skills Test even if you fail one part. Other states end the testing session if you fail one section.

Some states limit the number of retakes you can have. Most charge a fee for each retake. You should check with your local DMV to find out if this is the case in your state.

If you do fail a test the first time, don't give up. A few people, even well-prepared ones, do. Their nervousness about taking the test is so great it impairs their performance.

The same people find they pass the test easily on the second try. Taking the test the first time gave them the practice and familiarity with test-taking they needed to pass.

But hey, why worry about retaking the test? You're going to pass it the first time. We just know it.

Thank you for letting us help you prepare for the CDL tests. Please accept our best wishes for success.

Chapter 5 PASS Post-trip Answer And Self - Scoring Form

Test taken on: SCORE

Start Time:
End Time:

Time spent on test:

Instructions: Mark the date you took the PASS Post-trip at the top of this form. Note the time you started and finished the test. Calculate the time spent taking the test. Circle the letter of the answer you choose. Then, use the Answer Key to score your test. Mark your final score at the top.

Test Item	Answer Choices		Self - Scoring: Correct	Self - Scoring: Incorrect
1.	A	B	☐	☐
2.	A	B	☐	☐
3.	A	B	☐	☐
4.	A	B	☐	☐
5.	A	B	☐	☐
6.	A	B	☐	☐
7.	A	B	☐	☐
8.	A	B	☐	☐
9.	A	B	☐	☐
10.	A	B	☐	☐

Cut Here

Chapter 6 PASS Post-trip Answer And Self - Scoring Form

Test taken on:

SCORE

Start Time:
End Time:

Time spent on test:

Instructions: Mark the date you took the PASS Post-trip at the top of this form. Note the time you started and finished the test. Calculate the time spent taking the test. Circle the letter of the answer you choose. Then, use the Answer Key to score your test. Mark your final score at the top.

Test Item	Answer Choices				Self - Scoring Correct	Self - Scoring Incorrect
1.	A	B	C	D	☐	☐
2.	A	B	C	D	☐	☐
3.	A	B	C	D	☐	☐
4.	A	B	C	D	☐	☐
5.	A	B	C	D	☐	☐
6.	A	B	C	D	☐	☐
7.	A	B	C	D	☐	☐
8.	A	B	C	D	☐	☐
9.	A	B	C	D	☐	☐
10.	A	B	C	D	☐	☐

Cut Here

Chapter 7 PASS Post-trip Answer And Self - Scoring Form

Test taken on: SCORE

Start Time: Time spent on test:
End Time:

Instructions: Mark the date you took the PASS Post-trip at the top of this form. Note the time you started and finished the test. Calculate the time spent taking the test. Circle the letter of the answer you choose. Then, use the Answer Key to score your test. Mark your final score at the top.

Test Item	Answer Choices				Self - Scoring Correct	Self - Scoring Incorrect
1.	A	B	C	D	☐	☐
2.	A	B	C	D	☐	☐
3.	A	B	C	D	☐	☐
4.	A	B	C	D	☐	☐
5.	A	B	C	D	☐	☐
6.	A	B	C	D	☐	☐
7.	A	B	C	D	☐	☐
8.	A	B	C	D	☐	☐
9.	A	B	C	D	☐	☐
10.	A	B	C	D	☐	☐

Cut Here

Chapter 8 PASS Post-trip Answer And Self - Scoring Form

Test taken on:

SCORE

Start Time:
End Time:

Time spent on test:

Instructions: Mark the date you took the PASS Post-trip at the top of this form. Note the time you started and finished the test. Calculate the time spent taking the test. Circle the letter of the answer you choose. Then, use the Answer Key to score your test. Mark your final score at the top.

Test Item	Answer Choices				Self - Scoring Correct	Self - Scoring Incorrect
1.	A	B	C	D	☐	☐
2.	A	B	C	D	☐	☐
3.	A	B	C	D	☐	☐
4.	A	B	C	D	☐	☐
5.	A	B	C	D	☐	☐
6.	A	B	C	D	☐	☐
7.	A	B	C	D	☐	☐
8.	A	B	C	D	☐	☐
9.	A	B	C	D	☐	☐
10.	A	B	C	D	☐	☐

Cut Here

Chapter 9 PASS Post-trip Answer And Self - Scoring Form

Test taken on:

SCORE

Start Time:
End Time:

Time spent on test:

Instructions: Mark the date you took the PASS Post-trip at the top of this form. Note the time you started and finished the test. Calculate the time spent taking the test. Circle the letter of the answer you choose. Then, use the Answer Key to score your test. Mark your final score at the top.

Test Item	Answer Choices				Self - Scoring Correct	Self - Scoring Incorrect
1.	A	B	C	D	☐	☐
2.	A	B	C	D	☐	☐
3.	A	B	C	D	☐	☐
4.	A	B	C	D	☐	☐
5.	A	B	C	D	☐	☐
6.	A	B	C	D	☐	☐
7.	A	B	C	D	☐	☐
8.	A	B	C	D	☐	☐
9.	A	B	C	D	☐	☐
10.	A	B	C	D	☐	☐

Cut Here

Chapter 10 PASS Post-trip Answer And Self - Scoring Form

Test taken on:

SCORE

Start Time:
End Time:

Time spent on test:

Instructions: Mark the date you took the PASS Post-trip at the top of this form. Note the time you started and finished the test. Calculate the time spent taking the test. Circle the letter of the answer you choose. Then, use the Answer Key to score your test. Mark your final score at the top.

Test Item	Answer Choices				Self - Scoring Correct	Self - Scoring Incorrect
1.	A	B	C	D		
2.	A	B	C	D		
3.	A	B	C	D		
4.	A	B	C	D		
5.	A	B	C	D		
6.	A	B	C	D		
7.	A	B	C	D		
8.	A	B	C	D		
9.	A	B	C	D		
10.	A	B	C	D		

Cut Here

Chapter 11 PASS Post-trip Answer And Self - Scoring Form

Test taken on:

SCORE

Start Time:
End Time:

Time spent on test:

Instructions: Mark the date you took the PASS Post-trip at the top of this form. Note the time you started and finished the test. Calculate the time spent taking the test. Circle the letter of the answer you choose. Then, use the Answer Key to score your test. Mark your final score at the top.

Test Item	Answer Choices				Self - Scoring: Correct	Self - Scoring: Incorrect
1.	A	B	C	D	☐	☐
2.	A	B	C	D	☐	☐
3.	A	B	C	D	☐	☐
4.	A	B	C	D	☐	☐
5.	A	B	C	D	☐	☐
6.	A	B	C	D	☐	☐
7.	A	B	C	D	☐	☐
8.	A	B	C	D	☐	☐
9.	A	B	C	D	☐	☐
10.	A	B	C	D	☐	☐

Chapter 12 PASS Post-trip Answer And Self - Scoring Form

Test taken on: SCORE

Start Time: Time spent on test:
End Time:

Instructions: Mark the date you took the PASS Post-trip at the top of this form. Note the time you started and finished the test. Calculate the time spent taking the test. Circle the letter of the answer you choose. Then, use the Answer Key to score your test. Mark your final score at the top.

Test Item	Answer Choices				Self - Scoring Correct	Self - Scoring Incorrect
1.	A	B	C	D	☐	☐
2.	A	B	C	D	☐	☐
3.	A	B	C	D	☐	☐
4.	A	B	C	D	☐	☐
5.	A	B	C	D	☐	☐
6.	A	B	C	D	☐	☐
7.	A	B	C	D	☐	☐
8.	A	B	C	D	☐	☐
9.	A	B	C	D	☐	☐
10.	A	B	C	D	☐	☐

Chapter 13 PASS Post-trip Answer And Self - Scoring Form

Test taken on:

SCORE

Start Time:
End Time:

Time spent on test:

Instructions: Mark the date you took the PASS Post-trip at the top of this form. Note the time you started and finished the test. Calculate the time spent taking the test. Circle the letter of the answer you choose. Then, use the Answer Key to score your test. Mark your final score at the top.

Test Item	Answer Choices				Self - Scoring Correct	Self - Scoring Incorrect
1.	A	B	C	D	☐	☐
2.	A	B	C	D	☐	☐
3.	A	B	C	D	☐	☐
4.	A	B	C	D	☐	☐
5.	A	B	C	D	☐	☐
6.	A	B	C	D	☐	☐
7.	A	B	C	D	☐	☐
8.	A	B	C	D	☐	☐
9.	A	B	C	D	☐	☐
10.	A	B	C	D	☐	☐

Chapter 14 Review
Answer And Self - Scoring Form

Test taken on: SCORE

Start Time: End Time: Time spent on test:

Instructions: Mark the date you took the Review test at the top of this form. Note the time you started and finished the test. Calculate the time spent taking the test. Circle the letter of the answer you choose. Then, use the Answer Key to score your test. Mark your final score at the top.

Test Item

General Knowledge

Test Item	Answer Choices				Self - Scoring Correct	Incorrect
1.	A	B	C	D	☐	☐
2.	A	B	C	D	☐	☐
3.	A	B	C	D	☐	☐
4.	A	B	C	D	☐	☐
5.	A	B	C	D	☐	☐
6.	A	B	C	D	☐	☐
7.	A	B	C	D	☐	☐
8.	A	B	C	D	☐	☐
9.	A	B	C	D	☐	☐
10.	A	B	C	D	☐	☐
11.	A	B	C	D	☐	☐
12.	A	B	C	D	☐	☐
13.	A	B	C	D	☐	☐
14.	A	B	C	D	☐	☐
15.	A	B	C	D	☐	☐
16.	A	B	C	D	☐	☐
17.	A	B	C	D	☐	☐
18.	A	B	C	D	☐	☐
19.	A	B	C	D	☐	☐
20.	A	B	C	D	☐	☐

Cut Here

Chapter 14 Review
Answer And Self - Scoring Form

Cut Here

Test Item	Answer Choices				Self - Scoring: Correct	Self - Scoring: Incorrect
21. ______	A	B	C	D	☐	☐
22. ______	A	B	C	D	☐	☐
23. ______	A	B	C	D	☐	☐
24. ______	A	B	C	D	☐	☐
25. ______	A	B	C	D	☐	☐
26. ______	A	B	C	D	☐	☐
27. ______	A	B	C	D	☐	☐
28. ______	A	B	C	D	☐	☐
29. ______	A	B	C	D	☐	☐
30. ______	A	B	C	D	☐	☐
31. ______	A	B	C	D	☐	☐
32. ______	A	B	C	D	☐	☐
33. ______	A	B	C	D	☐	☐
34. ______	A	B	C	D	☐	☐
35. ______	A	B	C	D	☐	☐
36. ______	A	B	C	D	☐	☐
37. ______	A	B	C	D	☐	☐
38. ______	A	B	C	D	☐	☐
39. ______	A	B	C	D	☐	☐
40. ______	A	B	C	D	☐	☐

Chapter 14 Review Answer And Self - Scoring Form

Test Item	Answer Choices				Self - Scoring Correct	Incorrect
41.	A	B	C	D	☐	☐
42.	A	B	C	D	☐	☐
43.	A	B	C	D	☐	☐
44.	A	B	C	D	☐	☐
45.	A	B	C	D	☐	☐
46.	A	B	C	D	☐	☐
47.	A	B	C	D	☐	☐
48.	A	B	C	D	☐	☐
49.	A	B	C	D	☐	☐
50.	A	B	C	D	☐	☐
51.	A	B	C	D	☐	☐
52.	A	B	C	D	☐	☐
53.	A	B	C	D	☐	☐
54.	A	B	C	D	☐	☐
55.	A	B	C	D	☐	☐
56.	A	B	C	D	☐	☐
57.	A	B	C	D	☐	☐
58.	A	B	C	D	☐	☐
59.	A	B	C	D	☐	☐
60.	A	B	C	D	☐	☐

Cut Here

Chapter 14 Review
Answer And Self - Scoring Form

Cut Here

Test Item	Answer Choices				Self - Scoring	
					Correct	Incorrect
61. ______	A	B	C	D	☐	☐
62. ______	A	B	C	D	☐	☐
63. ______	A	B	C	D	☐	☐
64. ______	A	B	C	D	☐	☐
65. ______	A	B	C	D	☐	☐
66. ______	A	B	C	D	☐	☐
67. ______	A	B	C	D	☐	☐
68. ______	A	B	C	D	☐	☐
69. ______	A	B	C	D	☐	☐
70. ______	A	B	C	D	☐	☐
71. ______	A	B	C	D	☐	☐
72. ______	A	B	C	D	☐	☐
73. ______	A	B	C	D	☐	☐
74. ______	A	B	C	D	☐	☐
75. ______	A	B	C	D	☐	☐
76. ______	A	B	C	D	☐	☐
77. ______	A	B	C	D	☐	☐
78. ______	A	B	C	D	☐	☐
79. ______	A	B	C	D	☐	☐
80. ______	A	B	C	D	☐	☐

Chapter 14 Review
Answer And Self - Scoring Form

Test Item	Answer Choices				Self - Scoring Correct	Self - Scoring Incorrect
81. ______	A	B	C	D	☐	☐
82. ______	A	B	C	D	☐	☐
83. ______	A	B	C	D	☐	☐
84. ______	A	B	C	D	☐	☐
85. ______	A	B	C	D	☐	☐
86. ______	A	B	C	D	☐	☐
87. ______	A	B	C	D	☐	☐
88. ______	A	B	C	D	☐	☐
89. ______	A	B	C	D	☐	☐
90. ______	A	B	C	D	☐	☐
91. ______	A	B	C	D	☐	☐
92. ______	A	B	C	D	☐	☐
93. ______	A	B	C	D	☐	☐
94. ______	A	B	C	D	☐	☐
95. ______	A	B	C	D	☐	☐
96. ______	A	B	C	D	☐	☐
97. ______	A	B	C	D	☐	☐
98. ______	A	B	C	D	☐	☐
99. ______	A	B	C	D	☐	☐
100. ______	A	B	C	D	☐	☐

Cut Here

Chapter 14 Review
Answer And Self - Scoring Form

Test Item	Answer Choices				Self - Scoring Correct	Self - Scoring Incorrect
101.	A	B	C	D	☐	☐
102.	A	B	C	D	☐	☐
103.	A	B	C	D	☐	☐
104.	A	B	C	D	☐	☐
105.	A	B	C	D	☐	☐
106.	A	B	C	D	☐	☐
107.	A	B	C	D	☐	☐
108.	A	B	C	D	☐	☐
Air Brakes						
1.	A	B	C	D	☐	☐
2.	A	B	C	D	☐	☐
3.	A	B	C	D	☐	☐
4.	A	B	C	D	☐	☐
5.	A	B	C	D	☐	☐
6.	A	B	C	D	☐	☐
7.	A	B	C	D	☐	☐
8.	A	B	C	D	☐	☐
9.	A	B	C	D	☐	☐
10.	A	B	C	D	☐	☐

Cut Here

Chapter 14 Review
Answer And Self - Scoring Form

Test Item	Answer Choices				Self - Scoring Correct	Self - Scoring Incorrect
11.	A	B	C	D	☐	☐
12.	A	B	C	D	☐	☐
13.	A	B	C	D	☐	☐
14.	A	B	C	D	☐	☐
15.	A	B	C	D	☐	☐
16.	A	B	C	D	☐	☐
17.	A	B	C	D	☐	☐
18.	A	B	C	D	☐	☐
19.	A	B	C	D	☐	☐
20.	A	B	C	D	☐	☐
21.	A	B	C	D	☐	☐
22.	A	B	C	D	☐	☐
23.	A	B	C	D	☐	☐
24.	A	B	C	D	☐	☐
25.	A	B	C	D	☐	☐
26.	A	B	C	D	☐	☐
27.	A	B	C	D	☐	☐
28.	A	B	C	D	☐	☐
29.	A	B	C	D	☐	☐
30.	A	B	C	D	☐	☐

Cut Here

Chapter 14 Review
Answer And Self - Scoring Form

Cut Here

Test Item Tractor-Trailer/ Bus Questions	Answer Choices				Self - Scoring Correct	Incorrect
1. ____	A	B	C	D	☐	☐
2. ____	A	B	C	D	☐	☐
3. ____	A	B	C	D	☐	☐
4. ____	A	B	C	D	☐	☐
5. ____	A	B	C	D	☐	☐
6. ____	A	B	C	D	☐	☐
7. ____	A	B	C	D	☐	☐
8. ____	A	B	C	D	☐	☐
9. ____	A	B	C	D	☐	☐
10. ____	A	B	C	D	☐	☐
11. ____	A	B	C	D	☐	☐
12. ____	A	B	C	D	☐	☐
13. ____	A	B	C	D	☐	☐
14. ____	A	B	C	D	☐	☐
15. ____	A	B	C	D	☐	☐
16. ____	A	B	C	D	☐	☐
17. ____	A	B	C	D	☐	☐
18. ____	A	B	C	D	☐	☐
19. ____	A	B	C	D	☐	☐
20. ____	A	B	C	D	☐	☐

Chapter 14 Review Answer And Self - Scoring Form

Test Item	Answer Choices				Self - Scoring Correct	Self - Scoring Incorrect
21.	A	B	C	D	☐	☐
22.	A	B	C	D	☐	☐
23.	A	B	C	D	☐	☐
24.	A	B	C	D	☐	☐
25.	A	B	C	D	☐	☐
Transporting Passengers Questions						
1.	A	B	C	D	☐	☐
2.	A	B	C	D	☐	☐
3.	A	B	C	D	☐	☐
4.	A	B	C	D	☐	☐
5.	A	B	C	D	☐	☐
6.	A	B	C	D	☐	☐
7.	A	B	C	D	☐	☐
8.	A	B	C	D	☐	☐
9.	A	B	C	D	☐	☐
10.	A	B	C	D	☐	☐

Cut Here

Chapter 14 Review
Answer And Self - Scoring Form

Test Item	Answer Choices				Self - Scoring Correct	Self - Scoring Incorrect
11. ______	A	B	C	D	☐	☐
12. ______	A	B	C	D	☐	☐
13. ______	A	B	C	D	☐	☐
14. ______	A	B	C	D	☐	☐
15. ______	A	B	C	D	☐	☐
16. ______	A	B	C	D	☐	☐
17. ______	A	B	C	D	☐	☐
18. ______	A	B	C	D	☐	☐
19. ______	A	B	C	D	☐	☐
20. ______	A	B	C	D	☐	☐

Cut Here

APPENDIX A
Answer Keys

CHAPTER 5

Pre-trip
1. B **2.** B **3.** B

Post-trip
1. B (Page 50)
2. B (Page 59)
3. B (Page 54, 61)
4. B (Page 55)
5. B (Page 50)
6. B (Page 61)
7. B (Page 60)
8. B (Page 61)
9. B (Page 66)
10. B (Page 61)

CHAPTER 6

Pre-trip
1. B **2.** A **3.** B

Post-trip
1. B (Page 70)
2. A (Page 70)
3. B (Page 70)
4. B (Page 107)
5. C (Page 112)
6. A (Page 114)
7. B (Page 118)
8. C (Page 105)
9. A (Page 96)
10. B (Page 105)

CHAPTER 7

Pre-trip
1. B **2.** B **3.** A

Post-trip
1. A (Page 153)
2. B (Page 150)
3. D (Page 174)
4. B (Page 153)
5. C (Page 153)
6. C (Page 155)
7. D (Page 152)
8. B (Page 159)
9. C (Page 161)
10. B (Page 166)

CHAPTER 8

Pre-trip
1. A **2.** B **3.** A

Post-trip
1. A (Page 181)
2. C (Page 185)
3. A (Page 189)
4. C (Page 190)
5. D (Page 192)
6. A (Page 193)
7. D (Page 197)
8. A (Page 159)
9. B (Page 202)
10. A (Page 209)

CHAPTER 9

Pre-trip
1. B **2.** B **3.** B

Post-trip
1. C (Page 213)
2. D (Page 215)
3. B (Page 227)
4. D (Page 215)
5. B (Page 215)
6. A (Page 215)
7. B (Page 216)
8. B (Page 218)
9. D (Page 214)
10. C (Page 223)

CHAPTER 10

Pre-trip
1. A **2.** A **3.** B

Post-trip
1. A (Page 230)
2. D (Page 233)
3. B (Page 234)
4. D (Page 234)
5. D (Page 234)
6. B (Page 235)
7. B (Page 236)
8. B (Page 236)
9. A (Page 237)
10. A (Page 238)

CHAPTER 11

Pre-trip

1. B **2.** B **3.** B

Post-trip

1. B (Page 254)
2. C (Page 255)
3. B (Page 258)
4. C (Page 261)
5. D (Page 261)
6. C (Page 264)
7. B (Page 264)
8. C (Page 270)
9. C (Page 282)
10. A (Page 282)

CHAPTER 12

Pre-trip

1. B **2.** A **3.** A

Post-trip

1. C (Page 286)
2. C (Page 289)
3. A (Page 286)
4. C (Page 288)
5. B (Page 299)
6. A (Page 288)
7. D (Page 286, 290)
8. A (Page 299)
9. A (Page 297)
10. C (Page 299)

CHAPTER 13

Pre-trip

1. B **2.** A **3.** B

Post-trip

1. C (Page 307)
2. D (Page 307)
3. B (Page 311)
4. B (Page 308)
5. D (Page 308)
6. B (Page 311)
7. C (Page 312)
8. A (Page 312)
9. B (Page 313)
10. B (Page 313)

CHAPTER 14 REVIEW

General Knowledge Questions

1. A (Chapter 5) (Page 52)
2. D (Chapter 5) (Page 57)
3. A (Chapter 5) (Page 57)
4. B (Chapter 5) (Page 57)
5. B (Chapter 5) (Page 60)
6. A (Chapter 5) (Page 55)
7. D (Chapter 5) (Page 55)
8. B (Chapter 5) (Page 56)
9. C (Chapter 5) (Page 56)
10. B (Chapter 5) (Page 54)
11. C (Chapter 5) (Page 56)
12. B (Chapter 5) (Page 57)
13. B (Chapter 5) (Page 59)
14. C (Chapter 6) (Page 70)
15. C (Chapter 6) (Page 76)
16. B (Chapter 6) (Page 71)
17. D (Chapter 6) (Page 73)
18. D (Chapter 6) (Page 74)
19. A (Chapter 6) (Page 74)
20. B (Chapter 6) (Page 76)
21. C (Chapter 6) (Page 79)
22. B (Chapter 6) (Page 80)
23. D (Chapter 6) (Page 97)
24. A (Chapter 6) (Page 98)
25. B (Chapter 6) (Page 103)
26. B (Chapter 6) (Page 112)
27. A (Chapter 6) (Page 113)
28. D (Chapter 6) (Page 113)
29. B (Chapter 6) (Page 116)
30. A (Chapter 7) (Page 121)
31. A (Chapter 7) (Page 121)
32. A (Chapter 7) (Page 150)
33. C (Chapter 7) (Page 154)
34. D (Chapter 7) (Page 153)
35. A (Chapter 7) (Page 153)
36. C (Chapter 7) (Page 159)
37. D (Chapter 7) (Page 161)
38. B (Chapter 7) (Page 161)
39. D (Chapter 7) (Page 162)
40. B (Chapter 7) (Page 173)
41. A (Chapter 7) (Page 174)
42. D (Chapter 8) (Page 181)
43. A (Chapter 8) (Page 181)
44. D (Chapter 8) (Page 183)
45. B (Chapter 8) (Page 184)
46. D (Chapter 8) (Page 186)
47. B (Chapter 8) (Page 186)
48. C (Chapter 8) (Page 187)

49. B (Chapter 8) (Page 188)
50. B (Chapter 8) (Page 192)
51. D (Chapter 8) (Page 195)
52. C (Chapter 8) (Page 195)
53. C (Chapter 8) (Page 198)
54. B (Chapter 8) (Page 199)
55. C (Chapter 8) (Page 200)
56. D (Chapter 8) (Page 200)
57. C (Chapter 8) (Page 202)
58. D (Chapter 8) (Page 202)
59. B (Chapter 8) (Page 204)
60. A (Chapter 8) (Page 205)
61. C (Chapter 8) (Page 207)
62. C (Chapter 8) (Page 207)
63. A (Chapter 8) (Page 209)
64. A (Chapter 8) (Page 210)
65. A (Chapter 8) (Page 209)
66. D (Chapter 9) (Page 219)
67. D (Chapter 9) (Page 213)
68. C (Chapter 9) (Page 214)
69. D (Chapter 9) (Page 215)
70. A (Chapter 9) (Page 215)
71. A (Chapter 9) (Page 215)
72. D (Chapter 9) (Page 216)
73. D (Chapter 9) (Page 216)
74. B (Chapter 9) (Page 218)
75. C (Chapter 9) (Page 218)
76. B (Chapter 9) (Page 219)
77. A (Chapter 9) (Page 221)
78. B (Chapter 9) (Page 222)
79. B (Chapter 9) (Page 222)
80. D (Chapter 9) (Page 222)
81. D (Chapter 9) (Page 223)
82. C (Chapter 9) (Page 224)
83. D (Chapter 10) (Page 229)
84. B (Chapter 10) (Page 229)
85. A (Chapter 10) (Page 230)
86. C (Chapter 10) (Page 230)
87. B (Chapter 10) (Page 234)
88. D (Chapter 10) (Page 234)
89. C (Chapter 10) (Page 235)
90. C (Chapter 10) (Page 237)
91. D (Chapter 10) (Page 237)
92. B (Chapter 10) (Page 238)
93. D (Chapter 10) (Page 240)
94. B (Chapter 10) (Page 240)
95. D (Chapter 10) (Page 244)
96. A (Chapter 10) (Page 246)
97. B (Chapter 10) (Page 246)
98. A (Chapter 10) (Page 251)
99. D (Chapter 10) (Page 246)
100. B (Chapter 10) (Page 251)
101. B (Chapter 7) (Page 154)
102. A (Chapter 7) (Page 154)
103. C (Chapter 7) (Page 153)
104. D (Chapter 7) (Page 153)
105. C (Chapter 9) (Page 215)
106. D (Chapter 9) (Page 215)
107. B (Chapter 9) (Page 215)
108. A (Chapter 9) (Page 215)

Air Brake Questions

1. D (Chapter 11) (Page 254)
2. D (Chapter 11) (Page 255)
3. C (Chapter 11) (Page 258)
4. D (Chapter 11) (Page 261)
5. D (Chapter 11) (Page 261)
6. C (Chapter 11) (Page 261)
7. B (Chapter 11) (Page 263)
8. B (Chapter 11) (Page 263)
9. C (Chapter 11) (Page 263)
10. C (Chapter 11) (Page 264)
11. B (Chapter 11) (Page 264)
12. D (Chapter 11) (Page 265)
13. C (Chapter 11) (Page 265)
14. A (Chapter 11) (Page 266)
15. D (Chapter 11) (Page 268)
16. C (Chapter 11) (Page 268)
17. A (Chapter 11) (Page 268)
18. B (Chapter 11) (Page 269)
19. C (Chapter 11) (Page 269)
20. C (Chapter 11) (Page 269)
21. D (Chapter 11) (Page 270)
22. C (Chapter 11) (Page 270)
23. D (Chapter 11) (Page 270)
24. D (Chapter 11) (Page 270)
25. D (Chapter 11) (Page 271)
26. A (Chapter 11) (Page 272)
27. B (Chapter 11) (Page 272)
28. C (Chapter 11) (Page 272)
29. A (Chapter 11) (Page 272)
30. B (Chapter 11) (Page 272)

Transporting Passengers Questions

1. C (Chapter 13) (Page 306)
2. B (Chapter 13) (Page 306)
3. B (Chapter 13) (Page 306)
4. A (Chapter 13) (Page 307)
5. D (Chapter 13) (Page 308)
6. A (Chapter 13) (Page 308)
7. B (Chapter 13) (Page 308)
8. A (Chapter 13) (Page 308)
9. A (Chapter 13) (Page 308)
10. A (Chapter 13) (Page 310)
11. C (Chapter 13) (Page 310)
12. C (Chapter 13) (Page 311)
13. A (Chapter 13) (Page 312)
14. A (Chapter 13) (Page 312)
15. D (Chapter 13) (Page 313)
16. C (Chapter 13) (Page 313)
17. B (Chapter 13) (Page 313)
18. A (Chapter 13) (Page 312)
19. A (Chapter 13) (Page 313)
20. D (Chapter 13) (Page 313)

Tractor-trailer Bus Questions

1. B (Chapter 12) (Page 285)
2. B (Chapter 12) (Page 286)
3. D (Chapter 12) (Page 286)
4. D (Chapter 12) (Page 288)
5. B (Chapter 12) (Page 287)
6. B (Chapter 12) (Page 286)
7. D (Chapter 12) (Page 288)
8. D (Chapter 12) (Page 288)
9. A (Chapter 12) (Page 289)
10. C (Chapter 12) (Page 299)
11. B (Chapter 12) (Page 298)
12. A (Chapter 12) (Page 286)
13. D (Chapter 12) (Page 286)
14. B (Chapter 12) (Page 289)
15. D (Chapter 12) (Page 290)
16. B (Chapter 12) (Page 290)
17. D (Chapter 12) (Page 290)
18. D (Chapter 12) (Page 297)
19. D (Chapter 12) (Page 298)
20. B (Chapter 12) (Page 299)
21. B (Chapter 12) (Page 299)
22. D (Chapter 12) (Pages 290, 299)
23. C (Chapter 12) (Page 285)
24. A (Chapter 12) (Page 287)
25. D (Chapter 12) (Page 297)

APPENDIX B

Motor Vehicle Office Addresses

Alabama Department of Public Safety
Montgomery, AL 36130

Alaska Division of Motor Vehicles
Juneau, AK 99802

Arizona Motor Vehicle Division
Phoenix, AZ 85007

Arkansas Office of Driver Services
Little Rock, AR 72203

California Department of Motor Vehicles
Sacramento, CA 95818

Colorado Motor Vehicle Division
Denver, CO 80204

Connecticut Department of Motor Vehicles
Wethersfield, CT 06109

Delaware Division of Motor Vehicles
Dover, DE 19903

District of Columbia
Bureau of Motor Vehicle Services
Washington, DC 20001

Florida Division of Driver Licenses
Neil Kirkman Building
Tallahassee, FL 32399-0575

Georgia State Patrol
Atlanta, GA 30316

Hawaii Motor Vehicle Safety Office
Honolulu, HI 96813

Idaho Motor Vehicle Bureau
Boise, ID 83731-0034

Illinois Driver Services Department
Springfield, IL 62723

Indiana Bureau of Motor Vehicles
Indianapolis, IN 46204

Iowa Office of Driver Services
Des Moines, IA 50319

Kansas Division of Vehicles
Topeka, KS 66626

Kentucky Department of Vehicle Regulation
Frankfort, KY 40622

Louisiana Office of Motor Vehicles
Baton Rouge, LA 70806

Maine Motor Vehicle Division
Augusta, ME 04333

Maryland Motor Vehicle Administration
Glen Burnie, MD 21062

Massachusetts Registry of Motor Vehicles
Boston, MA 02114

Michigan Department of State
Lansing, MI 48918

Minnesota Driver and Vehicle Service Division
St. Paul, MN 55155

Mississippi Highway Safety Patrol
Jackson, MS 39216

Missouri Division of Motor Vehicle and
Drivers Licensing
Jefferson City, MO 65105

Montana Motor Vehicle Division
Helena, MT 59620

Nebraska Department of Motor Vehicles
Lincoln, NE 68509

Nevada Department of Motor Vehicles
Carson City, NV 89711

New Hampshire Division of Motor Vehicles
Concord, NH 03305

New Jersey Division of Motor Vehicles
Trenton, NJ 08666

New Mexico Motor Vehicle Division
Santa Fe, NM 85703

New York Department of Motor Vehicles
Albany, NY 12228

North Carolina Division of Motor Vehicles
Raleigh, NC 27697

North Dakota Drivers License Division
Bismarck, ND 58505

Ohio Bureau of Motor Vehicles
Columbus, OH 43233

Oklahoma Department of Public Safety
Oklahoma City, OK 73136

Oregon Motor Vehicles Division
Salem, OR 97314

Pennsylvania Department of Transportation
Harrisburg, PA 17120

Rhode Island Division of Motor Vehicles
Providence, RI 02903

South Carolina Motor Vehicle Division
Columbia, SC 29216

South Dakota Division of Motor Vehicles
Pierre, SD 57501-2080

Tennessee Department of Safety
Nashville, TN 37219

Texas Department of Public Safety
Austin, TX 78752

Utah Driver License Division
Salt Lake City, UT 84119

Vermont Department of Motor Vehicles
Montpelier, VT 05603-0001

Virginia Department of Motor Vehicles
Richmond, VA 23269

Washington Department of Licensing
Olympia, WA 98504

West Virginia Department of Motor Vehicles
Charleston, WV 25317

Wisconsin Division of Motor Vehicles
Madison, WI 53702

Wyoming Field Services Division
Cheyenne, WY 82002

APPENDIX C

Motor Transport Associations

Alabama
Alabama Trucking Association
660 Adams Avenue
Montgomery, AL 36104
(205) 834-3983

Alaska
Alaska Trucking Association
3443 Minnesota Drive
Anchorage, AK 99503
(907) 276-1149

Arizona
Arizona Motor Transport Association
2111 W. McDowell Road
Phoenix, AZ 85009
(602) 252-7559

Arkansas
Arkansas Motor Carriers Association
P.O. Box 2798
Little Rock, AR 72203
(501) 372-3462

California
California Trucking Association
1251 Beacon Boulevard
West Sacramento, CA 95691
(916) 373-3500

Colorado
Colorado Motor Carriers Association
4060 Elati Street
Denver, CO 80216
(303) 433-3375

Connecticut
Motor Transport Association of Connecticut
60 Forest Street
Hartford, CT 06105
(203) 520-4455

Delaware
Delaware Motor Transport Association
1201 College Park Drive, Suite 102
P.O. Box 343 (Zip 19903)
Dover, DE 19901
(302) 678-5306

Florida
Florida Trucking Association
350 E. College Avenue
Tallahassee, FL 32301
(904) 222-9900

Georgia
Georgia Motor Trucking Association
500 Piedmont Avenue, N.E.
Atlanta, GA 30308
(404) 876-4313

Hawaii
Hawaii Transportation Association
2850 Paa Street, Suite 244
P.O. Box 30166
Honolulu, HI 96820
(808) 833-6628

Idaho
Idaho Motor Transport Association
P.O. Box 550
Boise, ID 83701
(208) 342-3521

Illinois
Illinois Trucking Associations
2000 Fifth Avenue
River Grove, IL 60171
(312) 452-3500

Indiana
Indiana Motor Truck Association
1 North Capitol Ave, Suite 460
Indianapolis, IN 46204
(317) 630-4682

Iowa
Iowa Motor Truck Association
700 Second Avenue
Des Moines, IA 50309
(515) 244-5193

Kansas
Kansas Motor Carriers Association
2900 S. Topeka Boulevard
P.O. Box 1673
Topeka, KS 66601
(913) 267-1641

Kentucky
Kentucky Motor Transport Association
134 Walnut Street
Frankfort, KY 40601
(502) 695-4055

Louisiana
Louisiana Motor Transport Association
4838 Bennington Avenue
P.O. Box 80278
Baton Rouge, LA 70898
(504) 928-5682

Maine
Maine Motor Transport Association
524 Western Avenue
P.O. Box 857
Augusta, ME 04330
(207) 623-4128

Maryland
Maryland Motor Truck Association
3000 Washington Boulevard
Baltimore, MD 21230
(301) 644-4600

Massachusetts
Massachusetts Motor Transportation Association
14 New England Executive Park
Burlington, MA 01803
(617) 270-6880

Michigan
Michigan Trucking Association
5800 Executive Drive
Lansing, MI 48910
(517) 939-2053

Minnesota
Minnesota Trucking Association
Griggs-Midway Building, Room 134N
1821 University Avenue
St. Paul, MN 55104-2994
(612) 646-7351

Mississippi
Mississippi Trucking Association
767 N. President Street
Jackson, MS 39202
(601) 354-0616

Missouri
Missouri Motor Carriers Association
201 E. Capitol Avenue
Jefferson City, MO 65102
(314) 634-3388

Montana
Montana Motor Carriers Association
P.O. Box 1714
Helena, MT 59624-1714
(406) 442-6600

Nebraska
Nebraska Motor Carriers Association
1701 K. Street
Lincoln, NE 68508
(402) 276-8504

Nevada
Nevada Motor Transport Association
P.O. Box 7320
Reno, NV 89510
(702) 331-6684

New Hampshire
New Hampshire Motor Transport Association
4 Park Street
Concord, NH 03301
(603) 224-7337

New Jersey
New Jersey Motor Truck Association
160 Tices Lane
East Brunswick, NJ 08816
(201) 254-5000

New Mexico
New Mexico Motor Carriers Association
4809 Jefferson N.E.
Albuquerque, NM 87113
(505) 884-5575

New York
New York State Motor Truck Association
1234 Western Avenue
Albany, NY 12203
(518) 438-8184

North Carolina
North Carolina Trucking Association
219 W. Martin Street
Raleigh, NC 27602
(919) 834-0387

North Dakota
North Dakota Motor Carriers Association
1031 E. Interstate Avenue
Bismarck, ND 58502
(701) 223-2700

Ohio
Ohio Trucking Association
50 W. Broad Street, Suite 1111
Columbus, OH 43215
(614) 221-5375

Oklahoma
Associated Motor Carriers of Oklahoma
P.O. Box 14607
Oklahoma City, OK 73113
(405) 843-9488

Oregon
Oregon Trucking Associations
5940 N. Basin Avenue
Portland, OR 97217
(503) 289-6888

Pennsylvania
Pennsylvania Motor Truck Association
P.O. Box 128
Camp Hill, PA 17001-0128
(717) 761-7122

Rhode Island
Rhode Island Truck Owners Association
1240 Pawtucket Avenue
Rumford, RI 02916
(401) 438-0410

South Carolina
South Carolina Trucking Association
P.O. Box 50166
Columbia, SC 29250
(803) 799-4306

South Dakota
South Dakota Trucking Association
P.O. Box 89008
Sioux Falls, SD 57105
(605) 334-8871

Tennessee
Tennessee Trucking Association
212 Capitol Boulevard
Nashville, TN 37219
(615) 255-0558

Texas
Texas Motor Transportation Association
P.O. Box 1669
Austin, TX 78767
(512) 478-2541

Utah
Utah Motor Transport Association
1615 West 2200 South, Suite B
Salt Lake City, UT 84119
(801) 973-9370

Vermont
Vermont Truck & Bus Association
P.O. Box 271
Barre, VT 05641
(802) 479-1778

Virginia
Virginia Trucking Association
104 W. Franklin Street
Lexington Tower, Suite 5
Richmond, VA 23220
(804) 649-9311

Washington D.C.
Washington D.C. Area Trucking Association
2200 Mill Road
Alexandria, VA 22314
(703) 838-1885

Washington
Washington Trucking Associations
P.O. Box 81086
Seattle, WA 98108
(206) 682-0250

West Virginia
West Virginia Motor Truck Association
P.O. Box 5187, Capitol Station
Charleston, WV 25311
(304) 345-2800

Wisconsin
Wisconsin Motor Carriers Association
125 West Doty Street
Madison, WI 53703
(608) 255-6789

Wyoming
Wyoming Trucking Association
555 N. Poplar Street
P.O. Box 1909
Casper, WY 82602
(307) 234-1579

Regional
Eastern Central Motor Carriers Association
P.O. Box 4540
Akron, OH 44310
(216) 929-2901

National
American Trucking Associations
2200 Mill Road
Alexandria, VA 22314
(800) ATA-LINE
(703) 838-1880

American Bus Association
1015 15th Street, N.W., Suite 250
Washington, DC 20005

United Bus Drivers of America
1300 L Street N.W., Suite 1050
Washington, DC 20005
(800) 424-UBOA

APPENDIX D

Transportation Agencies

Office of Motor Carrier Standards
Washington, D.C. 20590

Regional Offices of Motor Carrier and Highway Safety of the Federal Highway Administration

Region	**Including:**	**Address:**
Region 1	Connecticut, Maine, Massachusetts, New Jersey, New Hampshire, New York, Rhode Island, Vermont, Puerto Rico, and the Virgin Islands. Also, the part of Canada east of Highways 19 and 8 from Port Burwell to Goderich, then a straight line running north through Tobermory and Sudbury, and then due north to the Canadian border	Leo W. O'Brien Federal Office Building Room 719 Albany, NY 12207-2334
Region 2	Delaware, District of Columbia, Maryland, Pennsylvania, Virginia, and West Virginia	31 Hopkins Plaza Federal Building Room 1615 Baltimore, MD 21201-2819
Region 3	Alabama, Florida, Georgia, Kentucky, Mississippi, North Carolina, South Carolina, and Tennessee	1720 Peachtree Road., NW Suite 210 Atlanta, GA 30367-2349
Region 4	Illinois, Indiana, Michigan, Minnesota, Ohio, and Wisconsin. Also, Canada west of Highways 19 and 8 from Port Burwell to Goderich, then a straight line running north through Tobermory and Sudbury, and then due north to the Canadian border, and east of the boundary between the provinces of Ontario and Manitoba to Hudson Bay and then a straight line north to the Canadian border	18209 Dixie Highway Homewood, IL 60430-2294
Region 6	Arkansas, Louisiana, New Mexico, Oklahoma, and Texas. All of Mexico, except the States of Baja California and Sonora and the Territory of Baja California Sur, Mexico. Also, all nations south of Mexico	Room 8A00 Federal Building 819 Taylor Street Ft. Worth, TX 76102-6115
Region 7	Iowa, Kansas, Missouri, and Nebraska	6301 Rockhill Rd. P.O. Box 419715 Kansas City, MO 64141-6715

Region 8	Colorado, Montana, North Dakota, South Dakota, Utah, and Wyoming. Also, Canada west of the boundary between the Provinces of Ontario and Manitoba to Hudson Bay and then a straight line due north to the Canadian border, and east of Highway 95 from Kingsgate to Blaeberry and then a straight line north to the Canadian border	555 Zang Street Room 400 Lakewood, CO 80228-1014
Region 9	Arizona, California, Hawaii, Nevada, Guam, American Samoa, and Mariana Islands. The States of Baja California and Sonora, Mexico, and the Territory of Baja California Sur, Mexico	211 Main Street Room 1108 San Francisco, CA 94150-1926
Region 10	Alaska, Idaho, Oregon, and Washington. Also, Canada west of Highway 95 Kingsgate to Blaeberry and then a straight line due north to the Canadian border and all the Province of British Columbia	Mohawk Building Room 312 708 SW Third Ave. Portland, OR 97204-2491

Glossary

Definitions and explanations of terms used in your text and in the industry.

A

AC. Alcohol concentration.
Agent. A person authorized to transact business for and in the name of another. For instance, a driver becomes an agent of the trucking company when signing for freight.
Air bag suspension. Trailer suspension system using air bags for a greater cushion than conventional leaf spring.
Air brakes. Brakes that use compressed air instead of fluid.
Air compressor. Builds up and maintains required air pressure in the brake system reservoir.
Air line. Carries compressed air from one part of the air brake system to another, and from tractor to trailer.
Air reservoir. Storage tank for compressed air.
Alcohol concentration (AC). A measure of how much alcohol is in a person's blood or breath. You may also see the term "blood alcohol concentration (BAC)" used.
Alcohol (or alcoholic beverage). Beer, wine, and distilled spirits (liquor).
Alternator. Produces electricity for the battery and electric power to operate lights, radio, and other items when the engine is running.
Ammeter. Measures the amount of current flowing in an electrical current.
Amphetamines. "Bennies," "speed," or "pep pills." Stimulant drugs.
Application pressure air gauge. Indicates pressure being applied by brakes during brake operation.
Articulated. Refers to the ability to move or bend, as a tractor-trailer articulates when it turns.
Axle. The bar that connects opposite wheels.
Axle temperature gauge. Indicates temperature of lubricant in an axle.
Axle weight. How much weight the axle (or set of axles) transmits to the ground.

B

Battery. Converts chemical energy into electricity.
Bias. A type of tire with diagonal body plies and narrow plies under the tread going in the same direction.
Blasting agents. Material designed for blasting. Not likely to explode by accident.
Blocking. Supports that keep cargo from shifting during transport.
Brake drum. The rotating unit of the brake that is attached to the wheel.
Brake lining. Material attached to the brake shoe that creates friction.
Brake shoe. Non-rotating part of the brake that contacts the brake lining and supplies braking force.
Braking distance. Perception time plus reaction time plus brake lag.
Bridge formula. Determines how much weight is put on any point by any group of axles.
Bridge law. Regulates how much weight can be put on a bridge at any one point.
Bus. Any motor vehicle designed, constructed, and/or used to transport passengers, including taxicabs. (Note: Although taxicabs are "buses," they are not usually subject to CDL regulations because of their weight and seat rating.)

C

Cab. Part of the vehicle where the driver sits.
Cabover. Vehicle with most of its engine under the cab.
Cargo. Freight.
Cargo tank. Any bulk liquid or compressed gas packaging. Cargo tanks can be portable or permanently attached to any motor vehicle. They can be loaded or unloaded without being removed from the motor vehicle. Packaging built to specifications for cylinders is not cargo tanks.
Carrier. A person who transports passengers or property by land or water as a

common, contract, or private carrier, or by civil aircraft.
CDL. Commercial Driver's License.
Centrifugal force. The natural force that pulls objects in motion outward from the center of rotation.
Check valve. Seals off one part of the air brake system from another.
Chock. A block placed in front of a tire to keep the vehicle from moving.
Circuit. A closed electrical path.
Circuit breaker. Breaks and opens an electrical circuit in an overload.
Class A Explosives. The most hazardous explosives.
Class B Explosives. Explosives that are dangerous because they burn rapidly rather than explode.
Class C Explosives. The least dangerous explosives.
Combination vehicle. One that articulates. It has joined sections that can move independently of each other.
Combustible. Able to ignite and burn.
Combustible liquid. A liquid with a flash point at or above 100 degrees and below 200 degrees Fahrenheit.
Commerce. Trade, traffic, or transportation in the United States (or any area controlled by the United States). The trade can be between a place in a state and a place outside the state, even outside the United States.
Commercial vehicle. Commercial vehicles are vehicles with gross vehicle weights of 26,001 pounds or more; trailers with gross vehicle weights of 10,001 pounds or more; vehicles that transport hazardous materials requiring placards; and buses designed to carry 16 or more people (including the driver).
Compressed gas. Compressed gases are held under pressure. When in the container, compressed gases have an absolute pressure of more than 40 psi (that is, 40 psia) at 70 degrees Fahrenheit. Or if measured at 130 degrees Fahrenheit, they have a pressure of 104 psia. A liquid flammable material with a vapor pressure over 40 psia at 100 degrees Fahrenheit is also a compressed gas.
Conductor. A material through which electricity flows.
Controlled intersection. An intersection with a traffic light or signs that control traffic.
Controlled substance. A substance listed on Schedules I through V of the Code of Federal Regulations.
Convex mirror. "Spot mirror" that shows a wider area than a flat mirror of the same size.
Coolant. The liquid that reduces engine heat.
Corrosive material. A corrosive is a solid or liquid that harms human skin on contact.
Couple. Connect two sections of a vehicle combination.

D

Deceleration. To slow down, to come to a stop (the opposite of acceleration).
Department of Transportation (DOT). The federal department that establishes the nation's overall transportation policies.
Differential. A system of gears that permits each wheel to turn at different speeds on the same axle, as occurs when going around a curve.
Disc brakes. Brakes that function by causing friction pads to press on either side of a disc rotating along with the wheel.
Disc wheel. A single unit that combines a rim and a wheel. The most common type is the Budd wheel.
Disqualification. Suspension or complete loss of driving privileges.
Dock. A platform where trucks are loaded and unloaded.
Driveaway-towaway operation. A hauling operation in which the cargo is one or more vehicles with one or more sets of wheels on the roadway.
Drive axle. An axle that transmits power to the wheels and actively pulls the load.
Driver's record of duty status. Form submitted by driver to carrier for each 24-hour period of work.
Drive shaft. A heavy-duty tube that connects the transmission to the rear end assembly of the tractor.
Drive train. A series of connected mechanical parts for transmitting motion.
Duals. A pair of wheels and tires mounted together on the same side of one axle.

DUI. Driving a commercial motor vehicle while under the influence of alcohol.
Dummy coupler. A fitting used to seal the opening in an air brake hose connection (gladhands) when the connection is not in use. Sometimes called a dust cap.
Dunnage. The material used to protect or support freight in trucks.

E

Eighteen-wheeler. A combination of tractor and trailer with five axles and dual wheel combinations totaling 18 rims and tires.
Electrical system. Consists of starter, wiring, battery, generator, alternator, and generator regulator, all of which work together to crank the engine for starting.
Employee. Anyone who operates a CMV either directly for or under lease to an employer.
Employer. Anyone who owns or leases a CMV or assigns employees to operate one.
Endorsement. A special allowance added to your CDL which permits you to drive certain vehicles or haul certain cargo.
Engine retarder. An auxiliary device added to the engine to reduce its speed. Also referred to as an engine brake.
En route. On the way.
EPA. The U.S. Environmental Protection Agency.
Etiologic agents. Microorganisms (germs). They cause disease.
Explosives. Explosives are chemical compounds, mixtures, or devices that explode. Class A explosives are the most dangerous. Class B explosives are less dangerous. They don't explode. Instead, they burn rapidly. Of the three, Class C explosives present the least danger. They contain only small amounts of Class A or B explosive.

F

F. Fahrenheit. A scale for measuring temperature.
Fan belt. A belt attached to the engine block that drives the fan.
Federal Motor Carrier Safety Regulations (FMCSR). Govern the operation of trucks and buses operated in interstate or foreign commerce by common, contract and private motor carriers.
Felony. A crime that is punishable by death or a prison term of more than one year.
Fifteen-hour rule. Department of Transportation regulation in which no driver is allowed to be on duty for more than 15 hours following eight hours of off-duty time.
Fifth wheel. Part of the locking device used to connect a semitrailer and tractor.
First aid. Immediate and temporary care given the victim of an accident or sudden illness until the services of a medical professional can be obtained.
Fishyback. Transporting motor truck trailers and containers by ship.
Flammable. A substance that easily bursts into flame (also "inflammable").
Flammable compressed gas. Compressed gas is said to be flammable if a mixture of 13 percent or less will form a flammable mixture when combined with air or if it passes any one of three Bureau of Explosives tests for flammability.
Flammable liquid. A liquid with a flash point below 100 degrees Fahrenheit.
Flammable solids. A flammable solid is a solid material, other than an explosive, that can cause fire.
Flatbed. Truck or trailer without sides or top.
FMCSR. The Federal Motor Carrier Safety Regulations.
Foot brake valve. Foot operated valve that controls the amount of air pressure delivered to or released from the brake chambers.
Freight container. A reusable container with a volume of 64 cubic feet or more. It's designed and built so it can be lifted with its contents intact. It's mainly used to hold packages (in unit form) during transport.
Friction. Resistance between the surfaces of two objects.
Fuel pump. In a vehicle, the pump that moves fuel from the fuel tank to the engine.
Fuel tank. A tank other than a cargo tank used to transport flammable or combustible liquid. It's also a tank that holds compressed gas used to fuel the transport vehicle it's attached to or the equipment on that vehicle. This is different from a tank semitrailer that transports fuel as cargo.

G

GCWR. Gross combination weight rating.
Generator. In a vehicle, the device that changes mechanical energy into electrical energy to run lights and battery.
Glad hands. Air hose brake system connections between tractor and trailer.
Governor (air). Device to automatically control the air pressure being maintained in the air reservoirs. Keeps the air pressure between 100 and 125 psi and prevents excessive air pressure from building up.
Groove. On a tire, the space between adjacent tread ribs.
Gross combination weight (GCW). The total weight of the power unit or tractor, plus any trailers, plus the cargo. (This also applies to a vehicle towing another vehicle as cargo.)
Gross combination weight rating (GCWR). Gross combination weight rating is the value stated by the manufacturer as being the loaded weight of a combination vehicle.
Gross vehicle weight (GVW). The total weight of a single vehicle, plus its load.
Gross vehicle weight rating (GVWR). The value stated by the manufacturer as the loaded weight of a single vehicle.
Gross weight. The weight of a packaging plus the weight of its contents.
GVWR. Gross vehicle weight rating.

H

Hand throttle. A manually set throttle in a tractor that is used to maintain a certain engine speed.
Hazardous material. A substance or material, including a hazardous substance, that the Secretary of Transportation judges to pose an unreasonable risk to health, safety, and property when transported in commerce.
Hazardous substance. A material listed in the Appendix to Part 172.101 of the Hazardous Materials Regulations.
Hazardous waste. Any material that is subject to the Hazardous Waste Manifest Requirement of the U.S. Environmental Protection Agency, specified in 40 CFR Part 262.
Hazardous waste manifest. A document (shipping paper) on which all hazardous waste is identified and which must accompany each shipment of waste from the point of pickup to its destination.
Highway. A public roadway that carries through traffic.
Hydraulic brakes. Brakes that depend on the transmission of hydraulic pressure from a master cylinder to the wheel cylinders.

I

Ignition switch. Allows current to flow from the battery to the starter motor.
Import. To receive goods from a foreign country.
Inertia. The tendency of an object to remain in the same condition (that is, to stay still or keep moving).
Injector. In a diesel engine, the unit that sprays fuel into the combustion chamber.
Intermodal container. A freight container designed and built to be used in two or more modes of transport.
Intersection. The place where two roadways intersect.
Intrastate traffic. Traffic within one state only.
Irritating material. When exposed to air or flames, it gives off dangerous fumes.

J

Jacking. Changing the direction of the trailer.
Jake brake. (slang) The Jacobs engine brake that is used as an auxiliary braking device on a tractor.

K

Kingpin. Hardened steel pin on a semitrailer that locks into the fifth wheel for coupling.

L

Landing gear. Supports the front end of semitrailer when not attached to a tractor.
Leaf spring suspension. Conventional type of suspension system.
Load lock. A pole-shaped piece of equipment used to hold cargo in place during transport by way of a tension spring.

Log book. A book carried by truck drivers that contains daily records of hours, route, and so forth, which is required by the Department of Transportation.
Low air warning device. A mechanical warning of brake failure by means of buzzer, flashing red light, or small red flag that drops into the driver's line of vision.

M

Manifest. A document describing a shipment or the contents of a vehicle or ship.
Marker lights. Clearance or running lights.
Marking. Putting the descriptive name, instructions, cautions, weight, or specification marks required by regulations on outer containers of hazardous materials.
Mixture. A material composed of more than one chemical compound or element.
Mode. Any of the following transportation methods: rail, highway, air, or water.
Motor vehicle. A vehicle, machine, tractor, trailer or semitrailer, or any combinations of these. This term assumes the vehicle is driven or drawn by mechanical power, is on the highway, and is transporting passengers or property. It doesn't refer to vehicles used on rail. It also doesn't include a trolley bus running on a fixed overhead electric wire and carrying passengers.
Mph. Miles per hour.

O

Oil pressure gauge. Instrument that measures pressure of engine lubricating oil.
Operator. A person who controls the use of an aircraft, vessel, or vehicle.
ORM. Other Regulated Materials.
Other Regulated Materials. "Other Regulated Materials" are those that don't meet any of the other hazardous materials class definitions but that are dangerous when transported in commerce. There are five classes of ORM: A, B, C, D, and E. ORM A is irritating or toxic. If it leaks during transport, it can make people in the area very uncomfortable. ORM B is harmful to the vehicle if it leaks. ORM C has different features from A and B, but is still dangerous to transport. ORM D is an ordinary consumer item. It's dangerous in transport because of its form or amount or because of the way it's packaged. ORM E is neither A, B, C, nor D. But in some cases it can be dangerous, and then it must be regulated. Hazardous waste is an example of ORM E.
Outage. The amount by which a packaging falls short of being full of liquid. Usually expressed as a percent of volume. Outage allows for liquids to expand as they warm.
Out-of-service driver. Driver declared out of service by a government representative because of violations.
Out-of-service vehicle. A vehicle that cannot pass the government safety inspection and is declared out of service until the problems are corrected.
Oversized vehicle. Any vehicle whose weight and/or dimensions exceed a state's regulations.
Oxidizer. Oxidizers cause other materials to react with oxygen.

P

Piggyback. Intermodal transportation system in which trailers or containers are carried by rail.
Pigtail. Cable used to transmit electrical power to the trailer.
Placards. Signs placed on tanker or trailer during shipment to identify hazardous material and which must be visible from all angles.
Ply ratings. The number of ply cords in the sidewall and tread of a tire (from two for cars up to as many as 20 for large off-the-road trucks).
Point of origin. The terminal at which a shipment is received by a transportation line from the shipper.
Poison. There are two classes of poison: A and B. Poison A can be gas or liquid. Of the two classes, A is the more dangerous. Just a small amount in the air can kill. Poison B can be liquid or solid, in a paste or semisolid gel. These are so harmful to humans they are dangerous to transport. They can kill when swallowed or inhaled or when absorbed by the skin.
Poison A. The more dangerous of the hazardous materials classed as poison.
Poison B. The less dangerous of the hazardous materials classed as poison.

Portable tank. Any packaging (except a cylinder having a 100-pound or less water capacity) with a capacity of over 110 U.S. gallons. This definition includes tanks designed to be loaded into or on or temporarily coupled to a transport vehicle or ship. These tanks are equipped with skids, mounting or other parts that make mechanical handling possible.
Pot torches. Safety equipment used on a highway to warn traffic of an obstruction or hazard.
Preferred route (or preferred highway). A highway for shipment of highway route controlled quantities of radioactive materials. These routes are named by state routing agencies. When there is no other option, any interstate system highway can be named a preferred route.
Private carrier. A company that maintains its own trucks to ship its own freight.
Progressive shifting. Shifting technique whereby the vehicle is taken up to highway speed by using the least horsepower needed to get the job done, thereby saving fuel.
Proper shipping name. The name of the hazardous material shown in Roman print (not italics) in Part 172.101 of the Hazardous Materials Regulations.
Psi (or p.s.i.). Pounds per square inch.

R

Radial. Tires constructed with the cords running directly across the top to better mold and flex their way around objects on the road, thereby offering less rolling resistance and increased mileage.
Radiator. Part of the cooling system that removes engine heat from the coolant passing through it.
Radiator cap. A cap that protects the radiator from impurities, allows pressure to build up, and releases excess pressure from the engine.
Radioactive material. Material that gives off rays, usually harmful.
Reaction time. The time that elapses between the point that a driver recognizes the need for action and the time the driver takes that action.
Rearward amplification. The "crack-the-whip" effect found on tractors with trailers.
Recap. Restoring a tire by putting new tread on the carcass (body).
Reciprocity. Mutual action; exchange of privileges such as between two states.
Reefer. Commonly used industry term for refrigerated truck or trailer that hauls perishables.
Reflectors. Light reflectors that, when placed along the road, warn motorists of an emergency.
Regulation. A law designed to control behavior. A governmental order with the force of law.
Relay emergency valve. A combination valve in an air brake system that controls brake application and that also provides for automatic trailer brake application should the trailer become disconnected from the towing vehicle.
Representative vehicle. One that stands for the type of motor vehicle that a CDL applicant plans to drive.
Rev. To operate an engine at a high speed.
Road. The traveled part of a roadway and any shoulder alongside it.
Roadside. The part of a highway or street that is not used by vehicles and is not a sidewalk.
Roadway. A general term that refers to any surface on which vehicles travel.
Rocky Mountain double. Combination consisting of a tractor and two trailers.
Runaway ramp. A ramp on a steep downgrade that can be used by a truck driver to stop a runaway truck when brakes have failed. Sometimes called an escape ramp.
Rural. The countryside.

S

Saddle tanks. Barrel-type fuel tanks that hang from the sides of the tractor's frame.
School bus. A passenger motor vehicle designed or used to carry more than ten passengers in addition to the driver. School buses have been determined by the Secretary of Transportation to be largely used to transport preprimary, primary, or secondary school students to these schools from their homes or from their homes to these schools.
Seal. In the shipping industry, a security device to assure that truck doors have not been opened in transit.

Semitrailer. Truck trailer equipped with one or more axles and constructed so that the front end rests upon a truck tractor.
Serious traffic violations. These are going more than 15 miles over the posted speed limit; reckless driving; improper or erratic lane changes; following the vehicle ahead too closely; traffic violations that result in fatal accidents.
Shipping paper. A shipping order, bill of lading, manifest, or other shipping document serving the same purpose. These documents must have the information required by Parts 172.202, 172.203 and 172.204 of the Hazardous Materials Regulations.
Shoulder. The part of a roadway that runs along next to it and can be used by stopped vehicles.
Sidewalk. The part of a roadway that is to be used by people who are walking (pedestrians).
Sight glass or gauge. Glass window for determining fluid levels, as in a radiator.
Sight side. The side of the tractor visible to driver, opposite the blind side.
Sixty-hour/seven-day or seventy-hour/eight-day rule. Department of Transportation regulation stating that no driver is allowed to be on duty for more than 60 hours in any seven-day period; if carriers are operating the vehicles every day of the week, they may permit drivers to be on duty not more than 70 hours in any eight-day period.
Skid. Failure of the tires to grip the road due to loss of traction.
Slack adjuster. An adjustable device located on the brake chamber push rod that is used to compensate for brake shoe wear.
Sleeper berth. Area in a tractor where a driver can sleep.
Sleeper. Truck cab with a sleeping compartment.
Slider. Nickname for a sliding fifth wheel.
Sliding tandem. A semitrailer tandem suspension that can be adjusted forward and backward.
Sludge. Thickened oil and sediment.
Spotter mirror. Small, convex mirror mounted on the mirror frame that gives a different view from the larger part of the mirror.
Spring brake. Conventional brake chamber and emergency or parking brake mechanism for use on vehicles equipped with air brakes.
Spring brake control. Controls spring-loaded parking brakes.
Starter motor. The motor that cranks the engine to get it started.
Starting system. Made up of the starter battery, cables, switch, and controls.
State of domicile. Your home state. This is the place you plan to return to when you are absent. It's where you have your main, permanent home.
Steering axle. An axle that steers the vehicle. Can be powered or non-powered.
Stopping distance. The distance the vehicle travels between the time the driver recognizes the need to stop and the time the vehicle comes to a complete stop.
Straight truck. A truck with the body and engine mounted on the same chassis (rather than a combination unit such as a tractor-semitrailer).
Street. The entire width of a roadway that is maintained with public funds, including the shoulder, sidewalk, and roadway.
Suspension. The system of springs and other supports that hold a vehicle on its axles.

T

Tailgating. Following another vehicle too closely so that, if the need arises, there is not enough room to come to a safe stop.
Tandem. Semitrailer or tractor with two rear axles.
Tandem axle. An assembly of two axles, either of which may be powered.
Tank vehicle (or tanker). One that transports gas or liquids in bulk. Portable tanks that carry less than 1,000 gallons are not included in this definition.
Tarp. Tarpaulin cover for an open-top trailer.
Technical name. A recognized chemical name currently used in scientific and technical handbooks, journals, and text. Some generic descriptions are used as technical names.

Ten-hour rule. Department of Transportation ruling in which no driver shall drive for more than ten hours following eight consecutive hours of off-duty time (a driver's carrier is not allowed to let a driver break this rule).
Throttle. Controls the engine speed.
Tire load. The most weight a tire can carry safely.
Traffic. Anything using the roadway for the purpose of travel, including vehicles, pedestrians, herded animals, or streetcars.
Trailer. Freight-hauling part of a rig, designed to be pulled by a tractor, that is generally divided into three groups: semitrailer, full trailer, and pole trailer.
Trailer brake. Hand-operated remote control brake located on the steering column or dashboard for the trailer only.
Transmission. Mechanical device that uses gearing or torque conversion to change the ratio between engine rpm and driving rpm.
Triple. Combination rig consisting of tractor, semitrailer, and two full trailers coupled together. Also called triple headers or triple bottoms.
Trolley brake. A hand valve used to operate the trailer brakes independently of tractor brakes. Also called trailer brake.
Trucking industry. The business of carrying goods by truck, including carrier, drivers, warehouse and terminal employees, and all others involved in any phase of trucking.

U

Uncontrolled intersection. An intersection without any form of traffic control, such as stop signs or stop signals.
Uncouple. To disconnect sections of a trailer combination.
United States. The fifty states, the District of Columbia, the Commonwealth of Puerto Rico, the Virgin Islands, American Samoa, and Guam.
Urban. The city or referring to the city (the opposite of rural).

V

Vacuum brake system. A brake system in which the brake mechanism is activated by a vacuum.
Valve. A device that opens and closes openings in a pipe, tube, or cylinder.
Volt. A unit of measurement of electrical potential.

W

Water pump. Part of the cooling system that circulates coolant between the engine's water jackets and the radiator.
Wedge. In a truck, a commonly used type of brake.
Wet tank. Part of the air brake system with a tank that must be drained at least once a day.
Wrecker. Truck designed for hoisting and towing disabled vehicles.

Y

Yield. Give way to a driver with the right-of-way.

Index

C

D

Q

R

S